Acts and Paul's Letters

Handbooks on the New Testament

Benjamin L. Gladd, series editor

HANDBOOK ON

Acts and Paul's Letters

Thomas R. Schreiner

Baker Academic

a division of Baker Publishing Group
Grand Rapids, Michigan

Published by Baker Academic
a division of Baker Publishing Group
PO Box 6287, Grand Rapids, MI 49516-6287
www.bakeracademic.com

Printed in the United States of America

Library of Congress Cataloging-in-Publication Data
Names: Schreiner, Thomas R., author.
Title: Handbook on Acts and Paul's Letters / Thomas R. Schreiner.
Description: Grand Rapids : Baker Academic, a division of Baker Publishing Group, 2019. | Series: Handbooks on the New Testament | Includes bibliographical references and index.
Identifiers: LCCN 2019005930 | ISBN 9781540960177 (cloth)
Subjects: LCSH: Bible. Acts—Introductions. | Bible. Epistles of Paul—Introductions.
Classification: LCC BS2625.52 .S37 2019 | DDC 227/.06—dc23
LC record available at https://lccn.loc.gov/2019005930

Baker Publishing Group publications use paper produced from sustainable forestry practices and post-consumer waste whenever possible.

21 22 23 24 25 26 27   8 7 6 5 4 3 2

To Eric Johnson,
Faithful Servant of Christ,
Beloved Friend

Contents

Series Preface

The Handbooks on the New Testament are the counterpart to the well-received, four-volume set Handbooks on the Old Testament by Baker Academic. With the myriad of New Testament commentaries and introductions, why pen yet another series? The handbooks stand unique in that they are neither introductions nor commentaries. Most New Testament commentaries work in the trenches with verse-by-verse expositions, whereas introductions fly at 40,000 feet above the biblical text. This series lies between these two approaches. Each volume takes a snapshot of each New Testament passage without getting bogged down in detailed exegesis. The intent is for the reader to be able to turn to a particular New Testament passage in the handbook and quickly gain a grasp of the sense of the passage without having to read a considerable amount of the preceding and following discussion. This series is committed to summarizing the content of each major section of the New Testament. Introductory issues are not ignored (authorship, dating, audience, etc.), but they are not the focus. Footnotes, too, are used sparingly to keep the readers attuned to the passage. At the end of each chapter, the author includes a brief, up-to-date bibliography for further investigation.

Since the handbook focuses on the final form of the text, authors pay special attention to Old Testament allusions and quotations. The New Testament writers quote the Old Testament some 350 times and allude to it well over a thousand. Each author in this series notes how a good portion of those Old Testament allusions and quotations shape the passage under discussion. The primary audience of the handbook series is lay people, students, pastors, and professors of theology and biblical studies. We intend these volumes to find a home in the classroom and in personal study. To make the series more accessible, technical jargon is avoided. Each volume is theologically and pastorally informed. The authors apply their observations to contemporary issues within the church and to the Christian life. Above all, our prayer and desire is that this series would stimulate more study and serious reflection on God's Word, resulting in godly living and the expansion of the kingdom.

Benjamin L. Gladd

Author's Preface

It has been a delight to reflect on and write about the content of Acts and the Pauline Letters. Many introductions effectively discuss author, date, setting, and other critical questions. Many readers, however, desire an introduction that in a simple and nontechnical way discusses the content of the NT. It is comparable to having a class on Shakespeare in which most of the discussion centers on whether Shakespeare wrote his plays, the situation and background to each play, other literary influences on Shakespeare, and so on. What may be neglected, however, is significant discussion and reflection on what Shakespeare actually wrote, and thus here the focus is on the content of the books studied. The descriptive outlines are intended to give the big picture and are overly simplistic, but the intention is to help readers get a quick grasp of the contours of the book in question.

I am grateful to Ben Gladd for asking me to contribute to this series, for his vision for biblical theology, and for his helpful comments on this work. Bryan Dyer and Eric Salo deserve thanks for shepherding this book expertly through the publication process, sharpening and correcting what has been written. I am also thankful to Andrés Vera, who arranged and formatted each bibliography, which I sent to him in a most unorganized form! I am so thankful for Andrés's friendship, his careful work, and how he models Christ every day. Since this book is nontechnical and an introduction, there are no footnotes, but I hope the bibliography for each book will introduce readers to other resources worth consulting. In one sense every line could be footnoted, for I am indebted to a plethora of scholars who have shaped me in lectures and through their writings. There are places in the book where I draw on what I have written elsewhere, especially on Romans, 1 Corinthians, and Galatians. Since there are no footnotes, I did not quote myself, and even when I drew on what I wrote elsewhere, I revised what had been written earlier. The bibliographies, of course, are also selective, and in a day in which so much has been written, many other works could have been included.

I dedicate this book to my dear friend for many years, Eric Johnson. Eric has been a model of a Christian psychologist and one of the godliest and wisest people I know. I am eternally grateful for his love and friendship.

Abbreviations

Old Testament

Gen.	Genesis
Exod.	Exodus
Lev.	Leviticus
Num.	Numbers
Deut.	Deuteronomy
Josh.	Joshua
Judg.	Judges
Ruth	Ruth
1 Sam.	1 Samuel
2 Sam.	2 Samuel
1 Kings	1 Kings
2 Kings	2 Kings
1 Chron.	1 Chronicles
2 Chron.	2 Chronicles
Ezra	Ezra
Neh.	Nehemiah
Esther	Esther
Job	Job
Ps(s).	Psalm(s)
Prov.	Proverbs
Eccles.	Ecclesiastes
Song	Song of Songs
Isa.	Isaiah
Jer.	Jeremiah
Lam.	Lamentations
Ezek.	Ezekiel
Dan.	Daniel
Hosea	Hosea
Joel	Joel
Amos	Amos
Obad.	Obadiah
Jon.	Jonah
Mic.	Micah
Nah.	Nahum
Hab.	Habakkuk
Zeph.	Zephaniah
Hag.	Haggai
Zech.	Zechariah
Mal.	Malachi

New Testament

Matt.	Matthew
Mark	Mark
Luke	Luke
John	John
Acts	Acts
Rom.	Romans
1 Cor.	1 Corinthians
2 Cor.	2 Corinthians
Gal.	Galatians
Eph.	Ephesians
Phil.	Philippians
Col.	Colossians
1 Thess.	1 Thessalonians
2 Thess.	2 Thessalonians
1 Tim.	1 Timothy
2 Tim.	2 Timothy
Titus	Titus
Philem.	Philemon

Heb.	Hebrews
James	James
1 Pet.	1 Peter
2 Pet.	2 Peter
1 John	1 John
2 John	2 John
3 John	3 John
Jude	Jude
Rev.	Revelation

Other Primary Texts

Apostolic Fathers

1 Clem.	1 Clement
Did.	Didache

Apuleius

Metam.	Metamorphoses (The Golden Ass)

Aratus

Phaen.	Phaenomena

Athenaeus

Deipn.	Deipnosophistae (Banquet of the Learned)

Bible: Texts and Versions

CSB	Christian Standard Bible
ESV	English Standard Version
KJV	King James Version
LXX	Septuagint (the Greek OT)
MT	Masoretic Text (of the Hebrew Bible)
NASB	New American Standard Bible
NET	New English Translation
NIV	New International Version (2011)
NKJV	New King James Version
NRSV	New Revised Standard Version
NT	New Testament
OT	Old Testament
RSV	Revised Standard Version

Tg. Onq.	Targum Onqelos (Aramaic translation of the Pentateuch)

Cicero

Cael.	Pro Caelio
Clu.	Pro Cluentio
Off.	De officiis (On Obligations)

Dead Sea Scrolls

4QMMT	Halakhic Letter (4Q394–399)
4QpNah	Pesher Nahum, from Cave 4 of Qumran
11QTemple	Temple Scroll, from Cave 11 of Qumran

Diogenes Laertius

Vit. phil.	Vitae philosophorum (Lives of Eminent Philosophers)

Epictetus

Diatr.	Diatribai/Dissertationes

Josephus

Ant.	Jewish Antiquities
J.W.	Jewish War

Juvenal

Sat.	Satirae (Satires)

Old Testament Apocrypha

Bar.	Baruch
2 Esd.	2 Esdras
1–4 Macc.	1–4 Maccabees
Sir.	Sirach
Tob.	Tobit
Wis.	Wisdom of Solomon

Old Testament Pseudepigrapha

2 Bar.	2 Baruch
Jos. Asen.	Joseph and Aseneth
Jub.	Jubilees
LAB	Liber antiquitatum biblicarum (Pseudo-Philo)
Pss. Sol.	Psalms of Solomon
Sib. Or.	Sibylline Oracles

T. Benj.   Testament of Benjamin
T. Sol.   Testament of Solomon

Other Rabbinic Works

m. Avod. Zar.   Avodah Zarah
m. Demai   Demai
m. Kiddushin   Kiddushin
Num. Rab.   Numbers Rabbah
Sifre Num.   Sifre Numbers
t. Sukkah   Sukkah

Papyri

P.Oxy.   Oxyrhynchus Papyri

Philo

Creation   On the Creation of the World
Decalogue   On the Decalogue
Embassy   On the Embassy to Gaius

Plato

Leg.   Leges (Laws)

Plutarch

Conj. praec.   Conjugalia praecepta (Advice to Bride and Groom)
Lib. Ed.   Pseudo-Plutarch, De liberis educandis (Educating the Virtuous Citizen)
Mor.   Moralia (Moral Essays)

Xenophon

Mem.   Memorabilia

Modern Works

AB   Anchor Bible
ABCS   Asia Bible Commentary Series
ABR   Australian Biblical Review
AcBib   Academia Biblica
ACCS   Ancient Christian Commentary on Scripture
ACNT   Augsburg Commentary on the New Testament
ACT   Ancient Christian Texts
AGJU   Arbeiten zur Geschichte des antiken Judentums und des Urchristentums
AnBib   Analecta Biblica
ANTC   Abingdon New Testament Commentaries
BBC   Blackwell Bible Commentaries
BBR   Bulletin for Biblical Research
BCBC   Believers Church Bible Commentary
BDAG   Danker, Frederick W., Walter Bauer, William F. Arndt, and F. Wilbur Gingrich. *Greek-English Lexicon of the New Testament and Other Early Christian Literature.* 3rd ed. Chicago: University of Chicago Press, 2000.
BDF   Blass, Friedrich, Albert Debrunner, and Robert W. Funk. *A Greek Grammar of the New Testament and Other Early Christian Literature.* Chicago: University of Chicago Press, 1961.
BECNT   Baker Exegetical Commentary on the New Testament
BETL   Bibliotheca Ephemeridum Theologicarum Lovaniensium
BHGNT   Baylor Handbook on the Greek New Testament
BHT   Beiträge zur historischen Theologie
Bib   Biblica
BIS   Biblical Interpretation Series

Abbreviations

BNTC	Black's New Testament Commentaries
BSac	*Bibliotheca Sacra*
BST	Bible Speaks Today
BT	*The Bible Translator*
BTCB	Brazos Theological Commentary on the Bible
BTCP	Biblical Theology for Christian Proclamation
BZNW	Beihefte zur Zeitschrift für die neutestamentliche Wissenschaft
CBET	Contributions to Biblical Exegesis and Theology
CBQ	*Catholic Biblical Quarterly*
CBR	*Currents in Biblical Research*
CCSS	Catholic Commentary on Sacred Scripture
CGTC	Cambridge Greek Testament Commentaries
CPNIVC	College Press NIV Commentary
CRINT	Compendia Rerum Iudaicarum ad Novum Testamentum
CTJ	*Calvin Theological Journal*
CTR	*Criswell Theological Review*
DSBS	Daily Study Bible Series
EEC	Evangelical Exegetical Commentary
EGGNT	Exegetical Guide to the Greek New Testament
ETL	*Ephemerides Theologicae Lovanienses*
EvQ	*Evangelical Quarterly*
ExpTim	*Expository Times*
FRLANT	Forschungen zur Religion und Literatur des Alten und Neuen Testaments
FSS	Five Solas Series
GNC	Good News Commentary
GTJ	*Grace Theological Journal*
HBT	*Horizons in Biblical Theology*
HDR	Harvard Dissertations in Religion
HNTC	Harper's New Testament Commentaries
HTR	*Harvard Theological Review*
IBC	Interpretation: A Bible Commentary for Teaching and Preaching
ICC	International Critical Commentary
IVPNTC	IVP New Testament Commentary
JAAR	*Journal of the American Academy of Religion*
JBL	*Journal of Biblical Literature*
JETS	*Journal of the Evangelical Theological Society*
JPTSup	Journal of Pentecostal Theology Supplement
JSJ	*Journal for the Study of Judaism*
JSJSup	Supplements to Journal for the Study of Judaism
JSNT	*Journal for the Study of the New Testament*
JSNTSup	Journal for the Study of the New Testament Supplement Series
JSOT	Journal for the Study of the Old Testament
JSPL	*Journal for the Study of Paul and His Letters*
JTS	*Journal of Theological Studies*
LNTS	Library of New Testament Studies
LTP	*Laval théologique et philosophique*
LTPM	Louvain Theological and Pastoral Monographs

LW	Luther's Works
MNTC	Moffatt New Testament Commentary
NAC	New American Commentary
NACSBT	New American Commentary Studies in Bible and Theology
NCB	New Century Bible
NCBC	New Cambridge Bible Commentary
NCCS	New Covenant Commentary Series
NIBC	New International Biblical Commentary
NICNT	New International Commentary on the New Testament
NIGTC	New International Greek Testament Commentary
NIVAC	NIV Application Commentary
NovT	*Novum Testamentum*
NovTSup	Supplements to Novum Testamentum
NSBT	New Studies in Biblical Theology
NTC	New Testament in Context
NTL	New Testament Library
NTM	New Testament Monographs
NTOA	Novum Testamentum et Orbis Antiquus
NTS	*New Testament Studies*
NTT	New Testament Theology
PBM	Paternoster Biblical Monographs
PCNT	Paideia: Commentaries on the New Testament
PGNT	Phoenix Guides to the New Testament
PNTC	Pillar New Testament Commentary
Presb	*Presbyterion*
ResQ	*Restoration Quarterly*
RevExp	*Review and Expositor*
RNTS	Reading the New Testament Series
RTR	*Reformed Theological Review*
SBLDS	Society of Biblical Literature Dissertation Series
SBLMS	Society of Biblical Literature Monograph Series
SEJC	Studies in Early Judaism and Christianity
SHBC	Smyth & Helwys Bible Commentary
SJT	*Scottish Journal of Theology*
SNTSMS	Society for New Testament Studies Monograph Series
SNTSU	Studien zum Neuen Testament und seiner Umwelt
SNTW	Studies of the New Testament and Its World
SOGBC	Story of God Bible Commentary
SP	Sacra Pagina
ST	*Studia Theologica*
SUNT	Studien zur Umwelt des Neuen Testaments
THNTC	Two Horizons New Testament Commentary
TJ	*Trinity Journal*
TNTC	Tyndale New Testament Commentaries
TPINTC	TPI New Testament Commentaries
TTE	*The Theological Educator*
TUGAL	Texte und Untersuchungen zur Geschichte der altchristlichen Literatur

TynBul	*Tyndale Bulletin*
TZ	*Theologische Zeitschrift*
WBC	Word Biblical Commentary
WTJ	*Westminster Theological Journal*
WUNT	Wissenschaftliche Untersuchungen zum Neuen Testament
ZECNT	Zondervan Exegetical Commentary on the New Testament
ZIBBC	Zondervan Illustrated Bible Backgrounds Commentary
ZNW	*Zeitschrift für die neutestamentliche Wissenschaft und die Kunde der älteren Kirche*

CHAPTER ONE

The Acts of the Apostles

Introduction

Author and Date

In the book of Acts we are not told the identity of the author, nor are we told when Acts was written. It is quite clear, however, that it was written by the same person who wrote the Gospel of Luke. A number of reasons could be listed, but I will restrict myself to three: (1) Both books are addressed to Theophilus (Luke 1:3; Acts 1:1). (2) Acts refers to "the first narrative" (1:1), and that is obviously the Gospel of Luke. (3) The table illustrates some common themes that conclude the Gospel of Luke and are picked up at the beginning of Acts.

Theme	Texts
Proof of Jesus's resurrection	Luke 24:1–43; Acts 1:3
Promise of the Spirit	Luke 24:49; Acts 1:4–5, 8
Waiting in Jerusalem	Luke 24:52–53; Acts 1:4
Commission to proclaim the gospel	Luke 24:47–48; Acts 1:8
Jesus's ascension	Luke 24:51; Acts 1:9–11

The bridge between the end of Luke and the beginning of Acts shows the hand of the same author at work.

Theophilus knew the author, but how can we know who wrote the Gospel of Luke and Acts? It isn't my purpose to delve into this matter in detail, but we derive the conclusion from tradition and the internal evidence in Acts—the famous "we" passages, where the author of Acts traveled with

Paul (Acts 16:10–16; 20:5–15; 21:1–12; 27:1–28:16). From the earliest times the early church agreed that Acts was written by Luke. It is quite unlikely that this tradition was invented, for when we read the NT, Luke plays a nearly invisible role. In fact, he only appears in three verses (Col. 4:14; 2 Tim. 4:11; Philem. 24). The only reason we notice Luke when reading those verses today is because we know the tradition that Luke wrote a gospel and the book of Acts. Luke's fame did not lead the early church to identify Luke as the author. It was just the opposite: Luke became famous because the tradition identified him as the author. The "we" passages of Acts, though not altogether determinative, also lead us to Lukan authorship. By a process of elimination in studying the "we" passages in Acts, Luke is shown to be the most likely author.

The date of the Acts of the Apostles is a much more difficult matter. It is tied up with how we date the Gospels, since Acts was clearly written after Luke. Also, most scholars think that Luke used Mark when writing his Gospel, and so the date is linked with a thicket of issues we can't explore here. I believe there are good reasons to think that the Gospels were written early enough so that Acts was written in the 60s, before the destruction of the temple in Jerusalem in AD 70. Perhaps Luke completed Acts before Paul was freed from prison (Acts 28:30–31). On the other hand, it is also possible that Acts was written in the 70s or 80s. In any case, the interpretation of the book remains the same, whatever date we assign.

Structure and Central Themes

There are a number of different ways to structure Acts. Here are three possibilities.

Major Persons

Peter	1:1–12:25
Paul	13:1–28:31

Geography

Jerusalem	1:1–8:3
Samaria and Coastal Regions of Palestine	8:4–11:18
South Galatia	11:19–15:35
Philippi, Thessalonica, Berea, Athens, Corinth, and Ephesus	15:36–19:20
Jerusalem and Rome	19:21–28:31

Summary Statements

6:7	"So the *word of God* spread, the disciples in **Jerusalem** increased greatly in number, and a large group of priests became obedient to the faith."
9:31	"So the church throughout all **Judea, Galilee, and Samaria** had peace and was strengthened. Living in the fear of the Lord and encouraged by the Holy Spirit, it increased in numbers."
12:24	"But *the word of God* flourished and multiplied."
16:5	"So the churches were strengthened in the faith and grew daily in numbers."
19:20	"In this way *the word of the Lord* flourished and prevailed."
28:30-31	"Paul stayed two whole years in his own rented house. And he welcomed all who visited him, *proclaiming the kingdom of God* and *teaching about the Lord Jesus Christ* with all boldness and without hindrance."

The outline below is overly simplistic and uses some modern categories, but it helps us get a big picture of Acts.

Outline

The gospel spreads in Jerusalem	1:1-6:7
The gospel spreads in Judea, Samaria, and Galilee	6:8-9:31
The gospel spreads to the gentiles	9:32-12:24
The gospel spreads to what now is Turkey	12:25-16:5
The gospel spreads to Europe	16:6-19:20
The gospel spreads from Jerusalem to Rome	19:21-28:31

The first structure presented above clearly doesn't work, since the book isn't fundamentally about Peter and Paul. In fact, Peter doesn't even appear in Acts 7, and he plays a minor role in chapters 8–9. The geographical structure is more promising but not very illuminating, and to be honest, is a bit boring. No structure is without faults, but I believe the summary statements in the third table nicely structure the book. The summary statements fit well with the theme of the book, which is found in 1:8, "But you will receive power when the Holy Spirit has come on you, and you will be my witnesses in Jerusalem, in all Judea and Samaria, and to the end of the earth."

The summary statements in the table are marked to denote three themes. First, the **bold** in the summary statements notes the geographical spread of the gospel. In Acts 1:8 we see that the gospel begins in Jerusalem, then spreads to Judea, to Samaria, and then goes to the ends of the earth. If we look at the bold in the summary statements, we see that the only two summary statements that mention geography are in 6:7 and 9:31. In 6:7 the first part of the promise in 1:8 is fulfilled: the gospel spreads in Jerusalem. These chapters center on the Jerusalem temple, and the gospel is proclaimed in Jerusalem and in the temple courts. The prophecy of Isaiah begins to be fulfilled here, "For instruction will go out of Zion and the word of the LORD from Jerusalem" (Isa. 2:3; cf. Mic. 4:2). The second summary statement in Acts 9:31 records the extension of the gospel to Judea, Galilee, and Samaria. We are not told much about how the gospel spread in Judea and Galilee, but the spread of the gospel to Samaria indicates that Judea and Galilee have also been reached. Later we will consider why it is so important that Samaria is included here.

Three other comments about the structure of 1:1–9:31 should be noted. First, why does the encounter with Stephen in 6:8–8:4 occur after the summary statement in 6:7, especially since Stephen was martyred *in Jerusalem*? Moreover, Stephen was appointed as one of the seven chosen to serve in 6:1–6, and so placing the story of his death (6:8–8:4) after the summary statement about the gospel spreading *in Jerusalem* seems to break up the narrative. I suggest that the story of Stephen's speech and death are placed after the summary statement in 6:7 because Stephen's death "scattered" the disciples "throughout the land of Judea and Samaria" (8:1), and "those who were scattered went on their way preaching the word" (8:4; cf. 11:19). Stephen's speech and martyrdom, in other words, became the impetus for the gospel being proclaimed *outside Jerusalem* in Judea, Samaria, and Galilee. It is the catalytic event for the spread of the gospel outside Jerusalem.

Second, why is the conversion of Paul (9:1–30) placed before the second summary statement (9:31) since Paul's ministry was mainly to the gentiles and to the Jews in the diaspora? In a sense the conversion of Paul seems to complete reaching the Jews in Jerusalem and Judea, Galilee, and Samaria. It is crucial to see that this observation is being made from the Lukan narratival perspective, from the way Luke crafts the story. Certainly Jewish Christians continued to preach the gospel in Jerusalem and in Judea, Galilee, and Samaria after Paul's conversion, but Luke doesn't continue to rehearse that story after the conversion of Paul. Thus, the conversion of Paul represents a significant shift in redemptive history. From that point on, the Lord guides Peter (10:1–11:18) and commissions Paul to proclaim the good news about Jesus to the gentiles.

Third, this brings us to our final observation. Why are geographical references missing in the summary statements after 9:31? We noticed that 1:1–6:7 centers on Jerusalem, and 6:8–9:31 focuses on Judea, Samaria, and Galilee, but in the summary statements that follow, geographical references are absent. There is no need to mention specific locales because, from 9:32 on, the gospel goes to the gentiles to the ends of the earth, which includes the farthest reaches of the world. Every locale in Acts from this point on represents the spread of the gospel as it goes to the "end of the earth" (1:8). The word of the Lord emanating from Jerusalem was going to all nations (Isa. 2:2–3; Mic. 4:1–2). It is fitting, then, that the book ends with Paul in Rome, not because Rome *is* the ends of the earth, but because it symbolizes that the church was carrying out Jesus's mission to go to the ends of the earth, even by bringing the gospel to the capital of the Roman Empire. Thus Rome becomes a new launching point for mission.

The second feature of the summary statements is highlighted in *italics*. We see in three of the summary statements that the church grew by *the word* of the Lord or *the word* of God (6:7; 12:24; 19:20). The content of the word is "the kingdom of God," and the kingdom focuses on Jesus Christ (28:31). The church in Acts grows and expands by the power of the word, which is a way of saying that "the gospel . . . is the power of God for salvation" (Rom. 1:16). Here is the place to make a very important observation. The message of salvation in Acts, the message that has an inherent power, is the message of the end-time kingdom. Some have said that the kingdom isn't important in Acts in comparison to the Gospels, but this judgment is mistaken. The word "kingdom" isn't used often, but the theme of the kingdom actually plays a central role in the book. The kingdom frames the entire book, for after Jesus's ascension when he met with the apostles for forty days, he spoke to them "about the kingdom of God" (Acts 1:3). And the book closes, as was just noted, with Paul "proclaiming the kingdom of God" (28:31).

Furthermore, it is imperative to see that the kingdom centers on Jesus Christ. In the last story of the book, as Paul explains the gospel to the Jews while under house arrest in Rome (cf. Acts 28:16, 23), he "testified about the kingdom of God," which means that he "tried to persuade them about Jesus from the Law of Moses and the Prophets" (28:23). The kingdom and the gospel of Jesus Christ, the gospel Paul proclaimed in Rome to Jewish Christians, were not two different messages. The kingdom promises of the OT were fulfilled in Jesus Christ, in his death and resurrection. The close connection between gospel, kingdom, and the message about Jesus Christ is confirmed by Acts 8:12. When Philip was in Samaria, he "proclaimed the good news [*euangelizomenō*] about the kingdom of God and the name of Jesus Christ." Furthermore, when Luke summarized Paul's three months of preaching in Ephesus, he says that he was "persuading them about the kingdom of God" (19:8). Similarly, Paul described his ministry among the Ephesians as "preaching the kingdom" (20:25). The word of the Lord, which has such power, is the gospel, the message of the kingdom, the good news about Jesus Christ.

The third theme in the summary statements (presented in the summary statement chart above), indicated by the underlined statements, is the growth of the gospel, the expansion of the word. Two words stand out for the growth of the church: *increase (auxanō)* and *multiply (plēthynō)*, and in the chart immediately below they are italicized.

6:7	"the word of God *continued to increase*, and the number of the disciples *multiplied* greatly" (ESV)
12:24	"But the word of God *increased* and *multiplied*" (ESV).
19:20	"So the word of the Lord continued to *increase*" (ESV)

We see these same two words, increase and multiply, in the LXX creation account where God says to the human race: "Be fruitful [*auxanesthe*] and multiply [*plēthynesthe*]" (Gen. 1:28 ESV). The creation mandate is being fulfilled in a distinctive manner in the gospel. Human beings were created to rule the world for God, and the rule over the world is restored through the gospel of Jesus Christ. As the gospel spreads, God's rule over human beings is restored. The remarkable "number" of those who are converted is noted in two summary statements (Acts 6:7; 16:5), and the growth in numbers is recorded elsewhere in the book as well, as the table below shows.

Church Growth in Acts

Text	Reference to Growth
2:41	"That day about three thousand people were added to them."
2:47	"Every day the Lord added to their number those who were being saved."
4:4	"But many of those who heard the message believed, and the number of the men came to about five thousand."
5:14	"Believers were added to the Lord in increasing numbers—multitudes of both men and women."
6:1	"In those days, as the disciples were increasing in number . . ."
9:35	"So all who lived in Lydda and Sharon saw him and turned to the Lord."
9:42	"And many believed in the Lord."
11:21	"The Lord's hand was with them, and a large number who believed turned to the Lord."
11:24	"And large numbers of people were added to the Lord."
14:1	"A great number of both Jews and Greeks believed."
17:4	"Some of them were persuaded and joined Paul and Silas, including a large number of God-fearing Greeks, as well as a number of the leading women."
17:12	"Consequently, many of them believed, including a number of the prominent Greek women as well as men."
18:8	"Many of the Corinthians, when they heard, believed and were baptized."
21:20	"You see, brother, how many thousands of Jews there are who have believed."

The creation mandate to rule the world for God was being fulfilled as the *church* increased and multiplied. But we can take another step. The promise given to Abraham that "all the peoples on earth will be blessed through you" (Gen. 12:3) is a central theme in the covenant made with Abraham. In fact, this promise of universal blessing is repeated regularly in Genesis to Abraham, Isaac, and Jacob (18:18; 22:18; 26:4; 28:14). The universal blessing promised to Abraham is the means by which the original creation mandate to rule God's world will be fulfilled, and thus the increasing number of believers and the extension of belief to the ends of the earth (the inclusion of the gentiles) fulfills the promise of universal blessing given to Abraham.

One last point should be made. Psalm 72 is a messianic psalm, which looks forward to the realization of the promises made to David in the Davidic covenant. One petition in the psalm is, "May all nations be blessed by him and call him blessed" (72:17). The promise of universal blessing made to Abraham will become a reality through a Davidic king, and in Acts that king is clearly Jesus Christ. All these themes are pulled together in Peter's second sermon in Jerusalem. "In addition, all the prophets who have spoken, from Samuel and those after him, have also foretold these days. You are the sons of the prophets and of the covenant that God made with your ancestors, saying to Abraham, 'And all the families of the earth will be blessed through your offspring.' God raised up his servant and sent him first to you to bless you by turning each of you from your evil ways" (Acts 3:24–26). The creation mandate to human beings, to rule the world for God, would become a reality through the covenant with Abraham, and the covenant of Abraham was fulfilled through a son of David, Jesus Christ.

Preparation for Pentecost (1:1–26)

Acts 1 functions as the preparation for Pentecost (AD 30) and for the gift of the Spirit that Jesus promised the disciples. We see from its first verse (1:1) that the book of Acts will continue Jesus's words and works. The disciples, however, will only be able to do what Jesus did and to speak his words if they are empowered by the Holy Spirit; thus Jesus instructs the apostles to wait for the promise of the Spirit (1:4–5).

The promise of the Spirit is inextricably intertwined with the coming of the kingdom (1:4–6). The kingdom of God plays a central role in Jesus's preaching in the Synoptic Gospels, and it is clearly one of the central themes in Scripture. The Prophets (e.g., Isa. 9:2–7; 32:1–5; 33:15–24; Amos 9:11–15; Obad. 21; Zeph. 3:8–20; Zech. 14:9) and the Psalms (e.g., 2; 72; 89; 102:15–22) anticipate the day when God's kingdom will come and prevail over the earth.

In the OT the fulfillment of the covenant promises and the coming of the kingdom will become a reality when God pours out his Spirit (e.g., Isa. 32:15; 44:3; Ezek. 36:26–27; Joel 2:28–29).

We are not surprised, then, to find that the promise of the Spirit in Acts 1:4–5 provoked the disciples to ask if the kingdom was about to be restored to Israel. The restoration of Israel is found in many texts in the OT, especially in texts that promise return from exile (e.g., Isa. 11:11–15; 40:3–11; 42:16; 43:2, 5–7, 16–19; 48:20–21; 49:6–11; 51:10; Jer. 31:27–34; Ezek. 34–37; Amos 9:11–15). Israel's return from exile and the gift of the Spirit are two dimensions of the same promise, which is also described as "a new covenant" (cf. Jer. 31:31–34). The new covenant is also described as a "covenant of peace" (Isa. 54:10; Ezek. 34:25; 37:26) and an "everlasting covenant" (ESV: Isa. 55:3; 61:8; Jer. 32:40; 50:5; Ezek. 16:60; 37:26). It is clear from Isaiah 52:13–53:12 that the return from exile is based on the sacrifice of the servant of the Lord, who suffers death for the sake of his people's sins. Since Jesus, the servant of the Lord, was crucified and risen, the new covenant (i.e., the gift of the Spirit) became a reality on Pentecost. We see at Jesus's baptism that he was anointed with the Spirit (Luke 3:21–22), and now at Pentecost he pours out the Spirit on those who belong to him.

When the disciples asked whether Israel would be restored, Jesus directed them to their responsibility to witness, beginning in Jerusalem and even to the ends of the earth, instructing them that it wasn't theirs to know the precise time of restoration. What Jesus meant by Israel's restoration is debated. Some think the disciples asked the wrong question, but Jesus doesn't criticize the notion that Israel would be restored. He corrects the idea that the time of the restoration can be calculated. Others believe that there will be a literal restoration of the kingdom to ethnic Israel, and so there will be a future kingdom in the millennium, where Jesus will reign over the earth from Jerusalem along with Jewish believers.

When we examine the text more closely, however, we see that the restoration of true Israel includes gentile believers in Christ. The kingdom includes Jewish believers, of course, and the Twelve (see below) constitute the foundation and nucleus of restored Israel. The phrase "the end of the earth" (*eschatou tēs gēs*, 1:8) provides the clue to what is going on. The "end of the earth" (ESV) represents the areas where gentiles live, denoting those who live outside Israel and the land of promise (Deut. 28:49; Isa. 8:9; 48:20; 62:11; Jer. 6:22; 16:19; 25:31). Jesus promised that the disciples would witness to "the end of the earth" (Acts 1:8), and this means that gentiles would be folded into the people of God. Isaiah invites all nations to come and to believe: "Turn to me and be saved, all the ends of the earth" (Isa. 45:22). Isaiah also prophesies that the servant of the Lord, who is Jesus Christ, will restore more than Israel: "It is not enough for you to be my servant raising up the tribes of Jacob and restoring the protected ones of Israel. I will also make you a light for the nations, to be my salvation to the ends of the earth" (Isa. 49:6). Here we have a hint that the restored Israel includes gentiles. The timing of restoration is not the only surprise, for the nature of restored Israel also confounds expectations. This reading is confirmed in Acts 13:47, which quotes Isaiah 49:6. The Jews in Pisidian Antioch largely rejected the gospel proclaimed by Paul and Barnabas, and so they turned to the gentiles so that the light of salvation shines "to the end of the earth." We see, then, that the church of Jesus Christ, composed of both Jews and gentiles, constitutes the restored Israel.

Rounding out Acts 1 are three other themes, which we will look at briefly. First, before the Spirit is given, Jesus must be exalted, and hence we have the account of the ascension (1:9–11). For forty days after the resurrection, Jesus appeared to the disciples at various times. During those forty days they never knew when Jesus would suddenly be in their presence. The ascension clarifies that the period of appearances had ended; they would not see Jesus again until the kingdom came in its fullness. Most importantly, however, the Spirit would not be poured out, the new era would not be inaugurated, until Jesus ascended and ruled on high. We see this clearly in Acts 2:33: "Since [Jesus] has been exalted to the right hand of God and has received from the Father the promised Holy Spirit, he has poured out what you both see and hear." Since the Spirit is only given after Jesus has been crucified and has risen, the Spirit glorifies Jesus in his ministry, death, and resurrection.

The second theme is the prayer of the disciples (1:12–14). The 120 disciples gathered for prayer before the coming of the Spirit. The waiting for the Spirit in Jerusalem wasn't passive (1:4; Luke 24:49), for the disciples spent the time in prayer. Often in Luke-Acts the Spirit comes when there is prayer. Jesus was praying when the Spirit came down on him like a dove (Luke 3:21–22). After the disciples were threatened for proclaiming Jesus and the resurrection, they prayed together and "were all filled with the Holy Spirit" (Acts 4:31). Similarly, Peter and John prayed that the Samaritans would receive the Spirit (8:14–15). The account where Cornelius and his friends receive the Spirit is attributed in part to the prayers of Cornelius (10:2, 4, 30, 31). Here we see the confluence of the Spirit, the coming of the kingdom, and prayer.

Third, in 1:15–26 we see that the apostles selected the twelfth apostle before Pentecost. In popular circles it is often said that a mistake was made here and that the apostles should have waited for the selection of Paul. This reading is certainly wrong. Luke gives no indication that he believed the apostles went awry. On the contrary, he emphasizes that Scripture was fulfilled, since the betrayal of Judas was foretold by the Holy Spirit (1:16). Here Luke likely sees a fulfillment of Psalm 41:9, which states that one of David's closest friends turned against him. The treachery of David's friend isn't, strictly speaking, a prophecy, since it records an incident in David's life. Indeed, in the psalm David confesses his own sin (41:4). What we have here is typology, but it isn't arbitrary, for the text needs to be interpreted along the lines of the Lord's covenants with his people. The Lord made a covenant with David, promising that his dynasty would endure forever and that a descendant of David would reign on the throne (e.g., 2 Sam. 7; 1 Chron. 17; Pss. 2; 89; 132). David's life, then, functioned as a prophetic pattern and anticipation for the life of Jesus Christ. Just as David suffered before he gained the throne, so did Jesus. Just as David was abandoned by a close friend, so too was Jesus. Typology is not merely retrospective, as if the parallels are only present after the fact; the correspondences and patterns were planned by God from the beginning, and in this sense typology is prophetic, even though as readers we may only see the parallels retrospectively. Another feature of typology is escalation, which means that the fulfillment is greater than the type. The fulfillment outstrips the type; this is evident in the case of OT sacrifices, for the sacrifice of Jesus is clearly greater than the sacrifice of animals. According to Psalm 41, David was a sinner, but Jesus is greater than David, and thus he was without sin. He is the perfect messianic king.

Two OT psalms are quoted in 1:20, which function quite similarly (69:25; 109:8). Both psalms recount experiences in the life of David. Psalm 69 describes a time of great crisis in David's life, where his life was in danger, and he faced enemies who hated him for no reason. David pleaded for the Lord to deliver him and prayed that the Lord would judge his enemies for mistreating him. In 69:25 David prayed that his enemies would be destroyed and have no place to live, and Peter sees this prayer as fulfilled in Judas being removed from apostolic ministry and in his death (Acts 1:18–20). Clearly, Davidic typology is at work since the psalm is not an overt prophecy, and we see again that David in the psalm confesses his sins (Ps. 69:5). The hatred and opposition to king David points typologically to Judas's opposition to and betrayal of Jesus the Messiah. We again have an instance of escalation, and interestingly many NT writers see Psalm 69 as being ultimately fulfilled in the life and death of Jesus (e.g., Ps. 69:4 in John 15:25; Ps. 69:9 in John 2:17 and Rom. 15:3; Ps. 69:22 in Matt. 27:34, 48; Mark 15:23, 36; Luke 23:36; and John 19:29; Ps. 69:23–24 in Rom. 11:9–10).

Psalm 109 is similar in many respects to Psalm 69. David was once again beset by enemies, and there was no reason for their hatred of him. David prays that the Lord will show his faithfulness to him and have mercy on him despite the fierce opposition against him. In the midst of the psalm, David prays against his adversary, asking God to judge him (Ps. 109:6–20). The appropriation of the psalm in Acts 1 shows that we can't dismiss the prayer as if it reflected a bad attitude. David prays for God's righteousness to be manifested in the world by repaying the wicked what they deserve (Ps. 109:20). As David prays against his enemy, one of the petitions is, "Let another take over his position" (Ps. 109:8; Acts 1:20). Again, this verse isn't a prophecy but a prayer, and it is about David's enemy, not Jesus's adversary. Still, Peter takes up what is said in the psalm and applies it typologically to Judas. What David prayed is fulfilled supremely in the relationship between Jesus and Judas.

We have seen, then, that Luke portrays the greatest treachery in the world (betraying Jesus) as a fulfillment of Scripture, and Scripture is also fulfilled in Judas losing his apostolic rank and another filling it. Did the apostles fall short of the ideal in casting lots to choose the twelfth apostle, or is it the case that after the Spirit is given, casting lots is shown to be inferior? Neither of these conclusions convinces. Casting lots had a respectable pedigree from the OT (e.g., Josh. 18:6, 8, 10; 1 Chron. 24:31; 25:8; Neh. 11:1). Where the lot falls reflects the Lord's will (Prov. 16:33) since there is ultimately no random event in the universe. Nor does Luke indicate that such an activity is otiose now that the Spirit has come, as if those who have the Spirit are always certain of God's will. Luke isn't attempting to provide a pattern for discerning God's will in the future; he indicates that the church could not discern which of the two to choose as an apostle, and thus the believers trusted God to choose which of the two should serve in the apostolic office. The apostles did the right thing in choosing Matthias, and the number twelve is significant before Pentecost since the twelve apostles represent the nucleus of restored Israel. Just as the twelve tribes represented Israel under the old covenant, the twelve apostles are the nucleus of the restored Israel—the Israel to whom the kingdom will be restored (Acts 1:6).

Expansion in Jerusalem (2:1–6:7)

Pentecost (2:1–41)

One of the most significant events in Christian history occurred on the first Pentecost after Jesus's resurrection. The Holy Spirit was poured out on the 120 believers who were gathered, and they spoke in tongues. The gift of the Spirit was accompanied by "a violent rushing wind from heaven" (2:2), and "tongues like flames of fire . . . separated and rested on each one of them" (2:3). Pentecost, which celebrated the grain harvest, was also connected with the giving of the law on Mount Sinai in Jewish tradition. Thus, the giving of the Spirit on this occasion suggests that the new covenant (Jer. 31:31–34; Ezek. 36:26–27) had arrived, and the era in which God's people lived under the Mosaic covenant and law had come to an end. The phenomena accompanying the gift of the Spirit confirm this reading since they echo what happened at Sinai. The rushing of the wind may be analogous to "the very loud trumpet sound" (Exod. 19:16) on Mount Sinai. The tongues of fire remind us of the "thunder and lightning" on Sinai (Exod. 19:16), and often in Scripture fire denotes God's presence (e.g., Gen. 15:17; Exod. 3:2; 13:21–22; 14:20, 24; Ps. 104:4; Isa. 5:24). The connections to Sinai point to the inauguration of the new covenant, to the gift of the Spirit, promised so often in the OT (Isa. 32:15; 44:3; Ezek. 36:26–27; Joel 2:28–29).

What is the significance of speaking in other tongues, which clearly in Acts 2 is speaking in foreign languages? It is connected with the Jews and proselytes who were visiting Jerusalem from a wide array of regions. We likely have here a reversal of the tower of Babel (Gen. 11:1–9). At Babel the tongues of human beings were confused because of human sin. At Pentecost people who spoke different languages understood one another when the Spirit descended, and thus we have here an anticipation of the new creation, where the separation of peoples due to their inability to understand one another has ended.

Proclaiming the Gospel in Jerusalem (2:1–6:7)

Since Jesus as the crucified one was raised from the dead and reigns at God's right hand, he pours out his Spirit on his disciples. Two long speeches are given by Peter in Jerusalem (Acts 2:14–40; 3:12–26) and two shorter ones (4:8–12; 5:29–32). I have divided the speeches into seven themes: (1) prophecy fulfilled in (2) Jesus's ministry; (3) his death; (4) his resurrection; (5) his ascension; and (6) the gift of the Spirit. Therefore, (7) people should repent. First, the days of fulfillment have arrived in the ministry, death, resurrection, and ascension of Jesus Christ, and such prophecy is fulfilled in the gift of the Spirit as well. The pouring out of the Spirit fulfills what Joel wrote (Acts 2:16–21; Joel 2:28–32). The culmination of redemptive history, the fulfillment of all that Israel longed for, has come in Jesus Christ: "all the prophets . . . have foretold . . . these days" (Acts 3:24). Moses prophesied that a prophet like him would arise to whom the people must listen (Deut. 18:15), and Jesus is the prophet like Moses (Acts 3:21–22). The covenant made to Abraham, pledging blessings for all peoples everywhere (Gen. 12:3), has been realized in Jesus Christ (Acts 3:25). This is Luke's way of saying that the eschatological kingdom has come, the covenants are fulfilled, the new creation has dawned, the new exodus has occurred, and the new and final David sits on his throne.

Second, prophecy is fulfilled in the ministry of Jesus. We actually find only one verse devoted to Jesus's ministry: "This Jesus of Nazareth was a man attested to you by God with miracles, wonders, and signs that God did among you through him, just as you yourselves know" (2:22). We recognize that Luke has abbreviated Peter's speech (2:14–36); there was no need to expand upon Jesus's ministry since Theophilus could fill in the details from the Gospel of Luke. The miracles and signs Jesus did were sufficient to accredit him as the Messiah. Here we can pick up a similarly abbreviated account, where in the speech to Cornelius and his friends, Peter summarizes Jesus's ministry by reminding them "how God anointed Jesus of Nazareth with the Holy Spirit and with power, and how he went about doing good and healing all who were under the tyranny of the devil, because God was with him" (Acts 10:38). Jesus was the Spirit-anointed Messiah, and his ministry is summarized in terms of doing good and healing.

Third, God was also working out his purposes in Jesus's death. Jesus's death was no accident but fulfilled God's predestined plan (2:23; cf. 4:27–28) in that it fulfilled prophecy (3:18). As readers we would love to see which prophecies were fulfilled according to Peter. Certainly, Peter's sermons were much longer than the abbreviated (but accurate) synopses we have here, and thus for the listeners Peter must have expounded the prophecies he had in mind. We have a clue in 3:26, which identifies Jesus as God's "servant" (see also 3:13; 4:27–28). Luke doesn't explain precisely why Jesus was put to death, but the reference to the servant almost certainly refers to Isaiah 52:13–53:12. It is quite clear in Isaiah that the servant died for the sake of his people and in place of his people, to atone for their sins. Luke provides other hints that Jesus's death was atoning when he calls upon them to repent "for the forgiveness of your sins" (2:38; cf. also 5:30–31), which is presumably based on Jesus's death. Similarly, Jesus's suffering and the wiping away of sins are closely tied together in 3:18–19. Peter claims that Jesus's name is the only means of salvation, and this salvation is tied to his death and resurrection (4:10–12).

Fourth, the Petrine speeches especially emphasize the resurrection (2:24–32; 3:15, 22, 26; 4:10; 5:30), which is scarcely surprising since the claim that Jesus was the Messiah was verified by his resurrection. The resurrection represented God's vindication of Jesus, for governing leaders among both Jews and gentiles declared that Jesus was guilty and thus put him to death for being a messianic pretender (2:23; 4:27–28). Naturally, a particular responsibility for putting Jesus to death was assigned to Jewish leaders since Jesus fulfilled their Scriptures and prophetic hopes (2:36; 3:13–15; 4:10; 5:30). The resurrection of

Jesus constituted a decisive rejection of the verdict that Jesus was guilty and instead declared that Jesus was God's anointed one and the cornerstone of God's new temple, the restored Israel (4:11; Ps. 118:22; Isa. 28:16), and thus he is the only hope for salvation (Acts 4:12; 5:31). Mercifully, the resurrection of Jesus wasn't followed by immediate judgment for those who condemned him, but forgiveness was offered to those who turned from evil (3:26).

The language of 3:13 is particularly interesting, for there we read that God "glorified his servant Jesus." The servant, as noted earlier, takes us back into the orbit of the suffering servant of Isaiah 52:13–53:12. The servant died for the sake of and in the place of his people (53:4–6, 10, 12), but his own people rejected and despised him (53:3) and did not believe in him (53:1). They actually thought that God was punishing him (53:4). The glorification of Jesus (i.e., his resurrection), however, represents his vindication. The same verb "glorify" (*doxazō*) occurs in Acts 3:13 and Isaiah 52:13. The servant will be "lifted up and glorified exceedingly" (my translation of the LXX). Jesus's death did not end in humiliation but was the pathway to his glorification.

The longest explanation of Jesus's resurrection comes in the first speech on the day of Pentecost (Acts 2:24–32), where Peter quotes Psalm 16:8–11 to support the claim that Jesus is risen from the dead. He also emphasizes that he and others were witnesses to the resurrection (Acts 2:32); what the Scriptures prophesied is verified in the empirical world. The reference to Psalm 16:8–11 in support of Jesus's resurrection is fascinating because the psalm clearly records an event in David's life. In the context of the psalm, David asked the Lord to preserve his life and is full of praise because the Lord answered his prayers. The psalm doesn't seem to be a prophecy about the coming Messiah. We see here what was noted earlier. Psalms about David are read typologically in light of the Davidic covenant and the promise that an heir of David would reign forever. Peter specifically notes David's prophetic status and his realization that an heir would reign on his throne (Acts 2:30). David's prophetic status doesn't mean that he was conscious in Psalm 16 that he was writing about the Messiah. The point is that psalms about David function prophetically, and this is particularly true typologically. We also see another example of escalation in typology, for David was preserved from dying on the occasion in which the psalm was written, but Jesus was raised from the dead. Hence, the wording of the psalm particularly fits Jesus since he did not experience corruption in the grave (Acts 2:31).

Fifth, Jesus's resurrection signified his vindication, and his vindication is a permanent reality since he reigns as the ascended Lord. He "has been exalted to the right hand of God" (2:33), and as the exalted one he poured out the Holy Spirit. Peter cites one of the most famous psalms in the NT, Psalm 110, to support Jesus's exaltation. Jesus sits at God's right hand as Lord until his enemies are placed under his feet (Acts 2:34–35). God has "made this Jesus . . . Lord and Messiah" (2:36). We don't have adoptionistic Christology here, the idea that Jesus only became Lord and Messiah after his death. Instead, the point is that Jesus now reigns at God's right hand as Lord and Messiah, and such a reign only began after his resurrection. Indeed, Jesus's glorification (3:13), noted earlier, can't be separated from his ascension and exaltation. The servant "will be raised and lifted up and greatly exalted" (Isa. 52:13). Jesus's exaltation is also conveyed in his being identified as the cornerstone (4:11). Or, we read, "God exalted this man to his right hand as ruler and Savior" (5:31). The promise of the Davidic covenant that an heir would rule forever (2 Sam. 7:12–16; Ps. 89:29–37) is fulfilled by Jesus Christ, but the way the fulfillment came to pass was unexpected in that Jesus reigns now in heaven, at the right hand of the Father as the exalted Lord.

Sixth, as the crucified, risen, and exalted Lord, Jesus poured out the Spirit on his people (Acts 2:33). The baptism of the Spirit (1:5), which became a reality in the Pentecostal outpouring of the Spirit, fulfilled the promise of the book of Joel (2:16–21; Joel 2:28–32; cf. Acts 5:32). Similarly, "the times of refreshing" in Acts 3:20 (ESV) is probably another way of referring to the Spirit. Those who repent and are forgiven receive the Spirit in 2:38, and similarly those who repent and are forgiven experience refreshment in 3:19–20; this refreshment is the gift of the Spirit. As noted earlier, the Pentecostal gift of the Spirit represented the fulfillment of kingdom and covenant promises.

Finally, the hearers were summoned to respond. They must "repent and be baptized" to receive forgiveness of sins (2:38). Similarly, they are called upon to "repent and turn back" for their sins to be erased (3:19; cf. also 3:26). We see again in 5:31 that repentance and forgiveness of sins are linked, and the Spirit is given to those who are obedient (5:32). Those who want to be members of restored Israel must acknowledge their sins and turn from them.

The Solidarity of Life in the Early Church (2:42–46; 4:32–5:11; 6:1–6)

Another notable feature of life in the early church was its solidarity: love characterized the community. We see four elements of community life in 2:42. First, the church was devoted to the teaching of the apostles, and that teaching is probably summarized for us in the Petrine speeches. Corporately, they listened to and obeyed apostolic teaching. Second, believers were committed to fellowship with one another, which means that the church showed concern and commitment to one another. This fellowship is expanded upon in 2:44–46 and 4:32–37. One of the signs of such fellowship was that "all the believers were together" (2:44). Love between Christians manifested itself in that they spent time together. They met together daily in the temple and shared food together (2:46). Remarkably, they sacrificed for one another, even selling "possessions and property" (2:45) to assist those who were in need (2:44–45; 4:32–37). Such sharing was not mandatory or enforced but was entirely voluntary, testifying to the generosity that animated the early church.

Third, believers also broke bread together (2:42). The "breaking of bread" could refer to an ordinary meal (27:35), but it also denoted the sharing of the Lord's Supper (Luke 22:19; 24:30; Acts 2:42, 46; 20:7, 11). In this latter instance, the sharing of a meal and the Lord's Supper both took place on the same occasion. The meal that believers frequently celebrated together reminded them regularly of the death of Jesus on their behalf, and his death was the basis for their forgiveness of sins and their life together as Christians. Fourth, the believers were also devoted "to prayer" (2:42). The prayers were likely both spontaneous and memorized. Prayer signified the community's dependence upon God for maintaining their life together in truth and love.

Life in the community wasn't without its strains, and Luke gives two indications that it wasn't perfect. First, the sin of Ananias and Sapphira is recorded (5:1–11). The sin of Ananias and Sapphira was not that they failed to donate all their money, for Peter makes it clear that they were not required to sell their property, and after they sold it, there was no expectation that they would give all the proceeds to the church (5:4). Their sin, then, was lying; they pretended to give all the proceeds of the land sold to the church (5:1–3, 8–9). Their death symbolizes divine judgment upon blatant and intended hypocrisy in the church. Certainly, Luke isn't teaching that death invariably follows in such situations. At the inauguration of the new covenant, the Lord reveals his standards for the community. The sin of Ananias and Sapphira echoes the sin of Achan in the OT (Josh. 7), for Achan also sinned deceitfully and deliberately when Israel sacked Jericho and first entered the land of promise, and thus Achan was stoned and Israel was cleansed of evil. So too, at the inauguration of the new covenant we see an example of the Lord's response to blatant sin in the community. It is an example of escalation of judgment in the new age since Ananias and Sapphira sinned against the Spirit granted in the new covenant.

The other account has to do with the Hellenistic widows in Jerusalem who were being discriminated against in Jerusalem (Acts 6:1–6). The Hellenistic Jews spoke Greek, while the "Hebraic Jews" spoke Aramaic, the native language. The Hebraic widows were apparently receiving necessary food, but Hellenistic widows were overlooked. We see here that the early church was not free of the pettiness, prejudice, and cultural discrimination that has marked the church throughout the centuries. Luke probably includes the account to indicate how the church expended energy to resolve the problem. As the church continued to grow, new problems inevitably emerged. The apostles delegated the matter to others so that they could continue to concentrate on teaching and prayer. At the same time, it is remarkable that the seven appointed to care for the problem all have Greek names, which suggests that they were all diaspora Jews. Some of them (like Stephen and Philip) were probably bilingual, but the church appointed those from a Hellenistic background to avoid any sense of favoritism or discrimination. The story of the Hellenistic widows signifies how important it is to maintain the love of the community.

Suffering and Signs (4:1–31; 5:12–42)

It is also notable that the early church was marked by suffering and by signs and wonders. The apostles were arrested (4:1–3), questioned (4:5–7), and threatened (4:16–21) by the religious authorities. On a second occasion their lives were endangered, and they were beaten by the authorities (5:17–42), though they providentially escaped with their lives because of the counsel of Gamaliel. It is instructive to juxtapose signs and wonders and suffering, for those who believe in the former might think that they would be spared from the latter, but such was not the case in the early church. When the apostles were threatened by the authorities, they prayed that they would continue to boldly proclaim the gospel of Jesus Christ crucified and risen, and that God would heal and do signs and wonders through them (4:29–30). The remarkable signs and wonders and healings and exorcisms (5:12–16) accredited the message spoken by the apostles and drew people to hear God's word. The phrase "signs and wonders" echoes the exodus, where the Lord performed many "signs and wonders" in freeing Israel from Egypt (Exod. 7:3; Deut. 4:34; 6:22; 7:19; 26:8; 29:3; 34:11; Neh. 9:10; Pss. 78:43; 105:27; 135:9; Jer. 32:20–21). Still, Israel did not fully believe in the signs and wonders because of their hard hearts (Deut. 29:3–4). Just as the exodus was attested by the signs and wonders, so too the new exodus, accomplished by the death and resurrection of Jesus, was verified by signs and wonders. Both the suffering and the signs and wonders accredited the gospel proclaimed by the apostles.

Expansion in Israel (6:8–9:31)

Stephen's Speech (7:1–60)

I noted earlier how Stephen's speech became the catalyst for propelling the gospel outside of Jerusalem into Judea, Galilee, and Samaria (Acts 9:31).

Those "scattered" outside the land preached the word in various locales. We want to survey here the main themes of Stephen's speech, which may have been spoken around AD 31–32. Stephen was probably a diaspora Jew who faced opposition from Jews who came from synagogues in the diaspora (6:9). They leveled two charges against Stephen. First, they accused him of criticizing the Mosaic law (6:11, 13–14); second, they charged him with teaching that the temple was unnecessary and would be destroyed (6:11, 13–14). The law and the temple were two of the pillars of Judaism, and thus the charges were very serious.

At first glance, it might seem as though Stephen didn't answer the accusations. He seems to lapse into telling Bible stories that have nothing to do with the complaints lodged against him, but a closer look reveals that his speech represents a profound response to the charges. Two themes in the speech need to be explored. First, God has worked profoundly in Israel's history even when Israel was outside the land and there was no temple. For instance, Abraham had no inheritance at all in the land, "not even a foot of ground" (7:5), and yet Abraham was the father of the Jewish people. Certainly, there was the promise that Israel would eventually worship the Lord in the temple (7:7), but that was after four hundred years in Egypt (7:6). We see a similar theme in the life of Joseph. God was with him, even though he spent his life in Egypt—outside the land of promise. Indeed, God was with the people of Israel during their Egyptian sojourn, and we can conclude from this that God works in surprising ways. Along the same lines, the person whom God used to free people from Egypt, Moses, was "educated in all the wisdom of the Egyptians" (7:22). We could say that he attended a pagan university! And God further prepared him for leadership during the forty years he lived in the desert (7:29–30). The holy place, therefore, is wherever God meets his people, and sacred space isn't limited to the temple. As God was with Joseph in Egypt, so the holy place where Moses encountered the Holy One of Israel was in the Sinai wilderness, the fiery bush (7:30–34).

Furthermore, God did not even mandate from the outset that a temple should be built. Israel was instructed to build a moveable tabernacle, and with that moveable shrine they conquered the land of promise (7:44–45). The temple wasn't always God's mode of dwelling with his people, for it was only established in the days of David and Solomon (7:46–47). And Isaiah reminded the people (Isa. 66:1) that no temple can contain God since he transcends any building (Acts 7:48–49). Here we have a hint and a suggestion that a new temple was coming, a greater temple than the one in Jerusalem. Throughout his speech Stephen points to progressive revelation. God remains the same, but he deals with his people in different ways and with various covenants.

One segment of salvation history (when God gave the temple) must not be reified and treated as if it is the end point and culmination of God's plan.

The second theme uncovers a pattern in Israel's history where the people rejected God's messengers. For instance, Joseph was God's agent to preserve Israel from perishing during the Egyptian famine, but his brothers did not recognize that he was appointed by God and instead rejected him and sold him into slavery, though, we are told, the actions of the brothers were the means by which God accomplished his purposes (Gen. 45:4–7; 50:19–21). The theme is expanded upon in the case of Moses. The religious leaders of Stephen's day venerated Moses, but it was quite different when Moses was alive. The Israelite man who rejected Moses's leadership represented the typical response to his guidance (Exod. 2:13–14; Acts 7:26–28, 35). The law that Israel claimed to cherish was immediately rejected when it was given to Israel, for Israel broke the covenant in a dramatic fashion when the ink on the covenant (so to speak) was scarcely dry. Israel immediately flouted God's law by fashioning and worshiping the golden calf (Exod. 32; Acts 7:38–41). The wilderness generation and the history of Israel testified that Israel was often devoted to other gods and other temples. Since Israel flagrantly violated the covenant, the people were sent into exile (7:42–43).

Stephen's point, of course, is that the Israel of his day continued the pattern of their ancestors. The people claimed that they venerated Moses, but they were actually just like the people of Moses's day who ended up rejecting Moses. The same thing was happening, Stephen claims, with Jesus, for Jesus was the prophet Moses predicted would come (7:37). Stephen's hearers suffered from the same stubbornness and resistance to the Holy Spirit that had marked Israel's history (7:51). Their charge that Stephen didn't observe the law was ridiculous, for they, like their ancestors, killed and persecuted God's messengers (supremely Jesus!) and thus did not observe the law themselves.

Reading the law rightly means reading it in terms of redemptive history; it means reading it in terms of the whole story line. And those who failed to believe in Jesus revealed that they didn't understand how the temple pointed to something greater: Jesus as the true and final temple. Their claim to keep the law was contradicted by their refusal to believe in the one whom the law promised would come.

Stephen's speech enraged the people and ended up getting him killed (7:54–8:4). Before Stephen was stoned, he said, "Look, I see the heavens opened and the Son of Man standing at the right hand of God!" (7:56). The opening of the heavens symbolizes revelation from God (Isa. 64:1; Ezek. 1:1; Mark 1:10; Luke 3:21; John 1:51; Acts 10:11; Rev. 4:1; 11:19; 19:11). What Stephen saw was most astonishing since he saw Jesus as the Son of Man standing at God's right hand. Here we find the only instance in Acts where Jesus is identified as the Son of Man, though the title is quite common in the Gospels. The reference to the Son of Man alludes to Daniel 7:13–14, where the Son of Man is ushered into God's presence and receives a kingdom in which all people serve him. Stephen confessed that Jesus is the Son of Man (cf. Acts 7:59), the king of Israel and of the world. What is curious is that the Son of Man stands, instead of being seated, since elsewhere in the Gospels he is portrayed as sitting at God's right hand (Matt. 19:28; 25:31; 26:64; Mark 14:62; Luke 22:69), and elsewhere Jesus is depicted as one who sits and reigns (Matt. 20:21, 23; 22:44; Mark 10:37, 40; 12:36; Luke 20:42; Acts 2:34). Nowhere else do we read that he stands at God's right hand. Scholars have given various explanations for why Jesus was standing. Probably it indicates a vindication of Stephen's claims: Jesus stands as Stephen's advocate before the throne. Stephen's speech culminates, then, with a glorious vision of Jesus as the Son of Man. The promises of salvation and blessing have been fulfilled in Jesus Christ. The claims made by Stephen lead to his death; in his forgiveness of those who murdered him, Stephen reflects Jesus Christ, who forgave those who crucified him (Luke 23:34). Yet the martyrdom of Stephen didn't squelch the proclamation of the gospel, for now those scattered because of persecution preach the word outside Jerusalem (Acts 8:4).

Philip's Encounters in Samaria and with the Ethiopian Eunuch (8:4–40)

Chapter 8 records Philip's preaching the gospel in Samaria and his encounter with the Ethiopian eunuch (perhaps AD 31–32). The Philip in question is not Philip the apostle, but the Philip who was part of the seven appointed to help with the Hellenistic widows (6:5). We know it wasn't the apostle Philip, for the apostles had not left Jerusalem (8:1). Philip's preaching in Samaria had a tremendous effect: many believed as he proclaimed the gospel, which was attested by signs (8:5–8). The people were previously attracted to Simon the magician, but they changed their loyalties when Philip preached the gospel.

Curiously, even though the Samaritans believed and were baptized, they did not receive the Spirit when they believed (8:12, 15–16). There is no other instance in the NT where people believed in Jesus and did not receive the Spirit immediately, and so what we see here is not a pattern or model. Instead, the regular pattern is that those who believe receive the Holy Spirit upon believing (2:38). What stands out is that the Samaritans only received the Spirit later, when the apostles Peter and John laid hands on them (8:17). The story doesn't teach that laying on of hands is necessary to receive the Spirit, since others (Cornelius and his friends) received the Spirit without the laying on of hands (cf. 10:44–48). The question that must be asked is this: why is it the case that the Spirit could only be dispensed through apostles and not through Philip the evangelist? Probably because there was a cultural breach between the Jews and the Samaritans. The Samaritans had a long history in which they were separated from the Jews, worshiping, for example, on Mount Gerizim instead of in Jerusalem, and prizing the Pentateuch instead of the entirety of the OT. John Hyrcanus destroyed their temple on Mount Gerizim during his reign (134–104 BC). The tension between the Jews and the Samaritans is evident also in the NT (Luke 9:51–56; 10:33; 17:16; John 4:9; 8:48; cf. Acts 1:8; 9:31).

Since the Spirit is always given when people believe, the Lukan narrative would naturally provoke questions in the minds of readers, since otherwise it is unheard of for people to believe and not receive the Spirit! How can such a phenomenon be explained? The best answer is that God withheld the Spirit on this occasion to prevent a breach between the Jews and Samaritans, only granting the Spirit through the hands of the apostles so that the Samaritan church would not split off from Jerusalem. The church was united under the authority of the apostles.

Though there is no compelling evidence that the faith of the Samaritans was inauthentic, Simon's faith is shown to be deficient. Simon was astonished by "the signs and great miracles" performed by Philip (Acts 8:13). When he "saw that the Spirit was given" (probably evidenced by speaking in tongues; 8:18), he offered Peter and John money so that he could also have the power to dispense the Spirit. The words Peter used demonstrate that Simon did not belong to God, for the words "part" and "lot" (*meris oude klēros*) are used in the OT to denote possession of an inheritance (e.g., Deut. 10:9 LXX), which signifies that one has a place in the land and people of Israel. Typologically, the land of the OT points to the final inheritance of believers in the NT (e.g., Rom. 4:13). Such a reading is confirmed since Peter called upon Simon to "repent" (Acts 8:22). Furthermore, Peter charged Simon with being "poisoned by bitterness" and "bound by wickedness" (8:23). The words "poisoned by bitterness" reach back to Deuteronomy 29:18, which is a striking parallel. "Be sure there is no man, woman, clan, or tribe among you today whose heart turns away from the LORD our God to go and worship the gods of those nations. Be sure there is no root among you bearing poisonous and bitter fruit." It is clear that the person with a poisoned root is turning from the true God to false gods (see also Deut. 13:2); he is committing apostasy. Simon must truly repent to belong to the people of God.

What is the significance of the conversion of the Samaritans? Since Samaria was considered to be part of Israel and was part of the northern kingdom, the conversion of Samaria to Christ and its submission to the church in Jerusalem constitutes a fulfillment of the prophecy in Ezekiel 37. Ezekiel prophesied that there would come a day when "the stick of Ephraim" and "the stick of Judah" would become "a single stick" (37:15–28). The unification of Samaria and Judea/Galilee constitutes the fulfillment of the promise in Ezekiel, and the "one king" who will "rule over all of them" is Jesus (37:22), since they are cleansed from their sins through Jesus (37:23). "My servant David will be king over them, and there will be one shepherd for all of them" (37:24). In Acts, the servant David is Jesus Christ (Acts 3:13, 26; 4:27, 30), and "the dwelling place" is the promised Spirit (Ezek. 37:27).

The story of the Ethiopian eunuch (Acts 8:26–40) could be understood as the conversion of the first gentile, but more likely the eunuch was considered to be a proselyte (8:27), and thus Cornelius and his friends are set forth as the first gentile converts. It isn't certain if the eunuch was literally castrated or if he was simply a court official. In any case, the conversion of the eunuch was probably seen as the fulfillment of Isaiah 56:3, where eunuchs are included in the kingdom, indicating the arrival of the eschaton since he would be excluded from the Lord's assembly if he was castrated (Deut. 23:1). Interestingly, the eunuch was reading Isaiah 53, about the servant of the Lord, and Philip explained that the text was fulfilled in Jesus. The portion he was reading from (53:7–8) doesn't focus on Jesus's substitutionary death but on his innocent suffering. Why is the focus on Jesus's innocent suffering instead of his death for the sake of sinners? Probably because the early Christians had to regularly remind people that the death of Jesus was a miscarriage of justice, that he died as the innocent one. The first question people would ask is how it could be possible for God's anointed one to suffer and to be put to death, and upon reading Isaiah the early Christians found that Jesus's rejection was predicted from the beginning.

Paul's Conversion (9:1–30; 22:1–21; 26:1–32)

Luke recounts the conversion and calling of Saul/Paul three times in the book of Acts (9:1–30; 22:1–21; 26:1–32), and thus his conversion plays a central role in his narrative. Paul's call and ministry are one of the key means by which the gospel is proclaimed to the gentiles, and his conversion probably occurred in the early 30s, perhaps AD 32–33. The details of Paul's conversion are well known and do not need to be rehearsed here. What is striking is the sovereignty of God, for a zealous opponent of the Christian faith suddenly realized that Jesus was the Messiah. Paul could scarcely help being convinced, since Jesus as the risen Lord appeared to him and commissioned him. Paul's conversion represents a transition in Luke's narrative, for Paul was called to bring the gospel to the gentiles and to kings, though he continued to preach to Israel as well (9:15). What is striking in Paul's story is that the persecutor turns into the one persecuted. The Jews in Damascus could not tolerate his preaching about Jesus and were conspiring to kill him (9:19–25). The same story was replicated in Jerusalem, and thus the church sent him off to Tarsus for safekeeping (9:26–30). The rejection among Jews became the pathway for Paul to proclaim the gospel among the gentiles, so that Paul's preaching plays a fundamental role in fulfilling the promise of Abraham in bringing blessing to the ends of the earth (1:8).

Reaching Out to the Gentiles (9:32–12:24)

The Cornelius Story (10:1–11:18)

In the Lukan narrative in Acts, one of the central stories is the conversion of Cornelius and his friends (perhaps AD 37 or 38). We know that the account was very important to Luke because he tells the story twice: the first time the story is told in a more extended fashion (10:1–48), and in the second account, which is abbreviated, Peter defended his actions to critics in Jerusalem (11:1–18). This account is so important because here we find the first entry of gentiles into the people of God. Cornelius was probably a "God-fearer." God-fearers were attracted to the monotheism and moral principles of Judaism but were not proselytes (converts to Judaism), because they were not circumcised. An angel appeared to Cornelius, instructing him to summon Peter to visit him, though Peter was in Joppa, thirty-seven miles south of Caesarea. Meanwhile, when Cornelius's friends were about to find Simon the tanner's house where Peter was staying, Peter fell into a trance, seeing in a vision a great sheet with unclean animals, which he was instructed to kill and eat (10:9–16). The vision puzzled Peter since the law of Moses clearly taught that eating unclean animals was forbidden (Lev. 11:1–44; Deut. 14:3–21). We also learn from Peter's experience that Jesus never ate unclean food with his disciples, since Peter would not have been puzzled if he had often or ever eaten unclean food with Jesus. Peter emphasizes his observance of food laws in the strongest terms: "'No, Lord!' I said. 'For nothing impure or ritually unclean has ever entered my mouth'" (Acts 11:8). Jesus did say that foods entering the mouth can't defile a person (Mark 7:15), but the disciples apparently only understood the import of what Jesus said sometime after the resurrection. They slowly came to the realization that all foods were clean (7:19). The whole matter was puzzling to Peter since the vision was instructing him to violate commands given by God in the OT.

When the men from Cornelius arrived at the house where Peter stayed (and they were instructed where to find Peter by divine revelation), Peter began to comprehend the significance of the vision. The cleanness of the foods related to the cleanness of gentiles. Peter's insight is found in Acts 10:28, "You know it's forbidden for a Jewish man to associate with or visit a foreigner, but God has shown me that I must not call any person impure or unclean." Some Jews would never eat with gentiles (Jub. 22.16), and others may have eaten with gentiles if food was kosher, but most would avoid any contact because of fear of defilement. It was dawning on Peter, however, that purity laws (particularly regulations regarding food) were no longer required for gentiles to belong to the people of God, and thus fellowship with gentiles was permitted for Jewish Christians. Now all human beings in Christ are ritually pure and clean. To put it another way, gentiles did not have to become Jews and observe the Mosaic law to enter the people of God. The barriers that separated Jews and gentiles were coming down. This is not to say that the laws segregating Jews and gentiles in the OT were a mistake from the beginning. The Mosaic covenant and its laws were intended to be in force for a particular period of redemptive history, but now that Christ had come, a new era had arrived. Both Jews and gentiles belonged to God through faith in Jesus Christ.

The account of Peter's speech is abbreviated and summarized (10:34–43). The following themes are noted: (1) God doesn't show favoritism but accepts those from every nation who do what is right and fear him; (2) the message of good news, the message of peace, was sent to Israel first as the people of the promise; (3) Jesus is the Lord of all, both Jews and gentiles. The Christology of this statement is quite remarkable, showing that Jesus shares the same status as God; (4) Jesus was anointed with the Spirit at his baptism, and as a consequence Jesus healed the sick and cast out demons; (5) Peter and others are witnesses of what God did through Jesus, but despite Jesus's goodness, he was hung on a tree. The word "tree" points to Deuteronomy 21:23, suggesting that Jesus was cursed by God for the sake of his people; (6) God raised him from the dead, and many are witnesses of this truth; (7) Peter and others are called upon to proclaim the good news about Jesus and warn people about the coming judgment; (8) Jesus fulfills Scripture, and forgiveness of sins comes through him. Significantly, the speech was interrupted when Peter mentions forgiveness of sins in the name of Jesus Christ (10:43). At that moment something astonishing happened. The Spirit was suddenly poured out on Cornelius and his friends even though Peter did not ask them to repent or to believe (10:44–48). There could be no doubt for Jewish skeptics, as Peter explained in 11:15, that the gentiles had received the Spirit since they spoke in tongues just as the apostles did at Pentecost. Their sudden speaking in tongues certified that Cornelius and his friends had become believers. What happened here was a kind of second Pentecost, one where God had flung open the door of entrance into church for gentiles.

The significance of the vision of foods was now clear. The purity laws that constituted the people of God were no longer required. If the old covenant was marked by ethnic restrictiveness, the new covenant would be characterized by ethnic openness. One did not need to be part of the Jewish people or to follow regulations that segregated Jews from gentiles. It is hard to imagine anything that separates people more than rules that hinder them from sharing meals together. Peter and the Jews in Jerusalem recognized that a divine work had occurred. They all agreed that "God has given repentance resulting in life even to the gentiles" (11:18).

There was plenty of evidence in the OT that gentiles would enter the people of God, though in some texts it looked as if gentiles would still be subordinate to the Jews (Isa. 60:10–14; 61:5–7; Zech. 2:11–12; 8:22–23), while in others it seemed that they would occupy an equal place (Pss. 47:9; 87:4, 6; Isa. 11:10; 19:16–25; 25:6–7; 42:6; 49:6; 55:4–5; 56:6–7). The story of Cornelius and his friends clarifies that gentiles are equal members of the covenant community and equal recipients of the Spirit. God was doing a new thing and fulfilling his promises for a new covenant and a new creation.

Persecution (12:1–24)

The persecution of the church took a new turn with Herod Agrippa I, who ruled over Galilee beginning in AD 39; Idumaca and Judea were added to his reign in AD 41 until his death in AD 44. Probably the Jews in Jerusalem were becoming increasingly hostile toward believers in Christ, and Agrippa aided the cause, for he beheaded James the brother of John (Acts 12:2). When Agrippa saw that it pleased the Jews, he added Peter to the execution list and arrested him. Despite the many Jews becoming Christians, they must have still been a minority since Agrippa's actions were at least in part designed to curry political favor. Peter's miraculous deliverance by an angel stunned even the believers who had gathered to pray for him (12:6–17), and his deliverance demonstrates God's sovereignty; no believer dies before God wills it to happen. At the same time, God's ways are not calculable or easy to discern. Certainly God could have delivered James as well, but in his wisdom and sovereignty he rescued Peter but not James. Sometimes believers are rescued and sometimes they suffer, and advance notice is not given about what will happen to any particular person. The church and individuals are called upon to trust God whether their destiny is suffering or deliverance. The story concludes with God striking Herod dead for his pride, which is a story also told by Josephus (*Ant.* 19.343–346). During this present age the church is persecuted, but God will ultimately judge the persecutors. The account doesn't teach that judgment will necessarily come quickly on the wicked in this life. The Lord doesn't always strike evil rulers dead in their prime. Instead, the historical story should also be read parabolically, which means that those who persecute God's people will eventually and certainly face judgment.

Concentrated Mission to Gentiles (12:25–16:5)

First Missionary Journey (13:1–14:28)

The first planned and designed missionary journey undertaken to reach gentiles for the gospel of Jesus Christ was carried out by Paul and Barnabas (Acts 13–14) and probably occurred in AD 45–47. The Holy Spirit, through a prophecy, called Paul and Barnabas to mission; this call came as they were worshiping and fasting with some other believers (13:2). They visited the island of Cyprus, which was Barnabas's place of birth (4:36), and four cities in South Galatia, including Pisidian Antioch, Iconium, Derbe, and Lystra. Their practice, illustrated in the visit to Pisidian Antioch, was to preach to the Jews first in synagogues but to turn to gentiles if the Jews rejected the message (13:44–50). Remarkably, Paul and Barnabas, on the basis of Isaiah 49:6, are said to be a light to the gentiles as those who bring salvation to the ends of the earth (13:47). Certainly Luke believed that Jesus was *the* servant in Isaiah's prophecy (cf. Luke 4:16–21; 22:37; Acts 8:32–35), the servant of the Lord par excellence. Jesus as the servant of the Lord died for the sins of his people (Isa. 53:4–6, 10–12), and Paul and Barnabas did not atone for the sins of others. We should note that Isaiah explicitly says that the servant is Israel (41:8–9; 43:10; 44:1–2, 21; 45:4; 48:20; 49:3), but a close reading of Isaiah indicates that the servant transcends Israel since the servant also suffers *for* and *in place of* Israel and *restores* Israel (49:5–6; 53:4–6, 12). Jesus as *the* servant of the Lord is the true Israel, and thus all those who belong to Jesus also belong to the true Israel and continue to fulfill Isaiah's prophecy. Since Israel is the servant of the Lord, it follows that those who belong to Jesus are also, in a derivative sense, servants of the Lord, especially those who have a commission to bring the good news to the ends of the earth.

Paul's sermon in the synagogue at Pisidian Antioch (Acts 13:15–41) probably functions as a paradigm of the sermons he typically preached. The sermon has some features in common with Peter's sermon on Pentecost in Acts 2, which shows that the apostles proclaimed a common gospel (cf. 1 Cor. 15:11), though there are differences as well. Paul began by focusing on salvation history: the election of Israel, the deliverance from Egypt, and the appointment of David as king (Acts 13:16–22). What we see here is a covenantal reading of Israel's history, which includes the covenant with Abraham (Gen. 12, 15, 17), the Sinai covenant (Exod. 19–20), and the covenant with David (2 Sam. 7; 1 Chron. 17). The scriptural account isn't merely an isolated series of events but is read as a story, as a story that has meaning and purpose. The story of Israel is an account of how the creator God is faithful to his saving promises. The Davidic covenant is fulfilled with the coming of Jesus as the messianic king (Acts 13:23; cf. 2 Sam. 7:12), and thus Jesus is the climactic fulfillment of the story. John the Baptist's role as a forerunner is also noted (Acts 13:24–25), which means that there was a great royal announcement by the Baptist before the last curtain of God's saving acts was opened.

The death of Jesus fulfilled prophecy; it was God's plan all along, and thus must not be construed as accidental, as if evil people derailed God's purposes. Jesus's innocence is also stressed since some would be inclined to think that he died because of evil that he had done. Indeed, it would be scandalous for the Messiah to be hung on a tree (13:27–29). But the death of Jesus on a tree was God's plan, and Luke implies with the reference to the tree (see Deut. 21:23) that Jesus took the curse upon himself, the curse that sinners deserved. Referring to death by crucifixion as being hung upon a tree was not the way people described crucifixions in the ancient world! The reference to the tree is a deliberate allusion to Deuteronomy 21:23, which says that those hung on a tree are cursed by God. If that is where the story ended, Jesus would indeed be cursed, but Paul went on to say that God vindicated Jesus as the Messiah by his resurrection. The curse, then, was for our sake and for our salvation (cf. Gal. 3:13). The resurrection of Jesus was not a pious myth or wish fulfillment but was attested by eyewitnesses (Acts 13:30–31). The resurrection of Jesus also fulfilled prophecy, and Paul cites Psalm 2:7, Isaiah 55:3, and Psalm 16:10. The proof from prophecy played a major role for early Christians, and we already noted that Peter cited Psalm 16 as well in the defense of the resurrection, and thus the reference to Psalm 16 will not be explored here again.

The citation of Psalm 2 is particularly interesting. In its original context the nations of the world rejected the king whom Yahweh anointed, which was David himself. Nevertheless, Yahweh installed David as his king on Mount Zion (Ps. 2:6). Another way of expressing the same truth is that David had become God's son, and God had become his father through installing him as king (2:7). God had, so to speak, begotten David in installing him and exalting him as king. The promise that all nations would be blessed through Abraham would become a reality through the Davidic king (Gen. 12:3; Ps.

2:8–9). The use of this psalm is again typological since Jesus is the greater David and fulfilled the Davidic covenant. The covenant promises made to David (Isa. 55:3; cited in Acts 13:34) that he would become the "leader and commander for the peoples" (Isa. 55:4) and that the nations would run to the Davidic king in faith and obedience (55:5)—these promises are being fulfilled in Jesus. God has become Jesus's father by raising him from the dead and installing him as king at his right hand in heaven. Paul is not denying that Jesus was the Son of God from all eternity, nor is he denying that he was the Son of God on earth. But in this context, he reflects on when Jesus was *installed* as the risen and reigning king. The promise that Jesus would reign over the nations is being fulfilled as he rules at God's right hand (Ps. 110:1). Hence, the reference to Jesus being begotten here (Acts 13:33–34) does not refer to the incarnation or to Jesus's baptism, but to Jesus's status as the risen and reigning Lord.

As Paul concludes his speech by offering forgiveness of sins, a distinctive and remarkable Pauline theme is introduced (13:38–39): forgiveness of sins and justification are received through faith instead of by observing the Mosaic law. The law of Moses could not and did not accomplish forgiveness but instead revealed the sinfulness of human beings. The hearers are warned not to reject the message of the prophets (Hab. 1:5; Acts 13:40–41). In some ways the warning of Habakkuk 1:5 captures the message of the entire book of Habakkuk. The Lord used Babylon as an instrument to judge Judah because of the latter's sin, and yet in and through the judgment, he saved his people (Hab. 3). Salvation came to Israel on the other side of judgment. Habakkuk warned Israel to be perceptive, to see the Lord's work as he judged and saved his people. Paul saw the judgment and salvation proclaimed in Habakkuk as fulfilled in Jesus Christ, particularly in the cross and resurrection. In other words, the message of Habakkuk typologically anticipates the scandal of the cross (judgment) and vindication at the resurrection. Those who only see the judgment at the cross (and think Jesus was not worthy therefore to be the Messiah) need to read the whole of Habakkuk, for those who were judged were also vindicated. Again we see typological escalation since Jesus suffered judgment as the innocent one, suffering in the place of his people.

Influential Jews stirred people up against Paul and Barnabas during their first journey, and thus they fled from one town to another. The healing of the lame man in Lystra (Acts 14:8–10) is quite striking, for it reminds us of Peter and John healing the lame man in Jerusalem (3:1–10). In the latter case, the healing opened up the door to proclaim the gospel to the Jews in Jerusalem, while the healing of the lame man gave Paul and Barnabas the opportunity to proclaim the good news to gentiles (14:11–18).

We likely also see a pattern in the instructions given to the newly planted churches. Paul and Barnabas revisited the churches they planted in South Galatia on the return trip to Syrian Antioch, encouraging them to persevere and continue in the faith since entrance into the kingdom would come only through many difficulties and sufferings (14:22; cf. 11:23; 13:43). One of the first truths taught to new converts is that they must persevere and continue in the faith. Indeed, the newfound faith of their converts would be tested, which is why Paul and Barnabas prayed and committed the new believers to the Lord since they needed grace for their journey (14:23). Paul and Barnabas also appointed elders in every church (14:23) since the new churches needed leadership to guide them.

Jerusalem Council (15:1–35)

The first missionary journey of Paul and Barnabas brought many gentiles into the church (Acts 13–14). These gentile believers were counted as Christians apart from circumcision. Circumcision was clearly required in the OT for men to be part of the covenant people (Gen. 17:9–14), and those who did not submit to circumcision did not belong to the people of God. During the NT era some gentiles submitted to circumcision and became proselytes (converts) to the Jewish faith, but many gentiles who were attracted to Judaism are best described as God-fearers or as sympathizers with Judaism because they attended synagogue and were attracted by Jewish monotheism and morals but did not undergo circumcision. We can understand from the OT (Gen. 17:9–14) why some Jews, even those who identified with the Christian faith, insisted that circumcision was required for salvation (15:1, 5). A council was held at Jerusalem and included the apostles, elders, and the church in Jerusalem to adjudicate the matter (AD 48). The issue was of great significance, for if circumcision and the remainder of the law of Moses (see 15:5) were required for gentile believers, then the fledgling Christian movement would have remained a Jewish sect, for gentiles would be joining the Jewish people upon conversion.

The speech that tilted the assembly toward the viewpoint of Paul and Barnabas was uttered by Peter, and Luke gives an abbreviated version of Peter's words (15:7–11). Peter recalled the events of Acts 10–11, where Cornelius and his friends were converted. The Jerusalem council took place in AD 48 or 49, and the encounter with Cornelius probably occurred seven to ten years earlier. Peter reminded his hearers that God doesn't distinguish between Jews and gentiles, for he gave Cornelius and his friends, who were gentiles, the Spirit by faith. Imposing the law on the gentiles would lay a yoke on them that even the Jews could not bear. Even the Jewish people, the covenant people of God, could not keep the law sufficiently for salvation. Salvation, then, is through the grace of Christ instead of keeping the law since even the Jews did not keep the law.

James, the brother of Jesus, the James who wrote the epistle by the same name, and the James who played such a decisive role in Galatians 2, had the last word. James by this time had become the de facto leader in Jerusalem since he spent his entire life ministering in Jerusalem, and thus his advice was of massive importance. In contrast to James, Peter did not restrict himself to Jerusalem but ministered among both Jews and gentiles (cf. Gal. 2:11–14). James was later stoned to death in Jerusalem for his devotion to Christ at the behest of the high priest Ananus in AD 62 (Josephus, *Ant.* 20.9). Since James had such a strong influence in Jerusalem, his judgment on the controversy played a decisive role. He began by registering his agreement with Peter (Acts 15:14). More importantly, he argued that the Scriptures—the prophets—point in the same direction that Peter supported (15:15–18).

James cited Amos 9:11–12, but the prophecy from Amos is conflated with and read along with "the words of the prophets" (Acts 15:15). What James said, then, should not be restricted to the words of Amos alone. Amos looked forward to the day, after the judgment fell on Israel, when "the fallen shelter of David" would be rebuilt (9:11), which probably refers to the rebuilding of the temple and perhaps also to the restoration of Jerusalem. As a result Israel would "possess the remnant of Edom and all the nations that bear my name" (Amos 9:12). The translation is quite different in Acts 15:17: David's fallen tent will be rebuilt "so the rest of humanity may seek the Lord—even all the gentiles who are called by my name." According to Luke, God's temple is rebuilt through Jesus as the crucified and risen one; the people of God are defined by their relationship to him, and they constitute a new temple. Jews and gentiles together comprise God's temple, which has been rebuilt in the last days. The arrangement is not that gentiles are subordinate to Jews but that both are equally members of God's people.

James probably also alludes here to Jeremiah 12:15–16, where the Lord promises to return and have mercy on both Judah and gentile nations. The gentiles who learn the Lord's ways "will be built up among my people" (12:16). Together with the Jews they will constitute a new temple, the new people of God. In addition, the words "who makes these things known from long ago" (Acts 15:17–18) almost certainly allude to Isaiah 45:21, which is one of the great mission texts in the OT. Isaiah declares that there is only one God; all must turn to this God to be saved, and this invitation is given to "all the ends of the earth" (Isa. 45:22). Every knee will bow to the Lord and every tongue will confess allegiance to him (45:23), which is a text Paul picks up in Philippians 2:10–11.

James argued, then, that Peter's perspective was verified from the Scriptures. Jews and gentiles were God's new temple, and the days of fulfillment had arrived. Therefore, gentiles who turn to God by faith must not be burdened with the requirement of circumcision. Circumcision was not a prerequisite in the new people of God. What was required under the old covenant does not apply now that the new covenant has arrived. The apostles, elders, and the entire church agreed and sent a letter to gentile believers in Antioch, Syria, and Cilicia. The news was sent through Paul, Barnabas, and Judas; Barsabbas and Silas also traveled with them (Acts 15:22–28), presumably to verify the contents of the letter. The impact of this decision was explosive: gentiles did not need to become Jews or observe the law to be saved and to be part of God's people. They were members of God's new temple by faith alone.

The council agreed that circumcision and observing the law would not be required for salvation, but James also advised that four regulations should be kept by the gentiles (15:20, 29). Some think these regulations contradict the claim that gentiles could become part of God's people without being circumcised and keeping the law, but we shall see there is no contradiction. Certainly what James meant by these prohibitions is not easy to discern, and scholars have struggled to understand them and to see how they apply today. We have to admit that ascertaining what James said is difficult, and any solution must be tentative. I understand the first two requirements to prohibit eating food offered to idols and sexual immorality. These two prohibitions represent moral norms for all time for gentile Christians. It was common in the ancient world to eat food offered to idols in pagan temples, but Jews believed participation in such feasts constituted idolatry, and early Christians agreed (cf. Rev. 2:14, 20). Some believe that Paul disagrees in 1 Corinthians 8–10, but when we come to 1 Corinthians, I will explain how Paul actually held the same view (cf. also Did. 6.3). In addition, gentile Christians agreed that adultery was wrong, but the word for "sexual immorality" here (*porneia*) refers to sexual sin in general, which includes fornication, homosexuality, bestiality, and other sexual perversions. Such sins were commonly accepted in the gentile world, but we see here that they are not compatible with new life in Christ.

The last two stipulations probably have to do with eating food where the blood isn't properly drained or where the blood is still in the food. These stipulations may derive from Leviticus 17–18 (17:10–14; 18:26), and the references to eating food offered to idols (17:8–9) and to sexual sin may stem from Leviticus as well (18:6–20, 22–23). Perhaps Gentile Christians were not required to abstain from blood in every situation, but they were not to consume the blood when they had fellowship with Jewish Christians (Lev. 17:8–9, 10–14; 18:26). If Jewish Christians were present at table, then these requirements should be followed to facilitate fellowship between Jews and gentiles. Another possibility, which I incline toward slightly, is that the prohibition of eating blood stems from the command given to Noah (Gen. 9:4) and represents a moral norm, so that the prohibition to eat blood has the same binding character as the prohibitions against idol food and sexual immorality.

Remarkably, after it had been decided that circumcision was unnecessary for salvation, Paul circumcised Timothy (Acts 16:1–3). Actually, Paul agreed to circumcise Timothy precisely because it was determined that circumcision was not required for salvation. Since Timothy's mother was Jewish, he was probably considered to be Jewish if the matrilineal principle of the Mishnah was being followed (cf. m. Kiddushin 3:12), and thus it would be difficult for Paul to bring Timothy into Jewish synagogues with him to do evangelism if he were uncircumcised. If circumcision were required for salvation, as it was by some false brothers in the case of the gentile Titus (Gal. 2:3–5), Paul was inflexible; he didn't yield an inch. He was very happy, however, to live as a Jew for cultural reasons if it would advance the gospel (1 Cor. 9:19–23).

Expansion to Europe (Acts 16:6–19:20)

Philippi (*16:12–40*)

The gospel continued to advance through the Pauline mission, spreading to Philippi, Thessalonica, Berea, Athens, and Corinth, and it was solidified in Ephesus (Acts 16:6–19:20, ca. AD 49–54). In Philippi, the gospel captured the heart of the businesswoman Lydia (16:14–15), delivered a slave girl from a demon and from the clutches of her masters (16:16–18), and brought a jailer and his household to salvation (16:23–34). Philippi was a Roman colony, but it wasn't particularly large and probably had 5,000 to 10,000 inhabitants. The exorcism of the slave girl outraged her masters when they realized that their means of profit were gone. They brought Paul and Barnabas to the magistrates, complaining that Paul and Silas were detrimental to the order and peace of the city. They appealed to anti-Jewish bias, claiming that Paul and Silas were not loyal to Rome and that Roman laws were being subverted. Their charges seemed plausible, and both Paul and Silas were punished with *verberatio*, an incredibly severe flogging with a whip made of several strands or rods embedded with bones or metal.

Why didn't Paul and Silas appeal to their Roman citizenship to avoid being flogged (16:37)? Perhaps they didn't want to avail themselves of rights that most Philippian Christians didn't have, for most of the Philippians would not be able to appeal to Roman citizenship to avoid punishment. Paul and Silas functioned, then, as examples for the Philippians of those who face suffering. Despite suffering so shamefully, Paul and Silas sang praises to God when they were jailed (16:25), a remarkable indication of the grace of God in their lives. The sovereignty of God, which is a pervasive theme in Acts, manifests itself again in an earthquake that broke the chains of all the prisoners. The event led to the salvation of the Philippian jailor and his household, as Paul called upon him and his household to put their faith in Jesus. The authorities (for reasons not entirely clear to us) released Paul and Silas, entreating them to leave the city. Paul would not, however, leave without securing an apology for such shameful treatment. He probably wanted to clarify that the Christians in Philippi were not part of a subversive sect, and at the same time it would erase any precedent about his ministry being anti-Roman.

Thessalonica and Berea (17:1–15)

The gospel continued to advance through Paul's ministry. Paul arrived in Thessalonica and according to his usual practice explained from the Scriptures that Jesus was the Messiah, and that the Scriptures themselves prophesied that Jesus would suffer and rise again (17:1–3). Conflict ensued, for some, even some prominent members of society, were persuaded, and the Jews responded by whipping up anti-Christian sentiment. They suggested that Christians were devoted to another king, Jesus, instead of giving their allegiance to Caesar (17:7). It is quite ironic and self-refuting that Jews criticized Paul and his friends for believing Jesus was king since their very own Scriptures promised a Davidic king. In any case, Paul and Silas could not stay in the city; Jason posted bond for them, and they left the city (17:9). The synagogue in Berea comes in for special honor since those present searched the Scriptures diligently to verify Paul's teaching (17:10–11). The practice of the Bereans functions as the model for all who hear the gospel preached. In any case, many in Berea responded with faith, and some believers again came from the upper classes (17:12), but again the Jews inflamed the crowds, and Paul departed to Athens.

Paul's Speech in Athens (17:16–34)

Athens, of course, was the most famous city of ancient Greece. Some have argued that Paul didn't actually intend to do missionary work in Athens and that his preaching in Athens was not successful. Both of these conclusions are doubtful. There is no clear evidence that Paul desired to skip Athens as he journeyed (probably AD 50), and the trip to Athens was almost certainly intentional (17:15). Nor is it convincing to say that his preaching wasn't successful since Luke mentions two converts by name and says that there were others as well (17:34).

Since Athens was an ancient city, it had many idols and objects of worship. Paul wasn't inspired by the beautiful art but irritated and provoked by the idolatry that was rife in the city (17:16). He reasoned with Jews and God-fearers in the synagogue and also in the marketplace (17:17), trying to persuade them about Jesus Christ. Epicurean and Stoic philosophers dismissed Paul as far beneath their status intellectually. Still, some were stimulated enough (probably members of the Areopagus council) to bring Paul to the Areopagus so they could hear and assess his teaching (17:18–19). The Areopagus functioned as a governing authority in Athens.

Paul's speech (17:22–31) does not represent, as some have alleged, compromise with the philosophical groups of Paul's day. He did not avoid the point of sharpest conflict with those hearing him, since he emphasized that Jesus was raised from the dead (17:18, 31–32), which was a repugnant idea to many in the Greek world. Furthermore, he also taught that Jesus as the risen one would judge the world, which hardly fits with the idea that Paul was merely trying to please his hearers. This is not to deny that what Paul said on this occasion had much in common with Stoic and Epicurean thought, though the purpose here isn't to identify such common features. I will instead focus on the content of Paul's speech.

Paul established common ground with his hearers by identifying them as religious (17:22), even though they worshiped their gods in ignorance (17:23). Paul was irritated by their idolatry, yet he didn't begin with a strident attack on their idolatry but found a point of contact for discussion. When speaking with Jews who already believed in a creator God, Paul defended that Jesus was the Messiah from the Scriptures, but for pagan Athenians, he emphasized that the one God is the creator of the world and sovereign over all things (17:24). Before pagans can understand who Jesus is, they need to grasp that there is one creator God and that all the other so-called gods in the world are idols or phantoms. The notion that there is one God and that he created everything and is sovereign over all of life is repeatedly emphasized in the OT.

The implications of God being the sovereign creator must be understood. The one true God cannot be contained by temples, nor does he stand in need of anything. He is not dependent upon gifts or sacrifices or anything human beings do for him. God doesn't need human beings, but they need him since he gives life and breath to all (17:25–26). God is independent and self-sufficient, while human beings are utterly dependent on God.

In addition, the unity of the human race is emphasized (17:26). All people everywhere came from one person. Certainly for Paul this person would be Adam (Rom. 5:12–19; 1 Cor. 15:21–22), and thus there is no basis for racial or ethnic superiority since the human race is one family. Those who don't believe in a historical Adam as the one progenitor of the human race are faced with the daunting prospect that there could be a scientific basis for racism. On the other hand, those who believe all human beings derive from Adam and Eve have a biological and theological basis for the unity and equality of the human race.

The times in which people live and the places where they live have also been appointed by God. God made human beings to seek God, though he is not far from anyone (Acts 17:27). Incidentally, such a statement doesn't contradict Romans 3:11, where Paul says that "no one . . . seeks God," for Paul doesn't say here in Acts that people *do* seek God but they *should* seek him. God is near to human beings, but the idolatry of the Athenians, which Paul already observed, reveals that they turned away from God's revelation of himself.

Human beings are magnificent (the crown of creation, as Gen. 1:26–27 says) because they are God's offspring and are made in his image (Acts 17:28). Here Paul quotes the pagan poet Aratus (*Phaen.* 5), showing that the significance of human beings was recognized by both believers and pagans. The life of human beings is utterly dependent on God since their existence depends wholly upon him. The nature of God, then, is not communicated with gold or silver or any physical representation of who he is (Acts 17:29). Here Paul's understanding of the OT and its polemic against idolatry manifests itself. He continues to imply that the Athenians have gone astray from the revelation of God by crafting idols. Still, God has graciously overlooked the ignorance of past eras and now summons all people everywhere to repent and believe. Jesus as the risen Lord will judge all on the last day, and the Athenians must respond to the urgent call to turn from their sins.

Corinth (18:1–17)

Corinth was a bustling city near two harbors, with approximately 80,000 to 100,000 inhabitants. When Paul arrived, he came into contact with Priscilla and Aquila, who joined him in mission (Acts 18:1–3). In the synagogue Paul proclaimed that Jesus was the Messiah, but Paul turned to the gentiles when the Jews rejected his message (18:4–6). The tension between Paul and the Jews must have been intense since he took his message right next door and preached the gospel from the house of Titius Justus, and even the ruler of the synagogue, Crispus, believed in the gospel (18:7–8). The Lord assured

Paul that there would be significant fruit in the city and that he would protect him, and thus Paul stayed in the city for a year and a half (18:9–11, AD 50–51). The promise of protection was fulfilled under Gallio, the proconsul (18:12–17), who was the brother of the famous Stoic philosopher Seneca. The Jews tried to bring charges against Paul, but Gallio dismissed the charges as an intra-Jewish squabble, and his refusal to hear the accusations gave Paul space to continue his mission, fulfilling the promise that Paul would be protected. The Jews wanted to distinguish the early Christians from themselves since the Jews had legal protection to live out their faith in the Roman Empire. Gallio's decision, however, established another precedent where Christians could continue to operate under Jewish auspices and thus were protected from a formal ban in the empire. Of course, Gallio's decision did not represent an empire-wide decision, but it was still a significant precedent.

Ephesus (18:18–19:20)

Apollos burst upon the scene in Ephesus, and with his rhetorical brilliance and scriptural exposition, he proclaimed Jesus; then he did this even more effectively in both Ephesus and Achaia after Priscilla and Aquila instructed him more fully about the gospel of Christ (18:24–28).

When Paul arrived in Ephesus, where he stayed for three years (AD 52–55), he encountered twelve disciples of John the Baptist (19:1–7). From interactions with them, Paul discerned that they had not received the Spirit when they believed. They replied that they had not heard of the Spirit, but this should not be understood to say that they had never heard of the Holy Spirit, which is highly unlikely. Instead, it means that they had not heard that the Holy Spirit had been poured out in fulfillment of God's new-covenant promises (Isa. 32:15; 44:3; Ezek. 36:26–27; Joel 2:28–29). They were, so to speak, living in a salvation-historical time warp, as if the new age inaugurated by the gift of the Spirit had never come. Paul introduced these men to faith in Jesus and baptized them, and upon doing so they spoke in tongues and prophesied. The experience of the Ephesian twelve does not point to a second experience of the Spirit after conversion, for these men became Christians on this occasion. They were baptized and *believed in Jesus* for the first time. So even though Jesus Christ had already come and the Spirit had been given, these men, before Paul came, lived as if they were under the old covenant, as if Jesus had not died and been raised. Speaking in tongues and prophesying signified that they had received the same promises as the 120 on Pentecost and as Cornelius and his friends. Such phenomena attested that they had truly received the Spirit and also confirmed that Jesus was superior to John the Baptist.

Paul's experience in the synagogue in Ephesus (Acts 19:8–10) replicated what was becoming a common pattern. He proclaimed God's kingdom three months in the synagogue but moved from the synagogue to a lecture hall when his message was resisted and then continued preaching for two more years. Ephesus, therefore, became a launching pad for the gospel to spread throughout the Roman province of Asia, which is in modern-day Turkey. Delegates probably went out from Paul and evangelized smaller cities and towns in the region. We see an example of this in Colossians where Epaphras likely planted the church as Paul's ambassador, consulting Paul when problems arose. Paul specifically says that he had never met the Colossians (Col. 2:1), which suggests that Epaphras went out as a Pauline delegate.

Paul's ministry matches Peter's, in that amazing miracles were performed even from face cloths and aprons that he wore (Acts 19:11–12; cf. 5:15). Such extraordinary miracles attracted many and could easily lead to superstition: the problem of trying to imitate Paul immediately arose. The authentic power of the gospel stands in contrast to the Jewish exorcists who tried to put themselves under the banner of Jesus and Paul by attempting to expel demons in the name of Jesus and Paul (19:13–16). This superstitious attempt to wield miraculous power backfired as the demon in the man attacked the seven Jewish exorcists and left them bloodied and battered. The name of Jesus is not to be trifled with, and it doesn't work like a magic charm. As a result, people recognized the distinctiveness of the Christian faith and God's holiness. They renounced magic, even burning their magic books, which was a tremendous sacrifice, and the price has been calculated to be the yearly salary of 137 people. It is important to recognize that the people were not forced to burn books; they did so gladly and voluntarily. We don't have an example of coercion or repression of local culture; the people did what they wished to do.

Jerusalem and Rome (19:21–28:31)

The last section of Acts records Paul's travels by which he gets to Jerusalem and finally to Rome. The itinerary for the remainder of the book is sketched in for us, "After these events, Paul resolved by the Spirit to pass through Macedonia and Achaia and go to Jerusalem. 'After I've been there,' he said, 'It is necessary for me to see Rome as well'" (19:21). I will focus on and summarize some key events and themes in these chapters, as Paul travels to the center of the Jewish world (Jerusalem) and to the center of the Roman world (Rome). We should note that the church is described as "the Way" (9:2; 16:17; 18:25–26; 19:9, 23; 22:4; 24:14, 22; cf. Isa. 40:3). The Way is one of salvation, and the term is often used in contexts where opponents to the gospel are considered. Those who are of the Way belong to the true Israel, the true people of God.

Riot in Ephesus (19:21–41)

The riot in Ephesus (ca. AD 54–55), instigated by Demetrius, who made small replicas of the temple of Artemis, was precipitated by the success of Paul's preaching (Acts 19:23–41). Demetrius and those in his guild were worried about loss of profit, and at the same time they were concerned that the honor and reputation of Artemis and the temple constructed in her honor would be besmirched. The charge was serious since the cult of Artemis exercised significant influence not only in Ephesus but in many other places in the Greco-Roman world, though the temple resided in Ephesus. Certainly the lives of both Paul and his friends were in danger. Many rushed to the theater, which could hold 24,000 people. When the Jews put forward Alexander (presumably a Jewish leader), who was probably longing to explain that the controversy was caused by Paul and believers in Jesus instead of by those associated with the synagogue, the crowd erupted with the chant "Great is Artemis of the Ephesians!" Luke humorously quips that most of those gathered didn't even know the reason for the uproar, which perhaps reminds all of us of some controversies we have experienced. In any case, the city clerk of Ephesus, who was the most powerful person in the city, calmed the crowd by reminding them of the privilege they had of being guardians of Artemis's temple and by assuring them that Artemis's image had divine origin. Those criticized by Demetrius, the city clerk noted, were not guilty of robbing temples or of denigrating Artemis. In the ancient world, robbing temples was considered to be a heinous crime, warranting death or exile (cf. Rom. 2:22).

Apparently, Paul and his companions did not specifically speak against Artemis in proclaiming the good news about Jesus. The city clerk argued that if Demetrius or others desired to bring charges, they could appeal to the courts to adjudicate such matters. He made it quite clear that there was no basis for the riot and that if news of such reached Roman ears, there could be adverse consequences. The Lord used a secular executive figure to remind the people that the assembly wasn't lawful. In this account we see how the preached gospel can impact society where religious and social interests impinge on one another. Those who derived their profit from other gods worried that devotion to Jesus was undermining both their profits and their traditional way of life. Those who embrace the gospel live differently in society because their loyalties have changed. At the same time, Paul and his compatriots focused on preaching the gospel of Jesus crucified and risen. They preached judgment and salvation, yet did not specifically denigrate Artemis or the temple where her devotees worshiped. They proclaimed the gospel with wisdom and tact, with winsomeness and boldness, with love and truth.

Speech to Christian Leaders in Ephesus (20:17–35)

The first part of Acts 20 records Paul's travels from Ephesus to Macedonia, noting that he was anxious to arrive in Jerusalem by Pentecost. While he was en route to Jerusalem, he summoned the "elders" of Ephesus to the island of Miletus and instructed and admonished them (20:17–35). The elders are also identified as "overseers" (20:28), confirming that elders and overseers are two different ways of identifying the same office (cf. Titus 1:5, 7; 1 Pet. 5:1–2). Interestingly, they are called upon "to shepherd the church of God," and the infinitive "to shepherd" (*poimainein*) can be translated as "to pastor." We have a hint here that pastors, overseers, and elders all refer to the same office.

Paul presents himself as a model in this speech, emphasizing his humility and faithfulness while experiencing trials (Acts 20:18–19). He lived with integrity and did not use his preaching as a means to enrich himself but instead worked to provide for his own needs (20:33–34). Paul's ministry didn't cause him to prosper but led to suffering (20:22–23). His focus was on the gospel, which he proclaimed both in the public square and in house churches (20:20). The gospel centers on Jesus Christ, who purchased the church with his own blood (20:28). At the heart of the gospel was the cross, so that preaching Jesus's death and forgiveness for those who repent and believe in him (20:21) constitutes "the gospel of God's grace" (20:24). Another way of putting it is that the cross is the message of the kingdom (20:25), and it is also identified as "the whole plan of God" (20:27). In other words, those who understand the story line of the Scriptures, those who grasp what the kingdom is, proclaim the atoning death of Jesus as the fulfillment of God's plan. The gospel that Paul proclaimed represents the fulfillment of God's promise that the offspring of the woman would crush the serpent (Gen. 3:15). In other words, it fulfilled the promise to Abraham and David that blessing would come to the entire world through a Davidic king.

Paul's fearless preaching of forgiveness through Christ functioned as an example for the elders in Ephesus (Acts 20:20, 28). Like Ezekiel, the faithful discharge of his ministry meant that he was "innocent of the blood of all of you" (20:26; cf. Ezek. 3:17–21; 33:1–9). So too, the elders and overseers of Ephesus were charged to be ready to counter false teaching, which would arise even from the eldership (Acts 20:29–32). Thus they must be devoted to the gospel as that which builds up and secures a final inheritance. The gospel that Paul unflinchingly preached must be guarded and protected since there are always those who are trying to subvert it.

Paul in Jerusalem (21:1–23:35)

Chapters 21–23 depict Paul's trip to Jerusalem, the threat to his life, his arrest, and his transport to Caesarea (AD 57–59). We are reminded of Jesus's arrest and execution in Jerusalem, even though Jesus was innocent of the charges made against him. The point of 21:1–16 is that Paul's suffering in Jerusalem was prophesied, and yet Paul, compelled by the Holy Spirit, felt obligated to go to Jerusalem anyway and to suffer whatever he would face. Paul was accused of bringing a gentile into the temple, and the Jews descended upon him and began to batter him to death (21:17–36). The Roman tribune, however, rescued Paul from the clutches of the Jews. Luke explains that the attack upon Paul was completely unjustified, which is confirmed because Paul followed James's advice on how to mollify Jewish concerns about Paul's understanding of the law. Paul did not teach that Jews must abandon the law, for he was willing when with the Jews to follow the law's regulations himself and even to pay the necessary expenses for four other Jews who were being purified along with him (cf. 1 Cor. 9:19–23).

When Paul had the opportunity to speak in his defense, we read the second account of his conversion (cf. Acts 9:1–19), but there are distinctive elements here (22:1–21). Paul emphasized that he was a faithful Jew and not a renegade; he was zealous for the law and a disciple of the famous rabbi Gamaliel. Because of Paul's zeal, he traveled to Damascus to arrest and punish believers in Christ. Paul recounted his conversion, which clarified that it was a supernatural work of God; becoming a Christian was the furthest thing from Paul's mind. Paul particularly emphasized the role of Ananias since the latter observed the law and had a good reputation with the Jews. Paul was called by Christ to be a witness to all people, to proclaim the coming of Jesus as the Righteous One.

An incident in chapter 22 is particularly striking (22:17–21), for here we are told a story that appears nowhere else. Paul at some time after his conversion had another encounter with the Lord, a vision in the temple in Jerusalem, and the Lord instructed him to leave Jerusalem and to proclaim the gospel to the gentiles since the Jews would not accept his message. Paul protested and argued with the Lord, pointing out that he was the perfect messenger for the Jews. After all, they all knew he had approved of Christians being imprisoned, beaten, and in the case of Stephen, killed. Certainly they would be convinced by the remarkable change in Paul's life. The Lord, however, rejected Paul's plan and commissioned him to proclaim the good news to the gentiles (Isa. 42:6; 49:6). The moment Paul mentioned the gentiles, the crowd erupted into chaos, for the reference to the gentiles confirmed all their suspicions about Paul being an apostate. Paul probably hoped that his ministry to the Jews would be successful *after* his gentile mission (cf. Rom. 9–11), but the explosion that ensued provoked the tribune to interrogate Paul and to find out what was really going on by scourging him. Still, the tribune backtracked immediately upon discovering that Paul was a Roman citizen, for such a punishment could not be inflicted on a Roman citizen without a trial.

Paul was brought before the Sanhedrin in the next chapter (Acts 23:1–10). Luke continues to emphasize that Paul did nothing to warrant arrest. He carefully observed the law, even apologizing to the high priest when he inadvertently criticized him. Paul didn't violate the Jewish law but represented the Pharisaic position that there would be a resurrection (cf. Dan. 12:2). When Paul proclaimed advocacy of the Pharisaic position, the Sanhedrin erupted into a fierce debate between the Pharisees and Sadducees, and some Pharisees defended Paul's orthodoxy. As Luke demonstrates, the charge that Paul was anti-Jewish was not credible, for even Jews who did not believe in Jesus thought his view was within the confines of Jewish orthodoxy. Belief in a Messiah and in a future resurrection were compatible with Jewish beliefs; indeed, they fulfilled the promises made in the OT.

Luke reveals his narratival intent in Acts 23:11. The Lord had been orchestrating events so that Paul would testify about Christ in Jerusalem, and testimony about Christ would also take place in Rome. In other words, despite the plots against Paul's life, he would make it to Rome. The Lord's words in 9:15 were being fulfilled: Paul was taking Christ's "name to gentiles, kings, and Israelites." Some Jews from Jerusalem banded together, forming a plot to kill Paul, and the Sanhedrin colluded in their plot (23:12–15). Such actions confirmed Paul's innocence and Jewish deviousness since they were attempting to murder Paul by circumventing the law, for there was no basis in the Jewish Scriptures for murdering another person in this manner. Justice had to be administered in courts, and the evidence had to be carefully assessed before pronouncing someone guilty (Exod. 23:2–3, 6–8; Num. 35:30; Deut. 16:18–20; 19:15–19). Still, the Lord sovereignly protected Paul, and the plot was foiled since Paul's nephew heard about the plan and reported it to the tribune, Claudius Lysias (Acts 23:16–22). Claudius Lysias took pains to transport Paul safely to the Roman procurator, Felix (AD 52–59), in Caesarea (23:23–35). Claudius Lysias in his letter asserted Paul's innocence: "I found out that the accusations were concerning questions of their law, and that there was no charge that merited death or imprisonment" (23:29). To sum up: Paul proclaimed the gospel to religious leaders in Jerusalem; the charges against him were bogus; and God spared him from death, promising that he would go to Rome.

Paul in Caesarea (24:1–26:32)

The first scene in Caesarea was Paul's trial before the procurator Antonius Felix (24:1–23). The Jewish lawyer, Tertullus, is shown to be obsequious and vacuous in his prosecution (24:1–9). The charges against Paul were clearly groundless. Paul, in presenting his case, emphasized that the evidence for the charges against him were unsubstantiated (24:10–13, 17–20), demonstrating again that, like his Lord Jesus Christ, there was no basis for a trial (cf. Luke 23). At the same time, the promise that the gospel would be proclaimed to rulers was fulfilled (Acts 9:15), for Paul tells Felix about the Way, the Way that fulfills the promises in the Scriptures (24:16–18, 21). Paul particularly focuses on the resurrection of Jesus. Felix clearly had no legal basis for holding Paul in custody but apparently continued to do so to placate the Jews (24:22–27). Still, this led to further opportunities for Paul to proclaim the gospel, as he challenged Felix about faith in Christ, and instructed him about the judgment that was coming. Felix was spooked and fearful as he heard about the judgment. The procurator's fear reminds the reader that Felix was an ordinary and frail human being and that he too needed to reckon with God. No one is exempt from the judgment, and every person everywhere is called to repentance. At the end of the day, Felix desired money more than he sought after a right relationship with God, and thus he was hoping to receive a bribe from Paul.

Porcius Festus replaced Felix as procurator (AD 59–62), and Paul's case became his. When Festus traveled to Jerusalem, the Jewish plot to kill Paul reemerged, showing again the nefariousness of the Jewish leaders and the righteousness of Paul's cause (25:1–6). When the Jews came to Caesarea and charged Paul, it was again clear that the charges were without foundation (25:6–12). Festus, however, was a pusillanimous leader, and since he wanted to curry favor with the Jews, he proposed bringing Paul to Jerusalem for trial (25:9–12). Such a course of action would lead, as noted already, to Paul's murder on the way, which Festus himself would have known all too well since Paul was transferred to Caesarea for this very reason. Paul appealed to Caesar in Rome since Festus was clearly not granting him justice, and Festus granted his request. In the midst of all these circumstances, God was working out his purposes and plans.

King Herod Agrippa II, who in AD 53–93 reigned over various territories, arrived with his sister Bernice to visit Festus. Bernice was also the older sister of Drusilla, who was the wife of the procurator Felix, who had preceded Festus. Festus presented Paul's case to Agrippa and Bernice, though he shaded the story to exculpate himself from any charges of wrongdoing and made himself look noble and virtuous (25:13–22). As readers, however, we know that Festus acted corruptly, not with justice, for if he had done what was right, he would have released Paul after hearing the case. Agrippa, however, expressed interest in hearing Paul, and Festus turned it into an official event, one with pageantry and with many guests (25:23–27). Once again, God was working through venal rulers to accomplish his purposes by providing Paul with the opportunity to present his gospel to many prominent people in society. Remarkably, Festus admitted that he needed help in writing the emperor since he had no charges to send along against Paul! Such an admission was quite damning, showing that Festus's case against Paul was a radical miscarriage of justice. Certainly Festus should have freed Paul if he could not even think of charges to send to Caesar.

In Acts 26 Paul presented his case to Agrippa and the other military personnel and prominent people of the city (25:23). For the third time in Acts we are treated to the story of Paul's conversion. Agrippa, Paul realized, would be able to track his argument since he was familiar with the Jewish religion. Paul emphasized his Jewish credentials. From his youth onward Paul was devoted to the Jewish way of life, and he "lived as a Pharisee" (26:5). Amazingly, he was now on trial for believing in the promises of God, for believing in the resurrection of Jesus as the Messiah, for believing what the Jewish Scriptures taught! Paul's belief that these promises were fulfilled in Jesus was not superficial, for at the outset he was an ardent opponent of those devoted to the Nazarene, even imprisoning and agreeing with the death of believers. At one time Paul was convinced that those who followed Jesus were heretical and so dangerous that they must be stamped out. Paul then related the appearance of the risen Christ on the Damascus road, which turned him to faith in Christ. He emphasized not his conversion but his call. He was called to be a faithful witness and was summoned to proclaim the good news to the gentiles. In that way they would "turn from darkness to light and from the power of Satan to God, that they may receive forgiveness of sins and a share among those who are sanctified by faith in me" (26:18). The prophecy of Isaiah was being fulfilled in Paul's ministry where he was freeing "those sitting in darkness" (42:7) and turning "darkness to light in front of them" (42:16). As noted earlier, since Paul was united to Israel, he too was the servant of the Lord, and in a derivative sense he was bringing the promises of salvation to all people.

Paul's preaching was not limited to gentiles, for he also preached in Jerusalem and Judea. The reason for opposition to him, then, was the gospel itself.

Ironically, the Jews were opposing the fulfillment of the scriptural promise about the Messiah who "must suffer, and . . . as the first to rise from the dead, he would proclaim light to our people and to the gentiles" (Acts 26:23). We again think of the prophecies in Isaiah about those turning from darkness to light (Isa. 42:6; 49:6) and the many texts on gentile salvation (Isa. 2:1–4; 11:10; 19:16–25; 52:15; 55:3–5; etc.).

Festus interrupted Paul, thinking that he had become a religious fanatic and deluded because of excessive study, but Paul appealed to sober evidence to support his case. What Paul read in the books was verified by what happened in the real world (i.e., Jesus was truly risen). Paul's fundamental aim wasn't to defend himself but to persuade all present to become believers. His calling was to be a witness to Christ, and the promise that Paul would preach to Jews, gentiles, and kings (Acts 9:15) had become a reality. Agrippa put off the notion that he should become a believer, but by speaking to Agrippa about the good news of forgiveness of sins, Paul's hopes for his speech were realized. God was fulfilling his purposes in Paul's ministry. The gospel was on the way to the end of the earth through Paul (1:8), and believers after Paul (including us!) are called to continue the work Paul began. All those present in the auditorium recognized that the charges against Paul were without merit. Agrippa's final words were quite the indictment of Festus, for he said, "This man could have been released if he had not appealed to Caesar" (26:32). If Festus had done his job, Paul would not be going to Rome. Festus had to make up charges, but we readers see that they lacked substance.

Paul's Voyage to Rome (27:1–28:31)

Chapters 27–28 recount how Paul ended up in Rome (AD 60–62). Acts 27 is dominated by the shipwreck and the remarkable deliverance of every person on the ship, all 276 of them, onto the island of Malta. Paul stands out in the story for his leadership, receiving a revelation through an angel about the deliverance of everyone on board. We should especially observe that Paul was promised that he would appear before Caesar (27:24) to give testimony about Jesus before kings (9:15). On Malta, Paul suffered no harm from a snakebite and healed the father of the leading man on the island and many others as well (28:1–10). When Paul arrived in Rome (28:11–31), he met with the Jews, stressing his innocence, explaining that the kingdom of God, the fulfillment of the Scriptures, centers on Jesus. As readers we can fill in what Paul said from the other speeches in Acts. In any case, Paul proclaimed that the promises made to Abraham, Isaac, and Jacob and the promises made to David and the prophets were fulfilled in Jesus. The Jews in Rome, however, were divided over the gospel Paul preached, and Paul warned them with the words of Isaiah 6:9–10, predicting that the gentiles would listen to the good news. Isaiah 6 contains Isaiah's call to ministry and the content of his message. He would call Israel to repentance but, except for a remnant, Israel would refuse to believe. The Lord would blind their hearts and minds until judgment came. The refusal of many Jews to believe, which is a regular theme in Acts as Paul went to the synagogues (Acts 13:46–47; 18:6–7), fulfilled Isaiah's prophecy. Jewish unbelief was not an accident but was in accord with God's purposes. It is likely that Paul read this prophecy in light of other prophecies in Isaiah that predicted the salvation of gentiles (2:1–4; 11:9–10; 19:16–25; 42:6; 49:6–7; 52:15; 55:3–5; 66:18–19, 23). Here we have something very similar to Romans 9–11: the majority of the Jews disbelieved, while the fullness of the gentiles came in. At the same time Paul's words in Acts should not be read as if the Jews were abandoned. There is hope in the remnant for a fuller return (Isa. 6:13; cf. also Rom. 11:25–29). The book concludes with Paul preaching freely in Rome (Acts 28:30–31). The gospel hasn't reached the ends of the earth, but it is significant that Paul in Rome, the capital city of the empire, proclaimed the good news about Jesus, and Luke reminds the readers once more that teaching about Jesus fulfills the promises of God's kingdom.

Acts: Commentaries

Barrett, Charles. K. *The Acts of the Apostles*. 2 vols. ICC. Edinburgh: T&T Clark, 1994–98.

Bock, Darrell L. *Acts*. BECNT. Grand Rapids: Baker Academic, 2007.

Bruce, F. F. *The Acts of the Apostles: The Greek Text with Introduction and Commentary*. 3rd ed. Grand Rapids: Eerdmans, 1990.

———. *The Book of the Acts*. Rev. ed. NICNT. Grand Rapids: Eerdmans, 1988.

Conzelmann, Hans. *Acts of the Apostles*. Hermeneia. Philadelphia: Fortress, 1987.

Dunn, James D. G. *The Acts of the Apostles*. Epworth Commentary. London: Epworth, 1996.

Fitzmyer, Joseph A. *The Acts of the Apostles*. AB. New York: Doubleday, 1998.

Gaventa, Beverly R. *The Acts of the Apostles*. ANTC. Nashville: Abingdon, 2003.

Haenchen, Ernst. *The Acts of the Apostles*. Philadelphia: Westminster, 1971.

Hanson, Richard P. C. *The Acts in the Revisited Standard Version*. New Clarendon Bible. Oxford: Clarendon, 1967.

Johnson, Luke. *The Acts of the Apostles*. SP. Collegeville, MN: Liturgical Press, 1992.

Keener, Craig S. *Acts: An Exegetical Commentary*. 4 vols. Grand Rapids: Baker Academic, 2012–15.

Kistemaker, Simon J. *Exposition of the Acts of the Apostles*. New Testament Commentary. Grand Rapids: Baker, 1990.

Lake, Kirsopp, and Henry J. Cadbury. *The Acts of the Apostles: English Translation and Commentary*. Vol. 4 of *The Beginnings of Christianity*, edited by F. J. Foakes-Jackson and K. Lake. London: Macmillan, 1933.

Larkin, William J. *Acts*. IVPNTC. Leicester, UK: Inter-Varsity, 1995.

Longenecker, Richard N. "Acts." In *Luke-Acts*, vol. 10 of *The Expositor's Bible Commentary*, rev. ed., edited by Tremper Longman III and David E. Garland, 663–1102. Grand Rapids: Zondervan, 2007.

Marshall, I. Howard. "Acts." In *Commentary on the New Testament Use of the Old Testament*, edited by G. K. Beale and D. A. Carson, 513–606. Grand Rapids: Baker Academic, 2007.

Martin, Francis, ed. *Acts*. ACCS 5 (NT). Downers Grove, IL: InterVarsity, 1998.

Parsons, Mikeal C. *Acts*. PCNT. Grand Rapids: Baker Academic, 2008.

Pervo, Richard I. *Acts*. Hermeneia. Minneapolis: Fortress, 2009.

Peterson, David G. *The Acts of the Apostles*. PNTC. Grand Rapids: Eerdmans, 2009.

Polhill, John B. *Acts*. NAC 26. Nashville: Broadman, 1992.

Schnabel, Eckhard. *Acts*. ZECNT. Grand Rapids: Zondervan, 2012.

Spencer, F. Scott. *Acts*. Readings: A New Biblical Commentary. Sheffield: Sheffield Academic, 1997.

Walaskay, Paul W. *Acts*. Westminster Bible Companion. Louisville: Westminster John Knox, 1998.

Wall, Robert W. "The Acts of the Apostles." In *The New Interpreter's Bible*, edited by Leander E. Keck et al., 10:1–368. Nashville: Abingdon, 2002.

Williams, Charles S. C. A. *Commentary on the Acts of the Apostles*. BNTC. London: Black, 1969.

Williams, David J. *Acts*. NIBC. Peabody, MA: Hendrickson, 1990.

Witherington, Ben, III. *The Acts of the Apostles: A Socio-Rhetorical Commentary*. Grand Rapids: Eerdmans, 1998.

Acts: Articles, Essays, and Monographs

Alexander, Loveday C. A. "Acts." In *The Oxford Bible Commentary*, edited by J. Barton and J. Muddiman, 1028–61. Oxford: Oxford University Press, 2001.

———. *Acts in Its Ancient Literary Context: A Classicist Looks at the Acts of the Apostles*. LNTS 298. London: T&T Clark, 2005.

Anderson, Kevin L. *"But God Raised Him from the Dead": The Theology of Jesus' Resurrection in Luke-Acts*. Paternoster Biblical Monographs. Milton Keynes: Paternoster, 2006.

Barclay, John M. G. *Jews in the Mediterranean Diaspora: From Alexander to Trajan (323 BCE–117 CE)*. Edinburgh: T&T Clark, 1996.

Bauckham, Richard J. "James and the Gentiles (Acts 15.13–21)." In *History, Literature, and Society in the Book of Acts*, edited by Ben Witherington III, 154–84. Cambridge: Cambridge University Press, 1996.

———. "James and the Jerusalem Church." In *The Book of Acts in Its Palestinian Setting*, edited by R. J. Bauckham, 415–80. Vol. 4 of *The Book of Acts in Its First-Century Setting*, edited by Bruce W. Winter. Exeter: Paternoster, 1995.

———. "James and the Jerusalem Community." In *Jewish Believers in Jesus: The Early Centuries*, edited by O. Skarsaune and R. Hvalvik, 55–95. Peabody, MA: Hendrickson, 2007.

———. "James, Peter, and the Gentiles." In *The Missions of James, Peter, and Paul: Tensions in Early Christianity*, edited by B. D. Chilton and C. A. Evans, 91–142. NovTSup 115. Leiden: Brill, 2005.

Billings, Drew W. *Acts of the Apostles and the Rhetoric of Roman Imperialism*. Cambridge: Cambridge University Press, 2017.

Bock, Darrell L. *Proclamation from Prophecy and Pattern: Lucan Old Testament Christology*. JSNTSup 12. Sheffield: JSOT Press, 1987.

———. *A Theology of Luke and Acts: God's Promised Program, Realized for All Nations*. Grand Rapids: Zondervan, 2012.

Cunningham, Scott. *"Through Many Tribulations": The Theology of Persecution in Luke-Acts*. JSNTSup 142. Sheffield: Sheffield Academic, 1997.

Dibelius, Martin. *Studies in the Acts of the Apostles*. Edited by H. Greeven. New York: Scribner, 1956.

Dunn, James D. G. *Baptism in the Holy Spirit: A Re-examination of the New Testament Teaching on the Gift of the Spirit in Relation to Pentecostalism Today*. London: SCM, 1970.

Green, Joel B. *Conversion in Luke-Acts: Divine Action, Human Cognition, and the People of God*. Grand Rapids: Baker Academic, 2015.

Heil, John Paul. *Luke-Acts: Foundations for Christian Worship*. Eugene, OR: Cascade, 2018.

Hemer, Colin J. *The Book of Acts in the Setting of Hellenistic History*. Edited by C. H. Gempf. WUNT 49. Reprinted, Tübingen: Mohr Siebeck, 2001.

Hengel, Martin. *Acts and the History of Earliest Christianity*. London: SCM, 1979.

Jervell, Jacob. *The Theology of the Acts of the Apostles*. NTT. Cambridge: Cambridge University Press, 1996.

Jipp, Joshua W. "Hospitable Barbarians: Luke's Ethnic Reasoning in Acts 28:1–10." *JTS* 68 (2017): 23–45.

Kee, Howard C. *Good News to the Ends of the Earth: The Theology of Acts*. Philadelphia: Trinity Press International, 1990.

Keener, Craig. *The IVP Bible Background Commentary: New Testament*. Downers Grove, IL: InterVarsity, 1993.

Kim, Seyoon. *Christ and Caesar: The Gospel and the Roman Empire in the Writings of Paul and Luke*. Grand Rapids: Eerdmans, 2008.

———. *The Origin of Paul's Gospel*. Eugene, OR: Wipf & Stock, 1981.

Land, Darin H. *The Diffusion of Ecclesiastical Authority: Sociological Dimensions of Leadership in the Book of Acts*. Princeton Theological Monograph. Eugene, OR: Pickwick, 2008.

Lentz, John Clayton. *Luke's Portrait of Paul*. SNTSMS 77. Cambridge: Cambridge University Press, 1993.

Levinskaya, Irina A. *The Book of Acts in Its Diaspora Setting*. Vol. 5 of *The Book of Acts in Its First-Century Setting*, edited by Bruce W. Winter. Grand Rapids: Eerdmans, 1996.

Levinsohn, Stephen H. *Textual Connections in Acts*. SBLMS 31. Atlanta: Scholars Press, 1987.

Lierman, John. *The New Testament Moses: Christian Perceptions of Moses and Israel in the Setting of Jewish Religion*. WUNT 173. Tübingen: Mohr Siebeck, 2004.

Litwak, Kenneth D. *Echoes of Scripture in Luke-Acts: Telling the History of God's People Intertextually*. London: T&T Clark, 2005.

Lohfink, Gerhard. *The Conversion of St. Paul: Narrative and History in Acts*. Chicago: Franciscan Herald Press, 1976.

Macnamara, Luke. *My Chosen Instrument: The Characterisation of Paul in Acts 7:58–15:41*. Rome: Gregorian and Biblical Press, 2016.

Maddox, Robert. *The Purpose of Luke-Acts*. Edinburgh: T&T Clark, 1982.

Marguerat, Daniel. *The First Christian Historian: Writing the "Acts of the Apostles."* SNTSMS 121. Cambridge: Cambridge University Press, 2002.

Marshall, I. Howard. *The Acts of the Apostles*. New Testament Guides. Sheffield: Sheffield Academic, 1992.

Marshall, I. Howard, and David Peterson, eds. *Witness to the Gospel: The Theology of Acts*. Grand Rapids: Eerdmans, 1998.

Matson, David L. *Household Conversion Narratives in Acts: Pattern and Interpretation*. JSNTSup 123. Sheffield: Sheffield Academic, 1996.

Matthews, Christopher R. *Philip, Apostle and Evangelist: Configurations of a Tradition*. NovTSup 105. Leiden: Brill, 2002.

Menzies, Robert P. *The Development of Early Christian Pneumatology with Special Reference to Luke-Acts*. JSNTSup 54. Sheffield: JSOT Press, 1991.

Miller, John B. F. *Convinced That God Had Called Us: Dreams, Visions, and the Perception of God's Will in Luke-Acts*. Biblical Interpretation 85. Leiden: Brill, 2007.

Mitchell, Stephen. *Anatolia: Land, Men, and Gods in Asia Minor*. Oxford: Oxford University Press, 1995.

Miura, Yuzuru. *David in Luke-Acts: His Portrayal in the Light of Early Judaism*. WUNT 232. Tübingen: Mohr Siebeck, 2007.

Murphy-O'Connor, Jerome. *Paul: A Critical Life*. Oxford: Oxford University Press, 1996.

———. *St. Paul's Corinth: Texts and Archaeology*. Wilmington: Glazier, 1983.

———. *St. Paul's Ephesus: Texts and Archaeology*. Collegeville, MN: Liturgical Press, 2008.

Neagoe, Alexandru. *The Trial of the Gospel: An Apologetic Reading of Luke's Trial Narratives*. SNTSMS 116. Cambridge: Cambridge University Press, 2002.

Oschwald, Jeffrey. "The Word of the Lord Grew—and Multiplied—and Showed Its Strength: The Word of God in the Book of Acts." *Concordia Journal* 44 (2018): 41–60.

Padilla, Osvaldo. *The Speeches of Outsiders in Acts: Poetics, Theology and Historiography*. SNTSMS 144. Cambridge: Cambridge University Press, 2008.

Pao, David W. *Acts and the Isaianic New Exodus.* WUNT 130. Tübingen: Mohr Siebeck, 2000.

Penner, Todd C. *In Praise of Christian Origins: Stephen and the Hellenists in Lukan Apologetic Historiography.* Emory Studies in Early Christianity 10. New York: T&T Clark, 2004.

Penney, John M. *The Missionary Emphasis of Lukan Pneumatology.* JPTSup 12. Sheffield: Sheffield Academic, 1997.

Pereira, Francis. *Ephesus: Climax of Universalism in Luke-Acts. A Redaction-Critical Study of Paul's Ephesian Ministry (Acts 18:23–20:1).* Jesuit Theological Forum Studies 1. Anand, India: Gujarat Sahitya Prakash, 1983.

Pillai, C. A. Joachim. *Early Missionary Preaching: A Study of Luke's Report in Acts 13.* Hicksville, NY: Exposition Press, 1979.

Ramsay, William M. *St. Paul the Traveler and Roman Citizen.* Rev. ed. Edited by M. Wilson. Grand Rapids: Kregel, 2001.

Rapske, Brian M. *The Book of Acts and Paul in Roman Custody.* Vol. 3 of *The Book of Acts in Its First-Century Setting,* edited by Bruce W. Winter. Exeter: Paternoster, 1994.

Ravens, David A. S. *Luke and the Restoration of Israel.* JSNTSup 119. Sheffield: Sheffield Academic, 1995.

Riesner, Rainer. *Paul's Early Period: Chronology, Mission Strategy, Theology.* Translated by D. Stott. Grand Rapids: Eerdmans, 1998.

Rothschild, Clare K. *Paul in Athens: The Popular Religious Context of Acts 17.* WUNT 341. Tübingen: Mohr Siebeck, 2014.

Rowe, C. Kavin. *World Upside Down: Reading Acts in the Graeco-Roman Age.* Oxford: Oxford University Press, 2009.

Schnabel, Eckhard J. *Early Christian Mission.* 2 vols. Downers Grove, IL: InterVarsity, 2004.

———. *Paul the Missionary: Realities, Strategies, and Methods.* Downers Grove, IL: InterVarsity, 2008.

Seccombe, David P. *Possessions and the Poor in Luke-Acts.* SNTSU B6. Linz: Fuchs, 1982.

Shauf, Scott. *Theology as History, History as Theology: Paul in Ephesus in Acts 19.* BZNW 133. Berlin: de Gruyter, 2005.

Shelton, James B. *Mighty in Word and Deed: The Role of the Holy Spirit in Luke-Acts.* Peabody, MA: Hendrickson, 1991.

Shepherd, William H. *The Narrative Function of the Holy Spirit as a Character in Luke-Acts.* SBLDS 147. Atlanta: Scholars Press, 1994.

Sherwin-White, and Adrian Nicolas. *Roman Society and Roman Law in the New Testament.* Winona Lake, IN: Eisenbrauns, 2000.

Skinner, Matthew L. *Locating Paul: Places of Custody as Narrative Settings in Acts 21–28.* AcBib 13. Atlanta: Society of Biblical Literature, 2003.

Sleeman, Matthew. *Geography and the Ascension Narrative in Acts.* Cambridge: Cambridge University Press, 2009.

Soards, Marion L. *The Speeches in Acts: Their Content, Context, and Concerns.* Louisville: Westminster John Knox, 1994.

Spencer, F. Scott. *Journeying through Acts: A Literary-Cultural Reading.* Peabody, MA: Hendrickson, 2004.

———. *The Portrait of Philip in Acts: A Study of Roles and Relations.* JSNTSup 67. Sheffield: JSOT Press, 1992.

Squires, John T. *The Plan of God in Luke-Acts.* SNTSMS 76. Cambridge: Cambridge University Press, 1993.

Stenschke, Christoph W. *Luke's Portrait of Gentiles prior to Their Coming to Faith.* WUNT 108. Tübingen: Mohr Siebeck, 1999.

Steyn, Gert J. *Septuagint Quotations in the Context of the Petrine and Pauline Speeches of the Acta Apostolorum.* CBET 12. Kampen: Kok, 1995.

Tajra, Harry W. *The Trial of St. Paul: A Juridical Exegesis of the Second Half of the Acts of the Apostles.* WUNT 35. Tübingen: Mohr Siebeck, 1989.

Talbert, Charles H. *Reading Acts: A Literary and Theological Commentary on the Acts of the Apostles.* Rev. ed. RNTS. Macon, GA: Smyth, 2005.

Tannehill, Robert C. *The Narrative Unity of Luke-Acts: A Literary Interpretation.* Vol. 2 of *The Acts of the Apostles.* Philadelphia: Fortress, 1994.

Thompson, Alan. *The Acts of the Risen Lord: Luke's Account of God's Unfolding Plan.* NSBT 27. Downers Grove, IL: InterVarsity, 2011.

Turner, Max M. B. *"And So We Came to Rome": The Political Perspective of St. Luke.* SNTSMS 49. Cambridge: Cambridge University Press, 1983.

———. *Power from on High: The Spirit in Israel's Restoration and Witness in Luke-Acts.* JPTSup 9. Sheffield: Sheffield Academic, 1996.

Uytanlet, Samson. *Luke-Acts and Jewish Historiography: A Study of the Theology, Literature, and Ideology of Luke-Acts.* WUNT 2/366. Tübingen: Mohr Siebeck, 2014.

Walton, Steve. *Leadership and Lifestyle: The Portrait of Paul in the Miletus Speech and 1 Thessalonians.* SNTSMS 108. Cambridge: Cambridge University Press, 2000.

Watson, Alan. *The Trial of Stephen: The First Christian Martyr.* Athens: University of Georgia Press, 1996.

Weatherly, Jon A. *Jewish Responsibility for the Death of Jesus in Luke-Acts.* JSNTSup 106. Sheffield: JSOT Press, 1994.

Weaver, John B. *Plots of Epiphany: Prison-Escape in Acts of the Apostles.* BZNW 131. Berlin: de Gruyter, 2004.

Wenk, Matthias. *Community-Forming Power: The Socio-Ethical Role of the Spirit in Luke-Acts.* Sheffield: Sheffield Academic, 2000.

Williams, Margaret H. "Palestinian Jewish Personal Names in Acts." In *The Book of Acts in Its Palestinian Setting*, edited by R. J. Bauckham, 79–113. Vol. 4 of *The Book of Acts in Its First-Century Setting*, edited by Bruce W. Winter. Grand Rapids: Eerdmans, 1995.

Wilson, Benjamin R. "Jew-Gentile Relations and the Geographic Movement of Acts 10:1–11:18." *CBQ* 80 (2018): 81–96.

Wilson, Stephen G. *The Gentiles and the Gentile Mission in Luke-Acts.* SNTSMS 23. Cambridge: Cambridge University Press, 1973.

———. *Luke and the Law.* SNTSMS 50. Cambridge: Cambridge University Press, 1983.

Winter, Bruce W. "The Importance of the *Captatio Benevolentiae* in the Speeches of Tertullus and Paul in Acts 24:1–21." *JTS* 42 (1991): 505–31.

———. "In Public and in Private: Early Christian Interactions with Religious Pluralism." In *One God, One Lord in a World of Religious Pluralism*, edited by A. D. Clarke and B. W. Winter, 112–34. Cambridge: Tyndale, 1991.

———. "Official Proceedings and the Forensic Speeches in Acts 24–26." In *The Book of Acts in Its Ancient Literary Setting*, edited by Bruce W. Winter and A. D. Clarke, 305–6. Vol. 1 of *The Book of Acts in Its First-Century Setting*, edited by B. W. Winter. Exeter: Paternoster, 1993.

CHAPTER TWO

Romans

Introduction

The influence of Romans in the history of the church is remarkable. Augustine's understanding of grace was mined especially from Romans, though there were other sources as well. Martin Luther's entrance into the gates of paradise came as it dawned on him what Paul meant by the righteousness of God. The Reformation that swept through Europe and turned the Western world upside down was certainly shaped by the message of Romans. Then in the early part of the twentieth century, Karl Barth's commentary on Romans, as he noted, pulled on a bell that rang throughout the theological landscape and called into question the theological liberalism that was sweeping through the Western world.

No one seriously doubts Pauline authorship, and we know that Paul wrote the letter when he was in Corinth (Acts 20:2–3), and it should probably be dated in AD 55 or 56. In the past some scholars claimed that Romans was a treatise, a complete and full presentation of Paul's theology. Certainly Romans is a fuller exposition of Paul's theology than any other letter and is the most important Pauline letter for understanding his theology. Still, some important themes in his theology remain undeveloped in the letter. For instance, Ephesians represents a fuller exposition of the role of the church than we find in Romans or any other Pauline letter. Along the same lines, 1 Corinthians 12–14 says far more about spiritual gifts than we learn in Romans 12:4–8. Eschatology permeates Paul's theology and plays a critical role in Romans, but we see nothing like the extended reflections on Jesus's return that we find in 1 Thessalonians 4:13–5:11 and 2 Thessalonians 2:1–12. Christology isn't neglected in Romans, and we see an important christological confession at the inception of the letter (1:3–4), and yet virtually all would agree that we lack the depth of Christology found in Philippians 2:6–11 or Colossians 1:15–20. Other areas of Paul's theology could be explored, but it is clear that Romans isn't a comprehensive unfolding of Paul's thought.

We need to ask why Paul includes the subjects addressed in Romans. Is there an explanation that helps us understand every part of the letter? What strikes careful readers is the focus on issues pertaining to Jews and gentiles. Paul speaks of the Jew first and also the Greek (Rom. 1:16; 2:9–10). The sins of gentiles are revealed (1:19–32) but also the sins of the Jews (2:1–29). When it comes to righteousness by faith, one of the central affirmations is that both Jews and gentiles are justified in the same way (3:29–30; 4:9–16), and Paul emphasizes that both Jews and gentiles are children of Abraham (4:17–25). In addition, the letter often addresses the matter of the Mosaic law, which is a vital issue for Jew-gentile relations. Jews were apt to think that the law restrains sin, but Paul argues the opposite; the law doesn't damp down sin but exacerbates it (5:20; 6:14–15; 7:1–25). What changes people is God's grace in Jesus Christ and the power of the Holy Spirit (6:1–23; 7:6; 8:1–39). Nowhere else in his letters is there an extended reflection of God's promises to Israel, and in chapters 9–11 Paul explains how the destiny of Israel relates to the inclusion of the gentiles. Then in 14:1–15:13 the matter of clean and unclean foods comes to the forefront, and the weak were primarily Jews who believed that the purity laws regarding food were still important, while the strong were mainly gentiles who believed that they were free to eat any foods.

The Jew-gentile character of the letter helps us understand the purpose of Romans. It is likely that divisions plagued Jews and gentiles in the churches (cf. 14:1–15:13). Furthermore, Paul himself was a polarizing figure, especially among Jews and even Jewish Christians, as Acts 21:20–25 attests. Paul wanted the Roman Christians to be the launching pad for his mission to Spain, but they could hardly function as his base if they were divided over the role of the law, particularly when that was the very issue that raised concerns about Paul. Paul, then, in the letter gives a full explanation of his view of the law and the place of Israel and gentiles in God's plan. His aim was that they would embrace the gospel he proclaimed and support him as he took that same gospel to Spain. Here a rough outline of the letter is provided.

Outline

Introduction to God's saving righteousness	1:1–17
Need for God's saving righteousness	1:18–3:20
God's saving righteousness explained and experienced by faith	3:21–4:25

Hope as a result of God's saving righteousness	5:1–8:39
God's saving righteousness with reference to Israel	9:1–11:36
Living out God's saving righteousness	12:1–15:13
God's saving righteousness in the Pauline mission	15:14–16:27

Opening and Closing Romans (1:1–7; 16:25–27)

The first seven verses constitute the opening of Romans, and the opening is by far the longest of any of Paul's Letters. The opening is extended because Paul had never met the Roman Christians, and so he takes the opportunity to introduce himself and his gospel to them to secure their good will at the outset. Since the themes in the opening of the letter (1:1–7) are matched in the closing (16:25–27), both the opening and the closing will be discussed here. Some scholars argue that the closing wasn't included in the letter sent to the Romans; the discussion is complex and can't be adjudicated here, but it is likely that the verses are original. The opening and closing function like a sandwich for the rest of the letter, and the remaining contents of the letter are inside the sandwich. From the very first verse of the letter, we see that Romans centers on the gospel, which fulfills the OT Scriptures (1:2). The word "gospel" (*euangelion*) refers to good news and reaches back especially to Isaiah 40:9 and 52:7. The gospel proclaims that God reigns and rules, and this rule in Isaiah is manifested by Israel's return from exile, and the return from exile signifies that Israel's sins are forgiven so that the promises made to Abraham will be fulfilled. Israel went into exile because of its sin, and it will return from exile because its sins would be wiped away by the servant of the Lord (cf. Isa. 40:2; 42:24; 43:24–27; 44:22; 53:12; 57:17; 58:1; 59:2).

The gospel is central in Paul's theology (Rom. 1:1–5; 16:25), and it isn't a mere word, for in the proclamation of the gospel, God's creative and almighty power is at work (1:16). The relationship of the gospel to the OT Scriptures is reaffirmed in the closing; the gospel is a "mystery" revealed and a prophecy fulfilled (16:25–26). If the OT wholly conceals what is to come, then the understanding of the OT would be limited to the intellectual elite or to those who claimed to receive revelations directly from God. Conversely, one should not posit a simplistic and patently obvious continuity between the old covenant and the new, for it is also a mystery revealed. To paraphrase Augustine, what was concealed in the OT is now revealed in the NT.

We are also not surprised to learn that the gospel centers on Jesus Christ as God's Son (1:3–4; cf. 16:25): thus if the OT Scriptures are rightly interpreted, they point to Jesus Christ. We find a confessional statement about Jesus as God's Son in 1:3–4. First, Jesus is a descendant of David, which fulfills the OT promise that the Messiah would come from David's line (2 Sam. 7:12–16; Ps. 72:17; Isa. 11:1–5, 10; Jer. 23:5–6; 33:14–17; Ezek. 34:23–24; 37:24–25). The promises to Abraham, by which blessing would come to the entire world, are fulfilled in Jesus as David's son.

Second, Jesus was also "appointed" to be God's Son in power by the Holy Spirit at his resurrection (Rom. 1:4). Some English versions translate the word *horisthentos* as "declared" (NASB, ESV, NRSV) instead of "appointed," but the word never means "declared," and Paul teaches that Jesus was appointed as God's Son in power when he was raised from the dead and installed as the messianic king at God's right hand. Paul doesn't propound adoptionist Christology, as if Jesus were not the Son of God before the resurrection. If we look at verses 3–4 as a whole, we see that the one who was always God's Son, the one who preexisted as God's Son, was appointed at the resurrection to be God's Son *in power*. To put it another way: Paul is making a redemptive-historical point here. A new stage of redemptive history dawned with Jesus's resurrection, and he now reigns at God's right hand as God's Son and as the Davidic king, showing that Jesus Christ is Lord.

Paul also calls attention to his own ministry as an apostle of Jesus Christ. God "called" him "as an apostle," and he was "set apart for the gospel" (1:1; cf. 1:5) on the Damascus road. Paul's goal as a missionary and apostle was "the obedience of faith" among the gentiles (1:5; 16:26). What it means to be converted is to confess Jesus as Lord (10:9), and those who are saved *obey* the gospel (10:16). Paul speaks of the conversion of believers as "the obedience of the gentiles" (15:18). Obedience, which means submission to Jesus Christ, stems from and flows from faith. No one is converted who doesn't submit to Jesus as Lord and Savior.

Thanksgiving and Theme (1:8–17)

Paul usually places a thanksgiving after the opening of the letter, and Romans isn't any different (1:8–15). Several themes in the thanksgiving stand out. First, Paul gives thanks to God for the worldwide impact of the Romans' faith. Second, Paul had desired to visit the Romans for some time to encourage and strengthen them in the faith. As an apostle of Christ he felt a special obligation to proclaim the gospel to the gentiles. Paul's desire to proclaim the gospel can't be limited to a duty since he also indicates his eagerness to proclaim the gospel to all peoples, whether Jews or gentiles, whether foreigners or natives, whether wise or foolish. If believers proclaim the gospel only out of duty, their efforts will eventually wane, but for Paul preaching the gospel was a duty and a delight.

Most agree that the theme of the letter is found in 1:16–17. The ancient world was an honor-shame culture, and one might feel shame since the gospel was deemed by gentiles to be foolish and by Jews to be weak (1 Cor. 1:18–25). Paul was not ashamed, however, since the gospel is God's power, bringing salvation and delivering those who believe (both Jews and Greeks) from God's wrath, which will be poured out on the final day.

One of the most famous statements in Romans follows: in the gospel God's righteousness is revealed. Luther struggled mightily with this phrase and initially thought it referred to the righteousness by which God judged sinners. Luther came to realize that the righteousness of God refers here to the saving righteousness of God, not his judging righteousness. We see in the OT that God's righteousness often denotes his saving righteousness (Pss. 22:31; 31:1; 35:24, 28; 40:10; 69:27–29; 88:12; 119:123; Isa. 42:6, 21; 45:8, 13; 51:5–8; Mic. 6:5; 7:9). For instance, we read, "The LORD has made his salvation known and revealed his righteousness to the nations" (Ps. 98:2 NIV). The parallel between "righteousness" and "salvation" is apparent, showing that the psalmist is speaking of the saving righteousness of God.

Today scholars continue to debate over the significance of the phrase: does it refer to (1) an attribute of God, (2) a gift of God, (3) covenant faithfulness, or (4) God's righteousness as a transforming power? The discussion, of course, is technical, and we can't get into the details here. Righteousness should not be defined as covenant faithfulness; it *fulfills* God's covenant promises, but it *should not be defined as* covenant faithfulness. When Paul speaks of God's saving righteousness (cf. Rom. 3:21–22; 9:30–31; 10:3–6; 1 Cor. 1:30; 2 Cor. 3:9; 5:21; Gal. 2:21; 3:6, 21; 5:5; Phil. 3:9), the idea that God's righteousness is a transforming power is also unlikely. If we compare the contexts of Philippians 3:2–9 and Romans 10:1–4, we see that the subject matter discussed is virtually the same, and it is clear that the gift of righteousness is in view in Philippians. Furthermore, the verb (*dikaioō*) is clearly declarative, referring to the gift of righteousness, the declaration that one is in the right before God as judge (Rom. 8:33). It is quite unlikely that the related noun *dikaiosynē* has a different meaning since the noun and the verb are often used close to one another (e.g., Rom. 3:21–22, 24; Gal. 2:16, 21).

The righteousness of God, then, is both an attribute of God and the gift of God. It is an attribute that "is revealed" (Rom. 1:17) and "made known" (3:21 NIV). At the same time, it is a gift received by faith. Saying that God's righteousness is both a gift and an attribute is not a contradiction, nor is it hard to imagine readers having both ideas. For God gives believers *his* righteousness by faith. The phrase "from faith to faith" indicates that right standing with God is obtained by faith from first to last.

Righteousness by faith is affirmed from the quotation of Habakkuk 2:4. Paul's reading accords with the original context of Habakkuk, where the Lord threatened to punish Judah because they failed to keep the law (1:4). In the midst of judgment that would be imposed by Babylon, however, the Lord also promised final salvation (Hab. 3). God promised a future new exodus for Israel (Hab. 3), and the many allusions to the exodus in chapter 3 indicate the promise of a new exodus, a new deliverance for the people of God. Habakkuk's response functions as an example for Israel. He will continue to trust the Lord even if the fig tree doesn't blossom and vines are lacking fruit (3:17–18). He will continue to trust in and rejoice in God's promise of future salvation amid the impending judgment, and Paul's readers do the same as they put their faith in Christ crucified and risen.

The Sin of Gentiles and Jews (1:18–3:20)

The Sin of Gentiles (1:18–32)

God's saving righteousness is obtained by faith, and Romans 1:18–3:20 explains why both gentiles and Jews need God's saving righteousness. They need God's saving righteousness because of his judging righteousness, because of his wrath, which is revealed from heaven (1:18). Human beings suppress the truth about God because of their godlessness and unrighteousness. Most scholars agree that Paul concentrates on the sin of the gentiles in 1:19–31 and the sin of the Jews in 2:1–29, and the following arguments support this reading. First, in striking ways Paul's words in 1:19–32 match the typical Jewish view of gentile idolatry (see Wis. 11–15). Second, the appeal to creation (instead of the law) as a standard of judgment suggests a focus on gentiles. Third, the blatant idolatry described was common among gentiles but rare among Jews in Paul's day. Fourth, same-sex behavior was quite common in the Greco-Roman world, but consistently rejected by Jews.

The fundamental sin of gentiles is that they have suppressed the truth about God that has been revealed to them. Through the natural world, through the created order, God has revealed his power and divinity. The argument isn't that as they perceive the created world, those who are particularly gifted intellectually realize that God exists. Instead, Paul argues that all people everywhere, when they see the created world, intuitively recognize God's power and his Godness (1:18–20). They realize that the one true God deserves all glory and praise and thanksgiving, but they turn away from

God's lordship and construct an alternative version of reality, exchanging God's glory for images and idols (1:23), worshiping the creature rather than the Creator (1:25).

Paul alludes to Psalm 106:20 and Jeremiah 2:11 in Romans 1:23, and both of those verses describe Israel's idolatry. Psalm 106 contrasts God's faithful love and saving acts with Israel's treachery, affirming that God's faithfulness will prevail. Verse 20 represents a particularly egregious example of Israel's faithlessness, for right after the covenant was ratified on Mount Sinai and Israel agreed to be a faithful covenant partner, they exchanged the glory of God for an ox that eats grass (Exod. 32). Similarly, Jeremiah laments that Israel abandoned the Lord, exclaiming, "My people have exchanged their Glory for useless idols" (Jer. 2:11). Even though in historical context the verses applied to the Jews, Paul has gentiles in mind here. Perhaps he subtly anticipates Romans 2, where we discover that the Jews have the same problem as the gentiles. Idolatry isn't merely a gentile problem or a Jewish problem: it is a human problem.

Three times we are told that God has handed over the gentiles to evil (1:24, 26, 28), since they have rejected his lordship. They are handed over to sin because they "exchanged the truth of God for a lie" and thus "worshiped and served what has been created instead of the Creator" (1:25). They are given over because they didn't "acknowledge God" as God (1:28). Many other sins of human beings are noted here (1:26–31), but all sins come from the great sin, the fundamental sin, the root sin, which is the refusal to let God be Lord over our lives. We probably have an allusion to the account of Adam and Eve (Gen. 3:1–6) because their sin was the desire to be independent of God, to be their own gods instead of depending upon the all-glorious God.

Why does Paul bring up same-sex behavior here (Rom. 1:26–27)? Not because it is the worst sin imaginable. Instead, same-sex sin mirrors the rejection of God. What is natural for human beings—natural in the sense that it reflects what God *intended* human beings to do—is for human beings to worship the one who created them. Because of sin, human beings have turned from what is natural (worshiping the Creator) to what is unnatural (worshiping the creature). In the same way they have turned from natural sexual relations (with the opposite sex) to same-sex relations. The other sins listed in 1:28–31 show that all sin is unnatural, in the sense that all sin violates God's intention in creating human beings. The virulence of sin is evident in 1:32 in that people encourage others to sin, even though they realize that sin deserves judgment and death. Still they *applaud* others who sin, presumably because it makes them feel better about their own sin.

The Sin of Jews and Judgment according to Works (2:1–29)

The focus in Romans 2 is the sin of the Jews, as Paul drives to the conclusion that all people everywhere are sinners (3:9–20, 23). Paul doesn't specifically mention the Jews until 2:17, but there are good reasons for thinking that the Jews are the primary target in 2:1–16 as well. For instance, the sinful behavior described in 1:19–32 typically would be criticized by Jews. More important, 2:3–4 reflects Jews who believed that they were protected by their covenant relationship with God. Since they were in covenant with him, they thought that they would be spared from his wrath. Finally, the reference to the law in 2:12 almost certainly refers to the Jews who believed they had an advantage before God over against gentiles because they possessed the law. The emphasis on the Jew first and then the Greek (2:9–10) likewise suggests that the primary focus is on Jewish disobedience. When reading this chapter, we must also remember the distinction between the *audience* and the *target*. The *audience* for the letter is the Christians at Rome, but the *target* in chapter 2 is unbelieving Jews. We see, then, that Paul is not criticizing Jewish believers in Christ. Here we probably have a typical synagogue sermon that Paul preached to Jews as he proclaimed the gospel of Christ.

Romans 2 is an example of a diatribe, a mode of discourse where one reproves an opponent. Rhetorical questions and dialogue with an opponent were features of the diatribe style. Jews, reading the indictment of the gentiles in 1:19–32, would voice a hearty Amen! Paul surprises them, however, much as Nathan set a trap for David in 2 Samuel 12, or like Amos 1–2, which begins by declaiming against pagan nations but then turns to the sins of Judah and Israel. Through Paul's gospel the Lord was calling upon Israel to repent of its sins since those who fail to repent will face God's wrath on the day of eschatological judgment (Rom. 2:4–5).

Paul stresses that God's judgment is absolutely fair and impartial; he judges every person according to their works (2:6–11). In saying that judgment is according to works, Paul alludes to Proverbs 24:12 and Psalm 62:12. The notion that God judges according to works is a common OT theme (Job 34:11; Ps. 28:4; Jer. 17:10; 25:14; 32:19; 51:24; Ezek. 33:20). Romans 2:7–10 works out the thesis statement in verse 6 in more detail, and it clarifies that the final judgment and eternal life are at stake. The Jews can't rely on their covenant privilege if they don't actually keep the law. In verses 7 and 10 Paul also speaks of those who do good works and receive eternal life. Some interpreters argue that Paul speaks hypothetically: if anyone does good works, eternal life will be the reward; but since no one actually keeps the law sufficiently, the category of those who do good is empty. Such a conclusion is certainly possible, especially if one looks at the theme of the chapter as a whole and at the conclusion that all are sinners in 3:9–20. Still, there is no indication that Paul speaks hypothetically here, and so we should accept that good works are necessary for eternal life, and I will explain shortly how this fits with Paul's overall theme in this section.

Romans 2:12–16 is quite controversial. Still, the main point of the paragraph is clear: gentiles who sin without the law will perish because of their sin, and Jews who sin with the law will also be judged (2:12). God's impartiality shines through again; the Jews aren't spared simply because they are Jews and covenant members. Hearing the law doesn't justify; it is the doing of the law that justifies (2:13). The interpretation of 2:14–15 is contested: is the reference to believers or unbelievers? Good arguments can be adduced on both sides. If unbelievers are in view, Paul speaks of natural law and the conscience by which gentiles know what is right, even though they don't externally possess the law. More likely, Paul thinks of believing gentiles here. The CSB has it right in translating the first clause of verse 14 as "gentiles, who by nature do not have the law" instead of "when gentiles, who do not have the law, do by nature things required by the law" (NIV). The focus is on gentile identity, not whether one can do the law instinctively. The decisive argument for seeing a reference to Christians is verse 15: the law's work is inscribed on their hearts, and according to Jeremiah 31:33, this is the effect of the new covenant. Since accusing thoughts are noted, we recognize that Paul doesn't argue that *all* gentiles are justified in the final judgment; only those whose thoughts *excuse* them because they have received a new-covenant saving work will be vindicated (cf. also Ezek. 36:26–27). Those whose thoughts *accuse* them will be condemned.

In Romans 2:17–24 the privileges and the contradictions of unbelieving Jews are exposed. The Jewish privileges are genuine. Relying on the law isn't a fault but fits with the OT, where the law restores one's soul (Pss. 19:7–11; 119). Boasting in God is obviously a good thing, and it is certainly true that Jews knew God's will and ways because they were instructed in the law. Israel's role as a guide, a light, and an instructor—all fit with OT conceptions (cf. Isa. 42:6–7; 49:6) since God appointed Abraham and the Jews to be a blessing to all peoples (Gen. 12:1–3; cf. Exod. 19:5–6; Isa. 42:6). The problem with the Jews was hypocrisy (Rom. 2:21–24): they violated the law that they treasured and taught. Paul isn't saying that all Jews steal, commit adultery, and rob temples. Such charges would be ludicrous. Instead, he uses colorful examples (like any good preacher!) to illustrate his point: they don't keep the law themselves. The commandments referred to stem from the Decalogue

(Exod. 20:15, 14, 4–5; Deut. 5:19, 18, 8–9; cf. also Jer. 7:9–11), which prohibits stealing, adultery, and idolatry.

Paul quotes Isaiah 52:5 from the LXX in Romans 2:24. Some think Paul cites Ezekiel 36:20, since in Ezekiel 36 God's name is reviled because of the sin of Israel, while in the Isaiah text the blasphemy occurs because of oppression by foreign nations, and in context the Lord comforts and assures Israel. Some charge, then, that Paul misuses the OT text, but his use of Isaiah 52:5 is defensible when we place the Isaiah text onto the larger canvas of Isaiah's theology. In Isaiah 40–66 the people are in exile because of their sin (40:2; 42:24–25; 43:22–28; 50:1), and thus gentiles cast aspersions on Israel's God since Israel was in exile (which made them question Yahweh's power).

Romans 2 concludes with a reference to circumcision (2:25–29), which was the sign of the covenant (Gen. 17:9–14). Some Jews believed circumcision protected them from God's wrath even if they were disobedient, since it was the covenant sign. Paul rejects this understanding, claiming that those who fail to keep the law are uncircumcised in God's sight. In other words, if they were disobedient, they were not covenant members. On the other hand, gentiles who observe the law, even though they are uncircumcised, will be counted as circumcised, as covenant members.

Romans 2:28–29 clarifies that Paul isn't talking about hypothetical gentile obedience, but real obedience. The "for" in verse 28 connects verses 28–29 back to 26–27. The argument works like this: gentiles keep the law even though they are uncircumcised because they are spiritual Jews and truly circumcised by virtue of the work of the Holy Spirit. Ethnic Jews who trust in covenant signs and covenant privilege are deceived because true Jewishness and true circumcision aren't outward matters. Instead, gentiles who keep the law are true Jews, even though their true Jewishness is hidden from human beings. The mystery of the gospel is revealed: gentiles are equal members of the people of God with Jews; they are part of the restored Israel.

How can Paul speak of gentiles belonging to the people of God as those who keep and observe God's commands? Doesn't that contradict the theme of this section, which argues that no one is justified by works of the law? The obedience of the gentiles here is genuine, and verse 29 is decisive at this point. Circumcision of the heart fulfills the promise of Deuteronomy 30:6, and in the context of Deuteronomy such heart circumcision will occur *after* exile; thus Moses looked forward to an eschatological circumcision of the heart. This demand is met in the new covenant, where the Lord writes his law on the hearts by his Spirit (Jer. 31:33; Ezek. 36:26–27). Gentile obedience, then, isn't *the basis* of their relationship with God (for the basis is the death and resurrection of Christ) but *a consequence and result* of new life in the Spirit.

No one is right before God on *the basis of law obedience*, but Paul doesn't claim that the gentile obedience is the basis, for even though he speaks of gentile obedience and even though their lives are transformed, their obedience is still imperfect.

One last question must be answered. Why does Paul make the argument about gentile obedience in Romans 2? It seems confusing that an argument about gentile obedience, obedience that makes them covenant members, is inserted in the middle of an argument where all are said to be sinners and in need of justification. The answer is that Paul stresses the inclusion of gentiles into the people of God to motivate Jews to repent and to put their faith in Christ. He anticipates and forecasts here the theme of jealousy in Romans 10:19 and 11:11, 14, where he teaches that the inclusion of the gentiles will move Israel to turn to Christ.

All Are Sinners (3:1–20)

Romans 3:1–8 is one of the more difficult texts to interpret, probably because Paul touches on several themes but doesn't pursue them in detail, so threads are hanging that are not picked up until later in the letter. Paul again surprises readers as he begins the chapter. He finishes chapter 2 by affirming that gentile believers are truly circumcised and truly Jews, and he opens chapter 3 by asking whether there is any benefit in being an ethnic Jew or physically circumcised. We expect him to say: none at all, but instead he says, "Much in every way!" (3:2 NIV). The Jews have the advantage of possessing God's saving promises. God will remain faithful to his saving promises even though the Jews were unfaithful.

God's constancy is also revealed in judgment. In verse 4 Paul cites Psalm 51:4, which speaks of God as being "justified in your words and triumph[ing] when you judge" (Rom. 3:4). Psalm 51 represents David's confession of his sin in committing adultery with Bathsheba and then murdering Uriah; in verse 4 he confesses God's justice in judging him. Paul makes the same point: even though God promised to save Israel, he is also just in punishing Israel when the people sin. If God refused to judge Israel when its people sinned, then he couldn't judge anyone; he couldn't judge the world. There would be no justice, and a God without justice was inconceivable to Paul and to his Jewish opponents too! They weren't modern-day people who believed all should and would be saved. Paul refutes the charge that he teaches that people should actually pursue evil so that God's grace would be maximized in dispensing mercy, for such a view completely distorts his view; Paul takes up this matter again in chapter 6.

In Romans 3:9–20 the conclusion for 1:18–3:8 is given: all are sinners, and all need God's saving righteousness. The twists and turns of Paul's argument continue to confront us. In verse 9 he asks whether Jews are any better off, and we might expect from 3:1–4 that the answer is yes since they are the recipients of God's saving promises, but Paul firmly rejects such a conclusion. Instead, all, both Jews and gentiles, are charged with being under the power of sin. Verses 10–18 verify that all are under sin's dominion by citing a variety of OT texts. In verses 10–12 Paul quotes Psalm 14:1–3, and perhaps he calls upon Ecclesiastes 7:20 as well. Romans 3:13 contains citations from Psalms 5:9 and 140:3, while Romans 3:14 is an adaptation of Psalm 10:7. Romans 3:15–17 abridges and adapts Isaiah 59:7–8, with nearly the exact wording from the latter in Romans 3:16–17. Finally, verse 18 quotes Psalm 36:1.

The structure of the OT citations is illuminating. Romans 3:10–12 depicts the universality of sin: no person in the world is righteous; none seek God; all are corrupt; not even one does what is good and right and true. Verses 13–14 zero in on sins of speech. The corruption at the core of human beings reveals itself in poisonous speech and venomous words. Verses 15–17 go a step further from speech to action: murder, misery, and ruin are an all-too-common story in human history. Verse 18 functions as the ground and root cause of the sins described in verses 10–17, yet it also forms an *inclusio* with verses 10–12, reminding the reader again that the root of sin lies in a failure to reckon rightly with God, the refusal to fear God. The OT texts that in their original context distinguished between the righteous and the wicked are now applied to both Jews who believed they were righteous and gentiles. By removing the distinction between the righteous and the wicked, Paul overturns the Jewish concept of covenant protection. The sin of the Jews places them in the same situation as the gentiles: guilty before God.

Verses 19–20 conclude and summarize the argument. The law speaks to those who are in the realm of the law, namely, the Jewish people. If the covenant people did not and could not keep the law, then no one is able to observe it. The whole world is silenced before God, and everyone stands guilty before him. No one is justified "by the works of the law," for the law reveals human sins.

The new perspective on Paul, which has been influential since the late 1970s, argues that works of law focus on the boundary markers that separate Jews and gentiles, such as circumcision, food laws, and the Sabbath. The new perspective rightly sees that the Jew-gentile issue plays a major role in Paul's thought. Still, when Paul says justification isn't by works of the law, he doesn't concentrate on the boundary markers but on the entire law. In Romans 2–3 Paul doesn't criticize the Jews for excluding the gentiles. Instead, he indicts them for sinning in general, for not repenting (2:1–5), for not keeping the law (2:17–24), and for sin in thought, word, and deed (3:9–18). Justification can't be gained through works of law since all without exception fail to do all that the law commands.

The Saving Righteousness of God by Faith (3:21-4:25)

But Now! (3:21–26)

The words "But now" represent a dramatic shift in the argument and in redemptive history. A new age, which is "apart from the law," apart from the Sinai covenant and from the works of the law, has dawned with the coming of Jesus Christ. Now the saving righteousness of God has been manifested. Even though this saving righteousness is apart from the law covenant, it fulfills the OT in that it accords with what the OT prophesied. Romans 3:22 clarifies that God's saving righteousness, right standing with him, is given to those who put their faith in Jesus Christ. Paul particularly emphasizes the universality of the gift: it is for *all* those who believe, and God makes no distinction between Jews and gentiles.

Some interpreters argue that the phrase in 3:22 and elsewhere should be translated "the faithfulness of Jesus Christ" instead of "faith in Christ." Such a reading is certainly possible but is not the most likely translation for the following reasons: Some think it is redundant to speak of "faith in Jesus Christ" and believing in the same verse, but one person's redundancy is another person's emphasis! Paul repeats the idea of believing twice because it is imperative to see that righteousness is obtained by believing instead of by achieving, by resting instead of by working, by relying instead of by trying. Paul stands in contrast to Second Temple Judaism, which often put an emphasis on human achievement and obedience. Furthermore, the two expressions aren't exactly synonymous. In the first the emphasis is on "faith *in Jesus Christ*"; Christ as the object of faith is missing in the reference to believing. And in the second instance the focus is on "*all* who believe," which is a thought missing in the first phrase.

Justification (right standing with God, 3:24) is free; it is the result of God's grace. It is free for human beings but, as Dietrich Bonhoeffer said, it is costly grace since it came at the death of God's Son. The justifying work of God constitutes redemption (*apolytrōsis*) for the people of God. Redemption language is exodus language, evoking Israel's deliverance from Egypt (e.g., Deut. 7:8; 9:26; 15:15; 24:18). The first exodus from Egypt became a pattern and promise for a second exodus, for freedom from Babylonian exile (Isa. 41:14; 43:1, 14;

44:22–24; 51:11; 52:3; 62:12; 63:9), and in turn both the first and second exodus point forward to the great deliverance accomplished by Christ.

The paragraph before us is so important because it has key words that denote Christ's death: righteousness, redemption, and "atoning sacrifice." The meaning of the word translated by the CSB as "atoning sacrifice" (*hilastērion*; "sacrifice of atonement," Rom. 3:25 NRSV, NIV) is the subject of debate. Paul actually has in mind here "the mercy seat" or "the place of atonement." Some have argued that word should be translated "expiation" (RSV), while others have defended "propitiation" (see NASB, ESV). The word "expiation" means that sins are wiped away or erased by Christ's death. Those who defend expiation worry that propitiation, which means that God's wrath is appeased or satisfied by Christ's death, buys into pagan ideas of a bloodthirsty, vengeful, and arbitrary God who, like the pagan gods of the Greeks, needs to be appeased for his bad temper. The caution is salutary and helps us avoid unsavory notions of God's wrath that do not fit with the biblical witness. Even though the word refers to the mercy seat, we still have, given the entire context, a reference to propitiation. God judges sinners, as 1:18 shows, by pouring out his wrath upon them. His righteous judgment is described as his wrath (2:5; 3:5–6), yet such wrath isn't like the temper tantrums of the Greek gods but is holy, righteous, and the just response to human sin. God's wrath is not primitive, arbitrary, or capricious but is his holy and righteous response to human sin.

It would be a gross distortion of what is being stated here to say that Jesus persuades an angry God to stave off his anger, for God himself, because of his great love (cf. 5:6–10), put forth Jesus to appease his own anger. Actually, we should not pit expiation and propitiation against one another, for both ideas are present: God wiped away and forgave sins *and* he appeased and satisfied his wrath on the basis of Jesus's sacrifice. The background for the theology of atonement found here has a number of Old Testament strands. The great day of atonement in Leviticus 16 is almost certainly in view, as are Leviticus 17:11 and Isaiah 53. All these texts show that atonement comes through sacrifice, through the shedding of blood, and it all climaxes in Isaiah 53 with the guilt offering of the servant of the Lord as a substitutionary sacrifice (53:10).

The word *hilastērion* (atoning sacrifice) is rightly rendered "mercy seat," for just as the lid on the ark of the covenant in Leviticus 16 is the place where atonement was made, so too Jesus is the place of atonement. In the new age God now dwells with his people in and through Jesus Christ. Since Jesus is the definitive and final sacrifice, OT sacrifices are no longer necessary because they are fulfilled in Jesus's sacrifice. Such sacrifices foreshadowed the forgiveness achieved in Jesus Christ.

We come now to the last stage of the argument. What does the word "righteousness" mean in Romans 3:25–26? Some argue that it means "saving righteousness" as in 3:21–22, but the context supports the meaning "judging righteousness," judging according to God's holiness and justice. God set Jesus forth as an atoning sacrifice, as his mercy seat, to satisfy his wrath and to wipe away sin (v. 25). The key to interpreting these verses is the word translated as "passed over" (*paresis*). This word never means "forgiveness" but refers to God overlooking or passing over sin. God's act of passing over sin before Jesus died called into question his justice, but Jesus's death vindicates his righteousness since sin was punished in the person of Christ. Paul does not deny that God punished sin in the past; his point is that sin didn't receive the full and complete punishment deserved. In God's kindness he provided people with the opportunity to repent and to turn from their sins. Thus, in the cross of Christ, God's saving righteousness and judging righteousness meet, his love and justice converge, and his mercy and holiness come together.

Abraham and His Children (3:27–4:25)

As Romans 3 concludes, Paul makes three quick points. First, human beings can't boast of their right standing with God since justification is by faith alone and not by works of the law. Second, the oneness of God, as celebrated in the Jewish Shema (Deut. 6:4), has crucial implications for justification. Since there is only one God, the same way of salvation applies to both Jews and gentiles, and that way is by faith instead of works of law. Paul probably alludes to Zechariah 14:9, which also affirms God's oneness, for Zechariah anticipates the day when the Lord will be "King over the whole earth," and the eschatological promise in Zechariah is being fulfilled as the gospel goes to Jews and gentiles. Third, saying that justification isn't by works of law doesn't lead to the conclusion that the law has no role in the life of believers; it still functions as a moral norm, and how this is so will be explained later in the letter.

In Romans 4 Paul supports justification by faith by appealing to the life of Abraham. Abraham played a foundational role as the father of the Jewish people, and Jews in the Second Temple period focused on Abraham's obedience (1 Macc. 2:52; Sir. 44:19–21; cf. Jub. 16.28; 24.10–11; 2 Bar. 57.1–2). Paul's perspective on Abraham stands out as radically different (Rom. 4:1–5). If Abraham actually was justified by works, if he truly did what God required, then he could boast before God. Paul compares it to working for someone: if someone does the works required, they deserve to be paid. But Abraham did not do the works that God required! He was—a shocking claim to Jewish ears—ungodly. Abraham's pagan background is attested in Joshua 24:2, where we are told that Abraham and his ancestors "worshiped other gods." So, Abraham stood in the right before God not by obeying but by trusting, not by achieving but by believing. God justifies the ungodly who put their trust in him. The crucial verse for Paul is Genesis 15:6, where we are told that "Abraham believed God, and it was credited to him for righteousness" (Rom. 4:3). In Genesis 15 Abraham lamented that God had not given him an heir, concluding that his heir must be Eliezer his servant. The Lord told Abraham to go outside and to gaze at the night sky with its unending stars, promising him that his offspring would be as innumerable as the stars. Abraham believed this stunning promise and was counted as right before God.

David is introduced in Romans 4:6–8 as a secondary witness to support justification by faith and not works. Psalm 32:1–2 is quoted to support the case. Based on his own works, David did not stand in the right before God since he sinned grievously by committing adultery with Bathsheba and by murdering Uriah. Still, David knew the blessing of forgiveness, even though he was a lawbreaker. Righteousness by faith isn't confined to the NT; it is taught in the OT—in Genesis 15:6 and Psalm 32:1–2. Both Abraham and David were justified by faith and not by works.

In Romans 4:9–12 Paul asks the question whether righteousness belongs only to those who fit within the Jewish boundaries, whether Abraham's righteousness can be ascribed to his circumcision. Genesis 15:6 continues to play a major role in the discussion, where faith is counted as righteousness, though now Paul asks whether that faith which is counted as righteousness is confined to the circumcised. Here Paul appeals to the order of events in Genesis, since Genesis 15 (where Abraham's faith is counted as righteousness) precedes Genesis 17 (where Abraham was circumcised). Since Abraham's faith was counted as righteousness before circumcision, circumcision is not essential for righteousness; it is a sign and seal of righteousness by faith. Abraham, then, is the father of both Jewish and gentile believers.

In Romans 4:13–16 Paul considers the inheritance promised to Abraham and his offspring, namely, the promise that Abraham "would inherit the world" (4:13). The idea that Abraham would be heir of the world is surprising since God had promised Abraham that he would have offspring (Gen. 12:2; 13:16; 15:5; 17:4–6, 16–20; 18:18; 22:17), inherit the land of Canaan (12:7; 13:14–17; 15:7, 18–21; 17:8), and that all nations would be blessed through him (12:3; 18:18; 22:18). If we merge the three elements of the promise by taking universal blessing and land together, then the blessing extends to the entire world, and this is exactly what happens in the OT as the promise to Abraham is expanded upon. So, when we come to David, the entire earth will be under the king's rule (Ps. 2:8), and the messianic king will reign "from sea to sea, and from the River to the ends of the earth" (72:8 ESV). The "whole world" will be filled with Israel's fruit (Isa. 27:6), and thus the rule will be universal (Isa. 54:2–3).

Abraham's inheritance of the world wasn't based on his obedience but was given by virtue of his faith. If the inheritance is obtained by means of the law, faith is robbed of playing the decisive role in our relationship with God, and the focus is no longer on what God promises to give but on human effort to attain. Certainly, the law can't be the pathway to obtain the promise of a renewed creation because the law only brings wrath, not blessing. The law specifies what human beings are called to do, and since human beings transgress, God's wrath is the consequence of human sin. Receiving the promise by faith accords with God's grace in that the inheritance isn't obtained through human achievement but because God's mercy is extended to those who trust in him.

One of the central themes in Romans 4 is that Abraham is the father of both Jews and gentiles who believe, and 4:17–25 unpacks the nature of Abraham's faith, which saves. Faith alone saves, but what is the nature of the faith that saves? Abraham believed in the God who could give life where there was death: the creator God could call things into existence that didn't exist. Abraham's faith wasn't in faith itself, but in the promise that he would be the father of many nations (Gen. 15:5). Nor does faith close its eyes to the facts in a naive kind of wish fulfillment: Abraham acknowledged that he and Sarah were too old for the promise to be fulfilled; they had no ability to fulfill the promise.

We are surprised to read that Abraham didn't "waver in unbelief" since on reading the OT narrative it seems that he did waver and hesitate. When Paul says Abraham didn't waver, he doesn't mean that he never doubted or that he never strayed. His purpose is to say that Abraham's faith persisted and persevered through every obstacle. He became "fully convinced that what God had promised, he was also able to do" (Rom. 4:21). Faith gives "glory to God" (4:20) because it trusts that he will fulfill his promises, acknowledging that he is faithful and trustworthy (Gen. 15:6 again). Abraham's faith is a paradigm for all (Rom. 4:23–25), for believers also put their trust in the God who gives life to the dead, in the God who raised Jesus from the dead. When Jesus was raised from the dead, he was vindicated, declared to be in the right by God (1 Tim. 3:16). So too, those who believe are forgiven of their trespasses through Jesus's death (Isa. 53:12) and vindicated before God by virtue of his resurrection. His resurrection authenticates and confirms the justification of believers.

The Unshakeable Hope for Those Who Are Justified (5:1-8:39)

In the first four chapters of Romans, we see that God has fulfilled his saving promises through the death and resurrection of Jesus Christ. Those who put their faith in him are in the right before God. Some scholars think a major break should be placed after Romans 5, but it is more convincing to put the break after chapter 4. The fundamental reason for seeing a break here is thematic: in chapters 5–8 Paul emphasizes the hope of those who are justified.

The Blessings of Justification (5:1–11)

In chapters 1–4 righteousness by faith is featured, showing that human beings can't stand in the right before God by obedience (because all sin) but only through faith in Jesus Christ. Paul turns to the benefits of justification and begins with peace with God. Believers also enjoy access to God, just as in the old covenant there was access to God through the temple. Those who have access to God by faith stand in grace before God. The hope of believers is also secure because they have full confidence "in the glory of God" (5:2), which refers to the glory and splendor that God will grant to believers on the last day.

Astonishingly, believers are also filled with hope as they suffer from the pressures of life, and thus they rejoice in these pressures (5:3–4). We find similar teaching in 1 Peter 1:6–7 and James 1:2–4. Such rejoicing isn't because the struggles of life are pleasant but because suffering produces positive results in the lives of believers. The end result is that suffering produces hope, and hope springs up because believers see that they are being changed and transformed by God's grace. Nor will this hope bring shame on the last day, for even now the love of God has been poured out into the hearts of believers through the Holy Spirit (Joel 2:28–29).

Romans 5:6–11 provides objective evidence for the love of God, in that God's love is anchored to the cross of Christ, where he gave up his life for the sake of human beings. Christ died for those who are morally weak and helpless, for those who are ungodly, for those who are sinners, and for those who are his enemies. The love of Christ is contrasted with human devotion, for human beings may die for a righteous person or for a benefactor. In the ancient world, the story of the death of Alcestis for her husband, Admetus, was famous, and others died for friends or family members, but Christ's love stands out as being radically different since he died for those who hated him.

The death of Christ is the basis for assurance, confidence, and hope (5:9–10). Since Jesus has done the greatest thing imaginable, justifying believers through his blood, they can be confident of deliverance from wrath on the last day. A similar argument is made with respect to reconciliation. Since believers are now reconciled to God through the death of his Son, they will be saved on the last day by his resurrection life. The justification and reconciliation that believers enjoy gives unassailable hope for the future. When believers reflect on the wonder of God's love in Christ, they are filled with joy and rejoice in God through Christ (5:11), so that the giver is prized more than the gift.

Adam and Christ (5:12–21)

One of the most powerful and controversial texts in Paul is the discussion on Adam and Christ. There is no doubt that Paul believed Adam was a historical figure, and it is quite important for Christian theology. Sin isn't intrinsic and inherent to the human race: Adam and Eve were good when created. If the human race has many founders, how was sin introduced into the world? It seems difficult to believe they all fell as Adam did, and we come closer to the troubling and problematic notion that human beings were created sinful. If this is the case, sin is God's fault, and God's goodness is called into question.

Adam introduced sin, death, and condemnation into the world. All the devastation, all the misery, all the pain and horror in the world finds its root in Adam's sin. Sin and death are presented as two powers, as two mighty forces that overwhelm and conquer human beings. Anyone who has read history knows that the troubles in the world are massive. Why is the world the way it is? Why is there so much devastation, hatred, cruelty, and despair? The root cause is Adam's sin, his rejection of God's lordship in his life. Once we see the extent of Adam's sin, we could easily lose hope. Paul's argument in this section is that Christ has overcome the power of Adam's sin. Grace and life reign where sin and death previously ruled. Christ hasn't just reversed Adam's sin, but has gone beyond it, in that believers through Christ enjoy eternal life even in this present evil age, something that Adam never enjoyed. The discussion of Adam and Christ gives hope because we see that no evil, no matter how powerful, can withstand the power of God's grace in Christ. Life flourishes where death reigned!

A few details in the text will be considered. In Romans 5:12–14 Paul declares that sin and death entered the world through one man, Adam. Adam's sin didn't influence him alone but touched every human being after him. We think of the roll call of death in the genealogy in Genesis 5, where again and again we read: "then he died." Augustine believed that Romans 5:12 taught that all sinned in Adam, but he read the Scriptures to say "in whom" (his reading of the Latin *in quo*), but the translation "because" is a more likely meaning of the idiomatic Greek phrase *eph hō*. Paul refers in 5:12 to all people dying because they sinned individually, but this hardly leads to a Pelagian conclusion (the idea that all people are born into the world neutral and with the power to choose the good). Earlier in verse 12 Paul has already made it clear that Adam brought sin and death into the world, and he will hammer this home further in verses 15–19.

The role of verses 13–14 in the argument is disputed, and space is lacking to detail the various views, so I will explain what I think is most persuasive. Paul wants readers to see the distinctiveness of Adam's sin, its typological uniqueness. He sets up Adam and Christ as typological contrasts. The presence of sin in the world before the giving of the Mosaic law is acknowledged: who could doubt the presence of sin when one thinks of Cain's murder of Abel, of the human corruption that brought on the flood, and of the arrogance manifested at the tower of Babel? Sin before the law, however, was not counted against people in quite the same way, since it was not the violation of a specifically revealed commandment. This is not to say, however, that people weren't responsible for their sin since death reigned as king, and we already know that people die because of sin (5:12; 6:23). Paul has already said that those who don't have the law perish; they will face final judgment because they violate what they know to be right (2:12; cf. 1:32). But their sin wasn't like Adam's in that Adam violated a command made known to him, and thus there is a particular gravity and rebellion to Adam's transgression.

The impact of Adam's sin is set forth five times in 5:15–19, and the impact of Adam and Christ is contrasted. Because of Adam's sin, judgment, death, and condemnation have entered the world. Adam is the covenant representative, the covenant head for human beings. For individualistic cultures, such as is common in the West, the solidarity of the human race with Adam seems unfair. The human race, however, is an organic unity: what our first father did affects us all. We are one human family, organically related to one another.

Christ is also a covenant head, so that those who are united with him share the results of his triumph, which is also relayed in five statements. Paul especially emphasizes the lavish and bounteous grace poured out in Christ. The impact of Jesus's covenant headship is remarkable, since those who were dead, sinners, and condemned in Adam are now alive, righteous, and justified in Christ. All these blessings belong to those who are united to Jesus Christ, who is the covenant head of believers. The mess introduced into the world by Adam has been cleaned up through Jesus Christ, and he not only cleaned up the mess (forgave our sins) but also granted us life in Jesus Christ.

A few interpreters think Paul endorses universalism since he speaks of "all" in Adam and "all" in Christ, and the word "many" in these verses clearly means all (cf. also 1 Cor. 15:21–22), but universalism fails to persuade for three reasons. First, there are many texts in Paul that speak of final judgment, and it is hard to believe that no one will be judged when Paul speaks so often of a final judgment (cf., e.g., Rom. 2:12; 1 Cor. 1:18; 1 Thess. 1:10; 5:9; 2 Thess. 1:5–9). Second, we see in Romans 5:17 that one must "receive . . . the gift of righteousness" to "reign in life," and thus not all without exception belong to Jesus Christ. Third, 1 Corinthians 15:21–22 is also instructive. On first glance it seems that just as "all" are in Adam, so too "all" are in Christ, but verse 23 clarifies that the resurrected ones are "those who belong to Christ." The "all" in Christ, then, is not everyone without exception but is limited to those who trust in him, to those who belong to him.

Under the persons of Adam and Christ, Paul sketches in the broad sweep of history, but he has left out the law, and many Jews believed that the law was the means to life, thinking the pathway to righteousness, happiness, and holiness was the law. Paul, however, dissented (Rom. 5:20–21). The law wasn't the solution but part of the problem; it doesn't curb sin but exacerbates it; it doesn't limit transgressions but increases them. The grace of Christ, however, is sufficient, and so it conquers the sin that increased through the law. In the old era sin ruled through death, but now grace reigns in Jesus Christ the Lord.

Sin's Power Dethroned (6:1–23)

If grace is so powerful that it conquers sin, then was Paul teaching that people should sin all the more so that the power of grace would shine with luster? This perspective could stem from those who desired to find an excuse to sin. Such a misunderstanding of Paul's gospel has been common in history, but in the historical context in which Romans was written, something different was likely going on. Jewish critics of Paul's gospel rejected it because they alleged that Paul's teaching encouraged people to sin (see 3:7–8). They probably said something like this: "Any theology that encourages people to sin more isn't from God. Paul teaches that the more we sin, the more God pours out his grace. And the more God pours out his grace, the more glory God gets. And thus Paul encourages people to sin even more."

In Romans 6, Paul argues that this reading of his gospel is completely off the mark. The chapter can be divided into two parts: 6:1–14 and 6:15–23. The focus in 6:1–14 is that believers are dead to sin, and in 6:15–23 that they are no longer slaves of sin. The two sections overlap since what Paul teaches here represents two different ways of saying the same thing. Since sin is conquered in the lives of believers, they are full of hope as they see that God by his grace has changed and is changing them.

73

We return to the question raised by Paul's Jewish opponents: does Paul's theology of grace promote sin in the lives of believers? Paul answers with a categorical No. The reason given is that believers have "died to sin" (6:2). The metaphor of death might suggest that sin is impossible for believers since dead people are unable to sin. We must, however, let the text interpret the metaphor of death: as Paul proceeds, it becomes clear that by writing of death to sin, he doesn't mean that sin is impossible for believers.

When and how did believers die to sin? The answer: at baptism. Upon baptism, believers were immersed into or plunged into Jesus's death. After two thousand years of Christian history, we are apt to misread the meaning of baptism. Paul isn't teaching *ex opere operato*, which means that the act of baptism regenerates a person so that all those who are baptized are dead to sin. Baptism for Paul was part of the complex of events that took place at conversion. When people become Christians, they repent, believe, get baptized, confess Christ as Lord, receive the Spirit, and so forth. Baptism here is just another way of describing conversion, but it doesn't follow that a magical or sacramental version of baptism is being propagated. Paul answers the question, Who has died to sin? And his answer is that those who have died with Christ and have been raised with Christ have died to sin. Baptism, which most agree was by immersion in the ancient church, symbolizes well what it means to die with Christ (as one is submerged under the water) and to be raised with Christ (as one emerges from the water). The power of sin has been severed in the life of believers because they are united with Christ in his death and his resurrection. As a result they are enabled to live a new life, one that is pleasing to God. The grace of God in Jesus Christ does not only offer forgiveness; it also transforms those who belong to Jesus Christ.

What it means to die to sin is explained further in 6:6–10. The "old self," the old Adam, the unregenerate person, has been crucified with Christ. This is another way of saying that believers are united with Christ in his death, and the result is that believers are freed from sin's slavery. The language of slavery is helpful here, showing that before conversion, believers were subjugated to sin. Being dead to sin doesn't mean that sin is impossible for believers but that the dominion of sin has been broken through union with Christ; believers are no longer under sin's mastery and tyranny. Jesus Christ took sin and death upon himself and triumphed over them both through the cross and resurrection. The rule of death has been broken since Christ is the risen one, and Christ's victory over sin and death belongs to those united with Christ by faith.

The ethical implications of new life in Christ are considered in 6:11–14. Believers must realize that they are dead to sin and alive to God in Christ. Since they enjoy new life in Christ, sin must not rule and reign in their bodies.

We see again that sin and death are understood to be powers and forces that enslave and conquer human beings. Jesus Christ has conquered those powers through his cross and resurrection; believers are not free from all sin, but they are called upon to live lives free from the *rule* and *reign* of sin. The desire for sin remains, but they must not let those desires triumph. Since believers are alive in Christ, they are to give themselves to God and use their bodies as weapons for righteousness. The first part of the chapter concludes with a promise: sin "will not rule" over believers (6:14); its dominion, tyranny, and mastery have been broken. Since believers live in a new era of redemptive history, sin doesn't rule over them; they are not "under law" but "under grace."

The question of 6:1 is now asked from another perspective. Since Christians are no longer under the law but are under grace, should they give themselves to sin (6:15)? Again Paul emphatically rejects the idea and explains how this is so in verses 16–23. Believers are under the lordship either of God or of sin. If they give themselves to sin, the result will be death, physical death but also eternal death, final separation from God. No one can give oneself to sin and end up finding life.

The illustration in verse 16 could give the wrong impression, as if believers are poised neutrally between sin and God, between death and life. Paul interjects a thanksgiving in verse 17 to cast light on the new reality that has dawned in Christ. Believers are no longer what they were when they were previously enslaved to sin, but now they are free from sin's dominion since they have died and risen with Christ. The new obedience of believers is "from the heart." Paul doesn't summon believers to obey as if they had no inclination or desire to do what God commands. They have had a heart transformation. We almost certainly have an allusion here to the new covenant promised in Jeremiah 31:33, where the Lord says he will write his law "on their hearts."

We find an unusual expression in Romans 6:17, where Paul speaks of believers being "handed over" to a "pattern of teaching." The verb "handed over" doesn't refer to the passing on of traditional teaching but denotes being delivered over to another power, as a slave is handed over from one master to another. The passive verb indicates that God has handed over Roman believers to the imprint of teaching that they have obeyed from the heart. In other words, believers are now gladly under the dominion of a new lord: by God's grace they are enslaved to righteousness and free from sin.

The past and present life of believers is contemplated. As believers they rue and regret their past when they were enslaved to sin. The consequences of such a life were impurity and shame, and the final outcome is death itself. Now, however, they are set free from the dominion and mastery of sin. The consequence is sanctification and ultimately eternal life. Still, eternal life isn't earned but is God's gift, while those who give themselves to sin will suffer eternal death. Chapter 6 reveals that God's grace transforms those who are united with Christ in his death and resurrection; they have a new relationship to sin, in that sin is no longer their master and lord. By virtue of the power of grace, the rule of sin is dethroned in their lives.

The Role of the Law (7:1–25)

As we saw earlier, Jews believed that the law was the means to change human beings, but Paul argues that the law multiplied sin (Rom. 5:20) so that those who are under the law (6:14–15) are also under the power of sin. The law, then, is not the solution to the human dilemma but is part of the problem. The theme of chapter 7, then, is the law, and Paul explains in more detail the alliance between sin and the law.

In 7:1–6, Paul illustrates his view of the law by appealing to the law regarding marriage and divorce, and the illustration is designed to teach readers that the law only applies to people while they are alive. When Paul applies the illustration, he argues that believers have now died to the law by dying with Christ. Now they are united to Christ in his death and resurrection, and so they are enabled to bear fruit in their lives. Before believing, they were unregenerate, "in the flesh," and the law didn't restrain sin. Instead, the law "aroused" "sinful passions," leading to death. Believers, however, are now freed from the law since they have died with Christ, serving in the newness of the Holy Spirit.

Romans 7:7–25 contains some of the most controversial verses that Paul wrote. We will begin with verses 7–12. Scholars debate the identity of the "I" here, and I suggest that the reference is to Paul himself. Whatever one's view, the "I" has no inherent power to keep God's law. Three main views have been suggested on the identity of the "I": (1) the "I" refers to Adam's experience with God's command in the garden of Eden; (2) the "I" designates Israel's experience of receiving the law at Mount Sinai; (3) the "I" is autobiographical, denoting the experience of the apostle Paul.

Let's think first about Adam. The most powerful evidence for a reference to Adam is in verse 9. The claim "Once I was alive apart from the law" is, strictly speaking, true only of Adam since, apart from Adam, the entire human race is spiritually dead and condemned before God at birth (5:12–19). In the same way, the expressions "I died" (7:10) and "sin . . . killed me" (7:11) fit nicely with Adam's experience in the garden. If the reference is to Adam, then "apart from the law sin is dead" (v. 8) can be taken literally. Sin didn't exist among human beings before God gave the prohibition to eat from the tree of the knowledge of good and evil. The possibility of sin arose when God gave the commandment. Furthermore, the reference to coveting fits with Eve's desire to be wise (Gen. 3:6). At the same time, the reference to deceit (Rom. 7:11) accords with Eve's claim that she was deceived by the serpent (Gen. 3:13). A reference to Adam is very attractive, but the problem with this reading is that Paul refers to the tenth commandment in the Decalogue (Rom. 7:7), not to a command given to Adam in the garden. In addition, Paul specifically separates Adam from the era of the law in 5:13–14.

Other scholars think that the "I" refers to Israel's reception of the law at Sinai, their violation of the law, and the death that followed. The entrance of the law into salvation history provoked transgression (5:20). Israel's sin after Sinai can be described as transgression since specific commandments of God were violated. Because Israel was judged after receiving the law, this reading of Israel's history accords with the story of Israel's experience. A reference to Israel is also quite attractive and explains many features of the text. Still, the interpretation also has some defects that make it unconvincing. The fundamental problem is the interpretation of the phrases "I was alive" and "I died" (7:9–10). If death refers to eschatological death, then we must interpret life to refer to eschatological life, but it is hard to see how Israel had eschatological life at Sinai. Israel was physically delivered from Egypt, but the subsequent story reveals that only a remnant was regenerate.

It is most satisfying, then, to see a reference to Paul himself, which is the most natural way to interpret the "I," and to conclude that life and death aren't used to describe life and death before God but are to be interpreted experientially. Verses 14–25 support this reading with its intense experiential focus, especially in verse 24. What Paul writes in verses 7–11 is personal and confessional, reflecting his own experience with the law. Paul reflects on his own feelings about himself before he recognized his true state before God. Here Paul probably thinks of his coming maturity, perhaps his bar mitzvah, where the requirement of the law pierced his heart. Sin was "dead" in the sense that it was latent or hidden from Paul.

The most powerful objection to this reading is that Paul seems to say elsewhere that he didn't struggle with the law before his conversion. In fact, he claimed to surpass his contemporaries in obedience (Gal. 1:13–14) and said he was "blameless" as to righteousness from keeping the law (Phil. 3:6). How could Paul say he was blameless relative to the law and also have the struggle depicted in Romans 7:7–11? The answer is that neither in Galatians 1:13–14 nor in Philippians 3:6 is Paul claiming sinlessness: in these texts the focus is on outward obedience, external conformity to the requirements of the law; but in Romans 7 Paul focuses on the internal desires of the heart, on the prohibition against *coveting*. To sum up: Paul refers to himself, but Paul's experience also mirrors the experience of Adam and Israel, and thus in a sense the significance of determining who is in view could be exaggerated. Paul describes his own experience because it is paradigmatic, showing the fate of all those under the law.

The law itself is good and holy; there is nothing wrong with any of God's commands (7:12). The law, then, isn't sinful but beautiful in that it describes God's character. Still, the law is pulled into sin's orbit; sin is like a giant sun that draws the law under its influence, and thus the law doesn't dampen the desire for sin but actually precipitates the inclination to sin. Sin blazes up with more power and uses the law as its jumping-off point.

Romans 7:13–25 is one of the most controversial sections in Paul and in the Scriptures. Some think immature Christians are described here, Christians who are not walking in the Spirit, so that the point of the text is to instruct believers to say no to the flesh and yes to the Spirit. This reading isn't convincing since the purpose of the passage isn't to draw a portrait of how Christians move from victory to defeat. Instead, Paul focuses on the inherent capacities of human beings, which explains why the law can't transform them.

More plausible is the notion that Paul depicts pre-Christian experience in 7:14–25. A number of arguments support this reading. For example, the structure of the text is illuminating from this perspective, and we see this in the table below.

Life under the law in the flesh 7:5	Life under the law in the flesh elaborated 7:7-25
Life in the Spirit 7:6	Life in the Spirit elaborated 8:1-17

Along the same lines, the Holy Spirit is nowhere mentioned in 7:14–25 but is mentioned nineteen times in chapter 8, leading to the conclusion that the person described in 7:14–25 doesn't have the Spirit. Another structural argument relates to the role of the question in 7:13. Paul asks whether the law leads to death, answering that it isn't the law that kills, but sin. It seems, then, that 7:14–25 explains how a person dies, but death is the portion of the unbeliever, not the believer. Verse 25b is sometimes adduced as supporting Christian experience (see below), but the pre-Christian reading accounts for the tension in the verse in that it summarizes the main thesis of the text: those who are under the law are unable to obey.

Other arguments are used to support pre-Christian experience. For instance, the totality and depth of defeat in 7:14–25 contradicts Romans 6, which asserts that Christians are dead to sin and no longer slaves to sin. According to chapter 6 the tyranny of sin has been broken for believers so that they are now free from sin's rule, and 8:2 says that "the law of the Spirit of life in Christ Jesus has set you free from the law of sin and death." Could Paul truly say that a believer is "of the flesh" and "sold under sin" (7:14 ESV) after saying that believers are free from sin? Similarly, in 7:23 the "I" is said to be a "prisoner to the law of sin in the parts of my body." The picture is one of complete and absolute slavery to sin.

We can easily see why so many interpreters think we have a description of those who are not converted. On the other hand, some excellent arguments support a reference to Christian experience as well. The shift to the present tense (26 times!) is most naturally interpreted as a reference to Paul's experience as a believer. The present tense doesn't necessarily designate present time, but the shift in tense from the past in 7:7–11 to the present in 7:14–25 seems to be deliberate and intentional. It is also telling that the text doesn't end with victory and joy but with tension and ambiguity (7:25b), suggesting that believers still struggle with such experience in their everyday lives. A duality exists between the two "I's" in the text, which means that the flesh doesn't describe the whole of the person in view. The intense desire to keep God's law, which climaxes with the deep joy and delight in God's law, shows that Paul doesn't describe an unregenerate person (7:22). Pious Jews who refuse to put their faith and trust in Christ didn't truly delight in God's law but in establishing their own righteousness.

How do those who defend Christian experience do so when Paul talks about complete subjugation and bondage to sin? The answer is the already-but-not-yet character of Paul's theology. If we read Romans 6 and 8 carefully, we see that victory over sin isn't total; the dominion of sin has been broken, but sin continues to exercise influence in the lives of Christians, which is why they live in hope. The Pauline explanation of the role of sin in the lives of believers is not simplistic but complex. There is a sense in which we have been freed from the power of sin, and there is also a sense in which sin continues to have dominion over our lives, especially in terms of coveting: the desire to sin. Such an explanation makes sense of 7:24, which looks forward to the future day when believers will be freed "from this body of death." We see the same tension in 8:10–13, for believers fight against the sinful body until the day of redemption. As long as believers live in corruptible bodies, sin and desires for sin will remain (cf. 6:12), and freedom from the sinful body will take place on the final day (7:24; 8:11, 13, 23).

The arguments on both sides are remarkably strong. It is understandable why interpreters go both ways. Christians still experience what it is to be fleshly, for they are keenly aware of their inability in and of themselves to do what is right. In this section of Romans, Paul argues that the law is good, but it is impotent to conquer the power of sin. As long as believers are in the mortal body, they continue to experience their fleshiness. Such is part of the story for those who live in the realm of the already but not yet, for those who face the tension and incongruity of being new in Christ and yet living in a mortal body. Believers continue to feel their inherent wretchedness (7:24) and cry out for future deliverance. Some think the structural argument in which 7:7–25 elaborates on 7:5 is decisive, but actually in 7:14 "the law is spiritual," and thus the lines aren't drawn so simply between 7:7–25 and 8:1–17.

Paul considers whether the law has the ability to transform human beings, concluding that it does not. It would be a mistake to read the whole of Christian experience from this account, for as chapter 8 shows, believers by the power of the Spirit are enabled to keep God's law. And yet since believers have not yet experienced the consummation of their redemption, they are keenly aware of their inherent inability to keep God's law. When believers contemplate their own capacities, it is clear that they do not have the resources to do what God demands. In encountering God's demands, we are still conscious of our wretchedness and inherent inability.

Life in the Power of the Spirit (8:1–17)

The law can't transform human beings. What people need is new life in Christ and the power of the Spirit to live in a way that pleases God. Since believers are in Christ, they no longer face the condemnation that comes from the alliance of sin and the law. Believers are now set free by the Spirit from the principle of sin and death, which dominated them formerly. This freedom, however, is rooted in the work of Jesus Christ on the cross. Human beings don't have the capacity to live a new life since, as sons and daughters of Adam, they are fleshly and lack life. Victory over sin and death requires death, and thus Jesus, as God's Son, came in "the likeness of sinful flesh" (8:3). Certainly Paul did not believe Jesus committed sin (2 Cor. 5:21); he intends to say that Jesus came with a mortal body subject to all the difficulties of earthly life. Death and sin are conquered only through substitution; God condemned sin in the flesh of Jesus on the cross, and Jesus died as a sacrificial offering. The power of sin was broken in the judicial death of Jesus on the cross, which set believers free to live life in the Spirit (Rom. 8:2). The purpose of Jesus's death is expressed also in verse 4. Those who are free from sin's condemnation, those whose sins are judged in the death of the Son, are now by the Spirit enabled to keep "the law's requirement." The singular "requirement" probably refers to the command to love (13:8–10), which is the fruit of the Spirit's work. Believers are not perfected, but they are new, and their life reflects in substantial, significant, and observable ways the work of Christ and the Spirit.

In 8:5–11 the remarkable differences between those in the flesh and those in the Spirit are demarcated. Flesh doesn't stand here for the human body but for those who are still in Adam, for those who don't have new life in Christ, for those who are unregenerate. The entire ways of thinking and living, as we compare those of the flesh and those of the Spirit, are dramatically different. Life in the flesh leads to death, while those who live in the Spirit will find life and peace forever. The flesh is marked by hostility to God and a refusal to keep his law, but the problem is even deeper since those who are in Adam *cannot* keep God's law; they are slaves to sin. What it means to be a Christian is to have the Holy Spirit. Believers still struggle with the flesh (7:14–25), but they are no longer confined to the flesh. The Spirit indwells believers, and thus they have life, even though the bodies of believers are mortal, which testifies to the continuing struggle with sin until the day of resurrection.

Romans 8:12–13 draws the implications from the preceding paragraph. Since believers are in the Spirit and are new in Christ, they are free from slavery to the old Adam, from the dominion and tyranny of the flesh. Such a promise does not mean that there isn't a struggle and a battle. It does mean that those who give themselves over to the flesh, those who let sin reign and rule, will die: they will experience the final judgment. Believers are summoned to put to death "the deeds of the body" by the power of the Holy Spirit (8:13). They are to rely on the Spirit to conquer the flesh, and those who do such will experience eternal life. God's children are those who are "led by God's Spirit" (8:14), directed by the Spirit, governed by the Spirit, showing they are God's children by their obedience. Slavery and fear are associated with disobedience, but believers have received "the Spirit of adoption," and thus they exclaim "Abba, Father" (8:15). Obedience marks out one as an adopted son or daughter, and the Holy Spirit also imprints upon the heart and spirit of those who belong to God that they are God's children. An assurance of one's relation to God floods the heart, and this assurance is generated by the Spirit. Those who are God's children have an unshakeable hope—which is the theme of these chapters. They are guaranteed an inheritance as God's children, but the pathway to the inheritance is first suffering and then glory.

Indomitable Hope (8:18–39)

The theme of hope climaxes in these verses. Paul considers the created world in its fallenness (8:18–25), but also sets forth the glorious future for

God's children and for the created world. Currently, believers suffer, but the sufferings are trivial compared to the glory that will be revealed. When Paul refers to creation, he uses the language of personification to designate the physical universe created by God. The created world, so to speak, anticipates what God's children will be on the last day, when they are revealed in all their glory. Meanwhile, the created world is also subject to futility because of the sin Adam and Eve introduced into the world. The land was cursed because of their sin, and thorns and thistles sprang up from the ground (Gen. 3:17–18). The created world is beautiful, but there are also devastating hurricanes, tsunamis, tornadoes, floods, fires, and earthquakes. Still, there is the promise that the created world will also be transformed. Isaiah promised a new creation (Isa. 65:17; 66:22), a world where the groaning of the present world will be left behind. The created world will be liberated from the curse when the children of God come into the freedom pledged to them. A new world is coming, a world free from frustration and blight, from death and decay, from sorrow and sighing.

Believers also groan as they wait for this coming world, and the presence of the Spirit in their lives testifies that something better is impending. The indwelling Spirit doesn't suppress groaning but actually increases it as believers long for the future day when their bodies will be redeemed. We see from this that groaning centers on the mortal body because the body reminds believers of impending death; the body isn't evil but testifies to the continuing presence of sin in our lives. Believers live in the hope of God's promise, yet hope doesn't see or grasp what is to come but trusts the word of God and awaits the fulfillment of what has been promised.

Believers are also hopeful because the Spirit helps in prayer (Rom. 8:26–27). Hope doesn't blind its eyes to present reality but admits that we are beset by weakness. Weakness manifests itself in not knowing what to pray for. Paul isn't saying that believers don't know *how* to pray but that they don't always know *what* to pray for. Weakness manifests itself in the content of our prayers. In the midst of such weakness, the Spirit comes to our aid; and in the midst of our groaning and weakness, the Spirit prays with "groanings." Some interpreters say that the groanings represent speaking in tongues, but this interpretation can be dismissed, for we know from 1 Corinthians 12:30 that only some believers have the gift of tongues; yet the groanings of the Spirit are *for all* believers without exception. No one who belongs to God stands outside of the hope created by the Spirit. Believers have hope because they know by faith that the Spirit groans for them in prayer. The prayers of the Spirit fill believers with confidence and hope since God, who knows all and searches all, knows the requests of the Spirit. In other words, the prayers of the Spirit are always answered affirmatively since the Spirit invariably prays according to God's will.

Reasons for the hope of believers accumulate in Romans 8:28–30, in a passage that has been famously identified by the English Puritan William Perkins as *A Golden Chain* (1592). We see first that God works everything for good for the sake of believers. The claim that everything works together for good should not be interpreted in terms of immediate comfort or happiness. The good is defined as likeness to Jesus as God's Son, which means that the good is moral transformation and perfection, which will be realized fully at the eschaton, the very end of history. What Adam was called to be is now fulfilled in and through Jesus Christ. God's intention that many human beings would mirror his character is fulfilled in Jesus Christ and in those who belong to him. God works all for the good of those who love him, and loving God is one mark of genuine believers. Still, the emphasis isn't placed on the human subject, on our love for God. The added comment, "who are called according to his purpose," clarifies that our love for God has its roots in God's love for us, in his eternal purpose in calling believers to himself by his grace.

God's purpose in forming a people for himself who are like Jesus Christ is now unpacked with the golden chain: foreknew, predestined, called, justified, glorified. The word "foreknew" might at first glance suggest that God simply foresaw who would believe, and it certainly designates God's foresight, but the word has a thicker and deeper meaning. The background of the term is in the OT, where God's knowing refers to his covenant love, where he sets his affection on those whom he has chosen (cf. Gen. 18:19; Exod. 33:17; Ps. 18:43; Prov. 9:10; Jer. 1:5; Hosea 13:5; Amos 3:2). Romans 11:2 confirms the point, "God has not rejected his people whom he foreknew," which we can paraphrase as "God did not reject the people he selected."

The word "predestined" is closely related in meaning to the word "foreknew," indicating that God has preset or planned in advance those who would belong to him. Foreknowing and predestining took place before history began, but calling is next in the series and occurs in history during this life. The call comes to people through the gospel as it is proclaimed to them (2 Thess. 2:14). Some mistakenly think the term "calling" means an invitation, as if one could ultimately resist the call. When Paul uses the word, however, the calling is effectual in that it creates faith in the one called. We see this in the next line of Romans 8:30, where *all* those who are called are justified. It is certainly not true that all those who are invited to believe do so! Since justification is by faith (5:1), and since all those who are called are justified, the calling must create faith.

Justification is next in the chain. All those called by God are justified before him, which means that God as the judge declares that they stand in the right before him. And all those who are justified will be glorified. Glorification looks to the future, to the completion of God's work when those who belong to God will be all that they were created to be and all that God called them to be. We can see why believers are so full of hope since God has lovingly planned their destiny from eternity past to eternity future.

The theme of hope comes to a ringing conclusion in 8:31–39. In light of the gospel proclaimed in 1:16–8:30, Paul asks who can successfully be against believers, and the answer, of course, is no one. After all, God himself is *for* believers in Christ Jesus. God has given believers the greatest gift imaginable in graciously providing his Son for their sake and for their salvation. Since God has demonstrated the depth of his love in providing his dear Son for our sake and our salvation, we can be confident that God will give us everything else we truly need. The language of God not *sparing* his Son alludes to Abraham's willingness not to spare Isaac (Gen. 22:16). Still, there are significant differences since the Son of God willingly and gladly suffered for our sake and our salvation, and Isaac, unlike Jesus, was spared from death.

In Romans 8:33–34 the matter of condemnation is broached. Paul considers who could accuse those whom God has chosen as his own. God alone declares who stands in the right before him since he is the judge and the jury, and any charge against the elect is out of order because the penalty has been paid: Jesus died for his own, his resurrection signifies that his death for their sake was accepted (cf. 4:25), he reigns at God's right hand as the vindicated king, and he intercedes for believers on the basis of his atoning sacrifice. Believers can be assured that their sins are removed "as far as the east is from the west" (Ps. 103:12) and that their sins are thrown into the deepest sea (Mic. 7:19). These verses of Romans 8 make an allusion to Isaiah 50:8–9, where the servant of the Lord asks, "Who will contend with me?" and "Who will condemn me?" No one will finally bring a case against Jesus as the servant since God himself helps and vindicates him, and the same is true of those who belong to Jesus.

The chapter ends with an exalted meditation on God's conquering love. Paul exclaims that nothing can separate believers from the love of God and from the love of Christ. Such love isn't separated from the real world but manifests itself in the midst of a world where believers suffer from the pressures of the world, from lack of food and clothing, from persecution and death. Paul quotes from Psalm 44:22, affirming that believers are like sheep being slaughtered. The psalm is most interesting in that Israel suffered defeat from the hands of its enemies even though the people were faithful to the Lord!

The psalmist asked why God wasn't intervening on their behalf since they had not abandoned their God. The psalm suggests that God will ultimately answer, and the same can be said of its use in Romans. The elect of God may suffer in agonizing ways, but such suffering doesn't signal their unfaithfulness, nor does it suggest that God has abandoned them. God has appointed his people to suffer during this present evil age, but in the midst of their suffering he promises to flood them with his love, and thus the power of God's love shines forth in that it sustains and strengthens his own amid suffering, and it will ultimately carry them through to ultimate vindication and salvation.

God's Faithfulness to Israel (9:1–11:36)

In the past some scholars saw chapters 9–11 as a digression or as unimportant in the letter, but today almost all recognize that they play a vital role in the letter and that they flow from the previous chapters. We have seen that the end-time blessings promised to the Jews belong to gentile believers, who indeed are children of God, inheritors of the promise, God's elect people, righteous in his sight, and assured of glorification (Rom. 8:18–39). All of this raises the question of the promises made in the OT to ethnic Israel. Have the promises been rerouted to the church? And if God's promises to Israel have not been fulfilled, then how can one be sure that the promises made to the church will be fulfilled? The primary question raised in Romans 9–11, then, is God's faithfulness to his promises made to Israel.

God's Sovereign Promise (9:1–29)

Paul begins by sharing his intense grief and sorrow over the response of Israel to the gospel (9:1–5). He was willing to be cursed and cut off from Christ and to suffer final judgment for the sake of his people. Here we are reminded of Moses, who asked God to kill him to atone for the sin of Israel (Exod. 32:32). The Lord rejected Moses's request, and Paul knew his desire could not be realized, though it showed Paul's great love for Israel, and it also reveals that the issue causing Paul's grief was that the majority of ethnic Israel was unsaved. Such unbelief in Israel was disquieting and surprising, given Israel's privileges. In Romans 9:4 the privileges of Israel are listed with six items, best divided in two groups of three, pictured as follows.

A^1 adoption	A^2 the giving of the law
B^1 the glory	B^2 the temple worship
C^1 the covenants	C^2 the promises

Israel was adopted as God's people at Sinai, when the law was given to them. Later, God's glory dwelt in their midst in the temple. Most important, God's covenant promises were given to Israel, pledging future salvation. Now, however, it seems that these privileges belong to the gentiles instead of the Jews: they are God's adopted people; they enjoy the glory of God and the promise of glorification; and they enjoy God's covenant promises.

Israel's privileges continue: the patriarchs (Abraham, Isaac, and Jacob) were their ancestors. The supreme privilege is that the Christ comes from Israel, the Messiah promised in the OT Scriptures, the son of David who would reign forever (Pss. 72; 89; 132). Jesus is not only the Messiah but is also God himself, and thus the privileges given to Israel come to a stunning climax. Some scholars doubt that Christ is identified as "God" in Romans 9:5 since Paul rarely uses the term "God" with reference to Jesus. Still, this is the most natural way of understanding the grammar, and that Jesus is divine is taught elsewhere in Paul (esp. Phil. 2:6; Col. 1:15–20; Titus 2:13). Given all of Israel's privileges, it is tragic and astonishing that most of Israel did not believe in their Messiah, and it raises the question of God's faithfulness to his promises.

The thesis of all of Romans 9–11 is stated in 9:6: the word of God has not failed; God will be faithful to his promises. The rest of chapters 9–11 explain how this is so. We see in 9:6–9 that God never promised that all of the biological children of Abraham would be the children of God. Being a member of ethnic Israel didn't guarantee that one belonged to the true Israel. The children of Abraham are limited to those who received the promise, and the promise was given to Isaac, not Ishmael, as the citation of Genesis 21:12 in Romans 9:7 affirms.

In Genesis 21 Sarah was distressed when Ishmael was mocking Isaac, telling Abraham that since Ishmael was not the heir, he must be driven from the household. Abraham was distressed and grieved over Ishmael leaving, but the Lord affirms Sarah's words in 21:12, since the line of promise would be "traced through Isaac," not Ishmael. Paul also cites Genesis 18:10, which affirms that Sarah, after so many years of frustration and failure, would have a son (Rom. 9:9). Isaac, then, was the son of the promise, the child who came not from the flesh but from the powerful word of God, the child whose very existence is a miracle. Paul was confident that God would fulfill his promise to Israel because he kept his promise to Abraham and Sarah. Just as Isaac was born as the miracle child, so too the promise to ethnic Israel would be fulfilled by God's miraculous word.

The argument of 9:6–9 is reiterated, underscored, and clarified in 9:10–13. Perhaps some Jews would say it was obvious that Ishmael wasn't an heir of the promise, and so the principle that God's children are not of the flesh but of the promise is reaffirmed with reference to Isaac and Rebekah. In their case, the children (Esau and Jacob) were the sons of the same father and the same mother. Indeed, they were in the womb at the same time as twins. The promise upended social expectations; it was given to Jacob, the younger son, not to Esau, the older (Gen. 25:23). In ancient Near Eastern culture, primogeniture was the custom, but God reversed the cultural pattern to demonstrate that the promise depends on his word and accords with his sovereign freedom as the creator.

The content of the promise is reaffirmed in Malachi 1:2, which contrasts the Lord's love for Israel with his rejection of Esau. The Lord set his saving love upon Jacob, but he hated, that is, rejected Esau from his saving promise. Many scholars maintain that the promise relates to the historical destiny of nations (like Edom and Israel), and thus what is said here can't be applied to individual election and salvation. They point out that the subject of Malachi 1:2–5 is the historical destiny of nations, such as Edom and Israel. The argument is flawed because it separates what should be kept together. In other words, historical destiny and salvation can't be segregated from one another. Even if one thinks that Malachi refers only to historical destiny, in Romans 9 the issue is salvation since Paul's willingness to be cursed (9:1–5) stemmed from Israel's separation from Christ. Paul hasn't wandered from the subject that introduced the chapter but explains how God is faithful to the promise to save Israel.

Another controversy pertains to whether the salvation promised relates to individuals or groups. Certainly Paul thinks of Jews and gentiles as groups here, but individuals are also included. Groups are always composed of individuals, and one cannot have groups without including individuals. The selection of a remnant out of Israel requires the selection of some individuals out of a larger group. We also need to interpret Romans 9–11 together since the chapters are a unity. It is exegetically and logically flawed to say that chapter 9 is restricted to groups and not individuals and then to say that the choice of whether one believes or not in chapter 10 is an individual decision.

Why did God choose Jacob instead of Esau? Was it because he looked forward and saw that Jacob would be particularly righteous and godly? Hardly. Jacob's inclusion is grounded in God's electing and free purpose, not Jacob's noble choices. God's saving promise rests on himself alone, and thus he did not take into account Jacob's future actions. Indeed, Jacob's actions weren't in his purview at all because he chose Jacob instead of Esau before either were born or before they had "done anything good or bad" (9:11). Jacob wasn't included because of any works he had done but exclusively because of God's gracious and effectual call. In 9:10–13 Paul argues that God's promise to Israel will be fulfilled since it depends upon his grace alone.

Paul's argument, however, raises other questions, which he answers in 9:14–23. If God chooses some entirely apart from human works, is he unjust? Paul affirms God's unimpeachable justice and explains (in 9:15) how he is just with a citation from Exodus 33:19. We might expect that Paul would appeal to human free will to resolve the dilemma, but 33:19 affirms that God grants mercy to whomever he chooses. How does this fit with the claim that God isn't unjust? We need to put the quoted text in its historical context. Exodus 32–34 records the incident of the golden calf. Israel had just entered into covenant with the Lord (Exod. 24) but then violated the covenant in a flagrant way by committing idolatry with the golden calf. Moses shattered the tablets of the covenant, signifying that the covenant with Israel was broken. Moses interceded for Israel (as Paul does for Israel in Rom. 10:1), asking the Lord to forgive Israel and dwell with them so that the covenant would be renewed. Ultimately, the Lord answered Moses's petition, but we see in Exodus 33:19 that mercy wasn't given to all. The Lord grants mercy to whom he wishes. He acts in sovereign freedom as the Lord of all.

What is the answer, then, to the question of God's justice in Romans? The answer is that salvation is granted to sinners, to those who stand in need of mercy. God's mercy is his free prerogative; he gives it to whom he wishes as the sovereign God. No one deserves his mercy, and leaving Esau in his sin wasn't unjust. Thus as Romans 9:16 says, the promise doesn't depend upon human effort or human free will. Those who receive salvation depend utterly and totally upon God's mercy.

The example of Pharaoh is presented as another example of God's justice (9:17). All acknowledged that Pharaoh was evil, deserving immediate and full punishment. Still, the Lord did not destroy him immediately. Paul picks up Exodus 9:16, which is a most significant verse in the midst of the plague narrative (Exod. 7–10) and informs readers about God's purposes relative to Pharaoh and the plagues. The Lord works out his purposes in the most evil regimes and rulers; even in the case of Pharaoh, the Lord raised him up to accomplish his plan. Thereby his saving power was made known to Israel and his judging righteousness was poured out on Egypt.

Romans 9:18 draws the conclusion: God has mercy on some and hardens others. No one deserves his mercy, and in his freedom he chooses to show mercy to some and to harden others in their sin. The background here is the hardening of Pharaoh's heart in Exodus 4–10. Pharaoh hardens his own heart, and God hardens his heart as well. A careful analysis of the OT text reveals that God's hardening of Pharaoh precedes and undergirds Pharaoh's self-hardening, and it is an imposition on the text to conclude that God's hardening is a response to the hardening of human beings. Still, God hardens Pharaoh as one who was already a sinner; he is given over further to the sin that already ruled in his life.

The freedom and sovereignty of God has dominated the discussion; he shows mercy and hardens; he saves and rejects. If God's will stands behind all things, then, Paul asks, "Why . . . does he still find fault? For who can resist his will?" (9:19). We might expect Paul to appeal to free will, but instead he answers the question in an astonishing way, which suggests that the question asked stems from rebellion and rejection of God's freedom and sovereignty. Mere human beings, finite and frail, can't tell God how to run the world; they are the clay, and he is the potter, with freedom to make some for eschatological honor and others for eschatological dishonor. Paul isn't denying the reality and authenticity of human choices. Nor is it legitimate to appeal to the potter-and-clay illustration from Jeremiah 18 to say that free will is ultimate after all, for such a gambit violates and contradicts the flow of thought in Romans 9. Instead, we have an example of what we call "compatibilism." God is sovereign over all things—even where dice land! (Prov. 16:33)—and human choices are significant and authentic (cf. Acts 2:23; 4:27–28).

In Romans 9:22–23 Paul explains why God is patient with those prepared for eschatological destruction. God's patience reminds us of Romans 2:4, where his kindness is intended to bring people to repentance. God's patience with the wicked demonstrates that his wrath is just and deserved. At the same time, the mercy granted to those who will enjoy glory forever shines all the brighter when human beings realize that they truly deserve his wrath. Mercy is seen and felt as mercy when one is conscious that judgment has been averted because of God's kindness.

In Romans 9:24–29 we see the surprising and unexpected sovereign grace of God. God's freedom has been clear throughout: in choosing Isaac and not Ishmael, in choosing Jacob and not Esau. Once again we see the unexpected grace of God: the gentiles who deserve wrath were being shown mercy, while most of Israel failed to believe. Paul supports the inclusion of gentiles by quoting from Hosea 2:23 and 1:10. The application of these texts to gentiles seems strange since in historical context the verses clearly refer to Israel. We have more than a principle or illustration here. The church is the renewed and true Israel, the arena in which God's promises find their fulfillment. Gentiles who believe in Christ are part of restored Israel since Jesus is the true Israel, and thus those who belong to Christ are also true Israel (Gal. 3:16, 26–29; cf. Rom. 2:25–29). The restoration of Israel in the OT includes the calling of gentiles (e.g., Isa. 2:1–4; 11:1–12; 14:1; 19:19–25; 25:1–8; 49:6–8, 22–23; 56:3–8; 60:3–16; Zech. 2:11; 8:22–23; 9:7–8; 14:16–21).

In Romans 9:27 Paul conflates Isaiah 10:22–23 with Hosea 1:10. Many gentiles were being saved, while most of Israel disbelieved; there was only a remnant of Israel left, though the presence of a remnant pointed to a future salvation. Even the salvation of a remnant, however, is a miracle of grace (Isa. 1:9, cited in Rom. 9:29), for if God had not acted in Israel, no one would believe. Just as the Lord preserved a remnant in Isaiah's day, when Israel rebelled against the Lord, so he has preserved a remnant of Jewish believers in Paul's day.

Israel's Failure to Believe (9:30–11:10)

Thus far Paul has emphasized that God is faithful and that he will fulfill his promises to Israel in his sovereign freedom. In this new section Paul turns to Israel's refusal to believe, without denying in the least the emphasis on God's sovereignty. Biblical writers did not think God's sovereignty and the authenticity of human choices were incompatible but believed in both realities. Paul begins by speaking of gentile faith and Israel's unbelief (Rom. 9:30–33). Even though gentiles didn't pursue a right relationship with God, they stand in a right relationship with him by faith. At the same time, even though Israel pursued the law for righteousness, the people did not obtain a right relation with God through the law, for they pursued the law by works instead of through faith. Israel fell over the stone the Lord established. Paul quotes Isaiah 28:16 in Romans 9:33 to verify his point. In its historical context Isaiah prophesies that Samaria will be judged for its sins. The false prophets ridiculed Isaiah's message of judgment, but they themselves would not escape judgment. They thought they had made a covenant with death to spare themselves from disaster, but their so-called covenant would not avail. The Lord, however, had placed a "foundation," a "cornerstone" in Zion (Isa. 28:16). The one who believes will triumph over judgment. Paul understands Christ to be the cornerstone as the risen one; those who believe in him will be saved, but those who disbelieve will fall to their death.

The argument continues in Romans 10:1–13. Paul's desire for the Jews' salvation, which is the issue that pulsates throughout these chapters, is voiced. It isn't the case that unbelieving Jews lack zeal for God: the problem is that their zeal had become a cloak for self-righteousness so that instead of submitting to God's righteousness by faith, they tried to establish their own righteousness. They did not recognize that Christ is the end and the goal of the law for everyone who believes. The era of the law, the time period under the Mosaic covenant, had come to an end. The law pointed to and is fulfilled in Jesus Christ.

Paul contrasts law righteousness with righteousness by faith in 10:5–8, citing Leviticus 18:5 in Romans 10:5 and Deuteronomy 30:12–14 in Romans 10:6–8. The use of the OT in these verses is disputed and a difficult matter to assess. Some interpreters maintain that there is no contrast between Leviticus 18:5 and Deuteronomy 30:12–14. Seeing continuity between Romans 10:5 (from Lev. 18:5) and Romans 10:6–8 (from Deut. 30:12–14) is defended by pointing out that both texts envision obedience within the covenant. Furthermore, it seems strange to think that Paul would quote one OT text against another. Despite these impressive arguments, seeing a contrast is far more likely. First, a contrast between Romans 10:5 and 10:6–8 is supported by the antithesis between doing and believing, which permeates 9:30–10:13. Paul emphasizes that the way to obtain righteousness is not by achieving or doing but by believing, and nowhere in 9:30–10:13 is doing of the law ascribed to faith. In fact, when Paul cites Deuteronomy 30:12–14, all references to *doing* are removed and *faith* is inserted instead.

Second, Paul never speaks of righteousness that is *from* the law (Rom. 10:5; cf. Phil. 3:9) but repeatedly teaches that righteousness comes from God and is his gift. Righteousness cannot come *from* the law because the law incites people to sin (Rom. 5:20; 7:5, 7–13). Those who see 10:5 as a positive description of keeping the law fail to see the remarkable differences between what Paul says in 10:5 and other texts in which he speaks positively of keeping the law (Rom. 8:4; 13:8–10; Gal. 5:14).

Third, supporting the idea that Paul writes negatively of works righteousness in Romans 10:5 is his citation of Leviticus 18:5 in Galatians 3:12. It is improbable that Paul uses Leviticus 18:5 in a different way in Romans 10:5 and Galatians 3:12 since both texts treat the same theme: whether righteousness is available by the law.

The question still remains: does Paul wrongly pit Leviticus 18:5 against Deuteronomy 30:12–14? Some have said that Paul doesn't quote Leviticus 18:5 in context; he uses the wording to describe a legalistic attitude toward the law. It seems, however, that Paul's argument against Jewish opponents would not succeed if he doesn't cite the verse in context. This command, like the other commands in the Mosaic law, was given to a people in covenant with Yahweh by grace, and sacrifices could be offered to receive forgiveness when transgression occurred. Others suggest that Paul refers to the opponents' interpretation of Leviticus 18:5, and by citing other verses in the OT, he shows that the opponents' reading is wrong. The problem with this solution is that Paul doesn't follow this procedure anywhere else. He quotes the OT to *support* his argument, and it isn't clear that he cites verses the way opponents used the OT (cf. again Gal. 3:12).

We need, then, to read Leviticus 18:5 both in its historical context and in light of the fulfillment that has come in Christ. Life in the context of 18:5 doesn't refer to eternal life, but to life within the land of promise, to a life of blessing within God's covenant on this earth. Paul, however, applies the text to eternal life by arguing typologically. Life in the land is escalated to refer to eternal life under the new covenant. Paul teaches that those who have violated the law will not obtain eternal life, and thus any attempt to obtain righteousness by the law is misguided (cf. Gal. 3:12). At the same time, the arrival of the new covenant changes the role of the law. The law of Moses is no longer in force with the coming of Christ (Rom. 6:14–15; 7:4–6; 2 Cor. 3:4–18; Gal. 2:21; 3:15–4:7). Those who put themselves under the law must, therefore, keep it perfectly (Rom. 1:18–3:20; Gal. 3:10; 5:3), since OT sacrifices no longer had the power to forgive sins now that Christ is come. Only the cross of Christ provides forgiveness.

Paul appeals to Deuteronomy 30:12–14 to demonstrate that righteousness by faith should be contrasted with righteousness from the law. Again, Paul's use of the OT is controversial and not easy to explain. Some think Paul's use of the OT is arbitrary, but there are reasons to think that his quotation is rooted in the context of Deuteronomy. What is surprising about the Pauline usage is that he focuses on Jesus Christ rather than the law, since the law is clearly in view in Deuteronomy, and thus Paul reads the text in light of Christ's coming. Paul has prepared readers for this by claiming that Christ is both the goal and the end of the law in Romans 10:4. The narrative arc of Deuteronomy 29–30 also informs Paul's interpretation. Deuteronomy 27–30 records the blessings and cursings of the covenant, and it becomes clear in Moses's words that the cursings would become a reality in the history of Israel. Still, Israel is promised that it will return to the Lord following exile, after the Lord has circumcised their hearts and removed the hardness preventing them from keeping the Torah (30:6). Paul sees this prophecy fulfilled with the coming of Christ in that God has circumcised the hearts of his people so that they now keep the law (cf. Rom. 2:26–29; Phil. 3:3; Col. 2:11–12). The commandment in Moses's day was near in the sense that it was revealed clearly to Israel so that they had no excuse for failing to keep it (Deut. 30:11–14), but Moses himself says that the law would not be kept by Israel and would be fulfilled only in a coming age (Deut. 29:3–4; 30:6).

Righteousness by faith speaks in Romans 10:6, and Paul draws from Deuteronomy 9:4, where Israel is warned about thinking they would inherit the land because of their own righteousness (Deut. 9:4–5). Paul maintains that righteousness by faith rules out boasting in one's own righteousness. Paul interprets Deuteronomy 30:12–14 in Romans 10:6–8, taking what is impossible for human beings as contrasting with God's work in Christ. God sent the Messiah from heaven to earth in the incarnation. Human beings don't have any ability to bring Christ to earth or to raise him from the dead (cf. Ps. 107:26). In saying that the message is near, Paul probably has in mind the work of the new covenant (Jer. 31:31–34), where God writes his law upon the heart.

What it means to be a believer is to confess Jesus as the risen Lord, and such a confession points to his divinity (Rom. 10:9). In verse 11 Paul again quotes from Isaiah 28:16, which we explored at the end of the discussion on Romans 9 (in 9:33). In the midst of a discussion on God's faithfulness to the Jews, he reminds his readers that God doesn't make distinctions between Jews and gentiles: all who call upon him will be saved (10:12–13). He quotes Joel 2:32 here, and the context is significant since Joel prophesies about the coming of the Spirit on *all flesh* (Joel 2:28–32; cf. Acts 2:17–21). The promises made to Israel did not exclude the gentiles but included them within the circle of God's promises, and we are not surprised to learn this, given the universal blessing promised to Abraham from the outset (Gen. 12:1–3).

Those who call upon the Lord and believe in him are saved, and in Romans 10:14–21 Paul explains that Israel had heard the message and therefore should believe. In verses 14–15 the chain of events necessary to call on the Lord is traced out, but Paul begins with the end, the calling on the Lord for salvation, and in doing so he picks up the idea of calling on the Lord from verse 13. Those who call on the Lord will be saved, but no one will call on someone they don't believe in. Belief, however, is not possible without hearing, for no one can believe in someone they have never heard of. The means by which people hear the message about Christ is a preacher or herald, and preachers don't preach unless they are sent. Paul cites Isaiah 52:7 in Romans 10:15 to support the point. The feet of those who proclaim the good news are beautiful since they are coming to proclaim the fulfillment of Isaiah's promise that good news was at hand.

We see from Romans 10:16 that hearing is a necessary but not a sufficient condition for believing, since many who have heard, particularly in Israel, have not obeyed the message that summons them to repent and believe. The great servant song of Isaiah is quoted to make the point (Isa. 53:1). Isaiah prophesied that some would hear the message, which in context is the message about the servant's death and resurrection, and yet would fail to believe. Despite the fact that some or even many in Israel disbelieve, it is still the case that faith comes from hearing the message, and the message heard is specific: the gospel of Christ.

The main point Paul wants to establish is that Israel had heard the message about forgiveness of sins and return from exile as prophesied in Isaiah. The day of fulfillment had arrived. Remarkably, Paul quotes Psalm 19:4 to support his point, and the quotation surprises since Psalm 19:1–6 is about God's revelation of himself through the created order, through the natural world, and the subject of discussion in the Romans context is the gospel. Here Paul uses Psalm 19:4, which in its original context refers to natural revelation, to portray the dissemination of the gospel message to the ends of the earth. It should be noted, however, that when we look at Psalm 19 as a whole, both general revelation (vv. 1–6) and special revelation (vv. 7–14) are included. Paul believes that the progress and the course of the gospel is such that it now extends over the whole earth, so that the proclamation of the gospel is now comparable to the all-encompassing reach of general revelation. One of the remarkable features of the new age inaugurated by Christ is that the saving message is no longer restricted to Israel but encompasses the whole world.

As we come to Romans 10:19, Paul asks another question, which should be interpreted to mean that Israel should have known from the OT (Deut. 32:21) that gentiles would be saved and that Israel would resist Jesus's saving work. Paul also quotes Isaiah 65:1–2 to show that prophecy is being fulfilled in Israel's unbelief and the gentiles' belief. Most interpreters think that in the original context of Isaiah, both 65:1 and 65:2 were addressed to Israel, but that Paul has split up the prophecy by applying 65:1 to the gentiles and 65:2 to Israel. If this is the case, then Paul sees in Isaiah 65:1 a principle that applied to the gentiles, even though the verse related originally to the Jews. It is also possible that verse 1 referred to the gentiles in Isaiah's original context, and in that case we have in Paul an accurate interpretation of the original meaning of the verse. Alternatively, the verse related to the Jews in the historical context, but Paul reads the text in light of the promise in Isaiah that the nations would come to Zion in the last days (Isa. 2:2–5; 14:2; 45:14; 49:22; 55:5; 66:20).

The citation of Isaiah 65:2 in Romans 10:21 drives home the theme of Israel's unfaithfulness. What Isaiah prophesied has come to pass: Israel continues in its obstinacy despite God's continual invitation for them to return to him. We see here that Paul's belief in divine sovereignty does not lead him to minimize human responsibility and the seriousness of human choices and human freedom. All of Romans 9:30–10:21 emphasizes that Israel *should* believe and is held responsible for not doing so. The outstretched arms of God in Romans 10:21 reveal a genuine longing on his part that all will respond in faith (cf. 1 Tim. 2:4), and it indicates that Israel's history isn't over.

The rejection of the gospel by most in Israel raises the question whether God has abandoned Israel. The answer is that he has certainly not done so because a remnant has been spared, and Paul includes himself as an example of such (Rom. 11:1). God has not rejected Israel, for they are his covenant people. The account about Elijah in 1 Kings 19 is cited to demonstrate that God has chosen a remnant (Rom. 11:2–4). Elijah had given up all hope for Israel, because the prophets were killed by Ahab and Jezebel and because the altars of Yahweh were destroyed. Elijah concluded that he was the only prophet of the Lord left, and Jezebel and Ahab were trying to kill him as well. But the Lord corrected Elijah, showing him that his perspective was warped because the Lord had left 7,000 in Israel who had not compromised with Baal worship. The 7,000 who remained were no accident but were the result of God's gracious work.

The principle of election continued to apply in Paul's day (Rom. 11:5–6), and thus there was an elect remnant in Israel by God's grace, just as we saw a remnant of Jews believing in the Gospels and Acts. The presence of a remnant in the OT signals that God had not abandoned his people and that he would do more for them in the future. The survival of a remnant pointed to the *future*, to the full realization of God's promises. Such is the work of God's grace, and grace by definition excludes works from its orbit. Here we see that Paul's theology of election is another way of describing the gospel of grace, which is at the heart of his gospel.

In 11:7–10 Paul sums up the situation relative to Israel. Israel had not obtained a right relation with God. Still, God's promises are fulfilled among the elect, which includes a remnant in Israel and many gentiles. The scriptural quotations in 11:8–10 verify that the majority of the Jews were hardened by God, though such rejection doesn't mean that Israel was rejected forever. Paul cites verses from the Law (Deut. 29:4), the Prophets (Isa. 29:10), and the Writings (Ps. 69:22). Actually, Romans 11:8 contains a mixed citation from Deuteronomy 29:3 LXX and Isaiah 29:10. Paul strengthens the emphasis on the activity of God by inserting the phrase "spirit of stupor" from Isaiah 29:10. He adds from Deuteronomy 29:3 that God stupefies the people, and as a result they cannot hear or see.

The OT context of both quotations should be noted. In Deuteronomy 29–30 Moses rehearses and foretells the history of Israel, predicting that they will face exile for their sin and will be saved when God circumcises their hearts (30:6). Paul includes the words "to this day" from Deuteronomy 29:4, which shows that Israel continued to be hardened, but Deuteronomy 30 shows that a new day would come, a day of salvation. Isaiah 29 contains a judgment oracle against the prophets (29:9–16; cf. 6:9–10). Paul elsewhere applies Isaiah 29:14 to the blindness of the Jews in his day (cf. 1 Cor. 1:19), but Isaiah 29:17–24 also looks forward to the day in Israel when shame will be removed from Jacob and understanding will be granted to them. Thus Paul understands Israel to be under the judgment described in Deuteronomy and Isaiah, although the contexts of both prophecies indicate that this is not the last word for Israel.

The OT citation in Romans 11:9–10 comes from Psalm 69:22–23. Psalm 69 is often referred to in the NT with reference to the life, ministry, and death of Jesus Christ (Matt. 27:34, 48; Mark 3:21; 15:23, 36; Luke 13:35; 23:36; John 2:17; 15:25; 19:29; Acts 1:20; Rom. 15:3; Heb. 11:26; cf. also Phil. 4:3; Rev. 3:5; 16:1). As David relates his suffering and rejection, he includes a prayer that God would curse his enemies (Ps. 69:22–28). The curse pronounced upon David's enemies is applied to unbelieving Jews of Paul's day, who rejected Jesus as their Lord and oppressed the church. In Acts we noticed that Psalm 69 was used typologically, and we see another example of such typology and escalation here. That which the Jews trusted in has actually become their downfall and a vehicle of judgment. Even though God hardens, the Jews were still responsible for their sins. The two truths are compatible.

Israel's Future Hope (11:11–36)

The long discussion (Rom. 9:30–11:10), which emphasizes Israel's unbelief, might lead some to the conclusion that Israel had stumbled to such an extent that it had fallen irrevocably (11:11). Such was not the case (11:11–16). God planned that Israel's transgression and rejection would bring to the gentiles the riches of salvation and reconciliation with God. Israel, upon seeing gentiles included in the promises made to them, would become jealous and desire the same blessing. Paul anticipates a day when more than a remnant is saved, when the "fullness" of Israel will be saved (11:12), when Israel is accepted to a greater extent. When this happens, there will be "life from the dead" (11:15), which most naturally refers to the final resurrection. The fullness of Israel's salvation will be followed by the general resurrection.

In verse 16 two illustrations make the same point: God's choice of the patriarchs indicates that the people of Israel as a whole are consecrated to him. The idea of firstfruits is introduced to convey the notion of holiness, and Paul shifts to the illustration of the root and branches to describe the people of God as an olive tree. Both illustrations make the same point: the election of the patriarchs sanctifies Israel as a whole. Ethnic Israel is not cast off but still remains the elect people of God because of the promise made to the fathers (vv. 28–29).

In 11:17–24 the people of God are described as an olive tree, a comparison that reaches back to the OT (Jer. 11:16–19; Hosea 14:6–7). The Jewish branches were cut off because of unbelief, and now wild gentile branches have been grafted in so that there is one people of God made up of Jewish and gentile believers. Paul's concern was that the gentiles in Rome were boastful and proud about their inclusion in the people of God. Instead of boasting, the gentiles should fear when they contemplate the plight of Jews who disbelieved. Such fear serves as an antidote to conceit since gentile believers would be removed from the olive tree if they did not continue to believe. God's kindness is demonstrated in his grace toward those who have repented and believed, but his severity is experienced by those who turn away.

Since gentiles were grafted onto the olive tree, they were tempted to exalt themselves, but they also needed to realize that God could and would regraft onto the olive tree the natural branches, the ethnic Jews (Rom. 11:23–24). What Paul means by the mystery in 11:25–27 is the subject of considerable discussion. "Mystery" in Paul has an apocalyptic dimension (Rom. 16:25; 1 Cor. 2:1, 7; 4:1; 13:2; 14:2; 15:51; Eph. 1:9; 3:3–4, 9; 5:32; 6:19; Col. 1:26–27; 2:2; 4:3; 2 Thess. 2:7; 1 Tim. 3:9, 16), and it doesn't signify a riddle or a puzzle that surpasses human comprehension; instead, it designates a secret element of God's plan that had been hidden from human beings but has now been revealed. The mystery for Paul is revealed in the gospel of Christ (Rom. 16:25; 1 Cor. 2:1, 7; 15:51; Eph. 1:9; 3:3–4, 9; 5:32; 6:19; Col. 1:26–27; 2:2; 4:3; 1 Tim. 3:9, 16). Here Paul discloses the mystery to prevent the gentiles from being proud.

The mystery here in Romans 11:25–27 has at least three parts: (1) Part of Israel is hardened for a limited period of time. (2) The salvation of the gentiles will precede the salvation of Israel. And (3) all Israel will eventually be saved. Some have read Paul to say that Israel will be saved without putting their faith in Christ, but such a reading fails to understand 11:25–27 in context. After all, Paul is full of anguish because Israel is separated *"from Christ"* (9:3), and Israel is criticized for failing to believe in him (9:31–10:21). When Paul introduces himself as an example of the saved remnant (11:1–6), he qualifies as such because he believes in Christ. So, when Israel's unbelief is noted in 11:23, it clearly refers to failure to believe in Jesus.

The meaning of "all Israel" in 11:26 is disputed. Some maintain that Israel here refers to the church, so that it includes both Jews and gentiles who have believed in Jesus the Messiah. This fits with Paul's claim that believers are true Jews and the true circumcision (2:28–29; Phil. 3:3), the sons and daughters of Abraham (Rom. 4:1–17; Gal. 3:6–9, 26–29), and "the Israel of God" (Gal. 6:16). Gentiles are also included in Israel in the citations from Hosea in Romans 9:24–26 and are members of the olive tree (11:17–24). This reading is attractive in many ways, but it doesn't fit well with the context of Romans 9–11. The primary question that animates these chapters, the reason Paul was willing to be cursed, was the separation of *ethnic* Israel from Christ. In addition, the preceding verses in chapter 11 preserve a distinction between gentiles and ethnic Jews. It seems unlikely that the word "Israel" refers to ethnic Israel in 11:25 and then suddenly in verse 26 Paul switches the reference to the church. Indeed, the contrast between Jews and gentiles continues in verse 28, which suggests that the meaning of Israel doesn't change in verse 26, for Israel is an enemy with respect to the gospel but loved because of God's electing grace.

Others claim that Paul refers to the remnant of elect Jews throughout history who have believed. This interpretation fits with Paul's teaching about a Jewish remnant in these chapters (cf. 9:6–13, 27–29; 11:1–10). According to this view, seeing a future salvation for Israel in chapter 11 sits oddly with the emphasis on the remnant in the previous chapters. Paul doesn't look for the salvation of Israel in the future but "now" (11:31). The hardening "until" (*achri hou*, 11:25) all gentiles come in doesn't mean that anything will happen *after* all gentiles believe (cf. "until" in 1 Cor. 11:26). It means that the hardening of Israel will last until the very end of time. Romans 11:26 describes the manner (not the time) in which Israel will be saved. Paul refers to all elect Israelites throughout history.

Despite the strength of the remnant view, it is more convincing to say that Paul speaks of a future salvation of ethnic Israel near or at the return of Jesus Christ. One difficulty with limiting salvation to a Jewish remnant is that the mystery revealed at the end of Romans 11 is quite anticlimactic. Earlier I noted that the salvation of a remnant points to a great salvific work in the future; the remnant functions as a promise for the future. The salvation of a remnant isn't the solution but is the problem that has made these chapters necessary!

A future salvation of ethnic Israel also fits with the flow of thought in 11:25–27. The "fullness of the Gentiles" refers to the full number of gentiles who will be saved. The inclusion of the gentiles into the people of God probably stems from texts that describe the pilgrimage of gentiles to Zion (Isa. 2:2–4; 66:18–20; Mic. 4:1–5; Tob. 13:11–13; Pss. Sol. 17.30–31; T. Benj. 9.2). Meanwhile, Israel is hardened "until" and while the gentiles are believing. The word "until" implies that the hardening of the majority of Israel will be lifted *after* the full number of gentiles is saved. It seems unlikely that Paul merely says that the majority of Israel will be hardened for the rest of history, especially in chapters that denote God's faithfulness to his covenant people.

The words "and in this way" (Rom. 11:26) denote the manner in which Israel would be saved, but the way they will be saved also includes a temporal element. The content of the mystery, then, is not merely that Israel would be saved in the future (that was quite evident in the OT). What is new and distinctive is the revelation that all Israel would be saved only after the full number of gentiles had been included in the people of God. The OT citations in 11:26–27 also point to a future salvation: we have a conflation of Isaiah 59:20 and 27:9, and probably an allusion to Jeremiah 31:33 as well. In every one of these texts, Israel's salvation comes after a period of suffering because of its sin. Paul departs from the reading of the LXX and the MT in saying the redeemer will come "from Zion" instead of "to Zion" or "for the sake of Zion." Perhaps the change comes from an allusion to Psalm 14:7 (13:7 LXX). The merging of these texts indicates that they served a mutually interpretive function for Paul. By "Zion" Paul refers to the heavenly Jerusalem, from which the Lord comes. The future tense probably refers to Christ's second coming (cf. 1 Thess. 1:10). The conversion of the Jews here is similar to Paul's conversion when Jesus appeared to him. If this is correct, Paul teaches that Israel *will be saved*; the deliverer *will come*, and he *will turn* ungodliness from Jacob.

Israel's conversion is a divine work, and this accords with the last two lines of the OT citation. God overcomes the hardness of human hearts by putting his law within them per the new covenant (Jer. 31:31–34). He both removes the sin of his people and grants them a heart to know him. Thus the promises of salvation vouchsafed to Israel throughout the OT Scriptures are fulfilled in the last generation. We also see from Isaiah that the covenant will only be realized through the servant (Isa. 42:6; 49:6, 8; 52:13–53:12). The covenant reminds us that the salvation of Israel is the work of God himself.

"All Israel" refers to ethnic Israel and its future salvation at or near when Jesus returns. The "all" doesn't refer to every single Jewish person but to the majority of Israelites. Such a future salvation doesn't entail Israel ruling in Palestine in the millennium. Romans 11 says nothing about the fulfillment of such promises, and it views the church as a unified body consisting of Jews and gentiles together. The church itself should be understood to be the true and restored Israel. Jews who believe become members of the church of Jesus Christ. Nor does Paul argue that all ethnic Israelites throughout history will be saved. That would contradict the argument of Romans 9–11, which indicates that only a remnant is being saved. The revisiting of mercy upon Israel after such an interval reminds Israel that God's saving favor is truly mercy, not something they deserve because of their ethnic heritage. Just as God is merciful to the gentiles in the present era, so too, in accord with his promises, he pledges to shower his grace upon Israel again in the future (11:28–29).

God has designed salvation history in such a way that the extension of his saving grace surprises those who are its recipients as he exercises the freedom of his grace. Gentiles were elected to salvation when the Jews were expecting to be the special objects of his favor, and the Jews will be grafted in again at a time in which gentiles will be tempted to believe that they are superior to ethnic Israel (11:30–32). All is in place for Israel to "now" receive (11:31) the mercy that will conclude salvation history, but God alone knows the time of fulfillment. As God has arranged history, it is clear that both Jews and gentiles are enclosed under sin, and he designs history in such a manner that he can dispense his mercy to all, both Jews and gentiles.

Considering God's plan provokes Paul to break forth in praise to God for the riches of his wisdom and knowledge, and for the inaccessibility apart from revelation of his judgments and ways (11:33–36). Two OT texts are quoted to buttress Paul's case in the doxology. First, he cites Isaiah 40:13, where Isaiah asks if anyone knows the mind of the Lord or has become his counselor. The answer is obvious. No finite human being has enough wisdom to discern God's mind or to give him counsel on how to run the world. The OT context of the citation is important. In Isaiah 40 the second exodus from Babylon is promised, but Israel is filled with doubts and fears because the nation is so weak and Babylon is so strong. Yahweh assures Israel that he can accomplish his saving plan because all the nations are as nothing before him, a mere drop in the bucket or a speck on his scales.

The thematic connection to Romans 9–11 should be recognized. Just as the Lord promised to save Israel from Babylon when such deliverance seemed impossible and they had virtually given up, so too he has planned history in such a way that he fulfills the covenant promises made in Isaiah in an unexpected way. He has extended salvation to uncircumcised gentiles and at the end of history will again fold in unbelieving Jews. Does the inclusion of Israel again seem incredible? It is no more incredible than the pledge to rescue Israel from the dominion of Babylon. God effects salvation for the weak so that the glory of his strength is impressed upon all. Captive Israel in Babylon did not perceive the mind of the Lord, that it was his plan to rescue them from their plight; similarly, no human being could anticipate the wisdom of God's plan by which he has arranged history to bring about the salvation of both Jews and gentiles in a most improbable way.

Paul also teaches that no human being has the wisdom or knowledge to understand or to dictate to God the course that human history should take. His wisdom and plan are inaccessible to us, though Paul goes on to say that this inaccessible wisdom of God has been revealed to us, even though we are still unable to plumb the depths of it.

The second text is from Job 41:3. The meaning of the rhetorical question is not difficult: no one has first given to God, and therefore no one deserves repayment. The OT context must be considered. One of Job's major complaints during his suffering was that God was unjust. This led Job to doubt God's wisdom. In Job 38–41 God reveals himself to Job, rebuking him for questioning God's justice and mode of operation in the world. Job is too limited and finite to rule the world and all that is in it. God reminds Job that he indeed has the capacity to govern the world he has made. Job responds to God's speech (42:3) by admitting that he has been proud, that his knowledge is too limited, and that no one can thwart God's plan (42:2). Just as Job doubted God's wisdom and ability in his suffering, so too Christians might be inclined to question God's wisdom in terms of his saving plan for world history. Job's vision of God's greatness was limited. God accomplished his plan with respect to Job in wisdom and justice, and so too his plan to save some Jews and gentiles is wise and just. He is debtor to no one's wisdom, strength, or goodness, and he has accomplished his purposes by his own initiative. Since all things are from God, and all things are through God, then all things are to God: he deserves all the glory forever. God is the source, the means, and the goal of all things.

The Saving Righteousness of God in Everyday Life (12:1–13:14)

What God Requires (12:1–2)

In light of God's saving righteousness and saving mercy, which is explained in Romans 1:16–11:36, Paul calls upon people to give themselves completely to God. The grace of God in Christ is the foundation for all the exhortations so that the indicative (God's grace in Christ) undergirds the imperative (exhortations). We could say that 12:1–2 sums up all the exhortations in 12:1–15:13, in the sense that 12:3–15:13 unpacks what it means in everyday life to belong wholly to the Lord. Believers are to "present" their "bodies," their whole persons, to God. Their bodies are to be given as a "living sacrifice," since as those who are united with Christ, they now enjoy resurrection life. Unbelievers, by way of contrast, give their bodies to sexual sin (1:24, 26–27); they also fail to give thanks and praise to God, and they worship the creature rather than the Creator (1:21, 25). True worship means that God's rule is reinstated in the lives of his people. Believers are not to be shaped by the present evil age but are to "be transformed by the renewing of [their] minds." The thoughts of unbelievers are futile (1:21–22), but the minds of believers are reoriented and recalibrated, and as a consequence they are enabled to carry out God's good and pleasing will.

Life in the Body (12:3–8)

Those who give themselves to God also give themselves to one another in the body, the church of Jesus Christ. The greatest obstacle to living with one another in unity is pride, in cherishing illusions about oneself that don't accord with reality. Instead, believers are to think sensibly and in a realistic way about themselves. They are to consider and recognize the amount of faith they have so that they don't give in to impossible wishes and fantasies about their lives. Paul uses the metaphor of the body to describe the church, which is fitting since there are many different parts of the body, and yet the body is a unity. The diversity of parts indicates that various members of the church have different functions. They do not all excel at the same things. The church is Christ's body: diverse and yet unified.

God in his grace has bestowed gifts in the body, and the various gifts represent the diverse parts of the body, though Paul doesn't construct a one-to-one correspondence between the parts of the bodies and the gifts. A number of gifts are listed. The gift of prophecy is exercised through the reception of spontaneous revelations from God, where God communicates his will and his ways to his people. Those who have such a gift must not try to speak God's word beyond the faith given to them, for then they would begin to speak from their own imaginations instead of from God himself. Paul also emphasizes that believers must concentrate on their own gifts and not try to be what they are not. Those who have a gift of service should focus on serving, those who teach on teaching, and those who exhort in exhortation. Certainly, people should exercise gifts they don't possess, but they should concentrate on their strengths, their gifts. Paul also gives instructions about how gifts should be exercised. Those who give must be generous. Those who lead should be diligent and not give way to indolence since as leaders they may not be accountable to others. Finally, those who show mercy must continue to be cheerful and avoid resentment, guarding themselves lest their mercy be polluted by a spirit of reluctance.

Love in the Body (12:9–21)

Paul fleshes out further what it means to give oneself to God, and we have wide-ranging admonitions, which can't all be discussed here. Love heads up the list, and this is scarcely surprising since love is the heart and soul of Paul's ethic. As we examine the list of qualities, a few things stand out. Love must be genuine and must not be confused with flattery or being nice. At the same time, love is guided by moral norms so that it hates evil. The family affection for one another in the early church stands out, which means that believers form a new kinship group. Believers help those suffering financially and materially, providing hospitality to those who lack such. Authentic love manifests itself in truly caring about others so that people rejoice in the joys of others and weep with those who are in pain.

The impact of Jesus's teaching on loving enemies shows up as well (Matt. 5:43–48). Believers are to bless those who persecute and mistreat them. Instead of repaying evil for evil, believers should do what is honorable and Christlike. This difficult command can only be obeyed as believers regularly give themselves to God. At the same time, believers should rest in God's justice. He will pour out his wrath on those who don't repent of their hatred. Even though Paul speaks of believers "heaping fiery coals" (Rom. 12:20) on unbelievers, he is employing a manner of speaking here since God is the one who actually pours such coals upon them in the final judgment.

Most interpret the reference to the burning coals (Prov. 25:22) to refer to the remorse and shame enemies should experience for their hateful behavior when they see the love of Christians. The remarkable love of believers may, according to this reading, provoke unbelievers to repent and lead to their salvation. Others say that burning coals don't symbolize shame and remorse but the change of mind that occurs when good is returned for evil, and many find the source of the illustration in an Egyptian rite of repentance and remorse.

The problem with the above suggestions is that they depart from the most natural meaning of "coals of fire." We need not seek an obscure Egyptian ritual whose meaning is unclear, especially when we consider that Paul probably never heard of the rite. Actually, the OT itself provides clarity on the meaning of the metaphor. Coals of fire in the OT has a consistent meaning (2 Sam. 22:9, 13 = Ps. 18:8, 12; Job 41:20–21 [41:12–13 LXX]; Ps. 140:10; Prov. 6:27–29; Ezek. 24:11; cf. Sir. 8:10; 11:32; cf. also 2 Esd. 16:53), signifying God's judgment. Most scholars today reject this interpretation because it seems psychologically impossible to do good to others so that God will throw coals of fire on them on the last day! But the problem is no greater than what Paul already says in Romans 12:19, where believers refrain from revenge and leave unbelievers to the wrath of God. In both cases, believers are liberated from taking justice into their own hands and are free to do good because they know that God will right all wrongs in the end. Believers are to love enemies and pray for their repentance. At the same time, they know God is just: those who don't repent will experience God's wrath.

Submitting to Governing Authorities (13:1–7)

Paul's instructions on governing authorities match other texts in the NT on the same topic (Titus 3:1; 1 Pet. 2:13–17). Paul calls upon believers to submit since leaders are appointed and ordained by God. Paul even identifies pagan rulers (Nero was serving as emperor then) as God's servants, emphasizing that they punish evil and reward the good. Believers should obey rulers to avoid punishment and for the sake of conscience; in other words, it is the right thing to do. In particular, Paul calls upon readers to pay their taxes. Some have suggested that Paul wrote these words during the good part of Nero's reign, before he started to do horrific things, but Paul was not naive about governing authorities. The OT consistently teaches that God appoints rulers (2 Sam. 12:8; Prov. 8:15–16; Isa. 45:1; Jer. 27:5–6; Dan. 2:21, 37; 4:17, 25, 32; 5:21), and it is clear from the book of Daniel alone that many of the rulers were evil. Nor would Paul have forgotten that Jesus was unjustly crucified under a Roman prefect, and Paul himself suffered injustice from Roman governing authorities.

Readers have also wondered if there are any exceptions to what Paul says about submitting to the government. He doesn't mention governments doing what is evil. Does this mean that Paul countenances believers being complicit in evil perpetrated by the government? Unfortunately, this passage has been misunderstood so that some have used it to support injustice by governments, and others have protested that Paul supports injustice. We need to recognize, however, that Paul wasn't writing a treatise on government here! We have only a few lines of brief advice, and Paul's counsel has to do with what is ordinarily the case. Typically believers should obey the government and pay their taxes, even if the regime is evil. Governments restrain anarchy and preserve order in society. Deciphering whether there are exceptions must be gleaned from all of Scripture, and of course exceptions exist. Believers should not submit if authorities counsel believers not to preach the gospel (Acts 5:29) or to do what is evil (Exod. 1:15–21). Paul's purpose wasn't to consider the unusual but the usual, and we should refrain from reading more into the text than is warranted.

Living in Light of the End *(13:8–14)*

Giving oneself wholly to God means relating rightly to the government, and it manifests itself in loving one another. Here Paul argues that love fulfills the law, though it has often been noted that he leaves out the injunction to love God. Explaining why something is missing is a speculative endeavor, but perhaps Paul desired to emphasize that love for God reveals itself in love for others. It is a bit astonishing, given the Pauline emphasis on the temporary role of the Mosaic law, that the fulfillment of the law is described in terms of keeping commands from the Decalogue: the prohibitions against adultery, murder, stealing, and coveting are noted (Exod. 20:13–17; Deut. 5:17–21). How should we understand what Paul is doing in commending the fulfilling of the law? The most promising solution is to say that he believed that the moral norms of the Mosaic law are part of the law of Christ (Gal. 5:14; 6:2; 1 Cor. 9:21). Yes, the Mosaic covenant and its stipulations have passed away since the new covenant has come (Rom. 7:4–6; Gal. 3:15–4:7; 2 Cor. 3:4–18; Jer. 31:31–34). Clearly commands like circumcision (Rom. 4:9–12; 1 Cor. 7:19; Gal. 5:2–6), Sabbath (Rom. 14:5; Col. 2:16), and purity laws (Rom. 14:14, 20; Gal. 2:11–14) have passed away, but some of the laws in the OT are transcendent since they represent God's character.

It is instructive that love and commands are not seen by Paul to be enemies but friends. Particular commands delineate what love looks like in concrete circumstances. Love is more than keeping the law, but it is certainly not less than keeping the law, and no one is truly loving who violates moral norms. The focus isn't on the law but on love, since doing good to a neighbor (Lev. 19:18) envisions countless situations where no command applies. We could mistakenly count Paul as thinking that love is circumscribed totally by commands. On the other hand, specific commands avoid sentimentality where love collapses into feelings, and people show no concern for living a moral life.

Pauline ethics are animated by eschatology, and this is quite evident in Romans 13:11–14. Believers are to fulfill all the admonitions in 12:1–13:10 because the time of the end has drawn near, the time of salvation. The final day is at hand, and believers must live in light of the end. They are servants in the kingdom and must shed the weapons of darkness and wield the weapons of light. Believers aren't living in love if they give in to drunkenness and wild parties, sexual immorality, or fighting and quarreling. Even though believers are already "clothed with Christ" (Gal. 3:27), they are to clothe themselves anew every day with Christ so that they don't yield to the desires of the flesh.

The Weak and the Strong (14:1–15:13)

Living in Harmony (14:1–12)

From this larger section we see that dissension existed in Rome between the weak and the strong, and the dispute centered on foods. Scholars debate the nature of the difference between the weak and the strong, but it seems fair to say that the weak were mainly Jewish Christians, while the strong were mainly gentiles. Several lines of evidence point to this conclusion. First, when Paul sums up the entire discussion, he exhorts both Jews and gentiles (Rom. 15:7–13). Second, the words "unclean" (*koinos*, 14:14) and "clean" (*katharos*, 14:20) point to Jewish concerns about whether food is defiled (*koinos/koinoō*: 1 Macc. 1:47, 62; 4 Macc. 7:6; Josephus, *Ant.* 11.8.7 §346; Mark 7:2, 5; Acts 10:14–15, 28; 11:8–9; and LXX: Gen. 7:2–3, 8; 8:20; Lev. 11 passim; Deut. 14:7–8,

10, 19; Ezek. 4:13; Hosea 9:3; *katharos/katharizō*: Matt. 23:25–26; Mark 7:19; Luke 11:39, 41). Third, the reference to the observance of days (Rom. 14:5–6) fits with a Jewish background (cf. Gal. 4:10; Col. 2:16). Fourth, Paul's tolerance of such practices suggests a Jewish source. It is hard to imagine Paul being so sympathetic with practices that hailed from paganism.

The accent is on the strong accepting the weak, though admonitions are also given to the weak relative to the strong. In particular, the strong were to accept the weak and desist from arguing and contending with them. The temptation of the strong was to mock and ridicule the weak, thinking their restrictions were ludicrous. Conversely, the weak were prone to judge the strong, believing that their liberal stance on foods and days called into question whether they were true Christians. The weak didn't actually say that one must observe the food laws of the OT or the OT calendar to be saved, for if they did so, they would be guilty of proclaiming a false gospel. They probably said or thought that one would be a better or more mature Christian by adhering to these OT regulations. Paul assures the weak that the strong will stand on the day of judgment since the Lord will preserve their faith until the end. He leaves it to a person's conscience as to whether they should eat certain foods or observe particular days. Both the weak and the strong must remember that God is the judge: they live and die before him, and thus they are ultimately accountable to him (Isa. 45:23).

Building up the Weak (14:13–23)

Romans 14:13–23 is particularly directed to the strong. It is evident that Paul sides with the strong since he affirms that no food is unclean (14:14), and here he probably draws on the Jesus tradition that all foods are clean (Mark 7:19). Even though all foods are clean, Paul recognizes they are unclean for the person who thinks it is wrong to consume them (Rom. 14:20). The strong must beware so that they don't put an obstacle or a hindrance in the way of the weak, causing them to stumble or fall in their faith. One way the weak could fall is by returning to the synagogue if they felt that the strong were pressuring them. Love imitates Christ, who died for the salvation of others, and thus the strong should sacrifice for the sake of the weak and avoid eating foods that would scandalize them. The strong must recognize that Christian maturity is a process that takes time, and they must not force the weak to live like them.

The terms "stumbling" or "falling" (Matt. 13:20–21; 18:6–7; Luke 17:1; Rom. 9:32–33; 11:9; 16:17; 1 Cor. 1:23; Gal. 5:11; 1 Pet. 2:8; 1 John 2:10) and "destroying" (Rom. 2:12; 1 Cor. 1:18–19; 10:9–10; 15:18; 2 Cor. 2:15; 4:3; 2 Thess. 2:10) are regularly used in Scripture to designate eternal destruction and final judgment, and so the matter discussed here isn't trivial. If the weak begin to live contrary to their conscience and try to imitate what the strong do, even though the weak were convinced it was wrong, they would lose their footing as Christians since they would no longer be living according to their own conscience and convictions. If one acts apart from faith, sin is the result, since believers must live in accord with their faith in every circumstance and situation. All must realize that God's kingdom is not about what one eats and drinks but about righteousness, peace, and joy in the Holy Spirit, which means that all should live according to the Spirit in such a way that righteousness, peace, and joy flourish in the community.

Accepting One Another (15:1–13)

The strong are to help, support, and carry the weaknesses of those without strength (cf. Gal. 6:2). With an echo of Leviticus 19:18, the strong should please their neighbor, which means they should live to edify and build up their neighbors. In Romans 15:3 Christ is adduced as an example of what it means to please and build up one's neighbor. Paul quotes Psalm 69, which was widely used in the NT to interpret and explain the death of Jesus (see Matt. 27:34, 48; Mark 15:23, 36; Luke 23:36; John 2:17; 15:25; 19:29; Acts 1:20; Rom. 11:9). Jesus's death is the supreme example of one who forsakes his own pleasures to advance the honor of God. The psalm relates how David as a righteous sufferer was forsaken by his friends and attacked by his foes. So too, Christ took upon himself the reproaches that were directed against God because he lived for the glory and honor of God.

In Romans 15:4 Paul explains the instructive purpose of the OT Scriptures, anticipating the citations of Scripture in 15:9–12. The authority of the OT is clearly evident here (see 2 Tim. 3:16), verifying that the newness of the Pauline gospel does not nullify the OT. Believers are also consoled from the Scriptures in that they are nourished and strengthened in their spiritual lives and given hope. Hope also comes from endurance, as we have already seen in Romans 5:3–5. Here hope is linked to the unity of Jews and gentiles, which forecasts the eschatological unity of the people of God (15:5–6).

Verses 7–13 are the conclusion of 14:1–15:6 yet also summarize many of the main themes of the letter: they can thus be seen as the climax of the letter. Paul begins by calling upon the believers to accept one another. Paul wants the community to be filled with "joy and peace" in believing (15:13). The terms "joy" and "peace" reach back to 14:17, where Paul characterizes the kingdom of God as one of "joy" and "peace." Believers should accept one another to bring glory to God as they worship together. In this way the promises made to both the Jews and the gentiles will be fulfilled, promises first made to Abraham.

In 15:9–12 Paul quotes the Law, the Prophets, and the Psalms to support the notion that God's mercy has been poured out on both Jews and gentiles. The glorifying of God by the gentiles occurs in worship, when the name of God is lifted up in praise. Paul's first OT quotation (15:9) records David's words where he says he will sing praises among the gentiles, drawing on Psalm 18:49. Since gentiles in this psalm seem to be those conquered, not those being saved, does Paul cite the verse rightly? We need to recall that even in the OT context, David's victories anticipated the greater victories of Jesus. Thus Paul would have understood David's headship over his enemies and their service to him as fulfilled in a more profound way in Jesus the Messiah.

In Romans 15:10 the gentiles are called upon to rejoice along with God's people Israel. The LXX version of Deuteronomy 32:43 differs substantially from the MT, but the portion Paul lifts out is a sensible rendering from the MT as well. In this OT verse Paul discerns an indication that turning to Yahweh would not be restricted to Israel alone. Gentiles would rejoice along with Israel in the salvation accomplished. Thus the worship of Jews and gentiles together is fulfilled in the Pauline mission.

The third citation (Rom. 15:11) comes from Psalm 117:1 LXX, where the psalmist calls on all nations to "praise the LORD" for his "mercy" and "truth." In the Greek NT text, Paul moves the words "all nations" forward for emphasis in contrast to the psalm, where "all nations" follows "the LORD." The connection with Romans 15:8–9 is striking, for there God's covenant faithfulness and mercy are conveyed with these same two terms. True unity emerges when Jewish and gentile believers together voice their glad praise to God.

Paul closes out the OT quotations by citing Isaiah 11:10, which promises that a shoot of Jesse will come and rule over the nations, and "the nations will" put their hope in him. Paul obviously believed that this prophecy was fulfilled in Jesus Christ. Isaiah envisions a day when the promises for a transformed world will be fulfilled (11:1–9), and Israel will experience a second exodus (11:11–16). Jesus, as the shoot of Jesse, has inaugurated the salvation promised in Isaiah, and he has begun to rule over the gentiles. The rule of the son of Jesse over the gentiles involves their salvation, for the gentiles hope in him. Indeed, Isaiah often refers to the inclusion of the gentiles in the salvation that will be accomplished for Israel (e.g., 2:1–4; 12:4–5; 17:7–8; 19:18–25; 25:3–9; 42:4, 6, 10–12; 44:5; 45:14, 22; 49:6; 52:15; 55:3–5; 56:3–8; 59:19; 60:3; 65:1; 66:19–21). Paul prays that hope will fill the hearts of both Jews and gentiles as they trust in God. Harmony will exist between Jews and gentiles when both groups hope in the shoot of Jesse: Jesus Christ. Hope ultimately cannot be produced by human beings. Thus in Romans 15:13 Paul prays that the "God of hope" will grant hope, peace, and joy as they believe in God's promises.

Mission and Ministry (15:14–16:27)

Mission (15:14–33)

The fundamental concern that animates this section is mission. Paul wants the Roman church to rally together around his gospel and support his mission to Spain. Paul felt that his work in the east was finished, specifying the area from Jerusalem to Illyricum. How could he think that his work was finished when there were so many unconverted in the east and so many who had not heard the gospel? It seems that Paul's strategy was to establish churches in key cities and to send out delegates, such as Epaphras in Colossae, to reach smaller cities. His desire was to proclaim the gospel in unreached areas, and thus he felt compelled to go to Spain. In doing so Paul saw the prophecy of Isaiah 52:15 being fulfilled as the gospel was going to people who had never heard it (Rom. 15:21). It is difficult to know if Paul ever reached Spain. Clement says that Paul traveled to the farthest point of the west (1 Clem. 5.7), which may indicate that Paul made it to Spain.

Paul also reminded the Romans about the importance of the collection for the poor saints in Jerusalem (cf. also 1 Cor. 16:1–4; 2 Cor. 8–9). Again we see the solidarity of Jewish and gentile Christians, and Paul believed gentiles should support poor believers in Jerusalem since gentile believers owed them a spiritual debt, and salvation hails from the Jews (Rom. 1:16; 2:9–10).

Mutual Love (16:1–27)

The last chapter ends with greetings and an ascription of praise to God. We have already discussed the doxology (see Rom. 1:1–7), and so we will consider here the role of the greetings, but we should also note that Paul gives a final warning (16:17–20) to his readers not to veer away from the gospel at the impetus of false teachers. As readers we wonder about the role of such extensive greetings. Some maintain that the number of personal contacts demonstrates that Paul could not have written this chapter to Rome, but travel between various parts of the Roman Empire was more common than some have previously supposed. Further, Paul need not have known every single person greeted. He may send greetings to some because their reputation has reached him.

The main purpose of the greetings is to express the love that was the mark of the early Christian community (John 13:34–35). The greetings, then, should be appraised as authentic expressions of love in Christ, but the greetings also note the many supporters of the Pauline gospel in Rome. By sending his greetings to well-known and respected members of the Roman churches, Paul also indirectly commends his gospel since the persons named are in harmony with his teaching.

The number of women greeted also stands out, showing that women were involved in ministry in significant ways: Prisca, Mary, Junia, Tryphaena, Tryphosa, Persis, Rufus's mother, and Julia. The verb "to labor" (*kopiaō*) is used of four women—Mary (Rom. 16:6), Tryphaena, Tryphosa, and Persis (v. 12)—and for the ministry of Paul (1 Cor. 15:10; Gal. 4:11; Phil. 2:16; Col. 1:29; 1 Tim. 4:10) and others (1 Cor. 16:16; 1 Thess. 5:12; 1 Tim. 5:17). Here it probably denotes missionary work. Since Prisca is named first in some texts (Acts 18:26; Rom. 16:3; 2 Tim. 4:19), she was likely more prominent than her husband, Aquila; both were vitally involved in the early Christian movement.

The most controversial reference to a woman is found in the greetings given to Andronicus and Junia(s) (Rom. 16:7). Junia was certainly a woman, and she also had a significant ministry along with her husband. There is some dispute on the meaning of the words, but Junia is also probably said to be "outstanding among the apostles" (NASB, NIV). The word "apostle" is not necessarily a technical term (cf. 2 Cor. 8:23; Phil. 2:25), and Andronicus and Junia were likely itinerant evangelists or missionaries, and in a patriarchal world Junia probably worked especially among women.

The greetings also reveal that the Christian community in Rome was composed of a number of churches. Most scholars argue that the churches met in houses, but recent research has raised questions about whether churches met exclusively in houses. It seems that at least five different churches are greeted in Rome: the home of Prisca and Aquila (Rom. 16:5), those who belong to Aristobulus (v. 10), those who belong to Narcissus (v. 11), and in verses 14 and 15 the names probably represent members of two churches. Ultimately, we don't know how many churches existed in Rome. The presence of various churches, however, may also explain the tensions between the strong and the weak in Rome if differing customs were observed in the various churches.

The church is exhorted to greet one another with a holy kiss. The holy kiss was apparently a common greeting in early Christian communities (cf. 1 Cor. 16:20; 2 Cor. 13:12; 1 Thess. 5:26; 1 Pet. 5:14). Interestingly, there is no evidence for the practice in the Greco-Roman world, and thus it stemmed from the practice of the early church. Believers demonstrated their warm affection for one another as a new family.

Romans: Commentaries

Barrett, Charles K. *Commentary on the Epistle to the Romans*. HNTC. New York: Harper & Row; Peabody, MA: Hendrickson, 1957.

Bird, Michael F. *Romans*. SOGBC 6. Grand Rapids: Zondervan, 2016.

Black, Matthew. *Romans*. NCB. Grand Rapids: Eerdmans, 1973.

Bray, Gerald, ed. *Romans*. ACCS 6 (NT). Downers Grove, IL: InterVarsity, 1998.

Byrne, Brendan. *Romans*. SP. Collegeville, MN: Liturgical Press, 1996.

Cranfield, Charles E. B. *A Critical and Exegetical Commentary on the Epistle to the Romans: Introduction and Commentary on Romans I–VIII*. ICC. Edinburgh: T&T Clark, 1975.

———. *An Exegetical Commentary on the Epistle to the Romans: Commentary on Romans IX–XVI and Essays*. ICC. Edinburgh: T&T Clark, 1979.

Dodd, Charles H. *The Epistle of Paul to the Romans*. MNTC. London: Hodder & Stoughton, 1932.

Dunn, James D. G. *Romans 1–8*. WBC. Dallas: Word, 1988.

———. *Romans 9–16*. WBC. Dallas: Word, 1988.

Fitzmyer, Joseph A. *Romans: A New Translation with Introduction and Commentary*. AB 33. New York: Doubleday, 1993.

Godet, Frédéric L. *Commentary on the Epistle to the Romans*. Translated by A. Cusin. Translation revised by T. W. Chambers. Classic Commentary Library. Grand Rapids: Zondervan, 1956.

Hodge, Charles. *A Commentary on Romans*. Geneva Series of Commentaries. London: Banner of Truth Trust, 1972.

Hultgren, Arland J. *Paul's Letter to the Romans: A Commentary*. Grand Rapids: Eerdmans, 2011.

Jewett, Robert. *Romans: A Commentary*. Hermeneia. Minneapolis: Fortress, 2007.

Käsemann, Ernst. *Commentary on Romans*. Translated and edited by G. W. Bromiley. Grand Rapids: Eerdmans, 1980.

Keck, Leander. E. *Romans*. ANTC. Nashville: Abingdon, 2005.

Keener, Craig. S. *Romans: A New Covenant Commentary*. NCCS. Eugene, OR: Cascade, 2009.

Kruse, Colin. G. *Paul's Letter to the Romans*. PNTC. Grand Rapids: Eerdmans, 2012.

Leenhardt, Franz J. *The Epistle to the Romans: A Commentary*. Translated by H. Knight. London: Lutterworth, 1961.

Longenecker, Richard N. *The Epistle to the Romans*. NIGTC. Grand Rapids: Eerdmans, 2016.

Matera, Frank J. *Romans*. PCNT. Grand Rapids: Baker Academic, 2010.

Melanchthon, Phillip. *Commentary on Romans*. Translated by F. Kramer. St. Louis: Concordia, 1992.

Moo, Douglas J. *The Epistle to the Romans*. 2nd ed. NICNT. Grand Rapids: Eerdmans, 2018.

Morris, Leon. *The Epistle to the Romans*. Grand Rapids: Eerdmans, 1988.

Mounce, Robert H. *Romans*. NAC 27. Nashville: Broadman & Holman, 1995.

Murray, John. *The Epistle to the Romans: The English Text with Introduction, Exposition, and Notes*. Vol. 1, *Chapters 1–8*. NICNT. Grand Rapids: Eerdmans, 1959.

———. *The Epistle to the Romans: The English Text with Introduction, Exposition, and Notes*. Vol. 2, *Chapters 9–16*. NICNT. Grand Rapids: Eerdmans, 1965.

Nygren, Anders. *Commentary on Romans*. Translated by C. C. Rasmussen. Philadelphia: Fortress, 1949.

O'Neill, J. C. *Paul's Letter to the Romans*. Harmondsworth: Penguin, 1975.

Peterson, David G. *Commentary on Romans*. BTCP. Nashville: B&H, 2017.

Porter, Stanley. E. *The Letter to the Romans: A Linguistic and Literary Commentary*. New Testament Monographs 37. Sheffield: Sheffield Phoenix, 2015.

Schlatter, A. *Romans: The Righteousness of God*. Translated by S. S. Schatzmann. Peabody, MA: Hendrickson, 1995.

Schreiner, T. R. *Romans*. 2nd ed. BECNT. Grand Rapids: Baker Academic, 2018.

Stuhlmacher, P. *Letter to the Romans: A Commentary*. Translated by S. J. Hafemann. Louisville: Westminster John Knox, 1994.

Thielman, Frank. *Romans*. ZECNT. Grand Rapids: Zondervan, 2018.

Witherington, Ben, III, and D. Hyatt. *Paul's Letter to the Romans: A Socio-Rhetorical Commentary*. Grand Rapids: Eerdmans, 2004.

Wright, N. T. "The Letter to the Romans: Introduction, Commentary and Reflections." In *The New Interpreter's Bible*, edited by Leander E. Keck et al., 10:393–770. Nashville: Abingdon, 2002.

Ziesler, J. A. *Paul's Letter to the Romans*. TPINTC. Philadelphia: Trinity Press International, 1989.

Romans: Articles, Essays, and Monographs

Agersnap, Søren. *Baptism and the New Life: A Study of Romans 6:1–14*. Aarhus: Aarhus University Press, 1999.

Baldenas, R. *Christ, the End of the Law: Romans 10,4 in Pauline Perspective*. JSNTSup 10. Sheffield: JSOT Press, 1985.

Barclay, John M. G. *Paul and the Gift*. Grand Rapids: Eerdmans, 2015.

Barclay, John M. G., and Simon Gathercole, eds. *Divine and Human Agency in Paul and His Cultural Environment*. Library of Biblical Studies. London: T&T Clark, 2007.

Bassler, Jouette. *Divine Impartiality: Paul and a Theological Axiom*. SBLDS 59. Chico, CA: Scholars Press, 1982.

Baugh, S. M. "The Meaning of Foreknowledge." In *Still Sovereign: Contemporary Perspectives on Election, Foreknowledge, and Grace*, edited by T. R. Schreiner and B. A. Ware, 183–200. Grand Rapids: Baker Books, 2000.

Beale, G. K. "An Exegetical and Theological Consideration of the Hardening of Pharaoh's Heart in Exodus 4–14 and Romans 9." *TJ* 5 (1984): 129–54.

Bell, R. H. *No One Seeks for God: An Exegetical and Theological Study of Romans 1.18–3:20*. WUNT 106. Tübingen: Mohr Siebeck, 1998.

———. *Provoked to Jealousy: The Origin and Purpose of the Jealousy Motif in Romans 9–11.* WUNT 63. Tübingen: Mohr Siebeck, 1994.

Berkley, T. W. *From a Broken Covenant to Circumcision of the Heart: Pauline Intertextual Exegesis in Romans 2:11–29.* SBLDS 175. Atlanta: Society of Biblical Literature, 2000.

Berry, D. L. *Glory in Romans and the Unified Purpose of God in Redemptive History.* Eugene, OR: Pickwick, 2015.

Bird, Michael F. *The Saving Righteousness of God: Studies on Paul, Justification, and the New Perspective.* Eugene, OR: Wipf & Stock, 2007.

Bird, Michael F., and P. M. Sprinkle, eds. *The Faith of Jesus Christ: Exegetical, Biblical, and Theological Studies.* Peabody, MA: Hendrickson, 2009.

Blackwell, Ben C., John K. Goodrich, and Jason Maston, eds. *Reading Romans in Context: Paul and Second Temple Judaism.* Grand Rapids: Zondervan, 2015.

Blocher, Henri. *Original Sin: Illuminating the Riddle.* NSBT. Downers Grove, IL: InterVarsity, 1997.

Bornkamm, G. "The Letter to the Romans as Paul's Last Will and Testament." In *The Romans Debate*, edited by K. P. Donfried, rev. ed., 16–28. Peabody, MA: Hendrickson, 1991.

Brauch, M. T. "Perspectives on 'God's Righteousness' in Recent German Discussion." In *Paul and Palestinian Judaism: A Comparison of Patterns of Religion*, edited by E. P. Sanders, 523–42. Philadelphia: Fortress, 1977.

Bruno, Chris. *"God Is One": The Function of "Eis ho Theos" as a Ground for Gentile Inclusion in Paul's Letters.* LNTS 497. London: Bloomsbury T&T Clark, 2013.

Burk, Denny. "The Righteousness of God (*Dikaiosunē Theou*) and Verbal Genitives: A Grammatical Clarification." *JSNT* 34 (2012): 346–60.

Burke, T. J. *Adoption into God's Family: Exploring a Pauline Metaphor.* NSBT. Downers Grove, IL: InterVarsity, 2006.

Byrne, Brendan. *"Sons of God"—"Seed of Abraham": A Study of the Idea of the Sonship of God of All Christians in Paul against the Jewish Background.* AnBib 83. Rome: Pontifical Biblical Institute, 1979.

Campbell, Constantine R. *Paul and Union with Christ: An Exegetical and Theological Study.* Grand Rapids: Zondervan, 2012.

Campbell, W. S. *Paul's Gospel in an Intercultural Context: Jew and Gentile in the Letter to the Romans.* Studies in the Intercultural History of Christianity 69. New York: Peter Lang, 1992.

Carraway, George. *Christ Is God over All: Romans 9:5 in the Context of Romans 9–11.* LNTS 489. London: Bloomsbury T&T Clark, 2013.

Carson, D. A., P. T. O'Brien, and M. A. Seifrid, eds. *Justification and Variegated Nomism.* Vol. 1, *The Complexities of Second Temple Judaism.* WUNT 2/140. Tübingen: Mohr Siebeck, 2001.

———. *Justification and Variegated Nomism.* Vol. 2, *The Paradoxes of Paul.* WUNT 2/181. Tübingen: Mohr Siebeck, 2004.

Cranfield, Charles E. B. *On Romans and Other New Testament Essays.* Edinburgh: T&T Clark, 1998.

Crisler, Channing L. *Reading Romans as Lament: Paul's Use of Old Testament Lament in His Most Famous Letter.* Eugene, OR: Pickwick, 2016.

Das, Andrew A. *Paul, the Law, and the Covenant*. Peabody, MA: Hendrickson, 2001.

———. *Solving the Romans Debate*. Minneapolis: Fortress, 2007.

Davies, G. N. *Faith and Obedience in Romans: A Study in Romans*. JSNTSup 39. Sheffield: JSOT Press, 1990.

Deidun, T. J. *New Covenant Morality in Paul*. AnBib 89. Rome: Pontifical Biblical Institute, 1981.

de Roo, J. C. R. *"Works of the Law" at Qumran and in Paul*. NTM 13. Sheffield: Sheffield Phoenix, 2007.

De Young, J. B. "The Meaning of 'Nature' in Romans 1 and Its Implications for Biblical Proscriptions of Homosexual Behavior." *JETS* 31 (1988): 429–41.

Dickson, J. P. *Mission-Commitment in Ancient Judaism and in the Pauline Communities: The Shape, Extent, and Background of Early Christian Mission*. WUNT 159. Tübingen: Mohr Siebeck, 2003.

Donfried, Karl. *The Romans Debate*. Rev. ed. Peabody, MA: Hendrickson, 1991.

Dunn, James D. G. *The New Perspective on Paul: Collected Essays*. WUNT 185. Tübingen: Mohr Siebeck, 2005.

Elliot, Neil. *The Arrogance of Nations: Reading Romans in the Shadow of Empire*. Minneapolis: Fortress, 2008.

———. *The Rhetoric of Romans: Argumentative Constraint and Strategy and Paul's Dialogue with Judaism*. JSNTSup 45. Sheffield: JSOT Press, 1990.

Engberg-Pedersen, T. *Paul and the Stoics*. Edinburgh: T&T Clark, 2000.

Eskola, T. *Theodicy and Predestination in Pauline Soteriology*. WUNT 100. Tübingen: Mohr Siebeck, 1998.

Esler, P. F. *Conflict and Identity in Romans: The Social Setting of Paul's Letter*. Minneapolis: Fortress, 2003.

Fee, Gordon D. *God's Empowering Presence: The Holy Spirit in the Letters of Paul*. Peabody, MA: Hendrickson, 1994.

———. *Pauline Christology: An Exegetical-Theological Study*. Peabody, MA: Hendrickson, 2007.

Gaffin, Richard B., Jr. *"By Faith, Not by Sight": Paul and the Order of Salvation*. Waynesboro, GA: Paternoster, 2006.

Gagnon, R. A. J. *The Bible and Homosexual Practice: Texts and Hermeneutics*. Nashville: Abingdon, 2001.

Garlington, D. B. *Faith, Obedience, and Perseverance: Aspects of Paul's Letter to the Romans*. WUNT 79. Tübingen: Mohr Siebeck, 1994.

Gathercole, Simon. *Where Is Boasting? Early Jewish Soteriology and Paul's Response in Romans 1–5*. Grand Rapids: Eerdmans, 2003.

Grindheim, Sigurd. *The Crux of Election: Paul's Critique of the Jewish Confidence in the Election of Israel*. WUNT 202. Tübingen: Mohr Siebeck, 2005.

Gundry-Volf, J. M. *Paul and Perseverance: Staying In and Falling Away*. Louisville: Westminster John Knox, 1990.

Haring, James W. "Romans 5:12 Once Again: Is It a Grammatical Comparison?" *JBL* 137 (2018): 733–41.

Hays, Richard B. "Relations Natural and Unnatural: A Response to John Boswell's Exegesis of Romans 1." *Journal of Religious Ethics* 14 (1986): 184–215.

Hengel, Martin. *The Son of God: The Origin of Christology and the History of Jewish Hellenistic Religion.* Translated by J. Bowden. Philadelphia: Fortress, 1976.

Hill, David. *Greek Words and Hebrew Meanings: Studies in the Semantics of Soteriological Terms.* SNTSMS 5. Cambridge: Cambridge University Press, 1967.

Hvalvik, R. "A 'Sonderweg' for Israel: A Critical Examination of a Current Interpretation of Romans 11:25–27." *JSNT* 38 (1990): 87–107.

Irons, Charles Lee. *The Righteousness of God: A Lexical Examination of the Covenant-Faithfulness Interpretation.* WUNT 386. Tübingen: Mohr Siebeck, 2015.

Jacob, Haley Goranson. *Conformed to the Image of His Son: Reconsidering Paul's Theology of Glory in Romans.* Downers Grove, IL: InterVarsity, 2018.

Jarvis, L. A. *The Purpose of Romans: A Comparative Letter Structure Investigation.* JSNTSup 55. Sheffield: JSOT Press, 1991.

Jipp, Joshua W. *Christ Is King: Paul's Royal Ideology.* Minneapolis: Fortress, 2015.

Johnson, Elizabeth E. *The Function of Apocalyptic and Wisdom Traditions in Romans 9–11.* SBLDS 109. Atlanta: Scholars Press, 1989.

Johnson, Luke T. *Reading Romans: A Literary and Theological Commentary.* New York: Crossroad, 1997.

Johnson, S. L., Jr. "Romans 5:12—An Exercise in Exegesis and Theology." In *New Dimensions in New Testament Study*, edited by R. N. Longenecker and M. C. Tenney, 298–316. Grand Rapids: Zondervan, 1974.

Kaye, B. N. *The Argument of Romans: With Special Reference to Chapter 6.* Austin: Schola Press, 1979.

Kim, Seyoon. *Christ and Caesar: The Gospel and the Roman Empire in the Writings of Paul and Luke.* Grand Rapids: Eerdmans, 2008.

———. *Paul and the New Perspective: Second Thoughts on the Origin of Paul's Gospel.* Grand Rapids: Eerdmans, 2002.

King, Justin. *Speech-in-Character, Diatribe, and Romans 3:1–9: Who's Speaking When and Why It Matters.* BIS 163. Leiden: Brill, 2018.

Kirk, J. R. D. *Unlocking Romans: Resurrection and the Justification of God.* Grand Rapids: Eerdmans, 2008.

Kujanpää, Katja. *The Rhetorical Function of Scriptural Quotations in Romans: Paul's Argument by Quotations.* NovTSup 172. Leiden: Brill, 2019.

Kümmel, W. G. *Römer 7 und das Bild des Menschen in Neuen Testament: Zwei Studien.* Munich: Chr. Kaiser, 1974.

Laato, Timo. *Paul and Judaism: An Anthropological Approach.* Translated by T. McElwain. Atlanta: Scholars Press, 1995.

Lambrecht, Jan. *The Wretched "I" and Its Liberation: Paul in Romans 7 and 8.* LTPM 14. Louvain: Peeters, 1992.

Lampe, Peter. *From Paul to Valentinus: Christians at Rome in the First Two Centuries.* Translated by Michael Steinhauser. Edited by Marshall D. Johnson. Minneapolis: Fortress, 2003.

Linebaugh, Jonathan A. *God, Grace, and Righteousness in Wisdom of Solomon and Paul's Letter to the Romans: Texts in Conversation.* NovTSup 152. Leiden: Brill, 2013.

Longenecker, Bruce W. *Eschatology and the Covenant: A Comparison of 4 Ezra and Romans 1–11.* JSNTSup 57. Sheffield: JSOT Press, 1991.

Longenecker, Richard N. *Introducing Romans: Critical Issues in Paul's Most Famous Letter.* Grand Rapids: Eerdmans, 2011.

Luther, Martin. *Lectures on Romans: Glosses and Scholia.* Edited by C. Oswald. LW 25. Philadelphia: Muhlenberg, 1972.

Madueme, Hans, and M. Reeves, eds. *Adam, the Fall, and Original Sin: Theological, Biblical, and Scientific Perspectives.* Grand Rapids: Baker Academic, 2014.

Marshall, I. Howard. "Romans 16:27: An Apt Conclusion." In *Romans and the People of God: Essays in Honor of Gordon D. Fee on the Occasion of His 65th Birthday*, edited by S. Soderlund and N. T. Wright, 170–84. Grand Rapids: Eerdmans, 1999.

Martin, B. L. *Christ and the Law in Paul.* NovTSup 62. Leiden: Brill, 1989.

Matthew, S. *Women in the Greetings of Romans 16.1–16: A Study of Mutuality and Women's Ministry in the Letter to the Romans.* LNTS 471. London: Bloomsbury T&T Clark, 2013.

McFadden, Kevin W. "Does ΠΙΣΤΙΣ Mean 'Faith(fulness)' in Paul?" *TynBul* 66 (2015): 251–70.

———. *Judgment according to Works in Romans: The Meaning and Function of Divine Judgment in Paul's Most Important Letter.* Emerging Scholars. Minneapolis: Fortress, 2013.

McKnight, Scot, and Joseph Modica, eds. *Jesus Is Lord, Caesar Is Not: Evaluating Empire in New Testament Studies.* Downers Grove, IL: InterVarsity, 2012.

Merkle, Benjamin L. "Romans 11 and the Future of Ethnic Israel." *JETS* 43 (2000): 709–21.

Meyer, Jason C. *The End of the Law: Mosaic Covenant in Pauline Theology.* NACSBT 6. Nashville: Broadman & Holman, 2009.

Miller, J. C. *The Obedience of Faith, the Eschatological People of God, and the Purpose of Romans.* SBLDS 177. Atlanta: Society of Biblical Literature, 2000.

Minear, Paul S. *The Obedience of Faith: The Purposes of Paul in the Epistle to the Romans.* Studies in Biblical Theology, 2nd ser., 19. Naperville, IL: Allenson, 1971.

Moo, Douglas J. "'Law,' 'Works of the Law,' and Legalism in Paul." *WTJ* 45 (1983): 73–100.

Munck, Johannes. *Christ and Israel: An Interpretation of Romans 9–11.* Translated by I. Nixon. Philadelphia: Fortress, 1967.

Nanos, Mark D. *The Mystery of Romans: The Jewish Context of Paul's Letter.* Minneapolis: Fortress, 1996.

Naselli, Andrew D. *From Typology to Doxology: Paul's Use of Isaiah and Job in Romans 11:34–55.* Eugene, OR: Pickwick, 2012.

Novenson, Matthew V. *Among the Messiahs: Christ Language in Paul and Messiah Language in Ancient Judaism.* Oxford: Oxford University Press, 2012.

Oakes, Peter. *Reading Romans in Pompeii: Paul's Letter at Ground Level.* Minneapolis: Fortress, 2009.

O'Brien, Peter T. "Romans 8:26, 27: A Revolutionary Approach to Prayer?" *RTR* 46 (1987): 65–73.

Ortlund, Dane C. "Justified by Faith, Judged according to Works: Another Look at a Pauline Paradox." *JETS* 52 (2009): 323–39.

———. "What Does It Mean to Fall Short of the Glory of God? Romans 3:23 in Biblical-Theological Perspective." *WTJ* 80 (2018): 121–40.

Packer, J. I. "The 'Wretched Man' Revisited: Another Look at Romans 7:14–25." In *Romans and the People of God: Essays in Honor of Gordon D. Fee on the Occasion of His 65th Birthday*, edited by S. Soderlund and N. T. Wright, 70–81. Grand Rapids: Eerdmans, 1999.

Pao, David W. *Thanksgiving: An Investigation of a Pauline Theme*. NSBT. Downers Grove, IL: InterVarsity, 2002.

Patte, D., and C. Grenhold, eds. *Modern Interpretations of Romans: Tracking Their Hermeneutical/Theological Trajectory*. Romans through History and Culture Series. New York: T&T Clark, 2013.

Piper, John. *The Justification of God: An Exegetical and Theological Study of Romans 9:1–23*. 2nd ed. Grand Rapids: Baker, 1993.

Quarles, Charles L. "From Faith to Faith: A Fresh Examination of the Prepositional Series in Romans 1:17." *NovT* 45 (2003): 1–21.

———. "The Soteriology of R. Akiba and E. P. Sanders' *Paul and Palestinian Judaism*." *NTS* 42 (1996): 1–21.

Rainbow, Paul A. *Way of Salvation: The Role of Christian Obedience in Justification*. Waynesboro, GA: Paternoster, 2005.

Räisänen, Heikki. *Paul and the Law*. WUNT 29. Tübingen: Mohr Siebeck, 1983.

Rapa, R. K. *The Meaning of "Works of the Law" in Galatians and Romans*. Biblical Literature 31. New York: Peter Lang, 2001.

Reasoner, Mark. *The Strong and the Weak: Romans 14.1–15.13 in Context*. SNTSMS 103. Cambridge: Cambridge University Press, 1999.

Reumann, J. H. Paul, J. A. Fitzmyer, and J. D. Quinn. *Righteousness in the New Testament: Justification in the United States Lutheran-Roman Catholic Dialogue*. Philadelphia: Fortress, 1982.

Rhyne, C. T. *Faith Establishes the Law*. SBLDS 55. Chico, CA: Scholars Press, 1981.

Ribbens, Benjamin J. "Forensic-Retributive Justification in Romans 3:21–26: Paul's Doctrine of Justification in Dialogue with Hebrews." *CBQ* 47 (2012): 486–99.

Ridderbos, H. *Paul: An Outline of His Theology*. Translated by J. R. de Witt. Grand Rapids: Eerdmans, 1975.

Riesner, Rainer. *Paul's Early Period: Chronology, Mission Strategy, Theology*. Translated by D. Stott. Grand Rapids: Eerdmans, 1998.

Robinson, J. A. T. *Wrestling with Romans*. Philadelphia: Westminster, 1979.

Rodriguez, R. *If You Call Yourself a Jew: Reappraising Paul's Letter to the Romans*. Eugene, OR: Cascade, 2014.

Roetzel, Calvin J. *Judgement in the Community: A Study of the Relationship between Eschatology and Ecclesiology in Paul*. Leiden: Brill, 1972.

Rosner, Brian. *Paul and the Law: Keeping the Commandments of God*. NSBT. Downers Grove, IL: InterVarsity, 2013.

Sanders, E. P. *Paul and Palestinian Judaism: A Comparison of Patterns of Religion.* Philadelphia: Fortress, 1977.

———. *Paul, the Law, and the Jewish People.* Philadelphia: Fortress, 1983.

Schliesser, B. *Abraham's Faith in Romans 4: Paul's Concept of Faith in Light of the History of Reception of Genesis 15:6.* WUNT 224. Tübingen: Mohr Siebeck, 2007.

Schnabel, Eckhard J. *Law and Wisdom from Ben Sira to Paul: A Tradition Historical Enquiry into the Relation of Law, Wisdom, and Ethics.* WUNT 16. Tübingen: Mohr Siebeck, 1985.

Schnelle, Udo. *Apostle Paul: His Life and Theology.* Translated by M. E. Boring. Grand Rapids: Baker Academic, 2005.

Schoeps, Hans Joachim. *Paul: The Theology of the Apostle in Light of the Jewish Religious History.* Translated by H. Knight. Philadelphia: Westminster, 1961.

Schreiner, Thomas R. "Did Paul Believe in Justification by Works? Another Look at Romans 2." *BBR* 3 (1993): 131–58.

———. "Does Romans 9 Teach Individual Election unto Salvation?" In *Still Sovereign*, edited by T. R. Schreiner and B. K. Ware, 89–106. Grand Rapids: Baker Books, 2000.

———. *Faith Alone: The Doctrine of Justification; What the Reformers Taught . . . and Why It Still Matters.* FSS. Grand Rapids: Zondervan, 2015.

———. *The Law and Its Fulfillment: A Pauline Theology of Law.* Grand Rapids: Baker, 1993.

———. "'Works of Law' in Paul." *NovT* 33 (1991): 217–44.

Scott, J. M. *Adoption as Sons of God: An Exegetical Investigation into the Background of ʿΥἱοθεσία in the Pauline Corpus.* WUNT 48. Tübingen: Mohr Siebeck, 1992.

———. *Paul and the Nations: The Old Testament and Jewish Background of Paul's Mission to the Nations with Special Reference to the Destination of Galatians.* WUNT 84. Tübingen: Mohr Siebeck, 1995.

Seifrid, Mark A. *Christ, Our Righteousness: Paul's Theology of Justification.* NSBT 9. Downers Grove, IL: InterVarsity, 2000.

———. *Justification by Faith: The Origin and Development of a Central Pauline Theme.* NovTSup 68. Leiden: Brill, 1992.

———. "Paul's Turn to Christ in Romans." *Concordia Journal* 44 (2018): 15–24.

———. "Paul's Use of Righteousness Language against Its Hellenistic Background." In *Justification and Variegated Nomism*, edited by D. A. Carson, P. T. O'Brien, and M. A. Seifrid, vol. 2, *The Paradoxes of Paul*, 39–74. WUNT 2/181. Tübingen: Mohr Siebeck, 2004.

———. "Righteousness Language in the Hebrew Scriptures and Early Judaism." In *Justification and Variegated Nomism*, edited by D. A. Carson, P. T. O'Brien, and M. A. Seifrid, vol. 1, *The Complexities of Second Temple Judaism*, 415–22. WUNT 2/140. Tübingen: Mohr Siebeck, 2001.

Shum, S.-L. *Paul's Use of Isaiah in Romans: A Comparative Study of Paul's Letter to the Romans and the Sibylline and Qumran Sectarian Texts.* WUNT 156. Tübingen: Mohr Siebeck, 2002.

Snodgrass, Klyne R. "Justification by Grace—to the Doers: An Analysis of the Place of Romans 2 in the Theology of Paul." *NTS* 32 (1986): 72–93.

———. "Spheres of Influence: A Possible Solution to the Problem of Paul and the Law." *JSNT* 32 (1988): 93–113.

Soards, M. L. *Scripture and Homosexuality: Biblical Authority and the Church Today.* Louisville: Westminster John Knox, 1995.

Southall, David. J. *Rediscovering Righteousness in Romans: Personified "Dikaiosynē" within Metaphoric and Narratorial Settings.* WUNT 240. Tübingen: Mohr Siebeck, 2008.

Sprinkle, Preston M. *Law and Life: The Interpretation of Leviticus 18:5 in Early Judaism and in Paul.* WUNT 241. Tübingen: Mohr Siebeck, 2008.

———. *Paul and Judaism Revisited: A Study of Divine and Human Agency in Salvation.* Downers Grove, IL: InterVarsity, 2013.

Stanley, C. D. *Paul and the Language of Scripture: Citation Technique in the Pauline Epistles and Contemporary Literature.* SNTSMS 69. Cambridge: Cambridge University Press, 1992.

Stendahl, Krister. *Paul among Jews and Gentiles and Other Essays.* Philadelphia: Fortress, 1976.

Still, Todd D., ed. *God and Israel: Providence and Purpose in Romans 9–11.* Waco: Baylor University Press, 2017.

Stowers, Stanley K. *A Rereading of Romans: Justice, Jews, and Gentiles.* New Haven: Yale University Press, 1994.

Thielman, Frank. *From Plight to Solution: A Jewish Framework for Understanding Paul's View of the Law in Galatians and Romans.* NovTSup 61. Leiden: Brill, 1989.

———. *Paul and the Law: A Contextual Approach.* Downers Grove, IL: InterVarsity, 1994.

Thiselton, Anthony C. *Discovering Romans: Content, Interpretation, Reception.* Grand Rapids: Eerdmans, 2016.

Thompson, M. B. *Clothed with Christ: The Example and Teaching of Jesus in Romans 12.1–15.3.* JSNTSup 59. Sheffield: JSOT Press, 1991.

Timmins, Will N. *Romans 7 and Christian Identity: A Study of the "I" in Its Literary Context.* Cambridge: Cambridge University Press, 2017.

———. "Why Paul Wrote Romans: Putting the Pieces Together." *Themelios* 43 (2018): 387–404.

Tomson, P. J. *Paul and the Jewish Law: Halakha in the Letters of the Apostle to the Gentiles.* CRINT 1. Minneapolis: Fortress, 1990.

Toney, C. N. *Paul's Inclusive Ethic: Resolving Community Conflicts and Promoting Mission in Romans 14–15.* WUNT 252. Tübingen: Mohr Siebeck, 2008.

Vickers, Brian. *Jesus' Blood and Righteousness: Paul's Theology of Imputation.* Wheaton: Crossway, 2006.

Wagner, G. *Pauline Baptism and the Pagan Mysteries: The Problem of the Pauline Doctrine of Baptism in Romans VI.1–11, in the Light of Its Religio-Historical "Parallels."* Translated by J. P. Smith. Edinburgh: Oliver & Boyd, 1967.

Wagner, J. R. *Heralds of the Good News: Isaiah and Paul in Concert in the Letter to the Romans.* NovTSup 101. Leiden: Brill, 2002.

Watson, Francis. *Paul and the Hermeneutics of Faith.* New York: T&T Clark, 2004.

———. *Paul, Judaism, and the Gentiles: Beyond the New Perspective.* Rev. ed. Grand Rapids: Eerdmans, 2007.

———. *Paul, Judaism, and the Gentiles: A Sociological Approach.* SNTSMS 56. Cambridge: Cambridge University Press, 1986.

Wedderburn, A. J. M. *The Reasons for Romans.* Edited by J. Riches. SNTW. Edinburgh: T&T Clark, 1988.

Weima, Jeffrey A. D. *Neglected Endings: The Significance of the Pauline Letter Closings.* JSNTSup 101. Sheffield: JSOT Press, 1994.

Westerholm, Stephen. *Israel's Law and the Church's Faith: Paul and His Recent Interpreters.* Grand Rapids: Eerdmans, 1988.

———. *Perspectives Old and New on Paul: The "Lutheran" Paul and His Critics.* Grand Rapids: Eerdmans, 2004.

Wilk, F., and J. R. Wagner, eds. *Between Gospel and Election: Explorations in the Interpretation of Romans 9–11.* WUNT 257. Tübingen: Mohr Siebeck, 2010.

Williams, Jarvis J. *Christ Died for Our Sins: Representation and Substitution in Romans and Their Jewish Martyrological Background.* Eugene, OR: Pickwick, 2015.

———. *Maccabean Martyr Traditions in Paul's Theology of Atonement: Did Martyr Theology Shape Paul's Conception of Jesus's Death?* Eugene, OR: Wipf & Stock, 2010.

Williams, Sam K. *Jesus' Death as Saving Event: The Background and Origin of a Concept.* HDR 2. Missoula, MT: Scholars Press, 1975.

Wilson, W. T. *Love without Pretense: Romans 12.9–21 and Hellenistic-Jewish Wisdom Literature.* WUNT 46. Tübingen: Mohr Siebeck, 1991.

Wright, N. T. *Justification: God's Plan and Paul's Vision.* Downers Grove, IL: InterVarsity, 2009.

———. "The Meaning of περὶ Ἁμαρτίας in Romans 8.3." In *Studia Biblica 1978: Sixth International Congress on Biblical Studies, Oxford, 3–7 April 1978*, vol. 3, *Papers on Paul and Other New Testament Authors*, edited by E. A. Livingstone, 453–59. JSNTSup 3. Sheffield: JSOT Press, 1980.

Yinger, Kent L. *Paul, Judaism, and Judgment according to Deeds.* SNTSMS 105. Cambridge: Cambridge University Press, 1999.

Ziesler, J. A. *The Meaning of Righteousness in Paul: A Linguistic and Theological Enquiry.* SNTSMS 20. Cambridge: Cambridge University Press, 1972.

Zoccali, C. "'So All Israel Will Be Saved': Competing Interpretations of Romans 11.26 in Pauline Scholarship." *JSNT* 30 (2008): 289–318.

CHAPTER THREE

1 Corinthians

Introduction

The city of Corinth, at the base of the Acrocorinth, was strategically located near two harbors. The city was destroyed by Rome in 146 BC and rebuilt as a Roman city in 44 BC. It was bustling with commerce and, like other cities in the Greco-Roman world, was full of gods and temples. Magic, mystery religions, and merchants were present in the city, and the imperial cult devoted to the Roman emperor also played a role. Like any seaport town, there was greed, corruption, and sexual immorality. Obviously, the city was much smaller than present-day cities, but comparisons to cities like San Francisco and New York are apt.

Jews were also present in the city, and Paul started his missionary work in the synagogue when he visited Corinth in AD 50 on his second missionary journey (Acts 18:1–17). Paul enjoyed significant success, and a good number became believers. His converts were from the upper and lower classes, both the rich and the poor (cf. 1 Cor. 1:26). Scholars have disputed whether the congregation was mainly lower or upper class. Most would agree that the congregation was socially diverse but comprised mainly of those who belonged to the lower class. Still, the presence of some from the upper class is attested by the desire for wisdom: that desire, as argued here, was tied to prizing Greek rhetoric (cf. 1 Cor. 2:1–5). In the same vein, it was the rich who could afford lawsuits (6:1–8), ate sumptuously at the Lord's Supper, and ignored the hunger of the poor at the same meal (11:17–34). Perhaps the congregation overlooked the man committing incest because he was wealthy (5:1–13).

The First Letter to the Corinthians was probably written during the spring of AD 54. Reports about the church were sent to Paul from Chloe's people and also from Stephanas, Fortunatus, and Achaicus (1 Cor. 1:11; 16:15–17). The Corinthians also sent Paul a letter, likely asking questions, and in the letter we see Paul's answers to their questions.

We can divide most of the letter into the reports Paul received and the questions he was asked.

Reports About . . .

Divisions	1:10–4:21
Incest	5:1–13
Lawsuits	6:1–11
Sexual immorality	6:12–20
Adornment of women	11:2–16
Behavior at the Lord's Supper	11:17–34
The resurrection	15:1–58

Questions/Now About . . .

Marriage	7:1–24
Virgins	7:25–40
Food offered to idols	8:1–11:1
Spiritual gifts	12:1–14:40
Apollos	16:12

Scholars have also suggested that the letter can be divided into issues of conflict and compromise. Another way of putting it is that the issues in 1 Corinthians are unity and purity.

Conflict Situations

Divisions	1:10–4:21
Lawsuits	6:1–11
Lord's Supper	11:17–34
Spiritual gifts	12:1–14:40
Apollos	16:12–14
Stephanas and his co-workers	16:15–18

Compromise Situations

Incest	5:1–13
Sexual sin	6:12–20
Marriage	7:1–24
Virgins	7:25–40

Food offered to idols	8:1–11:1
Head coverings	11:2–16
The resurrection	15:1–58

A brief outline follows, which can be filled in by looking at the subjects in the tables above.

Outline

Prologue	1:1–9
Divisions in the church	1:10–4:21
Problems in the church	5:1–6:20
Questions in the church	7:1–16:4
Epilogue	16:5–24

Paul tackles these various issues from the standpoint of his gospel, the truth that Jesus is the crucified and risen Lord. The Corinthians need the grace of God for the matters affecting the church, and in this letter Paul reminds them of God's grace in Christ.

Scholars have postulated various backgrounds for the problems affecting the Corinthians. Two popular proposals have postulated gnosticism or over-realized eschatology as the false teaching that informs what was going on in the church. The gnostic hypothesis has almost breathed its last breath, and very few hold such a view today. Overrealized eschatology is more promising, but many of the issues in the letter are not clearly related to overrealized eschatology: a fascination with Greek rhetoric (1 Cor. 1:10–2:16), toleration of incest (5:1–13), lawsuits (6:1:8), sexual sin (6:12–20), food offered to idols (8:1–11:1), and lack of love at the Lord's Supper (11:1–34). It is more convincing to claim that the Corinthians were influenced by paganism, by the mores and convictions of the society they lived in. Thus they were fascinated by Greek rhetoric, fell prey to sexual sin, grasped after wealth and position, desired to compromise on food offered to idols, and rejected a bodily resurrection. Paul tries to pull them back from their errors by recalling for them the gospel.

The Opening (1:1–9)

What is striking in the greeting (1:1–3) is that Paul identifies the Corinthians as "sanctified" and as "saints." The attributions astonish us when we consider that the church was plagued by divisions, compromised by sexual sin, and riven by pride. Still, in Christ they are holy and perfect since their righteousness doesn't reside in themselves. At the same time we have a foreshadowing of

1 Corinthians 6:1–11, where Paul warns the believers as those who are washed, sanctified, and justified that they won't inherit the kingdom if they don't live according to their standing in Christ. The other interesting feature in the opening is the reference to "all those in every place who call on the name of the Lord Jesus" (1:2). Such words aren't found in the greetings in other Pauline letters, and so we are provoked to ask why it is included here. If we scan the entire letter, it is evident that the Corinthians were suffused with pride, and Paul reminds them that they aren't the only Christians in the world, that there are many believers all over the Greco-Roman world, and thus the believers at Corinth should not overestimate themselves.

Given the problems at Corinth, we might be surprised that Paul includes a thanksgiving (1:4–9). After all, he omits the thanksgiving in the Letter to the Galatians, presumably because he wasn't thankful for what was happening in the church. Despite all the messiness in the Corinthian church, despite all the expressions of sin and selfishness, Paul gives thanks for the work of grace in the congregation. We must not fail to see that the accent is on God's grace: "the grace of God" was "given to you" (1:4). The passive verbs also point to God's work: "You *were enriched* in him" (1:5); "The testimony about Christ *was confirmed* among you" (1:6). Even though the Corinthians were misunderstanding and even abusing spiritual gifts, Paul was thankful for the gifts they exercised (1:5, 7). God's grace was working despite and in the midst of the Corinthians' faults, which reminds us of our own lives. Paul also assures the Corinthians that the grace that was theirs would be completed and perfected. They will be fortified and strengthened "to the end" (1:8), not because they were virtuous but because "God is faithful" to continue the fellowship they enjoyed with Jesus Christ (1:9).

Divisions (1:10–4:21)

One of the fundamental problems in the church is confronted in 1:10–4:21: the church was divided over various ministers, some following Paul, others Apollos, and others Peter. The phrase about belonging to Christ (1:12) is quite difficult to interpret and could be read to say that there was a Christ party as well. But being a partisan of Christ is a good thing, and so it seems better to interpret the last phrase as Paul's response. He doesn't align himself with the previously named ministers but with Christ alone. It is imperative to see that the divisions were not caused by *theological* differences among Paul, Apollos, and Peter. The fault for the divisions was placed entirely at the feet of the Corinthians. Actually, Paul, Peter, and Apollos agreed theologically. Paul encouraged Apollos to visit the Corinthians (16:12), and he would hardly do so if he thought Apollos's theology was defective! Similarly, in 15:11 Paul in the clearest terms affirms that he and Peter proclaimed the same gospel. We will see shortly that the reason for divisions has to do with style instead of substance. Paul begins to take on those who follow him, showing them the absurdity of such a course of action. Paul wasn't crucified for them, nor were they baptized into his name. Paul's fundamental purpose wasn't to baptize but to proclaim the gospel, which suggests that baptism must be interpreted in light of the gospel and not vice versa.

What precipitated the divisions? We see a hint in 1:17, and it is confirmed in the discussion that follows (1:18–2:16). The Corinthians became partisans of Paul, Apollos, or Peter based on their rhetorical ability. Rhetoric was a common feature in the Greco-Roman world, as public speeches were regularly made for various reasons. Handbooks on rhetoric were written by the likes of Quintilian and Cicero, where the structure and elements of effective speeches were set forth. Speakers would be evaluated in terms of the effectiveness of their rhetoric, and apparently the Corinthians were aping the culture in which they lived as they assessed Paul, Apollos, and Peter. The standard for appraising ministry became the brilliance and inventiveness and creativity of the speaker, which means that the medium became more important than the message. Entertainment rather than the substance of what was said functioned as the criterion for determining the value of the discourse.

The discussion on wisdom that follows (1:18–2:16) flows out of the preoccupation with the rhetorical ability of the various ministers. The "wisdom" of the various ministers was adjudicated by their speaking ability. Paul's concern is that the Corinthians had inadvertently fallen prey to a secular paradigm. The message he preached was foolish to the world (1:18–25) since it centered on the cross of Jesus Christ. Speech that is entrancing and beautiful brings praise to the human being who crafts it, but the message of the cross is the power of God and brings salvation (cf. Rom. 1:16), and this message was rejected by those heading toward eschatological judgment.

Paul quotes Isaiah 29:14 in 1 Corinthians 1:19 to demonstrate that God has rejected the wisdom of the wise. In chapter 29 of Isaiah the prophet predicts that Jerusalem would be besieged but would escape destruction. The so-called prophets and those who were thought to be wise failed to discern what the Lord was doing. Since their hearts were far from God (Isa. 29:13, cited also in Matt. 15:8–9; Mark 7:6–7), the Lord prevented them from understanding his plans. Paul applies the prophecy of Isaiah to his own day. God determined, just as he did in Isaiah's day, to frustrate the wisdom of those who claim knowledge since their hearts were cold toward God. By acting in this way God ensures that human beings will have no basis for pride in

125

their own wisdom, as if their wisdom is the pathway by which one comes to know the truth about God.

Paul asks the readers to consider the wise, those who teach the law, and those who were renowned for their ability to debate and adjudicate matters in the public square. In terms of the standards "of this age" (1 Cor. 1:20), they were celebrated and praised. The contrast between "this age" and "the age to come" played an important role both in Jesus's teaching (e.g., Matt. 12:32; 13:39, 40, 49; 24:3; 28:20; Mark 10:30; Luke 18:30; 20:35) and in Paul's writings (Rom. 12:2; 1 Cor. 2:6, 7, 8; 10:11; 2 Cor. 4:4; Gal. 1:4; Eph. 2:2; 1 Tim. 6:17; Titus 2:12). God subverts what is prized by human beings, and his subversion of human wisdom reflects his wisdom, for otherwise the path to God, the way to salvation, would be charted by the intellectuals, by the philosophers. God delights in saving those who believe the "foolish" message of the cross, for in doing so all the glory in salvation goes to him.

Human beings look for standards in believing that exalt human beings, and thus Jews demand signs and wonders that display overwhelming power and force, while Greeks were fascinated with wisdom and philosophy that testified to the brilliance and mastery of the world through the human mind (1 Cor. 1:22). By way of contrast, Paul's message focused on Christ as the crucified one: such a message was a scandal to the Jews because the cross represented weakness and a curse (Deut. 21:23). To the Greeks, the notion that the salvation of the world would come through a person dying on a cross was ludicrous. This, of course, was Paul's point: in the cross, God's wisdom and power are displayed and unleashed (Rom. 1:24). The world is rescued through a man forsaken on the cross (1 Cor. 1:23–24), and thus the "foolish" message is wiser than any philosophy, and God's weakness surpasses all human strength.

Paul makes an interesting point here: the message of the cross is preached and proclaimed to all (1:23), but only those who are "called" grasp and understand it (1:24). The use of the word "called" fits with what we have found in Romans. The message is proclaimed to all people everywhere, but those who are called by God embrace and understand that "Christ crucified" is the only hope of salvation. Why do the called, those who hail from both Jewish and gentile backgrounds, understand it? Not because they are skilled at assessing the quality of Greek rhetoric. They understand the message because God's grace has been granted to them.

What troubled Paul was that the Corinthians, by becoming enamored by the rhetorical abilities, particularly of Paul and Apollos, were falling into secularism. They had forgotten the message of the cross and were imitating the world's standards and criteria instead of adhering to the gospel. Paul isn't suggesting that speakers should be as boring as possible in their presentation.

Certainly Apollos was a gifted speaker, and his abilities were evident when he proclaimed the gospel (Acts 18:24–28). Paul's point is that one must not rely on human eloquence and make it the standard for assessing the effectiveness of one's message. The focus must remain on the message of the cross instead of the manner of presentation.

The Corinthians' penchant for Greek rhetoric betrayed a secularizing influence, and so Paul reminds them of who they are (1 Cor. 1:26–31). He picks up on the word "calling" from 1:24 and expands upon it in these verses. The word "calling" (1:26) is unpacked with the threefold refrain "God has chosen" (1:27–28), indicating that the transformation of their lives should be ascribed entirely to God. The Greco-Roman world was an honor-shame culture, and the social contrasts between the haves and the have-nots were striking. Paul reminds the Corinthians that most of them were not from the intellectual class of society, nor did they enjoy political and cultural power, nor were they from the social elite. God chose those who were deemed to be foolish, those who had little or no influence in society; he chose the "nothings," the nobodies in the world instead of the somebodies, the cultured elite. Those who now are socially honored will experience eschatological shame on the day of judgment, and their societal status will be nullified forever. Why has God structured the world in this way? Why has he mainly called to salvation those from the lower rungs of society? To rule out all human boasting.

To put it another way, God's work accounts for people being "in Christ Jesus" (1:30). The Corinthians were drawn toward human wisdom as it was displayed in Greek rhetoric, but they should see, they must see, that Christ Jesus is their wisdom. Paul then defines this wisdom in terms of salvation, saying that Christ is their "righteousness, sanctification, and redemption" (1:30). Righteousness should be defined as standing in the right before God, being acquitted before him. Sanctification here doesn't mean progress in holiness, but has a positional or definitive sense. Believers are holy (cf. 1:2!) before God in Christ; they are perfect before him. And they are redeemed, freed, and liberated from the guilt and tyranny of sin. True wisdom resides in those who are changed by God's grace, in those who are freed from their sins by the cross.

Paul fittingly ends by saying that all boasting should be "in the Lord" (1:31). Boasting in human beings is forbidden (1:29), and boasting in the Lord represents the heart and soul of what it means to belong to Christ. He deserves all the praise since he has done the saving. Paul cites the OT here, and though the wording isn't exact, he clearly draws on Jeremiah 9:23–24 (cf. also 1 Sam. 2:10). It is hard to imagine better verses to make his point: "This is what the Lord says: The wise person should not boast in his wisdom; the strong should not boast in his strength; the wealthy should not boast in his wealth. But the one who boasts should boast in this: that he understands and knows me—that I am the LORD, showing faithful love, justice, and righteousness on the earth, for I delight in these things." The entire citation remarkably matches the themes in 1 Corinthians. Paul restricts himself to the wording about boasting, but Jeremiah admonishes the wise, the strong, and the rich to desist from boasting. These three categories of people fit perfectly with the description of the wise, the influential, and the upper class in 1 Corinthians 1:26–28. Paul brings up the Corinthians' lowly status to remind them that all praise goes to God; they had clearly forgotten this since they were entranced with the so-called wisdom, meaning the rhetorical ability, of those who ministered to them.

Now that Paul has set the scene in 1:18–31, he is prepared to describe his own approach to proclaiming the gospel in 2:1–5, emphasizing that he did not come to show off his brilliant and inventive rhetoric. In doing so, the message of the cross would be muted; Paul's purpose was to preach Jesus Christ as the crucified one. Paul's weakness, fear, and trembling should not be ascribed to natural human nervousness. Rather, Paul feared that he would trust in himself rather than in the cross, because his work would be futile if the Corinthians trusted in wisdom and rhetoric instead of relying on the message of the cross, where the Spirit's power is located.

The repudiation of human wisdom could lead to a misunderstanding, as if the gospel Paul preached was bereft of wisdom, and thus Paul explains in 2:6–16 that true wisdom is revealed in the message of the cross. When Paul says that wisdom is for the "mature," he doesn't refer to an elite group of believers in contrast to those who are at a substandard level. The mature are those who are saved (1:18), are believers (1:21), are called (1:24), and are spiritual (2:13). In other words, it refers to all believers. The wisdom that Paul preaches does not belong to "this age" or to "the rulers of this age" (2:6). The Corinthians were dazzled by secular wisdom, but the world doesn't grasp or see true wisdom. Indeed, "the rulers of this age," which probably refers to political rulers (though perhaps behind the political rulers are demonic powers) were so out of touch with reality that they crucified Jesus Christ, who is the Lord of glory. It is not astonishing that these rulers "are coming to nothing" (2:6), for they were clearly on the wrong side of history if they put to death the one who is Lord of all. Paul's point is that the Corinthian believers were paradoxically throwing in their lot with those who crucified Jesus by lusting for human approval in their partisan divisions. God's wisdom is a "mystery" and "predestined" for believers (2:7), and thus it isn't disclosed to all without exception. The mystery centers on the cross, which wasn't clearly disclosed or understood in the OT era, even though it was predicted by the OT Scriptures.

The Corinthians have perceived "what no eye has seen, no ear has heard, and no human heart has conceived" (2:9). It is difficult to know what OT text Paul cites, but he probably has in mind Isaiah 64:4, "From ancient times no one has heard, no one has listened to, no eye has seen any God except you who acts on behalf of the one who waits for him." The citation belongs to a prayer where Isaiah asks God to renew his saving work in Israel, to save his people as he did in the first exodus. For Paul this prayer was fulfilled in the life, death, and resurrection of Jesus Christ. The great promises of salvation and blessing from the OT were now fulfilled. What no one had seen or heard had become a reality.

What Paul emphasizes in 1 Corinthians 2:10–16 is that God's wisdom, God's salvation, is *revealed* to believers through the Holy Spirit. They didn't *discover* such wisdom; God graciously made it known to them. Only the Spirit of God knows the things of God, just as only the human heart knows its own reflections and thoughts. If we desire to know the thoughts of another, that person must tell us what they are thinking. So too, the only way to know God's thoughts is if he discloses his will and ways through the Spirit. Believers, therefore, know what wisdom is because the Spirit has disclosed such truth to us. Conversely, unbelievers, natural people, those without the Spirit, find the things revealed by the Spirit to be foolish. They don't welcome or receive the truths about God and Jesus Christ because such truths don't accord with their perception of reality. All of this is another way of saying that true wisdom is a miracle of grace where the Spirit opens eyes to spiritual realities.

Paul isn't saying that believers understand all truth about science or history or mathematics, nor is he saying that no one can ever criticize a believer about anything. His point is that believers are able to assess the truth about God and Jesus Christ; they see that true life is in Jesus Christ crucified and risen. Paul appeals to Isaiah 40:13 to support the idea that unbelievers don't know the mind of the Lord, while believers have the mind of Christ. The context of the verse is fascinating, for in Isaiah 40 the Lord pledges to return Israel from exile in Babylon. Israel can scarcely believe this promise since it felt like a drop in the bucket compared to the superpower Babylon. But the point in Isaiah is that God can and will do what no one expects. He is the Lord and governor of history. The thoughts of the Lord are not accessible to human beings. Since believers "have the mind of Christ," they are able to assess all of reality. Still, this shouldn't lead to boasting since all knowledge is revealed by the Spirit.

It might seem as if the divisions of the church have been left behind in 1 Corinthians 1:18–2:16, but the discussion on wisdom provides the platform by which Paul can return more directly to the divisions over the ministers in chapters 3–4. The Corinthians may have been tempted to pat themselves on the back as people of the Spirit, given what Paul taught in 2:6–16. In 3:1–4, however, Paul splashes cold water in their faces, saying that he could not address them as people of the Spirit, but like those who are in the flesh, as babes in Christ. They weren't spiritual giants but spiritual pygmies, needing milk instead of solid food. The evidence of the immaturity was the quarreling and strife centering on different ministers, so that some aligned themselves with Paul and others with Apollos. The Corinthians doubtless thought their choice of Paul or Apollos reflected their wisdom and discernment, but for Paul it was a sign of their immaturity.

These verses have played a significant role in Christian interpretation and have often been used to defend the notion that there are levels or classes of Christians. Some Christians are spiritual, according to this scheme, and some are carnal or fleshly. Such a reading veers away from the Pauline purpose and intention here. He wrote to shock the Corinthians by describing them as if they were fleshly. But we know from 2:6–16 that those who are fleshly are unbelievers, those who don't have the Spirit (1 Cor. 2:14; cf. Rom. 8:9). We have to understand the rhetorical force and import of the text. The Corinthians were living as if they were not Christians; they were in a spiritual no-man's-land, and they could not continue to occupy that space. They could be either people of the flesh or people of the Spirit, and Paul wants them to see that they can't stay where they are.

Instead of quarreling over which minister is best by assessing their rhetorical skills, they should recognize that Paul and Apollos were servants of God, and that God had assigned a distinct role to each of them (3:5–9). Paul, for instance, established the church, and he uses the image of planting a field to express this idea. Apollos strengthened the church by watering the crop that had already sprouted. Both Paul and Apollos had the same function: to do what is assigned to them by the Lord, which means they were called to strengthen the Corinthians. Still, the focus is on God, not Paul and Apollos, for all growth comes from him.

Paul shifts from portraying the Corinthians as a field and turns to describing them as a building (3:10–17), and he probably does so because he conceives of the Corinthians (3:16) as God's temple, the place where the Holy Spirit resides. Since the image changes, Paul shifts from talking about planting to laying a foundation. Planting and laying a foundation are two different ways of talking about establishing the church as the eschatological temple of God. Paul has had the privilege of laying the foundation, and the foundation of the church is Jesus Christ crucified and risen. What is crucial is how one builds on the foundation. In the previous paragraph Paul noted that Apollos watered what was already planted, but he leaves Apollos out of the picture here since he gives an exhortation about the need to build well on the foundation, and he doesn't want to give any impression that Apollos's work was defective. The reference to the stones reminds us again of the temple (cf. Exod. 28:17–20; 1 Kings 5:17; 6:20–21; 1 Chron. 29:2; Isa. 54:11–12; Ezek. 28:13; Rev. 21:18–21). The point of the illustration is clear. One may build on the foundation of the temple with worthless materials like wood, hay, and straw or with precious materials like gold, silver, and costly stones. On the day of the Lord, which is the day of judgment, the fire will destroy wood, hay, and straw, but gold, silver, and costly stones will survive (cf. Mal. 3:1–3; 4:1).

Three different kinds of ministries are contemplated here. First, some build on the foundation with gold, silver, and costly stones. Their teaching is in harmony with the gospel of Christ crucified and risen, and thus they are rewarded for their ministry; their ministry has significant and long-lasting fruit. Second, Paul considers ministers who are saved but their ministry is built with wood, hay, and straw. They didn't build sufficiently on the foundation of the gospel with truth, and so their ministry doesn't have enduring value. Third, the ministry of a person who destroys God's temple is contemplated. God's temple is the church of Jesus Christ, where he resides (2 Cor. 6:16; Eph. 2:19–22; 1 Pet. 2:5), just as the Lord dwelt in the tabernacle/temple under the old covenant (Exod. 25:8; 29:45; Lev. 26:11–12; Ps. 114:2). The minister who destroys God's temple, a minister who corrupts and ruins a local church, will be destroyed by God. In the OT we see instances where God's temple was desecrated (Ps. 79:1; Isa. 64:11; Ezek. 23:29). The destroying of a particular church doesn't contradict Matthew 16:18, for "the gates of Hades will not" conquer the church of Jesus Christ as a whole, but this doesn't mean that particular local churches can't lose their witness. The minister who tears out and destroys the foundation of God's temple, who corrupts a particular church, will be destroyed by God. The concept is similar to the practice of *herem* in the OT, where those who touch what is dedicated to God are destroyed (cf. Exod. 22:19; Lev. 27:28; Deut. 7:26; Josh. 6:17; 7:11, 25). Paul reminds the Corinthians that leaders will be assessed and judged at the very end of history; the quality of their ministries doesn't go unnoticed, and they are responsible to God for their work and will be judged accordingly.

In 1 Corinthians 3:18–23 Paul returns to the fundamental problem with the Corinthians: the divisions that were rending the congregation. The Corinthians went off the rails because they wanted the prestige and status that belonged to the wisdom of this age, but in doing so they had become fools, for those who are wise understand that the wisdom of this world contradicts the message of the cross.

Two OT quotations, from Job 5:13 and Psalm 94:11, demonstrate that Paul isn't merely saying that God considers worldly wisdom to be foolish. It is more than this: God *makes* the world's wisdom to be foolish. Even though Job 5:13 is from the lips of Eliphaz, who is ultimately mistaken in his opinions about Job, his words here represent truth about God. Not everything that Eliphaz says is mistaken. The wisdom and intelligence of the wicked, in accord with God's sovereign purposes, becomes the means by which they go astray. Their great intellect, in which they take so much pride, veers from the truth. The point of the citation is that, according to the designs of the Lord, the intelligence of the wicked proves to be their undoing. The second citation comes from Psalm 94:11, but Paul inserts the word "wise" instead of "mankind," fusing it more closely to the circumstances facing the Corinthians. "The Lord knows that the reasonings of the wise are futile" doesn't mean that the Lord merely recognizes that their thoughts are futile. The word "knows" in Hebrew often means that God ordains, chooses, or determines what will happen. For instance, the Lord has "known only [Israel] out of all the clans of the earth" (Amos 3:2) means that they are the only people "chosen" by the Lord. In the same way, the "LORD knows the way of the righteous" (Ps. 1:6 ESV). God's knowing is active and produces a good outcome for the righteous. But in 1 Corinthians 3:20 the Lord ordains that "the reasonings of the wise" will not prevail.

Boasting in human leaders, then, particularly in their rhetorical ability, is profoundly foolish. In doing so the Corinthians weren't gaining an advantage but were shortchanging themselves. For indeed, already everything was for their sake! In other words, there was no need to be partisans or to take sides, for Paul, Apollos, and Peter were all for their benefit. How shortsighted to latch on to one when they had all, when the ministry of each person was for their benefit. Nor is the statement "Everything is yours" hyperbole, for in words that remind us of Romans 8:35–39, the promise is explained in terms of "the world or life or death or things present or things to come" (1 Cor. 3:22). Certainly this is one of the most radical things Paul ever wrote: to say that the entire world is for the benefit of the Corinthians, and that even death is for their sake, not to mention the present and the future, is nothing short of amazing. Paul isn't denying that death is the last enemy (15:26), and so what is said here should not be misinterpreted. Paul is scarcely saying (and the parallel in Romans 8:35–39 is helpful here) that death and everything faced in the present and future are delightful and pleasant. His point is that God uses everything in one's life, even death, to make believers more like Christ. The enemies of life are pressed into God's service and made to serve his purposes, and in that sense they become friends, even if in and of themselves they are painful. Everything is theirs, for in Christ they possess all things.

The Corinthians are then admonished as to how they are to estimate ministers (1 Cor. 4:1–5). Ministers are "servants of Christ" and "managers" of God's mysteries (4:1), and these mysteries center on Christ crucified and risen (cf. 2:7). They aren't masters but ministers and helpers, and they minister before God; thus their responsibility is to be faithful to their calling. Since God is the final judge, the Corinthians' estimate and judgment of Paul is insignificant in his eyes. Paul isn't rejecting any and all evaluation and criticism. After all, he assesses Peter's actions in Galatians 2:11–14 and judges the man committing incest according to 1 Corinthians 5. In saying that he doesn't even assess himself, Paul isn't decrying self-evaluation (cf. 2 Cor. 13:5). His point is that neither the Corinthians nor Paul have the requisite knowledge to determine how faithful Paul was before God. To put it another way, the Corinthians couldn't decipher whether Paul or Apollos or Peter was a better Christian! Human beings lack enough knowledge to determine how faithful one truly is in ministry. Paul wasn't aware of anything that called into question his faithfulness, but his own subjective thoughts and feelings aren't the final arbiter, for it is the Lord's judgment that is necessary to acquit him. Thus the Corinthians should cease and desist from pronouncing final judgment on people like Paul and Apollos before the Lord returns, for only the Lord can truly see the secret, hidden things, and only the Lord can truly evaluate the motives that lie deep in the hearts of human beings. The reward for each person, the reward for each minister, will come from the Lord on the last day.

Paul informs the Corinthians that the discussion regarding him and Apollos has been for the sake of the Corinthians (1 Cor. 4:6). He and Apollos didn't need to hear the discussion because there was no division between them! Paul wrote what he did so that the Corinthians wouldn't go beyond what was written. What Scripture or Scriptures Paul has in mind here has been long debated. The best solution is probably that Paul has in mind the OT texts already cited in the letter (Isa. 29:14 in 1 Cor. 1:19; Jer. 9:23–24 in 1 Cor. 1:31; Isa. 64:4 in 1 Cor. 2:9; Job 5:13 in 1 Cor. 3:19; Ps. 94:11 in 1 Cor. 3:20). In any case, the Corinthians have gone beyond what is written in their inflated views of themselves. The debates about whether Paul or Apollos are superior are actually a cloak, a pretext for pride and self-promotion. Such self-promotion stands in total contradiction to Jesus's self-giving love on the cross.

Paul asks rhetorical questions in 1 Corinthians 4:7 to puncture the recipients' pride. Apparently they thought they were superior to others, and they had clearly forgotten that everything they had is a gift. There is nothing in their life about which they can boast since everything was given to them. Paul responds sarcastically to their claims to superiority, which some understand as evidence of their overrealized eschatology, but it is more likely that their stance reflects their worldliness and paganism. For instance, the Stoic Epictetus says, "Who, when he lays eyes upon me, does not feel that he is seeing his king and master?" (*Diatr.* 3.22.49). Their estimation of themselves was off-center in that they thought they were full, rich, and reigning.

The truth is that Christians during this present evil age seem to be on the wrong side of history. Like their Lord they suffer and are despised. The apostles, for instance, are on death row. They are a "spectacle," and Paul probably has in mind the picture of a Roman triumphal procession (cf. 2 Cor. 2:14; Col. 2:15). Victorious generals paraded defeated captives through the streets in a victory celebration, and at the end of the procession the enemies of the emperor were put to death. In a series of striking and sarcastic contrasts, we see the upside-down reality of the gospel: the Corinthians were so wise, but the apostles were fools; the Corinthians were so strong, but the apostles were weak; the apostles were shamed, but the Corinthians were honored. But here's the problem: it is those who are honored now who will be despised on the last day. The Corinthians were taking the side of the world, but Paul and the other apostles lined up behind Christ crucified, for it is those who suffer with Christ who will truly rule as kings. Paul goes on to record what it means to be a messenger of Christ. He suffers hunger, thirst, cold, and mistreatment (cf. 2 Cor. 11:23–25).

Paul emphasizes the toil and labor of his work, for he often supported his ministry with manual labor, which was considered to be unsuitable for those who were of the upper class (cf. Acts 18:3; 1 Thess. 2:9; 2 Thess. 3:8). Cicero says, "Unbecoming to a gentleman, too, and vulgar are the means of livelihood of all hired workmen whom we pay for mere manual labour, not for artistic skill; for in their case the very wage they receive is a pledge of their slavery" (Cicero, *Off.* 1.42). All of this is to say that Paul's life was a corollary of Christ's: he blessed others when they criticized him, endured persecution, and responded graciously to slander. He was considered to be like the scum and garbage that people cast away. The point of all this is that the Corinthians had joined forces with the world, and Paul reminds them what it looked like to be a disciple of Christ.

Paul's words in 1 Corinthians 4:8–13 are sarcastic and strong, and we might even say shaming, but in 4:14–21 Paul explains that he didn't write to shame them. We should recall again the powerful role of shame in the ancient world. Still, Paul writes not to shame them but because of his love for them since he was their spiritual father who brought them to faith in Jesus Christ. He calls upon the Corinthians to imitate him in the way of the cross instead of trying to live like the world. It is fascinating that Paul calls upon the Corinthians to imitate him. He could hardly have instructed them to imitate him at the outset of the letter: given their partisanship, they would have surely misunderstood such an admonition. But by this stage in the argument, they would not misconstrue his meaning, as if he were exalting himself over against Peter and Apollos.

Timothy had become Paul's ambassador because he would teach and model his "ways in Christ Jesus" (4:17). Still, the root problem of arrogance had reared its ugly branches in the church, and when Paul came, he would address the problem. Yet he would do so not with secular methods but with the power of God, which is nothing other than the power of the kingdom. It has often been remarked that Paul doesn't often refer to the eschatological kingdom or the kingdom of God in his writings (cf. Rom. 14:17; 1 Cor. 6:9, 10; 15:24, 50; Gal. 5:21; Eph. 5:5; Col. 1:13; 4:11; 1 Thess. 2:12; 2 Thess. 1:5; 2 Tim. 4:1, 18). The kingdom, however, is more important in Paul's theology than most scholars have acknowledged, and here we see significant support for this contention. The kingdom is the place of power: and power (perhaps alluding here to Dan. 2), as Paul argues in 1 Corinthians 1:18–25, centers on the cross. The kingdom and the cross, then, are both the places where God's power is displayed. If the Corinthians don't repent, Paul will come with a rod of discipline, but if they humble themselves, he will come with love and gentleness.

Incest! (5:1–13)

The Corinthians tolerated egregious sexual sin in their midst in that they allowed someone committing incest to stay in the congregation. The man's stepmother is almost certainly in view: Paul doesn't say that he has sexual relations with his mother but with "his father's wife." The prohibition against such an action is found in Leviticus 18:8, "Do not have sexual relations with your father's wife" (NIV; cf. also Deut. 22:30; 27:20). Paul was scandalized because even pagans thought such behavior was despicable, but the Corinthians were tolerating such sin. Cicero records an instance of incest: "Oh! to think of the woman's sin, unbelievable, unheard of in all experience save for this single instance! To think of her wicked passion, unbridled, untamed! To think that she did not quail, if not before the vengeance of Heaven, or the scandal among men" (*Clu.* 6.14–15). Some think the Corinthians were proud of tolerating incest, but this is unlikely since even pagans thought incest was outrageous. The point is that the Corinthians were proud, even though a sin such as incest was present in their congregation. The incongruity between pride and incest is Paul's point.

Grief and mourning should be the experience of the congregation, and such grief should lead to action: they should remove the person from the church.

As an apostle, Paul summons the church to action. Calling on the words of Jesus, the church, when assembled in the name of Jesus (see Matt. 18:15–20), is commanded to deliver the offender to Satan so that his flesh would be destroyed and his spirit saved. Those who aren't part of the church belong to the world, to Satan's sphere, since Satan is "the god of this world" (2 Cor. 4:4; Eph. 2:2). Some think the destruction of the flesh refers to physical death, as in 1 Corinthians 11:29–32. More likely, though, the flesh refers here to the sin-principle in the man, for it is difficult to see how physical death could save him. The death of the offender isn't envisioned because Paul calls upon the church not to eat with him (5:11), which implies his ongoing life. The salvation of the offender isn't guaranteed but hoped for, and such salvation will be evidenced by his repentance.

In 5:6–8 Paul lays down an illustration from the Feast of Passover and Unleavened Bread as an OT foundation for his instructions. He picks up the notion that all leaven must be removed from houses during Passover and the Feast of Unleavened Bread and nothing leavened should be eaten (Exod. 12:14–20; 13:6–7). Here leaven stands for what is evil and corrupting (Gal. 5:9; cf. Matt. 16:6). Paul's main concern isn't with the man committing incest, though of course he was concerned about him. Still, the main problem was with the congregation that tolerated such a sin. The proverb about a little leaven spreading through the entire lump of dough reveals the problem, for if the Corinthians allowed sin to exist in the community unchecked, it opened the door for sin to flourish (1 Cor. 5:6). Once blatant sin is tolerated, the floodgates of sin are likely to be opened, and the church would lose its distinctive witness.

The admonition to clean out the old leaven appropriates the OT instruction to remove all leaven from houses during the Feast of Passover and Unleavened Bread (Exod. 12:19; 13:7). For Paul it means that the evil person must be purged and removed from the congregation. By removing the man committing incest, the Corinthians would be the pure unleavened community they were called to be. The tension between the indicative and the imperative in Paul's theology surfaces here. On the one hand, they must remove the person committing sin to be a new and pure lump, but, on the other hand, they "are" *already* "unleavened" (1 Cor. 5:7) in Christ. The indicative (they are unleavened in Christ) is the foundation and the basis for the imperative (clean out the old leaven). They aren't instructed to clean out the old leaven so that they will for the first time become a new lump. They are already a pure lump of dough in Christ.

The reason or the basis for believers being unleavened is that "Christ our Passover lamb has been sacrificed" (5:7). When Israel was freed from Egypt, the blood on the houses of Israelites ensured that the Lord would pass over them so that their firstborn would be spared a death inflicted by the destroyer

(Exod. 12:13, 22–23, 27). So too, the blood of Christ frees believers from divine judgment and cleanses them from sin so that they are a pure batch before God. The call to remove leaven is grounded in Christ's redeeming work, and thus grace precedes demand. And yet the demand must be heeded for the Corinthians to be truly pure and a new lump before the Lord. The grace of Christ doesn't just echo in an empty room but changes believers.

What it means to live the Christian life is to celebrate the feast, just as Israel in the OT was called upon to celebrate the Festivals of Passover (Exod. 12:14) and Unleavened Bread (23:14–15). The basis for such celebration is that Christ has been sacrificed as the Passover Lamb; his death frees believers from the wrath of God and from the dominion of sin. Believers observe the feast by not allowing what is leavened to infect the community. Truth and sincerity should mark their lives together instead of malice and wickedness.

Before Paul closes the discussion (1 Cor. 5:12–13), he turns to a misunderstanding in a previous letter he wrote. The letter in question has been lost to history, and all we know about it is found here. Apparently Paul previously wrote a letter instructing the Corinthians not to associate with those who were sexually immoral, with those who were living in blatant sin. The Corinthians interpreted this to mean, perhaps intentionally, that believers could not associate with unbelievers. Such advice, of course, was completely impractical, and thus the Corinthians responded by ignoring it entirely. Here Paul corrects any misapprehensions. When he said that believers must not associate with those who were immoral, he meant that they should not associate with those who claimed to be brothers and sisters and yet lived in blatant sin. Paul gives some examples of what he has in mind: sexual immorality, idolatry, verbal abuse, drunkenness, and stealing. He also mentions greed, but surely such greed would have to manifest itself in concrete and identifiable ways. The list of sins stems from Deuteronomy: sexual immorality (22:21–22, 30), idolaters (13:1–5; 17:2–7), slanderers (19:16–19), drunkards (21:18–21), swindlers (24:7).

If a brother or sister gives oneself to such sins and doesn't repent, then believers should not eat with such. Does Paul have the Lord's Supper in mind or ordinary meals? Perhaps both. The fellowship, partnership, and friendship with the one in blatant sin has been disrupted, and the church needs to indicate that such a disruption has occurred; refusing to eat is a specific way to signal the change in circumstances.

As paraphrased below, 1 Corinthians 5:12–13 may be portrayed with a table:

A[1] Believers should not judge outsiders.	A[2] God will judge outsiders on the last day.
B[1] Believers should judge insiders.	B[2] Believers should purge the wicked from the church.

Superficial Bible readers sometimes say that the Bible only instructs people not to judge (cf. Matt. 7:1–5; Rom. 2:1), but the picture is nuanced. Proud and censorious judgment is forbidden, but there is a kind of judgment that is loving (Gal. 6:1). Believers are not to judge unbelievers. This doesn't mean that believers never assess the lifestyles of unbelievers; it does mean that they don't take any actions against unbelievers, for they realize that God will judge them on the last day. On the other hand, believers have a responsibility to judge insiders. They are called upon to judge and assess Christian brothers and sisters, and this is part of what it means to be a holy and loving community. Judgment of blatant sin means that those who sin in grievous ways are purged from the church.

Here the use of the OT is fascinating. The last line is a clear allusion from the OT, where we read repeatedly, "You must purge the evil from you" (Deut. 17:7; 19:19; 21:21; 22:21, 22, 24; 24:7; cf. 13:6, 10). In the OT these verses refer to criminal cases, where Israel is commanded to put to death those committing idolatry (17:7), a stubborn and rebellious son (21:21), those engaged in sexual sin (22:21, 22, 24), and kidnappers (24:7). Paul sees an authoritative word of God from OT texts that require the death penalty for those guilty of outrageous sin. And yet the OT text isn't literally applied to the church of Jesus Christ. The OT text is still the word of God, yet instead of death, the penalty for the offender is excommunication. The people of God in the OT were a theocracy, a kind of church-state, where the penalty for egregious sins was death. The church is not a civil entity, and thus sin in the community isn't punished with death, but those who sin and fail to repent are expelled from the church, with the hope and desire that the person will repent and be saved.

Lawsuits (6:1–11)

Paul was scandalized (the first word in verse 1 in the Greek is "dare") that the Corinthians took their disputes with one another to secular courts for adjudication. The Greco-Roman courts were known for favoritism and corruption. The lawsuits in Corinth weren't criminal cases, such as murder, rape, or theft, but the kind of minor matters that lead to litigation, what we call civil cases. Perhaps the rich were taking the poor and socially disadvantaged to court since the rich would have the resources to go to court. We see the concern about the rich taking advantage of the poor in a passage in Petronius: "Of what avail are laws to be where money rules alone, and the poor suitor can never succeed? The very men who mock at the times by carrying the Cynic's wallet have sometimes been known to betray the truth for a price. So a lawsuit is nothing more than a public auction, and the knightly juror who sits listening to the case approves, with the record of his vote, something bought" (*Satyricon* 14).

What annoys Paul isn't that there are conflicts in the community, for difficulties and disagreements are to be expected. Paul's complaint is that the Corinthians ran to unbelievers, the unrighteous, to adjudicate their controversies. After all, the conflicts facing the Corinthians were ultimately trivial, and they should be able to resolve them. Paul argues from the lesser to the greater. As saints (which they are not acting like currently) they will judge the world, and so they should be able to arbitrate their disputes. The notion that believers will judge the world reaches back to Daniel 7:22 (cf. Matt. 19:28; Rev. 20:4). Judging the world carries the idea of ruling and governing the world and should not be restricted to judicial decisions. The notion that human beings should rule the world for God was his intention from the beginning (Gen. 1:26–28; 2:15). Adam and Eve were to be God's vice-regents in the world, managing and administrating the world for his glory.

Given the future responsibilities of the believers, Paul laments that they are appointing those who are "scorned" in the church to adjudicate the lawsuits (1 Cor. 6:4 NIV). Recognizing the rhetorical force of Paul's words is imperative, for he doesn't write these words to unbelievers, nor for a moment would he countenance scorning or despising unbelievers. He writes hyperbolically to shock the Corinthians so that they would refrain from suing one another.

The rhetorical force of his words shines through in verse 5, for now, in stunning contrast to 4:14, he says that he writes to shame them. In an honor-shame society such words would cut deeply, as would the next thing he says. We know that the Corinthians were impressed with their own wisdom, with their ability to discriminate between truth and error. Paul asks, though, whether there is even one *wise* person in the entire congregation! Apparently not, for they could not resolve the lawsuits among themselves and were going to unbelievers for help.

The Corinthians were suing each other to gain victory, to claim their rights, but instead of a victory, the very fact that they were having legal disputes constituted a "defeat" for them (6:7). They had already lost the case, according to Paul. Paul calls upon them to follow the way of Jesus, to suffer wrong and even be cheated. Paul's admonition here accords with the words of Jesus in Matthew 5:39, where he instructs his disciples to turn the other cheek (cf. also Rom. 12:17; 1 Thess. 5:15). Instead of turning the other cheek, however, the believers engaging in lawsuits were striking other believers, so to speak, on the cheek. They were not suffering wrong but doing wrong; they were not being cheated but were cheating themselves. They were acting like the unrighteous (1 Cor. 6:1), like unbelievers in the way they were treating brothers and sisters.

Nor were the legal disputes waged against other believers a minor matter (6:9–11). Paul reminds the Corinthians that "the unrighteous will not inherit God's kingdom" (6:9; cf. Gal. 5:21; Eph. 5:5). The NIV forges the connection well between 1 Corinthians 6:8 and 9: the Corinthians "do wrong" (*adikeite*, 6:8), and "wrongdoers [*adikoi*] will not inherit the kingdom of God." There is no doubt, then, that Paul warns the Corinthians in the strongest possible terms. If they continue to live unrighteously, they won't enter the kingdom. He anticipates that they might wave off what he says, so he cautions them about being deceived.

We find in 6:9–10 a vice list, and they are quite common in Paul (Rom. 1:29–31; 1 Cor. 5:10–11; 2 Cor. 12:20; Gal. 5:19–21; Eph. 4:31; 5:3–5; Col. 3:5, 8; 1 Tim. 1:9–10; 6:4–5; 2 Tim. 3:2–4; Titus 3:3). Vice lists are used for various purposes, but they consistently denote that one is an unbeliever or that one is headed for eschatological destruction. Here sexual sins and sins that involve coveting and stealing dominate, showing that this vice list is crafted to speak to the Corinthian situation. The "sexually immoral" (*pornoi*) designates those who practice sexual immorality in a wide variety of ways; it is the general term for sexual immorality. Idolatry is, of course, a major concern in the OT, and in Paul it is the fundamental sin (cf. Rom. 1:18–25; see also 1 Cor. 5:10, 11; 10:7, 14; Gal. 5:20; Eph. 5:5; Col. 3:5; see also Exod. 20:3–6). The term "adulterers" describes those unfaithful to marriage vows (cf. Exod. 20:14; Lev. 20:10; Rom. 2:22; 7:3; 13:9). Interestingly, all these issues concern Paul in 1 Corinthians, and so their listing is no accident (cf. 5:1–13; 6:12–20; 10:14–22).

The next two words are translated as "males who have sex with males." The first word *malakoi* refers to "passive homosexual partners" (NET), while the word *arsenokoitai* (cf. 1 Tim. 1:10) comes from Leviticus: "Do not have sexual relations with a man as one does with a woman" (18:22 NIV), and "If a man has sexual relations with a man as one does with a woman, both of them have done what is detestable" (20:13 NIV). Some think Paul criticizes pederasty (which refers to a man having sex with a young boy), but this is unconvincing, for then Paul would have almost certainly used the word "pederasty" (*paiderastēs*). Both the passive and the active partner are condemned, showing that Paul isn't discussing cases of abuse or pederasty.

The vice list continues in 1 Corinthians 5:10. "Thieves" refers to those who steal secretly, whereas "swindlers" refers to those who forcibly steal from others. Tucked into the middle of these is the term "greedy," which identifies the motive that would incite someone to bring a legal case against another. "Drunkards" and those who are verbally abusive are also mentioned, showing that blatant and remarkable sins, from which people don't turn, exclude them from the kingdom. The list matches what Paul says about church discipline in 5:10–11, where he notes flagrant sins, which lead to one's exclusion from the church. If the Corinthians continued to give themselves over to sin, they would not inherit the kingdom.

The incongruity between how the Corinthians were living and what they were in Christ is set forth. Their past life was marked by such sins, and such sins characterized their lives before conversion. But such should no longer be the case since the Corinthians were "washed," "sanctified," and "justified." All three of these realities belong to believers in Christ's name and by the Spirit. The death of Christ, the cross (1:18), the great Passover sacrifice (5:7), has delivered believers from the rule of sin. The Holy Spirit is the means by which the work of Christ is applied to believers. The words "washed," "sanctified," and "justified" all refer to the time of conversion. Paul isn't thinking of three distinct times in the lives of believers. Washing refers to baptism but doesn't refer to baptismal regeneration. Baptism is part of a series of events that occur at conversion; those who are converted also repent, believe, confess Jesus as Lord, and so on. The washing takes place upon conversion, when one repents and believes in Jesus Christ, and thus baptism symbolizes cleansing from sin.

It is common to read the word "sanctified" (*hagiazō*) in terms of progressive growth in holiness in the Christian life. If that is the case, Paul seems to follow the wrong order here, putting sanctification before justification! We need to read the term "sanctification" in context, for here Paul refers to the definitive status of holiness given to believers in Christ at conversion. The term often has this definitive and positional significance in Paul (1 Cor. 1:2; Eph. 5:26; cf. also Heb. 10:10, 29; 13:12). Such a reading also fits with the attribution of the word "saints" to believers (Rom. 1:7; 1 Cor. 1:2; 2 Cor. 1:1; Eph. 1:1; Phil. 1:1; Col. 1:2; 2 Thess. 1:10; Philem. 5). Believers are holy before God by virtue of Christ's atoning work and the Spirit's work in setting them apart.

Believers are also justified. The word "justify" in Paul has a forensic meaning (e.g., Rom. 2:13; 3:4, 20, 24, 26, 28; 4:2, 5; 5:1; 8:33; 1 Cor. 4:4; Gal. 2:16, 17; 3:8, 11, 24; 5:4; 1 Tim. 3:16; Titus 3:7; cf. Exod. 23:7; Deut. 25:1; LXX: 1 Kings 8:32; 2 Chron. 6:23), in that believers are declared righteous before God by virtue of the atoning work of Jesus Christ on the cross. The three terms Paul uses communicate in different ways the new status of believers: they are washed and cleansed of their sins, holy before God and part of the true temple, and declared to be in the right before him. Paul's purpose is to underscore how incompatible taking legal action against other believers is with their new status in Christ. The Corinthians are different now; they are new and clean and holy and righteous before God. Therefore, there is no place in their lives for selfish grasping after their own rights, for cheating brothers and sisters. Such actions contradict the cross.

Sexual Immorality (6:12–20)

Sexual immorality was quite common and accepted in the Greco-Roman world, as it is in ours. We see this attitude in the words of Cicero, "However, if there is anyone who thinks that youth should be forbidden affairs even with courtesans, he is doubtless eminently austere (I cannot deny it), but his view is contrary not only to the license of this age, but also to the custom and concessions of our ancestors. For when was this not a common practice? When was it blamed? When was it forbidden? When, in fact, was it that what is allowed was not allowed?" (*Cael.* 20.48). Paul argues, however, that sexual immorality does not accord with new life in Christ and doesn't fit with the new life purchased by the cross of Christ.

Interpreting these verses is bedeviled by determining if and where Paul cites words of the Corinthians. Most scholars think that the words "Everything is permissible for me," quoted twice in 1 Corinthians 6:12, reflect a Corinthian slogan. The slogan was probably used to excuse doing whatever they wished sexually with their bodies (cf. 10:23). Perhaps the slogan comes from Stoic sources and was picked up by believers. Paul doesn't reject the slogan entirely but qualifies it since it could be applied in misleading and destructive ways (so also in 10:23). Even though "everything is permissible," not everything is "beneficial." Some matters that are permissible are not helpful. At the same time, there is the danger of being "mastered" by what is permitted. Some might find themselves enslaved by something that is not necessarily wrong in and of itself. Freedom, as Paul teaches elsewhere (Gal. 5:13), may be abused and should be used for the sake of love.

Most interpreters believe that Paul quotes the church at Corinth again in 1 Corinthians 6:13, but the details are disputed. If we read the text according to the CSB, the Corinthians were claiming that God gave our stomachs an appetite for food, and we should satisfy that appetite when we so desire. Paul responds that God will put an end to both food and the stomach. The appetites that characterize the present age will not last forever: a new world is coming. In the new creation, the bodies of believers will be raised, just as Jesus was raised from the dead. We know from chapter 15 that this was an issue for the Corinthians since at least some of them rejected the resurrection of the body. The connection between the resurrection of Christ and the resurrection of believers finds its roots in the union between believers and Christ. Believers are united to Jesus Christ by faith, and thus his life is their life, and so they are members of Christ. It is completely off-center and incompatible for them, then, to take their bodies, which belong to Christ, and join themselves with a prostitute.

Nor can one say that union with a prostitute is of no consequence, as if it bears no greater significance than eating a meal. Many in the Greco-Roman world viewed visiting prostitutes as entirely normal. Athenaeus remarked, "We keep mistresses for pleasure, concubines for daily concubinage, but wives in order to produce children legitimately and to have a trustworthy guardian of our domestic property" (*Deipn.* 13.573B). Paul has an entirely different perspective. When one has sexual relations with a prostitute, one is united to her in a profound psychophysical way. Paul cites Genesis 2:24, where the sexual union of a man and a woman means that they have become one flesh. Sexual relations can't be limited to a physical act; there is a profundity and depth to sexual union that involves the whole person. Still, the union with the Lord is even deeper, and thus it is completely incongruous for someone who is united with Christ to form a sexual union with a prostitute.

The central thesis of 1 Corinthians 6:18–20 is now stated: "Flee sexual immorality!" (6:18). The story of Joseph and Potiphar's wife depicts in a narrative what it means to run from sexual sin (Gen. 39:6–18). Sexual sin is uniquely and distinctively harmful. We can think of other sins against one's own body such as drunkenness, drug addiction, or suicide, though in all these instances some other substance or tool must be used. In the case of sexual sin, the sin is committed in and with one's own body.

Earlier we have seen that the church in Corinth is a temple of the Holy Spirit (1 Cor. 3:16). Remarkably the same is said about individual believers and their physical bodies. When we think of how the Lord's presence was limited to the most holy place in the tabernacle/temple, this reality is truly astonishing. Since the Spirit indwells believers, they belong entirely to God. Their lives and their bodies are no longer their own. They have been "bought with a price" (6:20). They are the ransomed, the redeemed, the ones purchased with Christ's blood. They are like slaves who have been manumitted, purchased from slavery, which was quite common in the Greco-Roman world. More profoundly, the language of purchasing echoes Israel's exodus from Egypt, from which they were delivered by God's mercy. Since the Corinthians have been freed through the cross of Jesus Christ, they are to flee sexual sin. Or, to put it positively, their bodies are now to be used for the glory of God. They are to use their bodies to bring him praise and honor in every situation.

Marriage Matters (7:1–24)

Paul turns to a letter from the Corinthians, and the matters introduced with the words "now about" (*peri de*) could refer to subjects Paul desired to discuss, but as mentioned earlier, they probably reflect a letter the Corinthians wrote to Paul in which they posed various questions to Paul. Their first question relates to marriage and sexuality (7:1–24).

The interpretation of verse 1 is difficult and controversial. The NIV and the CSB reflect two different interpretations. The NIV says, "It is good for a man not to have sexual relations with a woman." According to this interpretation, some of the Corinthians supported asceticism and desired to refrain from sexual relations in marriage. Alternatively, the CSB says, "It is good for a man not to use a woman for sex." Deciding between these interpretations isn't easy. Those supporting the reading of the CSB maintain that the Greco-Roman parallels show that the Corinthians were saying, "It is good for a man not to use women" sexually. If one supports the CSB, then the problem in Corinth isn't asceticism, and this reading fits with 6:12–20, where sexual immorality is rampant. In the remainder of chapter 7, according to this interpretation, Paul supports singleness and asceticism more than the Corinthians do.

The translation by the CSB may be correct, but the NIV should be preferred for the following reasons. First, the idiom "touching a woman" clearly refers to sexual relations, but it isn't apparent that it invariably refers to using another person for sexual gratification. The examples from Greco-Roman literature aren't entirely clear. Second, the concern for asceticism seems to come from the Corinthians, not from Paul, as we shall show in the remainder of chapter 7. Most important, the question from the Corinthians about divorcing an unbelieving spouse and Paul's claim that the unbeliever is "sanctified" most likely counters an ascetic desire from the Corinthians to abstain from sex with an unbeliever because of fear of defilement (v. 15). Third, Paul would certainly agree with the notion that women should not be used for recreational sex, but elsewhere when he cites the Corinthians' letter to him, he has some disagreement with the quoted material. We are left wondering why he cites the saying at all since it would reflect his view. Fourth, the situation at Corinth reflects the complexity of life; some Corinthians were guilty of sexual sin (1 Cor. 6:12–20) while others supported asceticism, though asceticism, as we shall see, may lead one into sexual sin.

We follow the NIV, then, and conclude that some of the Corinthians were applying the notion of not touching a woman to marriage and were abstaining from sexual relations in marriage, presumably because they thought it was more pleasing to God to abstain. Paul encourages, on the contrary, regular sexual relations in marriage, for abstaining from sexual relations could open the door to sexual immorality. The mutuality between the husband and the wife in this text is striking. Both the husband and the wife have a conjugal, sexual duty to one another, and they must be sexually available to one another. Indeed, neither the husband nor the wife has authority over the other's body, but their bodies belong to one another. Neither the husband nor the wife can declare that they have decided to live a life free of sex, for now their bodies belong to the other. They are not to deprive themselves of sexual relations unless they both agree, and the period of abstention must be limited to a short time. Otherwise, temptation might arise, and Satan might draw them into sexual sin (cf. 6:12–20!). Some have thought that Paul's view of marriage seems rather crass here, but we need to remember that he responds to a specific situation, and this isn't his only perspective on marriage (cf. Eph. 5:22–33).

The meaning of 1 Corinthians 7:6 has been contested in church history. Augustine understood the concession to be the permission to marry and to engage in sexual relations, but this is a dramatic misreading of the verse. The concession isn't permission to marry and to have sex: the concession is that married couples may abstain from sex for a limited time for the purpose of prayer. In other words, Paul doesn't instruct husbands and wives to abstain from sexual relations, but if the couple wants to do so, he allows it as long as they abstain for a limited period of time. The Augustinian reading, then, gets the verse exactly backward! Now Paul does say (7:7) that he wishes all people were single, but we need to recognize that this statement is made after he forcefully emphasizes the good of marriage and sexual relations. Paul wants to show that he doesn't entirely and completely disagree with the Corinthians. We will see something similar when it comes to Paul's positive statement about tongues after he gives precedence to prophecy over tongues (14:5). Paul acknowledges and agrees that singleness is a good gift, but he immediately recognizes that people have different gifts; some have the gift of marriage, and some have the gift of singleness. It is likely that Paul, who was familiar with the creation narrative in Genesis 2, would acknowledge that most are called to be married.

Paul applies the discussion in 1 Corinthians 7:8–9 to those who are unmarried and who are widows. He agrees with the Corinthians (see 7:1) that remaining single is a good thing. Still, the rule isn't absolute. If they have strong sexual desires, then it is preferable to marry instead of burning with sexual passion. Obviously, some people with strong sexual passions are still unable to find a marriage partner, and in such cases they must exercise self-control. Paul addresses the situation where a person has strong sexual desires but feels an external constraint to refrain from marriage. Those who have such desires should not be plagued with guilt but recognize that they are called to marry if possible. We think of the parallel in 1 Timothy 5:11–14, where younger widows are encouraged to marry and have children.

In 1 Corinthians 7:10–11 the discussion turns to divorce. When Paul says that he isn't giving the command, but the command stems from the Lord, he has the words of the historical Jesus on divorce and remarriage in mind (Matt. 5:31–32; 19:3–12; Mark 10:2–12; Luke 16:18). If one were to summarize Jesus's teaching, divorce is not an option. Wives must not leave their husbands, and husbands must not separate from their wives. Incidentally, the word translated "separate" in some versions (e.g., NIV, ESV, CSB, NRSV) should not be read in terms of Western culture, where there is often a period of separation before divorce. The words "separate" and "leave" here are synonyms; in the Greco-Roman world, marriages ended when spouses left their marriage partners. Paul, then, is not drawing a distinction between the words "separate" (1 Cor. 7:10) and "leave" (v. 15), since they both designate divorce. Someone who divorces should not remarry but be reconciled to the spouse. Are there any exceptions to what Paul says here? Actually, Paul doesn't answer that question, and our answer will depend upon how we read other texts. Jesus declares that divorce is wrong except in the case of sexual infidelity (Matt. 5:32; 19:9), and Paul allows such if one is abandoned or deserted (1 Cor. 7:12–16).

In 7:12–16 a new situation is envisioned where believers are married to unbelievers. Perhaps one spouse became a believer, but the other refused the faith, and thus a mixed marriage resulted. When Paul says he gives his own opinion, that he is speaking rather than the Lord, he is not suggesting that his words aren't authoritative. Paul, as an apostle of Jesus Christ, thinks his instructions are authoritative. His point is that the historical Jesus never addressed the matter of a believer married to an unbeliever, and thus he speaks to this particular situation as an apostle of Christ. Paul addresses both the believing husband and the believing wife, instructing them not to divorce the unbelieving spouse. The mutuality of Paul's instructions is again striking. Paul's counsel stands out particularly with reference to the wife. In the ancient world the wife was expected to follow the religion of her husband. Plutarch said: "A wife ought not to make friends of her own, but to enjoy her husband's friends in common with him. The gods are the first and most important friends. Wherefore it is becoming for a wife to worship and to know only the gods that her husband believes in, and to shut the front door tight upon all queer rituals and outlandish superstitions" (*Conj. praec.* 19). Clearly, Paul dissents from Plutarch's view, for the wife's first commitment is to Christ, not her husband.

Why did this matter of mixed marriages come up? A hint appears in 1 Corinthians 7:14–15. The believers probably began to think that sexual relations with an unbeliever were unclean. Perhaps they even appealed to OT precedents, for Ezra summoned Jewish believers to "separate yourselves from the peoples around you and from your foreign wives" (Ezra 10:11 NIV; cf. Neh. 13:3). According to Jewish tradition, Joseph refused even to kiss Aseneth while she was an idolater (Jos. Asen. 8.5–7). In the OT, that which is unclean usually defiles that which is clean (Hag. 2:11–13), and we can imagine believers thinking that sexual relations with an unbeliever, even if one is married, were particularly defiling, so that a divorce was warranted. Paul, however, responds in a surprising way. The unbelieving spouse is sanctified or made holy through their marital union with the believing spouse. An interesting parallel is where Jesus touches the leper and makes him clean, heals him (Matt. 8:1–4). Touching a leper should make Jesus unclean, according to Leviticus 13–14, but in Jesus's case his cleanness purifies the one who is unclean. Something similar happens in the marriage of a believer to an unbeliever. Now this doesn't mean that the unbelieving spouse is saved, since 1 Corinthians 7:16 makes it clear that salvation of the unbelieving spouse isn't guaranteed. It is harder to know what Paul means by saying the unbelieving spouse is sanctified: perhaps they are holy in that the possibility of salvation is increased through union with a believer (cf. 1 Pet. 3:1–5). We see as well that the children of a mixed marriage are holy in the same way that an unbelieving spouse is sanctified.

Unbelieving spouses, however, may choose to leave a marriage and divorce their believing partner. In such instances, the believer is no longer tied to the marriage and should live in peace, not fretting about a marriage that has been severed. Is remarriage in such instances permitted? Commentators disagree since Paul doesn't speak to the issue directly. I suggest that remarriage is permitted for the following reasons. First, according to Jewish and Greco-Roman tradition, divorce implies freedom to remarry, and Paul would need to make it quite clear if he dissented from the tradition. Second, the most likely reading of Matthew 5:32 and 19:9 is that Jesus permitted remarriage in the case of sexual infidelity. Third, even though some Corinthians were interested in asceticism, we can scarcely say that all of them were ascetics, and in any case Paul, as a wise servant of Christ, knew human nature. He would recognize that some would desire to remarry. Fourth, the word "bound" (*douloō*) used here (in 1 Cor. 7:15) and "bound" (*deō*, 7:39) belong to the same semantic range and thus are roughly synonymous. Hence, Paul thinks married women are *bound* (*dedetai*) while their husband lives (Rom. 7:2; 1 Cor. 7:39), but they are "free" (CSB, ESV: Rom. 7:3; 1 Cor. 7:39; *eleuthera*) when their husband dies. So too here, a person is bound to the marriage until the unbelieving spouse chooses to initiate a divorce.

In 1 Corinthians 7:16 Paul speaks of the salvation of the unbelieving spouse. The main question that has been posed here is whether Paul speaks optimistically or pessimistically. A case can be made for both, but the optimistic view is more likely. Paul, of course, doesn't guarantee the conversion of unbelieving spouses. Still, the fundamental purpose of the paragraph is to encourage believers to remain in their marriages with unbelievers. An optimistic reading fits that purpose well. One reason a believer should continue in a marriage to an unbeliever is that the marriage may become a means by which the unbeliever is saved.

Stay Where You Are (7:17–24)

The overriding principle for 1 Corinthians 7, with respect to both marriage and virgins, is found here. Believers should stay in the situation in which they find themselves. Three times in the paragraph the admonition that believers should not change their circumstances is articulated (vv. 17, 20, 24). Structurally, these words introduce and close the paragraph, and they are also tucked into the middle of the paragraph. Hence it would be difficult to miss the main thesis. The Corinthians must not think they would be more pleasing to God if they could change their circumstances and situation. Nor is this command limited to the Corinthians but represents what Paul teaches "in all the churches" (7:17). Since believers are to remain in the circumstances in which they were called, they can rest in God's sovereignty since he has appointed the circumstances of their lives.

The first example given of changing one's situation relates to circumcision. When called to salvation, some were circumcised, but others were uncircumcised. The person who was uncircumcised should not remove the marks of circumcision. In the ancient world circumcision could be reversed, and an athlete who performed in the nude in the Greco-Roman world might want to remove the cultural reproach of being Jewish and draw the foreskin back over so that it wasn't evident that he was previously circumcised. One author notes that some Jews, departing from their ancestral customs, "built a gymnasium, . . . removed the marks of circumcision, and abandoned the holy covenant" (1 Macc. 1:14–15 NRSV; cf. Josephus, *Ant.* 12.241). Perhaps some would also be motivated to remove the marks of circumcision, concluding that they would be more pleasing to God since they had learned from Paul that circumcision doesn't avail for salvation (Rom. 4:9–12; Gal. 2:3–5; 5:2–4; 6:12–13; Phil. 3:2–3; Col. 2:12).

Paul wasn't opposed to circumcision in and of itself. He circumcised Timothy (Acts 16:3) for cultural reasons since it was clear after the apostolic council of Acts 15 that circumcision wasn't required for salvation. On the other hand, those who weren't circumcised should not think that circumcision was more pleasing to God, even though it was the sign of the covenant in the OT (Gen. 17:9–14). Paul made it clear that circumcision and obeying the law were not required for salvation.

Paul's overarching stance on circumcision emerges in 1 Corinthians 7:19. From Galatians, one might think that Paul was opposed to circumcision, but actually whether one was circumcised or uncircumcised was irrelevant to him. He opposed it when one said circumcision was necessary for salvation, but he also resisted the idea that uncircumcision was more pleasing to God. Both circumcision and uncircumcision were unimportant; what matters is keeping God's commands. It has often been noted that this is an astonishing statement from Paul, who grew up as a Jew nurtured in the OT because circumcision was one of God's commandments (Gen. 17:9–14; Lev. 12:3). Clearly, Paul operates now with a reframed understanding of God's commands. Believers now observe the law of Christ (1 Cor. 9:21; Gal. 6:2) since they are no longer under the Mosaic covenant. Paul's declaration here matches Galatians 5:6 and 6:15, where he says, respectively, that circumcision and uncircumcision don't matter, but what is important is faith that expresses itself through love, and what really matters is the new creation. Those who keep God's commands do so because they are a new creation in Christ. Another way of putting it is that they keep God's commands as an expression of their faith.

The second situation considered is slavery, and here we see that the Pauline rule about not changing one's situation isn't inflexible. Slavery was exceedingly common in the Greco-Roman world. One-third of those in Corinth were probably slaves. People could be born as slaves, sell themselves into slavery to pay debts, be sold into slavery, or become slaves by being captured in war. Many slaves lived terrible lives, particularly those who served in the mines. Other slaves served as doctors, teachers, managers, musicians, artisans, barbers, cooks, shopkeepers, and could even own other slaves. In some instances slaves were better educated than their masters. Those familiar with slavery from the history of the United States must beware of imposing our historical experience upon NT times, since slavery in the Greco-Roman world was not based on race and American slave owners discouraged the education of slaves. Still, slaves in the Greco-Roman world were under the control of their masters and had no independent existence. Ancient slavery was cruel and often oppressive, but it does not follow that all masters were cruel. Slaves could purchase their freedom in the Greco-Roman world with the help of their masters, a procedure called manumission.

Paul addresses those called to salvation when serving as slaves, and by addressing slaves directly, he values their personhood and dignity. They must not worry about being slaves, as if being a slave would make them less useful and effective as Christians. One's status in life isn't a matter of great concern, according to Paul. What Paul says next (1 Cor. 7:21), however, is a matter of significant debate. Is Paul instructing slaves to remain as slaves or to get their freedom? The NIV interprets Paul as counseling slaves to get their freedom: "If you can gain your freedom, do so." The NRSV represents another interpretation, that slaves should remain as slaves, even if freedom becomes possible: "Even if you can gain your freedom, make use of your present condition now more than ever." Some support the idea that slaves should renounce freedom and continue as slaves since the theme of the paragraph is that one should remain in one's life situation, and thus the simplest view, in their eyes, is that Paul tells slaves to remain slaves.

It is much more likely, however, that Paul advises slaves to get their freedom for the following reasons. First, the extra words (i.e., the qualifying comment) are superfluous unless Paul offers an exception to this general rule. Second, the rule of remaining in one's station is not inflexible, and that is apparent from the entire chapter since Paul repeatedly assures the Corinthians that it isn't a sin to get married. The principle that Paul enunciates was never intended to be an inflexible rule, applying in every circumstance. Third, the admonition "Do not become slaves of human beings" (7:23) supports the idea that remaining as a slave isn't ideal. Fourth, this reading fits with the OT, where enslaving a fellow Hebrew is frowned upon (e.g., Exod. 21:2–11; Neh. 5:5).

Paul returns to his fundamental point. A slave is a freedperson in the Lord, and a free person is Christ's slave. One's social standing and position should not be a matter of concern. Each one should live out their life before God regardless of their station in life. As in 1 Corinthians 6:20, the readers are said to be "bought by a price" (7:23). The fundamental reality in their life is that they belong to Jesus Christ, that they have been redeemed and ransomed by his blood from the sin that dominated their lives.

Singleness and Virgins (7:25-40)

Paul turns to the matter of being engaged to virgins in 7:25–40, and the principle of 7:17–24 continues to inform the discussion. One should not think that changing status is important to God. Each person should bloom where they are planted. When Paul says he doesn't have a "command from the Lord" (7:25), he is not saying that his advice isn't authoritative, but once again he distinguishes his counsel from the words of the historical Jesus. Still, his admonitions, as an apostle of Jesus Christ, are authoritative (7:40; 14:37). Paul prefers singleness on account of "the present distress" (7:26 ESV). It isn't easy to decipher what the present distress is. Many commentators think it was a famine that affected Corinth at this time, and such a reading is certainly possible. More likely Paul has in mind eschatology (7:29–31). Luke 21:23 also refers to the end-time distress, and the afflictions and woes of the last time are noted elsewhere (e.g., Jer. 30:7; Dan. 8:19; 12:1; Luke 21:23). Paul believed that Christians were living in the times of fulfillment, that the end had dawned in Jesus Christ (Gal. 4:4–5; 1 Cor. 10:11).

Those who are engaged, following the principle of 1 Corinthians 7:17–24, should not seek to sever their engagement, and those who aren't pledged to a woman for marriage shouldn't seek marriage. We should recognize again that Paul particularly responds to those who were inclined toward asceticism. He doesn't want to be misunderstood, and so he affirms that those who marry haven't sinned. Paul speaks negatively ("You have not sinned," v. 28) instead of positively (It's good to marry) because he responds to ascetics. He simply wants people to have a realistic estimate about marriage and its struggles and temptations.

What drives Paul especially is eschatology (7:29–31). The new age has come in Jesus Christ, and all of history should be assessed in terms of the nearness of the end. The next great act in redemptive history is Christ's return. The coming of Christ relativizes all of life. Paul's remarks about marriage and relationships could be misunderstood in dramatic ways, as if he were a world-denying person instead of affirming the world. When he says that husbands should live as if they didn't have wives, he is scarcely denying what he wrote about loving one's wife and sacrificing for her in Ephesians 5:25–33. His purpose is to remind the readers that marriage doesn't last forever: marriage is temporary, and thus one should not sink all of one's hopes and desires into marriage. The same applies to joy and sorrow. Paul is scarcely saying that one should not weep at a funeral or rejoice with those who are blessed. Indeed, elsewhere he commands believers, "Rejoice with those who rejoice; weep with those who weep" (Rom. 12:15). Joy and sorrow must be swept up into eschatology. In other words, as wonderful as joys are in this world, and as painful as sorrows are, they are both temporary. No joy or sorrow will end up defining our lives because they are part of this present world order that is passing away. Buying and obtaining things isn't evil, but every single thing we own, every possession, is a wisp of air, a thread of smoke that doesn't last. The world as we know it "is passing away" (1 Cor. 7:31), and a new world is coming; believers should set their sights on the new creation.

Practical reasons for remaining single are given in 7:32–35. Unmarried persons are enabled to concentrate solely on pleasing the Lord, but those who are married need to think about how to please their spouses. No alien restrictions are placed on believers since these instructions are given for their own good and service to the Lord. Advice regarding virgins follows in 7:36–38, where the NASB translates the text so that it refers to a man and his virgin daughter, which is supported by the following reasons: (1) The words "his virgin" (NASB) may suggest the father since the daughter belongs to his family. (2) The plural verb "they can get married" (*gameitōsan*) may point to a father granting permission for his (future) son-in-law and daughter to get married. (3) The words "keep his own virgin" (*tērein tēn heautou parthenon*, 7:37 NASB) could refer to a father who has determined to keep a daughter in his family. (4) The participle *gamizōn* (7:38) may designate a father *giving* his daughter in marriage (so NASB).

It is more likely that the relationship is between a fiancé and one to whom he is engaged, for the following reasons. First, in the previous verses in this section (vv. 25–35), Paul addresses men facing the decision about getting married, and it isn't apparent that the subject has changed in these verses. Second, the remark that the virgin who marries hasn't sinned makes better sense if a virgin and her fiancé are intended. In other words, she has a voice in the decision about marriage, and her father isn't deciding her fate. Third, the words "his virgin" may refer to a man and the virgin to whom he is engaged; the wording is perfectly natural. Fourth, the words "keep his own virgin" don't mean that she remains in the man's possession permanently. The words convey that the woman will remain a virgin and will not get married. Fifth, the verb *gamizō* doesn't always mean "given in marriage" but may also mean "marry" (so NIV, BDAG, BDF §101). Sixth, the words "they can get married" (*gameitōsan*) may reflect Paul's comment about the fiancé and his virgin.

Paul closes the chapter with some final words (7:39–40). A wife is bound to her marriage while her husband is alive, but if the husband dies, remarriage is permitted (cf. Rom. 7:1–3) as long as he marries a believer. Yet Paul, as an authoritative apostle, thinks that singleness is preferable.

Food Offered to Idols (8:1–11:1)

The Situation (8:1–13)

In 8:1–11:1 the issue of food offered to idols is introduced, and Paul probably responds to Corinthian questions. The word for "food sacrificed to idols" (*eidōlothytōn*, 4 Macc. 5:2; Sib. Or. 2.96; Acts 15:29; 21:25; 1 Cor. 8:4, 7, 10; 10:19; Rev. 2:14, 20) reflects a Jewish view of the food offered in temples, for this term is never used in pagan sources. Pagans used the word "food sacrificed to a divinity" (*hierothytos*). The term used here adopts the negative perspective about such food that was common in Jewish circles (see also Exod. 23:13, 24, 32–33; 34:12–16; Deut. 7:1–6, 23–26; 12:2–3; m. Demai 6:10; m. Avod. Zar. 5:3–7; Acts 10:28; 11:3).

In a city like Corinth, there were many temples and many gods, and it was common to attend the temple where food was offered to idols. Food was offered to the idol via a sacrifice, but some of the food was saved for those celebrating in the temple, and any leftover food would be sold in the marketplace. An invitation to a temple found in the Oxyrhynchus Papyri reads: "Apollonius requests you to dine at the table of the Lord Serapis on the occasion of the coming of age of his brothers in the temple of Thoeris" (P.Oxy. 1484).

Associations were popular in the Greco-Roman world, and people who shared the same trade would join together for a meal and sacrifices. Some feasts were given in honor of a god, but one could also attend a temple for private events like birthdays, funerals, the birth of a child, and so forth. In the ancient world the social and the religious weren't neatly separated from one another. The Western conception of separating religion from the social world wasn't present in the Greco-Roman world. For Christians to refuse to eat in such settings would strike unbelievers as antisocial and could lead others to think that Christians weren't good citizens and as a consequence they might be treated as social outcasts. Christians debated whether it was permissible to eat food sacrificed to idols. It will be argued here that Paul bans the eating of such food in temples, and if believers were informed that the food was offered to idols, they must refrain from eating it. Believers weren't required, however, to search out and discover if food was offered to idols. If they were unaware of the origin of food, they were free to eat it. Paul's rule was much more lax than the rules followed in the Judaism of his day, for Jews would often refrain from eating gentile food out of fear that it was contaminated, even if they weren't sure about whether the food was offered to idols.

In our discussion of Romans 14:1–15:13 we noted that the matter differs from what is discussed here in 1 Corinthians 8–10. Paul particularly addresses a group I will call the "knowers." He never calls them the strong in 1 Corinthians. Paul warns about the dangers of knowledge in 8:1–3. He picks up on one of his favorite words in the letter: knowledge without love "puffs up" (4:6, 18, 19; 5:2; 13:4, my translation), and thus we see that the knowers were using their knowledge as a weapon, as a means of self-exaltation instead of as a means of edification. Paul obviously does not propound philosophical relativism in 8:2, as if people don't know anything at all about life and truth! He is simply saying that those who truly have knowledge adorn that knowledge with humility and love. The issue finally isn't what believers know, but whether they love God, for that is the fundamental issue in life (8:3). In other words, what matters isn't what believers know but whom God knows, and those whom he knows (cf. Jer. 1:5; Amos 3:2; Rom. 8:29; Gal. 4:9), those whom he has chosen, are those who love him. There is no basis for pride in knowledge when we realize that we haven't come to the knowledge of God based on our virtue.

Paul reflects on the Shema in 1 Corinthians 8:4–6, the great statement in the OT that the Lord is one (Deut. 6:4). Those who know this truth realize that idols are nothing, that they are fantasies and illusions. Paul probably draws on many OT texts that ridicule idols as nonentities since they are completely ineffectual and helpless (e.g., Isa. 41:28; 44:5–28; Jer. 14:22; 16:19; Hab. 2:18; Ps. 115:4–8). In the pagan world, of course, there were many gods and lords, but believers acknowledge only the one true God, the Father, who is the creator of all. The nothingness of idols is evident because they did not and cannot create anything. At the same time, as has often been pointed out, Paul modifies the Shema without compromising monotheism. The being of God has more complexity than one might think, for the oneness of God includes Jesus Christ as Lord. Jesus Christ is the agent of creation, and thus he is also the creator (John 1:3; Col. 1:16; Heb. 1:2).

The full implications of there being one God and of the truth that Jesus Christ shares in God's identity did not dawn fully on the weak (1 Cor. 8:7). Certainly they recognized that God is the creator and Jesus Christ is Lord (12:3), for otherwise one could not be a believer. They didn't understand, however, how to integrate their confession with their experience of idols. They still felt and believed that idols were real. On the other hand, the knowers should not become proud (8:8). Eating food is of no advantage before God; the weak were not at any disadvantage just because they didn't eat food, perhaps even abstaining from food in the marketplace because of the fear that it was offered to idols.

According to many interpreters, Paul says that eating food offered to idols is a "right" (8:9), but such a reading is unpersuasive for a number of reasons. Actually, Paul uses the word "right" ironically in verse 9, and thus he has in mind the so-called right of the knowers. We need to remember that the situations in Romans 14–15 and 1 Corinthians 8–10 are distinct. Romans addresses whether believers may eat unclean food prohibited in Leviticus 11 and Deuteronomy 14, but 1 Corinthians deals with whether they may eat food offered to idols. Thus the permission to eat unclean food in Romans can't be transferred to 1 Corinthians. There is also universal condemnation of eating food offered to idols in the NT (see Acts 15:20, 29; 21:25; Rev. 2:14, 20) and in early church history. For instance, Didache 6.3 says, "Keep strictly away from meat sacrificed to idols, for it involves the worship of dead gods."[1]

---

1. Translation from Michael W. Holmes, ed. and trans., *The Apostolic Fathers: Greek Texts and English Translations*, 3rd ed. (Grand Rapids: Baker Academic, 2007), 355.

Paul doesn't immediately state his objection to eating food offered to idols because the Corinthians were already aware of Paul's stance on the matter, which he regularly taught in synagogues and other places where he preached. The knowers realized that they were expressing their "freedom" in a way that contradicted Paul's instructions, and they probably ate idol food because they would suffer social discrimination if they didn't eat. They likely justified their right to eat on the grounds that friends and business partners invited them to eat in the temple of idols. Paul approaches the issue pastorally in that he doesn't immediately condemn what the knowers were doing. He sets up a theological and pastoral context before he gives his judgment on the matter in 1 Corinthians 10.

The "right" to eat in 8:9 is followed up immediately by a reference to eating in idols' temples, but we know from 10:19–22 that eating in such temples is forbidden, and thus we have good exegetical reasons for thinking that the "right" here is ironic. Paul's right to be remunerated financially isn't parallel in every respect to the so-called right of the knowers to eat idol food. Why does Paul establish a parallel if the two rights aren't equivalent? He does so because he wants the knowers to think of others before they consider their own so-called rights. Paul wants them to be others-centered and to have a pastoral attitude toward other believers. The knowers need to become like Christ (8:11) and Paul (9:15–22), to live sacrificially for the sake of others, and thus the knowers are summoned to live in such a way that they love others and give up their so-called rights for the sake of others.

The issue at stake here for the weak is of the utmost importance, for Paul mentions the weak being "ruined" by the strong's *knowledge!* (8:11). Clearly, their "knowledge" is being wielded in destructive ways. In Pauline use, the word "ruined" refers to the final judgment, to final destruction (Rom. 2:12; 1 Cor. 1:18, 19; 10:9, 10; 15:18; 2 Cor. 2:15; 4:3; 2 Thess. 2:10). Paul is deadly serious here because eating in the temples of idols constitutes idolatry, and no one who makes a practice of committing idolatry will "inherit God's kingdom" (1 Cor. 6:9; Gal. 5:20–21; Eph. 5:5).

How can Paul contemplate the eternal ruin of those "for whom Christ died" (cf. Rom. 14:15)? Some understandably maintain that those who truly belong to Christ can apostatize, but a better reading of the entire fabric of the Scriptures is available. Paul teaches that those who are called to salvation will be preserved to the end in 1 Corinthians 1:8–9 (cf. Rom. 8:28–39; Phil. 1:6; Eph. 1:13–14). We need to recognize that we have a pastoral warning here; Paul asks if the knowers are willing to act in a way that leads to the damnation of brothers and sisters. From elsewhere in Paul and elsewhere in the NT, we know that if someone actually falls away and apostatizes, they show that they weren't genuine in the first place (1 Cor. 11:19; 2 Tim. 2:18–19; 1 John 2:19). The knowers are to imitate Christ and to live for the sake of brothers and sisters who are weak. Indeed, if they sin against the weak, they sin against Christ, and thus they should be willing to refrain from meat or any other food forever if it helps brothers or sisters not to fall to perdition.

Paul's Example (9:1–27)

Paul uses his life as an illustration of what it looks like to yield one's rights, to live for the sake of others, to live so others will be saved. The specific example is his right to be paid for his apostolic ministry, a right that he relinquished for the sake of the gospel. In 1 Corinthians 9:1–14, though, Paul establishes that he had a right to financial support. He begins by noting his freedom, which forges a connection with the knowers who think they are free to eat idol food. Paul is clearly an apostle, and his apostleship is established because the Lord Jesus appeared to him on the road to Damascus and commissioned him as an apostle (Acts 9:1–19; 1 Cor. 15:8). Furthermore, his apostolic credentials are verified because Paul established the Corinthian church. If they denied Paul's apostleship, they would deny their own conversion! Paul's apostleship was sealed and authenticated by the Corinthians themselves.

Paul doesn't write this because his apostleship was questioned or under an attack. In 1 Corinthians 9:3–14 he gives a battery of reasons indicating that he deserved financial support. When Paul says he has the right "to eat and drink" (9:4), he means he has the right to be supported in his ministry with the necessary food and drink. He notes that the Lord's brothers and Peter were supported financially in their travels, along with their wives (9:5), and thus he and Barnabas also have the right to be supported so that they could refrain from manual work (9:6).

In verse 7 examples are given from ordinary life to indicate that Paul deserves financial support. Soldiers are paid for their labor, those who plant vineyards "eat its fruit," and shepherds consume milk from their flock. Here we see how Paul argued as a rabbi, and he turns to the OT law to make his case in 9:8–10. The proof he uses is somewhat surprising because he appeals to Deuteronomy 25:4, which says that an ox treading out grain should be allowed to eat while working. Some think Paul uses the OT allegorically since he says the text was meant for human beings instead of oxen. Other explanations are given, but it is quite unlikely that Paul intends to deny the literal sense of the text here (cf. Prov. 12:10). Paul uses a typical rabbinical argument from lesser to greater. If oxen should be fed when they are working and treading out grain, how much more is this true of those who proclaim the gospel! Paul's illustration fits with the notion that those who plow and thresh do so to partake of the crop. And those who sow "spiritual things" should "reap material benefits" (1 Cor. 9:11). Paul anticipates what is to come when he says that he doesn't want to avail himself of the right to be paid. Still, he gives two more examples that support the right to payment. Those who work in the temple share in the offerings of the temple. For instance, a portion of the offerings brought by Israel was to be eaten by Aaron and his sons (Num. 18:8, 18; cf. also Deut. 18:1–4). The final and climactic example comes from Jesus himself, for he instructed that those who proclaim the gospel should be supported by the gospel they proclaim (Matt. 10:8–10; Luke 10:7).

Paul has given a litany of reasons why he deserves pay, but in 1 Corinthians 9:15–18 he turns the corner, insisting in the strongest terms that he will not take pay. In fact, he would rather die than be paid! Paul can't boast in preaching the gospel because in a sense he had no choice in the matter. Certainly, the language here is hyperbolic, but Paul's point is that he was called supernaturally on the road to Damascus (Acts 9:1–19; Gal. 1:15–16) and was pressed into service to proclaim the gospel. The compulsion to preach the gospel was so overwhelming that he could not resist it. We think of Jeremiah whose sufferings moved him to the point where he didn't want to prophesy any longer, but God's word was like a burning fire in his heart, and he had to speak (Jer. 20:9). Paul's call to preach was like this. Paul's "reward" (1 Cor. 9:17), Paul's "boast" (9:15–16), then, was to proclaim the gospel without charging. In this way he didn't avail himself of all his rights in the gospel and functioned as an example to the Corinthians.

Paul further explains his rationale for not receiving pay in 9:19–23, and here we see that what drove him was a missionary impulse: he acted the way he did for the sake of the salvation of others. Paul's love was such that he made himself a slave to others to win them to Christ (cf. Gal. 5:14). Paul gives several examples of the principle by which he lived. For instance, when he was with the Jews, he lived like a Jew. How remarkable that Paul, who was an ethnic Jew, speaks of becoming like a Jew! His identity had changed; now he was a Christian, even though he was ethnically Jewish. Still, when he was with the Jews, he lived like the Jews. He put himself "under the law," even though he wasn't under the law as a believer (1 Cor. 9:20; cf. Rom. 6:14–15; Gal. 3:23; 4:4–5, 21; 5:18). He was willing to circumcise Timothy for evangelistic purposes (Acts 16:1–5), to take a Nazirite vow (18:18), and to pay for expenses in the temple (21:20–25). Paul adapted the way he lived, even though the Mosaic covenant and law had passed away, so that he could identify with those under the law to win them to faith in Jesus Christ.

Paul also lived flexibly when he was with those who were without the law (1 Cor. 9:21). In such cases, Paul himself didn't abide by the law. He didn't remind gentiles of his Jewish heritage and customs but adapted to their cultural setting to win them to Christ. Still, Paul cautions, he was not entirely without law. He was subject to the law of Christ (cf. Gal. 6:2). He wasn't subject to the law of Moses, for the Mosaic covenant and law had passed away and had been fulfilled in Christ. But it didn't follow that he was free from any moral constraints; "the law of Christ," which is summarized in the call to love one another (Gal. 5:14), was not abandoned by Paul. Being free from the Mosaic law didn't mean that he lived as an antinomian.

When Paul was with the weak, which is the issue for the Corinthians, he became weak to win the weak. He remarks, "I have become all things to all people, so that I may by every possible means save some" (1 Cor. 9:22). Such a statement is an expression of the law of Christ. As Paul structures his life for evangelistic purposes he adapts the way he lives, without compromising moral or doctrinal principles, to win others to Christ. Still, Paul's actions weren't just instrumental: they are not merely for the sake of others. His actions benefited himself as well, for if he did not act in accord with the gospel, he would not share in the benefits of the gospel, which means that he would not be saved himself.

Verse 23 functions as a transition to 9:24–27, which itself is a transition to 10:1–12. Verses 24–27 stress that one must run the race until the end to receive the eschatological prize. Here too Paul functions as an example for the Corinthians because they could not commit idolatry and eat food offered to idols yet still be assured of eternal life. Paul almost certainly has the Isthmian games in view here, which were played every other year just outside Corinth. Here Paul picks up the image of a race where there are many runners, but only one receives the prize, exhorting the Corinthians to run to win. His point isn't that only one believer will win the prize, but the illustration presses on the readers the importance of persevering in the faith. Athletes compete for a crown that perishes, often made of celery or pine leaves. Believers compete for a crown that never passes away, and the crown isn't a reward above and beyond eternal life, but eternal life itself. Thus the believers must run to reach the goal; they must fight like a boxer who doesn't punch at the air. Paul exerts self-discipline so that he won't be "disqualified" after he has proclaimed the gospel to others. The word "disqualified" (*adokimos*) always refers to disqualification from eternal life (cf. Rom. 1:28; 2 Cor. 13:5, 6, 7; 2 Tim. 3:8; Titus 1:16; Heb. 6:8). Paul wasn't worried or anxious that he would fall away from the faith. He knew the promises that God would keep him (Rom. 8:28–39; 1 Cor. 1:8–9; Phil. 1:6; 1 Thess. 5:23–24). Perseverance is a gift of God, but it works itself out through the actions of human beings, through their faith that expresses itself in love (Gal. 5:6).

Run to Avoid Danger! *(10:1–22)*

Paul continues the stream of thought from 1 Corinthians 9:23–27, warning the hearers, especially the knowers, by adducing OT examples of those who were judged. We see from 10:11 that the OT Scriptures were written for the sake of believers. The "ends of the ages" have dawned in Jesus Christ, but that doesn't mean that the OT stories and accounts are irrelevant. Instead, they play an important instructional role for believers. The stories are typological in nature. Typology exists when there is correspondence between events, institutions, and people in the OT and the NT. Another feature of typology is escalation, which means that the fulfillment is greater than the type. The sacrifice of Christ is the prime example of this feature of typology, in that his sacrifice is far superior to the sacrifice of animals. Typology may be retrospective from the standpoint of human beings: we may only see the typological connection after the fact. But from God's perspective typology is prospective: the typological connections were planned before history began. The types are not merely arbitrary connections but represent events, institutions, and persons that God intended to foreshadow what we find in the NT.

The Corinthians are instructed about the lines of continuity between the experiences of Israel and the church. He identifies Israel as "our ancestors" (10:1), even though most of the Corinthians were gentiles (cf. 5:1!), indicating that believers in Jesus Christ are part of restored Israel. Israel's story, Israel's history, is their history. Paul refers to the pillar of cloud that guided Israel during the day and provided light at night (Exod. 13:21). Their experience "under the cloud" indicates that Israel was protected by God (Ps. 105:39), evidenced by Israel's deliverance when it "passed through the sea" (cf. Exod. 14:21).

Paul draws parallels between Christian baptism and the Lord's Supper and the experiences of the wilderness generation. The language of baptism seems odd since Israel didn't get wet but walked on dry land, with water on the left and the right. Paul argues typologically. There is a sense in which Israel, through the great redemptive event of the exodus, was incorporated into Moses and established as the people of God. Some think the Corinthians had a magical and sacramental view of baptism and the Lord's Supper (1 Cor. 10:3–4): the Corinthians imagined that the sacraments protected them from any possibility of judgment. But we don't see any evidence anywhere else of a magical understanding, so it is better to think that Paul responds to the notion that those who are delivered by God's grace and enjoy his mercy will be spared from judgment regardless of what they do.

If Israel enjoyed a kind of baptism, they also had experiences that prophetically anticipated the Lord's Supper. The reference is to the manna that sustained Israel forty years in the wilderness (Exod. 16:4, 35; Neh. 9:20; Ps. 78:24–25). Paul also says the food was "spiritual," forging a connection between believers and Israel (1 Cor. 10:3). We see the same thing in 10:4: Israel also "drank the same spiritual drink." The parallel between eating the bread and drinking the cup at the Lord's Supper is completed. Israel had sacramental experiences that anticipated the experience of believers in eating the bread and drinking the wine at the Lord's Supper.

Then Paul says one of the most astonishing and difficult things in his letter. Israel "drank from the spiritual rock that followed them" (10:4). The idea of a following rock, if taken literally, may come from a rabbinic tradition of a well that followed Israel in the wilderness (LAB 10.7; 11.15; t. Sukkah 3.11–12; Sifre Num. 11.21; Tg. Onq. on Num. 21:16–20; Num. Rab. 1.5 on 21:17). An allusion may also exist to Numbers 21:17, "Spring up, well—sing to it!" It is probable, however, that the word "followed" isn't meant literally. Moses provided water for the people out of a rock (Exod. 17:6; Num. 20:7–11; Ps. 78:15–16), and Paul saw a connection between this text and the confession that God is "the Rock" of Israel (Deut. 32:4, 15, 18, 30, 31). The water given to them in the wilderness came from the Rock, meaning the one and only true God (Deut. 32:31), and Paul identifies the rock as Christ. The high Christology here has already been anticipated in 1 Corinthians 8:6.

Even though Israel received so many blessings, they experienced judgment: they "were struck down in the wilderness" (10:5). Other NT writers refer to this same incident and admonish believers by reminding them of Israel's failure (Heb. 3:17; Jude 5). The account of Israel's failure to believe and enter the land is found in Numbers 14. The history of Israel is sobering, reminding the Corinthians to be vigilant; they must not think they are exempt from God's judgment.

In 1 Corinthians 10:6–10 we find five examples of Israel's sins in the wilderness. Paul frames the discussion to highlight the importance of Israel's history for the Corinthians, and thus the stories from the wilderness generation function as *examples* (*typoi*) for the Corinthians. The history of Israel isn't merely of antiquarian interest but is appropriated and applied to the church of Paul's day, relating specifically to the issue of idol food. The first example (10:6) centers on evil desires. Paul alludes to Numbers 11:4 (cf. Ps. 106:14), where some among Israel had "greedy desires" (NASB). The people craved meat, and the Corinthians also desired food, and thus a connection is forged with food offered to idols. Such craving was not a minor matter, for Israel was judged severely, and the Corinthians will be as well if they eat food offered to idols.

In 1 Corinthians 10:7 the believers are exhorted not to be idolaters. Paul recalls the most blatant example of idolatry in the Scriptures. Israel had just entered into covenant with the Lord, agreeing to the covenant stipulations (Exod. 24:3–8). When Moses went up onto Mount Sinai, Israel turned quickly away from the covenant requirements and made a golden calf (32:8; cf. 20:4). Paul selects a verse where Israel committed idolatry while eating and drinking! The warning to the Corinthians is clear: they too will be guilty of idolatry if they eat and drink in an idol's temple.

The next warning from the journey of Israel in the wilderness comes from Numbers 25 (1 Cor. 10:8). The Corinthians are warned about following the example of Israel by indulging in "sexual immorality." The account in Numbers 25 applies to the Corinthian situation in a fascinating way. The men of Israel engaged in sexual relations with Moabite women (Num. 25:1). Remarkably, "The women invited them to the sacrifices for their gods, and the people ate and bowed in worship to their gods" (25:2). Their sexual sin is closely tied with idolatry, and particularly with eating sacrifices offered to other gods. The Lord's judgment led to the death of 24,000. Paul uses the number 23,000. Various reasons are given as to why Paul uses a different number. We need to remember that biblical writers were content with generalizations and were not always as precise as we are in our calculations.

In 1 Corinthians 10:9 Paul warns about the danger of testing Christ, as Israel did, drawing on the story where many were bitten by snakes and died (Num. 21:5–9). The word used for judgment, "destroyed" (*apōllynto*), has to do with physical death in Numbers 21, but the word is often used by Paul to denote eschatological destruction (Rom. 2:12; 14:15; 1 Cor. 1:18, 19; 8:11; 15:18; 2 Cor. 2:15; 4:3; 2 Thess. 2:10). Israel was punished physically; Paul warns the Corinthians about the final eschatological judgment here. The judgment of Israel in redemptive history points to and anticipates a greater and more serious judgment, one that is eternal and not merely temporal. Paul forges a tight connection between the testing of Israel and the danger facing the Corinthians, saying that they tested Christ. The Corinthians would be testing Christ as well if they ate food in a temple devoted to idols, and judgment would be the consequence.

The final example calls on the Corinthians not to grumble and complain as Israel did (1 Cor. 10:10; cf. Phil. 2:14). Israel grumbled about lack of food (Exod. 16:1–3, 7, 8) and water (15:24; 17:7); about the difficulty of traveling in the wilderness (Num. 11:1); about the leadership of Aaron (16:11); about the death of Korah, Dathan, Abiram, and their families (16:41); and especially about the Lord's promise that he would bring them into the land of promise (14:2, 27, 29, 36; Deut. 1:27; Ps. 106:24). Grumbling is not a minor sin, for those who grumbled in the OT were "killed by the destroyer" (1 Cor. 10:10). Again, Paul uses the word "destroyed" (*apōlonto*) to designate the judgment, which points again to the eschatological judgment of believers if they give in to sin as Israel did.

The church must be warned, then, against presumption, thinking that they could blatantly sin against the Lord by eating food offered to idols and still escape judgment (10:12). Paul doesn't address those who are paralyzed by fear of falling, but those who think that they are safe no matter what they do. He warns them that they can't presume they will be safe from judgment if they fall prey to idolatry.

Although Paul warns the Corinthians in verse 12, he comforts them in verse 13. The temptation they were facing was not atypical or extraordinary but accords with the experience of all people everywhere (cf. James 1:13–14). The Lord doesn't abandon his people in the midst of temptations. The focus here isn't on temptation in general but the temptation to apostatize, as the failure of Israel (1 Cor. 10:1–10) and the following verses (10:14–22) demonstrate. God's faithfulness is such that he provides believers with the ability to withstand the temptation, and his faithfulness, as we saw in 1:9, is always linked with his promise to sustain his people until the end, keeping them from apostasy.

Paul now comes to the main point in the entire discourse beginning in chapter 8: "Flee from idolatry" (10:14). The Corinthians would fall prey to idolatry by knowingly eating food offered to idols. Paul is confident that they will understand what he is saying, using examples from the Lord's Supper and the sacrifices of Israel (10:15–18). When believers drink the cup and eat the bread, they celebrate the blessings and benefits of Christ's death on their behalf. So too, those in Israel who partake of the sacrifices benefit from what is sacrificed. When the people of Israel sacrificed food, often part of the sacrifice was spared and eaten by priests (Lev. 7:6) or by the person making the sacrifice (7:15). Those who ate of the food enjoyed fellowship with God and benefited from what was offered in the temple. Perhaps Paul also has in mind the eating of the tithe by all the people as well (Deut. 14:23–26).

The whole argument has been pointing toward the admonition about fleeing idolatry (1 Cor. 10:14), and now Paul gives the primary argument supporting his warning (10:19–22). The examples from the Lord's Supper and the sacrifices of Israel might suggest to the Corinthians that Paul thinks idols are real after all. Paul utterly rejects such a conclusion, but then he pulls out an argument that he has been holding in reserve, the argument that shatters any defense of eating food offered to idols. Idols don't exist, but demons do. In Deuteronomy 32 we see that the wilderness generation stirred up the Lord's jealousy and angered him with their idols (32:20–21). Even though the false gods are helpless, they are also identified as "demons" (*daimoniois*, 32:17 LXX). Idols are fantasies and don't exist, but demons exist and can inflict damage on human beings (cf. Lev. 17:7; Ps. 106:37; Bar. 4:7). If believers eat in the temple of idols, they participate in what is offered to demons and expose themselves to demonic powers, which for Paul is tantamount to idolatry (1 Cor. 10:14; cf. Isa. 65:11 LXX). Believers can't have fellowship with demons and escape unscathed. Paul doesn't imply that eating idol food is fine if one eats with the right motives or if one has the right knowledge. Eating idol food, if it is known to be idol food, is objectively wrong. By eating they join with demonic powers and come under their influence.

There can be no compromise. Believers can't benefit from the Lord and demons. They can't eat at the Lord's Supper and eat in the temples of idols. Eating in the temple of idols is blatant idolatry and provokes the Lord to jealousy: no one will survive a contest with the Lord, as the OT testifies. The Lord's jealousy is regularly linked with idolatry in the OT (Exod. 34:14; Deut. 4:24; 6:14–15; 29:18–20; 32:16, 21; Josh. 24:19–20; 1 Kings 14:22–23; Ps. 78:58; Ezek. 8:3–6). God's jealousy inevitably leads to punishment, to the pouring out of his wrath on those who have worshiped other gods. Thus Paul concludes by asking whether believers think they are stronger than God, since those who are acquainted with the OT recognize that the Lord's jealousy breaks out in wrath and judgment.

Counsel for Eating Food Sold in the Marketplace (10:23–11:1)

Eating food offered to an idol in the temple is always wrong, but what should believers do about food sold in the marketplace? Should believers inquire about whether the food is offered to idols and refuse to eat it? Paul picks up the discussion from 1 Corinthians 6:12 again, noting that not everything that is permitted is beneficial, nor does it necessarily build up others. The rule here is that believers should seek to build up and strengthen others. Believers aren't required to know whether food sold in the market was offered to idols. They can eat with confidence since God is the creator: the earth and all that is in it (including food) belongs to him (Ps. 24:1). Believers, then, may eat the food offered to them when unbelievers invite them over, without asking questions. Still, if someone informs them that the food was offered to idols, they should not eat the food for the sake of the person's conscience who informed them. When Paul speaks of the freedom to eat (1 Cor. 10:29), he returns to what he said in verse 27, stressing that believers don't need to determine whether food has been offered to idols. They are free to eat as long as they eat with thanksgiving, though if they discover that the food was offered to idols, then they should not eat the food. In any case, when people "eat or drink" and in every situation they should "do everything for the glory of God" (10:31). Living for the glory of God means that believers consider what will lead to the salvation and edification of others, and thus they will not do anything to cause offense.

Adornment of Women (11:2-16)

One of the most controversial and difficult passages in the Pauline Letters is found here. Paul begins by praising the Corinthians because they were mainly following his instructions, though apparently they weren't doing what he said about the adornment of women.

The theological foundation for the discussion is found in 11:3. We are told that (1) Christ is the head of man; (2) man is the head of woman; and (3) God is the head of Christ. But what does Paul mean by "head"? Does it mean (1) authority, (2) source, or (3) preeminence? I argue that the meaning "authority" is most convincing. There may be a couple of examples where head means "source" (e.g., Eph. 4:15; Col. 2:19), but in most instances the word "authority" fits the context better (cf. Eph. 1:22; 5:23; Col. 1:18; 2:10). The most important evidence here is the parallel in Ephesians 5:23, where Paul discusses the relationship of husbands and wives. Wives are called upon to submit to their husbands since husbands are head (Eph. 5:22–23). The word "head" here clearly designates authority, for contextually the notion of authority fits with the call for wives to submit. Husbands aren't the physical source of their wives, since, as Paul teaches in 1 Corinthians 11:11–12, all men come from women. Paul guards against a misunderstanding of his teaching in verses 11–12. Men and women are interdependent, and thus men are not superior to women. In the Lord there is equality. Nor are husbands the spiritual source of their wives since that honor goes to Jesus Christ. Some think that Paul means the husband is socially preeminent, but such a reading brackets out the theological contribution of the text. The social and theological can't be so neatly separated from one another. God being the head of Christ isn't merely a social reality!

Women dishonor their head if they prophesy without proper adornment (11:4–6). Many argue that the text is limited to husbands and wives, and not men and women in general, for in the social world of the first century, wives veiled themselves for the sake of their husbands. Still, it seems odd to envision single women or widows praying or prophesying in the assembly without wearing a head covering (11:5), while those who were married were required to wear a veil of some kind. The comment about wearing veils "because of the angels" (11:10) applies more convincingly to women in general and not just wives.

Paul's reflections also suggest that he casts the net more widely than marriage, for he reflects on the creation account where Eve came from Adam. Paul probably alludes to marriage in verse 11, but he moves outside the orbit of marriage in his discussion (11:12). The argument from nature (11:13–15) also supports the notion that Paul doesn't confine himself to marriage. If nature teaches women to wear long hair, such a state of affairs isn't limited to married women. Paul's instructions naturally apply to marriage, but his main concern in this text is not marriage but the adornment of women in the corporate assembly. So, he thinks of men and women in general, and not merely husbands and wives.

How should we understand the relation between the Father and the Son in verse 3? Is the authority functional or ontological? The reference to Christ in 11:3 suggests that the emphasis is on the economic Trinity (the work of the Trinity in the world) instead of the immanent Trinity (the inner relations among the persons of the Trinity). If the verse constructs a parallel between God's relation to Christ and the relationship of men to women, how should we formulate what is being said with respect to the relationship between men and women? The headship of the Father over the Son (the functional submission of the Son), grounds the relationship between men and women. The scriptural and confessional testimony is that the Son is of the same nature with the Father and coequal with him. We have an analogy between the Trinity and male-female relationships, but not an exact parallel. We are not surprised to discover that there is discontinuity because the relationship of the incarnate Son (the Second Person of the Trinity) to his Father can't be completely analogous to any human relationship, given the uniqueness of the relationship between the Father and the Son. Still, an analogy is drawn. Jesus is the God-man, and as the eternal Son of God, he shares every attribute that belongs to the Father. And yet as the eternal Son he voluntarily and gladly submits to the Father. So too, the different role for women in the church doesn't call into question the essential dignity, value, and worth of women, just as Christ's functional submission doesn't contradict his essential unity with the Father.

Paul applies what he has written to the cultural issue of veils. If a man prays or prophesies in the assembly, that is, during a worship gathering, and he has a veil on his head, he *dishonors his head*, which is Christ. The central concern in this text is the behavior of women. Perhaps some women felt that they were liberated from social and cultural limitations because of the equality of men and women in Christ (Gal. 3:28). The matter addressed here pertains to the public gathering of the church since he refers to women praying or prophesying, which are activities that would take place when the church was gathered. Some scholars, seeing a contrast with 14:33b–36, think that private home meetings are under consideration in 11:2–16 and formal church assemblies in 14:33b–36. We have no evidence, however, for separate private meetings, especially since the church typically gathered for their meetings in homes. There is no basis, then, for distinguishing the gathering here from what we find in 14:33b–36. Paul assumes that women will pray and prophesy when the church gathers (cf. Acts 21:9). If she prays or prophesies with her *head uncovered*, however, she brings shame on her head. The shame and dishonor are such that she might as well shave her head if she isn't going to wear a covering.

Scholars debate whether there actually was a covering. Many maintain that women didn't wear a head covering or a veil. Instead, the issue addressed is the hairstyle of women. The argument is complicated, but most agree that a veil or a head covering is in view rather than long hair. Paul describes Roman customs here, and a covering fits with what we find on statues, grave reliefs, and coins, and the word "covering" fits most naturally with the verbs used in 1 Corinthians 11:6–7. Verse 15 seems to support long hair, but the point is probably that the long hair of women makes a suitable covering. For a woman not to wear such a covering in public in the first century had sexual connotations, suggesting that the woman was sexually available. For instance, in the work by Apuleius, Lucius says about the hair of women, "My exclusive concern has always been with a person's head and hair, to examine it intently first in public and enjoy it later at home" (*Metam.* 2:8), and the context makes it clear that there are sexual connotations here (*Metam.* 2:8–9). The issue in 1 Corinthians is one of honor and shame: if the women didn't each wear a veil, it sent a signal in Paul's day about how women related to male leadership.

It is clear from 11:7–10 that the cultural and theological collide here. Men should not wear a veil or covering since they are made in God's image and bring glory to him (cf. Gen. 1:26–27). Woman is the glory of man, that is, she was created to bring him honor. Paul doesn't deny that women are the image and glory of God but concentrates on their distinctive role in bringing glory and honor to men. Woman is the glory of man because of the order of creation: woman came from man (so Gen. 2:21–23; cf. 1 Tim. 2:13). Man isn't ontologically superior to woman, nor does he have more dignity and value; but a different role and function is enunciated for woman, and those differences are rooted in the created order (1 Cor. 11:3). This fits with the idea that man was not created "for the sake of woman, but woman for the sake of man" (11:9). Wearing veils in the culture of the first century communicated this relationship between men and women.

Some interpreters think verse 10 means that women have the authority to prophesy, but such a reading is unlikely. Paul emphasizes what the woman ought to do, not her freedom. The qualification in verses 11–12 fits best if Paul responds to a possible overreaction to the call for women to submit to male authority. It is natural to read *exousia* in verse 10 as "symbol of authority" (NRSV, ESV, NASB, NET, CSB). One can see why something worn on the head could function as a sign or symbol of something (cf. Rev. 12:3; 19:12). Diodorus Siculus (1.47.5, ca. 60–30 BC) refers to a stone statue that has "three kingdoms on its head" (*echontōn treis basileias epi tēs kephalēs*), which in the context means that the statue has three crowns, which are symbols of governing kingdoms. Something on the head, then, may be a symbol of something else. In 1 Corinthians 11:10 Paul gives a new reason for wearing the coverings: "because of the angels." We aren't really sure about what Paul means here, but he probably has in mind good angels who assist in worship and desire to see the order of creation maintained.

The argument for coverings is cultural and theological. Paul appeals to nature to make his case in 11:14–15. It seems that creation and culture coalesce here. The hair of men and women, generally speaking, is quite different, and hence for a man to wear his hair long disgraces (*atimia*) him. What long hair means isn't defined, but Paul probably has in mind a man wearing his hair so that he looks like a woman. Pseudo-Phocylides (200–212) writes, "If a child is a boy, do not let locks grow on his head. Do not braid his crown nor cross knots at the top of his head. Long hair is not fit for boys, but for voluptuous women." Nature functions as an instructor that teaches human beings about distinctions between men and women. The distinctions are echoed in culture, and thus a man with long hair elicits repugnance and brings shame upon himself. Hence, both men and women should adorn themselves in an honorable way.

The universal practice of the churches was important to Paul since he mentions it several times in 1 Corinthians (4:17; 7:17; 14:33). Freedom that departs from the tradition of the churches isn't commended by Paul but is seen as a serious departure. The "custom" that the churches practice is certainly the veiling of women. According to some scholars, at the conclusion of the text Paul teaches that neither he nor the churches follow the custom of women being veiled. Such a reading, however, is clearly mistaken and actually quite bizarre since it contradicts the teaching of the remainder of the text.

The Lord's Supper (11:17–34)

If Paul praises the Corinthians about holding some traditions, he doesn't have the same compliment when it comes to the Lord's Supper (11:17–34). Divisions during the supper, which was a meal concluding with a celebration of the Lord's Supper, were surfacing in almost unbelievable ways. The conflict was between the haves and have-nots. Some have thought that the rich ate their meal *before* the poor arrived, but a closer look at the text (see 11:21) indicates that everyone ate at the same time. They are not called upon to wait for each other (so ESV), but they are to "welcome one another" (11:33). The rich were probably eating in the triclinium (the dining room of the house), and the poor were relegated to the atrium. The rich enjoyed a wonderful meal and drank so freely that they got drunk, while the poor didn't have enough to eat. Paul was scandalized that such was happening. Whatever they wanted to call the meal, it certainly wasn't a supper for the Lord! (11:20). The behavior of the rich humiliated the poor and despised the gathering of the saints (11:21).

The divisions in the church also revealed who was "approved" (*dokimoi*) in the church (11:19). The word "approved" refers to those who were truly believers (2 Cor. 13:7), and those "unapproved" were unbelievers (Rom. 1:28; 1 Cor. 9:27; 2 Cor. 13:5, 6, 7; 2 Tim. 3:8; Titus 1:16; cf. Heb. 6:8). Paul wasn't thinking of the social standing or the social elite but of those who are approved by God.

Paul recounts the tradition of the Lord's Supper in 1 Corinthians 11:23–26. He doesn't do this for liturgical purposes but to demonstrate that the church's meetings contradicted the purpose and meaning of the Supper. Jesus broke the bread, which was intended to memorialize his self-giving love, but the rich in the church were using the Supper for gluttonous purposes. Obviously, the Supper wasn't being held in Jesus's remembrance! In the same way, the cup symbolized the shedding of Jesus's blood, which testifies to his death as a sacrifice and to his great love for sinners. Incidentally, the church has long debated the meaning of Jesus saying, "This is my body." We have an important clue that the wording is symbolic in the words "This cup is the new covenant" (11:25). Surely the cup itself isn't the new covenant but symbolizes it, and thus there is no idea of transubstantiation here. The Supper is also eschatological, proclaiming Jesus's death *until* he returns, yet the Corinthians weren't proclaiming his death but their own selfishness.

The Corinthians were eating and drinking in an unworthy manner because they were abusing fellow believers at the Supper; they were guilty of blatant sin. Paul calls for self-examination at the Supper so that believers will discern whether they are living according to the cross. They must discern "the body" (11:29), which probably means both the significance of the cross and the unity of the church. Some were sick and some had even died because of their sinful behavior at the Supper. Paul apparently teaches that the Lord took the life of some because of their sin, but we have a severe mercy, for in doing so, he spares them from eternal death, from a condemnation that lasts forever.

Spiritual Gifts (12:1–14:40)

Unity and Diversity (12:1–31a)

Paul addresses spiritual gifts in a long discussion (12:1–14:40), and here we find a different version of the haves and have-nots. Apparently those who had the gift of tongues believed their gift was superior, indicating that they were specially filled with the Spirit. Paul tries to recalibrate the way they think about the gifts so that love for others instead of a flashy manifestation of gifts receives preeminence.

He sets the scene and lays the foundation in 12:1–3. Once again, Paul uses the word "gentiles" to refer to the former life of believers (cf. 5:1), suggesting again that Christians in Corinth are part of restored Israel. He contrasts paganism with submission to Jesus as Lord. "Pagans" are "enticed" and "led" by idols. The reference isn't to ecstasy; the point is that unbelievers lived under the sway of demonic powers. On the contrary, what it means to be a believer is to confess Jesus as Lord. A genuine confession of those words indicates the work of the Spirit. It is doubtful that the contrasting words (despite the contention of some scholars) "Jesus is cursed" were actually spoken in the congregation. If anyone were saying such in the assembly, Paul would have had a lot more to say about such blasphemy.

In 12:4–7 we see that the various gifts, ministries, and activities are from "the same Spirit," "the same Lord," and "the same God." We have a remarkable trinitarian reference here. Spiritual gifts aren't the manifestation of the self, but the "manifestation of the Spirit"! (12:7). They are the work of God, not the product of the human being. Nor are they given so that people will be amazed at the gift but for "the common good," for the edification of others.

Paul lists a number of gifts in chapter 12, and it should prove helpful here to have a table of the gifts and then provide brief definitions.

Spiritual Gifts in Paul's Letters

Romans 12:6–8	1 Corinthians 12:7–10	1 Corinthians 12:28	Ephesians 4:11
"According to the grace given to us, we have different gifts"	"A manifestation of the Spirit is given to each person for the common good"	"And God has appointed these in the church"	"And he himself gave"
		Apostles	Apostles
Prophecy	Prophecy	Prophets	Prophets
			Evangelists
	Ability to distinguish between spirits		
Teaching	Word of wisdom and word of knowledge	Teachers	Pastors and teachers
Exhorting			
	Working of miracles	Miracles	
	Gifts of healing	Gifts of healing	
Service		Helping	
Leading		Administrating	
	Various kinds of tongues	Various kinds of tongues	
	Interpretation of tongues		
Giving			
	Faith		
Mercy			

The definitions of the various gifts will be given in the order they are presented in 1 Corinthians 12, and Paul especially emphasizes repeatedly that these gifts come from the Spirit; the gifts are sovereignly given (12:11).

What is meant by "a message of wisdom" and "a message of knowledge" is difficult. Some modern-day charismatics understand the "message of knowledge" to refer to the ability to discern someone else's situation, thoughts, or sins, but the definition isn't supported with clear evidence. Though it is hard to be certain, both wisdom and knowledge probably refer to the gift of teaching. Teaching isn't mentioned in 1 Corinthians 12:8–10, but this vital gift is noted in every other list of spiritual gifts (Rom. 12:6–8; 1 Cor. 12:28–30; Eph. 4:11), and thus Paul probably refers to it here. Wisdom in Paul (cf. 1 Cor. 1:18–2:16) centers on the message of the cross proclaimed and taught. The parallels between "the word of wisdom/knowledge" and the message Paul preached are notable: he refers to "the word of God" (Rom. 9:6; 1 Cor. 14:36; 2 Cor. 2:17; 4:2; Eph. 6:17; Phil. 1:14; Col. 1:25; 1 Thess. 2:13; 1 Tim. 4:5; 2 Tim. 2:9; Titus 2:5), "the word of faith" (Rom. 10:8), "the word of truth" (Eph. 1:13; Col. 1:5; 2 Tim. 2:15), "the word of life" (Phil. 2:16), "the word of the Lord"

(1 Thess. 1:8), and "the word of Christ" (Col. 3:16) (all references here are from the NASB). Knowledge is also closely related to teaching—to the gospel that is proclaimed (cf. Rom. 15:14; Phil. 1:9; Col. 1:9–10; 2:2–3; 2 Tim. 2:4, 25; 3:7; Titus 1:1). All of this suggests that both wisdom and knowledge refer to teaching. Paul doesn't sharply distinguish the words from one another; they overlap in meaning and are different facets of the same reality.

The gift of faith can't be identical with saving faith since all believers possess the latter, and the gift of faith is reserved for only some Christians. The gift of faith must refer to extraordinary faith—faith that "can move mountains" (1 Cor. 13:2). The gift of healing refers to the healing of those who suffer from sickness, disease, and infirmities such as being blind, lame, and deaf.

Perhaps the gift of miracles should be distinguished from healing. If that is the case, miracles may refer to exorcising demons or even nature miracles. Or perhaps we aren't intended to distinguish sharply between the gifts of healing and miracles. Distinguishing of spirits represents a gift where one is able to discern between what is true and what is false.

The meaning of prophecy is quite controversial. It has been understood as charismatic exegesis and as preaching, but both of these are flawed. The gift of prophecy is typically more occasional and spontaneous (cf. Agabus, Acts 11:28; 21:10; and Caiaphas, John 11:51–52). Those who prophesy communicate revelations from God in a spontaneous utterance. The spontaneity is evident in 1 Corinthians 14:29–32, as a revelation comes to a prophet sitting in the assembly, and the one speaking must give way to the one sitting (see also Acts 11:27–28; 13:2).

Some suggest that NT prophecy is fallible, unlike OT prophecy, so that it may be mixed with error, but this is unconvincing. Judging prophecies, according to this interpretation, demonstrates that prophets could err. The problem with this line of reasoning is that the only way to determine whether someone was a true prophet was by assessing prophecies. If the prophecies were mistaken, the person wasn't a true prophet (see Deut. 18:21–22; 1 Sam. 3:19–20). Agabus was not mistaken in Acts 21:11, as some allege, since when Paul recounts the story of his arrest in 28:17, he appeals to the very word Agabus used (*paradidōmi*) to describe Paul being handed over to the Romans. Agabus, like OT prophets, used prophetic symbolism in binding his own hands and feet, imitating here the kind of prophetic symbolism we find in the OT (e.g., Isa. 20:1–6; Jer. 13:1–11; Ezek. 4:1–5:17). In addition, the words of Agabus reflect a prophetic formula, "This is what the Holy Spirit says" (Acts 21:11). We have good reason to think, then, that NT prophecy is infallible, like OT prophecy.

The nature of the gift of tongues is debated as well. Most scholars think that the gift in 1 Corinthians 12–14 differs from what we find in Acts, and many think that "ecstatic utterances" are in view. It is more likely that the gift is in foreign languages, as in Acts. The reference to the "tongues . . . of angels" in 1 Corinthians 13:1 is probably a rhetorical flourish on Paul's part, for 13:2 is also rhetorical when it speaks of knowing "all mysteries and all knowledge." Some think 14:2 proves that ecstatic utterances are in view since in Acts people understand the tongues, but in 1 Corinthians 14:2 tongues are directed to God. Furthermore, no one understands in 1 Corinthians, but they do understand in Acts. Still, foreign languages are probably in view. First, there is no evidence that the word "tongue" (*glōssa*) means ecstatic utterances in Hellenistic literature; the term refers to languages. Second, we have to take into account how the situation in 1 Corinthians 14:2 differs from the scene in Acts 2. Paul remarks that people can't understand tongues if they don't know the language and if there is no interpreter. In these instances, tongues are spoken to God since he alone understands what is being communicated. It isn't that the nature of tongues is different, but that the two contexts are different: in Acts those present knew the languages spoken, but in 1 Corinthians no one knew the language or the interpretation.

In 1 Corinthians 12:12–31a the unity and diversity of the body is emphasized. The church is the body of Christ, and every member has been baptized into the body at conversion. The gift of every single member matters and makes a difference. No member is inferior even if they put themselves down for being a "foot" or an "ear." Nor is any member of the body comprehensive; imagine how grotesque the body would be if it were made up entirely of an eye or an ear. God has sovereignly planned the place and role of each member in the body, and thus there is no place for feelings of superiority and pride. No member can say to another, "I don't need you!" (12:21 NIV). The diversity of the body represents God's wisdom, and the intention is that the members would care for and love one another, so that they suffer with those suffering and rejoice with those rejoicing. Another way of putting it is that it was never God's intention that everyone would have the same gift. From the beginning he planned that there would be different gifts so that the body could meet the various needs arising. Paul does say to seek greater gifts, but he doesn't mean by this that some people are greater than others. The point is that some gifts edify the body more directly.

The Way of Love (12:31b–13:13)

Chapter 13 isn't a digression but reveals what is most important of all, which is not gifts but love. In verses 1–3 we see that gifts without love are worthless. Even if one could speak in the languages of human beings or angels, without love such remarkable gifts are like an annoying clanging sound that doesn't stop. Similarly, someone may have an extraordinary gift of prophecy so that they know "all mysteries" and "all knowledge." Or perhaps their faith is so remarkable that mountains are moved. But if these gifts are exercised without love, the person with the gifts is "nothing!" It is even possible to die for the sake of others and give everything one has for the sake of others without love. In these cases the motive is to bring glory to oneself, and such sacrifices don't avail one whit if a person isn't motivated by love for others.

Paul describes love in action in verses 4–7. It isn't as clear in the English translation that these are all verbs. Love acts! Love shows up in concrete ways. I am not going to define all these words here, but we will note how Paul selects themes that connect to the rest of the letter. The centrality of love in the Pauline ethic is evident. When it comes to what foods one may eat, love considers the good of fellow believers (Rom. 14:15; 1 Cor. 8:1–3), which helps explain why Paul says, "Do everything in love" (1 Cor. 16:14). Paul particularly warns the Corinthians about envy in their divisions (1 Cor. 3:3; see also Gal. 5:20).

Love doesn't boast: the word "boastful" here (*perpereuetai*) points to bragging, where people praise themselves. Perhaps Paul thinks here of those who boast about their knowledge (8:1–3) or those who are proud of their spiritual gifts. Love isn't "arrogant," which is Paul's favorite word for describing the arrogance of the Corinthians. He uses the verb (*physioō*) five other times besides here in the letter (4:6, 18, 19; 5:2; 8:1). The word is often translated "puffed up" (KJV, NET, NKJV), denoting those who are full of themselves.

Love isn't "rude" but acts in appropriate ways (1 Cor. 7:36). The word-group is often used of appropriate behavior in sexual matters (e.g., Lev. 18:6–8; Ezek. 23:29; Rom. 1:27; 1 Cor. 12:23; cf. Sir. 29:21), and this connects in 1 Corinthians to the case of incest (5:1–13) and sin with prostitutes (6:12–20). Paul goes on to say that love isn't "self-seeking," which fits with 1 Corinthians 10:24, "No one is to seek his own good, but the good of the other person."

Love finds pleasure in virtue and what is good: love doesn't delight in evil. Love doesn't tolerate incest (5:1–13), selfish lawsuits (6:1–11), or sex with prostitutes (6:12–20). The righteous rejoice in the progress of the gospel whether it is furthered through Paul or Apollos, and they don't become partisans who quarrel over which minister is more effective.

Paul concludes with a rhetorical flourish: love bears, believes, hopes, and endures. We see in 1 Corinthians 9:12 that Paul uses himself as an example of a person who bears everything for the gospel's sake. Love isn't naive in believing and hoping in all things. At the same time, love isn't cynical and despairing, for it believes in "the God who gives life to the dead" (Rom. 4:17). Love believes and hopes for the best since it looks to God, who can forgive sins and grant a new beginning to those "dead in . . . trespasses and sins" (cf. Eph. 2:1–7). Belief and hope don't exist in a vacuum: they are anchored to the God of the promise.

Love is better than any spiritual gift, for love lasts forever, and all the spiritual gifts will pass away (1 Cor. 13:8–13). The Corinthians prized spiritual gifts and viewed them as the *summum bonum* of the Christian life, but the gifts actually testify to the truth that "we know in part, and we prophesy in part" (13:9). When "the perfect comes" (13:10), the spiritual gifts will pass away. There is dispute over what is meant by "the perfect." Some have said that the perfect refers to the completion of the NT canon or even spiritual maturity, which is only realized after the canon has been completed. Both of these readings are flawed. The perfect, as verse 12 makes plain, refers to the second coming, when Jesus is seen "face to face." Here we have the language of theophany, of God appearing to people (Gen. 32:30; Judg. 6:22; Deut. 34:10). Furthermore, it is scarcely true that believers after the completion of the NT canon "know fully" (1 Cor. 13:12). Lack of knowledge still afflicts believers, even though everything that one needs to know for salvation and sanctification has been revealed. The Corinthians were entranced with the gifts, but Paul compares the gifts to childhood, to the period of immaturity. Paul wasn't criticizing the gifts in the least, but reminding the Corinthians that the period of adulthood, the time of consummation, awaited Christ's coming.

The last verse restates the permanence and preeminence of love. It is more difficult to decipher what is being said about faith and hope. Many think that faith and hope also cease at the second coming since we will then "walk . . . by sight" (2 Cor. 5:7). Hope will no longer be necessary, for we will see what we hoped for (Rom. 8:24–25). This indeed may be what Paul is saying. But I slightly lean toward the notion that faith and hope continue in some fashion in the future as well. After all, Paul contrasts faith, hope, and love with spiritual gifts, which pass away. There may be a sense, then, in which trust in God continues for all of eternity, even though we now see Christ. And yes, hope is realized, but hope continues to animate God's people as well for all eternity. Faith and hope remain, but they are experienced in a new octave and in a different way. Still, love reigns supreme, because the purpose of all of life is the love of God, knowing and enjoying him forever.

Tongues and Prophecy: Edification (14:1–40)

In 1 Corinthians 14, the last of the three chapters on spiritual gifts, Paul gets to the nub of the issue affecting the Corinthians. We have seen this approach often in 1 Corinthians. Paul sets the table theologically first, and then he concludes by applying his theology to the situation at hand. It is evident that the Corinthians treasured tongues, seeing it apparently as an indication of spiritual strength and exalted power. Paul, however, prefers prophecy to tongues (14:1–5). No one can understand those who speak in tongues, but those who prophesy strengthen, encourage, and console those hearing. Those who speak in another language build themselves up, but those who prophesy edify the church. Functionally, then, prophecy is superior to tongues, and tongues only match prophecy if there is an interpreter who can explain and strengthen others.

Verses 6–19 give a long explanation on why prophecy is better than tongues. The fundamental point is that speaking in other languages doesn't edify when one doesn't understand what is being said. Many examples are adduced to make the point. No one will recognize a melody on a musical instrument if the melody is mangled. Similarly, if the one who sounds a bugle for war doesn't produce the proper sound, the army won't prepare for war. After all, if someone speaks a foreign language, it is of no benefit if we don't know the language they speak. Those who pray or sing in tongues, then, should pray for the gift of interpretation so that others will understand and be helped. Paul thinks that the gift of tongues is a wonderful gift; he himself speaks in tongues more than all the Corinthians, but he would rather say a few words that are understood than thousands of words that are incomprehensible to his hearers.

Verses 20–25 are one of the more difficult paragraphs in the letter, and we only have space here to suggest a solution. Paul calls upon the readers to be mature in their thinking and to avoid being childish in their understanding. He quotes Isaiah 28:11–12, which in its historical context refers to the Assyrians coming to Samaria for judgment against Israel. The so-called prophets in Samaria lampooned Isaiah's threat of impending judgment, comparing his words to baby talk! But Isaiah replied that the words of Assyria, when they are destroying the city, would be like baby talk to Israel because they wouldn't understand a word of it.

Paul applies this text to tongues and prophecy. Tongues are a sign for unbelievers, but prophecy is designed to help believers. What Paul means about tongues being a sign for unbelievers becomes clear when he paints a scenario where an outsider or unbeliever enters the church and all the people speak in tongues. The outsider turns away in disgust, thinking that the believers have left their senses. In other words, tongues have become a means of judgment because the one hearing the tongue-speaker rejects the gospel. Paul's point is that the believers should not desire such an outcome!

And therefore they should not speak in uninterpreted tongues in the assembly. Meanwhile, prophecy does exactly what one would wish. When unbelievers or outsiders enter, they hear, understand, are convicted, and see God's presence in the congregation (Isa. 45:14; Zech. 8:23). It is a bit confusing when Paul says that prophecy is for believers and then gives an example of it helping unbelievers! The scenario, however, makes sense, for Paul's point is that prophecy brings people to belief and faith, while tongues drive them away.

In the last segment of the chapter (1 Cor. 14:26–40) some rules are given regarding order in the congregation. The rule for meeting together is to pursue what edifies and builds up the church. Various people can contribute, but no one must dominate the meeting. If there is tongue-speaking, the number doing so must be limited to two or three, and only one should speak at a time. If there is no interpreter, then speaking in tongues should not be allowed. The rules for prophets are similar. Apparently Paul realized that church meetings can go too long! Only two or three prophets should speak, and the congregation should evaluate and assess what is said to discern whether they are false prophets. If a revelation is given to one who is seated, the first one speaking should sit down and give room for the next to speak so that more can participate and all may be encouraged and built up. Spiritual gifts can and should be controlled; the person speaking can't just go on and on.

The order of the church also applies to the behavior of women when the church meets (14:33b–36). The meaning of these verses is the subject of intense controversy, and again we can't adjudicate here all the different suggestions. Some have even said that the verses aren't authentic, that they represent a later interpolation, but this view is almost certainly wrong. The verses are present in the entire manuscript tradition. In a few manuscripts they are placed after verse 40, but they are still present in the text. Paul's concern is that some of the wives weren't being submissive, and thus acting contrary to the law. The law here, as is the case elsewhere in Paul, is the Mosaic law, and he probably has in mind Genesis 2–3, where there are certain indications of male leadership (e.g., the man was created first, and woman was created to be a helper). Perhaps the specific thing forbidden was that the women were judging prophecies, but I think it is more convincing to say that the wives were asking questions in a way that challenged the male leadership of the church and perhaps their own husbands' leadership as well. Paul instructs them to ask their husbands at home, and to avoid the shame and dishonor of contravening both a biblical and a social norm. The word of God, after all, did not originate with the Corinthians, and they should follow the practice of all the churches.

Paul's counsel in these matters is not just his private opinion (1 Cor. 14:37–38). His words, as an apostle of Christ, take precedence over the words of any prophet. Those who flout and ignore his commands will be ignored by God himself. Paul sums up the chapter by noting that prophecy is to be preferred, tongue-speaking isn't to be despised, and everything is to be done in order.

The Resurrection (15:1–58)

The last major issue addressed in the letter relates to the resurrection. Some of the Corinthians denied a physical resurrection from the dead. They didn't adopt such a stance because of overrealized eschatology. Instead, they were influenced by the common Greek way of thinking, which prized the immortality of the soul but despised the body. For many Greeks the resurrection of the body would have been grotesque. Here Paul explains that belief in the physical resurrection is nonnegotiable: it is essential for orthodoxy and for the Christian faith.

In 15:1–11 Paul begins by showing that there are excellent reasons for believing in the resurrection and that such was the common confession of the church. Such a belief is a constituent element of the gospel that was handed down to him and that Paul preached. All the apostles, all those who saw the risen Christ, preached this same gospel (15:11). And no one is saved by this gospel unless they hold fast in belief until the end of their lives. The gospel centers on Christ's death and resurrection. Christ's death was verified by his burial, and Christ's resurrection by the appearances of the risen Lord. Furthermore, this gospel is attested by the Scriptures. For Christ's death, Paul certainly had in mind Isaiah 53 and perhaps Psalm 22, but many other Scriptures were included. The resurrection is attested by Psalm 16, Psalm 22, Daniel 12:1–2, and probably Hosea 6:1–3, and other texts as well.

Since the resurrection was a matter of dispute, Paul focuses on Jesus's appearances that vindicate the claim that he was raised from the dead. He appeared to Peter, the Twelve (which may be a conventional way of speaking of the Twelve or may include Matthias), and to more than 500 brothers and sisters at once. Paul remarks that many of those who saw Jesus were still alive. Clearly, his point is that the readers can have confidence that Jesus was raised physically from the dead since many saw the risen Lord, and it is highly doubtful that more than 500 people at once suffered from a hallucination.

Jesus also appeared to his brother James, and his final and last resurrection appearance was to the apostle Paul. Paul was the freak apostle, so to speak, and he thought of himself as the least of the apostles because he persecuted the church. Still, he was transformed by God's grace, and the incredible work he did was by virtue of God's grace working in him.

In 1 Corinthians 15:12–19, Paul affirms four times that there is an indissoluble connection between the resurrection of Christ and the resurrection of believers. The Corinthians cannot say that they believe in the resurrection of Christ and at the same time deny belief in their own bodily resurrection. If they deny the latter, then, according to Paul, they deny the former. The logical consequences of denying Christ's resurrection are communicated with devastating force. For instance, Paul's preaching would be futile, and thus he would be a false witness, preaching something that is false if the resurrection isn't true. The faith of the Corinthians would also be futile, showing that faith for Paul can't be equated with pious wishes only. Faith must be based on truth. And if their faith was a pious fantasy and Christ wasn't raised, then they aren't forgiven of their sins. Similarly, if there is no resurrection, those who have "fallen asleep" (15:18 NASB) in Christ are not forgiven but are eternally ruined, destined to face final judgment. Indeed, those who put their hope in Christ for this life only are to be pitied. Paul doesn't think it is noble and wonderful to be a Christian even if it isn't true. He thinks believing what is false, even if it brings comfort, is pitiful.

Christ, however, has certainly risen from the dead, but the temporal interval and the temporal implications of Christ's resurrection need to be explained (15:20–28). Christ is the "firstfruits," the guarantee that the remainder of the harvest will be reaped. In Adam came death, but in Christ came the resurrection. And the resurrection is limited to those who belong to Christ and will become a reality for believers when Jesus returns. When Christ comes, history will also be at an end; the kingdom will be handed over to the Father. The most natural way of reading the text is that the end and Christ's coming are at the same time. In verse 25 Paul alludes to Psalm 110:1, affirming that Christ will reign until all enemies are put below his feet, and death is identified as the last and final enemy. Paul also refers to the great creation psalm (Ps. 8:6) in saying that everything will be put under Christ's feet. God the Father, however, will not subject himself to Christ, but the Son, as the God-man, as the last Adam, as the risen and reigning one, will subject himself to the Father.

Further practical arguments supporting the resurrection are given in 1 Corinthians 15:29–34. First, if there is no resurrection, baptism for the dead should be abandoned. It is almost impossible to know what Paul means by baptism for the dead, and that is not surprising since the topic is the resurrection, not baptism for the dead! Many guesses have been propounded, but the most likely scenario is that some believers died very soon after conversion, and other believers were baptized for them. Second, if there is no resurrection, there is no point in suffering now. Instead, believers should follow the example of the godless and eat and drink and rejoice before death strikes (cf. Isa. 22:13). The Corinthians' failure to see things rightly on this matter is shameful, showing that they were associating with the wrong people. They are admonished to wake up because their stance on the resurrection only shows their ignorance of God.

In the remainder of the chapter, Paul takes on the idea that the resurrection of the dead is foolish (1 Cor. 15:35–58), and the objections raised by some Corinthians fit with Greek notions of the resurrection of the body. Paul chastises as foolish those who reject the resurrection, as he engages in a polemic against those who ridicule and mock the idea of a bodily resurrection. The natural world is brought in as a witness to the transforming power of God. Marvelous plants spring forth from seeds that appear to be lifeless. The diversity of flesh in the present era demonstrates that God can produce a resurrection body; God's creativity is evident in the flesh of humans, animals, fish, and birds. Along the same lines, he made heavenly bodies like the sun and the moon, and earthly bodies like humans and giraffes. Even the stars differ from one another in their beauty and their splendor. The God who has created a world with such beauty and with such diversity can surely raise the dead.

Certainly, there is discontinuity between the present body and the future body. The body will not be the same: from corruption to incorruption, from dishonor to glory, from weakness to power, from a natural body to a spiritual body. A "spiritual body" doesn't mean that the body to come isn't physical; it means that the future body is animated and empowered by the Holy Spirit. There is a typological progression from Adam to Christ, in that the first gives natural life but the second grants supernatural life from the Spirit.

Believers in their present bodies, believers in their corruptible bodies, cannot inherit the kingdom. Those who are living when Christ returns will be instantaneously transformed, the believing dead will be raised, and all believers will have incorruptible bodies. When that day arrives, the promises of Isaiah 25:8 and Hosea 13:14 will be fully realized. Isaiah 25 anticipates the day when God will judge the wicked city and will prepare an end-time banquet for his people on the mountain of the Lord. The Lord will save his people, and they will be full of joy. The Lord "will swallow up death forever," and tears will be wiped away (Isa. 25:8 ESV).

The words of Hosea 13:14 will be fulfilled at the same time. Paul's use of the OT here is difficult to grasp. Hosea promises that judgment will come upon Israel because of their idolatry and pride. In the midst of these words of judgment, words of comfort are given. "I will deliver this people from the power of the grave; I will redeem them from death. Where, O death, are your plagues? Where, O grave, is your destruction?" (13:14 NIV). The promise seems to be withdrawn, however, in the next lines (13:14–15). Perhaps in light of Hosea's entire message, we can say that judgment will certainly come, though it is also the case that the Lord will finally restore Israel (14:7–9). Paul sees the promise of redemption in Hosea fulfilled in Jesus Christ. The victory and sting of death have been removed, and thus Paul rhapsodically celebrates the defeat of death. This victory, however, is not yet fully experienced. Believers still await the realization of what is promised. The victory over sin and death is accomplished in Jesus Christ, and thus believers should continue gladly in their work.

Collection for Poor Saints in Jerusalem (16:1–4)

The collection for the poor was important to Paul. He brings it up here, in 2 Corinthians 8–9, and in Romans 15:25–28. The collection was intended to help the poor believers in Jerusalem who were suffering from a famine. The Corinthians should give in a disciplined way ("first day of the week") and generously ("in keeping with how he is prospering"). Paul is open to send to Jerusalem those whom the Corinthians commend in the delivering of the gift.

Final Words (16:5–24)

Paul communicates his plans to come and visit them, for he is convinced that face-to-face contact and ministry is the most effective. Paul asks them to receive Timothy graciously, for he fears they might mistreat him, not because Timothy was timid, but because he was Paul's representative. On the other hand, Apollos didn't feel it was the time to visit the Corinthians, and though Paul thinks otherwise, he leaves that decision to Apollos. Final exhortations for alertness, strength, and love are given. Paul commends Stephanas and friends, who have arrived to visit Paul, urging the Corinthians to submit to them and to recognize them. They would reinforce Paul's message to the Corinthians, and thus the Corinthians' response to them would signal their response to Paul and to the gospel. The letter closes with greetings and the admonition to greet one another with a holy kiss. Paul calls down a curse on anyone who doesn't love the Lord Jesus and prays that the Lord will return. The letter closes with a grace benediction and the expression of Paul's love.

─── 1 Corinthians: Commentaries ───

Ambrosiaster. *Commentaries on Romans and 1–2 Corinthians.* Translated and edited by Gerald L. Bray. ACT. Downers Grove, IL: InterVarsity, 1999.

Barclay, William. *The Letters to the Corinthians.* Rev. ed. DSBS. Philadelphia: Westminster, 1975.

Barnett, Paul. *1 Corinthians.* Ross-shire, UK: Christian Focus, 2000.

Barrett, Charles K. *The First Epistle to the Corinthians.* HNTC. New York: Harper & Row, 1968.

Blomberg, Craig L. *1 Corinthians.* NIVAC. Grand Rapids: Zondervan, 1994.

Brookins, Timothy A., and Bruce W. Longenecker. *1 Corinthians 1–9: A Handbook on the Greek Text.* Waco: Baylor University Press, 2016.

———. *1 Corinthians 10–16: A Handbook on the Greek Text.* Waco: Baylor University Press, 2016.

Bruce, F. F. *1 and 2 Corinthians.* London: Marshall, Morgan & Scott, 1971.

Calvin, J. *Commentary on the Epistles of Paul the Apostle to the Corinthians.* Translated by J. Pringle. Calvin Translation Society. Grand Rapids: Baker, 1981.

Ciampa, Roy E., and Brian S. Rosner. "1 Corinthians." In *Commentary on the New Testament Use of the Old Testament*, edited by G. K. Beale and D. A. Carson, 695–752. Grand Rapids: Baker Academic, 2007.

———. *The First Letter to the Corinthians.* PNTC. Grand Rapids: Eerdmans, 2010.

Collins, Raymond F. *First Corinthians.* SP. Collegeville, MN: Liturgical Press, 1999.

Conzelmann, Hans. *1 Corinthians.* Hermeneia. Philadelphia: Fortress, 1975.

Edwards, T. C. *A Commentary on the First Epistle to the Corinthians.* Minneapolis: Klock & Klock, 1979.

Fee, Gordon D. *The First Epistle to the Corinthians.* 2nd ed. NICNT. Grand Rapids: Eerdmans, 2014.

Fisk, Bruce. *First Corinthians.* Interpretation Bible Studies. Louisville: Westminster John Knox, 2000.

Fitzmyer, Joseph A. *First Corinthians.* Rev. ed. AB. New Haven: Yale University Press, 2008.

Gardner, Paul D. *1 Corinthians.* ZECNT. Grand Rapids: Zondervan, 2018.

Garland, David E. *1 Corinthians.* BECNT. Grand Rapids: Baker Academic, 2003.

Godet, Frédéric L. *Commentary on St. Paul's First Epistle to the Corinthians.* 2 vols. Edinburgh: T&T Clark, 1886–87.

Grosheide, Frederick W. *Commentary on the First Epistle to the Corinthians.* NICNT. Grand Rapids: Eerdmans, 1953.

Harrisville, Roy H. *First Corinthians.* ACNT. Minneapolis: Augsburg, 1987.

Hays, Richard B. *First Corinthians.* IBC. Louisville: John Knox, 1997.

Héring, Jean. *The First Epistle of St. Paul to the Corinthians.* London: Epworth, 1962.

Hodge, Charles. *Exposition of the First Epistle to the Corinthians.* Grand Rapids: Eerdmans, 1976.

Horsley, Richard A. *1 Corinthians.* Nashville: Abingdon, 1998.

Johnson, Alan F. *1 Corinthians*. IVPNTC. Downers Grove, IL: InterVarsity, 2010.

Keener, Craig S. *1–2 Corinthians*. NCBC. Cambridge: Cambridge University Press, 2005.

Kistemaker, Simon. *Exposition of the First Epistle to the Corinthians*. Grand Rapids: Baker, 1993.

Lockwood, Gregory. *1 Corinthians*. Concordia Popular Commentary. St. Louis: Concordia, 2000.

Lull, David. *1 Corinthians*. St. Louis: Chalice, 2007.

Mare, W. H. "1 Corinthians." In *Romans through Galatians*, vol. 10 of *The Expositor's Bible Commentary*, edited by F. E. Gaebelein, 173–297. Grand Rapids: Zondervan, 1976.

Merklein, Helmut, and Marlis Gielen. *Erste Brief an die Korinther Kapitel 1–4*. Gütersloh: Gütersloher Verlagshaus, 2005.

Meyer, H. A. W. *Critical and Exegetical Handbook to the Epistles to the Corinthians*. Winona Lake, IN: Alpha, 1979.

Moffatt, James. *The First Epistle of Paul to the Corinthians*. London: Hodder & Stoughton, 1938.

Montague, George T. *First Corinthians*. CCSS. Grand Rapids: Baker Academic, 2011.

Morris, Leon. *The First Epistle of Paul to the Corinthians*. TNTC. London: Tyndale, 1958.

Murphy-O'Connor, Jerome. *1 Corinthians*. New York: Doubleday, 1998.

Oropeza, B. J. *1 Corinthians*. Eugene, OR: Cascade, 2017.

Orr, W. F., and J. A. Walther. *1 Corinthians: A New Translation*. Garden City, NY: Doubleday, 1976.

Oster, Richard. *1 Corinthians*. Joplin, MO: College Press, 1995.

Powers, B. Ward. *First Corinthians: An Exegetical and Explanatory Commentary*. Eugene, OR: Wipf & Stock, 2008.

Prior, David. *The Message of 1 Corinthians: Life in the Local Church*. Leicester, UK: Inter-Varsity, 1985.

Robertson, A. T., and A. Plummer. *A Critical and Exegetical Commentary on the First Epistle of St. Paul to the Corinthians*. ICC. Edinburgh: T&T Clark, 1911.

Ruef, J. S. *Paul's First Letter to Corinth*. Baltimore: Penguin, 1971.

Sampley, Paul. "1 Corinthians." In *The New Interpreter's Bible*, edited by Leander E. Keck et al., 10:771–1003. Nashville: Abingdon, 2001.

Schreiner, Thomas R. *1 Corinthians*. TNTC. Nottingham: Inter-Varsity, 2018.

Talbert, Charles H. *Reading Corinthians: A Literary and Theological Commentary*. Rev. ed. RNTS. Macon, GA: Smyth & Helwys, 2003.

Taylor, Mark Edward. *1 Corinthians*. NAC. Nashville: B&H, 2014.

Theodoret of Cyrus. *Commentary on the Letters of St. Paul*. Vol. 1. Translated by Robert Charles Hill. Brookline, MA: Holy Cross Orthodox Press, 2001.

Thiselton, Anthony C. *1 Corinthians: A Shorter Exegetical and Pastoral Commentary*. Grand Rapids: Eerdmans, 2006.

———. *The First Epistle to the Corinthians*. NIGTC. Grand Rapids: Eerdmans, 2000.

Witherington, Ben, III. *Conflict and Community in Corinth: A Socio-Rhetorical Commentary*. Grand Rapids: Eerdmans, 1995.

Wright, N. T. *Paul for Everyone: 1 Corinthians*. Louisville: Westminster John Knox, 2004.

─── 1 Corinthians: Articles, Essays, and Monographs ───

Aune, David E. *Prophecy in Early Christianity and the Ancient Mediterranean World.* Grand Rapids: Eerdmans, 1983.

Bartchy, Scott S. *"Mallon Chrēsai": First-Century Slavery and the Interpretation of 1 Corinthians 7:21.* Missoula, MT: Society of Biblical Literature, 1973.

Bauckham, Richard J. *Jesus and the God of Israel: God Crucified and Other Studies on the New Testament's Christology of Divine Identity.* Grand Rapids: Eerdmans, 2009.

Baur, F. C. *Paul the Apostle of Jesus Christ: His Life and Work, His Epistles and Teachings.* 2 vols. Peabody, MA: Hendrickson, 2003.

Beale, G. K. *The Temple and the Church's Mission: A Biblical Theology of the Dwelling Place of God.* Downers Grove, IL: InterVarsity, 2004.

Bedale, S. "The Meaning of *Kephalē* in the Pauline Epistles." *JTS* 5 (1954): 211–15.

Blattenberger, David E. *Rethinking 1 Corinthians 11:2–16 through Archaeological and Moral-Rhetorical Analysis.* Lewiston, NY: Mellen, 1997.

Blomberg, Craig. "Degrees of Reward in the Kingdom of Heaven?" *JETS* 35 (1992): 159–72.

Bockmuehl, Markus N. A. *Revelation and Mystery in Ancient Judaism and Pauline Christianity.* Tübingen: Mohr Siebeck, 1990.

Boswell, John. *Christianity, Social Tolerance, and Homosexuality: Gay People in Western Europe from the Beginning of the Christian Era to the Fourteenth Century.* Chicago: University of Chicago Press, 1980.

Bradley, K. R. *Slavery and Society at Rome.* Cambridge: Cambridge University Press, 1994.

———. *Slaves and Masters in the Roman Empire: A Study in Social Control.* Oxford: Oxford University Press, 1987.

Brookins, Timothy. *Corinthian Wisdom, Stoic Philosophy, and the Ancient Economy.* SNTSMS 159. Cambridge: Cambridge University Press, 2014.

Bullmore, Michael A. *Theology of Rhetorical Style: An Examination of 1 Corinthians 2:1–5 in Light of First Century Graeco-Roman Rhetorical Culture.* San Francisco: International Scholars, 1995.

Byers, Andrew. "The One Body of the Shema in 1 Corinthians: An Ecclesiology of Christological Monotheism." *NTS* 62 (2016): 517–32.

Byron, John. *Slavery Metaphors in Early Judaism and Pauline Christianity: A Traditio-Historical and Exegetical Examination.* Tübingen: Mohr Siebeck, 2003.

Callan, Terrance. "Prophecy and Ecstasy in Greco-Roman Religion and in 1 Corinthians." *NovT* 27 (1985): 125–40.

Carson, D. A. *The Cross and Christian Ministry: An Exposition of Passages from 1 Corinthians.* Grand Rapids: Baker, 1993.

———. "Pauline Inconsistency: Reflections on 1 Corinthians 9.19–23 and Galatians 2.11–14." *The Churchman* 100 (1986): 6–45.

———. *Showing the Spirit: A Theological Exposition of 1 Corinthians 12–14.* Grand Rapids: Baker, 1987.

Cervin, Richard S. "Does *Kephalē* Mean 'Source' or 'Authority' in Greek Literature? A Rebuttal." *TJ* 10 (1989): 85–112.

Chester, Stephen J. *Conversion at Corinth: Perspectives on Conversion in Paul's Theology and the Corinthian Church*. Edinburgh: T&T Clark, 2003.

Cheung, Alex T. *Idol Food in Corinth: Jewish Background and Pauline Legacy*. Sheffield: Sheffield Academic, 1999.

Chow, John K. *Patronage and Power: A Study of Social Networks in Corinth*. Sheffield: JSOT Press, 1992.

Clarke, Andrew D. *Secular and Christian Leadership in Corinth: A Socio-Historical and Exegetical Study of 1 Corinthians 1–6*. Leiden: Brill, 1993.

Collins, A. Y. "The Function of 'Excommunication' in Paul." *HTR* 73 (1980): 251–63.

Davidson, Richard M. *Typology in Scripture: A Study of Hermeneutical Typos Structures*. Berrien Springs, MI: Andrews University Press, 1981.

de Boer, Martinus C. *The Defeat of Death: Apocalyptic Eschatology in 1 Corinthians 15 and Romans 5*. Sheffield: JSOT Press, 1988.

Deming, Will. *Paul on Marriage and Celibacy: The Hellenistic Background of 1 Corinthians 7*. Cambridge: Cambridge University Press, 1995.

DeSilva, David A. *Honor, Patronage, Kinship and Purity: Unlocking New Testament Culture*. Downers Grove, IL: InterVarsity, 2000.

Dunn, James D. G. *Baptism in the Holy Spirit: A Re-examination of the Testament Teaching on the Gift of the Spirit in Relation to Pentecostalism Today*. Philadelphia: Westminster, 1970.

———. *1 Corinthians*. New Testament Guides. Sheffield: Sheffield Academic, 1995.

Dutch, Robert S. *The Educated Elite in 1 Corinthians: Education and Community Conflict in Graeco-Roman Context*. London: T&T Clark, 2005.

Ellis, E. Earle. *Prophecy and Hermeneutic in Early Christianity: New Testament Essays*. Grand Rapids: Eerdmans, 1978.

Enns, Peter E. "The 'Moveable Well' in 1 Corinthians 10:4: An Extra-Biblical Tradition in an Apostolic Text." *BBR* 6 (1996): 23–38.

Fee, Gordon D. "*Eidōlothyta* Once Again: An Interpretation of 1 Corinthians 8–10." *Bib* 61 (1980): 172–97.

———. *God's Empowering Presence: The Holy Spirit in the Letters of Paul*. Peabody, MA: Hendrickson, 1994.

Finney, Mark. "Honour, Head-Coverings and Headship: 1 Corinthians 11:2–16 in Its Social Context." *JSNT* 33 (2010): 31–58.

Fisk, Bruce N. "Eating Meat Offered to Idols: Corinthian Behavior and Pauline Response in 1 Corinthians 8–10 (A Response to Gordon Fee)." *TJ* 10 (1989): 49–70.

———. "*Porneuein* as Body Violation: The Unique Nature of Sexual Sin in 1 Corinthians 6.18." *NTS* 42 (1996): 540–58.

Fitzmyer, Joseph A. "Another Look at *Kephalē* in 1 Corinthians 11:3." *NTS* 35 (1989): 503–11.

———. "A Feature of Qumran Angelology and the Angels of I Cor. xi.10." *NTS* 4 (1958): 48–58.

Forbes, Christopher. *Prophecy and Inspired Speech in Early Christianity and Its Hellenistic Environment*. WUNT 2/75. Tübingen: Mohr Siebeck, 1995.

Fotopoulos, John. *Food Offered to Idols in Roman Corinth: A Social-Rhetorical Reconsideration of 1 Corinthians 8:1–11:1*. WUNT 2/151. Tübingen: Mohr Siebeck, 2003.

Furnish, Victor P. *The Theology of the First Letter to the Corinthians*. Cambridge: Cambridge University Press, 1999.

Gardner, Paul D. *The Gifts of God and the Authentication of a Christian: An Exegetical Study of 1 Corinthians 8–11:1*. Lanham, MD: University Press of America, 1984.

Gill, David W. J. "Erastus the Aedile." *TynBul* 40 (1989): 293–301.

———. "The Importance of Roman Portraiture for Head-Coverings. 1 Corinthians 11:2–16." *TynBul* 41 (1990): 245–60.

———. "The Meat-Market at Corinth (1 Corinthians 10:25)." *TynBul* 43 (1992): 389–93.

Gillespie, Thomas W. *First Theologians: A Study in Early Christian Prophecy*. Grand Rapids: Eerdmans, 1994.

Gladd, Benjamin L. *Revealing the* Mysterion: *The Use of Mystery in Daniel and Second Temple Judaism with Its Bearing on First Corinthians*. BZNW 160. Berlin: de Gruyter, 2008.

Glancy, Jennifer A. *Slavery in Early Christianity*. Minneapolis: Fortress, 2006.

Gooch, Peter D. "'Conscience' in 1 Corinthians 8 and 10." *NTS* 33 (1987): 244–54.

———. *Dangerous Food: 1 Corinthians 8–10 in Its Context*. Waterloo, ON: Wilfrid Laurier University Press, 1993.

Grudem, Wayne A. "Does *Kephalē* ('Head') Mean 'Source' or 'Authority Over' in Greek Literature? A Survey of 2,336 Examples." *TJ* 6 (1985): 38–59.

———. "1 Corinthians 14:20–25: Prophecy and Tongues as Signs of God's Attitude." *WTJ* 41 (1979): 381–96.

———. *The Gift of Prophecy in 1 Corinthians*. Washington, DC: University Press of America, 1982.

———. "The Meaning of *Kephalē* ('Head'): A Response to Recent Studies." *TJ* 11 (1990): 3–72.

———. "The Meaning of *Kephalē* ('Head'): An Examination of New Evidence, Real and Alleged." *JETS* 44 (2001): 25–65.

Gundry, Robert H. "'Ecstatic Utterance' (N. E. B.)?" *JTS* 17 (1966): 299–307.

Gundry-Volf, Judy. "Affliction for Procreators in the Eschatological Crisis: Paul's Marital Counsel in 1 Corinthians 7.28 and Contraception in Greco-Roman Antiquity." *JSNT* 39 (2016): 141–68.

———. "Gender and Creation in 1 Corinthians 11:2–16: A Study in Paul's Theological Method." In *Evangelium, Schriftauslegung, Kirche: Festschrift für Peter Stuhlmacher zum 65 Geburtstag*, edited by J. Adna et al., 151–71. Göttingen: Vandenhoeck & Ruprecht, 1997.

Hill, Charles E. "Paul's Understanding of Christ's Kingdom in 1 Corinthians 15:20–28." *NovT* 30 (1988): 297–320.

Hill, David. *New Testament Prophecy*. London: Marshall, Morgan & Scott, 1979.

Hock, Ronald F. *The Social Context of Paul's Ministry*. Philadelphia: Fortress, 1980.

Hooker, Morna D. "Authority on Her Head: An Examination of 1 Cor. 11:10." *NTS* 10 (1963–64): 410–16.

———. "'Beyond the Things That Are Written': St. Paul's Use of Scripture." *NTS* 27 (April 1981): 295–309.

Horrell, David. *The Social Ethos of the Corinthian Correspondence: Interest and Ideology from 1 Corinthians to 1 Clement*. Edinburgh: T&T Clark, 1996.

Houston, Graham. *Prophecy: A Gift for Today?* Downers Grove, IL: InterVarsity, 1989.

Hurley, James B. *Man and Woman in Biblical Perspective*. Grand Rapids: Zondervan, 1981.

Instone-Brewer, David. *Divorce and Remarriage in the Bible: The Social and Literary Context*. Grand Rapids: Eerdmans, 2002.

———. "1 Corinthians 9:9–11: A Literal Interpretation of 'Do Not Muzzle the Ox.'" *NTS* 38 (1992): 554–65.

———. "1 Corinthians 7 in the Light of the Graeco-Roman Marriage and Divorce Papyri: Part 1." *TynBul* 52 (2001): 101–15.

———. "1 Corinthians 7 in the Light of the Jewish Greek and Aramaic Divorce Papyri: Part 2." *TynBul* 52 (2001): 225–43.

Johanson, Bruce C. "Tongues, a Sign for Unbelievers? A Structural and Exegetical Study of I Corinthians XIV.20–25." *NTS* 25 (1979): 180–203.

Kroeger, Catherine C. "The Classical Concept of *Head* as 'Source.'" In *Equal to Serve*, edited by G. G. Hull, 267–83. London: Scripture Union, 1987.

Kubo, Sakae. "1 Corinthians VII.16: Optimistic or Pessimistic?" *NTS* 24 (1978): 539–44.

Kuck, David W. *Judgment and Community Conflict: Paul's Use of Apocalyptic Judgment Language in 1 Corinthians 3:5–4:5*. Leiden: Brill, 1992.

Litfin, Duane. *St. Paul's Theology of Proclamation: 1 Corinthians 1–4 and Greco-Roman Rhetoric*. Cambridge: Cambridge University Press, 1994.

Martin, Dale B. *The Corinthian Body*. New Haven: Yale University Press, 1995.

———. *Slavery as Salvation: The Metaphor of Slavery in Pauline Christianity*. New Haven: Yale University Press, 1990.

———. "Tongues of Angels and Other Status Indicators." *JAAR* 59 (1991): 547–89.

Martin, Ralph P. *The Spirit and the Congregation: Studies in 1 Corinthians 12–15*. Grand Rapids: Eerdmans, 1984.

Massey, Preston T. "Veiling among Men in Roman Corinth: 1 Corinthians 11:4 and the Potential Problem of East Meeting West." *JBL* 137 (2018): 501–17.

May, Alistair Scott. *"The Body, for the Lord": Sex and Identity in 1 Corinthians 5–7*. JSNTSup 278. London: T&T Clark, 2004.

McDonough, Sean M. "Competent to Judge: The Old Testament Connection between 1 Corinthians 5 and 6." *JTS* 56 (2005): 99–102.

Meeks, Wayne A. "'And Rose Up to Play': Midrash and Paraenesis in 1 Corinthians 10:22." *JSNT* 16 (1982): 64–78.

Mickelsen, Alvera, and Berkeley Mickelsen. "What Does *Kephalē* Mean in the New Testament?" In *Women, Authority and the Bible*, edited by A. Mickelsen, 97–110. Downers Grove, IL: InterVarsity, 1986.

Mitchell, Alan C. "Rich and Poor in the Courts of Corinth: Litigiousness and Status in 1 Corinthians 6.1–11." *NTS* 39 (1993): 562–86.

Mitchell, Margaret. "Concerning *peri de*, in 1 Corinthians." *NovT* 31 (1989): 229–56.

———. *Paul and the Rhetoric of Reconciliation: An Exegetical Investigation of the Language and Composition of 1 Corinthians.* Louisville: Westminster John Knox, 1993.

Murphy-O'Conner, Jerome. "1 Corinthians 11:2–16 Once Again." *CBQ* 50 (1981): 265–74.

Naselli, Andrew David. "Is Every Sin outside the Body except Immoral Sex? Weighing Whether 1 Corinthians 6:18b is Paul's Statement or a Corinthian Slogan?" *JBL* 136 (2017): 969–87.

Niccum, Curt. "Voice of the Manuscripts on the Silence of Women: The External Evidence for 1 Cor. 14:34–35." *NTS* 43 (1997): 242–55.

Oropeza, B. J. *Paul and Apostasy: Eschatology, Perseverance and Falling Away in the Corinthian Congregation.* WUNT 11. Tübingen: Mohr Siebeck, 2000.

Oster, Richard E., Jr. "When Men Wore Veils to Worship: The Historical Context of 1 Corinthians 11:4." *NTS* 34 (1988): 481–505.

Perriman, A. C. "The Head of a Woman: The Meaning of *Kephalē* in 1 Cor. 11:3." *JTS* 45 (1994): 602–22.

Phua, Richard Liong-Seng. *Idolatry and Authority: A Study of 1 Corinthians 8:1–11:1 in the Light of the Jewish Diaspora.* LNTS 299. London: T&T Clark, 2005.

Pogoloff, Stephen M. *Logos and Sophia: The Rhetorical Situation of 1 Corinthians.* Atlanta: Scholars Press, 1992.

Poythress, Vern S. "Linguistic and Sociological Analysis of Modern Tongues Speaking: Their Contributions and Limitations." *WTJ* 42 (1980): 367–88.

———. "The Nature of Corinthian Glossolalia: Possible Options." *WTJ* 40 (1977): 130–35.

Richardson, Peter. "Judgment in Sexual Matters in 1 Corinthians 6:1–11." *NovT* 255 (1983): 37–58.

Robertson, O. Palmer. "Tongues: Sign of Covenantal Curse and Blessing." *WTJ* 38 (1975): 43–53.

Rosner, Brian S. *Paul, Scripture, and Ethics: A Study of 1 Corinthians 5–7.* Grand Rapids: Baker, 1999.

Schreiner, Thomas R., and Ardel B. Caneday. *The Race Set before Us: A Biblical Theology of Perseverance and Assurance.* Downers Grove, IL: InterVarsity, 2001.

Smith, David R. *"Hand This Man Over to Satan": Curse, Exclusion and Salvation in 1 Corinthians 5.* New York: T&T Clark, 2008.

Stuhlmacher, Peter. "The Hermeneutical Significance of 1 Cor 2:6–16." In *Tradition and Interpretation in the New Testament: Essays in Honor of E. Earle Ellis for His 60th Birthday,* edited by G. F. Hawthorne and O. Betz, 328–47. Grand Rapids: Eerdmans, 1987.

Sweet, J. P. M. "Sign for Unbelievers: Paul's Attitude to Glossolalia." *NTS* 13 (April 1967): 240–57.

Thielman, Frank. "Coherence of Paul's View of the Law: The Evidence of First Corinthians." *NTS* 38 (1992): 235–53.

Thiselton, Anthony C. "The 'Interpretation' of Tongues? A New Suggestion in the Light of Greek Usage in Philo and Josephus." *JTS* 30 (1979): 15–36.

———. "The Meaning of *SARX* in 1 Corinthians 5.5: A Fresh Approach in the Light of Logical and Semantic Factors." *SJT* 26 (1973): 204–28.

———. "Realized Eschatology at Corinth." *NTS* 24 (1977–78): 510–26.

Turner, Max. *The Holy Spirit and Spiritual Gifts: Then and Now*. Grand Rapids: Baker, 1996.

Verbruggen, Jan. "Of Muzzles and Oxen: Deut. 25:4 and 1 Cor. 9:9." *JETS* 49 (1996): 699–711.

Vlachos, Chris A. "Law, Sin, and Death: An Edenic Triad? An Examination with Reference to 1 Corinthians 15:56." *JETS* 47, no. 2 (2004): 277–98.

Wagner, J. R. "'Not Beyond the Things Which Are Written': A Call to Boast Only in the Lord (1 Cor. 4:6)." *NTS* 44 (1998): 279–87.

Wasserman, Emma. "Gentile Gods at the Eschaton: A Reconsideration of Paul's 'Principalities and Powers' in 1 Corinthians 15." *JBL* 136 (2017): 727–46.

Weima, Jeffrey A. D. "What Does Aristotle Have to Do with Paul? An Evaluation of Rhetorical Criticism." *CTJ* 32 (1997): 458–68.

Westfall, Cynthia Long. *Paul and Gender: Reclaiming the Apostle's Vision for Men and Women in Christ*. Grand Rapids: Baker Academic, 2016.

Williams, H. H. Drake. *The Wisdom of the Wise: The Presence and Function of Scripture within 1 Corinthians 1:18–3:23*. Leiden: Brill, 2001.

Willis, Wendell L. *Idol Meat in Corinth: The Pauline Argument in 1 Corinthians 8 and 10*. Chico, CA: Scholars Press, 1985.

Wilson, Andrew J. *The Warning-Assurance Relationship in 1 Corinthians*. WUNT 2/452. Tübingen: Mohr Siebeck, 2017.

Wimbush, Vincent L. *Paul, the Worldly Ascetic: Response to the World and Self-Understanding according to 1 Corinthians 7*. Macon, GA: Mercer University Press, 1987.

Winter, Bruce W. *After Paul Left Corinth: The Influence of Secular Ethics and Social Change*. Grand Rapids: Eerdmans, 2001.

———. *Philo and Paul among the Sophists: Alexandrian and Corinthian Responses to a Julio-Claudian Movement*. Grand Rapids: Eerdmans, 2002.

———. *Roman Wives, Roman Widows: The Appearance of New Women and the Pauline Communities*. Grand Rapids: Eerdmans, 2003.

———. *Seek the Welfare of the City: Christians as Benefactors and Citizens*. Grand Rapids: Eerdmans, 1994.

Wire, Antoinette C. *The Corinthian Women Prophets: A Reconstruction through Paul's Rhetoric*. Minneapolis: Fortress, 1990.

Witherington, Ben, III. "Not So Idle Thoughts about *Eidōlothyton*." *TynBul* 44 (1993): 237–54.

Wright, David F. "Homosexuality: The Relevance of the Bible." *EvQ* 61 (1989): 291–300.

Yamauchi, Edwin M. *Pre-Christian Gnosticism: A Survey of the Proposed Evidence*. Grand Rapids: Eerdmans, 1973.

CHAPTER FOUR

2 Corinthians

Introduction

No one doubts that Paul wrote 2 Corinthians, but many agree that it is the most difficult letter to analyze. Paul clearly responds to adversaries in the letter, and he is more personal, vulnerable, and emotional than in any other letter. We are given a valuable window into Paul's ministry and the nature of the Christian life in the letter.

Some tables about the letter may help us get a picture of the situation.

146 BC	Ancient Corinth destroyed in war with Rome
44 BC	Corinth founded as a Roman colony
AD 50–51	Paul spends eighteen months in Corinth (Acts 18:11)
AD 51–52	Gallio is proconsul of Achaia (cf. Acts 18:12–17)
AD 54	Paul writes 1 Corinthians from Ephesus (1 Cor. 16:8)
AD 55	Paul writes 2 Corinthians from Macedonia (2 Cor. 7:5)

Paul's Letters to the Corinthians

Letter before I Corinthians	"My letter" (1 Cor. 5:9)
1 Corinthians	
Letter between 1 and 2 Corinthians	"I wrote to you" (2 Cor. 2:4). The minority view identifies this letter as 1 Corinthians.
2 Corinthians	

Outlining 2 Corinthians isn't easy, but one simple way to divide up the book is as follows.

Outline

Past: Titus returned after severe letter	1:1–7:16
Present: Paul's exhortation to give money for the poor in Jerusalem	8:1–9:15
Future: a minority was still against Paul	10:1–13:13

Another outline with the same chapter divisions could be divided as follows.

Paul's joy over the repentance of the Corinthians	1:1–7:16
The Corinthians' repentance will be demonstrated by their generous gift	8:1–9:15
The Corinthians' repentance will be demonstrated by rejecting the false teachers	10:1–13:13

Some scholars think 2 Corinthians is composed of several different letters that were stitched together later into one letter. In particular, many maintain that chapters 10–13 were added later since there the tone of the letter changes dramatically. However, I will argue, when we come to the various sections, that the letter was a unity from the beginning and that it is actually carefully and intentionally structured.

If we think of the letter as a whole, in chapters 1–7 Paul rejoices that the Corinthians repented at the reception of his severe letter, and Titus conveyed this good news to him. In chapters 8–9 the Corinthians are exhorted to prove their repentance by contributing to the collection for the poor saints in Jerusalem. They will also prove their repentance (chaps. 10–13) by repudiating the opponents who advocate a false gospel.

Scholars have also labored to understand the opponents in the letter. Were they Judaizers who emphasized the importance of observing the law? Against this, apart from 2 Corinthians 3 the law doesn't figure much in the discussion, and circumcision doesn't seem to be an issue. Other suggestions have been made, but it seems better to describe the opponents generally. Clearly, they questioned Paul's apostolic legitimacy, and their complaint seems to have been that he suffered excessively. They seemed to promote what we would today call a health-wealth gospel: those who belonged to Christ, they claimed, would prosper and not suffer. Paul sees such a gospel as a contradiction of the message of the cross, for first comes suffering and then glory (though of course there is also glory and strength in the midst of suffering), and the Lord manifests his strength through the weakness of believers.

Comfort in Suffering (1:1–11)

The greeting is quite ordinary, but as in 1 Corinthians, Paul widens the scope of their vision, mentioning "all the saints" in Achaia (2 Cor. 1:1). Paul likely reminds the Corinthians again that they aren't the only believers in the world to ward off their pride. At the end of the letter we will see that 2 Corinthians is the only letter in which we have a greeting from "all the saints" (13:12). At the beginning and the end of the letter Paul staves off Corinthian provincialism.

Instead of a thanksgiving, Paul begins, as in Ephesians 1:3–4, with a blessing (2 Cor. 1:3–7). He blesses God the Father for being the source of mercy and comfort. When Paul says "us," he thinks especially of himself as an apostle, praising God for comforting him in his sufferings (cf. Isa. 40:1; 51:12). The purpose of such comfort is so that he can pass on the same comfort to others when they suffer. Just as the sufferings of Christ flow into their lives, so does the comfort of Christ. Afflictions and troubles are for the comfort and salvation of others, and the comfort passed on to others encourages those suffering to bear their own troubles with endurance. The experience of suffering, then, doesn't dampen hope but strengthens it. For those who suffer for Christ's sake will also enjoy his comfort. The content of this paragraph (2 Cor. 1:3–7) is most interesting when we consider the letter as a whole. We know that the opponents questioned Paul's legitimacy since he suffered, yet Paul doesn't come out of the gate fighting but praising. He doesn't begin with a battle but with a blessing (the battle will come soon enough). He wants the Corinthians to recognize the benefits of sufferings and thus see that God uses such sufferings both in their lives and in the lives of others. The opponents thought suffering undercut one's legitimacy, but Paul says just the opposite! Suffering brings hope.

In 1:8–11 Paul shares a suffering in which God comforted and delivered him, giving an example of what he was talking about in 1:3–7. We would love to know what event Paul discusses here; one interesting guess is that he refers to the riot in Ephesus in Acts 19, but Paul may be referring to a severe illness, an imprisonment, or an attack from opponents. At the end of the day, we have to confess that we aren't given enough information to be certain. The suffering he experienced was almost completely paralyzing and disabling, and Paul despaired of living. The purpose of the suffering was to dash self-confidence so that Paul would put his trust in the God who raises the dead. Suffering reminds believers that their only hope is the cross and resurrection of Christ. Situations of suffering and death are the experience of believers so that hope will be put in Christ for deliverance. The deliverance is also mediated through the prayers of others, and thus Paul receives strength from God through their prayers. Again, Paul anticipates the criticism of opponents who think that spiritual power means that there is no weakness in our lives. At the outset Paul shows that such a stance contradicts the fundamental message of the gospel.

Paul's Defense of His Integrity (1:12–2:11)

Paul turns from blessing God to defending his ministry, and we will see later why he defends himself (12:19). Paul isn't asserting perfection in his personal life, but he is claiming that his ministry was conducted with "godly sincerity and purity" (1:12). No one could point to a moral defect or sin that disqualified Paul from ministry. Paul boasts about his integrity, and boasting seems strange since Paul himself emphasizes that believers should "boast in the Lord" (1 Cor. 1:31). Boasting, awkward as it is, has a place when it is for Christ's sake and when the intention is to advance the gospel. Instead of criticizing him, the Corinthians should rejoice in him, as he rejoices in them, for they will find great pride and joy in one another on the day of Christ. Apparently the criticism of Paul stemmed from his communicated intention to visit them twice, then changing his plans, deciding not to visit them at all (2 Cor. 1:15–17).

Did the change of plans call into question Paul's fundamental honesty and integrity? Did he say that he would visit yet all the while planning not to come? In 1 Corinthians 16:5–9 we see that Paul intended to spend a significant amount of time in Corinth, but he does qualify his intention, noting that a future visit depends on God's will. Paul ties his faithfulness to the faithfulness of God (2 Cor. 1:18). If he denied his identification with Christ, he would deny the gospel, and so Paul is placed in a position where he had to defend himself to defend the gospel. After all, Jesus Christ does not say "Yes" *and* "No" to believers, but God's word is always "Yes" in Christ. All of God's "promises" are "Yes" in Christ.

The whole fabric of biblical revelation, beginning with the promise of victory over the serpent (Gen. 3:15), the promises of blessing in Abraham (Gen. 12:1–3), the everlasting dynasty pledged to David (2 Sam. 7), and a new covenant based on the death of the servant (Isa. 52:13–53:12; Jer. 30–33; Ezek. 36–37) are all fulfilled in Jesus Christ and, by extension, the church (e.g., 2 Cor. 7:1). Believers respond by uttering "Amen": they rejoice in the fulfillment of the promises and pray that they will be realized in all their fullness. All this brings glory to God since it is evident that the promises are fulfilled by his strength.

Paul doesn't shrink back from his authority as an apostle. The Lord established (a legal term) and anointed him for the ministry, just as he established and anointed Christ. Paul is hardly suggesting that he is on the same plane as Christ himself, but he is putting himself forward as a corollary of Christ, as one who represents Christ in his ministry. God has sealed Paul, authenticating him as a believer and as an apostle. The Spirit granted to him is the guarantee of the final inheritance. It is quite astonishing that a question of a change in travel plans becomes a full-blown theological defense of the authenticity of Paul's apostleship, but that is exactly what Paul does. It is possible that Paul also addresses all believers here, for it is certainly true that God establishes, anoints, seals, and gives the down payment of the Spirit to all believers. I suspect that Paul's ministry is particularly in view, but the meaning doesn't change dramatically if all believers are intended.

Paul tacks back to why he didn't make the visit to Corinth that was originally planned (1:23–2:4). The seriousness of the matter is evident because Paul uses an oath formula to signal his truthfulness, which shows, incidentally, that taking oaths isn't absolutely forbidden. Paul refrained from visiting Corinth because he wanted to spare the church. He immediately inserts a word to avoid a misunderstanding. Despite his apostolic authority, he didn't "lord it over" their "faith" (1:24). If he does any good, he is a coworker for their joy, and that joy is manifested as they continue in faith, which shows that Paul's fundamental goal in ministry was to encourage people to put their trust in God. Paul's goal wasn't to bind the Corinthians to himself so that they put their trust in him rather than in Jesus Christ. He wrote to them so that they would give themselves completely to Christ, and he didn't want to do anything that would limit their joy or faith.

In any case, to avoid another painful visit, Paul didn't go to Corinth. Paul judged that it was best to refrain from making a visit, precisely because he wanted to give the Corinthians time and space to repent. We see another indication that Paul's intention wasn't to rule over the Corinthians. Nor did he want to discipline them since that would bring him grief. The ideal context for growth in faith is joy, not punishment. The severe letter Paul wrote was produced with tears and anguish, and such pain was felt because of Paul's love for the Corinthians.

Paul addresses a discipline case in 2:5–11, and it is possible that the person in question was guilty of the incest discussed in 1 Corinthians 5. Most scholars believe, however, that the severe letter can't be 1 Corinthians and that here the person referred to resisted Paul's authority in some way. Certainty on this matter is impossible, though I slightly prefer the minority view that the person in view is the same one who committed incest (1 Cor. 5). Fortunately, resolving this issue is not crucial for our purposes. Whatever the situation, the person who sinned didn't just grieve Paul but also the entire congregation (2 Cor. 2:5). The discipline administered by the church as a whole was appropriate and fitting. Interestingly, the discipline wasn't just the decision of the leaders but was carried out by the entire congregation. Evidently the offender had repented, and thus the congregation should forgive and comfort him, because they could fall into the trap of being excessively harsh and severe so that the person who sinned would fall into irreparable despair. The Corinthians thus are enjoined to affirm their love for the offender, who has responded in a fitting way to the discipline administered.

The call to discipline was a test for the Corinthians to determine whether they would be responsive to Paul's apostolic authority. Paul assures the Corinthians that he had forgiven the offender, just as they had. The failure to forgive would represent an overreaction, and if harshness and rigidity settled in the congregation, then the believers would demonstrate that Satan himself had won a victory. Casual toleration of sin has no place, but the other extreme must also be eschewed: the church must extend forgiveness to all who repent.

A Defense of Paul's New-Covenant Ministry (2:12–5:19)

Paul begins with his arrival in Troas, where a remarkable opportunity for evangelism presented itself. Nevertheless, he left Troas quickly because of his anxiety over the spiritual state of the Corinthians. He had sent Titus to meet the Corinthians, calling them to repentance through Titus. Paul was filled with anxiety about the Corinthian response, and thus he rushed across the Aegean from Troas to meet Titus, even though a wide door for effective ministry was available to him in Troas (2:12–13). Paul doesn't pick up this account again until 7:5, where he resumes the story of arriving in Macedonia, bedeviled by conflicts and fears, to meet Titus. We read there that God comforted Paul with news of the Corinthians and their repentance upon receiving the severe letter. So all of chapters 1–7 are shaped by Paul's voyage across the Aegean to see Titus and by the good news of the Corinthians' repentance upon receiving the Pauline letter. We understand, then, why chapter 7 ends with Paul's relief and joy at hearing about what was happening in Corinth.

Some scholars think the long separation (2:14–7:4) between the accounts of what happened when Paul left Troas for Macedonia to meet Titus (2:12–13 and 7:5–7) supports the notion that 2 Corinthians is composed of a number of letters stitched together. Actually, the disruption is intentional, and we have no manuscript evidence of distinct letters that were put together in such a complicated fashion. It is far better to conclude that Paul deliberately inserted a long discussion of his new-covenant ministry between the accounts of his meeting with Titus. The Corinthians had reconciled with Paul, but there are indications that he was concerned about their ongoing faithfulness, and thus he wanted them to understand the nature of his ministry over against the opponents (who will take center stage in chaps. 10–13). From 2:14–5:19 Paul explains his new-covenant ministry; in 5:20–7:4 he exhorts his hearers to be reconciled to him and to God on the basis of this ministry; and then in 7:5–16 he rejoices that they have taken a decisive step in being reconciled to him in their response to Titus's visit.

In giving thanks to God (2:14), probably in part because of the good news that Titus brought, Paul interrupts the full explanation of what occurred when Titus visited, and he delays the full report until 7:5–16. Here he gives thanks for being led in a triumphal procession and for the aroma of the knowledge of Christ being wafted through him everywhere he goes. What Paul means by the triumphal procession is quite controversial. When the Romans triumphed over enemies in military battles, they would have a triumphal procession, a parade through the streets of Rome, where they would display the wares they captured and some of the leading men of the opposition. At the end of the procession, the opponents were put to death. Many interpreters think that it hardly makes sense for Paul to have this meaning in mind in 2 Corinthians, for it seems strange to speak of Christ leading Paul to his death! That doesn't seem like something that one would be thankful for!

The image does make sense, however, if Paul describes his suffering as an apostle. Paul's new-covenant ministry is hardly what one would expect it to be, and Paul's opponents rejected it for this very reason. Paul was called to suffer as an apostle of Christ; he was being led to suffering and death. Yes, he would ultimately be raised from the dead, but life comes from death, or as he said earlier in the letter, comfort flows through sufferings. We already saw that God rescued him from death in his sufferings (1:8–11). The reference to a fragrance and aroma verifies the interpretation suggested here, for the aroma and fragrance comes from the world of sacrifices. Paul's life and ministry, like the sacrifices offered in the OT, are a fragrant and pleasing aroma to God (cf. Gen. 8:21; Exod. 29:18; Lev. 1:9, 13, 17; etc.). The metaphor for sacrifice, however, suggests suffering and death. The pleasing aroma of the knowledge of God is conveyed through Paul's ministry, in which he suffers for the sake of the gospel. Paul's suffering, then, is a corollary of Christ's suffering. The saving message is disseminated to others through his suffering.

Both those who are being saved and those who are perishing, those who are heading to eschatological judgment, smell the aroma in Paul's life, but the response to the fragrance differs. Unbelievers smell death and reject the message of the gospel proclaimed by Paul as one that is life denying. Believers think that the message is entrancing and embrace it as life giving. In 2 Corinthians 2:16 Paul asks, Who is adequate? Who is sufficient to proclaim the message? In 3:5 he will tell us that no one is adequate in themselves, but first he contrasts himself with the opponents. And here in 2:17 he suggests that he is adequate in contrast to the adversaries. The opponents are those who "market the word of God." They are health-wealth preachers and preach to pad their bank accounts. Here Paul anticipates his attack on the adversaries, which will be amped up to full force in chapters 10–13. Now they appear for the first time in the letter, but Paul wants to make his case positively before dealing with them in more detail later in the letter. We do see an indication, however, that Paul was aware of his adversaries from the outset of the letter. It is not as if sudden news reached him about the opponents after he wrote chapters 1–9. In contrast to the opponents, Paul has suffered for the sake of the gospel and speaks with sincerity and integrity. He was adequate to proclaim the good news because he was a person of integrity.

Paul responds to the demand that he provide "letters of recommendation" (3:1–6), and such letters were probably requested by his opponents. Perhaps they pointed out that Paul wasn't one of the original twelve apostles and that he never walked and talked with the historical Jesus. They may have raised questions about Paul since he didn't have letters from Jerusalem, particularly from the Jerusalem apostles. Paul deftly answers the need for references. The Corinthians themselves were his letter! (3:2). They were the only reference he needed, the only letter he had to provide, and everyone could read the letter. Paul is talking about, of course, their conversion. The Corinthians could scarcely deny the point, for if they did, they would be denying their own salvation. Letters with pen and ink can hardly compare with the changed lives that were the result of Paul's ministry.

Paul backs up in the discussion so that he won't be misunderstood. Actually, the Corinthians were a letter of Christ and the Holy Spirit, and Paul served as a minister (3:3). We are back to 1 Corinthians 3:5–9 again, where Paul emphasizes that he and Apollos were God's servants. We also see how Paul's fertile mind was saturated with the OT, for as he thought about letters of recommendation, he began to reflect on the difference between the old covenant and the new covenant. The Corinthian letter (i.e., the changed lives of the Corinthians) was not written with ink and not inscribed on stone tablets but on human hearts. The tablets written with ink had the Ten Commandments inscribed on them (Deut. 10:2–5), but the Pauline ministry was deeper and more profound, for now the law is written on human hearts. Clearly, Paul has in mind Ezekiel 36:26–27 and probably Jeremiah 31:31–34 as well. In Ezekiel the Lord promises to remove "your heart of stone and give you a heart of flesh" (36:26). Such transformation is ascribed to the Holy Spirit. When the Spirit is given, God's people will keep his statutes and ordinances. Or, as Jeremiah says, the law will be written "on their hearts" (31:33).

Paul's confidence as a minister derived from the fact that he was ministering under the new covenant, and thus God was working supernaturally in and through him. Ultimately, of course, he recognized that he was nothing in himself (2 Cor. 3:5). His strength and adequacy came from God. Paul was a minister of the new covenant and not the old. The old was characterized by the letter, but the new by the Holy Spirit. Paul uses the letter-Spirit contrast on two other occasions (Rom. 2:29; 7:6). Some have understood the contrast between the letter and the Spirit hermeneutically, as if Paul were giving an operating principle for interpreting the OT. Despite the popularity of this reading, it veers away from Paul's intention. In every instance the contrast between the letter and the Spirit isn't hermeneutical but redemptive-historical. Paul contrasts the old and new ages, the old covenant and the new, the old creation and the new creation. There is nothing wrong with the content of the law (cf. Rom. 7:12); what was written on the stony tablets was holy and good. Still, the law is an external letter with no power to transform. As Paul says in 1 Corinthians 15:56, "The power of sin is the law." Because the law doesn't transform the heart, the letter of the law "kills." People hear the commands and instead of being enabled to keep them, sin pulls the law into its orbit and produces sin (cf. Rom. 7:7–11). By way of contrast, however, the Spirit produces new life and grants believers the desire and the ability to do God's will.

In 2 Corinthians 3:7–18 Paul contrasts his new-covenant ministry with Moses's old-covenant ministry, showing that his ministry was superior to Moses's. We could say he was a new and better Moses! Moses's ministry, which was in service of the old covenant, is contrasted with Paul's ministry, which was in service of the new covenant. We see three contrasts: (1) the ministry of death and the ministry of the Spirit, (2) the ministry of condemnation and the ministry of righteousness, (3) the ministry that ends and the ministry that endures. The old covenant brought spiritual death. Most of Israel, as the wilderness generation indicates (1 Cor. 10:1–12; cf. Heb. 3:7–4:11), were spiritually dead, which was verified by their rebellion in the wilderness. As Israel's history progresses, the exile to Assyria (722 BC) and to Babylon (586 BC) testified to Israel's inability to keep the law. They were exiled because of their transgression of the law. If Moses's ministry is one of death, we expect Paul to say his ministry is one of life, but instead he refers to the Spirit, because he wants to stress that believers in the new covenant have the indwelling Spirit, the power of God, in a way that wasn't typically present under the old covenant.

The second contrast is between the ministry of condemnation and the ministry of righteousness. Moses's ministry under the old covenant brought condemnation; people were declared to be guilty by virtue of their disobedience. The new-covenant ministry, however, which is based on Christ's blood

(1 Cor. 11:25), effects righteousness, meaning right standing with God. Righteousness here is forensic, not transformative; we clearly have a declaration of righteousness since righteousness stands in contrast to condemnation. Third, the old covenant was temporary and had a built-in obsolescence, but the new covenant is a permanent reality, and this fits with Jeremiah's claim that the new covenant is *new* (Jer. 31:31–34). The old covenant was beautiful in so many ways, but its glory is inferior to the glory of the new. It has often been explained that the glory of the old covenant is like the light of the moon eclipsed by the glory of the sun. The difficult statement in 2 Corinthians 3:7 about the light on Moses's face being "set aside" (more on this below) points to the temporary nature of Moses's ministry. Even though many scholars cast doubt on this point, the word for "set aside" (*katargeō*) in this context designates that which is coming to an end (cf. 3:11), that which is fading.

The contrast between the ministries of Paul and Moses, the contrast between the new covenant and the old covenant, underscore Paul's boldness and hope in ministry (3:12). The new covenant brings hope because it unleashes the ministry of the Spirit, it brings unbelievers into a right relation with God, and it lasts forever. Moses, by way of contrast, put a veil over his face to prevent the Israelites from seeing the glory of God reflected on his face. The story comes from Exodus 34:29–35. Aaron and Israel fled from Moses when they saw the glory on his face, fearing judgment from being in the glorious presence of God. The story in Exodus is quite difficult to interpret, and scholars dispute over exactly what is going on. It seems that Moses continued to be unveiled when he relayed God's commands to Israel, and then put the veil on after he talked with them. A pattern ensued: Moses would remove the veil when he spoke with the Lord, and then would put the veil on until he was in the Lord's presence again.

Understanding what is going on in Exodus is puzzling enough, but it is even more perplexing to decipher how Paul understands the text. He contrasts the boldness and openness of his ministry with the ministry of Moses, who veiled his face so that the Israelites couldn't look at what was passing away (*katargeō* again! 2 Cor. 3:13). Perhaps we have two thoughts here. Paul was bold in his ministry because he knew that his ministry would permanently endure, in contrast to Moses's temporary ministry. Also, Israel could not look at the glory of God persistently without being judged because of its sin, but those who belong to Christ can see God's glory without being judged. Israel saw God's glory, but their hearts and minds "were hardened" (3:14–15). The veil on Moses's face, which kept them from seeing God's glory, still lies on Israel today, and it is only removed when one turns to Christ in conversion. In verse 16 Paul picks up the words of Exodus 34:34, where Moses would go into the Lord's presence and remove the veil to see God's glory. Many scholars, therefore, think turning to the Lord in 2 Corinthians 3:16 refers to turning to Yahweh. Such an interpretation is possible, but a reference to Christ is more likely since Paul says the veil "is set aside only in Christ" (3:14). It is quite common for Paul to take texts that refer to Yahweh and to apply them to Jesus Christ (e.g., Rom. 10:13; 14:11; 1 Cor. 1:31; 2:16; 10:22, 26; 2 Cor. 10:17; Phil. 2:10–11; 1 Thess. 3:13; 4:6; 2 Thess. 1:7–8; 2 Tim. 2:19).

Some suggest that "the Lord" in 2 Corinthians 3:16 is the Spirit because of what Paul says in 3:17, but this is doubtful. The text has a trinitarian cast, featuring the work of the Father, the Son, and the Spirit. Saying "the Lord is the Spirit" is not an ontological statement: Paul speaks functionally of the Spirit's work, which circles us back to the work of the Spirit in the earlier part of the chapter (3:3–8). The work of the Spirit frees those who are in Christ from condemnation. Those who are righteous in Christ are also free from the dominion of sin, and this too is the new-covenant work of the Spirit. Believers, then, enjoy an access to God not granted to Israel. All believers see "the glory of the Lord" in Jesus Christ. As they see his glory, beauty, and splendor, they are transformed into "the same image" as Jesus Christ (cf. Rom. 8:29). The process of transformation is gradual and not immediate; it is "from glory to glory" until it consummates on the day of resurrection with perfection. Believers are transformed as they look at Christ, but it is the work of the Spirit that enables believers to truly see Christ, so that he has a transforming impact on their lives.

Paul continues to explain the nature of his ministry, which he has received because of God's mercy (2 Cor. 4:1–6). He didn't become discouraged in the ministry, given the realities of a new-covenant ministry traced out in chapter 3. He trusted the power of God in the proclamation of the gospel and did not resort to what is "shameful" (4:2) or turn toward deception or distort the message of the gospel. Again we see an anticipation of the opponents who will be addressed more fully in chapters 10–13. Paul, in contrast to the adversaries, spoke the truth plainly, appealing to each person's conscience.

Paul responds, perhaps, to criticisms that his gospel wasn't effective enough in 4:3, picking up the language of veiling from chapter 3. The gospel is veiled to some; to those who "are perishing," to those headed toward eschatological ruin, to those who don't see the glory of Christ in the gospel. In this case "the god of this age" (4:4), Satan (cf. Eph. 2:2; 1 John 5:19), "has blinded" unbelievers from seeing the beauty and splendor of Christ in the gospel. They don't realize that Christ represents who God is (cf. Col. 1:15). The fault, then, isn't Paul's; there is satanic influence. Paul's calling was not to proclaim his own virtue or qualifications: he was called to proclaim the truth that Jesus Christ is the Lord of all, and he was a servant of such a message. What happens in conversion is relayed in a beautiful appropriation of Genesis 1:3, where on the first day of creation the world was muffled in darkness until the Lord called light into existence. Paul applies this text to God's new-creation work in Jesus Christ (2 Cor. 4:6). God shines in the darkness that shrouds the hearts of sinners, showing them God's glory in Jesus Christ. There may also be a reference to Isaiah 9:2, a famous messianic text that speaks of the light that "has dawned on those living in the land of darkness." Paul could not dispel the darkness in unbelievers, but God can turn the light on and shine into hearts so that people see that Jesus is lovely and beautiful.

Paul labors to show that the effectiveness of his ministry can't be attributed to him; he was just a servant (2 Cor. 4:5). Sometimes one wonders if the Corinthians had really learned anything from 1 Corinthians! The treasure of the gospel is found in "jars of clay" (4:7 ESV), meaning that Paul was just a clay pot, a piece of fragile pottery. The fragility and weakness of human beings reveals that power stems from God instead of from human beings. Paul's weakness is sketched in with some remarkable contrasts in 4:8–9. Paul suffered from the pressures of life, but he was "not crushed" by them. He didn't have all the answers; sometimes he was "perplexed," but the perplexity and puzzlement never led to despair. He was "persecuted" and rejected by human beings, but in the midst of such he was not "forsaken" by God (4:9 ESV; cf. Ps. 37:24). The presence of God sustained him in the midst of suffering. He was often "struck down" but was not ultimately "destroyed" (2 Cor. 4:9).

When Paul says, "We always carry the death of Jesus in our body" and "We who live are always being given over to death for Jesus's sake" (4:10–11), he refers again to his suffering as an apostle. He embodied the "mystery" of the cross (1 Cor. 2:7). He didn't lead a serene life where he sailed above the troubles and pains of this world. He was led along the path of suffering so that Jesus's life would reveal itself in the midst of suffering, just as it did with Jesus as the crucified one. The opponents rejected Paul's ministry because he suffered, but for Paul his suffering qualified him as an apostle, verifying that he was following the pathway of his Lord. The suffering Paul experienced, which he characterizes as "death," became the vehicle for "life" for the Corinthians (2 Cor. 4:12). Again we see the programmatic character of 1:3–7, where the comfort Paul receives in sufferings becomes the means by which others are comforted.

In 4:13 Paul cites Psalm 116:10, where the one who believes also speaks. Psalm 116 addresses a situation where the psalmist was suffering and indeed near death. The Lord rescued him from death, and the psalmist will fulfill his vows and offer thanksgiving for the Lord's compassion and goodness in his suffering. The content of verse 10 is fascinating, for here the psalmist continues to trust the Lord even as he announces that he is under severe oppression from enemies. The context fits Paul's situation well. Paul also continued to trust in the Lord despite his sufferings. He was confident of final deliverance, but for Paul the deliverance would come at the resurrection (2 Cor. 4:14), when Paul would be presented with the fruit of his ministry: the Corinthians. Paul's afflictions were for their "benefit," and ultimately more glory goes to God as thanks for his saving power is voiced (4:15).

Paul reflects on his ministry, declaring again that he wasn't discouraged and had not lost heart (4:16). If we follow the thread of thought, he was encouraged in his sufferings, even as he was given over to death, for the death he suffered brought life to the Corinthians. The pattern of Christ's resurrection is replicated in Paul's ministry: out of death comes life. The adversaries criticized Paul for suffering, but such suffering was the means by which his ministry was truly effective. The "outer person" is being destroyed, but the "inner person" is renewed daily through the resurrection power of Christ. Paul doesn't mean that the inner person improves a little each day, but that the Lord renews us each day. The sufferings of the present may seem heavy to us (because they *are* heavy now!), but they are "light" and temporary and will yield an "incomparable weight of glory" (4:17). Sufferings aren't trivial now, but looking back they will seem light, and it will be clear that every pain was worth it. As believers, then, our attention must not be fixed on what is temporary, but on what is eternal, even though now it "is unseen" (4:18).

The prime example of falling apart outwardly while waiting for what is unseen relates to our physical bodies (5:1–10). The body we live in presently is compared to a tent, a temporary residence. When that tent is destroyed, believers will have something far more stable, not a mere tent but a building. The "tent" represents the corruptible body that believers have now, and the building indicates the resurrection body to come. The present tense of the verb "we have" doesn't mean that believers will be raised immediately after death, as some scholars claim. The notion that Paul changed his idea of when the resurrection would occur needs more evidence than this; the present tense signifies the certainty that there will be a future resurrection. The reference is to the stability and eternal nature of the resurrection body. Life in our corruptible bodies is characterized by groaning and longing, for we look forward to being clothed with "our heavenly dwelling" (5:2, 4).

The better reading in 5:3 is reflected in the NIV and ESV over against the CSB. When believers put on the resurrection body, they will no longer be "naked." They will finally experience the fullness of life for which human beings were created from the beginning. "Nakedness" here doesn't refer to lack of good works, but to the awkwardness of living apart from one's resurrection body, for human beings were meant to live in bodies that were eternal from the outset, but Adam's sin and the consequent death frustrated that possibility. Existence without a body, existence as a soul apart from the body, lacked wholeness for Paul. Greeks may have prized life without a body, but biblical writers look forward to the resurrection of the soul and the body. We have an allusion here to Isaiah 25:8, for both Paul and Isaiah use the verb "swallow," and the context in Isaiah is the resurrection. Death will be swallowed up, and God will wipe away every tear. The Spirit functions as the guarantee and down payment of the final inheritance (2 Cor. 5:5). Believers can be sure that a new body will be theirs.

While the body is perishing, believers remain confident because they look to the unseen, even though suffering will not end as long as this life lasts. Home isn't found in the present incorruptible body but will be realized when believers are with the Lord forever and have new incorruptible bodies (5:6). Believers can't prove that they will receive new bodies. When people die, they remain in the grave, and thus the new body promised can't be proved empirically, which explains why believers live by faith instead of by sight (5:7). Faith fills believers with confidence that the future promises will be secured, and thus believers desire to be home with the Lord now (5:8). Given the eschatological hope, believers make it their aim in life to please the Lord in all things (5:9). Ultimately, each person will stand before Christ to give an account of their lives; those who do what is good will receive eternal life, but those who have given themselves to evil will suffer judgment (5:10). Such a statement doesn't contradict the Pauline teaching on justification by faith alone, for as we have seen elsewhere, true faith expresses itself in love and good works (Gal. 5:6).

The fear of the Lord, the prospect of the final judgment, impelled Paul as a missionary, and his desire was to persuade people to embrace the gospel he proclaimed (5:11). Paul's hope and desire was that the Corinthians would recognize his authenticity as an apostle, especially because the opponents were trying to lodge themselves in the affections of the Corinthians. Paul was placed in a sensitive situation where it looked as though he was commending himself (5:12), but he needed to speak on his own behalf since the opponents were focused on outward appearance. We have an allusion to 1 Samuel 16:7, where Samuel was about to anoint a king to replace Saul and relied on outward appearance, thinking that Jesse's oldest son would certainly be the king. The Lord, however, sees the heart and probes more deeply, and so too the Corinthians must beware of superficial judgments. They could come to the false conclusion that the adversaries were favored over Paul.

It is difficult to know what Paul has in mind in 2 Corinthians 5:13. Does the statement of Paul being out of his mind reflect the charge of adversaries? Paul claims that if he experiences spiritual ecstasy, it is for God's sake, and if he speaks the sober truth, "it is for you." In 5:14–19 the nature of the gospel Paul proclaimed is sketched in, and surely this is one of the most important soteriological texts in Paul's writings. Reconciliation is particularly featured here, and clearly this theme plays an important role in Paul's soteriology (cf. Rom. 5:1, 10–11; Eph. 2:11–22; Col. 1:20–21). Justification clarifies that we are right with God, but reconciliation assures us that we are friends with God, that he loves us as his children. What drives Paul in his ministry is Christ's love, and Christ's love is expressed particularly in his death.

Jesus as the crucified one "died for all," and so "all died" (2 Cor. 5:14). Most interpreters take this to mean that all died potentially, and such a reading may be on target. It is preferable, however, to understand "all died" not as hypothetical but actual. The "all" on this schema doesn't refer to everyone without exception but to all those who belong to Christ without distinction, both Jews and gentiles. The ones who died, then, are also the ones who "live," not merely physically; they have new life in Christ (5:15). Christ's death rescued them from alienation with God and made them friends with God. Their lives no longer orbit around themselves, but now they live for the sake of the one who gave his life for them and was raised for them. Those who have died with Christ live radically new lives; they are transformed and live for the glory of God.

Because the grace of God in Christ is transformative, Paul didn't estimate anyone in terms of who they are in Adam. He recognized that the grace of Christ dramatically, though not perfectly in this life, changes people. At one time Paul viewed Christ from a secular perspective, not understanding his death for sinners. Paul believed that Jesus was cursed by God because he suffered on the cross (Gal. 3:13; Deut. 21:23). The blindness in his life was lifted, however, so that he saw Christ as he really was. At the same time, Paul recognized, picking up new-creation language from the OT (Isa. 65:17; 66:22), that those in Christ are a new creation (cf. 2 Cor. 4:6). They are no longer marked fundamentally by the old order but by the new creation in Christ (cf. Gal. 6:15). Knowing the transforming grace of Christ in the gospel filled Paul with hope and optimism as a minister of the gospel, as he saw the new covenant, the new creation, and the new exodus realized in Jesus Christ.

The new creation is characterized by reconciliation. Some scholars have seen the background in the diplomacy of the Greco-Roman world, and this may have played a role, but the fundamental background comes from the new-creation contexts in the OT, especially from the prophet Isaiah. When Israel was freed from exile, they were reconciled to Yahweh (Isa. 65–66). Reconciliation with God, peace with God, and fellowship with God are ours through Jesus Christ, and this ministry of reconciliation was given in a particular way to Paul (2 Cor. 5:18). The message of reconciliation is expressed in 5:19, though it will also be unpacked further in 5:21. Through the work of Christ via the cross, God took the initiative to reconcile "the world to himself." The "world" here doesn't mean the entire world, as if it referred to every person without exception. The reference is to the whole world without distinction, both Jews and gentiles. Reconciliation is based on forgiveness, on God not "counting their trespasses against them" (5:19). Reconciliation can only take place when guilt is removed, and in 5:21 we shall see further how this takes place. What Paul emphasizes here is that God gave him the ministry of reconciliation, the new-covenant ministry of urging people to surrender their enmity toward God.

Exhortations to Reconciliation (5:20–7:4)

The Corinthians repented at the visit of Titus and sided with Paul, but their repentance was recent, and Paul wanted to solidify it. Their alignment with him must be deepened and strengthened, rooted in an understanding of his new-covenant ministry. There is still the danger that they will side with the opponents, who are a dangerous minority in the church. Here Paul makes it clear that those who are reconciled with God are also reconciled with Paul. The two can't be separated from one another ultimately, and thus if the Corinthians sided with the false teachers, they would be separated from God.

In 5:20 Paul explains his role as Christ's ambassador, as one who speaks for the king. On God's behalf, he exhorts all to "be reconciled to God." We might think that Paul simply represents what he preaches to unbelievers so that he is not addressing the Corinthians. The words do capture his message to unbelievers, but as the argument progresses, it becomes plain that he addresses the Corinthians. The admonition to be reconciled with God reveals that human beings are alienated from God because of their sin. Verse 21 unpacks the basis for such reconciliation in one of the most famous verses in Pauline literature. On the cross God made Christ, who was sinless, to "be sin" for the sake of believers. God counted Christ as a sinner; he placed the sin of human beings upon him. Since Christ took the sin of human beings upon himself, those who trust in him, those who are reconciled with him, enjoy God's righteousness when they are united with Christ. We have here what is called "the Great Exchange." Christ took our sins, which he didn't deserve to bear, but he bore them because of his great love, and he gave us the righteousness of God. We think of the parallel in Galatians 3:13, where Christ was cursed for us, even though he didn't deserve to be cursed since he was sinless.

The Corinthians were already reconciled with God; they had embraced the message that Paul preached. Still, as an ambassador of Christ, Paul appealed to them, imploring them not to receive God's grace in vain. The exhortation fits with what Paul says elsewhere as he exhorts believers to persevere until the end to be saved (cf. Rom. 11:22; 1 Cor. 15:2; 1 Thess. 3:1–5). It will be evident that the Corinthians didn't receive God's grace in vain if they continue to embrace the Pauline gospel. In 2 Corinthians 6:2 Paul quotes Isaiah 49:8, which refers to the time of God's favor, the day of his salvation. In the context of Isaiah 49, the servant of the Lord is the means by which Israel is restored to the Lord, and the nations are drawn to him. The time of favor is the return from exile, and God's people will come from all over the world to Zion. Paul sees this great promise as fulfilled in Jesus Christ, when the return from exile is fulfilled through the atoning death of God's servant (Isa. 52:13–53:12).

It may seem odd that Paul launches into a defense of his ministry in 2 Corinthians 6:3–10, but if we are following the argument, it makes perfect sense. If the Corinthians wanted to be reconciled with God, they must also embrace the Pauline ministry and reject the false teachers. Paul commended his ministry so that the Corinthians would understand that they should continue to be reconciled with him. Paul anticipates the "fool's speech" of chapter 11, for his apostolic credentials are his endurance, his suffering, and his deprivation (sleeplessness and hunger). The opponents, on the other hand, believed that true servants of Christ would be spared such experiences. Paul's character also attests to the legitimacy of his ministry. The character qualities evident in his life are due to the work of the Spirit, not his own strength. Life as an apostle was paradoxical, as Paul was often slandered and attacked. The world didn't recognize him, but God did! In his suffering he was "dying" (6:9), and yet in Christ he lived. In the midst of sorrow, he found joy, and though he was poor, many were enriched through his ministry. Of the world's goods he had little, and yet he had what really mattered in life.

In 6:11–13 and 7:2–4 Paul calls upon the Corinthians to reconcile with him. Here we find a vulnerable and personal yearning for the Corinthians, a heartfelt desire for them to continue to be reconciled with Paul. As noted before, it seems that the Corinthians had reconciled with Paul, and yet there was a minority that still opposed Paul (chaps. 10–13), so the direction in which the Corinthians would go wasn't completely settled.

One of the striking elements here is that 6:11–13 and 7:2–4 fit together beautifully, but they are interrupted by the strong exhortation not to be unequally yoked with unbelievers (6:14–7:1). Some scholars think that these intervening verses represent a distinct letter and were later added by an editor. And some scholars have even argued that the verses are inauthentic, that Paul did not write them at all. But there is no manuscript evidence that 6:14–7:1 was written as a distinct letter. It is included here in all the manuscripts we have of 2 Corinthians. As noted previously, Paul sandwiches 2:14–7:4 into the story of meeting Titus, which begins in 2:12–13 and is picked up in 7:5–7. In other words, we see this sandwich technique elsewhere in 2 Corinthians. The insertion of 6:14–7:1 between 6:11–13 and 7:2–4, therefore, is deliberate. In heartfelt words 6:11–13 calls upon the Corinthians to open their hearts to Paul, to show him full affection. Paul continues this theme in 7:2–4: the Corinthians are to make room for Paul, and they should do so because of the integrity of his ministry. Paul communicates with the Corinthians in such a way because of his intense love for them. They are his pride and joy and encouragement in the midst of his sufferings. What then is the reason for 6:14–7:1 being inserted into the middle of this discussion? The Corinthians must make room either for Paul or for the false teachers. They can't choose both. They can't belong to both. No compromise is allowed on this matter.

A few more words should be said about the content of 6:14–7:1. The admonition to refuse to "become partners with those who do not believe" (6:14) isn't addressed to those considering marrying unbelievers (but see 1 Cor. 7:39). Paul had in mind the false teachers, whom he identified as satanic (see 2 Cor. 11:13–15). Therefore, he posited a sharp disjunction between himself and these so-called apostles. The differences are as sharp as those between "righteousness and lawlessness," "light" and "darkness," "Christ" and "Belial" (the latter was a name for Satan). The Corinthians must not make peace with such false apostles because the latter were unbelievers.

In 6:16–18 a number of OT texts are introduced to support the admonition to refuse to have any partnership or fellowship with the false teachers. God's temple, which is the church at Corinth (cf. 1 Cor. 3:16; 6:19), can't dwell together with idols, with false gods, which are fantasies. Paul cites Leviticus 26:11–12 (cf. also Ezek. 37:27) in support, where Moses explains the purpose of the tabernacle, the sacrifices, and the purity regulations. The various instructions were given so that God could dwell with his people. The covenant formula has become a reality in Jesus Christ. The people at Corinth, Christian believers, were God's people, and he was their God. The new covenant reiterates that the Lord will dwell among his people and that he will be their God (2 Cor. 6:16; Jer. 31:33; 32:38; Ezek. 36:26–27). As their God, he will be with them in every circumstance, strengthening them in every difficulty.

Paul (2 Cor. 6:17) brings in Isaiah 52:11 (cf. also Ezek. 20:34) to support his case. Isaiah 52 is placed in Isaiah 40–66, which promises Israel that they will return from exile to Babylon. Indeed, Isaiah 52:13–53:12 sets forth the basis upon which the return will occur: the substitutionary death of the servant of the Lord (cf. 2 Cor. 5:21!). In Isaiah 52 Israel is revealed to be unclean, but the prophet proclaims good news (gospel! 52:7). The Lord reigns, he will return to Zion, and everyone will see God's great salvation. Israel, however, must leave Babylon and refuse to touch what is unclean there. For Paul, the good news of Isaiah is realized in Jesus Christ as the servant of the Lord, and the church of Corinth would fulfill Paul's command by refusing to join with the false teachers. The false teachers represented false and demonic religion; they represented what is unclean, and the Corinthians must decisively break with them. If they turn away from such teachers, they would be welcomed by God himself.

The Corinthians, as those who are reconciled with God, are the sons and daughters of the Father. Here Paul alludes to the promise in the Davidic covenant (2 Sam. 7:14). In 2 Samuel 7 an eternal covenant was made with David, a covenant promising that the dynasty of David would endure forever. If a son of David sins, he will be disciplined, but the Lord will not withdraw the promise of the covenant; the dynasty will not be wiped out. The covenant promise of a son ruling on David's throne is fulfilled in Jesus Christ; he is the son of David, the Messiah, the king of Israel. At the same time those who belong to Jesus Christ are God's sons and daughters. They are the children of the covenant. We probably also have an allusion to Isaiah 43:6, where the Lord promises to bring back his sons and daughters from exile, and this is in a context where the true God is clearly differentiated from idols (see Isa. 44). At the same time Paul draws on Deuteronomy 32:19, which also explains the use of the term "daughters." In the context of Deuteronomy 32, those who are God's sons and daughters are judged if they give way to idolatry. The covenant "promises" (2 Cor. 7:1), the promises of God's presence among his people, the promises that they are his covenant children and he is their faithful God, have been fulfilled among the Corinthians through Jesus Christ. As God's temple, as God's holy dwelling place, they are to remove that which is defiling and unclean and live in holiness. Certainly there are a number of implications for the readers, but above all, they must not partner with the false apostles, and they must stay true to the apostle Paul and his message.

Paul's Joy and Confidence Explained (7:5–16)

Paul exhorted the Corinthians to reconcile with him, but the call to reconciliation could be misunderstood as if he thinks they weren't making any progress at all. In chapters 1–7 Paul stresses that he was encouraged by their repentance at the visit of Titus. With 7:5 he picks up the story of his encounter with Titus from 2:12–13, when he crossed the Aegean Sea from Troas to meet Titus in Macedonia. Paul rushed to meet Titus because Titus had news about the Corinthians. As Paul traveled, he was besieged with difficulties: opposition and conflicts on the outside and fears on the inside. Paul was discouraged, but Titus's visit cheered him up, especially because of the good news that Titus brought from Corinth.

Paul learned that the Corinthians were filled with longing for him and were grieved because of their sin, which is an indication of true repentance. As Paul reflected on the previous letter he wrote them, at one level he regretted sending it because he knew it would bring them sorrow. But eventually the letter did them good and brought joy because their grief led to repentance. Worldly sorrow produces grief, but it is evident that the sorrow is superficial when one's life isn't changed by the sorrow, whereas true repentance brings a grief that leads to a change in one's life. In the repentance of the Corinthians, Paul saw the indignation and zeal and passion that verified their repentance as genuine. It seems that Paul had especially in mind the person who was disciplined (2:5–11), which could possibly refer to the man guilty of incest (1 Cor. 5:1–13). The Corinthians acted, showing their devotion to Paul, which is another way of showing their devotion to the Lord. Paul, circling back to the very beginning of the letter (2 Cor. 1:3–7), was comforted and strengthened by the Corinthians' repentance. Their obedience to Titus filled Paul with joy and confidence since it showed that they were giving themselves to God and were truly reconciled with God.

The Gift for the Poor Saints in Jerusalem (8:1–9:15)

How do chapters 8–9 fit with the letter as a whole? The repentance of the Corinthians, Paul believed, would be evident if they gave generously to the collection for the poor saints in Jerusalem, to which they had previously promised to contribute. The collection isn't a new topic; arrangements for saving and collecting were set forth in 1 Corinthians 16:1–4. Paul's passion for the collection also surfaces in Romans 15:24–28. The collection shows the solidarity between Jewish and gentile believers, and the gentile believers owed a special debt to Jewish believers since they shared in their spiritual blessings.

The encouragement for the Corinthians to contribute to the collection begins with an appeal to the example of the Macedonians (2 Cor. 8:1–6). The generosity of the Macedonians is characterized as "the grace of God" (8:1). Paul uses the word "grace" ten times in chapters 8–9, and it communicates both God's grace in Christ and the effect of that grace in the lives of others. Grace gives birth to grace. God's generous gift in Christ frees up our hearts so that we desire to give to others. What was so striking to Paul was that the Macedonians gave generously and beyond their ability even though they were suffering from poverty. The Macedonians weren't compelled to give: instead they begged for the opportunity to give, revealing that their generosity was animated by joy. Paul didn't expect or hope that they would give so remarkably, probably because they suffered from poverty, and so their giving proved to be a special encouragement to him. At the same time, the Macedonian example functioned as an example to the Corinthians as well. Paul encouraged Titus, therefore, to solicit the Corinthians so that they would give what they initially promised. Paul wasn't compelling the Corinthians to give but encouraging them to complete what they had started.

In 8:7–15 Paul diplomatically encourages the Corinthians to contribute to the poor believers in Christ in Jerusalem. Paul handles the matter of giving deftly, sensitively, and often indirectly, showing again his pastoral inclinations. The Corinthians are commended for their faith, speech, knowledge, diligence, and love; all these virtues are evidence of God's grace in the community. Paul asks them, then, to excel in the "grace" of giving as well (8:7). Just as money is a delicate matter today, so it was in the ancient world. Since Paul had to avoid misunderstanding in requesting their aid, he adjudicated the whole matter with care. Paul didn't command the Corinthians but challenged them, since they had already offered to give, by comparing their diligence in fulfilling their promise to the Macedonians, who had given sacrificially.

The supreme example of self-giving love is the Lord Jesus Christ. Giving is an act of sacrificial love, but it is rooted in and finds its motivation from the greatest act of costly love in history. Just as financial giving can be designated as "grace," so too the love of Christ is the supreme example of grace. He "was rich" (8:9), which, if we compare with Philippians 2:6–7, probably means that he shared equality with God. In other words, we have a clear example here of Jesus's preexistence. Though Jesus was rich, he "became poor": as one who was fully God, he took on humanity, he became incarnate, "for your sake" (8:9). By virtue of "his poverty," which includes the incarnation and his suffering on the cross (Phil. 2:7–8), he enriched the Corinthians. Their giving to the collection, then, constitutes a response to Jesus's self-giving love.

Paul reminded them again (2 Cor. 8:10–11) that his counsel was nothing new; he wasn't suddenly sending them a new request for funds. The desire and plan to give stemmed from the Corinthians themselves, and it was now about a year old. Paul simply encouraged them to bring their commendable desire to completion, to give the promised gift. Paul anticipated another misunderstanding (8:12–15). He wasn't trying to wrest money from them that they didn't have. Paul didn't want to impoverish them and enrich others. The goal is unity of the church and equality, which doesn't mean that everyone has the same income, but that everyone has enough to eat so that no one in the church of Jesus Christ is going hungry. If some have more than enough to provide for their own sustenance, but others lack such, then those who are blessed with abundance should provide for the needs of those who are suffering. In the future the tables might be turned, and others may be blessed with more than they need so that they are able to assist the Corinthians. Paul spies a lesson in Israel's gathering manna (Exod. 16:18). Some collected more manna and some less, but in the end everyone had enough. The same should be true in the church of Jesus Christ, and believers should share their substance so that no one suffers want.

Paul gives thanks that Titus shared the same concern and diligence about the gift, and then he proceeds to explain how the gift would be managed (2 Cor. 8:16–24). Titus was not the only person sent to administer the gift, but also "the brother" praised among the churches for his ministry. The decision to send this one was affirmed by the churches as well (8:18–19). Apparently the Corinthians knew the identity of this person, but as readers today we can't be certain who he was. Paul wanted to administer the gift "for the glory of the Lord" (8:19), and the Lord would be glorified if the gift were managed by people of integrity (8:21). Otherwise, there could be warrant for thinking that the gift was a means by which the Corinthians were swindled so that Paul and his friends could pad their own pockets. Paul enunciates the principle that they must "do what is right" both in the Lord's sight and in the estimation of human beings (8:21). Such a practice follows the maxim found in Proverbs 3:4. Paul did not wish to carry the gift alone, for it was crucial that those who examined how the gift was handled were satisfied about the integrity of the project. The right handling of the gift must be publicly verified, and thus a team of people with the highest credentials and unimpeachable integrity should handle the gift. Such a concern explains why the brother named in 8:22 is commended for being "diligent," after being "tested" on many occasions. Once again, we would love to know the name of the person, but his identity remains a mystery to us. Clearly, if enough people administered the gift, then one or two people could not abscond with the money. Paul had sent Titus as his "coworker" to help in this situation, along with the brothers who were recommended by the churches. Since the gift was being administered with integrity and wisdom, Paul closes the chapter by encouraging the Corinthians to demonstrate their love to the churches and to verify his confidence in them by giving the gift they promised (8:24).

In chapter 9 Paul revisits the matter of the gift. Some have thought that we have two distinct letters about the need for the Corinthians to give, one in chapter 8 and one in chapter 9, but there is no manuscript evidence for distinct letters. Instead, Paul continues the discussion begun in chapter 8. There are new dimensions to the discussion, but we lack compelling evidence for seeing two letters. In 9:1–5 Paul pulls back a bit and reassures the Corinthians that he was well aware that they wanted to contribute. He mentioned such in chapter 8, but he clarifies that he was fully confident of their generosity. So, in one sense, it was unnecessary for him to speak to them about the gift for the poor in Jerusalem (9:1). After all, Paul realized that the Corinthians had been planning to give for a year, and Paul mentioned this desire to the Macedonians, which in turn motivated them to give (9:2). Having made this boast to the Macedonians, he didn't want the Macedonians, when they arrived in Corinth, to find the Corinthians unprepared, which would embarrass both Paul and the Corinthians. Such embarrassment would be no little matter in an honor-shame culture. This state of affairs explains why he sent the brothers in advance to collect the gift. He was not trying to compel or force them to give in an awkward way. He simply wanted to ensure that the gift they promised was ready.

The discussion on giving comes to a close in 9:6–15, and motivations for giving and the joy of giving are communicated. An image from the world of farming is introduced, and giving is compared to sowing and reaping. One receives in proportion to what one gives. Reaping isn't the promise of riches in this life as health-and-wealth preachers today claim but is eschatological reaping. Giving that pleases God comes from a joyful heart, representing the glad and authentic will of the giver. Paul had no desire to compel or force someone to give so that they end up giving reluctantly. Generosity is a response to the grace of God, for he grants gifts so that believers stand out for their good works. The life of the righteous person is described in 9:9. One might think that Paul describes what God does here, but the OT context makes it clear that the righteous person is intended. Psalm 112 commends "the person who fears the LORD" and keeps "his commands." God pours his blessings on such persons. Indeed, the righteous live a life that is patterned after God himself, for they are "gracious, compassionate, and righteous" (Ps. 112:4). They "[lend] generously" and are righteous in their business (112:5). Because they trust the Lord, the righteous don't fear the future, knowing that they will be vindicated (112:7–8). Then we come to a verse that is quoted in 2 Corinthians 9:9: the godly give generously to the poor and their "righteousness endures forever" (Ps. 112:9). Here we see that the reaping enjoyed by the generous is an eschatological reward (see 2 Cor. 9:10). The Corinthians will be enriched for their generosity, and the saints who are helped will give thanks to God (9:11–12).

The obedience of the Corinthians and their submission to the gospel of Christ give glory to God (9:13). Their joy will be maximized as others see concrete evidence "of the surpassing grace of God in you" (9:14). For Paul, the generous gift of the Corinthians demonstrates the genuineness of their faith and the reality of their repentance. Indeed, their generosity, as we have already seen (8:9), points back to the greatest gift of all, to the "indescribable gift" of God's Son (9:15).

Preparation for Paul's Visit: Unmasking the Opponents (10:1–13:13)

In chapters 1–7 Paul was full of relief and joy because the Corinthians repented when Titus visited. At the same time, Paul in chapters 1–7 interleaves his new-covenant ministry, for in reconciling with Paul they were turning their backs on false teachers. The Corinthians had repented and were headed in the right direction. Still, clouds were on the horizon. Some false apostles, in the minority, were promulgating a different gospel. If the Corinthians were going to continue to be reconciled with Paul and with God, they must repudiate such pseudo-apostles and their message. Paul was ready to target these false teachers, for he had now explained the nature of his ministry to the Corinthians. He had also explained that he was full of joy over the direction they were heading and confident that they would do the right thing. The exposition of his new-covenant ministry in previous chapters provided a foundation for the discussion in chapters 10–13.

A Spiritual Battle (10:1–6)

The opening in 10:1 is serious and solemn, as Paul earnestly begins his plea with the congregation. The exhortation, however, isn't coercive but humble and gentle, though the adversaries complained that Paul wrote harsh letters but acted like a wimp when he was present with the Corinthians. Paul didn't want to minister with the swaggering confidence that marked the ministry of the false apostles. They may have looked impressive, but their behavior actually betrayed a trust in the flesh, in human ability. Of course, Paul lived "in the flesh" as well, but he didn't want "to wage war according to the flesh" (10:3) but to rely on the Spirit and on the "foolish" message of the cross (1 Cor. 1:18–25). The false teaching would be dismantled through the proclamation of the cross, through a message that proclaims life through the crucified and risen Lord. Pride in the flesh, which exalts human strength and represents the core teaching of the false apostles, runs directly counter to the message that Paul preaches. Paul countered such notions because they obstructed the "knowledge of God" (2 Cor. 10:5). He would deal fully with the opponents once the congregation as a whole demonstrated its obedience, when it sided fully with Paul over against the opponents. Once the congregation was ready, he could discipline the adversaries.

Paul's Legitimacy (10:7–11)

The opponents questioned Paul's legitimacy as an apostle, and so he began by asking the Corinthians to consider the facts. If some were confident that they belonged to Christ, that they were truly believers, Paul was in the same category. Boasting is an unseemly business, precisely because praise is given to the human subject instead of to God himself. Still, Paul wasn't ashamed of pointing to his authority, for it was given to him by the Lord. Interestingly, Paul says that his authority is for edification and not destruction (10:8). We have a clear allusion to Jeremiah's ministry: he was appointed "to uproot and tear down, to destroy and demolish, to build and plant" (Jer. 1:10; cf. 24:6). In Jeremiah's ministry, first came judgment, uprooting and destroying, and then came building and planting. We see in Jeremiah 31:28, in what is often called the "book of comfort" (Jer. 30–33), that Jeremiah builds and plants after judgment has fallen. What is fascinating is that Paul had the ministry of building up and not tearing down. He had a new-covenant ministry, fulfilling the saving promises found in Jeremiah.

Since Paul's ministry was fundamentally edifying, he didn't want to incite fear in the Corinthians by his letters (2 Cor. 10:9), for his primary work was not judgment but salvation! The opponents complained that Paul wrote letters full of sound and fury and thunder and lightning, but when he arrived among them, he was as meek and gentle as a lamb. In other words, they claimed that he was a hypocrite. But they radically misunderstood Paul, for he wrote with threats to move them to repentance (7:8–10) so that when he was present with them, he would not need to wield a sword of judgment. Still, if there wasn't repentance, if the Corinthians tolerated the false teachers, he would judge and discipline when he arrived (10:11).

False Comparisons (10:12–18)

The mindset of the false apostles was flawed because they exalted and prized human beings and human abilities instead of focusing on God. Because of this, they engaged in comparisons, assessing and evaluating themselves in terms of others. Such an enterprise, however, fails from the outset, demonstrating a profound lack of understanding. They failed to see that God works through human weakness (the burden of the entire letter!), not human strength. The paragraph is filled with irony because Paul eschews comparisons, but in the paradoxical and wonderful world of 2 Corinthians, he immediately plunges into a comparison of himself with the opponents! Paul engages in comparisons for the sake of the Corinthians. In contrast to the false apostles, Paul did not boast beyond the sphere God had granted to him. The pseudo-apostles were quite impressed with their ministry, and yet, Paul reminds the readers, it was Paul who established and planted the church at Corinth. It was not the adversaries who brought the Corinthians to Christ but Paul himself, and thus the agitators should be classed as interlopers. Paul's hope was that through the Corinthians his ministry would expand further so that he could proclaim the gospel in other regions where Christ wasn't named.

Paul desired to do evangelistic work where the name of Christ had not been heard before, but the pseudo-apostles showed up where the work of evangelism had already been done (in Paul's mission field!) and tried to claim as their own those who were already converted. In doing so, they were subverting the message of the gospel. Again (in 2 Cor. 10:17) Paul picks up the words of Jeremiah 9:24, which he also cited in 1 Corinthians 1:31 (see there). He did not want the readers to be mistaken about the source of his strength and power; it came wholly from the Lord and not from himself. The problem was that the opponents were commending themselves, but what people think of themselves is utterly irrelevant. What matters is whether the Lord commends someone.

Why the Corinthians Should Put Up with and Embrace Paul (11:1–6)

Paul implores the hearers in 2 Corinthians 11–12 to put up with his foolishness, and his foolishness shows up in his self-commendation. Paul explains why they should bear with him in such an enterprise; he had their best interests at heart. He burned for their welfare with a divine jealousy, a divine zeal. As the founder of the church, as the evangelist who won the Corinthians to Christ, he had played the role of a matchmaker: he had engaged them to Christ.

Paul desired that they would be a pure virgin on the day of the Lord and would be a worthy bride for Jesus Christ. He feared for the Corinthians' welfare, hoping that they would not be moved off-center from a clear and "pure devotion to Christ" (11:3). The account of Eve being deceived by the serpent in the garden (Gen. 3:1–6, 13) reminds us about the danger of deception, for she was deceived because of the serpent's "cunning." Now the serpent was speaking through the false apostles, trying to lure the Corinthians from their true husband, Jesus Christ. The opponents spoke of Jesus and the gospel and the Spirit, but it was not the same Jesus, the same gospel, and the same Spirit. The Corinthians needed to exercise discernment, for they (at least some of them) had embraced the adversaries' message gladly.

Paul wasn't inferior to the "super-apostles" (2 Cor. 11:5). Scholars debate the identity of the super-apostles. Some think they were the Jerusalem apostles. This interpretation is quite possible, but it is more likely that the super-apostles represent the false teachers. The first mention of them comes immediately after a reference to the unorthodox views being promulgated in Corinth. The term appears again in 12:11, and once again Paul defends his legitimacy in a context where he is engaged in a polemic with false teachers. Another reason for seeing a reference to the agitators is that they are later identified as those who masquerade as apostles (11:13), and this is probably just another way of talking about the super-apostles. From 11:6 it seems that the super-apostles were rhetorically gifted and that they criticized Paul (back to 1 Corinthians again! cf. 1:10–4:21) since he lacked eloquence. Focusing on style, however, is flawed because the issue is substance, and Paul's knowledge is in accord with the gospel.

Finances and Fakes (11:7–15)

In 1 Corinthians 9 Paul's practice of not taking money when in Corinth while he preached the gospel functions as an example for the Corinthians. We have no evidence in 1 Corinthians that the refusal to receive pay was controversial. In fact, Paul uses it as an illustration of not availing oneself of one's rights precisely because it wasn't a matter of dispute. By the time we come to 2 Corinthians, however, the situation had changed. Now the refusal to accept support had become contentious. The opponents probably accused Paul of refusing to take funds because he knew he couldn't get them directly, and thus he was using the collection as a way to siphon off funds for himself and his coworkers (12:16–18). We are reminded of the importance of 8:16–24, where Paul sets forth how the collected funds were being administered and managed so that no one could claim that money was being skimmed off dishonestly.

Some feelings of frustration also bubble over as Paul asks the Corinthians if he sinned by proclaiming the gospel "free of charge" (11:7). He resorts to hyperbole by saying he "robbed other churches" so that he could minister without charging the Corinthians (11:8). It seems that Paul refused to accept financial help when establishing a church, but he did take money for ongoing support after a church was planted, which explains why he accepted contributions from the Macedonians. The situation in Corinth is such, however, that he refused to accept any contributions. The rhetoric is rather astonishing since Paul claims that no one could stop him from boasting about not accepting pay. Still, once one is under suspicion, once one is under attack, everything is interpreted from a skeptical perspective. The Corinthians could engage in comparisons and say that Paul accepted money from the Macedonians but not from them. Why? Because he didn't love them! He loved the Macedonians more! What can one say to such accusations? Paul simply appealed to God himself: God knows that he loved them (11:11).

The key paragraph is 11:12–15, for now Paul explains why he would not receive a contribution from the Corinthians. He didn't receive money from them because of the opponents. By refusing to accept money, it became evident that the super-apostles weren't on the same level as he was. We remember earlier that the false apostles were indicted as those who market God's word (2:17). They engaged in ministry, as so many have all through history, for financial gain. Paul wanted it to be completely clear that he and the opponents were not working together. Indeed, it is clear from 11:13 that they were unbelievers since they were "false apostles, deceitful workers, disguising themselves as apostles of Christ." Indeed, they were satanic, for Satan also appeared as "an angel of light" (11:14). Paul may have in mind Genesis 3, for Satan appeared as a teacher of enlightenment to Eve, promising her that if she ate from the tree of the knowledge of good and evil, she would be like God. In the same way, the false apostles claimed that they were giving instructions in the way of righteousness. In truth, however, their teaching promoted evil, and thus they would be rejected by God on the final day since their works were evil (11:15).

Fool's Speech (11:16–29)

Paul was placed in an awkward position of boasting about himself for the sake of the gospel and for the sake of the Corinthians. He confessed that in doing so, he had become a fool, for no one who is wise would exalt human beings. Nevertheless, boasting was necessary because the false apostles also boasted, and the Corinthians were attracted to them. Paul needed to play their game to awaken those in Corinth who had become dazzled by the pseudo-apostles. The Corinthians were being taken advantage of, and yet they seemed to enjoy it (11:20). We might say they were codependent on the false apostles. They were willing to take directions, to be exploited, taken advantage of, and even struck (the language is probably hyperbolic) by the opponents. We have all seen situations where authoritative people exercise an almost cult-like control over others, using them for their own advantage, and those being exploited happily submit. Paul confesses sarcastically and ironically that he was too weak to act in such a way (11:21). True leaders don't coerce or exploit those who are under their leadership.

Paul listed his qualifications to win the Corinthians' affection. Apparently the opponents boasted about their ethnic credentials as Hebrews, as Israelites, as Abraham's children (11:22). It isn't clear how or whether we should distinguish these three descriptions, but we do see from this that the opponents were Jewish and claimed to have the right genealogy and the right connections. Those in the West might find this argument irrelevant, but in most cultures throughout history, one's lineage plays an important role in determining one's role in society. Paul could match the opponents in every respect, for he shared all the same credentials they had in terms of his ethnic background.

The adversaries claimed to be "servants of Christ" (11:23). Paul protested that he had been drawn into this insane world of comparisons, for it sends all the wrong messages. But if they could match Paul in terms of ethnic credentials, they could not match him as a servant of Christ. We are surprised, however, because Paul doesn't list his signs, wonders, and miracles but his sufferings. He qualified as an apostle because he had suffered, not because he had triumphed. What commends Paul are his labors, his imprisonments, his beatings, and his many near-death experiences. Five different times the Jews gave him thirty-nine lashes (cf. Deut. 25:3), presumably because they judged him to be heretical or in violation of the Mosaic law. Three times he was "beaten with rods" (cf. Acts 16:22–23), and such beatings could be brutal enough to cause death. On one occasion adversaries stoned Paul and left him for dead, but he survived (14:19–20). He was "shipwrecked" three times, and we know from Acts 27, which took place after 2 Corinthians was written, that the number of shipwrecks was at least four. Once Paul was on the sea a night and day before being rescued.

Paul lived a life fraught with danger, being exposed to "rivers," "robbers," Jews, and pagans (2 Cor. 11:26). He faced danger whether he was in the city or in the wilderness, and he often faced the opposition of "false brothers," which includes the opponents in Corinth, of course. Paul labored intensely, was often weary from lack of sleep, faced "hunger and thirst," and was often cold (11:27). Paul's concerns weren't limited to physical deprivation: he also suffered psychologically, feeling constant pressure about the welfare of the churches he established (11:28). His love surfaced in his passion for his converts: he felt the weakness of the weak, and he burned with "indignation" when some fell from the faith (11:29).

Boasting in Weakness (11:30–12:13)

If one has understood the substance of Paul's argument throughout the letter, we aren't surprised that he boasts about his weakness instead of his strength. He recounts his escape from the ruler of Damascus under King Aretas, by being lowered over the city wall (11:32–33). How is this an example of weakness? We need to remember that Paul was an intellectual, a Roman citizen, and he was used to being a respected member of society. Brave warriors scaled city walls to capture cities, but Paul fled from the city like a criminal, like the dregs of society.

Paul continues to think that boasting is necessary for the sake of the Corinthians, though it is spiritually dangerous if anyone begins to admire stories about their own spiritual experiences. Paul proceeds to talk about accounts of "visions and revelations of the Lord" (12:1). The story is told in the third person and recounted in such a way that for a while we don't know as readers that Paul refers to himself. He probably shared the experience in this way to distance himself from the account. Even in telling the story, he didn't want to exalt himself, for he didn't want the readers to be impressed with his spiritual experiences.

The third heaven (12:2) is the same place as paradise (12:4), and Paul was transported there fourteen years earlier. Twice Paul mentions that he didn't know if he was in or out of the body (12:2–3); the experience transcended ordinary human experiences to such a degree that he didn't even know whether the revelation was in his physical body or not. When he was transported, Paul heard "inexpressible words," which no human being can utter. It is difficult to know for sure what Paul means here. Perhaps they could not be spoken because they exceeded human capacity to understand, or perhaps he was forbidden to relay what he saw in paradise. In any case, Paul was reluctant to share the revelation because he feared that people would overestimate him. Still, it was a fact that he had "extraordinary revelations" (12:7), which we would love to know more about as readers, but perhaps in desiring this we fall into the same error as the Corinthians. We want to be dazzled with the amazing, the unusual, the provocative, and to dismiss the ordinary and prosaic.

Paul, however, zeroed in on his weaknesses (12:5) so that people would not think more highly of him than is warranted. He wanted the Corinthians to assess him based on what they actually saw and heard of him in his life. The amazing revelations given to Paul could prompt him to pride, to self-exaltation, and so he was given "a thorn in the flesh" (12:7). The verb is actually passive: the thorn "was given" to him, which means that it was given to him by God. At the same time, we are told that the thorn was a "messenger of

Satan" (12:7). These two ideas are not contradictory but actually fit together. We think of Job 1–2, where Satan brought disaster upon disaster on Job and also struck him with a disease, and yet all that happened to Job represents God's will. The same is true in this instance: Satan's malevolence and agency were a reality in the affliction that Paul experienced. God also permitted and ruled over what happened to Paul. The overarching sovereignty of God doesn't negate Satan's role, showing that reality is thick instead of thin.

All through history people have tried to discern what the thorn in the flesh was, though no consensus has emerged. Some have understood the thorn to be Paul's opponents, who made life so difficult for Paul. It is more likely, however, that the thorn was a physical malady of some kind, for this is the most likely interpretation of the words "in the flesh." We know that Paul suffered from some kind of sickness in Galatia (Gal. 4:13–14). All kinds of guesses have been made, such as malaria, epilepsy, and eye trouble. Whatever the problem, Paul's physical strength was extraordinary, especially when we consider the lashings and beatings mentioned in 2 Corinthians 11. He also traveled an amazing amount, and so the physical problem bedeviled him but did not derail his ministry. From God's perspective, the purpose of the thorn was so that Paul would not "exalt" himself, and thus the thorn kept him humble.

Still, Paul pleaded with the Lord "three times" for the thorn to be removed (12:8), and three times may symbolize a significant period of time. It surely isn't wrong to ask the Lord to remove sufferings and difficulties from us. In this instance, the Lord made it clear to Paul that the answer was "No." Incidentally, the Lord here is Jesus Christ, which shows that Paul prayed to Christ. Some have said that prayers should only be offered to the Father, but the NT doesn't bear out such a dogmatic judgment. Jesus assured Paul that his grace is sufficient, that his "power" would be "perfected in weakness" (12:9). In many ways, this statement summarizes the message of 2 Corinthians and forms a striking contrast to the view of Paul's critics. These opponents looked for glory, power, triumph, success, health, and wealth. Paul's new-covenant ministry, however, reveals the way God works: he grants strength and grace in the midst of weakness. The inadequacy of human beings reveals the adequacy and power of God, and so God receives the glory and praise instead of human beings. Suffering becomes the vehicle by which God's grace manifests itself.

As a result Paul exulted in his weaknesses so that he could experience and display the power of Christ in his life. Such is the character of a new-covenant ministry and life. The super-apostles did not understand and embrace such a perspective, and thus they fostered a distorted gospel, which exalted human beings. Paul's understanding of weakness fits with the message of the cross, for God grants life where there is death. Weaknesses aren't pleasant in and of themselves, and yet Paul embraced them for Christ's sake (12:10). It is important to recognize that weaknesses aren't sins. Paul lists "insults, hardships, persecutions, and . . . difficulties." And we have already seen a reference to sickness; none of these are sins. They are the difficulties of life that oppress and weigh us down. But Paul embraced such hardships, because strength comes through weakness, comfort through suffering, joy through sorrow, and life through death.

Paul's boasting had been forced upon him by the Corinthians (12:11), but he thinks it is a foolish endeavor since it exalts human beings instead of God. The whole enterprise could have been avoided if the Corinthians had commended Paul, but instead they were in danger of being lured away from the gospel by the super-apostles, which explains why Paul had to resort to playing the fool. Paul had to show that his ministry accorded with the gospel rather than the ministry of the super-apostles, but in doing so he ran the danger of exalting himself, which is why he adds, "I am nothing." Still, there was evidence of his apostolic ministry, for it was accredited by "signs and wonders and miracles" (12:12). Paul emphasized his weakness and sickness, but it doesn't follow that there were no displays of power in his ministry. Nevertheless, the ministry isn't fundamentally marked by glory but by weakness. Even signs and wonders are performed by "cracked pots" (cf. 4:7). The Corinthians were apparently feeling injured because Paul took money from other churches but not from them! (12:13). Paul sarcastically says, "Forgive me for this wrong!" Since the charge against Paul was so ridiculous, there was really nothing else to say.

Impending Visit: Call to Repentance (12:14–13:10)

Paul announces his impending third visit, reiterating that he would not burden them financially. He acted the way he did because of a parental affection for the Corinthians, for he didn't desire their things but loved them for Christ's sake. Like most parents, Paul gladly sacrificed himself for the sake of his spiritual children (12:15). The Corinthians should not respond to Paul's love for them by refusing to love him in turn.

The argument turns the corner and most likely stems from certain accusations made by opponents. Paul didn't take any money from them and burden them by asking for support, yet, it was whispered, he was actually playing a savvy game where he got money from them by other means (12:16). Paul confronted the charge head-on. He had already indicated that the collection would be administered by a number of trusted men to preclude any suggestion of financial impropriety (8:16–24). Here he asks whether there is any evidence of corruption. None of those he sent took financial advantage of them; they were all persons of impeccable integrity (12:17). The Corinthians themselves could attest that Titus and the brother he sent with him acted in a godly way.

As Paul draws the letter to a close, he makes one of the most astonishing statements in the entire epistle (12:19). He queries whether they were wondering if the entire letter was written to defend his own integrity and ministry. We might be forgiven for saying "Yes"! Paul replies with one of the most important comments in the letter. He spoke in Christ and in God's sight: he wrote what he did for the edification of the Corinthians. Paul's motive, then, wasn't to defend himself; his apologetic for his ministry in the letter was for the sake of the Corinthians. As Paul anticipated his visit, he was concerned that he might find them to be in significant sin, marked by dissension, quarreling, envy, anger, sinful speech, disorder, and sexual sin (12:20–21). If such things turned out to be true, Paul would be filled with grief and would have to discipline those who failed to repent (cf. 1:23–2:4). The majority had repented (chaps. 1–7), but the fullness and genuineness of that repentance would be measured by their response to the false apostles who were still wielding some influence in the congregation.

If discipline must be administered, no precipitous or rash action should take place. Any charge against a person must be verified with compelling evidence; as the OT says, accusations must be attested "by the testimony of two or three witnesses" (13:1; cf. Num. 35:30; Deut. 17:6; 19:15). Paul feared that the report of his leniency, as spread by some, would be misunderstood; upon arriving, he would discipline if needed, and thus he warns them in advance so that problems will be resolved before he came (2 Cor. 13:2). Some of the Corinthians apparently wanted evidence of Christ's power in Paul by seeing him come with authority! As usual in the letter, he tied his message and ministry to Jesus Christ. Christ was "not weak" with them but "powerful among" them (13:3). Still, his power should not be misconceived because "he was crucified in weakness" (13:4). We return again to the message of 1 Corinthians (as in 1:18): "The word of the cross is foolishness" to the world since the salvation of the world comes through a crucified man. No power and glory here! But weakness wasn't the end of the story, for Christ also "lives by the power of God" (2 Cor. 13:4). He is both crucified and risen. First comes suffering, but then comes glory and power and splendor. The opponents wanted splendor, glory, and power now, and they failed to see the sequence. Paul's weakness, which has been a central theme in the letter, is a corollary of Christ's weakness; the servant is like his master. The weakness characterizing Paul's ministry and life is one indication that he belonged to God. Still, Paul's weakness isn't the only dimension of his ministry. Since Paul belonged to Christ, he was also strong in him, and he would exercise that strength in discipline if necessary when he arrived for a third visit.

Paul challenged the Corinthians, then, to test and "examine yourselves" to determine whether they were "in the faith" (13:5). If they sided with the pseudo-apostles (11:13–15), then they were certainly not part of the people of God. If Jesus Christ truly indwelt them, they were believers (cf. Rom. 8:9–10). The divisions among them indicate who among them is truly "approved" (*dokimoi*), truly saved (1 Cor. 11:19). Those who "fail the test" (*adokimoi*) are the "unapproved," those who are disqualified from receiving the prize (cf. 1 Cor. 9:24–27).

Paul hopes that the Corinthians recognized that he didn't "fail the test," that he wasn't unapproved or disqualified (*adokimoi*, 2 Cor. 13:6). In the letter we have seen that Paul's ministry was linked with the Corinthians' own standing with God, and thus Paul's hope here wasn't trivial. If they thought that Paul didn't belong to God, it called into serious question their own relationship with God. The same is true today, incidentally. If someone thinks their understanding is better than that of the apostles, they raise serious questions about their own claim to be believers.

When Paul says he prayed that the Corinthians would not do anything evil (13:7), this isn't just a general maxim. In context it has to do with the matter before them. He prays that they won't side with the masquerading apostles, with the false teachers who were undercutting Paul. Paul's fundamental concern wasn't that the Corinthians believe that he has "[passed] the test," as if his approval was his paramount concern (*dokimos*). He would be quite happy if the Corinthians did what was right in the whole matter, even if they thought he "failed" (*adokimos*). Unfortunately, it wasn't that simple. If they rejected Paul's ministry, if they believed Paul was disqualified as an apostle, it impinged on their own salvation, and we are back to why Paul had to defend himself so passionately in the letter.

Finally, Paul could not "do anything against the truth, but only for the truth" (13:8). This general maxim could be taken out of context, for there are certainly contexts in which people say and do things that hinder the truth. Paul is thinking ultimately, however, and from the perspective of God's sovereignty. No one can thwart God's intentions, for they will certainly be realized. As Jesus taught, the "gates of Hades will not overpower" the church (Matt. 16:18). Still, human beings have the privilege of supporting and extending the truth. Like Paul, God may give human beings the role of conveying the truth of the gospel to others. In 2 Corinthians 13:9 Paul returns to his favorite theme in the letter, one that we find at the outset of the epistle, where he informs the readers that his sufferings were for their comfort (1:3–7). Here he rejoices when he is "weak" but they are "strong." Such a theme is the heart and soul of a new-covenant ministry, as we have seen, and it is the burden of Paul's fool's speech in chapters 11–12. Most important, it reflects the heart of the gospel, for Jesus was weak as the crucified one but gives strength to his people as the risen Lord. Paul prays, then, that the Corinthians will fully appropriate the message he has shared and "become fully mature."

In 13:10 we again see the main purpose of the letter. He wrote while absent so that when he came to them, he would not need to use his authority to discipline them for departing from the gospel, which would manifest itself especially if they sided with the false apostles. Paul picks up again what he said in 10:8, alluding again to Jeremiah 1:10 (cf. 24:6), saying that the Lord gave him authority "for building up and not for tearing down." Salvation and not discipline is the heart of a new-covenant ministry. Paul's ministry wasn't like Jeremiah's, which focused mainly on judgment. The minister of the new covenant edifies and builds the church, though there are occasions where discipline is necessary.

Final Words (13:11–13)

The closing of the letter is remarkably brief, but it captures some of the central concerns of the letter. Five exhortations are in 2 Corinthians 13:11. The Corinthians are summoned to rejoice. The verb "become mature" (*katartizesthe*) comes from the same root as the noun in 13:9, where Paul prays that they will "become fully mature" (*katartisin*). What Paul prays for he also exhorts the Corinthians to realize in their lives. They will be mature and restored if they say no to the false teachers and embrace Paul and his gospel. They were on the road to doing so, and Paul encouraged them to take the final steps. The next three commands focus on unity: they are to "be encouraged, be of the same mind, be at peace." The church has been divided in the past (as in 1 Corinthians), and those divisions still exist, as the presence of the false apostles proves. Paul exhorts them to be unified in the gospel. If they act rightly, "the God of love and peace will be with you." This is the only place where Paul adds love to the attribution that God is a God of peace. Both love and peace come from God, and Paul's desire is to see such love and peace flourish in the congregation.

The theme of unity continues since believers as family members are to "greet one another with a holy kiss" (2 Cor. 13:12). This is the only occasion where Paul says that all the believers with him send greetings, and this fits with the reference to other believers in 1:1 and in 1 Corinthians 1:2 as well.

Paul reminds the Corinthians once again that they were not the only believers in the world. There was a worldwide church that transcended Corinth.

The letter concludes with one of the most beautiful benedictions in the Scriptures (2 Cor. 13:13). How is the church going to unify? How will they repudiate the false teachers and embrace Paul and his gospel? They need the grace that comes from the Lord Jesus Christ, the love that comes from God, and the fellowship that they enjoy with the Holy Spirit. In other words, they need divine strength in their weakness to carry out what they are instructed to do. The order reflects the experience of believers. First, they receive Christ's grace, and as a result they enjoy the love of God and fellowship with the Spirit. The trinitarian character of the statement is quite striking as well. The Corinthians were weak in themselves, but the Son, the Father, and the Spirit can and will give them strength.

2 Corinthians: Commentaries

Barnett, Paul. *The Second Epistle to the Corinthians*. NICNT. Grand Rapids: Eerdmans, 2008.

Barrett, Charles K. *The Second Epistle to the Corinthians*. BNTC. London: Black. Reprinted, Peabody, MA: Hendrickson, 1973.

Belleville, Linda L. *2 Corinthians*. IVPNTC. Downers Grove, IL: InterVarsity, 1996.

Best, E. *Second Corinthians*. Interpretation. Atlanta: John Knox, 1987.

Bray, Gerald. *1–2 Corinthians*. ACCS 7 (NT). Downers Grove, IL: InterVarsity, 1999.

Bruce, F. F. *1 and 2 Corinthians*. Greenwood, SC: Attic Press, 1971.

Calvin, John. *The Second Epistle of Paul the Apostle to the Corinthians and the Epistles to Timothy, Titus and Philemon*. Calvin's Commentaries 10. Edinburgh: Oliver & Boyd, 1964.

Danker, F. W. *II Corinthians*. Minneapolis: Augsburg Fortress, 1989.

Furnish, Victor P. *II Corinthians: A New Translation with Introduction and Commentary*. AB. Garden City, NY: Doubleday, 1984.

Garland, David E. *2 Corinthians*. NAC 29. Nashville: Broadman & Holman, 1999.

Guthrie, George H. *2 Corinthians*. BECNT. Grand Rapids: Baker Academic, 2015.

Hafemann, Scott J. *2 Corinthians*. NIV Application Commentary. Grand Rapids: Zondervan, 2000.

Hanson, R. P. C. *The Second Epistle to the Corinthians: Introduction and Commentary*. Torch Bible Commentaries. London: SCM, 1961.

Harris, Murray J. "2 Corinthians." In *Romans–Galatians*, vol. 11 of *The Expositor's Bible Commentary*, rev. ed., edited by Tremper Longman III and David E. Garland, 415–545. Grand Rapids: Zondervan, 2008.

———. *The Second Epistle to the Corinthians: A Commentary on the Greek Text*. NIGTC. Grand Rapids: Eerdmans, 2005.

Hodge, Charles. *Commentary on the Second Epistle to the Corinthians*. Grand Rapids: Eerdmans, 1994.

Hughes, P. E. *Paul's Second Epistle to the Corinthians: The English Text with Introduction, Exposition and Notes*. NICNT. Grand Rapids: Eerdmans, 1962.

Keener, Craig. S. *1–2 Corinthians*. NCBC. Cambridge: Cambridge University Press, 2005.

Kruse, Colin G. *The Second Epistle of Paul to the Corinthians: An Introduction and Commentary*. TNTC. Leicester, UK: Inter-Varsity, 1987.

Lambrecht, Jan. *Second Corinthians*. SP. Collegeville, MN: Liturgical Press, 1999.

Martin, Ralph P. *2 Corinthians*. WBC. Waco: Word, 1986.

Matera, Frank J. *II Corinthians: A Commentary*. NTL. Louisville: Westminster John Knox, 2003.

McCant, Jerry W. *2 Corinthians*. Readings: A New Biblical Commentary. Sheffield: Sheffield Academic, 1999.

Plummer, A. *A Critical and Exegetical Commentary on the Second Epistle of St. Paul to the Corinthians*. ICC. Edinburgh: T&T Clark, 1915.

Roetzel, Calvin J. *2 Corinthians*. ANTC. Nashville: Abingdon, 2007.

Scott, J. M. *2 Corinthians*. NIBC. Peabody, MA: Hendrickson, 1998.

Stegman, T. J. *Second Corinthians*. CCSS. Grand Rapids: Baker Academic, 2007.

Talbert, C. H. *Reading Corinthians: A Literary and Theological Commentary*. Macon, GA: Smyth & Helwys, 2002.

Thrall, Margaret E. *A Critical and Exegetical Commentary on the Second Epistle to the Corinthians*. Vol. 1, *Introduction and Commentary on II Corinthians I–VII*. ICC. Edinburgh: T&T Clark, 2000.

———. *A Critical and Exegetical Commentary on the Second Epistle to the Corinthians*. Vol. 2, *Commentary on II Corinthians VIII–XIII*. ICC. London: T&T Clark, 2000.

Witherington, Ben, III. *Conflict and Community in Corinth: A Socio-Rhetorical Commentary on 1 and 2 Corinthians*. Grand Rapids: Eerdmans, 1995.

2 Corinthians: Articles, Essays, and Monographs

Adewuya, J. A. *Holiness and Community in 2 Cor 6:14–7:1: Paul's View of Communal Holiness in the Corinthian Correspondence*. Studies in Biblical Literature 40. New York: Lang, 2003.

Amador, J. D. H. "Revisiting 2 Corinthians: Rhetoric and the Case for Unity." *NTS* 46 (2000): 92–111.

Andrews, S. B. "Too Weak Not to Lead: The Form and Function of 2 Cor 11:23b–33." *NTS* 41 (1995): 263–76.

Baird, W. R., Jr. "Letters of Recommendation: A Study of II Cor. 3:1–3." *JBL* 80 (1961): 166–72.

Baker, W. R. "Did the Glory of Moses' Face Fade? A Reexamination of *Katargeō* in 2 Corinthians 3:7–18." *BBR* 10 (2000): 1–15.

Barrett, Charles K. "Paul's Opponents in II Corinthians." *NTS* 17 (1971): 233–54.

Beale, G. K. "The Old Testament Background of Reconciliation in 2 Corinthians 5–7 and Its Bearing on the Literary Problem of 2 Corinthians 6.14–7.1." *NTS* 35 (1989): 550–81.

Becker, E. M. *Letter Hermeneutics in 2 Corinthians.* Edinburgh: T&T Clark, 2004.

Belleville, Linda L. "A Letter of Apologetic Self-Commendation: 2 Cor. 1:8–7:16." *NovT* 31 (1989): 142–63.

———. *Reflections of Glory: Paul's Polemical Use of the Moses-Doxa Tradition in 2 Corinthians 3.1–18.* JSNTSup 52. Sheffield: JSOT Press, 1991.

Betz, Hans Dieter. "2 Cor 6:14–7:1: An Anti-Pauline Fragment?" *JBL* 92 (1973): 88–108.

Betz, Hans Dieter, and G. W. MacRae. *2 Corinthians 8 and 9: A Commentary on Two Administrative Letters of the Apostle Paul.* Hermeneia. Philadelphia: Fortress, 1985.

Bieringer, R. *The Corinthian Correspondence.* BETL 125. Leuven: Leuven University Press/Peeters, 1996.

Bieringer, R., and Jan Lambrecht. *Studies on 2 Corinthians.* BETL 112. Leuven: Leuven University Press/Peeters, 1994.

Blomberg, Craig. "The Structure of 2 Corinthians 1–7." *CTR* 4 (1989): 3–20.

Boers, Hendrikus. "2 Corinthians 5:14–6:2: A Fragment of Pauline Christology." *CBQ* 64 (2002): 527–47.

Bowens, Lisa M. *An Apostle in Battle: Paul and Spiritual Warfare in 2 Corinthians 12:1–10.* WUNT 2/433. Tübingen: Mohr Siebeck, 2017.

Dahl, Nils. "A Fragment in Its Context: 2 Corinthians 6:14–7:1." In *Studies in Paul: Theology for the Early Christian Mission,* 62–69. Minneapolis: Augsburg, 1972.

Dalton, W. J. "Is the Old Covenant Abrogated (2 Cor. 3.14)?" *ABR* 35 (1987): 88–94.

Danker, F. W. "2 Corinthians." *JBL* 107 (1988): 550–53.

Derrett, J. "2 Cor. 6:14: A Midrash on Dt 22:10." *Bib* 59 (1978): 231–50.

Dewey, A. "A Matter of Honor: A Social-Historical Analysis of 2 Corinthians 10." *HTR* 78 (1985): 209–17.

Duff, P. B. "Glory in the Ministry of Death: Gentile Condemnation and Letters of Recommendation in 2 Cor 3:6–18." *NovT* 46 (2004): 313–37.

———. "Metaphor, Motif, and Meaning: The Rhetorical Strategy behind the Image 'Led in Triumph' in 2 Corinthians 2:14." *CBQ* 53 (1991): 79–92.

Dumbrell, W. J. "The Newness of the New Covenant: The Logic of the Argument in 2 Corinthians 3." *RTR* 61 (2002): 61–84.

———. "Paul's Use of Exodus 34 in 2 Corinthians 3." In *God Who Is Rich in Mercy: Essays Presented to Dr. D. B. Knox,* edited by P. T. O'Brien and D. Peterson, 179–94. Homebush, Australia: Lancer Books, 1986.

Dunn, James D. G. "2 Corinthians 3:17: The Lord Is the Spirit." *JTS* 21 (1970): 309–20.

Fee, Gordon D. "Χάρις in II Corinthians 1:15: Apostolic Parousia and Paul-Corinth Chronology." *NTS* 24 (1978): 533–38.

Fitzgerald, J. T. *Cracks in an Earthen Vessel: An Examination of the Catalogues of Hardships in the Corinthian Correspondence.* SBLDS 99. Atlanta: Scholars Press, 1988.

Fitzmyer, Joseph A. "Glory Reflected on the Face of Christ (2 Cor 3:7–4:6) and a Palestinian Jewish Motif." *Theological Studies* 42 (1981): 630–44.

———. "Qumran and the Interpolated Paragraph in 2 Cor 6:14–7:1." *CBQ* 23 (1961): 271–80.

Fredrickson, D. E. "Paul's Sentence of Death (2 Corinthians 1:9)." *Word and World* 4 (2000): 99–107.

Garland, David E. "Paul's Apostolic Authority: The Power of Christ Sustaining Weakness (2 Corinthians 10–13)." *RevExp* 86 (1989): 371–89.

Garrett, Duane A. "Veiled Hearts: The Translation and Interpretation of 2 Corinthians 3." *JETS* 53 (2010): 729–72.

Gignilliat, Mark S. *Paul and Isaiah's Servants: Paul's Theological Reading of Isaiah 40–66 in 2 Corinthians 5:14–6:10*. London: T&T Clark, 2007.

Goulder, M. D. "2 Cor. 6:14–7:1 as an Integral Part of 2 Corinthians." *NovT* 36 (1994): 47–57.

Guthrie, George H. "Paul's Triumphal Procession Imagery (2 Cor 2.14–16a): Neglected Points of Background." *NTS* 61 (2015): 79–91.

Hafemann, Scott J. "Adam Christology as the Exegetical and Theological Substructure of 2 Corinthians 4:7–5:21." *JBL* 113 (1994): 346–49.

———. "The Glory and Veil of Moses in 2 Cor. 3:7–14: An Example of Paul's Contextual Exegesis of the OT—A Proposal." *HBT* 14 (1992): 31–49.

———. *Paul, Moses, and the History of Israel: The Letter/Spirit Contrast and the Argument from Scripture in 2 Corinthians 3*. WUNT 81. Tübingen: Mohr Siebeck, 1995.

———. "Paul's Argument from the Old Testament and Christology in 2 Cor. 1–9: The Salvation-History/Restoration Structure of Paul's Apologetic." In *The Corinthian Correspondence*, edited by R. Bieringer, 277–303. BETL 125. Leuven: Leuven University Press/Peeters, 1996.

———. "'Self-Commendation' and Apostolic Legitimacy in 2 Corinthians: A Pauline Dialectic?" *NTS* 36 (1990): 66–88.

———. *Suffering and Ministry in the Spirit: Paul's Defense of His Ministry in II Corinthians 2:14–3:3*. Grand Rapids: Eerdmans, 1990.

———. *Suffering and the Spirit: An Exegetical Study of 2 Cor. 2:14–3:3 within the Context of the Corinthian Correspondence*. WUNT 2/19. Tübingen: Mohr Siebeck, 1986.

Hall, D. R. *The Unity of the Corinthian Correspondence*. London: T&T Clark, 2003.

Hanson, A. T. "The Midrash in 2 Corinthians 3: A Reconsideration." *JSNT* 9 (1980): 2–28.

Harvey, A. E. *Renewal through Suffering: A Study of 2 Corinthians*. SNTW. Edinburgh: T&T Clark, 1996.

Hemer, Colin J. "A Note on 2 Corinthians 1:9." *TynBul* 23 (1972): 103–7.

Hock, Ronald F. *The Social Context of Paul's Ministry*. Philadelphia: Fortress, 1980.

Hood, J. B. "The Temple and the Thorn: 2 Corinthians 12 and Paul's Heavenly Ecclesiology." *BBR* 21 (2011): 357–70.

Hooker, Morna D. "On Becoming the Righteousness of God: Another Look at 2 Cor. 5:21." *NovT* 50 (2008): 358–75.

Hubbard, Moyer V. *New Creation in Paul's Letters and Thoughts*. SNTSMS 119. Cambridge: Cambridge University Press, 2002.

———. "Was Paul Out of His Mind? Re-reading 2 Corinthians 5.13." *JSNT* 70 (1998): 39–64.

Kim, Seyoon. *The Origin of Paul's Gospel*. 2nd ed. WUNT 4. Tübingen: Mohr Siebeck, 1984.

———. "2 Cor. 5:11–21 and the Origin of Paul's Concept of 'Reconciliation.'" *NovT* 39 (1997): 360–84.

Lambrecht, Jan. "Dangerous Boasting: Paul's Self-Commendation in 2 Corinthians 10–13." In *The Corinthian Correspondence*, edited by R. Bieringer, 325–46. Leuven: Leuven University Press, 1996.

———. "Structure and Line of Thought in 2 Cor 2: 14–4:6." In *Studies on 2 Corinthians*, edited by R. Bieringer and J. Lambrecht, 257–94. Leuven: Leuven University Press, 1984.

———. "Transformation in 2 Cor 3:18." *Bib* 64 (1983): 243–54.

Lincoln, A. T. "Paul the Visionary: The Setting and Significance of the Rapture to Paradise in II Corinthians 12:1–10." *NTS* 25 (1979): 204–20.

Long, Frederick J. *Ancient Rhetoric and Paul's Apology: The Compositional Unity of 2 Corinthians*. SNTSMS 131. Cambridge: Cambridge University Press, 2004.

Longenecker, Bruce W. *Remember the Poor: Paul, Poverty, and the Greco-Roman World*. Grand Rapids: Eerdmans, 2010.

Marshall, Peter. *Enmity in Corinth: Social Conventions in Paul's Relations with the Corinthians*. WUNT 23. Tübingen: Mohr Siebeck, 1987.

———. "A Metaphor of Social Shame: *Thriambeuein* in 2 Cor 2:14." *NovT* 25 (1983): 302–17.

Morray-Jones, C. R. A. "Paradise Revisited (2 Cor 12:1–12): The Jewish Mystical Background of Paul's Apostolate." *HTR* 86 (1993): 265–92.

Murphy-O'Connor, Jerome. "The Date of 2 Corinthians 10–13." *ABR* 39 (1991): 31–43.

———. *Keys to Second Corinthians: Revisiting the Major Issues*. Oxford: Oxford University Press, 2010.

———. "Paul and Macedonia: The Connection between 2 Corinthians 2:13 and 2:14." *JSNT* 25 (1985): 99–103.

———. *St. Paul's Corinth: Texts and Archaeology*. Good News Studies 6. Wilmington, DE: Michael Glazier, 1983.

———. *The Theology of the Second Letter to the Corinthians*. Cambridge: Cambridge University Press, 1991.

Neyrey, J. H. "Paul's Use of Ethos, Pathos, and Logos in 2 Corinthians 10–13." *CBQ* 59 (1997): 375–76.

O'Collins, G. G. "Power Made Perfect in Weakness: 2 Cor 12:9–10." *CBQ* 33 (1971): 528–37.

Park, D. M. "Paul's Σκόλοψ τῇ Σαρκί: Thorn or Stake? (2 Cor. XII 7)." *NovT* 22 (1980): 179–83.

Pate, C. M. *Adam Christology as the Exegetical and Theological Substructure of 2 Corinthians 4:7–5:21*. Lanham, MD: University Press of America, 1991.

Philpot, Josh M. "Exodus 34:29–35 and Moses' Shining Face." *BBR* 23 (2013): 1–11.

Price, R. M. "Punished in Paradise (An Exegetical Theory on 2 Corinthians 12:1–10)." *JSNT* 7 (1980): 33–40.

Riesner, Rainer. *Paul's Early Period: Chronology, Mission Strategy, Ideology*. Grand Rapids: Eerdmans, 1998.

Sampley, J. P. "Paul, His Opponents in 2 Corinthians 10–13, and the Rhetorical Handbooks." In *The Social World of Formative Christianity and Judaism: Essays in Tribute to Howard Clark Kee*, edited by J. Neusner, 162–77. Philadelphia: Fortress, 1988.

Savage, T. B. *Power through Weakness: Paul's Understanding of the Christian Ministry in 2 Corinthians*. SNTSMS 86. Cambridge: Cambridge University Press, 1996.

Schmeller, T. "No Bridge over Troubled Water? The Gap between 2 Corinthians 1–9 and 10–13." *JSNT* 36 (2013): 73–84.

Scott, J. M. "The Triumph of God in 2 Cor 2.14: Additional Evidence of Merkabah Mysticism in Paul." *NTS* 42 (1996): 260–81.

Stegman, T. D. "Ἐπίστευσα, διὸ ἐλάλησα (2 Corinthians 4:13): Paul's Christological Reading of Psalm 115:1a LXX." *CBQ* 69 (2007): 725–45.

Stockhausen, Carol K. *Moses' Veil and the Glory of the New Covenant: The Exegetical Substructure of II Cor. 3,1–4, 6*. AnBib 116. Rome: Pontifical Biblical Institute, 1989.

Stowers, Stanley K. "*Peri Men Gar* and the Integrity of 2 Cor. 8 and 9." *NovT* 32 (1990): 340–48.

Sumney, Jerry. *Identifying Paul's Opponents: The Question of Method in 2 Corinthians*. JSNTSup 40. Sheffield: JSOT Press, 1990.

Thierry, J. J. "Der Dorn im Fleische (2 Kor. 12:7–9)." *NovT* 5 (1962): 301–10.

Thrall, Margaret E. "The Problem of II Cor 6:14–7:1 in Some Recent Discussion." *NTS* 24 (1977): 132–48.

———. "'Putting On' or 'Stripping Off' in 2 Corinthians 5:3." In *New Testament Textual Criticism: Its Significance for Exegesis; Essays in Honor of Bruce M. Metzger*, edited by E. J. Epp and G. D. Fee, 221–37. Oxford: Clarendon, 1981.

———. "2 Corinthians 1:12: ΑΥΙΟΤΗΤΙ or ΑΠΛΟΤΗΤΙ." In *Studies in New Testament Language and Text: Essays in Honour of George D. Kilpatrick on the Occasion of His Sixty-Fifth Birthday*, edited by F. S. Kilpatrick, 366–72. NovTSup 44. Leiden: Brill, 1976.

———. "A Second Thanksgiving Period in II Corinthians." *JSNT* 16 (1982): 101–24.

Unnik, W. C. van. "With Unveiled Face: An Exegesis of 2 Corinthians 3:12–18." *NovT* 6 (1963): 153–69.

Vegge, Ivar. *2 Corinthians: A Letter about Reconciliation*. WUNT 2/239. Tübingen: Mohr Siebeck, 2008.

Walker, D. D. *Paul's Offer of Leniency (2 Cor. 10,1): Populist Ideology and Rhetoric in a Pauline Letter Fragment*. WUNT 2/152. Tübingen: Mohr Siebeck, 2002.

Wallace, J. B. *Snatched into Paradise (2 Cor. 12:1–10): Paul's Heavenly Journey in the Context of Early Christian Experience*. BZNW 179. Berlin: de Gruyter, 2011.

Wanamaker, Charles A. "'By the Power of God': Rhetoric and Ideology in 2 Corinthians 10–13." In *Fabrics of Discourse: Essays in Honor of Vernon K. Robbins*, edited by D. B. Gowler, L. G. Bloomquist, and D. F. Watson, 194–221. Harrisburg, PA: Trinity Press International, 2003.

Watson, Francis. "2 Cor. 10–13 and Paul's Painful Letter to the Corinthians." *JTS* 35, no. 2 (October 1984): 324–46.

Webb, William J. *Returning Home: New Covenant and Second Exodus as the Context for 2 Corinthians 6.14–7.1*. JSNTSup 85. Sheffield: Sheffield Academic, 1993.

Weima, Jeffrey A. D. "Neglected Endings: The Significance of the Pauline Letter Closings." JSNTSup 101. Sheffield: JSOT Press, 1994.

Welborn, L. L. "The Dangerous Double Affirmation: Character and Truth in 2 Cor 1,17." *ZNW* 86 (1995): 34–52.

———. "The Identification of 2 Corinthians 10–13 with the 'Letter of Tears.'" *NovT* 37 (1995): 138–53.

———. "Like Broken Pieces of a Ring: 2 Cor 1.1–2.13; 7.5–16 and Ancient Theories of Literary Unity." *NTS* 42 (1996): 559–83.

———. "Paul's Appeal to the Emotions in 2 Corinthians 1.1–2.13; 7.5–16." *JSNT* 82 (2001): 31–60.

———. "Paul's Caricature of His Chief Rival as a Pompous Parasite in 2 Corinthians 11.20." *JSNT* 32 (2009): 39–56.

Wenham, David. "2 Corinthians 1:17, 18: Echo of a Dominical Logion." *NovT* 28 (1986): 271–79.

Wilson, Jim. "The Old Testament Sacrificial Context of 2 Corinthians 8–9." *BBR* 27 (2017): 361–78.

Young, Frances M., and David Ford. *Meaning and Truth in 2 Corinthians*. Grand Rapids: Eerdmans, 1998.

CHAPTER FIVE

Galatians

Introduction

We begin Galatians with some tables for historical purposes. The dates are disputed, but they are relatively close. Some of the dates reflect more controversial historical judgments, such as when Paul was converted and when Galatians was written. The time line assumes that Paul wrote to the south Galatian churches, which Paul evangelized in Acts 13–14, instead of the north Galatian churches. The matter is intensely debated, but it actually doesn't make a great difference, fortunately, for interpreting Galatians. Resolving the destination of the letter has more to do with Pauline chronology and history, which is an important matter in its own right. One advantage, if the south Galatian hypothesis is on target, is that we have a record of the evangelization of the churches in Acts 13–14. If Paul wrote to north Galatia, we don't have a record of his proclaiming the gospel to them.

Galatians Time Line

31/32	Paul's conversion
33/34	First visit to Jerusalem (Gal. 1:18; Acts 9:26–29)
44–46	Fourteen years after conversion (Gal. 2:1; Acts 11:29–30)
47/48	Paul evangelized south Galatia (Acts 13–14)
48	Paul writes the letter to the Galatians
48/49	Jerusalem council (Acts 15)

Paul's Visits to Jerusalem

Galatians	Acts
1:15–17—Paul's conversion	9:1–19—Paul's conversion
1:18—First visit to Jerusalem, 3 years after conversion	9:26–30—In Jerusalem with Barnabas
2:1–10—Fourteen years after conversion—meets pillars	11:27–30—Famine relief visit to Jerusalem
2:11–14—Dispute in Antioch	
Paul writes Galatians	
	15:1–29—Jerusalem council

The situation that precipitated the letter should be sketched in briefly. Scholars propose many different theories about the opponents in the letter and the theology they propounded. I think it is fair to say that the mirror reading proposed here has been the majority view, but readers should consult commentaries for other reconstructions.

From the outset of the letter it is clear that the Galatians were straying from Christ's grace "to a different gospel" (1:6). What caused their defection? Some persons were disturbing and troubling the Galatians and distorting the gospel (1:7; 5:11; 6:12–13). It seems likely that these individuals or "agitators" came from the outside, and perhaps even from Jerusalem. Some think they are the same group who came to Antioch. "Some men came down from Judea and began to teach the brothers: 'Unless you are circumcised according to the custom prescribed by Moses, you cannot be saved'" (Acts 15:1). They may be the same group, but it is impossible to know for certain. They clearly held the same theology.

What was the message of the false teachers who arrived in Galatia? We have seen a hint from the men who came down from Jerusalem to Antioch and argued that gentiles must be circumcised and observe the law of Moses to be saved. The adversaries have often and rightly been identified as "Judaizers," which means that one must adopt the Jewish way of life according to the OT: the term points to their belief that one must observe the OT law to be saved. From Galatians 6:12–13 we see that they were trying to coerce the Galatian gentiles to be circumcised. We understand, then, why Paul warns against accepting circumcision in incredibly strong terms in 5:2–4. A story about false brothers in Jerusalem who wanted to compel Titus to be circumcised is relayed in 2:3–5, and clearly Paul tells the story because the opponents in Galatia wanted to impose the same regimen upon the gentiles whom Paul evangelized.

The Judaizers almost certainly appealed to Genesis 17:9–14 in demanding circumcision. The covenant, which was to be in force for all generations, required circumcision. The covenant wasn't just for Abraham but was for "your offspring after you" (17:10). And there were no exceptions: "Every one of your males must be circumcised" (Gen. 17:10; cf. 17:12). Spiritual circumcision alone isn't sufficient, for they "must circumcise the flesh of your foreskin" (17:11). It is "the sign of the covenant" (17:11), and the "covenant . . . in your flesh" was "a permanent covenant" (17:13). Those who refuse circumcision "will be cut off from his people," and they have "broken my covenant" (17:14). We can see from Genesis 17:9–14 why the Judaizers troubled the Galatians. They pointed to the OT and said that one must be circumcised to belong to the covenant people of God. If the gentile Galatians refused circumcision, they could not belong to God's covenant people.

The focus on the OT law is also evident in Galatians 2:11–14, where Peter initially ate foods with gentiles that were prohibited by the OT law, but he turned back from eating with gentiles when the men from James arrived. Apparently the Galatians were also beginning to observe feasts, festivals, and days from the OT calendar (4:10). Claiming that the issue was obedience to the law fits with the six references to "the works of the law" (2:16 [3×]; 3:2, 5, 10), and the more than twenty references to the Mosaic law in the rest of the letter. Since Paul taught that believers weren't under the law and didn't have to be circumcised, the adversaries probably argued that Paul wasn't a true apostle and that he proclaimed freedom from the law out of a desire to please people. Thus Paul defends his apostleship in Galatians 1–2.

One outline of Galatians, overly simplistic yet helpful for getting a handle on the letter as a whole, can be presented as follows.

Outline

Defense of Paul's apostleship	1:1–2:21
Defense of Paul's gospel	3:1–4:31
Application of the gospel to everyday life	5:1–6:18

Another rough outline follows:

The independence of Paul's gospel	1:1–24
The confirmation of Paul's gospel	2:1–14
The summary of Paul's gospel	2:15–21
The explication of Paul's gospel	3:1–4:11
The response to Paul's gospel	4:12–6:10
Final summary of Paul's gospel	6:11–18

Introduction (1:1–10)

The greeting in the letter is actually quite long by Pauline standards (1:1–5), and we want to spy out particularly what stands out in the greeting. Paul asserts his apostleship, but he is immediately on the defensive, saying his apostleship was "not from men or by man" (1:1). The defensive reaction is unique, suggesting that Paul responds to opponents who disputed his apostleship, and this suspicion is borne out by the discussion that ensues in the remainder of chapters 1–2. We should also mention here the reference to "all the brothers" present with Paul (1:2) and ask why they are included in the greeting. Paul probably brings them up to demonstrate that those who were with Paul agreed with the Pauline gospel. Paul's gospel wasn't the minority view: it was the view espoused by the worldwide church, and it was the Galatians who were getting offtrack.

The other striking feature in the greeting is its eschatological dimension. Paul doesn't typically bring up Christ's resurrection in the greeting, but he mentions it in the first verse of the letter (1:1). The resurrection signals the arrival of the age to come, the coming of the new creation (Isa. 25:7–8; 26:19; Ezek. 37:12–13; Dan. 12:2–3). In other words, the promises made to the patriarchs are being fulfilled in the new era. The confession-sounding statement in Galatians 1:4 has the same significance: Christ "gave himself for our sins to rescue us from this present evil age." We see another eschatological reference here. If we put the two statements together, the cross and the resurrection have rescued believers from the old age and transferred them to the new age. We could say that in the forgiveness of sins, the exile is over. Here is the crucial point: if the new age has arrived, circumcision is no longer necessary, for circumcision belonged to the old age, to the old creation, and the old covenant. Now that the new age, the new creation, the new covenant, and the new exodus have come, believers are free from circumcision and other national particulars of the Mosaic law. Paul will explain how this is so in the remainder of the letter, but he has set up the whole discussion in the greeting.

The greeting in Paul is typically followed by a thanksgiving, but not in Galatians, for Paul apparently wasn't very thankful! Instead of a thanksgiving, we have a rebuke statement. He is astonished that they have so quickly defected from the true gospel to another gospel (1:6). We have an allusion to the golden-calf episode in Israel's history, where Israel entered into covenant with the Lord and "quickly turned from the way [the Lord] commanded them" (Exod. 32:8). The ink, so to speak, was hardly dry on the covenant documents when Israel sinned. Paul sees the Galatians moving in a similar direction in shifting away from the gospel so soon after their conversion.

In the most uncompromising terms, Paul also insists that there is no other gospel, that the alternative gospel that the Galatians were embracing was no gospel at all. To avoid any misunderstanding, Paul declares that even if he or an angel were to proclaim a variant gospel, they would be cursed (Gal. 1:8; cf.

Rom. 9:3; 1 Cor. 16:22). The word for "cursed" has its roots in the OT word "destruction" (*herem*), which refers to something devoted to God (e.g., Lev. 27:28–29; Num. 18:14; Deut. 7:26), and Paul draws upon OT contexts where the term means destruction (Exod. 22:20; Num. 21:2–3; Josh. 6:17). Nor are there any defects in the gospel the Galatians received; if they give heed to any other gospel, they will be cursed. The curse stands here for final destruction, eschatological judgment. In Paul's eyes the message proclaimed by the troublemakers wasn't just slightly off-center: it was an entirely different gospel. Galatians 1:10 is a transitional verse, fitting with both this section and the section that follows. Paul disavows the notion that he left out difficult commands (like circumcision) just because he wanted to please people.

Paul's Independent Gospel (1:11–24)

Starting in 1:11 Paul explains why he was a servant of Christ, why he wasn't a people-pleaser. The good news he proclaimed, the gospel he preached, did not come from human beings. Paul didn't receive the gospel from anyone else, nor was he taught it. The gospel was disclosed to him independently on the road to Damascus when Jesus Christ appeared to him (1:12; cf. Acts 9:1–19).

In Galatians 1:13–14 Paul explains that his desire to proclaim the gospel of Jesus Christ did not originate with him, rehearsing here his "former way of life in Judaism" (1:13), when he "persecuted God's church and tried to destroy it." Incidentally, some scholars maintain that Paul was *called* as an apostle but not *converted* on the Damascus road. Such a reading stumbles at the wording Paul uses here. It is quite fascinating that the period of time before the revelation of Jesus Christ on the road to Damascus is described as his *former life in Judaism*. Apparently he believed that he was no longer part of Judaism and that Judaism characterized his past life. Furthermore, it is hard to imagine that Paul could have thought of himself as a believer while trying to destroy God's assembly.

Before meeting Jesus Christ, Paul was the bright young rabbinic star, outshining his contemporaries, presumably because of his zeal and his intellectual ability (1:14). Paul remarks on his zeal for the ancestral traditions, and such traditions should not be equated with the OT. The traditions represent later Jewish commentary and application of the Jewish text. Many of these traditions were codified in the Mishnah (ca. AD 200), and later Jews developed the traditions further with the Babylonian and Palestinian Talmuds in the following centuries. When Paul refers to zeal, his heroes were almost certainly Phinehas, Elijah, and Mattathias. Phinehas is commended for his zeal in slaying the Israelite man having sex with a Midianite woman (Num. 25:11). Elijah's zeal for the Lord manifested itself in killing the prophets of Baal (1 Kings 19:10, 14), while Mattathias burned with zeal for the Lord, slaying both the Jew who was about to offer an illegitimate sacrifice along with the king's officer (1 Macc. 2:23–25). Mattathias and those who followed him clearly saw themselves as exercising the same kind of zeal as Phinehas and Elijah (1 Macc. 2:24, 26, 27, 50, 54, 58). Zeal and violence went together, and thus Paul would not have felt any guilt about putting to death and persecuting those whom he considered to be heretical. On the contrary, he was proud of his zealous commitment to the law.

We need to zero in on Paul's main point here. If he wanted to please people, he would not have become Christ's slave. He would have remained in Judaism, for he was praised in Judaism for his extraordinary devotion and zeal. He was the bright young rabbinic student, and everyone was watching that young man because he would have an amazing future. The reason Paul became Christ's slave, then, wasn't to garner human praise. Indeed, serving Christ never entered his mind, but something amazing happened to him on the Damascus road. The God who formed him from conception had decided to reveal Jesus Christ to him (Gal. 1:15–16). Paul couldn't take any credit for proclaiming Christ, for God had ordained his destiny before he was born. Then God called Paul in a dramatic and striking way on the Damascus road. Paul never dreamed or thought of becoming a believer in Jesus; he suffered from no guilt feelings over persecuting Christians, but suddenly he saw and realized that Jesus was the Messiah, the king of Israel, and the King of the world.

The language Paul uses here resonates with the call of both Isaiah and Jeremiah as prophets. Isaiah said, "The LORD called me before I was born. He named me while I was in my mother's womb" (Isa. 49:1). The Lord said to Jeremiah when he was called to be a prophet, "I chose you before I formed you in the womb; I set you apart before you were born. I appointed you a prophet to the nations" (Jer. 1:5). Like Isaiah and Jeremiah, Paul's destiny was determined before he was born, while he was in his mother's womb, and like them he was called as the Lord's spokesman, though he was called as an apostle. So Paul's argument thus far is that if he wished to please people, he would have remained in Judaism. Jesus Christ launched him in a completely different direction than he would have chosen himself.

When Jesus Christ met Paul on the Damascus road, he called him to proclaim the gospel to the gentiles, and in this way Paul functioned as the servant of the Lord (Isa. 49:6). Paul didn't "consult with anyone" (Gal. 1:16) about whether he should preach to the gentiles. He had been independently called by Christ himself. The opponents may have charged that Paul was *dependent* upon the Jerusalem apostles, but Paul shows that he received the gospel from Christ himself. Since Paul's call was independent, he didn't travel to Jerusalem to receive validation from the apostles (1:17). He went immediately to Arabia and then came back to Damascus. What did Paul do in Arabia? Some have argued that he spent his time reading and meditating on the OT Scriptures, and doubtless he spent some time doing this. At the same time, he almost certainly proclaimed the gospel as well. When he came back to Damascus, people wanted to kill him, and such a plot was probably concocted because of his missionary work in Arabia and Damascus (Acts 9:23–25).

Paul didn't travel to Jerusalem for three years but then went up to the city to get to know Peter (Gal. 1:18). This is likely the same visit recorded in Acts 9:26–29. The three-year interval certifies that Paul wasn't dependent on Peter for the substance of his gospel. Still, in his two-week stay Paul certainly talked to Peter, as C. H. Dodd famously said, about more than the weather. Doubtless Peter passed on to Paul much about the Jesus tradition. The only other apostle Paul saw was James, the Lord's brother (Gal. 1:19). This is the same James who wrote the letter in the NT by that name and who played such a major role in the apostolic council in Acts 15. And as we shall see, he also plays an important role in Galatians 2. It is also obvious from this verse that the apostolic circle included more than twelve members since James is identified as an apostle.

Suddenly the narrative is interrupted with an oath formula where Paul declared that he wasn't lying (1:20). Such a statement is inexplicable and very strange if Paul were not under attack by opponents. The adversaries claimed that Paul's gospel was dependent upon others, and so Paul carefully chronicles his contact with apostolic leaders in Jerusalem. Since Paul needed to establish his independence, he informs the readers that he traveled to "Syria and Cilicia" after seeing Peter and James. When Paul wrote Galatians, Syria and eastern Cilicia belonged to one Roman province (Syria-Cilicia). Paul's relocation to Syria and Cilicia matches Acts 9:30, where Paul was sent off to Tarsus (in Cilicia) after a short time in Jerusalem.

Paul's argument for independence continues. The Judean churches were unacquainted with him. Judea was constituted as a Roman province when Galatians was written and included both Galilee and Samaria. Therefore, Paul refers here to a rather large area. What we have here is a generalization, for it is likely that some believers knew him personally from his days in Jerusalem. The point is that the majority of believers in Palestine and Jerusalem were unacquainted with him, but they were reporting on his remarkable transformation, declaring that their former persecutor was now proclaiming the faith (Gal. 1:23–24).

Ratification of Paul's Gospel (2:1–10)

Paul establishes the independence of his gospel from the Jerusalem apostles in 1:11–24. He received his gospel directly from Jesus Christ on the Damascus road and did not run to the Jerusalem apostles to receive validation. Still, what the Jerusalem apostles thought about Paul's gospel was an important question. The Judaizers probably claimed that Paul's gospel was *dependent* on the Jerusalem apostles and that he *distorted* what they taught. Paul argued just the opposite. His gospel was *independent* of Jerusalem, but it was also *ratified and recognized* by the Jerusalem apostles. That's the story Paul tells in these verses.

Paul rehearses an event where he traveled to Jerusalem, fourteen years after his conversion, with Barnabas and the gentile believer Titus. Scholars dispute whether the event matches Acts 11:27–30 (the famine relief visit) or Acts 15 (the apostolic council). Good arguments can be made on both sides. The matter is too complicated to get into the details here, but it is more likely that the account here matches the famine relief visit of Acts 11:27–30. If this is correct, Paul doesn't omit any of his visits to Jerusalem in Galatians, and Galatians 2:1–10 rehearses a private meeting with Peter, James, and John—and the public discussion (which occurred after Gal. 2:10) takes place in Acts 15. The subject was the same (circumcision), but the events were distinct. We are not surprised that a controversial subject was discussed more than once. For instance, the christological controversies of the fourth century AD were revisited repeatedly in the 300s.

Paul went up to Jerusalem in response to a revelation. Some have wondered if he refers to the revelation given by Agabus (Acts 11:27–28), but it is equally possible that he received the revelation himself. In any case, the Lord instructed Paul to go up to Jerusalem and to share privately the gospel he proclaimed to the gentiles. Perhaps he brought Titus as a test case. What follows is one of the most astonishing statements in Paul's Letters. He communicated his gospel in private to James, Peter, and John in case his missionary efforts were "in vain" (Gal. 2:2). The statement is astonishing because it seems to indicate that Paul had private doubts about the truth of his gospel, and it seems to undercut his confident declaration about the independence of his gospel in chapter 1. What do we make of this? Paul was certainly not retracting what he wrote in chapter 1. He makes a practical point, acknowledging a pragmatic reality. Paul knew his gospel was the truth because Jesus Christ revealed it to him on the Damascus road. He didn't need anyone else to verify its truth to him. Still, there were practical realities that he acknowledged. If the apostles in Jerusalem (Peter, James, and John) disagreed with Paul's gospel, Paul's apostolic work would be irreparably damaged. He would be followed everywhere he traveled by messengers announcing that the Jerusalem apostles dissented from what Paul preached. Paul knew his gospel was the truth, but for practical reasons he needed the agreement of the apostles in Jerusalem. Since his gospel was becoming controversial, he shared it with recognized leaders in Jerusalem, knowing that agreement was crucial for his ongoing work.

In 2:3–5 Paul describes a controversy that erupted in Jerusalem over Titus. The first mention of circumcision in the letter appears here, yet we should notice that the controversy didn't take place in Galatia but in Jerusalem. Rhetorically, Paul doesn't criticize the Galatian attraction to circumcision; he waits for Galatians 5:2–4 to do that. He tells a story about what happened in Jerusalem to set up the readers for his more pointed words later. In the meeting with the leaders in Jerusalem, some "false brothers" wormed their way into the meeting and insisted that Titus be circumcised since he was a gentile believer in Christ. Clearly, Paul did not view this as a mere difference of opinion on a minor matter since he calls out those who disagreed with him as "false brothers." He notes that he didn't cave in for even a moment to the demand for circumcision "so that the truth of the gospel would be preserved for you" (2:5). Evidently, the false brothers insisted that circumcision was required for salvation, and Paul rejected the imposition of the law and circumcision as a false gospel. At the end of the day, they lost the argument. The decision made was that Titus should not be "compelled to be circumcised" (2:3). Titus was not circumcised and didn't feel forced or coerced to do so. Rather, the leaders in Jerusalem and Paul agreed that imposing circumcision violated the freedom of the gospel.

Paul shifts the focus to the role played by the pillars of the church, Peter, James, and John (2:6–10). They are probably called pillars because they are the foundation of the church, God's temple (cf. 1 Cor. 3:16; 2 Cor. 6:16). In Ephesians 2:20 the apostles and prophets are the foundation of the church. Such language doesn't contradict the claim that Jesus is the foundation of the church (1 Cor. 3:10) since metaphors can be used in different ways without being contradictory. Paul walks a tightrope in these verses, as he shows respect to the pillars of the church, those who are recognized as leaders, without venerating them. Yes, they walked and talked with the historical Jesus (cf. Gal. 2:6), but Paul wasn't filled with worshipful awe of them, for he realized that God doesn't show favoritism and isn't impressed with human beings. Furthermore, as a matter of fact, these recognized leaders "added nothing" to Paul's gospel (2:6), confirming what he taught in chapter 1; he independently received the gospel from Jesus Christ.

The pillars, those esteemed as leaders, didn't contribute to Paul's gospel. His gospel was true regardless of what they thought about it. In fact, however, James, Peter, and John recognized and affirmed the gospel that Paul and Barnabas preached, giving them "the right hand of fellowship" (2:9). Paul, then, had not run in vain because the pillars endorsed and ratified Paul's gospel. So the Judaizers were wrong on both counts: (1) Paul's gospel was *not dependent* upon the Jerusalem apostles; (2) his gospel was not repudiated by the pillars but *ratified* by them.

The Encounter at Antioch (2:11–14)

Paul goes on to tell a story about what happened in Syrian Antioch, the Roman Empire's third largest city, where many gentiles were becoming Christians (Acts 11:19–26). The population of the city was probably around 250,000, with around 10 percent of the residents being Jewish (25,000). It is difficult to be sure, but the event relayed here probably occurred before the apostolic council in Acts 15. The main point of the story is the gospel's authority over anyone, even an apostle, if they strayed from the truth of the gospel. Paul did not tell this story to criticize Peter but to affirm that the gospel he proclaimed was true and authoritative.

The pillar apostles ratified Paul's gospel in Jerusalem, but when Peter came to Antioch, Paul reproved him since Peter stood guilty before God for his actions. Before the men from James came, Peter was regularly eating with gentiles, which most likely means that he was eating unclean foods banned by the OT (Lev. 11:1–44; Deut. 14:3–21). The Lord had previously revealed to Peter that all foods were clean (Acts 10:1–11:18), and in Antioch the equality of Jews and gentiles in the church expressed itself at table. If believing Jews would not eat with gentiles who put their faith in Christ unless the latter observed the food laws, they were in essence saying that gentiles were not Christians unless they kept the law of Moses.

Peter initially ate with gentiles, presumably because of his visions in Acts 10–11, which indicated that foods previously declared unclean were now clean; he was eating with gentile believers food that was considered unclean according to the OT, but when men from James arrived, he abruptly withdrew and ceased eating with the gentiles (Gal. 2:12). We would love to know what the embassy from James said, and the account is frustratingly brief! We are left to conjecture, but they probably said that many Jews were scandalized upon hearing that Christian Jews in Antioch were abandoning the law in such a dramatic way. Many critical scholars contend that Peter *disagreed* with Paul, and that their disagreement led to the dramatic confrontation recorded here.

Such an interpretation, however, strays from the text, from what is actually written about the event. Paul tells the readers that Peter acted from fear and hypocrisy, not out of conviction. Revisionists claim that we are left with only Paul's version of the story, and it isn't quite accurate, but none of the revisionists were present, and even apart from inspiration of Scripture, why should we take their word for what happened over Paul's? It is one thing to propose possible reconstructions when the text is silent, but quite another thing to propose a reconstruction that contradicts the historical source that we have. In any case, Peter's fear and hypocrisy had a galvanizing effect, so that the remaining Jews withdrew from eating with the gentiles, even the generous and welcoming Barnabas. The men of the circumcision should probably not be identified with the men from James; the circumcision party probably stands for unbelieving Jews. James's ambassadors may have told Peter that his actions endangered other Jewish Christians in Jerusalem, that he was exposing them to the prospect of persecution and violence at the hands of unbelieving circumcised Jews. If this is the case, we can understand why Peter and the other Jews thought it was wise to cease eating with the gentiles.

Paul, however, publicly rebuked Peter for his change of behavior (Gal. 2:14). Was the public rebuke warranted? Should Paul have gone to Peter privately, as Jesus instructs in Matthew 18:15–17? It has often been noted, however, that public sins must be handled differently. I have often heard the saying, which is exactly right, that public sins that have public consequences deserve a public rebuke. Amazingly, Paul puts Peter in the same category as the "false brothers" who created such trouble in Jerusalem (Gal. 2:3–5), if he continues to avoid eating with the gentiles. Peter was wandering from "the truth of the gospel" (2:14). The false brothers wanted to *compel* Titus to be circumcised (2:3), and now Peter in effect would *compel* (same verb!) "gentiles to live like Jews" (2:14). The dispute, then, wasn't trivial: the gospel itself was at stake. Paul calls attention to Peter's hypocrisy, for he was willing to live like a gentile, but now he was requiring gentiles to become Jews (to keep Jewish food laws) for salvation. If Peter would not have table fellowship with them, he was in effect saying that they weren't Christians.

Scholars have speculated on whether Peter repented at Paul's words, and some have even maintained that Peter and Paul parted ways forever from this point onward. The textual evidence we have points in the other direction. In a later letter Paul says that he and Peter preached the same gospel (1 Cor. 15:5, 11). Furthermore, Paul's Letters are placed on the same level as Scripture in 2 Peter 3:15–16. Many scholars, of course, maintain that 2 Peter is inauthentic, and I dissent from that judgment. But even if 2 Peter was written by a later Petrine disciple, the verses attest that there was harmony between Peter and Paul. Why doesn't Paul mention Peter's response in Galatians? Because he wasn't interested in the encounter with Peter for its own sake. The story is recounted for the sake of the Galatians. Paul's purpose isn't to rehearse his history with Peter; he wrote so that the Galatians would adhere to the gospel he proclaimed.

There is another reason to think that Peter repented. In Galatians 2:1–10 Paul had just affirmed how important it was that the pillar apostles affirmed his gospel. But if, when the rubber met the road, Peter actually dissented from Paul, the argument in 2:1–10 is nullified and rendered worthless. It really doesn't matter that Peter agreed with Paul in 2:1–10 if he ended up disagreeing with him about the gospel later, for such news would have certainly reached the Galatians. To put it another way: Paul's argument in Galatians only works if Peter accepted Paul's rebuke, and Paul didn't mention Peter's repentance because that wasn't his purpose and because it was obvious that Peter didn't ultimately deny the gospel. What is clear is that Paul's authority, the gospel's authority, is absolute. No person, whether Paul, Peter, or an angel (1:8–9; 2:11–14) has more authority than the gospel.

The Gospel in Brief (2:15-21)

Verses 15–21 represent Paul's speech to Peter, and scholars differ as to where the speech ends. It probably extends all the way through verse 21. For historical purposes resolving the question of where the speech concludes is important, but interpretively the matter is of little consequence since, in any case, the speech is intended for the Galatian readers. The speech begins with the recognition that Paul and Peter were "Jews by birth" in contrast to gentiles who were "sinners" (2:15). Here Paul isn't denying that Jews are also sinners. His point is that Jews were in covenant with God from birth, marked by their circumcision on the eighth day. Gentiles, on the other hand, were outside the covenant and didn't stand in a right relationship with God.

As Christians, both Peter and Paul realized that no one is justified by the works of the law but only through faith in Jesus Christ. Three times in 2:16 faith in Christ is contrasted with works of the law. In Romans we noted that works of law refers to the entire law and can't be limited to identity markers like circumcision, food laws, and Sabbath. It was also seen in Romans that Paul likely speaks of faith in Christ rather than the faithfulness of Christ. In Galatians 2:16, Paul moves from the noun phrase "faith in Jesus Christ" to the verbal phrase "believed in Christ Jesus." The shift is for stylistic variety, and the threefold repetition constitutes emphasis.

Right standing with God does not come from observing the law but from trusting in Jesus Christ. We should also notice the subjects of the three phrases in the verse. First, we are told "a person" is justified by faith instead of works, which is a general way of including all people. Second, Paul shifts to "we," indicating that Jews aren't exempted from what is true of people generally. "Peter," Paul said, "you know that what is true of gentiles is also true of Jews." Finally, we are told that "no human being" is (lit., "all flesh is not") justified by doing the law. Here we have an allusion to Psalm 143:2, where David confesses that no living person "is righteous in your sight." Paul's argument here is both anthropological and redemptive-historical. It is anthropological: no one can be righteous apart from faith in Christ since all are sinners. It is redemptive-historical: the Mosaic law, the works of the law, are no longer in force now that Christ has come.

Verses 17–18 are intensely debated and remarkably difficult, but we don't have space to look at all the twists and turns, so I will defend a particular reading. In turning to Christ for justification, it was clear that both Peter and Paul were found to be sinners before God: they were no better than gentiles. They recognized that they could not be right before God through the Mosaic covenant or keeping the law but only through faith in Christ. Peter's refusal to have fellowship with gentiles unless they observed covenant regulations contradicted his own experience and theology (Acts 10–11) since Peter had himself confessed that salvation and forgiveness are found only in Christ, not the Mosaic law. Opponents charged that if the law is no longer necessary, then Christ actually promotes sin. Paul says that it is actually precisely the opposite. Now that the new age of salvation has dawned and salvation is through the Messiah, it would be sinful to turn the clock back in salvation history, as if Christ has not come. In effect, Peter was trying to turn the clock back by requiring the gentiles to follow the food laws.

The relationship of believers to the law is pursued further. Paul speaks representatively in saying that he "died to the law" "through the law" (Gal. 2:19). The statement is compact and could mean that Paul died to the law by disobeying the law, but a parallel statement in Romans provides a better lens for understanding: "You also died to the law through the body of Christ" (Rom. 7:4 NIV). Here the "body of Christ" stands for Jesus's death, and thus Paul died to the law when he was "crucified with Christ" (Gal. 2:20; so also 4:4–5). Dying to the law through Christ's death is the pathway to life, the only way to life, according to Paul. But Peter was attempting to undo Christ's work in requiring the gentiles to observe the law to be right with God. He was acting as if Christ hadn't even come.

The words in Galatians 2:20 are among the most famous that Paul wrote. Again, the "I" is representative. Now that Paul is crucified with Christ, the old I, the I that represents who Paul was in Adam, no longer lives. The law encourages moral reformation, but what is needed is death and resurrection! Now Christ lives in Paul. Usually Paul speaks of the Spirit indwelling, but he can alternate between Christ and the Spirit indwelling as well (cf. Rom. 8:9–11; Eph. 3:16–17). Now Paul and all Christians live in the new covenant established by Jesus Christ. Paul puts it in deeply personal terms: believers live by trusting Jesus as God's Son "who loved me and gave himself for me" (Gal. 2:20; cf. Eph. 5:2).

Peter's actions, however, were undermining the gospel. If the gentiles need to observe the law to be right with God, if the law is the means by which believers are right with God, then Christ's death is superfluous. Not eating with the gentiles was much more consequential than Peter realized!

How Did You Receive the Spirit? (3:1–5)

Paul's speech to Peter gets at the heart of the gospel, and now in the subsequent chapters Paul unpacks his gospel for the Galatians. He begins by asking them to consider their own experience, their initial encounter with God. The text is marked by a staccato series of rhetorical questions, intended as a kind of shock treatment so that the Galatians will realize what is at stake.

He begins by upbraiding the Galatians and calling them "foolish" (3:1). It is as if a spell had been cast over them, as if someone had waved a wand over them, causing them to forget the gospel. Magic was enormously popular in the ancient world, accompanied typically by a long string of invocations to attain the desired end. Though Paul would not put any stock in magic, it is as if someone wielded that kind of influence over the Galatians; for Paul such influence would have surely been satanic. Paul had publicly set forth the significance of Jesus Christ as the crucified one, and the Galatians seem to have entirely forgotten why Jesus's death mattered!

It is as if the Galatians swooned or went into a coma and forgot everything they had previously learned, and so Paul asks them twice in short compass how they received the Spirit. Did they receive "the Spirit by works of the law or by believing" the message they heard (3:2, 5)? Receiving the Spirit occurs at the inception of the Christian life, and thus Paul reminds the Galatians, with a rhetorical question, that they didn't receive the Spirit because they observed the law. They received the Spirit because they responded to the message of the gospel with faith. Paul elsewhere clarifies that the indwelling Spirit is *the sign* that one is a believer (Rom. 8:9). The Galatians should not have any doubts about their new life because they enjoyed the presence of the Holy Spirit. In Acts 10:44–48 Cornelius and his friends received the Spirit, proving that they were truly Christians, and thus Peter agreed that they must be baptized. The same event played a key role in the apostolic council, which met to discuss whether circumcision was necessary for salvation. Peter argued that the answer was no since Cornelius and his friends received the Spirit without being circumcised (Acts 15:7–11).

Paul wonders if the Galatians were going to continue in such a remarkable about-face. They rightly began their Christian lives in the Spirit, and a sudden turn to the flesh defies everything Paul taught them (Gal. 3:3). The flesh here refers to the ability and the strength of the human being, but the gospel teaches that there is no such virtue, that human beings need the power of God, that they need the Holy Spirit. After they were experiencing the latter, Paul is incredulous that they would turn back to human ability. If they kept going in this direction, they would be guilty of nothing less than apostasy. Paul doesn't guarantee final salvation for those who renounce the faith, and he wonders if the Galatians would throw away all they have experienced thus far.

Father Abraham (3:6–9)

Paul turns from experience to Scripture, from the Spirit to Abraham. Actually, that analysis is too simple, for an appeal to the gift of the Spirit in 3:1–5 is a scriptural argument, a covenantal argument. The presence of the Spirit in the Galatians' lives testifies that the covenant promises, the new-exodus promises, and the new-creation promises are fulfilled (cf. Isa. 32:15; 44:3; Ezek. 36:26–27; 37:14; Joel 2:28–29). As in Romans, Paul turns specifically to Abraham, the founder and progenitor of the Jewish people. In Second Temple Judaism, as we noticed in Romans 4, Abraham was regularly commended for his obedience. Paul, however, moves in a strikingly different direction.

As in Romans 4, Paul appeals to Genesis 15:6. In Genesis 15 Abraham lamented that he didn't have an heir, concluding that his heir would be Eliezer his servant. The Lord enjoined Abraham to go outside and to look at the stars, which were countless in the night sky, promising Abraham that his children would be as numerous as the stars. Abraham could have rejected such a promise as ridiculous, but he believed the Lord's promise, and his faith was counted to him as righteousness. He was righteous first and foremost not because he obeyed God but because he trusted the Lord. Abraham's family members, Abraham's sons and daughters, are those who exercise the same faith as Abraham. Abraham's sons and daughters aren't traced by genealogy and ethnicity; his children are those who trust in God's work as he did.

In verse 8 Paul merges two verses from the Abraham story, Genesis 12:3 and 18:18.

Genesis 12:3: "All the peoples on earth will be blessed through you."
Genesis 18:18: "All nations of the earth will be blessed through him."

The promise of Genesis 3:15, that the offspring of the woman will crush the serpent and his offspring, will be fulfilled through the promises made to Abraham. Here is the capstone of all the promises made to Abraham. All people groups everywhere will be blessed in and through Abraham. What is fascinating is that Paul identifies the promise of universal blessing as the gospel, the good news. The ancient promises made to Abraham were fulfilled in Jesus Christ as the crucified and risen Lord. Another way of putting it is this: Genesis 15:6 becomes the hermeneutical lens by which Genesis 12:3 and 18:18 are interpreted. The universal blessing for all peoples everywhere is only received by faith, and not by keeping the law! So Paul can say that those who exercise faith enjoy the blessing of the believing Abraham (Gal. 3:9).

Curse and Blessing (3:10–14)

Paul glides from the blessing of Abraham, the great covenant promise, to the opposite of blessing, which is the curse. Curses are what Adam experienced in the garden (cf. Gen. 3:17), and curses are pronounced on those in Israel who don't observe the law (Deut. 27:13–26; 28:15–20, 45, 46). In very compact form Paul explains his argument from the OT Scriptures in these verses. Galatians 3:10–13 is structured so that we have a Pauline statement first, and then a scriptural proof of the statement made. Here we encounter one of the most disputed sections of the letter, and certainly one of the most important. Paul had to show the Galatians from the OT that his understanding of the gospel and law was convincing.

The blessing of Abraham (3:8–9) belongs to those who have the faith of Abraham. In verse 10 Paul turns to the opposite of blessing, to the curse. All of those who adhere to works of law are "under a curse" (3:10). Paul quotes from Deuteronomy 27:26 to substantiate the claim that the curse falls upon those who are of the works of law. Before we look at Paul's argument more carefully, we should note the OT background of the citation. In Deuteronomy 27 the curses are pronounced on those who don't keep the law. Many of the sins listed here would be committed in secret and thus would avoid the notice of others: setting up an idol "in secret" (27:15); moving the neighbor's boundary (27:17); leading a blind person astray (27:18); having sex with one's father's wife, an animal, a sister, or a mother-in-law (27:20–23); secretly murdering a neighbor (27:24); and accepting a bribe (27:25). Verse 26 functions as a concluding and summary verse, indicating that a curse applies to all those who don't do the works of the law. The generalizing statement clarifies that the specific rules listed in 27:15–25 aren't comprehensive. The curse will fall on any infraction of the law, even if it isn't listed here.

In citing Deuteronomy 27:26, Paul depends upon the LXX, which adds the word "all," as already implicit in Deuteronomy 27:26. At the same time, Paul probably also has in mind the covenant curses threatened in Deuteronomy 28, and the word "all" may come from Deuteronomy 28:58, "If you are not careful to obey all the words of this law."

Paul's argument in Galatians 3:10, then, can be summarized as follows:

- One must keep *all* that is written in the law (3:10b).
- No one does everything the law commands (implicit proposition).
- Therefore, those who are of the works of the law are cursed (3:10a).

At this point several comments should be made. We see that works of the law are defined as doing *all* that is in the law, and thus we see further evidence that works of law refers to the entire law. The reason people are cursed is that they fail to keep the law and that they fail to keep it *perfectly*. They must do *all* the law commands.

Two objections are raised against this interpretation. First, Paul doesn't explicitly add the implicit proposition noted in the table above. Some think it is, therefore, wrongly introduced. But Paul doesn't write technical syllogisms: he often skips steps in the argument, and it was obvious that no one could keep the law perfectly because the OT often says this very thing (1 Kings 8:46; Eccles. 7:20; Ps. 143:2; Prov. 20:9). Second, some object that the argument being made here is ridiculous since the Sinai covenant provided forgiveness through OT sacrifices. Such an objection fails to see the redemptive-historical dimension of Paul's argument. Of course, OT sacrifices atoned for sin so that there was provision for those who sinned, but Paul believes that those sacrifices *no longer avail* since Christ has come. Now that Jesus has died, his death is the *only* means by which sin can be atoned for (Gal. 3:13). Those who put themselves under the law turn back the clock in redemptive history; they nullify Christ's death (Gal. 2:21). But after the coming of Christ, if one lives under the law, the old covenant, then perfect obedience is demanded since animal sacrifices *no longer* atone for sin.

Paul brings in another argument from the OT, and here I will be briefer since the same text was discussed in Romans 1:17. Righteousness does not come, as Habakkuk 2:4 teaches, from the law but by faith. In the book of Habakkuk, we see that Israel will be punished and sent into exile by Babylon (fulfilled in 586 BC) for failing to keep the law (Hab. 1:4). In chapter 2 the Lord promises that Babylon will eventually be punished, and then in chapter 3, which is full of references to what the Lord did for Israel in the first exodus, we find promises of a new exodus, a new deliverance after judgment. Those who trust in the Lord will see that the Lord will deliver his people after judging them. Habakkuk ends, then, with the prophet confidently waiting for the Lord's salvation. Israel's salvation is certainly by faith since it is granted by the Lord's grace to a sinful people.

The argument continues in Galatians 3:12, where the law is said to be contrary to faith, and Leviticus 18:5 is cited in support. The law is based on *doing*, but those who are right with God stand before him by *believing* rather than by *achieving*, by *trusting* rather than by *working*. Paul's use of Leviticus 18:5 has precipitated much discussion. Does Paul quote it correctly? In context the obedience necessary for life in Leviticus 18:5 is within the context of the Lord's covenant with Israel, and such obedience is a *response* to God's covenant grace. One possible answer is that Paul cites the verse apart from its OT context, appropriating its words for his own purposes. Another answer is that the verse is quoted because Paul refers to the *misinterpretation* by the opponents of Leviticus 18:5. The problem with both of these suggestions is that Paul typically makes a positive case from the OT for his theology.

In its OT context Leviticus 18:5 refers to obedience within the covenant, and that life refers to life in the land. Paul, however, reads life typologically (as did other interpreters in Second Temple Judaism). He also reads the verse redemptive-historically, and thus the comments made about Galatians 3:10 above apply here as well. Now that Christ has come, there is no covenant protection; there is no atonement in OT sacrifices. Thus those who put themselves under the law must keep it perfectly if they want to avoid the covenant curses. When Israel was under the law, its disobedience was so great that it went into exile. Faith in Christ, not keeping the law, is the means to a right relationship with God.

A curse is pronounced on all those who refuse to keep the law, which is everyone. Verse 13 explains how the curse is removed. "By becoming a curse for us," Christ freed and ransomed those who trusted in him. Clearly, Jesus's death was substitutionary in that he bore the curse that sinners themselves deserved. Paul introduces Deuteronomy 21:23 in support. In historical context the verse refers to those put to death and hung on a tree because of a crime. Others in Second Temple Judaism also believed that Deuteronomy 21:23 applies to those crucified (4QpNah 5–8; 11QTemple 64.6–13). Paul knew, of course, that some people who were crucified weren't cursed by God. Not all of the eight hundred crucified by Alexander Jannaeus were necessarily cursed by God!

(Josephus, *Ant.* 13.380). Still, before his conversion Paul was convinced that the *Messiah* would *never be crucified*; that would be an intolerable contradiction, "a stumbling block to the Jews" (1 Cor. 1:23). Paul failed to understand that Jesus, a righteous individual, was cursed "for us," and once he grasped this, he saw the cross as the place where God's love and justice meet.

Since Jesus took the curse that all deserved, "the blessing of Abraham" (Gal. 3:8–9, 14), in accord with the great promises in Genesis (e.g., Gen. 12:3), belongs to gentiles in Christ Jesus. The blessing doesn't come through the law but through Jesus Christ. Another way of referring to the blessing of Abraham is to speak of the promise of the "Spirit," as Isaiah 44:3 demonstrates (cf. Gal. 3:14). The "we" here refers to both Jews and gentiles who enjoy the blessing of Abraham if they have received the Spirit. The argument in Galatians 3:1–14 has come full circle. The gentiles don't receive the blessing of Abraham through law-obedience, and they are in the circle of those who are blessed since they are indwelt by the Holy Spirit.

An Interim Covenant (3:15–25)

Paul has argued that Christ rather than the law saves, that righteousness is by faith and not by works, and that the cross delivers from the curse of the law. Hovering in the background are Paul's convictions about redemptive history, and they move more clearly into view in these verses. Scholars dispute whether Paul speaks of a covenant or a will in verse 15, yet a covenant is probably in view, but in either case the point made in the illustration is the same. The original covenant with Abraham can't be supplemented with a law that was instituted 430 years later (3:16–18). The Sinai covenant and the Abrahamic covenant aren't of the same nature, for the covenant with Abraham is based on God's promise. The law teaches, however, that the inheritance is obtained through obedience. The law and promise, then, aren't complementary but represent two different pathways for receiving the promises made to Abraham: the promise of blessing, the promise of a new creation, the promise of a new world where evil is defeated and goodness reigns.

The promise is fulfilled through Abraham's singular offspring, Jesus Christ (3:19). We see again that the promises given to Abraham aren't realized through the law but in Christ. But how do we explain Paul's argument here? The word "offspring" (*sperma*) is already a collective noun, and Paul knows this. He uses it as a collective a few verses later, in 3:29. Scholars have proposed many solutions, which we don't have space here to examine. The use of the word "and" indicates that Paul cites Genesis 13:15 or 17:8. Some say that Paul's interpretation is unjustified and arbitrary, but there are better explanations. The promise of redemption in Genesis 3:15 includes the idea of a singular fulfillment, as we see in the births of Seth and Isaac (cf. Gen. 21:13). Paul elsewhere distinguishes between Isaac and Ishmael, seeing only Isaac as the true offspring (Rom. 9:6–9). Ultimately the promise in Genesis 3:15 is fulfilled through a singular descendant of David. We see from the OT that the seed narrows from Abraham to Isaac to a son of David. Such a view accords with typology and corporate solidarity as well. Paul interprets the OT text typologically and sees its crowning fulfillment in Jesus Christ. Jesus is *the representative* offspring of Abraham and David, and Jesus is the fulfillment of the original redemptive promise in Genesis 3:15. The promises made to Abraham have become a reality in Jesus Christ, and thus to move backward in salvation history to the Mosaic law and covenant is a serious mistake.

The stark contrast between the law and the promise (Gal. 3:15–18) raises the question of the law's purpose. Paul's answer is terse: "It was added for the sake of transgressions" (3:19). Some have said that the law was given to *limit* sin, or even to *define* sin, but the whole of Galatians and the context suggests that the law was given to *increase* sin. Such a reading fits with Romans 5:20 and 7:7–25 as well. Ironically, the law had a different effect than most anticipated, yet the problem isn't with the law but with human beings! The Mosaic law was never intended to last forever; once the Offspring, Jesus, arrived, the era of the law was over (Gal. 3:19): a new era in redemptive history dawned. Paul continues to downplay the Mosaic law, which was often viewed by Jews as the capstone of God's revelation to his people. He doesn't deny that the law ultimately came from God, but it was mediated through angels (cf. Deut. 33:2; Acts 7:53; Heb. 2:2). Since the law wasn't given directly by God but was mediated through angels and Moses, it is subordinate to the promise, and it needs to be interpreted in light of the covenant made with Abraham (Gal. 3:20).

Paul isn't always easy to follow in his arguments, and we might think he was teaching that the Mosaic law was contrary to God's promises since he just finished emphasizing the differences between promise and law. Still, he insists that the law doesn't contradict the promises (3:21). The law and the promise aren't identical, for the law isn't the source of life for believers; it doesn't give one right standing with God. The law and the promise are complementary in that the law reveals humanity's sin so that the promise of Abraham will be granted to those who put their faith in Jesus Christ (3:22). The Sinai covenant, the law given to Moses, functioned as our "guardian" until the coming of Christ (3:23–25). Now that the Christ has come, the era of the guardian (*paidagōgos*) has come to an end. The word "guardian" here doesn't mean "tutor," for the guardian in the ancient world wasn't a teacher but more of a child attendant or babysitter, keeping watch over children during the years of their immaturity. They would teach children morals and manners, attending to them in their daily lives. What comes to the forefront with the word "guardian" is the interim character of the law. Just as people had a guardian only as long as they were children, so too the law was intended to be in force for a limited time in the history of salvation. The law functioned as a kind of babysitter until the fullness of time came. Believers don't need to be circumcised or to keep the law, for the Mosaic covenant has come to an end!

Abraham's Offspring in Christ (3:26-29)

The new age has come, the promises made to Abraham are being fulfilled, and by faith believers are sons and daughters of God because they are united to Jesus Christ, the true offspring of Abraham. What stands out is how Paul emphasizes that the law points to and is terminated in Christ. Being "clothed with Christ" (3:27) means that one truly belongs to God, and all those who are baptized, all those who are converted, are clothed with Christ. Now that the promises of Abraham are being realized, what matters isn't one's ethnic background (whether one is Jew or Greek, circumcised or uncircumcised!), or one's social class (slave or free), or one's gender (male or female). Paul isn't saying that such things are completely irrelevant. Gender isn't abolished as a category by Paul, as many other texts show (e.g., Rom. 1:26–27; Eph. 5:22–33). The purpose is to say that there is equal access to salvation for all. Paul doesn't deny people's ethnic background; there are Jews and gentiles, but one's Jewishness or maleness doesn't qualify one for salvation. All believers are united in Christ Jesus. They are all Abraham's offspring and recipients of the promise if they "belong to Christ" (Gal. 3:29).

Adulthood! (4:1-7)

Paul's argument in 4:1–7 is in substance quite similar to 3:15–25, though it differs in particulars. In verses 1–2 we have an illustration, and the illustration is explained in 4:3–5 and applied in 4:6–7. Paul asks the readers to imagine an heir who is a minor. Even though he will inherit the entire estate, as a child "he differs in no way from a slave" (4:1). We see that Paul angles the illustration to make a particular point since most would not emphasize that an heir was like a *slave* when a child. The minor will only come into the inheritance at the time designated by the father, and in the meantime is under the care of "guardians and trustees" (4:2).

Paul explains the illustration in 4:3–5. The "we" here includes both Jews and gentiles since both Jews and gentiles are adopted as sons (4:5). Paul emphasizes that life under the law was a time of slavery, which would be quite shocking to any Jewish person who grew up being nurtured in the Torah. Those under the law need to be redeemed and freed from the law's bondage. Paul compares life under the law to being enslaved "under the elements of the world" (Gal. 4:9; Col. 2:8, 20). The word for "elements" (*stoicheia*) is the subject of considerable debate. When the word "world" is added, the phrase refers to the physical elements that make up the world, whether earth, air, fire, or water (Plato, *Timaeus* 48B; Diogenes Laertius, *Vit. phil.* 7.134–135; 4 Macc. 12:13; Philo, *Decalogue* 31; *Creation* 146; 2 Pet. 3:10, 12). The term "elements" alone also refers to the fundamental elements of a matter, whether of science, art, and so forth, and thus the term can be understood to denote the elementary or fundamental principles or rules of life (Plato, *Leg.* 7.790C; Xenophon, *Mem.* 2.1.1; Pseudo-Plutarch, *Lib. Ed.* 16.2; Heb. 5:12). Another possibility is that the elements refer to angelic powers, to demonic forces that rule unbelievers (T. Sol. 8.1–2; 18.1–2). Supporting a reference to the demonic powers is the personal nature of the language in Galatians 4:8–9, where the elements are linked with turning back to idols. Elsewhere in Paul, idols are identified as demons (1 Cor. 10:19–22). In Colossians the false teachers were entranced with angels (cf. 1:16; 2:10, 15, 18), and thus many see a reference to elemental spirits in Colossians.

A solid argument can also be made for a reference to fundamental principles or elementary principles in both Galatians and Colossians. The law is clearly center stage in Galatians, and Paul refers to specific traditions and regulations in Colossians 2:8 and 2:21–23. A decision is remarkably difficult. The phrase "elements of the world" has a long history of referring to the elements that make up the world: earth, air, fire, and water, which metaphorically could denote this present world order—the old creation; yet we also see that the elements making up the world were worshiped in Wisdom 13:1–5 (cf. also 7:17–19). Indeed, demonic powers may be included in the meaning inasmuch as they ruled over the elements of the old creation (cf. Eph. 2:2; 6:12).

God sent his Son at the right time, in the fullness of time, to ransom those who were enslaved under the law. The age of slavery, the time of subjection to the Mosaic covenant, has ended. The time for receiving the inheritance has come, and believers aren't minors or children but adults! The word "sons" here stands for full maturity, for adulthood, for the reception of all the privileges that accrue to one who has received the inheritance. The evidence of sonship is that the believers have the Spirit! (Gal. 4:6). Once again, the importance of the reception of the Spirit breaks through in the argument (cf. 3:1–5, 14). Now believers exclaim, "Abba, Father!" They are adult sons and daughters, heirs through Christ, and it makes no sense to revert back to being a minor, to life as a slave under the law.

Where Do They Stand? (4:8–11)

Paul rehearses the past, the days when the Galatians didn't know God, the time before their conversion, when they were enslaved to false gods, when they were subjugated to the elements of the world. The key words here are "But now" (4:9). The Galatians aren't what they were; now they "know God," which means that they are saved and converted and transformed. Paul pauses in the midst of his argument, however, to emphasize that they are "known by God." God always takes the initiative in salvation so that the reason people know God is that God has known them first (cf. Gen. 18:19; Jer. 1:5; Rom. 8:29; 11:2). No room is given for pride, even in choosing to belong to God.

Life is complex and multifaceted; we might think that those who are known by God would live serene and uncomplicated Christian lives. Instead, Paul was baffled because the Galatians seemed to be converting back to paganism! They were going back to their pre-Christian slavery and embracing "the weak and worthless elements" they repudiated when they were saved (Gal. 2:9). This shows up particularly in their observance of the calendar: "days, months, seasons, and years" (4:10; cf. Gen. 1:14). Paul piles up terms to denote their attraction to OT regulations pertaining to the Sabbath, new moons, Passover, and so forth. What is remarkable is that such a move on their part is classified as returning to paganism! Certainly this is one of the most shocking things ever written by Paul; it would offend Jews who were convinced that OT regulations were the furthest thing from paganism. Paul's intense concern for the Galatians surfaces as he wonders if his apostolic labor was in vain. Maybe they weren't Christians at all!

An Appeal Based on Friendship (4:12–20)

Thus far the argument has been deeply theological, but Paul switches things up and appeals to the Galatians based on the relationship forged between them, reflecting on their love and friendship with him in the past. Paul begins with an imperative, an entreaty: "Become like me" (4:12), and by this Paul means that they should live in freedom from the law, as Paul did. Paul "became like" them in not observing the law when he was with them, and now he asks them to do the same. Paul recalls the time when he preached the gospel to them, and when he did so, he was saddled with some physical ailment. We don't know what the problem was, yet the Galatians didn't turn against Paul but embraced him as a divine messenger (4:14).

In those days they received a "blessing," which probably refers to the gift of the Spirit (3:15; Isa. 44:3). The relationship between Paul and the Galatians was so close that they would have given anything to him, even their eyes, so to speak, if necessary (4:15). Now it seems as if things have changed. Paul was no longer viewed as a friend but an enemy, simply because he told them the truth of the gospel (4:16). The false teachers had zeal, and zeal for what is good is an excellent quality, yet the Judaizers were not zealous for the truth but wanted the Galatians to pursue and venerate them.

Paul uses a striking image in verse 19. He was like a mother suffering birth pains, wondering if the Galatians will truly be born alive—a common problem in the ancient world where many children didn't survive birth. In the middle of the verse the metaphor changes violently. Now the Galatians are pictured as giving birth, and the question is whether Christ will be formed in them. Paul uses striking metaphors to shake the Galatians out of their spiritual lethargy. Still, Paul was perplexed and didn't know what to do or say (4:20).

Argument from Allegory (4:21–5:1)

Paul is trying to do whatever he can to bring the Galatians back to their senses, and he ended the last section by saying that perhaps he needs to change his tone so that they see what is at stake. In the verses before us, that is exactly what Paul does. He appeals to them with a different kind of argument, utilizing an allegory so that they will understand.

The argument begins with a pointed question: if the Galatians love the Mosaic law so much, do they actually listen to what the law teaches (meaning the OT Scriptures)? If they listened, they would realize that they were no longer under the law! Paul returns to the story of Abraham and his two sons. One was born from the slave woman Hagar and the other by the free woman Sarah. The story of the birth of these two sons is instructive (see Gen. 16–21). Ishmael was born through "the flesh," but Isaac "through promise" (Gal. 4:23). Certainly this is a faithful account of the OT narrative, for Sarah and Abraham hatched the idea of having a son through the slave woman Hagar. On the other hand, the birth of Isaac was nothing short of a miracle since both Abraham and Sarah were far past the time of childbearing. The Lord promised a child (Gen. 18:10), and the birth of Isaac was entirely by his grace.

Paul reads and applies the story allegorically in Galatians 4:24–27. The reference to allegory has precipitated intense discussion since Paul usually argues typologically, and allegorical readings are often arbitrary and lack warrant for the parallels drawn. Space is lacking here to descend into the details. I suggest that Paul does argue allegorically, but what he does isn't remarkably different from typology in that he sees patterns that are truly present in the biblical text.

We are told that Hagar and Sarah "represent two covenants" (4:24). Hagar, as a slave woman, represents Mount Sinai, which leads to slavery. Now, strictly speaking, Hagar is an individual and doesn't stand for a distinct covenant; Paul draws a fascinating parallel between Hagar and Sinai. He goes on to say that "the present Jerusalem," which probably represents unbelieving Judaism and its leaders in Jerusalem, is ensconced in slavery like Hagar. Paul reads the story to say that unbelieving Jews are Hagar's children!

In contrast, believers are children of the heavenly Jerusalem, the "Jerusalem above" (4:26), the city of God. Elsewhere in the NT the heavenly Jerusalem (cf. Heb. 12:22; Rev. 3:12; 21:2, 10) represents the city awaiting believers; but according to Paul, the heavenly city has arrived, though not in its fullness, in the present evil age. The presence of the heavenly city instantiates the new creation (Isa. 65:17; 66:1). In Isaiah 66:7–11 Zion is portrayed as a mother in labor, and the birth of her sons indicates the fulfillment of God's saving promises. The mother of believers is not the church but the heavenly Jerusalem, showing that believers in Christ, both Jews and gentiles, are citizens of the heavenly city.

Isaiah 54:1 is introduced to support Paul's argument in Galatians 4:26, showing that the gentile Christians in Galatia are the children of the Jerusalem above, for they are the children of the barren woman from whom no children are expected. The connection between the Isaiah passage and what Paul says in Galatians is Sarah's barrenness, and her barrenness plays a major role in the story in Genesis. The context of Isaiah is one of return from exile. Israel in exile is like a barren woman whose children have been sent to Babylon, but the Lord promises that they will return and prosper and that he will have compassion on them again, fulfilling the "covenant of peace" (Isa. 54:10). Paul sees the fulfillment of this "covenant of peace" in the gospel of Jesus Christ. Hagar's child, Ishmael, seemed to Abraham and to Sarah to represent the fulfillment of the promise. Nevertheless, it was the miraculous child, Isaac, who was the true fulfillment of God's promise. According to Paul, the ultimate fulfillment of this promise has become a reality, not in the physical return of Israel from exile, but in the conversion of gentile Christians in places like Galatia.

The law did not produce God's children, for those under the law were enslaved by sin. The law puts to death, but the gospel liberates and gives life. And thus the Galatian Christians, not the Jewish false teachers, are the true children of Isaac (Gal. 4:28). This is borne out by persecution, for just as Ishmael persecuted Isaac (Gen. 21:8–9), so too those "born . . . of the flesh" persecute those "born . . . of the "Spirit" (Gal. 4:29). Amazingly, Paul quotes approvingly the words of Sarah, who angrily told Abraham to send away Ishmael because the son of the slave Hagar will not inherit with "the son of the free woman" (4:30). Abraham was grieved at what Sarah said, but the Lord, even though Sarah's motivations were wrong, ratified what she said. The inheritance would come through Isaac, not Ishmael (Gen. 21:12–13). Was Paul telling the Galatians to throw the Judaizers out of the church? Some have read it that way, but they weren't members of the church in any case since they were interlopers coming from the outside. More likely, he is informing the Galatians that if they joined the Judaizers, they would not receive the inheritance; they would be joining the slave woman and her children, the earthly Jerusalem, and would lose out on enjoying the heavenly city. Alternatively, Paul is saying that the readers should not allow the false teachers any place in the church or allow them to teach or enter the public assembly in Galatia.

Paul asserts that the believers in Galatia are the children of Sarah, not Hagar, though interestingly he never mentions Sarah but always refers to her in terms of her freedom (Gal. 4:22, 23, 30, 31). Christ liberated believers for the purpose of freedom (5:1), and so Paul calls on believers to live out who they are as children of the free woman. They must not subject themselves to the teaching of the Judaizers, which is inducing them to slavery.

Warning to the Galatians (5:2–6)

Paul has laid the foundation, and now for the first time in the letter he directly addresses the matter of circumcision. Earlier he recounted the dispute over circumcision in Jerusalem (2:3–5), but now he confronts the Galatians on the whole question. Clearly, Paul needed to defend his apostolic credentials and set forth his theology of law before tackling the specific issue. The paragraph opens with solemnity as Paul introduces himself, even naming himself, so that his words strike home with weight. He warns the Galatians that if they received circumcision, Christ would be of no saving benefit to them (cf. Rom. 2:25–29). The "again" in Galatians 5:3 probably recalls 3:10, for here Paul says that those who accept circumcision must keep the entire law. They could have responded to the challenge by accepting it! But Paul almost certainly has the argument of 3:10 in view, which teaches that such an endeavor would be futile since perfect obedience is required. It is important to understand that 5:4 is still part of the warning; Paul isn't declaring that some have already taken the step of getting circumcised. Aorist verbs aren't invariably past tense, and here the verbs probably denote timeless action. Those who attempt to gain justification by law, by receiving circumcision, no longer belong to Christ: they are cut off from the grace of the gospel. The warning is remarkably severe and is one of the means that God uses to keep believers from falling away.

Verses 5–6 portray what it looks like to heed the warning. Believers "eagerly await" what they hope for, meaning the fullness of righteousness, the public declaration that they are right with God before the whole world. Such waiting can't be accomplished in human strength but is only sustained by the work of the Spirit, and such waiting is by faith since believers haven't experienced the future declaration yet. What believers recognize is that both circumcision and uncircumcision are insignificant (cf. 1 Cor. 7:19; Gal. 6:15). There is no basis for pride in being circumcised, nor should we think that being uncircumcised impresses God. The important thing in life is that our lives are marked by continued trust in God, and such trust, such faith, plays a crucial role in the lives of believers since it expresses itself in love.

Warning about the False Teachers (5:7–12)

While Galatians 5:2–6 constitutes a personal warning to the Galatians, 5:7–12 points to the danger posed by the false teachers, the Judaizers. The Galatians were running the race of the Christian life (cf. 1 Cor. 9:24–27; Phil. 3:12–14), but the false teachers cut in on them in the race, hindering them from obeying the truth of the gospel. Paul flat-out says that their attempt to persuade the Galatians doesn't come from God, and they must be vigilant for "a little leaven leavens the whole batch of dough" (Gal. 5:9; cf. 1 Cor. 5:6). If the false teachers were allowed to infest the congregation, the purity of the entire congregation would be lost. Paul is quite confident that no such step will be taken, apparently believing that his explanations and admonitions in the letter will persuade the Galatians to refuse to be circumcised. The warnings (cf. Gal. 5:2–4) will have a salutary effect! Still, the false teachers (the singular "whoever" in 5:10 is generic) who "are troubling" the Galatians (see 1:7) will face judgment for the evil they are causing.

The Judaizers accused Paul of hypocrisy, probably by appealing to occasions when he circumcised Jews (cf. Acts 16:3). Even though Timothy's circumcision was later, it probably represented a standard practice of Paul, encouraging and permitting Jews to be circumcised for cultural and evangelistic reasons. Still, Paul was consistent; he never agreed to circumcise someone if circumcision was required for salvation (cf. Gal. 2:3–5), and that explains why he was persecuted by Jews. The opponents who promulgate circumcision are no better than pagans in Paul's eyes, which is quite astonishing for the former Pharisee to say. It would be better, says Paul, if they would cut off the penis altogether. In other words, he lumps circumcision with pagan castration (2:11–12; Deut. 23:1–2 LXX). We see the same thing in Philippians 3:2, where he views circumcision as mutilating. There is no basis for pride in our works before God; by humble faith we receive every good gift.

The Freedom of Love (5:13–15)

Freedom has been a major theme of the letter (2:4; 4:22, 23, 26, 30, 31; 5:1), and the Galatians must resist slavery, which is manifested in observing the law (4:1, 3, 7, 22–25, 30, 31; 5:1). Still, they must beware of abusing their freedom so that it becomes a launching pad for the selfish will of human beings. They are to *be enslaved (douleuete)* to one another in love (5:13). Freedom isn't freedom of self-expression but the freedom to do what is right, the freedom to serve and give oneself to others. Some have suggested that Paul includes this section because there was rampant moral confusion in Galatia before the Judaizers came since Paul didn't sufficiently emphasize the new life that believers must lead in the Spirit, which is why the Judaizers' insistence on the law was so influential. This reading, however, overlooks 5:21, which indicates that from the beginning Paul strongly admonished the Galatians about living a life pleasing to God. More likely, Paul wanted to guard against an overreaction to his teaching on freedom. Freedom from the law doesn't mean freedom from love; it doesn't mean there are no commands or exhortations.

The entire law, as we saw in Romans 13:8–10, is fulfilled in the maxim to love one's neighbor as oneself (Gal. 5:14). Believers can't be saved through keeping the law because one must *do* the entire law to be saved (5:3), but here the reference is to *fulfilling* the law, not *doing* it. And such fulfillment is the work of the Spirit, as the following verses will show. When believers are focused on meeting the needs of neighbors, the purpose of the law is realized. They are not to be like poisonous snakes, injecting venom into one another. The word "bite" is often used in the OT of serpents (Gen. 49:17; Num. 21:6, 8, 9; Deut. 8:15; Eccles. 10:8, 11; Jer. 8:17; Amos 5:19; 9:3). If these texts are echoed here (Gal. 5:15), Paul sharply distinguishes between life in the Spirit and that which is demonic. Hatred will destroy the church, for evil impulses will quench the power of love.

Live by the Spirit (5:16–24)

The injunction to live a life of love, to give oneself to one's neighbor, is impossible for human beings who are sons and daughters of Adam. The Spirit, whom believers received upon believing (3:1–5), is the agent of their new life. As believers they must live by the Spirit daily, and then they will not do what the flesh desires (5:16). The new life of believers is not free of conflict: there is an intense battle between the flesh and the Spirit (5:17). Paul doesn't envision the battle to be a stalemate where believers are caught in the middle. Believers are "led by the Spirit" (5:18), which means they are directed and governed by the Spirit and "are not under the law." In the letter we have already seen that those who are "under the law" are under the rule of sin, and this truth is conveyed in various ways (cf. 3:10, 22, 23, 25; 4:2, 4, 5, 21). Those who are directed by the Spirit, then, are free from the rule and dominion of sin.

It isn't difficult to decipher if one is living according to the flesh or the Spirit, as Paul contrasts "the works of the flesh" with "the fruit of the Spirit" (5:19–23). The works of the flesh can be divided into sexual sins, sins that have to do with idolatry, social sins, and sins of excess (like drunkenness). What stands out is the focus on social sins since eight different kinds of social sins are noted, while the largest category after this is sexual sin (with three sins listed). Paul was particularly concerned about sins that tore apart the social fabric of the church. The Letter to the Galatians trumpets the grace of God in Christ, but Paul also warns that those who persistently give themselves to sin won't inherit God's kingdom (5:21). The life of grace doesn't become a platform for a life of licentiousness.

It is more difficult to see any particular structure in the fruit of the Spirit, though we are not surprised that love heads the list. Certainly, these qualities aren't the product of human ability but are the result of the Spirit's supernatural work. What Paul means when he says that the law isn't against the fruit of the Spirit (5:23) is uncertain. Perhaps he means that no law prohibits the fruit of the Spirit or that the law can't produce these virtues. What human beings need in order to be changed is death and resurrection, and when believers are united with Christ by faith (2:20), they have "crucified the flesh with its passions and desires" (5:24). They are new in Jesus Christ.

Living by the Spirit Individually and Communally (5:25–6:10)

Life in the Spirit is both an individual and a community matter, and Paul toggles between both of these realities in these verses. Earlier we saw that the works of the flesh focus on social sins. Here Paul gives some indications of what life in the Spirit looks like. Believers have new life in the Spirit, and we have already seen they are to "walk by the Spirit" (5:16) and be "led by the Spirit" (5:18). Here they are exhorted to march in step with the Spirit (5:25). The evidence that they are doing so is in their relationships with others. Their life together will not be marked by pride, conflict, and jealousy (5:26). The new life of believers isn't perfect, and some will fall into sin. Those "who are spiritual" (which is all believers!) should gently restore those in sin and not think of themselves as superior to them since they are liable to fall into sin themselves and need the same assistance at some point (6:1). Believers "fulfill the law of Christ" when they "carry one another's burdens" (6:2). The law of Christ is the law of love (cf. 5:14), which is exemplified supremely in Christ's self-giving sacrifice on the cross. Jesus carried the burdens (the sins) of believers in his death (3:13), and in loving one another believers display the same sacrificial love as Jesus Christ.

The greatest danger in the community is pride, when someone begins to think oneself to be really something (6:3). On the one hand, believers are to care for and assist one another, but on the other hand, each person is responsible for their own life. On the day of judgment we will answer for ourselves, and no one else will be blamed or praised for the decisions we made about our own lives (6:4–5). What it means to be a community, to bear one another's burdens, and to live a life of love leads to supporting the teachers of the church financially (6:6). This spurs Paul to a larger principle: people will reap what they sow (6:7). Those who regularly sow to the flesh will experience eternal "destruction," but those who sow "to the Spirit will reap eternal life" (6:8). The new life in the Spirit is based on the grace of Christ and is supernatural, but it doesn't countenance moral laxity. By the Spirit believers are to continue to be generous and selfless, looking for opportunities to help unbelievers in need, but they should especially care for fellow believers.

Final Words (6:11–18)

The conclusion to Galatians reprises many of the central themes of the letter, as Paul strongly exhorts the believers about the dangers of the false teachers. The "large letters" don't indicate the awkwardness of Paul's handwriting but the importance of what he has to say (6:11). The opponents who advocate circumcision for salvation are doing so to curry favor with others and to avoid "being persecuted" (6:12). They actually don't keep the law themselves, but they want to add converts to their cause so that they can boast about the circumcised flesh of the Galatians (6:13). Paul's boast, on the other hand, is only in the cross, for the cross signals the deathblow to human pride and achievement (6:14). Paul's relationship to this present world has been decisively changed; it "has been crucified" to him, and he has died to the world. The world here stands for the old creation, the old order, so Paul returns to what he said at the outset of the letter. The new creation has come with the resurrection of Christ (1:1), and the cross has delivered believers from "this present evil age" (1:4).

Since the "new creation" has arrived (6:15), both circumcision and un-circumcision are irrelevant for Paul. They are both part of the old creation, the old order. Circumcision was required as long as the old creation, the old covenant, was in force, but now the old creation has passed away and the new creation "has come" (2 Cor. 5:17). We think of the two parallel statements about circumcision in 1 Corinthians 7:19 and Galatians 5:6, which tell us that the new creation makes possible the keeping of God's commandments and that faith expresses itself through love.

Paul prays for peace and mercy for all who follow the rule of the new creation, with a final comment on "the Israel of God!" (Gal. 6:16). Some scholars believe that "the Israel of God" represents only Jewish Christians here, while others see a reference to both gentile and Jewish Christians. The grammar can actually be read either way, but when read in light of the entire letter, the Israel of God must include both gentile and Jewish Christians. The whole point of the letter is that all those who trust in Christ are the true children of Abraham, which is another way of saying that they are the Israel of God. It would create confusion if, at this point in the letter, Paul were to say that the Israel of God is limited to Jewish believers, for such a claim could be read to support the theology of the Judaizers. At the end of the letter, Paul says what he has been saying throughout. Gentile and Jewish believers belong to the true Israel, they are the children of Isaac, and they are part of Abraham's family.

Paul closes the letter by saying that if someone wants marks on the body, then Paul has them (6:17). As a follower of Jesus, as one who bears Jesus's cross, he has the marks of persecution on his body, showing that he is a true follower of Christ. What the believers in Galatia need most is God's grace, and Paul prays that it is unleashed in their lives (6:18).

Galatians: Commentaries

Betz, Hans Dieter. *Galatians: A Commentary on Paul's Letter to the Churches in Galatia.* Hermeneia. Philadelphia: Fortress, 1979.

Bligh, John. *Galatians: A Discussion of St. Paul's Epistle.* London: St. Paul Publications, 1969.

Bruce, F. F. *The Epistle to the Galatians: A Commentary on the Greek Text.* NIGTC. Grand Rapids: Eerdmans, 1982.

Burton, Ernest De Witt. *A Critical and Exegetical Commentary on the Epistle to the Galatians.* ICC. New York: Scribner's, 1920.

Das, A. Andrew. *Galatians*. Concordia Commentary: A Theological Exposition of Sacred Scripture. St. Louis: Concordia, 2014.

de Boer, Martinus C. *Galatians: A Commentary*. NTL. Louisville: Westminster John Knox, 2011.

deSilva, David A. *The Letter to the Galatians*. NICNT. Grand Rapids: Eerdmans, 2018.

Duncan, George S. *The Epistle of Paul to the Galatians*. MNTC. New York: Harper, 1934.

Dunn, James D. G. *The Epistle to the Galatians*. BNTC. Peabody, MA: Hendrickson, 1993.

Esler, Philip F. *Galatians*. New York: Routledge, 1998.

Fee, Gordon D. *Galatians*. Pentecostal Commentary Series. Dorset: Deo, 2007.

Fung, Ronald Y. *The Epistle to the Galatians*. NICNT. Grand Rapids: Eerdmans, 1988.

Garlington, Don. *An Exposition of Galatians: A Reading from the New Perspective*. 3rd ed. Eugene, OR: Wipf & Stock, 2007.

George, Timothy. *Galatians*. NAC. Nashville: Broadman & Holman, 1994.

Guthrie, Donald. *Galatians*. NCB. Grand Rapids: Eerdmans, 1973.

Hays, Richard. "Letter to the Galatians: Introduction, Commentary, and Reflections." In *The New Interpreter's Bible*, edited by Leander E. Keck et al., 11:181–348. Nashville: Abingdon, 2000.

Longenecker, Richard N. *Galatians*. WBC. Dallas: Word, 1990.

Lührmann, Dieter. *Galatians*. Translated by O. C. Dean Jr. Continental Commentaries. Minneapolis: Fortress, 1992.

Luther, Martin. *Lectures on Galatians 1535: Chapters 1–4*. Edited by Jaroslav Pelikan. LW 26. St. Louis: Concordia, 1963.

———. *Lectures on Galatians 1535: Chapters 5–6. Lectures on Galatians 1519: Chapters 1–6*. Edited by Jaroslav Pelikan. LW 27. St. Louis: Concordia, 1964.

Martyn, J. Louis. *Galatians: A New Translation with Introduction and Commentary*. AB 33. New York: Doubleday, 1997.

Matera, Frank J. *Galatians*. SP. Collegeville, MN: Liturgical Press, 1992.

McKnight, Scot. *Galatians*. NIVAC. Grand Rapids: Zondervan, 1995.

Moo, Douglas J. *Galatians*. BECNT. Grand Rapids: Baker Academic, 2013.

Morris, Leon. *Galatians: Paul's Charter of Christian Freedom*. Downers Grove, IL: InterVarsity, 1996.

Riches, John. *Galatians through the Centuries*. BBC. Oxford: Blackwell, 2008.

Ridderbos, Herman N. *Epistle of Paul to the Churches of Galatia*. Translated by Henry Zylstra. NICNT. Grand Rapids: Eerdmans, 1953.

Schreiner, Thomas R. *Galatians*. ZECNT. Grand Rapids: Zondervan, 2010.

Silva, Moisés. "Galatians." In *Commentary on the New Testament Use of the Old Testament*, edited by G. K. Beale and D. A. Carson, 785–812. Grand Rapids: Baker Academic, 2007.

Stott, John R. W. *The Message of Galatians*. London: Inter-Varsity, 1968.

Williams, Sam K. *Galatians*. ANTC. Nashville: Abingdon, 1997.

Witherington, Ben, III. *Grace in Galatia: A Commentary on Paul's Letter to the Galatians*. Grand Rapids: Eerdmans, 1998.

—————— Galatians: Articles, Essays, and Monographs ——————

Abegg, Martin G., Jr. "4QMMT, Paul, and 'Works of the Law.'" In *The Bible at Qumran: Text, Shape, and Interpretation*, edited by Peter W. Flint, 203–16. Grand Rapids: Eerdmans, 2001.

Alexander, T. Desmond. "Further Observations on the Term 'Seed' in Genesis." *TynBul* 42 (1997): 63–67.

Arnold, Clinton E. "'I Am Astonished That You Are So Quickly Turning Away!' (Gal 1.6): Paul and Anatolian Folk Belief." *NTS* 51 (2005): 429–49.

———. "Returning to the Domain of the Powers: *Stoicheia* as Evil Spirits in Galatians 4:3, 9." *NovT* 38 (1996): 55–76.

Avemarie, Friedrich. "Paul and the Claim of the Law according to the Scripture: Leviticus 18:5, Galatians 3:12, and Romans 10:5." In *The Beginnings of Christianity: A Collection of Articles*, edited by Jack Pastor and Menachem Mor, 125–48. Jerusalem: Yad Ben-Zvi, 2005.

Baasland, Ernst. "Persecution: A Neglected Feature in the Letter to the Galatians." *ST* 38 (1984): 135–50.

Bachmann, Michael. *Anti-Judaism in Galatians? Exegetical Studies on a Polemical Letter and on Paul's Theology*. Translated by Robert L. Brawley. Grand Rapids: Eerdmans, 2008.

Bandstra, Andrew J. *The Law and the Elements of the World: An Exegetical Study in Aspects of Paul's Teaching*. Grand Rapids: Eerdmans, 1964.

Barclay, John M. G. "Mirror-Reading a Polemical Letter: Galatians as a Test Case." *JSNT* 31 (1987): 73–93.

———. *Obeying the Truth: Paul's Ethics in Galatians*. Minneapolis: Fortress, 1988.

Barrett, Charles K. "The Allegory of Abraham, Sarah, and Hagar in the Argument of Galatians." In *Rechtfertigung: Festschrift für Ernst Käsemann zum 70. Geburtstag*, edited by J. Friedrich, W. Pöhlmann, and P. Stuhlmacher, 1–16. Tübingen: Mohr Siebeck, 1976.

———. *Freedom and Obligation: A Study in the Epistle to the Galatians*. Philadelphia: Westminster, 1985.

———. "Paul and the 'Pillar' Apostles." In *Studia Paulina in Honorem J. de Zwaan*, edited by J. N. Sevenster and W. C. van Unnik, 1–19. Haarlem: Bohn, 1953.

Bauckham, Richard. "James, Peter, and the Gentiles." In *The Missions of James, Peter, and Paul: Tension in Early Christianity*, edited by Bruce Chilton and Craig Evans, 91–115. NovTSup 115. Leiden: Brill, 2005.

Baugh, S. M. "Galatians 3:20 and the Covenant of Redemption." *WTJ* 66 (2004): 49–70.

Beale, G. K. "The Old Testament Background of Paul's Reference to 'the Fruit of Spirit' in Galatians 5:22." *BBR* 15 (2005): 1–38.

———. "Peace and Mercy upon the Israel of God: The Old Testament Background of Galatians 6:16b." *Bib* 80 (1999): 204–23.

Belleville, Linda. "'Under Law': Structural Analysis and the Pauline Concept of Law in Galatians 3:21–4:11." *JSNT* 26 (1986): 53–78.

Betz, Hans Dieter. "The Literary Composition and Function of Paul's Letter to the Galatians." *NTS* 21 (1975): 352–79.

Black, David A. "Weakness Language in Galatians." *GTJ* 4 (1983): 15–36.

Bonneau, Normand. "The Logic of Paul's Argument on the Curse of the Law in Galatians 3:10–14." *NovT* 39 (1997): 60–80.

Borger, Peder. "Observations on the Theme 'Paul and Philo': Paul's Preaching of Circumcision in Galatia (Gal. 5:11) and Debates on Circumcision in Philo." In *The Pauline Literature and Theology*, edited by S. Pederson, 92–102. Göttingen: Vandenhoeck & Ruprecht, 1980.

Brawley, Robert L. "Meta-Ethics and the Role of Works of Law in Galatians." In *Lutherische und Neue Paulusperspektive: Beiträge zu einem Schlüsselproblem der gegenwärtigen exegetischen Diskussion*, edited by Michael Bachmann, 135–59. WUNT 182. Tübingen: Mohr Siebeck, 2005.

Brinsmead, B. H. *Galatians—Dialogical Response to Opponents*. SBLDS 65. Chico, CA: Scholars Press, 1982.

Bryant, Robert A. *The Risen Crucified Christ in Galatians*. SBLDS 185. Atlanta: Society of Biblical Literature, 2001.

Byrne, Brendan J. *"Sons of God"—"Seed of Abraham": A Study of the Idea of the Sonship of God of All Christians in Paul against the Jewish Background*. Rome: Pontifical Biblical Institute, 1979.

Calvert, Nancy L. "Abraham and Idolatry: Paul's Comparison of Obedience to the Law with Idolatry in Galatians 4.1–10." In *Paul and the Scriptures of Israel*, edited by C. A. Evans and J. A. Sanders, 222–37. JSNTSup 83. Sheffield: JSOT Press, 1993.

Campbell, R. A. "'Against Such Things There Is No Law'? Galatians 5:23b Again." *ExpTim* 107 (1996): 271–72.

Caneday, Ardel B. "The Faithfulness of Jesus Christ as a Theme in Paul's Theology in Galatians." In *The Faith of Jesus Christ: Exegetical, Biblical, and Theological Studies*, edited by Michael F. Bird and Preston Sprinkle, 221–46. Peabody, MA: Hendrickson, 2009.

Cavallin, H. C. C. "'The Righteous Shall Live by Faith': A Decisive Argument for the Traditional Interpretation." *ST* 32 (1978): 33–43.

Chibici-Revneanu, Nicole. "Leben im Gesetz: Die paulinische Interpretation von Lev 18:5 (Gal 3:12; Röm 10:5)." *NovT* 50 (2008): 105–19.

Choi, Hung-Sik. "PISTIS in Galatians 5:5–6: Neglected Evidence for the Faithfulness of Christ." *JBL* 124 (2005): 467–90.

Ciampa, Roy E. *The Presence and Function of Scripture in Galatians 1 and 2*. WUNT 102. Tübingen: Mohr Siebeck, 1998.

Collins, C. John. "Galatians 3:16: What Kind of Exegete Was Paul?" *TynBul* 54 (2003): 75–86.

———. "Syntactical Note (Genesis 3:15): Is the Woman's Seed Singular or Plural?" *TynBul* 48 (1997): 139–48.

Cosgrove, Charles H. "Arguing Like a Mere Human Being: Galatians 3:15–18 in Rhetorical Perspective." *NTS* 34 (1988): 536–49.

———. *Cross and Spirit: A Study in the Argument and Theology of Galatians*. Macon, GA: Mercer University Press, 1988.

Cowan, J. Andrew. "The Legal Significance of Christ's Risen Life: Union with Christ and Justification in Galatians 2:17–20." *JSNT* 40 (2018): 453–72.

Cranford, Michael. "The Possibility of Perfect Obedience: Paul and an Implied Premise in Galatians 3:10 and 5:3." *NovT* 36 (1994): 242–58.

Crownfield, Frederic R. "The Singular Problem of the Dual Galatians." *JBL* 64 (1945): 491–500.

Cummins, Stephen A. *Paul and the Crucified Christ in Antioch: Maccabean Martyrdom and Galatians 1 and 2.* SNTSMS 114. Cambridge: Cambridge University Press, 2001.

Dahl, Nils A. "Der Name Israel: Zur Auslegung von Gal 6,16." *Judaica* 6 (1950): 161–70.

Das, A. Andrew. "Another Look at ἐὰν μή in Galatians 2:16." *JBL* 119 (2000): 529–39.

———. "Galatians 3:10: A 'Newer Perspective' on an Omitted Premise." In *Unity and Diversity in the Gospels and Paul*, edited by Christopher W. Skinner and Kelly R. Iverson, 203–23. Atlanta: Society of Biblical Literature, 2012.

———. *Paul and the Stories of Israel: Grand Thematic Narratives in Galatians.* Minneapolis: Fortress, 2016.

Davis, Anne. "Allegorically Speaking in Galatians 4:21–5:1." *BBR* 14 (2004): 161–74.

Davis, Basil S. *Christ as Devotio: The Argument of Galatians 3:1–14.* Lanham, MD: University Press of America, 2002.

de Boer, Martinus C. "The Meaning of the Phrase τὰ στοιχεῖα τοῦ κόσμου in Galatians." *NTS* 53 (2007): 204–24.

de Roo, Jacqueline C. R. *"Works of the Law" at Qumran and in Paul.* NTM 13. Sheffield: Sheffield Phoenix, 2007.

Donaldson, T. L. "The 'Curse of the Law' and the Inclusion of the Gentiles: Galatians 3:13–14." *NTS* 32 (1986): 94–112.

Dunn, James D. G. "The Incident at Antioch (Gal 2:11–18)." *JSNT* 18 (1983): 3–57.

———. "Works of the Law and the Curse of the Law (Galatians 3:10–14)." *NTS* 31 (1985): 523–42.

———. "Yet Once More—'The Works of the Law': A Response." *JSNT* 46 (1992): 99–117.

Dunne, John Anthony. *Persecution and Participation in Galatians.* WUNT 2/454. Tübingen: Mohr Siebeck, 2017.

Eastman, Susan G. "'Cast Out the Slave Woman and Her Son': The Dynamics of Exclusion and Inclusion in Galatians 4.30." *JSNT* 28 (2006): 309–36.

———. "The Evil Eye and the Curse of the Law: Galatians 3.1 Revisited." *JSNT* 83 (2001): 69–87.

———. *Recovering Paul's Mother Tongue: Language and Theology in Galatians.* Grand Rapids: Eerdmans, 2007.

Elliott, Mark W., Scott J. Hafemann, N. T. Wright, and John Frederick, eds. *Galatians and Christian Theology: Justification, the Gospel, and Ethics in Paul's Letter.* Grand Rapids: Baker Academic, 2014.

Elliott, Susan. *Cutting Too Close for Comfort: Paul's Letter to the Galatians in Its Anatolian Cultic Context.* JSNTSup 248. London: T&T Clark, 2003.

Fairweather, Janet. "The Epistle to the Galatians and Classical Rhetoric: Parts 1–2." *TynBul* 45, no. 1 (1994): 2–38.

———. "The Epistle to the Galatians and Classical Rhetoric: Part 3." *TynBul* 45, no. 2 (1994): 213–43.

Filtvedt, Ole Jakob. "'God's Israel' in Galatians 6:16: An Overview and Assessment of the Key Arguments." *CBR* 15 (2016): 123–40.

Fredriksen, Paula. "Judaism, the Circumcision of Gentiles, and Apocalyptic Hope: Another Look at Galatians 1 and 2." *JTS* 42 (1991): 532–64.

Garlington, Don. "Role Reversal and Paul's Use of Scripture in Galatians 3.10–13." *JSNT* 65 (1997): 85–121.

Gathercole, Simon J. "The Petrine and Pauline Sola Fide in Galatians 2. In *Lutherische und Neue Paulusperspektive: Beiträge zu einem Schlüsselproblem der gegenwärtigen exegetischen Diskussion*, edited by Michael Bachmann, 309–27. WUNT 182. Tübingen: Mohr Siebeck, 2005.

———. "Torah, Life, and Salvation: Leviticus 18:5 in Early Judaism and the New Testament." In *From Prophecy to Testament: The Function of the Old Testament in the New*, edited by C. A. Evans and J. A. Sanders, 131–50. Peabody, MA: Hendrickson, 2004.

Gaventa, Beverly R. "Galatians 1 and 2: Autobiography as Paradigm." *NovT* 4 (1986): 309–26.

———. "The Maternity of Paul." In *The Conversation Continues: Studies in Paul and John in Honor of J. Louis Martyn*, edited by Robert Y. Fortna and Beverly R. Gaventa, 189–201. Nashville: Abingdon, 1990.

Gignilliat, Mark S. "Isaiah's Offspring: Paul's Isaiah 54:1 Quotation in Galatians 4:27." *BBR* 25 (2015): 205–23.

Goddard, A. J., and S. A. Cummins. "Ill or Ill-Treated? Conflict and Persecution as the Context of Paul's Original Ministry in Galatia (Galatians 4.12–20)." *JSNT* 52 (1993): 93–126.

Gombis, Timothy G. "The 'Transgressor' and the 'Curse of the Law': The Logic of Paul's Argument in Galatians 2–3." *NTS* 53 (2007): 81–93.

Gordon, T. David. "Abraham and Sinai Contrasted in Galatians 3:6–14." In *The Law Is Not of Faith: Essays on Works and Grace in the Mosaic Covenants*, edited by Bryan D. Estelle, J. V. Fesko, and David VanDrunen, 240–58. Phillipsburg, NJ: P&R, 2009.

———. "A Note on ΠΑΙΔΑΓΩΓΟΣ in Galatians 3.24–25." *NTS* 35 (1989): 150–54.

———. "The Problem at Galatia." *Interpretation* 41 (1987): 32–43.

Grindheim, Sigurd. "Apostate Turned Prophet: Paul's Prophetic Understanding and Prophetic Hermeneutic with Special Reference to Galatians 3.10–12." *NTS* 53 (2007): 545–72.

Gundry, Robert H. "Grace, Works, and Staying Saved in Paul." *Bib* 66 (1985): 1–38.

Hafemann, Scott J. "Paul and the Exile of Israel in Galatians 3–4." In *Exile: Old Testament, Jewish, and Christian Conceptions*, edited by James M. Scott, 329–71. JSJSup 56. Leiden: Brill, 1997.

Hahn, Scott W. "Covenant, Oath, and the Aqedah: Διαθήκη in Galatians 3:15–18." *CBQ* 67 (2005): 79–100.

Hall, R. G. "The Rhetorical Outline for Galatians: A Reconsideration." *JBL* 106 (1987): 277–88.

Hamilton, James M., Jr. "The Seed of the Woman and the Blessing of Abraham." *TynBul* 58 (2007): 253–73.

Hansen, G. Walter. *Abraham in Galatians: Epistolary and Rhetorical Contexts*. JSNTSup 29. Sheffield: Sheffield Academic, 1989.

Hardin, Justin K. *Galatians and the Imperial Cult: A Critical Analysis of the First-Century Social Context of Paul's Letter*. WUNT 237. Tübingen: Mohr Siebeck, 2008.

Hays, Richard B. *The Faith of Jesus Christ: An Investigation of the Narrative Substructure of Galatians 3:1–4:11*. 2nd ed. Grand Rapids: Eerdmans, 2002.

Hong, In-Gyu. *The Law in Galatians*. JSNTSup 81. Sheffield: Sheffield Academic, 1993.

Hove, Richard W. *Equality in Christ? Galatians 3:28 and the Gender Dispute*. Wheaton: Crossway, 1999.

Howard, George. *Paul: Crisis in Galatia; A Study in Early Christian Theology*. 2nd ed. SNTSMS 35. Cambridge: Cambridge University Press, 1990.

Hughes, John J. "Hebrews IX 15ff. and Galatians III 15ff.: A Study in Covenant Practice and Procedure." *NovT* 21 (1979): 27–96.

Hunn, Debbie. "The Baptism of Galatians 3:27: A Contextual Approach." *ExpTim* 115 (2005): 372–75.

———. "Galatians 3:13–14: Mere Assertion?" *WTJ* 80 (2018): 141–57.

Jobes, Karen H. "Jerusalem, Our Mother: Metalepsis and Intertextuality in Galatians 4:21–31." *WTJ* 55 (1993): 299–320.

Johnson, H. Wayne. "The Paradigm of Abraham in Galatians 3:6–9." *TJ* 8 (1987): 179–99.

Kern, Philip H. *Rhetoric in Galatians: Assessing an Approach to Paul's Epistle*. SNTSMS 101. Cambridge: Cambridge University Press, 1998.

Köstenberger, Andreas. "The Identity of the ἸΣΡΑΗΛ ΤΟΥ ΘΕΟΥ (Israel of God) in Galatians 6:16." *Faith and Mission* 19 (2001): 3–24.

Kwon, Yon-Gyong. *Eschatology in Galatians: Rethinking Paul's Response to the Crisis in Galatia*. WUNT 183. Tübingen: Mohr Siebeck, 2004.

Lambrecht, Jan. "Abraham and His Offspring: A Comparison of Galatians 5,1 with 3,13." *Bib* 80 (1999): 525–36.

———. "Critical Reflections on Paul's 'Partisan ἐκ' as Recently Presented by Don Garlington." *ETL* 85 (2009): 135–41.

Lee, Chee-Chiew. *The Blessing of Abraham, the Spirit, and Justification in Galatians: Their Relationship and Significance for Understanding Paul's Theology*. Eugene, OR: Pickwick, 2013.

Longenecker, Bruce W. *The Triumph of Abraham's God: The Transformation of Identity in Galatians*. Nashville: Abingdon, 1998.

———. "'Until Christ Is Formed in You': Suprahuman Forces and Moral Character in Galatians." *CBQ* 61 (1999): 92–108.

Longenecker, Richard N. "The Pedagogical Nature of the Law in Galatians 3:19–4:7." *JETS* 25 (1982): 53–61.

Lull, D. J. "'The Law Was Our Pedagogue': A Study in Galatians 3.19–25." *JBL* 105 (1986): 481–98.

Lutjens, Ronald. "'You Do Not Do What You Want': What Does Galatians 5:17 Really Mean?" *Presb* 16 (1990): 103–17.

Machen, J. Gresham. *Machen's Notes on Galatians: Notes on Biblical Exposition and Other Aids to Interpretation of the Epistle to the Galatians from the Writings of J. Gresham Machen*. Edited by John H. Skilton. Nutley, NJ: Presbyterian & Reformed, 1977.

Martin, Neil. "Returning to the *Stoichea tou Kosmou:* Enslavement to the Physical Elements in Galatians 4:3 and 9?" *JSNT* 40 (2018): 434–52.

Martin, Troy W. "The Covenant of Circumcision (Gen. 17:9–14) and the Situational-Antitheses in Galatians 3:28." *JBL* 122 (2003): 111–25.

———. "Whose Flesh? What Temptation? (Gal. 4.13–14)." *JSNT* 74 (1999): 65–91.

Martyn, J. Louis. "Apocalyptic Antinomies in Paul's Letter to the Galatians." *NTS* 31 (1985): 410–24.

Matera, Frank J. "The Culmination of Paul's Argument to the Galatians: Gal. 5.1–6:7." *JSNT* 32 (1988): 79–91.

Matlock, R. Barry. "PISTIS in Galatians 3:26: Neglected Evidence for 'Faith in Christ'?" *NTS* 49 (2003): 433–39.

———. "The Rhetoric of πίστις in Paul: Galatians 2.16, 3.22, and Philippians 3.9." *JSNT* 30 (2007): 173–203.

McEleney, Neil. "Conversion, Circumcision, and the Law." *NTS* 20 (1974): 319–41.

McLean, Bradley H. *The Cursed Christ: Mediterranean Expulsion Rituals and Pauline Soteriology.* JSNTSup 126. Sheffield: Sheffield Academic, 1996.

Meier, John P. "The Brothers and Sisters of Jesus in Ecumenical Perspective." *CBQ* 54 (1992): 1–28.

Mijoga, Hilary B. P. *The Pauline Notion of Deeds of the Law.* Lanham, MD: International Scholars Publications, 1999.

Mitchell, Stephen. *Anatolia: Land, Men, and God in Asia Minor.* Vol. 1, *The Celts in Anatolia and the Impact of Roman Rule.* Oxford: Clarendon, 1993.

———. *Anatolia: Land, Men, and God in Asia Minor.* Vol. 2, *The Rise of the Church.* Oxford: Clarendon, 1993.

Mitternacht, Dieter. "Foolish Galatians?—A Recipient-Oriented Assessment of Paul's Letter." In *The Galatians Debate: Contemporary Issues in Rhetorical and Historical Interpretation,* edited by Mark D. Nanos, 408–33. Peabody, MA: Hendrickson, 2002.

Moo, Douglas J. "'Law,' 'Works of the Law,' and Legalism in Paul." *WTJ* 45 (1983): 73–100.

Morales, Rodrigo J. *The Spirit and the Restoration of Israel: New Exodus and New Creation; Motifs in Galatians.* WUNT 282. Tübingen: Mohr Siebeck, 2010.

———. "The Words of the Luminaries, the Curse of the Law, and the Outpouring of the Spirit in Gal 3,10–14." *ZNW* 100 (2009): 269–77.

Morland, Kjell Arne. *The Rhetoric of Curse in Galatians: Paul Confronts Another Gospel.* Atlanta: Scholars Press, 1995.

Muddiman, John. "An Anatomy of Galatians." In *Crossing the Boundaries: Essays in Biblical Interpretation in Honour of Michael D. Goulder,* edited by Stanley E. Porter, Paul Joyce, and David E. Orton, 257–70. BIS 8. Leiden: Brill, 1994.

Nanos, Mark D. "Inter-and Intra-Jewish Political Context of Paul's Letter to the Galatians." In *The Galatians Debate: Contemporary Issues in Rhetorical and Historical Interpretation,* edited by Mark D. Nanos, 396–407. Peabody, MA: Hendrickson, 2002.

———. *The Irony of Galatians: Paul's Letter in First-Century Context.* Minneapolis: Fortress, 2000.

———. "What Was at Stake in Peter's 'Eating with Gentiles' at Antioch?" In *The Galatians Debate: Contemporary Issues in Rhetorical and Historical Interpretation*, edited by Mark D. Nanos, 282–318. Peabody, MA: Hendrickson, 2000.

Nolland, John. "Uncircumcised Proselytes?" *JSJ* 12 (1981): 173–94.

Oakes, Peter S. "*Pistis* as a Relational Way of Life in Galatians." *JSNT* 30 (2018): 255–75.

O'Brien, Kelli S. "The Curse of the Law (Galatians 3:13): Crucifixion, Persecution, and Deuteronomy 21:22–23." *JSNT* 29 (2006): 55–76.

Owen, Paul L. "The 'Works of the Law' in Romans and Galatians: A New Defense of the Subjective Genitive." *JBL* 126 (2007): 553–77.

Perriman, Andrew C. "The Rhetorical Strategy of Galatians 4:21–5:1." *EvQ* 65 (1993): 27–42.

Rainbow, Paul A. *The Way of Salvation: The Role of Christian Obedience in Justification.* Waynesboro, GA: Paternoster, 2005.

Räisänen, Heikki. "Galatians 2:16 and Paul's Break with Judaism." *NTS* 31 (1985): 543–53.

Rapa, Robert Keith. *The Meaning of "Works of the Law" in Galatians and Romans.* Studies in Biblical Literature 31. New York: Peter Lang, 2001.

Ray, Charles A., Jr. "The Identity of the 'Israel of God.'" *TTE* 50 (1994): 105–14.

Reicke, Bo. "The Law and This World according to Paul." *JBL* 70 (1951): 259–67.

Richardson, Peter. *Israel in the Apostolic Church.* SNTSMS 10. Cambridge: Cambridge University Press, 1969.

Robinson, D. W. B. "The Circumcision of Titus and Paul's 'Liberty'" *ABR* 12 (1964): 24–42.

Ropes, J. H. *The Singular Problem of the Epistle to the Galatians.* Cambridge: Harvard University Press, 1929.

Russell, Walter B. "The Apostle Paul's Redemptive-Historical Argumentation in Galatians 5:13–26." *WTJ* 57 (1995): 333–57.

———. "Rhetorical Analysis of the Book of Galatians." *BSac* 150 (1993): 341–58, 416–39.

Sanders, E. P. "Jewish Association with Gentiles and Galatians 2:11–14." In *The Conversation Continues: Studies in Paul and John in Honor of J. Louis Martyn*, edited by Robert T. Fortna and Beverly R. Gaventa, 170–88. Nashville: Abingdon, 1990.

Schnabel, Eckhard J. *Early Christian Mission.* 2 vols. Downers Grove, IL: InterVarsity, 2004.

Scott, Ian W. "Common Ground? The Role of Galatians 2.16 in Paul's Argument." *NTS* 53 (2007): 425–35.

Scott, James M. "'For as Many as Are of Works of the Law Are Under a Curse' (Galatians 3.10)." In *Paul and the Scriptures of Israel*, edited by C. A. Evans and J. A. Sanders, 187–221. JSNTSup 83. Sheffield: JSOT Press, 1993.

Silva, Moisés. "Faith versus Works of Law in Galatians." In *Justification and Variegated Nomism*, vol. 2, *The Paradoxes of Paul*, edited by D. A. Carson, P. T. O'Brien, and M. A. Seifrid, 217–48. Tübingen: Mohr Siebeck, 2004.

———. *Interpreting Galatians: Explorations in Exegetical Method.* 2nd ed. Grand Rapids: Baker Academic, 2001.

Smiles, Vincent M. *The Gospel and the Law in Galatia: Paul's Response to Jewish Christian Separatism and the Threat of Galatian Apostasy.* Collegeville, MN: Liturgical Press, 1998.

Smit, Joop. "The Letter of Paul to the Galatians: A Deliberative Speech." *NTS* 35 (1989): 1–26.

Smith, C. C. "Ἐκκλεῖσαι in Galatians 4:17: The Motif of the Excluded Lover as a Metaphor of Manipulation." *CBQ* 58 (1996): 480–99.

Smith, Michael J. "The Role of the Pedagogue in Galatians." *BSac* 163 (2006): 97–214.

Sprinkle, Preston. *Law and Life: The Interpretation of Leviticus 18:5 in Early Judaism and in Paul.* WUNT 241. Tübingen: Mohr Siebeck, 2008.

———. "Πίστις Χριστοῦ as an Eschatological Event." In *The Faith of Jesus Christ: Biblical, and Theological Studies*, edited by Michael F. Bird and Preston Sprinkle, 165–84. Peabody, MA: Hendrickson, 2009.

Stanley, Christopher D. "'Under a Curse': A Fresh Reading of Galatians 3.10–14." *NTS* 36 (1990): 481–511.

Stanton, Graham. "The Law of Moses and the Law of Christ: Galatians 3:1–6:2." In *Paul and the Mosaic Law*, edited by James D. G. Dunn, 99–116. WUNT 89. Tübingen: Mohr Siebeck, 1996.

Strelan, J. G. "Burden Bearing and the Law of Christ: A Re-Examination of Galatians 6:2." *JBL* 94 (1975): 266–76.

Thornton, T. C. G. "Jewish New Moon Festivals: Galatians 4:3–11 and Colossians 2:16." *JTS* 40 (1989): 97–100.

Tolmie, D. Francois. *Persuading the Galatians: A Text-Centred Rhetorical Analysis of a Pauline Letter.* WUNT 190. Tübingen: Mohr Siebeck, 2005.

Trudinger, L. Paul. "'ΕΤΕΡΟΝ ΔΕ ΤΩΝ ΑΠΟΣΤΟΛΩΝ ΟΥΚ ΕΙΔΟΝ, ΕΙ ΜΗ ΙΑΚΩΒΟΝ': A Note on Galatians i 19." *NovT* 17 (1975): 200–202.

Tyson, J. B. "Paul's Opponents in Galatia." *NovT* 10 (1968): 241–54.

VanLandingham, Chris. *Judgment and Justification in Early Judaism and the Apostle Paul.* Peabody, MA: Hendrickson, 2006.

Vos, Johan S. "Paul's Argumentation in Galatians 1–2." In *The Galatians Debate: Contemporary Issues in Rhetorical and Historical Interpretation*, edited by Mark D. Nanos, 169–80. Peabody, MA: Hendrickson, 2002.

Wakefield, Andrew H. *Where to Live: The Hermeneutical Significance of Paul's Citations from Scripture in Galatians 3:1–14.* AcBib 14. Atlanta: Society of Biblical Literature, 2003.

Wallace, Daniel B. "Galatians 3:19–20: A Crux Interpretum for Paul's View of the Law." *WTJ* 52 (1990): 225–45.

Wallis, Ian G. *Faith of Jesus Christ in Early Christian Traditions.* SNTSMS 84. Cambridge: Cambridge University Press, 1995.

Walter, Nikolaus. "Paul and the Opponents of the Christ-Gospel in Galatia." In *The Galatians Debate: Contemporary Issues in Rhetorical and Historical Interpretation*, edited by Mark D. Nanos, 62–66. Peabody, MA: Hendrickson, 2002.

Watson, Francis. *Paul and the Hermeneutics of Faith.* London: T&T Clark, 2004.

Watts, Rikk E. "'For I Am Not Ashamed of the Gospel': Romans 1:16–17 and Habakkuk 2:4." In *Romans and the People of God*, edited by S. Soderlund and N. T. Wright, 3–25. Grand Rapids: Eerdmans, 1999.

Weima, Jeffrey A. D. "Gal 6:11–18: A Hermeneutical Key to the Galatian Letter." *CTJ* 28 (1993): 90–107.

———. *Neglected Endings: The Significance of the Pauline Letter Closings.* JSNTSup 101. Sheffield: JSOT Press, 1994.

Westerholm, Stephen. "On Fulfilling the Whole Law (Gal 5:14)." *Svensk Exegetisk Årsbok* 51–52 (1986–87): 229–37.

———. *Perspectives Old and New on Paul: The "Lutheran" Paul and His Critics.* Grand Rapids: Eerdmans, 2004.

Wiarda, Timothy. "Plot and Character in Galatians 1–2." *TynBul* 55 (2004): 231–52.

Wilcox, Max. "The Promise of the 'Seed' in the New Testament and the Targumim." *JSNT* 5 (1979): 2–20.

———. "'Upon the Tree'—Deut. 21:22–23 in the New Testament." *JBL* 96 (1977): 90–94.

Wiley, Tatha. *Paul and the Gentile Women: Reframing Galatians.* New York: Continuum, 2005.

Williams, Sam K. "The Hearing of Faith: ΑΚΟΗ ΠΙΣΤΕΩΣ in Galatians 3." *NTS* 35 (1989): 82–93.

———. "Justification and the Spirit in Galatians." *JSNT* 29 (1987): 91–100.

Willitts, Joel. "Context Matters: Paul's Use of Leviticus 18:5 in Galatians 3:12." *TynBul* 54 (2003): 105–22.

———. "Isa 54,1 and Gal 4,24b–27: Reading Genesis in Light of Isaiah." *ZNW* 96 (2005): 188–210.

Wilson, R. McL. "Gnostics—in Galatia?" In *Studia Evangelica*, vol. 4, *Papers Presented to the Second International Congress on New Testament Studies Held at Christ Church, Oxford, 1961*, part 1, *The New Testament Scriptures*, edited by F. L. Cross et al., 358–67. Berlin: Akademie, 1968.

Wilson, Todd A. *The Curse of the Law and the Crisis in Galatia: Reassessing the Purpose of Galatians.* WUNT 225. Tübingen: Mohr Siebeck, 2007.

———. "The Law of Christ and the Law of Moses: Reflections on a Recent Trend in Interpretation." *CBR* 5 (2006): 123–44.

———. "'Under Law' in Galatians: A Pauline Theological Abbreviation." *JTS* 56 (2005): 362–92.

———. "Wilderness Apostasy and Paul's Portrayal of the Crisis in Galatians." *NTS* 50 (2004): 550–71.

Wisdom, Jeffrey R. *Blessing for the Nations and the Curse of the Law: Paul's Citation of Genesis and Deuteronomy in Gal 3.8–10.* WUNT 133. Tübingen: Mohr Siebeck, 2001.

Witherington, Ben, III. "Rite and Rights for Women—Galatians 3.28." *NTS* 27 (1981): 593–604.

Woyke Johannes. "Nochmals zu den 'schwachen und unfähigen Elementen' (Gal. 4.9): Paulus, Philo und die στοιχεῖα τοῦ κόσμου." *NTS* 54 (2008): 221–34.

Wright, N. T. "Paul, Arabia, and Elijah (Galatians 1:17)." *JBL* 115 (1996): 683–92.

Yeung, Maureen W. *Faith in Jesus and Paul: A Comparison with Special Reference to "Faith That Can Move Mountains" and "Your Faith Has Healed/Saved You."* WUNT 147. Tübingen: Mohr Siebeck, 2002.

Young, Norman H. "*Paidagogos*: The Social Setting of a Pauline Metaphor." *NovT* 29 (1987): 150–76.

———. "Pronominal Shifts in Paul's Argument to the Galatians." In *Early Christianity in Late Antiquity and Beyond*, 205–15. Vol. 2 of Ancient *History in a Modern University*, edited by T. W. Hillard, R. A. Kearsley, C. E. V. Nixon, and A. M. Nobbs. Grand Rapids: Eerdmans, 1998.

Ziesler, J. A. *The Meaning of Righteousness in Paul: A Linguistic and Theological Enquiry*. SNTSMS 20. Cambridge: Cambridge University Press, 1972.

CHAPTER SIX

Ephesians

Introduction

The account of Paul's time in Ephesus is recorded in Acts 19. Ephesians is written in an exalted style, representing a theologically rich meditation upon the gospel of Christ. The separation between theology and ethics is ultimately artificial, but chapters 1–3 set the theological foundation, and chapters 4–6 apply the theology to the readers. Many scholars believe that the letter was originally an encyclical letter sent to many churches, and this is certainly possible, but it is more likely that the letter was originally sent to Ephesus, and the words "in Ephesus" were accidentally deleted in some manuscripts. We have no definite textual evidence that the letter was sent to other churches. It should also be noted that some scholars reject Pauline authorship. It is not my purpose here to adjudicate such questions, but I suggest that there are good reasons for seeing Paul as the author.

The specific topics covered in Ephesians are indicated below, but we can divide the letter as a whole into two larger sections.

Outline

Praising God for our salvation	1:1–14
Praying to understand our salvation	1:15–23
The wonder and greatness of our salvation	2:1–10
Jews and gentiles reconciled in one body	2:11–3:13
Prayer to be filled with God's fullness	3:14–21
Exhortation to unity	4:1–16
Exhortation to godliness in all realms of life	4:17–6:9
Stand against demonic powers	6:10–24

Praising God (1:1–14)

The introduction of the letter is unremarkable by Pauline standards, but then Paul breaks into one of the most remarkable texts in all his letters, as he praises God for the great salvation given in Jesus Christ (Eph. 1:3–14). In Greek verses 3–14 are one sentence, but it isn't hard to break it up into subsections, and the text is punctuated by "to the praise of his glorious grace" (1:6), "bring praise to his glory" (1:12), and "to the praise of his glory" (1:14). All three of these expressions are another way of saying, "Blessed be . . . God" (1:3 ESV). Paul begins this elegant letter with a God-centered pulse, which reverberates throughout the introduction. Unlike with many of his letters, Paul isn't initiating a debate but calling the readers to worship. The exalted style and meditative character of the letter fits the character and purpose of the letter from the outset.

Believers bless God because they enjoy "every spiritual blessing" (1:3) in the heavenly realms in Christ. One of the remarkable features of this paragraph is its trinitarian character. The Father blesses, elects, predestines, redeems, forgives, enlightens, plans, gives an inheritance, and seals. What is also striking is the repetition of prepositional phrases with Christ as the object: every spiritual blessing is ours "in Christ" (1:3), election is "in him" (1:4), predestination is "through Christ" (1:5), grace is lavished "in the Beloved One" (1:6), redemption is "in him" (1:7), God's will is "purposed in Christ" (1:9), all things are summed up "in Christ" (1:10), our inheritance is "in him" (1:11), hope is "in Christ" (1:12), and believers were sealed "in him" (1:13). The "spiritual" blessings given to believers are from the Holy Spirit. Believers are also "sealed with the promised Holy Spirit" (1:13), and the Spirit "is the down payment of our inheritance" (1:14). We can say that salvation is from the Father, accomplished in and through the Son, and applied by the Spirit.

A few comments should be made on the spiritual blessings Paul identifies. First, God chose and predestined believers to salvation (1:4–5). Election isn't based on human choice: it took place "before the foundation of the world" (1:4). Nor is election disconnected from the everyday lives of believers since its goal and intention is a holy life. It is significant that election took place "in Christ," which means that God's predestinating love becomes a reality through the work of Jesus Christ on the cross. Paul is not teaching here that God chose Christ, and then believers choose to be in Christ. Instead, God chose *believers* in Christ, which is a different conception. Clearly, predestination results in salvation because those who are predestined are adopted so that they become members of God's family, God's beloved sons and daughters. The purpose of concentrating on election is not to precipitate theological arguments but to provoke believers to praise God for the grace poured out upon them in salvation.

The second blessing is redemption (1:7–8), and again the lavishness of God's grace is celebrated. Redemption focuses on God's great act of deliverance, recalling Israel's liberation from Egyptian slavery by God's power (Exod. 6:6). Here the deliverance is from our trespasses, our deliberate flouting of God's will. The deliverance took place at a price, through the blood of Christ; the word "blood," as with OT sacrifices (Lev. 17:11), points to his death, which freed believers from sin.

Third, God has planned history according to his infinite knowledge and wisdom (1:9–10). The "mystery of his will," meaning that which was hidden in the past but has now been revealed, centers on Jesus Christ. It is striking that God's plan brings God pleasure and joy, and it should fascinate believers as well since it reflects God's wise purposes for humanity. The mystery, the secret now declared to all, is that everything in heaven and on earth is summed up in Christ, both in heaven and on earth. All of history points to Christ and finds its organizing principle and rationale in him.

Fourth, believers have the hope of a future inheritance (Eph. 1:11–12). The first-person plurals aren't restricted to Jewish believers, for the many first-person plurals in the previous verses can't be restricted to Jews. What is emphasized is the assurance of receiving the inheritance since in God's sovereign purposes everything that occurs conforms to his will (cf. 1:10). Believers, then, look to the future with hope and confidence, anticipating the inheritance promised them.

Fifth, believers were sealed with the Spirit when they believed in the gospel (1:13–14). Sealing means that they were authenticated as truly belonging to God. At the same time and along the same lines, the Spirit "is the down payment" of the final "inheritance": the Spirit guarantees the final resurrection of those who are redeemed. The sealing has an irrevocable character and thus provides assurance that those whom God has elected and predestined will enjoy the final inheritance. The shift to the second-person pronoun probably doesn't refer to gentiles, as some interpreters suggest. Instead, Paul now addresses the readers directly, assuring them of the completion of their salvation.

Thanksgiving and Prayer (1:15–23)

We usually find a thanksgiving after the greeting in Pauline letters, but in Ephesians the blessing or praise is placed immediately after the opening (1:3–14). The thanksgiving, then, comes after the blessing, but the thanksgiving is rather abbreviated (1:15–16) and transitions to prayer (1:17–23). Elsewhere in Paul, we see thanksgiving (as in Phil. 1:3–8; Col. 1:3–8) followed by prayer (Phil. 1:9–11; Col. 1:9–12), though in these latter instances the thanksgiving is longer. It isn't as though Paul wasn't truly thankful in Ephesians. He is thankful for their faith in Christ and love for believers, which are staples of the Christian life (Eph. 1:15–16).

In verse 17 Paul prays that the Father would grant believers "the Spirit" (per the CSB: not just a human spirit) of wisdom and revelation in knowing God, which demonstrates that human beings don't have the capacity to know God unaided or through the power of the human intellect. The result of the Father and the Spirit giving such an understanding is that believers are enlightened with "the eyes of your heart" (1:18). They grasp in a profound way the wonder of what God has done for them. Paul prays three things for believers: that they would know (1) "the hope of his calling" (1:18), (2) the greatness of God's "inheritance in the saints" (1:18), (3) and God's amazing power, which is given to believers (1:19–23). We immediately see that Paul especially concentrates on the last request.

First, believers need to grasp the hope to which they are called. Calling refers to God's effective summons of believers to faith, a calling that is as powerful as God creating light where there was darkness (2 Cor. 4:6). The hope that believers await is the sure confidence that they will become like Christ, purified from all sin, and thus they will be all that they were created to be.

Second, believers should pray so they understand that God's inheritance is his people. The text doesn't speak of *our* inheritance but *God's* inheritance, and his inheritance, so to speak, is his people. Since saints are God's inheritance, it shows how God delights in and prizes and loves those who belong to him. Paul prays that believers will know how greatly they are loved by God.

Third, through prayer believers will come to know the extraordinary power of God (Eph. 1:19–23). This is the same power that raised Christ from the dead and placed him at God's right hand in the heavenly sphere. Paul clearly alludes to Psalm 110:1, where "the Lord" (Israel's God) declares that David's Lord will sit at his right hand until all enemies are placed under the feet of the king. The prophecy finds its fulfillment in Jesus Christ, and the power of Christ is such that he rules over every power, even all angels whether good or evil, and his rule is unending, pertaining both to this age and the coming age. Ephesians 1:22 picks up the words of Psalm 8, which is a creation psalm celebrating the subjection of the entire world to human beings. The psalm reflects the rule that Adam and Eve were to exercise as God's vice-regents. Since human beings sinned, the rule promised to human beings has been fulfilled in Jesus Christ as the sinless one. All things are now subjected to him as he rules at God's right hand. Jesus is now the "head," which here means the ruler and authority over the church. The church is Christ's body, and the church is filled with the fullness of Christ. Since the church belongs to Christ and he is its head, Christ's victory, Christ's power, Christ's triumph is the church's triumph. Just as Christ triumphed over death, the church will reign in victory as well.

Death and Resurrection (2:1–10)

Paul prays that the readers will truly understand the great power that is theirs in Christ, and he assists them by reminding them of the power that rescued them from death in 2:1–10. The text can be split into three parts: (1) the plight of human beings (2:1–3), (2) the new life granted to believers (2:4–7), and (3) the basis and the purpose of the new life (2:8–10).

The plight of humanity is drawn in bleak terms. Unbelievers are not merely weakened or enfeebled by sin, but "dead" in their sins, completely cut off from life (2:1). The death in which unbelievers live is expressed in three ways: (1) sociological, (2) spiritual, and (3) psychological. Sociologically, unbelievers live "according to the ways of this world" (2:2). Secular society with all its attractions holds sway over them, and they live to gain the world's approval and applause. They are under the dominion of the evil age and are being conformed to this world (Rom. 12:2; Gal. 1:4). Paul often uses the term "age" to contrast this present age with the coming age (Eph. 1:21; 2:7; 3:9, 11, 21). Spiritually, believers are under the rule of Satan, who is the ruler of the air (2:2). "The air" refers to the areas beneath the moon and earth. Christ, of course, still rules over Satan, but Satan is at work in those who are disobedient and unbelieving.

Third, the psychological dimension of sin is sketched in 2:3. Unbelievers live according to "fleshly desires." In other words, in their daily life they conceive of what will bring them pleasure, and they endeavor to carry out those desires. We should note that the plight of human beings isn't merely psychological, as if the human subject is the only reality that needs to be attended to. The problem is multifaceted since there is an invisible spiritual (satanic) dimension of evil, and evil is also promulgated by the environment (the world) in which we live. Nevertheless, human beings are still responsible for their choices: they are not puppets on the world stage. The decisions made are authentic and genuine. All human beings, then, enter the world as "children under wrath." Death has wrapped its tentacles around us, and it is hard to see how we can escape.

It has often been pointed out that two of the most amazing and glorious words in the Bible are right here: "But God" (2:4). We can't rescue ourselves, but God can rescue us. The astonishing truth here is that God is full of mercy and love for sinners, for those who rejected and despised him. The same God who raised Christ from the dead also grants life to those dead in sins (2:5). Paul pauses to exclaim that such life testifies to God's grace, to his kindness and favor and love to those who don't deserve it. Grace isn't only unmerited favor: it is also divine power, because believers are raised and seated in the heavenlies with Christ (2:6). We rule with him over death, over the secular world, and over Satan. Currently, believers' understanding of God's kindness and grace can fill a thimble, but "in the coming ages" (2:7) the oceans of God's love and mercy will sweep over us again and again so that believers will never tire of marveling over their great deliverance from death to life.

The basis and purpose of the new life is set forth in 2:8–10. The salvation of believers is entirely by grace and through faith. The word "this" (*touto*), which is neuter, embraces all that precedes it, and thus faith is included in what God gives to human beings (2:8). Faith stands fundamentally opposed to works, to what human beings accomplish. Salvation isn't obtained by doing but by believing, and we see here that faith is receptive, resting not on itself but on God's gift in Christ. Works open the door for human boasting, but faith casts itself entirely upon God for every good thing. Paul doesn't call for a quiescent life, where believers are passive. He reminds us that believers are the product of God's new-creation work (2 Cor. 5:17); they have been brought from death to life. Such new life, however, leads to "good works" (Eph. 2:10), not as a basis of salvation but as an expression and outflow of the gracious salvation given.

Jews and Gentiles United in Christ (2:11–22)

In some ways 2:11–22 is quite similar to 2:1–10, but the focus differs in that the reconciliation of Jews and gentiles in Christ is featured. The verses can again be split into three sections: (1) gentiles who were far off have been brought near (2:11–13); (2) the death of Christ as the basis of unity (2:14–18); and (3) Jews and gentiles are fellow citizens and God's new temple (2:19–22).

In verses 11–13 gentiles are enjoined to remember their covenant disadvantage; they were uncircumcised, which means that they were outside of God's covenant favor (cf. Gen. 17:9–14). Still, circumcision doesn't necessarily save since it was limited to a physical act, and thus circumcision apart from the circumcision of the heart didn't procure a right relation with God. Still, the focus is on the gentiles, and their plight is summarized with five statements in Ephesians 2:12: (1) As gentiles they had no promise of a Messiah, as the Jews did. (2) Nor did they have citizenship in Israel, the people of God. (3) The covenants promising salvation (probably including the Abrahamic, Mosaic, and Davidic covenants and the new covenant) were alien to them. (4) Gentiles, then, had no hope, and this doesn't mean that they didn't have feelings of hope but that they had no objective hope, no genuine grounds for hope. (5) They were separated from God and didn't belong to him. It is striking that Paul didn't think of gentiles before Christ as standing in a positive or even neutral relation with God. Instead, he claimed that they didn't belong to God (cf. Rom. 1:18–32). We encounter the striking words "But now," signaling that a new day has arrived, a new covenant has commenced (Eph. 2:13). Gentiles who were far from God have now "been brought near" through the blood of Christ. The fundamental need of gentiles was for forgiveness, and it was achieved through Christ's atoning death.

Verse 13 indicates the basis for gentiles being brought near, and 2:14–18 unpacks how both Jews and gentiles were reconciled with God and with one another through the death of Christ. Christ is the one who "is our peace," in that he has united Jews and gentiles together. The syntax here is complicated and controversial, but we don't need to unravel every thread and can concentrate on main points. What Paul means by the dividing wall of hostility is debated, and there are many suggestions. Some think Paul has in mind the fence in the temple separating Jews and gentiles, which had an inscription threatening gentiles with death if they transgressed the boundary. More likely the reference is to the law itself, which fits with what we read in the Letter of Aristeas (142–43). The law separating Jews and gentiles has been removed through Christ's death (Eph. 2:14). The next verse confirms this reading: the Mosaic law and its commands have been set aside (2:15). Some think Paul refers to the ceremonial law, but it is more likely, as Paul says elsewhere, that law as a whole is no longer in force (cf. Rom. 7:4–6; 2 Cor. 3:7–18; Gal. 3:15–4:7). It doesn't follow from this that there is no role for the commands in the law; Paul even cites a command later in Ephesians (6:2), and he likely views it as authoritative since it is part of Christ's law.

The setting aside of the law means that Jews and gentiles who belong to Christ are "one new man," and the consequence is that there is "peace" between them (2:15). The horizontal unity between Jews and gentiles is rooted in vertical realities since both are reconciled to God as "one body" through the cross of Christ (2:16). The social, cultural, and religious enmity that persisted between Jews and gentiles for hundreds of years had come to an end in Christ. They were now together in one body, "one new man," as Paul says.

Since the days of fulfillment have come, messengers are bringing the good news to places far (to the gentiles) and near (to the Jews, 2:17). The good news of peace with God and peace with one another, peace for all people groups and all ethnicities, has been won through Jesus Christ. Paul alludes to Isaiah 57:19; in the context of this chapter in Isaiah, the Lord reproves Israel for its sin and idolatry, promising judgment. But in the midst of the message of judgment, there is a promise of salvation for the humble and the oppressed. Those in Israel who are far from God will be brought near by virtue of his grace and mercy. The near and far in Isaiah 57 are both from Israel. Paul probably takes up the wider message of Isaiah, where we find many promises of gentile salvation (cf. Isa. 2:1–4; 11:10–12; 18:7; 19:18–25; 42:1, 4, 6; 45:21–22; 49:6–7; 52:15; 55:3–5; 56:3–8; 60:6–7, 10; 66:12–21), and uses the words of Isaiah 57 to communicate that both Jews and gentiles find peace through Jesus Christ. Through the Spirit both Jews and gentiles enjoy access to God (Eph. 2:18).

Because of Christ's reconciling work, which brings Jews and gentiles together in a saving relationship to God, gentiles are no longer considered to be outsiders. They are now part of the great company of saints and are members of God's new temple (2:19–22). The foundation of the temple is the teaching of the apostles and prophets. The prophets here are the NT prophets, not OT prophets. If the latter were in view, we would expect prophets to be listed first, and in 3:5 we will see that NT prophets are definitely in Paul's mind. Both the apostles and prophets are the authoritative messengers declaring the good news to the church. Christ is identified as the "cornerstone" of the temple (cf. Ps. 118:22); it is possible that the capstone is intended, but it is more likely (see Isa. 28:16) that we have a reference to the cornerstone. The entire temple takes its shape and direction from Christ crucified and risen. The church as God's new temple, as his place of residence, is growing! (Eph. 2:21). Temples don't grow, but this one does, and no metaphor adequately captures what the Lord is doing in the church. Jews and gentiles together comprise the Lord's temple; the Lord indwells the new temple by his Spirit.

Paul's Role in Administrating the Mystery (3:1–13)

Paul is driven to prayer because of the unity of Jews and gentiles in the church, because Christ has reconciled them to God and to one another in the church (3:1), but he digresses as he thinks of the particular role God has given him as the apostle to the gentiles. He doesn't identify himself as a prisoner of Rome but of "Christ Jesus." His imprisonment isn't hindering God's work; it is for the sake of the gentiles. As we have seen elsewhere, Paul's suffering is one of the means the Lord uses to advance the church. The revelation of the mystery, which was something previously hidden but is now revealed, was specially disclosed to Paul, and in 2:11–22 the Ephesians have already had a glimpse of Paul's understanding (3:3–4).

What is the content of the mystery? We saw in 1:9–10 that the mystery was that God's purpose for history centers on and finds its meaning in Jesus Christ. Here another dimension of the mystery is explored. Paul emphasizes that previous generations didn't grasp the mystery, but God's Spirit has revealed it to the apostles and prophets. It is clear, then, that the prophets are NT prophets because the mystery wasn't understood by previous generations, even by OT prophets! The mystery is now disclosed in the new era of redemptive history. The content of the mystery is disclosed in 3:6: gentiles are "coheirs" with Israel in Christ Jesus. The gentile Christians are not second-class citizens but are "members of the same body" (*syssōma*). Paul may have coined this word, which emphasizes the equality of Jews and gentiles in Christ. They share together with Israel the promises of salvation that begin with the protoevangelium in Genesis 3:15 and were confirmed to Abraham, David, and the prophets. When we read the OT, the status of gentiles who enter the people of God is unclear. In some texts they seem to occupy an inferior place (Isa. 60:10–14; 61:5–7; Zech. 2:11–12; 8:20–23), while in other texts they seem to have equal status (Pss. 47:9; 87:6; Isa. 11:10; 19:16–25; 25:6–7; 49:6; 55:5; 56:6–7). The apostles and prophets have clarified that Jews and gentiles are equal members of God's people, and thus there is no basis for racial or ethnic superiority in the people of God.

Paul didn't boast about his role but was humbled since he persecuted the church. God had given him the privilege of preaching the riches of Christ to gentiles (Eph. 3:8), of disclosing to all the plan of the mystery that was hidden in the past (3:9). The unity of Jews and gentiles in the church, accomplished through Christ's reconciling work, reveals the multifaceted wisdom of God. In particular, God's wisdom is displayed to "the rulers and authorities in the heavens" (3:10), which could refer to both good and evil angels. The church isn't plan B in God's purposes but represents the fulfillment of God's intentions in Christ Jesus for all of history (3:11). Both Jews and gentiles have bold and confident access to God in Christ and through faith in him (3:12). When Paul thinks of this plan, he asks the Ephesians not to be discouraged about his imprisonment, as if it represents a hindrance in God's plan. On the contrary, his imprisonment is for their "glory" (3:13). The Lord is using Paul's suffering to spread the gospel even more.

Prayer to Know Christ's Love (3:14–21)

Paul returns to what he intended to speak about before the digression (3:1–13). The unity of the Jews and gentiles in the church, the astonishing wisdom of God in the church, drove Paul to his knees in prayer (3:14). God as Father is the origin and authority over every social group, every ethnic group, and here he includes both human beings and angels, including demons. Another intriguing possibility is that every family refers to believers, those on earth and those who have died and are now in heaven, but since Paul doesn't often speak of deceased believers as in heaven, the former view is to be preferred. Paul prays to the God who has all the resources human beings need; he has "riches of . . . glory" (3:16). He prays that almighty God will strengthen believers internally through the Holy Spirit. The Spirit already indwells believers, of course, but here Paul prays that the Spirit would work in them with power. As a result of these believers being strengthened, Christ would live in their hearts as they trust in him. Certainly, Christ already dwells in believers (cf. Rom. 8:10; Gal. 2:20), but here Paul prays that they will experience the effect of his indwelling.

The syntax of Ephesians 3:17–19 is remarkably difficult, and we will have to make our way the best we can, realizing that there can't be complete certainty on the details. I understand Paul to be praying that believers—those who are rooted and grounded in God's love, who have known and received the love of God in the atoning death of Jesus Christ—would be able to comprehend in God's plan for history the greatness of his love. When believers truly see what God has done in Christ in reconciling Jews and gentiles with one another and with God himself, they will experience Christ's love, which transcends human experience. When believers are infused with such love, they are "filled with all the fullness of God" (3:19). Believers become what they were intended to be when the love of God penetrates their hearts and lives. Paul concludes chapter 3 with a doxology (3:20–21), praising God for his power since he does "beyond all that we ask or think." The church of Jesus Christ is a many-splendored reality, and Paul prays that God will be glorified in Christ and in the church forever.

Live Worthy of the Calling (4:1–6)

The letter shifts from an emphasis on what God has done in Christ to what believers are called to do, from the indicative to the imperative. The change is evident in the words "Therefore" and "I urge" (*parakalō*), with the latter especially signaling the beginning of the exhortation section of the letter. The substance of the admonition is found in the words "live worthy of the calling" (4:1). The grace of Christ in calling believers to faith is to be echoed in the way they live. When it comes to explaining what it means to live in a worthy way, the emphasis is on humility, gentleness, and forgiveness, qualities needed to preserve the unity of the body. Believers are *already* one, as 2:11–22 clearly teaches, but they must be diligent to maintain "the unity of the Spirit," which they now enjoy (4:3).

The line between the indicative and the imperative isn't neatly demarcated, because in 4:4–6 the basis of unity is sketched in, and the repetition of the word "one" seven times hammers home what believers share. Paul begins with "one body," which has been the focus of much of chapters 1–3 in proclaiming that Jews and gentiles are reconciled with each other through the work of Christ. The "one Spirit" has been a significant theme in the earlier chapters: believers are all sealed with the Spirit, and the Spirit is the down payment of the inheritance (1:13–14). Believers also have access to the Father through the "one Spirit" (2:18) and are together God's dwelling place in the Spirit (2:22). The Spirit also gives believers strength in the inner person (3:16).

Paul has elaborated upon the one hope of the believers' calling (1:18), and he prays that believers particularly understand this matter. Believers belong to one another, all have the same Holy Spirit, and all share the same destiny. Perhaps here is the place to mention the trinitarian nature of the unity believers enjoy: "one Spirit" (4:4); "one Lord," Jesus Christ (4:5); and "one God and Father" (4:6). Believers belong to the Triune God, and there is no true Christian unity that is not trinitarian. Believers also share the common experience of baptism, which is the induction into the Christian faith, the indication that one has left the world behind. The unity isn't just a feeling or an emotion, but believers share "one faith," which here doesn't refer to trust but to a common confession of faith, a shared doctrinal commitment to the fundamental truths of the Christian faith.

Gifts for Maturity (4:7–16)

The unity of the church is maintained and grows through the gifts given to the body of Christ. Each person, every believer, has been given grace by Christ to exercise their gift (4:7). The gifts believers enjoy are theirs because of Christ's triumph over demonic powers (4:8–10), though what Paul means here is controversial. Jesus as the risen Lord, as the one who triumphed over death, has ascended. His triumph signaled his victory over demonic powers, as their power was shackled at his death and resurrection (1:20–22). And as the risen and ascended Lord, he gave gifts to his people.

The controversy comes from the use of Psalm 68:18, which Paul quotes in Ephesians 4:8, for in the psalm God *received* gifts; he did not *give* gifts to people. A virtual industry has grown up in trying to explain what is going on here. The best solution is to recognize that Paul knew what the verse said and changed the verb intentionally. Such a procedure, however, isn't as arbitrary as it seems, for Paul's reading fits with the message of the psalm as a whole. Psalm 68 calls on God to arise and triumph over his enemies, and such triumph will cause Israel to praise the Lord. The Lord's ascent on Sinai demonstrates his victory over all his enemies and his grace to his people. The first part of the psalm celebrates God's victory and then moves to his provision for his people. Paul appropriates the psalm because he sees it as fulfilled in Christ: Christ has triumphed over enemies (especially demonic powers) and has blessed his people as a result of the victory he has won. The notion of God giving to his people is the thrust of the entire psalm, and the psalm ends on that note (Ps. 68:35).

The accent here is on Christ's victory, his ascending on high, and the gifts that are distributed in light of the victory achieved. Ephesians 4:9 is particularly difficult, where Christ is said to have ascended and descended. Some want to say that the Spirit is the one who descended when Christ ascended, but Paul makes it plain that the *same person* ascended and descended, and so Christ is clearly the referent. Discussion has centered on what it means for Christ to descend "to the lower parts of the earth" (4:9). One view is that "the lower parts" refers to the earth, but most in the ancient world would think of the underworld with this expression, and the phrase "the lower parts" could easily be omitted if the earth is in view. Others think that Jesus went to the realm of the dead to bring OT saints to faith in Christ, to allow a second chance for the dead, or to free saints in limbo who died before Christ. All these views, however, don't fit with any text in the Scriptures, and so the expression points to Christ's death, to Jesus being in the realm of the dead. Paul teaches that the one who died is also risen, and as the triumphant and victorious and reigning Lord, he fills everything (cf. 1:20–22).

The gifts granted to the church are gifted persons (4:11), and the list here is representative, not exhaustive (cf. 1 Cor. 12:8–10, 28–30; Rom. 12:6–8). The focus is on gifts where God's word is spoken and believers are strengthened through the spoken word. We have already seen that apostles and prophets are the foundation of the church (Eph. 2:20), that NT prophets are in view (3:5), and that the apostles and prophets are distinct from one another. Evangelists are those who proclaim the gospel to others (cf. Acts 21:8; 2 Tim. 4:5). How to understand the relationship between "pastors and teachers" is disputed, and the grammar doesn't resolve the matter decisively. They could certainly be distinct like "apostles and prophets," or perhaps they are two different ways of describing the same office. Perhaps the best solution is to say that pastors and teachers overlap in significant ways, but they are not completely identical.

The purpose of the gifts is to equip the saints to do "the work of ministry, to build up the body of Christ" (Eph. 4:12). Some argue that all three of these activities represent the role of the gifted persons so that, for instance, the ministry of pastors and teachers equips the saints, and the equipping of the saints constitutes the work of the ministry, and this work thereby builds up the body. Others think we have a chained argument here: the gifted persons equip the saints, the saints do the work of ministry, and the church is built up. I slightly lean toward the second view. Perhaps the change of prepositions from *pros* to *eis* in verse 12 supports the view preferred here. In any case, Paul emphasizes the role each person plays: gifts are given "to each one" (4:7, 11), and the body grows with "the proper working of each individual part" (4:16).

Christ came so that the church would be filled with God's fullness (3:19), and he came "to fill all things" (4:10), but this work won't be realized fully until the day of the Lord. Still, the reigning and ruling Christ grants gifts to his church so that the church enjoys "unity in the faith" (4:13), which means that there is confessional unity and stability in the "one faith" (4:5, 14). Another way of describing the church's growth is "the knowledge of God's Son" (4:13). Doctrinal stability and personal knowledge of Christ are not enemies but friends since teaching that is errant leads one away from a true knowledge of Jesus as God's Son. The church is to grow continually into the fullness enjoyed in Christ. Jesus is the head of the church (4:15); he is its ascended Lord and the source of its growth, and the church grows as the truth of the gospel is proclaimed in love and as each member plays their part.

Live as Those Who Know Christ (4:17–24)

Paul begins to give specific admonitions about what it means for believers to become mature and to grow up into the fullness of Christ, and these instructions continue until the end of the letter. The paragraph begins solemnly as Paul testifies about how they should live. He designates unbelievers as gentiles (4:17), which suggests that believers in Christ, both Jews and gentiles, constitute restored Israel (cf. 2:11–22; 3:5–6). We also see several contacts with Romans 1, though there are differences as well. Believers, since they are new in Christ, should no longer live like pagans, for unbelievers' whole way of thinking is futile, and their understanding (cf. 2:3) is darkened (see Rom. 1:21). The fundamental problem is that they don't have the life that God gives (cf. Eph. 2:1, 5!), and their separation from God is traced to culpable ignorance, to hearts that are hardened and cold toward God (4:18). Repeated giving of themselves to sin has made them "callous," and they have given themselves over to sensuality and "every kind of impurity" (4:19). In Romans, Paul emphasizes that God handed human beings over to evil (1:24, 26, 28), but here the active choice of human beings in giving themselves to evil is featured.

   Paul turns the corner in 4:20, using a rather strange expression: "But that is not the way you learned Christ!" (ESV). It isn't common to speak of learning a person, but Paul wants to impress that upon the readers: they didn't merely learn a code of ethics. They have come to know a person; they are transformed because they have fallen in love. After all, they know very well that the truth is in Jesus (4:21), and once again the personal character of their relation to Christ is stressed. They *know* Jesus. We find several infinitives in 4:22–24, and how they are functioning is disputed, but most agree that they have an imperatival function. Believers are to put off "the old self" (4:22), be "renewed" in their thinking (4:23), and "put on the new self" (4:24). Elsewhere Paul says that the old self is crucified (Rom. 6:6; cf. Gal. 2:20) and has already been put off (Col. 3:9). Along the same line, believers have already put on the new self (Col. 3:10). Some think these two different conceptions are contradictory, but they represent the tension between the already and the not yet, the indicative and the imperative, which is common in Paul. In Galatians 3:27 Paul says that believers have put on Christ in baptism, but in Romans 13:14 they are admonished to put on Christ. We see a similar phenomenon here. The old has been put off and the new has been donned, and yet believers are to live out that eschatological reality in their daily lives. They are daily to put off the old person and put on the new. No formula adequately grasps what Paul teaches here, but they are to be what they are in Christ, for as Ephesians 4:24 says, they are a new creation (cf. 2:10). Accordingly, their thinking must be renewed daily in the gospel (4:23; cf. Rom. 12:2).

Putting Off and Putting On in Daily Life (4:25–5:2)

Putting off the old and putting on the new may seem rather vague, but Paul gets down to particulars, and in almost every case he gives an example of what it means to put off evil *and* what it means to put on righteousness. Some end the section with chapter 4, and that is certainly a possibility, but I think 5:1–2 functions as the conclusion and summary of 4:25–32.

   Believers are to put off lying *and* put on truth (4:25). They are not merely to avoid lying but to embrace truth in all its beauty and clarity. The reason given is that the person with whom we speak is our "neighbor," and even more specifically, these persons are members of the body of Christ, fellow travelers in the gospel, members of the same family. Family members tell each other the truth.

   Verses 26–27 speak to anger. Surprisingly, believers are enjoined, "Be angry," yet "Do not sin." Some think we don't have an imperative here, but reading it as imperative also accords with Psalm 4, where David finds joy and peace in the Lord, even though some around him are insulting and liars. As he reflects on the character of such, he is to be angry but not to fall into sin (4:4). He avoids sin when he rests in the Lord, trusting God to vindicate him. Anger, it seems, turns to sin if it begins to dominate and consume a person. Righteous anger recognizes and hates evil, but it also trusts in God's sovereignty and protection, and thus a person does not become unduly vexed. We may have a hint, then, why we are told that the sun should not set on anger, because if anger begins to eat a person up, they can never let it go. And in doing so they are giving the devil a place in their lives (Eph. 4:27).

Paul then turns to work and labor (4:28). Stealing may have characterized one's life before salvation, but such a way of life should be a thing of the past (cf. Exod. 20:15). Still, Paul isn't satisfied with a life where evil is left behind; believers should also work hard at whatever they are doing, not only to provide for their own needs but also to give to those in need. Paul envisions a life that moves from stealing to generous giving.

In Ephesians 4:29 the topic turns to speech. What should be put off is rotten and putrid speech. The word for "foul" here is used for rotten fruit elsewhere (Matt. 7:17, 18; 12:33; Luke 6:43). Once again, however, merely putting aside evil isn't touted as righteousness. Believers haven't only put off the old: they have become new! So their speech should strengthen, edify, and build up others; as a result, speech can be a means of grace to others.

Verse 30 is a bit different, and we have here a more general idea. Believers are summoned not "to grieve" or sadden the Holy Spirit, which suggests that the Holy Spirit is a person. The Spirit has "sealed" them (see Eph. 1:13!) for redemption (1:14), for the consummation of salvation. Grieving the Spirit doesn't match their identity or destiny.

Ephesians 4:31–32 returns to the pattern of putting off and putting on, with verse 31 informing the readers what they should put off and verse 32 what they should put on. Bitterness, rage, angry shouting, and slander must be removed from their lives. Instead, believers should be characterized by kindness, compassion, and forgiveness. Paul doesn't call believers to goodness apart from the gospel. Forgiveness of others flows out of the forgiveness received from Christ himself. When believers truly realize their own evil, their forgiveness of those who injured them is rooted in their gratefulness to God for their own salvation and pardon.

Avoiding evil and pursuing what is good is another way of saying that believers are imitating God (5:1). And such imitation isn't an external duty but reflects a family relationship since believers are the beloved children of God. If one could summarize the new life of believers, it is the call to live a life of love, and the injunction to love is grounded in Christ's self-giving and sacrificial love. Such love, such a sacrifice, is a pleasing aroma to God (5:2). The OT sacrifices are often said to be a pleasing aroma (e.g., Gen. 8:21; Exod. 29:18; Lev. 1:9; 2:2; 3:5; 17:6), but the sacrifice of Christ, being greater than any animal sacrifice, surpasses them in procuring full atonement.

Transformative Lives (5:3–14)

Paul continues to set forth the kind of lives believers should live as those who are loved by God, as those for whom Christ sacrificed his life. Ephesians 5:3–7 centers on what they should avoid, and verses 8–14 feature the transforming power of the light. Verses 3–7 concentrate on the dangers of sexual sin and greed. Sexual immorality was very common in the Greco-Roman world, as is the case in our society. Sexual sin was often accompanied by greed, for in both cases people are living for comfort and pleasure instead of for the glory of God. Such behavior shouldn't exist among God's holy people since it is clearly not fitting. Obscene and foolish talk and turns of phrases with sexual innuendo or talk that belittles others for the sake of humor should also be left behind. Much more wholesome and life giving than the boredom that provokes such talk is a heart full of thanksgiving. Sexual sin and greed are not minor matters, for those who give themselves to such things have no inheritance in the kingdom, and they will face God's wrath on the last day (5:5–6). Many might be deceived, thinking that such a lifestyle could be pursued without consequences.

Verses 8–14 contrast light and darkness and highlight the transforming power of the light. It isn't as if darkness is alien to believers, for their existence was also once marked by darkness (cf. 4:18), but by virtue of Christ's love, their existence is now marked by light. Believers aren't just *in* the light: they *are* "light in the Lord," and they are to live out what they now are. Paul's common contrast in Ephesians between *then* (unbelieving) and *now* (believing) shows up again (cf. 2:1–6, 11–13; 4:17–24). The phrase "fruit of the light" (5:9) reminds us of the "fruit of the Spirit" in Galatians (5:22), and here we see the transforming power of light since the light produces "goodness, righteousness, and truth" (Eph. 5:9). Since believers are in the light, Paul doesn't give a detailed code of ethics, but he trusts that they will be able to assess and test what pleases the Lord (5:10). We are given broad outlines of behaviors that accord with light and darkness, but Paul doesn't provide a rule book for every circumstance.

Believers must be vigilant so that the darkness doesn't engulf them. Instead, they are to expose what is evil, showing evil for what it is (5:11). There is no need to linger over what is done in secret since such behavior is shameful.

But those upon whom the light shines are transformed (5:13); light doesn't just reveal: it also transforms and changes (5:14). The source of the quotation in 5:14 is a matter of controversy. Some think it is an early Christian hymn, which is certainly possible. More likely, the wording is woven together from Isaiah 60:1 and 26:19. It is clearly addressed to unbelievers who are, so to speak, sleeping in sin. They are to rise and let Christ shine on them with all his glorious power and thereby become children of light!

Live Wisely and by the Spirit (5:15–21)

The admonition to live wisely instead of foolishly accords with OT Wisdom literature, for those who are wise discern the Lord's will. When Paul contrasts getting drunk with being filled with the Spirit, he isn't implying, as some interpreters have thought, that the Ephesians were actually getting drunk, though the presence of the admonition indicates that the Ephesians, like all Christians, need these words (Eph. 5:18–21). What Paul means by the filling of the Spirit is disputed. Some think the Spirit is the agent by which we are filled (be filled *by* the Spirit). Others say that the Spirit is the content (be filled *with* the Spirit). And still others think the Spirit is the sphere in which the activity takes place (be filled in the sphere of the Spirit). I suggest that the contrast with wine affords the most help in interpreting what Paul says, and when people get drunk, they are drunk both by means of wine and with wine. Thus Paul probably is saying both things here: be filled with and by the Spirit.

Five participles are related to the main verb to be filled by/with the Spirit: (1) speaking, (2 and 3) singing and making music, (4) giving thanks, and (5) submitting. How are these participles to be understood? Do they designate result, or should they be interpreted as the means? Both options make good sense, and a decision is difficult. Perhaps the categories aren't helpful, for there is a sense in which both could be true, and our classifications may impose more precision than Paul intended. We see that life in the Spirit is attended by joy: singing hymns and songs and giving thanks. We see as well that believers submit to one another, which refers to the corporate life of the church, where believers defer to one another. Those who have the Spirit don't impose their selfish will on others and are full of praise and song.

Household Relationships (5:22–6:9)

Those who are filled with the Spirit relate to one another well in the household, whether they are husbands and wives (5:22–33), parents and children

(6:1–4), or slaves and masters (6:5–9). The longest section is on husbands and wives. Paul calls upon wives to submit to their husbands (5:22–24), and to many people in the West today, the admonition seems quite alien. Some argue that the admonition is culturally restricted to the first century, but that judgment seems off-center because the submission of the wife to the husband is compared to the submission of the church to Christ. Furthermore, the text concludes by citing Genesis 2:24, which is the signature text on marriage in the OT, locating marriage in creation. Marriage consists of leaving (but not abandoning) one's parents, being joined to one's spouse, and becoming one flesh (Eph. 5:31). Paul remarks that this statement in Genesis is a mystery that relates to Christ and the church (5:32). Marriage, in other words, discloses something that was hidden about Christ and the church, but now the mystery of marriage has been revealed. It isn't that Christ's relationship to the church mirrors marriage. Instead, marriage reflects Christ's relation to the church, and thus Christ's relation to the church is primary and fundamental. To put it another way, the call for a wife to submit to her husband is transcultural since it represents Christ's relation to the church.

The meaning of submission, of course, may be misunderstood profoundly, and some have wrongly understood it in a militaristic and rigid way. Mutuality also marks the marriage relationship (1 Cor. 7:2–5). Nor are husbands commanded to coerce or encourage wives to submit, for wives voluntarily submit to husbands as to the Lord. Paul grounds submission in the headship of husbands (Eph. 5:23). Some have argued that the word "head" means source, but we have seen elsewhere in Ephesians that the notion of authority is in the word "head" (1:22; 4:15; cf. Col. 1:18; 2:10, 19). Seeing a reference to the husband's authority fits clearly and logically with a call to submit. Furthermore, it is difficult to know how husbands are the source of their wives since they aren't the source of their wives physically or spiritually.

Paul modifies and qualifies the notion of hierarchy, which was present in the Greco-Roman world. The leadership of husbands is to be a loving authority, not a leadership that selfishly insists on its own way (Eph. 5:25). The model is Christ's love for the church, where he surrendered his life for the sake of the church. Husbands are to cherish, nourish, and care for their wives to the same extent that they care for themselves (5:28–29). It is important to recognize the discontinuity as well between Christ and husbands. Husbands don't save their wives, but Christ is the Savior of the church (5:23). The relationship between Christ and the church is featured here. Christ's distinctive role emerges in that he sanctifies the church and washes it clean (probably in baptism, 5:26). At the same time, he secures the eschatological presentation of the church, so that on the last day the church will be as beautiful and spotless as a bride (5:27).

Children are enjoined to "obey" their parents "in the Lord" (6:1). The words "in the Lord" modify the verb, not the term "parents." Even unbelievers typically agree that it is right to obey parents. In 6:2–3 the fifth commandment from the Decalogue is introduced (Exod. 20:12; Deut. 5:16). Why would Paul quote a command from the OT when he has argued that the OT law has been set aside (Eph. 2:15)? He does so because the moral norms of the law continue to be authoritative for the church of Jesus Christ as a constituent part of the law of Christ. Does Paul promise long life for children who obey? Possibly, but a better answer is that the land, as is usual in Paul (cf. Rom. 4:13), stands for the heavenly inheritance. The obedience of children is evidence that they belong to God, and those who obey will be part of the new creation forever. Fathers are to train their children in the things of the Lord, and at the same time they must beware of a perfectionism that sows frustration in children (6:4).

We discussed slavery in the Greco-Roman world in 1 Corinthians 7:17–24. Here Paul addresses the issue again (Eph. 6:5–9). Paul never endorses slavery, nor is it grounded in God's good creation; it is an evil human institution and is regulated. From our vantage point we wonder why early Christians didn't advocate a revolution, but we must remember that it wasn't a capitalist or democratic society where other jobs were awaiting those who were slaves. This is not to deny for a moment that the system was brutal and inhumane and evil. Clearly, slaves are called upon to obey their masters. Still, they are fundamentally serving the Lord, not their masters. Everything believers do should be for the glory of the Lord, as slaves of Christ. At the same time, masters are warned not to abuse their authority and not to threaten their slaves. After all, the human masters have a Lord in heaven, who holds them to account for what they do, and he will judge fairly.

Put On the Full Armor of God and Stand (6:10-24)

The letter closes with a call to put on God's armor and to stand against demonic and spiritual forces. Believers don't have the strength and power in themselves to withstand such forces. No doubt the foes that believers face are demonic: they are not "flesh and blood" but are "cosmic powers" and wicked "spiritual forces" (6:12). Some argue that literal demonic beings aren't in view, but such a reading represents a Western enlightenment mindset, which domesticates the biblical text and also imposes onto reality a particular scientific worldview. Paul clearly believed that there were invisible demonic powers and beings that oppress and stand against believers.

Since believers have died with Christ and have been raised with him (2:1–6), they are called upon to stand against the cosmic powers (6:11, 13, 14). They stand

291

by putting on the armor of God (6:11, 13; see Isa. 59:17). The armor includes truth as a belt, righteousness as a breastplate, "the gospel of peace" (Eph. 6:15) on the feet, the shield of faith, the helmet of salvation, the sword of the Spirit, and prayer. There is no need to be overly precise about which piece of armor goes with what, for in 1 Thessalonians 5:8 the breastplate is "faith and love," while here it is righteousness. Truth refers to the truth of the gospel and the life of truth pursued by believers. Righteousness is both the gift of righteousness granted to believers and the life of righteousness that follows from the divine gift. For footing, believers should be equipped with the good news of peace and be constantly prepared to share it. The shield that blocks all "flaming arrows" of Satan is faith (Eph. 6:16). God's word is the Spirit's sword and stands out as the one offensive weapon in the list. Some have questioned whether prayer is part of this armor since it isn't correlated with any particular piece of armor, but it should probably be included, for prayer is the means by which the word of the gospel and the perseverance of the saints are accomplished.

The letter closes with news about Tychicus, who would come to encourage the believers. Paul prays that the believers will know God's peace and his grace, and grace is reserved for those who have a love for Jesus Christ that will never be quenched.

Ephesians: Commentaries

Abbott, Thomas K. *A Critical and Exegetical Commentary on the Epistles to the Ephesians and to the Colossians*. 1897. Reprinted, Edinburgh: T&T Clark, 1985.

Aletti, Jean-Noël. *Saint Paul, Epître aux Ephésiens*. Études Bibliques, NS 42. Paris: J. Gabalda, 2001.

Arnold, Clinton E. *Ephesians*. ZECNT. Grand Rapids: Zondervan, 2010.

Arnold, Clinton E., Frank S. Thielman, et al. *Ephesians, Philippians, Colossians, Philemon*. ZIBBC 8. Edited by Clinton E. Arnold. Grand Rapids: Zondervan, 2002.

Barth, Markus. *Ephesians*. 2 vols. AB 34. Garden City, NY: Doubleday, 1974.

Baugh, S. M. *Ephesians*. EEC. Bellingham, WA: Lexham, 2016.

Best, Ernest. *A Critical and Exegetical Commentary on Ephesians*. ICC. Edinburgh: T&T Clark, 1998.

Bruce, F. F. *The Epistles to the Colossians, to Philemon, and to the Ephesians*. 2nd ed. NICNT. Grand Rapids: Eerdmans, 1984.

Cohick, Lynn H. *Ephesians*. NCCS. Eugene, OR: Cascade, 2010.

Donelson, Lewis R. *Colossians, Ephesians, First and Second Timothy, and Titus*. Louisville: Westminster John Knox, 1996.

Eadie, John. *A Commentary on the Greek Text of the Epistle of Paul to the Ephesians*. 3rd ed. Edinburgh: T&T Clark, 1883.

Foulkes, Francis. *Ephesians: An Introduction and Commentary*. TNTC. Reprinted, Downers Grove, IL: InterVarsity, 1956.

Fowl, Stephen E. *Ephesians: A Commentary*. NTL. Louisville: Westminster John Knox, 2012.

Hodge, Charles. *A Commentary on the Epistle to the Ephesians*. Reprinted, Grand Rapids: Eerdmans, 1994.

Hoehner, Harold W. *Ephesians: An Exegetical Commentary*. Grand Rapids: Baker Academic, 2002.

Kitchen, Martin. *Ephesians*. New Testament Readings. New York: Routledge, 1994.

Klein, William W. "Ephesians." In *Ephesians–Philemon*, vol. 12 of *The Expositor's Bible Commentary*, rev. ed., edited by Tremper Longman III and David E. Garland, 19–173. Grand Rapids: Zondervan, 2006.

Kreitzer, Larry J. *The Epistle to the Ephesians*. Peterborough, ON: Epworth, 1998.

Lincoln, Andrew T. *Ephesians*. WBC 42. Dallas: Word, 1990.

MacDonald, Margaret. *Colossians and Ephesians*. SP. Collegeville, MN: Liturgical Press, 2000.

Merkle, Benjamin L. *Ephesians*. EGGNT. Nashville: B&H Academic, 2016.

Moule, H. C. G. *The Epistle to the Ephesians*. Cambridge: Cambridge University Press, 1886.

Muddiman, John. *A Commentary on the Epistle to the Ephesians*. BNTC. New York: Continuum, 2001.

O'Brien, Peter. *The Letter to the Ephesians*. PNTC. Grand Rapids: Eerdmans, 1999.

Patzia, Arthur. *Ephesians, Colossians, Philemon*. GNC. San Francisco: Harper & Row, 1984.

Perkins, Pheme. *Ephesians*. ANTC. Nashville: Abingdon, 1997.

Roberts, Mark D. *Ephesians*. SOGBC. Grand Rapids: Zondervan, 2016.

Schnackenburg, Rudolf. *Ephesians: A Commentary*. Translated by Helen Heron. Edinburgh: T&T Clark, 1991.

Snodgrass, Klyne. *Ephesians*. NIVAC. Grand Rapids: Zondervan, 1996.

Stott, John. *The Message of Ephesians*. Downers Grove, IL: InterVarsity, 1979.

Swain, Lionel. *Ephesians*. Wilmington, DE: Michael Glazier, 1980.

Talbert, C. H. *Ephesians and Colossians*. PCNT. Grand Rapids: Baker Academic, 2007.

Thielman, Frank. *Ephesians*. BECNT. Grand Rapids: Baker Academic, 2010.

Westcott, Brooke Foss. *Saint Paul's Epistle to the Ephesians: The Greek Text with Notes and Addenda*. London: Macmillan, 1906.

Witherington, Ben, III. *The Letters to Philemon, the Colossians, and the Ephesians: A Socio-Rhetorical Commentary on the Captivity Epistles*. Grand Rapids: Eerdmans, 2007.

Wright, N. T. *Paul for Everyone: The Prison Letters: Ephesians, Philippians, Colossians, and Philemon*. 2nd ed. Louisville: Westminster John Knox, 2004.

Ephesians: Articles, Essays, and Monographs

Agnew, Francis H. "The Origin of the NT Apostle-Concept: A Review of Research." *JBL* 105 (1986): 75–96.

Allen, Thomas G. "Exaltation and Solidarity with Christ: Ephesians 1:20 and 2:6." *JSNT* 28 (1986): 103–20.

Arnold, Clinton E. "The 'Exorcism' of Ephesians 6:12." *JSNT* 30 (1987): 71–87.

———. *Power and Magic: The Concept of Power in Ephesians in Light of Its Historical Setting*. SNTSMS 63. New York: Cambridge University Press, 1989.

———. *Powers of Darkness: Principalities and Powers in Paul's Letters*. Downers Grove, IL: InterVarsity, 1992.

Asher, Jeffrey R. "An Unworthy Foe; Heroic Ἔθη, Trickery, and an Insult in Ephesians 6:11." *JBL* 130 (2011): 729–48.

Barth, Markus. *The Broken Wall: A Study of the Epistle to the Ephesians*. Valley Forge, PA: Judson, 1959.

Bauckham, Richard J. "Pseudo-Apostolic Letters." *JBL* 107 (1988): 469–94.

Baugh, S. M. "A Foreign World: Ephesus in the First Century." In *Women in the Church: A Fresh Analysis of 1 Timothy 2:9–15*, edited by A. Köstenberger and T. Schreiner, 2nd ed., 13–38. Grand Rapids: Baker Academic, 2005.

———. "Marriage and Family in Ancient Greek Society." In *Marriage and Family in the Biblical World*, edited by K. M. Campbell, 103–31. Downers Grove, IL: InterVarsity, 2003.

Beale, G. K., and Benjamin Gladd. *Hidden but Now Revealed: A Biblical Theology of Mystery*. Downers Grove, IL: InterVarsity, 2014.

Best, Ernest. "Ephesians i.1 Again." In *Paul and Paulinism*, edited by M. D. Hooker and S. G. Wilson, 273–79. London: SPCK, 1982.

Black, David. "The Peculiarities of Ephesians and the Ephesian Address." *GTJ* 2 (1981): 59–73.

Bockmuehl, M. *Revelation and Mystery in Ancient Judaism and Pauline Christianity*. Grand Rapids: Eerdmans, 1997.

Brannon, M. *The Heavenlies in Ephesians: A Lexical, Exegetical, and Conceptual Analysis*. LNTS. London: T&T Clark, 2011.

Caird, G. *Principalities and Powers: A Study in Pauline Theology*. New York: Oxford University Press, 1956.

Campbell, Constantine R. *Paul and Union with Christ: An Exegetical and Theological Study*. Grand Rapids: Zondervan, 2012.

Campbell-Reed, E. "Should Wives 'Submit Graciously'? A Feminist Approach to Interpreting Ephesians 5:21–33." *RevExp* 98 (2001): 263–76.

Caragounis, C. C. *The Ephesian Mysterion: Meaning and Context*. Lund: CWK Gleerup, 1977.

Carr, W. *Angels and Principalities: The Background, Meaning and Development of the Pauline Phrase "Hai Archai kai hai Exousiai."* SNTSMS 42. Cambridge: Cambridge University Press, 1981.

Cervin, R. "Does Κεφαλή Mean 'Source' or 'Authority Over' in Greek Literature? A Rebuttal." *TJ* 10 (1989): 85–112.

Collins, J. "Ephesians 5:18: What Does πληροῦσθε ἐν πνεύματι Mean?" *Presb* 33 (2007): 12–30.

Coutts, J. "Ephesians 1:3–14 and 1 Peter 1:3–12." *NTS* 3 (1957): 115–27.

Dahl, N. *Studies in Ephesians: Introductory Questions, Text-Critical Issues, Interpretation of Texts and Themes*. WUNT 131. Tübingen: Mohr Siebeck, 2000.

Darko, Daniel K. *No Longer Living as the Gentiles: Differentiation and Shared Ethical Values in Ephesians 4.17–6.9*. New York: T&T Clark, 2008.

Dawes, Gregory W. *The Body in Question: Metaphor and Meaning in the Interpretation of Ephesians 5:21–33*. Boston: Brill, 1998.

Easton, B. "New Testament Ethical Lists." *JBL* 51 (1932): 1–12.

Gibson, J. "Ephesians 5:21–33 and the Lack of Marital Unity in the Roman Empire." *BSac* 168 (2001): 162–77.

Gombis, T. "Being the Fullness of God in Christ by the Spirit: Ephesians 5:18 in Its Epistolary Setting." *TynBul* 53 (2002): 259–71.

———. "Cosmic Lordship and Divine Gift-Giving: Psalm 68 in Ephesians 4:8." *NovT* 47 (2005): 367–80.

———. *The Drama of Ephesians: Participating in the Triumph of God*. Downers Grove, IL: InterVarsity, 2010.

———. "Ephesians 2 as a Narrative of Divine Warfare." *JSNT* 26 (2004): 403–18.

Gordon, D. "'Equipping' Ministry in Ephesians 4?" *JETS* 37 (1994): 69–78.

Gosnell, P. "Ephesians 5:18–20 and Mealtime Propriety." *TynBul* 44 (1993): 363–71.

Grudem, Wayne. "Does ΚΕΦΑΛΗ ('Head') Mean 'Source' or 'Authority Over' in Greek Literature?" *TJ* 6 (1985): 38–59.

———. "The Meaning of Κεφαλή ('Head'): An Evaluation of New Evidence, Real and Alleged." *JETS* 44 (2001): 25–65.

———. "The Meaning of Κεφαλή ('Head'): A Response to Recent Studies." *TJ* 11 (1990): 3–72.

Harris, W. Hall, III. "The Ascent and Descent of Christ in Ephesians 4:9–10." *BSac* 151 (1994): 9–10.

———. *The Descent of Christ: Ephesians 4:7–11 and Traditional Hebrew Imagery*. AGJU 32. Grand Rapids: Baker, 1996.

———. "The 'Heavenlies' Reconsidered: Οὐρανός and Ἐπουράνιος in Ephesians." *BSac* 148 (1991): 72–89.

Heil, J. "Ephesians 5:18b: 'But Be Filled in the Spirit.'" *CBQ* 69 (2007): 506–16.

Jeal, R. "A Strange Style of Expression: Ephesians 1:23." *Filología Neotestamentaria* 10 (1997): 129–38.

Kerr, A. J. "ΑΡΡΑΒΩΝ." *JETS* 39 (1988): 92–97.

Klein, W. *The New Chosen People: A Corporate View of Election*. Grand Rapids: Zondervan, 1990.

Köstenberger, Andreas. "The Mystery of Christ and the Church: Head and Body, 'One Flesh.'" *TJ* 12 (1991): 79–94.

———. "What Does It Mean to Be Filled with the Spirit? A Biblical Investigation." *JETS* 40 (1997): 229–40.

Kreitzer, L. Joseph. "'Crude Language' and 'Shameful Things Done in Secret' (Ephesians 5.4, 12): Allusions to the Cult of Demeter/Cybele in Hierapolis?" *JSNT* 71 (1998): 51–77.

———. *Hierapolis in the Heavens: Studies in the Letter to the Ephesians*. London: T&T Clark, 2007.

Lau, Te-Li. *The Politics of Peace: Ephesians, Dio Chrysostom, and the Confucian Four Books*. Boston: Brill, 2010.

Lincoln, Andrew T. *Paradise Now and Not Yet*. SNTSMS. Cambridge: Cambridge University Press, 1981.

———. "The Use of the OT in Ephesians." *JSNT* 14 (1982): 16–57.

Lincoln, Andrew T., and A. Wedderburn. *The Theology of the Later Pauline Letters*. New York: Cambridge University Press, 1993.

Lunde, J., and J. Dunne. "Paul's Creative and Contextual Use of Isaiah in Ephesians 5:14." *JETS* 55 (2012): 87–110.

———. "Paul's Creative and Contextual Use of Psalm 68 in Ephesians 4:8." *WTJ* 74 (2012): 99–117.

McKelvey, R. *The New Temple: The Church in the New Testament*. New York: Oxford University Press, 1969.

Miletic, S. *"One Flesh": Eph. 5:22–24, 5.31, Marriage and the New Creation*. AnBib 115. Rome: Pontifical Biblical Institute, 1988.

Moritz, Thorsten. *A Profound Mystery: The Use of the Old Testament in Ephesians*. NovTSup 85. New York: Brill, 1996.

Page, S. "Whose Ministry? A Re-Appraisal of Ephesians 4:12." *NovT* 47 (2005): 26–46.

Petrenko, Ester A. G. D. *Created in Christ Jesus for Good Works: The Integration of Soteriology and Ethics in Ephesians*. PBM. Milton Keynes, UK: Paternoster, 2011.

Reinhard, D. "Ephesians 6:10–18: A Call to Personal Piety or Another Way of Describing Union with Christ?" *JETS* 48 (2005): 521–32.

Sampley, J. Paul. "'And the Two Shall Become One Flesh': A Study of Traditions in Ephesians 5:21–35." Cambridge: Cambridge University Press, 1971.

Schlier, Heinrich. *Christus und die Kirche im Epheserbrief*. BHT 6. Tübingen: Mohr Siebeck, 1930.

Smith, Gary. "Paul's Use of Psalm 68:18 in Ephesians 4:8." *JETS* 18 (1975): 181–89.

Strelan, Rick. *Paul, Artemis, and the Jews in Ephesus*. BZNW 80. New York: de Gruyter, 1996.

Stuhlmacher, Peter. "'He Is Our Peace' (Eph. 2:14)—On the Exegesis and Significance of Eph. 2:14–18." In *Reconciliation, Law, and Righteousness: Essays in Biblical Theology*, 182–200. Philadelphia: Fortress, 1986.

Taylor, R. "The Use of Psalm 68:18 in Ephesians 4:8 in Light of the Ancient Versions." *BSac* 148 (1991): 319–36.

Wallace, Daniel. "Ὀργίζεσθε in Ephesians 4:26: Command or Condition?" *CTR* 3 (1989): 353–72.

Wansink, C. *Chained in Christ: The Experience and Rhetoric of Paul's Imprisonments*. JSNTSup 130. Sheffield: Sheffield Academic, 1996.

White, R. Fowler. "Gaffin and Grudem on Eph 2:20: In Defense of Gaffin's Cessationist Exegesis." *WTJ* 54 (1992): 303–20.

Wiles, G. *Paul's Intercessory Prayers: The Significance of the Intercessory Prayer Passages in the Letters of Paul*. SNTSMS 24. Cambridge: Cambridge University Press, 1974.

Wink, Walter. *Engaging the Powers: Discernment and Resistance in a World of Domination*. Minneapolis: Fortress, 1992.

————. *Naming the Powers: The Language of Power in the New Testament.* Vol. 1 of *The Powers.* Philadelphia: Fortress, 1984.

————. *Unmasking the Powers: The Invisible Forces That Determine Human Existence.* Vol. 2 of *The Powers.* Philadelphia: Fortress, 1986.

Winter, Bruce. *Roman Wives, Roman Widows: The Appearance of New Women and the Pauline Communities.* Grand Rapids: Eerdmans, 2003.

Yee, Tet-Lim N. *Jews, Gentiles and Ethnic Reconciliation: Paul's Jewish Identity and Ephesians.* SNTSMS 130. Cambridge: Cambridge University Press, 2005.

CHAPTER SEVEN

Philippians

Introduction

The Philippian church was established when Paul visited Philippi, and the account is found in Acts 16:11–40. The date and place from which Philippians was written is debated. Some have argued for Caesarea, others for Ephesus, and still others say from Rome. Space is lacking to adjudicate this matter, but I favor the traditional view that Philippians was written from Rome sometime during his imprisonment (AD 60–62). What precipitated Paul to write the letter? Apparently the Philippians had sent Paul a financial gift to help him in his ministry, and Paul sends his thanks (Phil. 1:3–6; 4:10–20). The financial gift alone doesn't account for sending the letter. It seems evident from 1:12–2:30 and 4:2–9 that lack of unity plagued the congregation, and Paul wrote to unify the congregation in the spread of the gospel. When we come to 3:2–4:1, the tone changes abruptly: we find a warning against false teachers. Some think two different opponents are addressed in these verses, but the simpler hypothesis is to be preferred. The opponents throughout this section were Judaizers whose teaching was similar to what we find in Galatians. We should also mention that a few scholars argue that the different topics addressed in the letter indicate that Philippians contains several independent letters, which were later combined together. Such theories aren't convincing, and I will attempt to show how the letter fits together. Before examining the letter, two themes that are prominent in Philippians are portrayed in the tables below.

Joy in Philippians

1:4	Paul prays with joy
1:18	Paul rejoices that Christ is proclaimed
1:25	Paul will continue to live for the Philippians' joy in the faith
2:2	Paul asks the Philippians to complete his joy
2:17–18	Paul is glad and rejoices with the Philippians and asks the same of them
2:28	Paul sends Epaphroditus that the Philippians might rejoice
2:29	Paul commands the Philippians to receive Epaphroditus with joy
3:1	Paul tells the Philippians to rejoice in the Lord
4:1	Paul relays to the Philippians they are his joy
4:4	Paul enjoins the Philippians twice to rejoice in the Lord
4:10	Paul rejoices in the Lord at the Philippians' concern for him

Partnering in the Gospel

1:5	"your partnership in the gospel"
1:7	"you are all partners with me in grace"
1:27	"contending together for the faith of the gospel"
2:22	"served with me in the gospel ministry"
2:25	"my brother, coworker, and fellow soldier"
3:17	"Join in imitating me"
4:3	"true partner, . . . help these women who have contended for the gospel at my side, along with Clement and the rest of my coworkers"
4:15	"shared with me in the matter of giving and receiving"

The outline here is a bit different from the headings below, but I am offering a complementary way of looking at the letter in the outline.

Outline

Joy in thanksgiving and prayer for fruitfulness	1:1–11
Joy in sharing the gospel and seeing it shared	1:12–26
The joy of living like Christ	1:27–2:30
The joy of knowing Christ keeps one from false teachers	3:1–4:1
The joy of peace and of giving sacrificially	4:2–23

Introduction (1:1–11)

The letter begins with a greeting (Phil. 1:1–2), thanksgiving (1:3–8), and prayer (1:9–11). Several features stand out in the greeting. Paul and Timothy are listed together as cosenders, though Paul clearly wrote the letter. What is striking, however, is that in contrast to virtually every other letter he wrote, Paul says nothing about his apostolic authority. Instead he and Timothy are designated as "servants" (*douloi*). Why would Paul fail to mention his apostolic authority? I suggest that it is because the church was suffering from disunity, and Paul commences the letter with a major theme (service) that will inform the rest of the epistle. He and Timothy were servants, and their goal was to build up others in the faith. Perhaps the fissures in the church also explain why the "overseers and deacons" are included, for we see no mention of leaders in the introduction of any of the other Pauline letters. Paul doesn't give any indication elsewhere that the leaders were at fault, unless Euodia and Syntyche were deacons (4:2–3). Perhaps he addresses them because they have a particular responsibility in pursuing unity and harmony.

The thanksgiving brims with joy (1:3–8) as Paul rejoices in the Philippians, and that joy even percolates into his prayers. He is full of joy because of their "partnership in the gospel" (1:5), a partnership that was there from the outset. This partnership was marked by financial assistance, but, of course, can't be reduced to such. In any case, their participation made it clear that they belonged to God, signifying that God had initiated the "good work" (1:6) of conversion, and what he began he will faithfully complete so that the Philippians can be assured of final salvation. The fellowship of the Philippians, who were partners in the grace of the gospel, was such that they identified with Paul in his imprisonment. Their love for God and love for Paul bound him to them with deep affection. The love and joy that mark this paragraph testify to the beauty of relationships in the early church.

The Philippians have made an excellent start as Christians, and Paul prays that the love so evidently characterizing their lives will increase, and particularly that their love will become wise and discerning (1:9–11). If they grow in knowledge, they will be able to discern what is truly loving and right in every situation and will lead lives that are pleasing to God and without blame until the last day. They will live righteous and beautiful lives, and such a way of life comes from the strength Christ gives and brings glory to God.

Paul as an Example of Living for the Gospel (1:12–26)

The problems with unity in the congregation were not over false teaching, nor was it similar to what we find in Corinthians, where the church was taking sides over various ministers, nor do we have evidence that the rich and the poor were divided. From what we can discern, it seems that the petty annoyances of everyday life were creating problems. Paul shares an account of what happened to him when he was imprisoned (probably in Rome). The story isn't randomly selected: it is introduced as a model and example for the Philippians.

Paul lived for the sake of the gospel, and he shares how his imprisonment became the impetus for the gospel being shared with the imperial guard and with others as well. The imperial guard presumably refers to soldiers who guarded Paul while he was in prison. Other believers, seeing Paul's boldness despite his imprisonment, were galvanized to proclaim the gospel without fear. Still, the situation was complicated because there was division in Rome among Christians over Paul. Some, perhaps resenting the fact that Paul was more prominent than they were, proclaimed Christ with a spirit of jealousy and competition. It is impossible to be certain, but in some way they hoped to distress Paul or perhaps cause the authorities to oppress him more in his imprisonment. Others, however, proclaimed Christ with a genuine love for Paul, knowing that God had specially appointed him to suffer for the gospel. How did Paul respond to this state of affairs? With joy! For whether the motives were good or ill, Christ was being proclaimed. Since Paul rejoices over the proclamation of Christ even from those who envied him, it is evident that they were preaching the true gospel, and there was no doctrinal deviation present. Why did Paul share this story? Paul gives the Philippians an example of how to love those who are difficult to love. Paul didn't live for the approval of others. He lived for the sake of the gospel, and thus when the gospel was advancing, he could overlook petty conflicts with those who tried to make life miserable for him.

Verses 19–26 center on what animates Paul's life. Paul didn't regret or rue his circumstances because they led to his deliverance, which is not deliverance from prison, but eschatological salvation. Salvation is obtained through means, including the help of the Spirit and the prayers of the saints. Verse 19 alludes to Job 13:16, where Job affirms that his suffering will lead to his salvation, and Paul's hope is similar. Paul's aim is that in both life and death he would live to bring honor to Christ. In one of the most remarkable statements ever written, Paul says, "For me, to live is Christ and to die is gain" (Phil. 1:21). Paul doesn't merely give his life for a cause: he gives his all for a person. At the end of the day love controls how we live and what we do. Dying is gain because it will lead to a deeper and more intimate relationship with Christ.

Dying is the pathway to the greatest joy, but while Paul lived he was engaged in ministry to assist others, and since he wanted to glorify Christ both now and forever, he was divided about whether to desire life or death. Death meant departing and being with Christ, which is the greatest good. Still, Paul was persuaded that he would continue to live so that he could minister to the Philippians and to others. Paul lived so that others would advance in the joy of faith. Once again, Paul functions as a model and example. His preference was to leave this life and be with Christ, but he lived to honor Christ and to serve others by helping them progress in faith.

Live Worthily of the Gospel as Heavenly Citizens (1:27–2:4)

Believers are citizens of heaven, and in what is perhaps the central admonition in this letter, they are exhorted to live in a way that accords with the gospel (1:27). What this means specifically is that the church is to be *united*: one in the Spirit and united in the faith (1:28). Unity comes from devotion to the gospel and allegiance to Christ. Outside pressure, opponents with all the stress they cause, may also fray and harm relationships inside the community. We are not told who the opponents are, but given what happened to Paul in Philippi (Acts 16:11–40), the opposition could be political and/or religious. In any case, Paul comforts the believers by assuring them that they will be saved, while the opponents will experience eschatological destruction (Phil. 1:29). God rules over all things, for he has granted the Philippians faith and the privilege (remarkably!) of suffering for Christ. The Philippians were "engaged in the same struggle," the same kind of suffering Paul faced for the sake of the gospel (1:30).

In 2:1–4 the church is summoned to unity, and Paul piles up the terms to emphasize the importance of harmony. Paul will be full of joy if they are humble and others-centered instead of living for the sake of themselves, if they look to the interests of others instead of their own concerns. The pronounced emphasis on unity suggests that the church was struggling with divisiveness. The call to unity is rooted in the resources they have in Christ, the encouragement, the "consolation of love," the "fellowship with the Spirit," and the "affection and mercy" (2:1). The indicative grounds the imperative.

The Example of Christ (2:5–11)

Philippians 2:5–11 is famous and intensely debated, and for good reason, since it is one of the most exalted and beautiful texts in the Pauline corpus. A few scholars have seen in the text only the story of Christ's saving work and deny that Christ plays an exemplary role, but most rightly discern that such a reading is a false dichotomy. Indeed, the most natural reading of 2:5 is that Paul calls upon the readers to imitate Christ, and so the call to imitate Christ is the main point of the passage! The church is to be united and to live for others, and Jesus functions as the supreme example. Certainly the imitation of Christ is analogous and not exact, for believers who humble themselves won't be exalted as Lord. Nevertheless, those who suffer as believers will be raised with Christ (3:10–11, 20–21).

Most agree that verses 6–11 constitute a hymn or confessional statement, and some think it is pre-Pauline, though I suspect Paul wrote it himself. In any case, our task is to interpret the text before us. The text falls nicely into two stanzas: verses 6–8 denote Christ's humiliation and verses 9–11 his exaltation. We begin with Jesus humbling himself, and the question of what it means that he was "in the form of God" (2:6). The expression doesn't mean that he only appeared to be God externally or that he had the splendor of God without being God. We see in verse 7 that Jesus took "the form of a servant," and this clearly means, as the context demonstrates, that he became a human being. His humanity, however, wasn't merely external; he was truly and fully human. So too, Jesus was truly and fully divine.

We have another important clue in verse 6 that Jesus was fully God. The CSB (cf. also NIV and NRSV) rightly translates the verse to say that Jesus "did not consider equality with God as something to be exploited." In other words, Jesus was fully equal with God but didn't take advantage of his divinity. Jesus being in the form of God is another way of saying that he was (and is!) fully equal with God.

Jesus functions as an example because he didn't cling to his rights. He was fully God (2:6), but "emptied himself" by becoming a "servant," by taking on humanity (2:7). The reference to the servant may allude to the servant of the Lord of Isaiah 53. Some in the history of interpretation have understood the emptying to mean that Jesus gave up his divinity, surrendering his divinity to become a man. The text, however, says nothing about Jesus relinquishing his divinity; it says he *added* or *assumed* humanity. If we look at the participles modifying the verb "emptied," he emptied by *adding*, not by *subtracting*. For God to take on humanity is to lower himself. The divine attributes of Jesus were veiled or not always exercised when he was on earth, but he didn't relinquish his divinity.

The Son of God did not take advantage of his deity but emptied himself by becoming human. As a human being, he could have been feted and prized as a king. Instead, he "humbled himself" by consenting to die, and not only was he willing to die, but he died the most shameful and agonizing death imaginable, death on a cross. Cicero said the cross was the "cruelest and most disgusting penalty" (*Against Verres* 2.5.169). Josephus said it was "the most pitiable of deaths" (*J.W.* 7.203) The Philippians were called upon to love one another, and the model and supreme exemplar is Christ's self-giving love on the cross.

As a consequence of Jesus's self-giving love, God "exalted him," giving him "the name that is above every name" (Phil. 2:9). Thus all of creation, both angelic and human, submits to Jesus Christ and confesses his lordship (2:10–11). The exaltation of Jesus as Lord doesn't diminish the Father, but actually magnifies him and brings him glory. When we investigate the OT text to which Paul alludes here, two truths stand out. First, the deity of Jesus is delineated with clarity. The text Paul draws on is Isaiah 45:20–25. One of the striking things about Isaiah and this text in particular is its uncompromising monotheism. Any and all idolatry is scorned, and Yahweh is confessed as the one and only true God (45:20–21). Since there is only one God, there is only one way to salvation (45:22). Since Yahweh is Lord, "Every knee will bow to me, every tongue will swear allegiance" (45:23). Clearly, Paul draws on this verse from Isaiah, applying it to Jesus of Nazareth. Jesus Christ, then, shares the same identity as Yahweh. Just as Yahweh is worshiped, so Jesus is worshiped. Paul as a Pharisee knew very well that there was only one God, and thus we see clear evidence not that monotheism is surrendered but that monotheism is more complex than we might initially think. There is complexity in the being of God.

The OT text also helps regarding the question of universalism. Does Paul in Philippians think that eventually every creature in the universe will embrace Jesus as Lord and be saved? The many affirmations of judgment in his writings demonstrate that such a reading misinterprets the Pauline intention. We also receive help on this score from the next two verses in Isaiah 45. Every knee will bow and every tongue confess, but those who "are enraged against him" will "be put to shame" (45:24). Yes, all will swear allegiance, but neither Isaiah nor Paul envision glad subjection by all: some will still hate his rule but will face eschatological humiliation and eternal shame. Yet others, those who belong to the restored Israel, "will be justified" (Isa. 45:25). They will gladly confess Jesus as Lord and will stand as right before him based on Christ's atoning death and resurrection. We need to return to the main point that Paul has made. Jesus's glad willingness to give up his rights as God and to suffer humiliation for the sake of the salvation of others is the reason God exalted him. No one who loves so radically is ever forsaken but is always rewarded. So too the readers, though they won't be exalted as Lord, will be rewarded if they give themselves up for the sake of others.

The Necessity of Obedience (2:12–18)

Christ's humility functions as an example for believers and also points to the necessity of obedience. Such obedience means believers are to "work out" their "salvation" (Phil. 2:12). In this verse salvation is clearly future, and the language of accomplishing salvation is quite startling, especially from the pen of Paul! Certainly he doesn't retrench on the gracious gift of salvation, which is received by faith instead of being based on one's own righteousness (cf. 3:9). Still, those who have received the gift of righteousness are to live righteous lives. Indeed, without such lived-out righteousness, which is clearly imperfect (cf. 3:12–16), one will not be saved. Paul expected that there was evidence of new life in Christ—a new obedience. Also, such obedience is not self-generated, as 2:13 clarifies. The good work accomplished comes from God's work within a person. Indeed, God grants even the desire to do what is good and righteous, showing that all the glory goes to God for the good that human beings carry out.

Part of what it means to obey and to work out salvation is not to grumble and argue (2:14). Grumbling marked Israel in the wilderness (Exod. 16:7–9, 12; Num. 17:20, 25), and they ultimately didn't make it into the land of promise. Paul's citation of Deuteronomy 32:5 in Philippians 2:15 constitutes a wallop. In the Song of Moses, Israel's sin means that they are to be blamed (*mōmēta*, LXX). In fact, the wilderness generation "are not his children but a devious and crooked generation." Paul picks this up, saying that the Philippians must obey to be "children of God" and "without fault" (*amōma*) in the midst of "a crooked and perverted generation" (Phil. 2:15). Certainly Paul doesn't think believers achieve their salvation, but if obedience isn't present, they show that they belong to the world rather than to God. Saying that believers will "shine like stars" alludes to Daniel 12:3, and there the righteous stand out from the wicked as those whose names are written in God's book (12:1), as those who shine forth in an evil world (12:3). In a world full of stress and suffering, believers are to persevere and endure to the end, holding on to "the word of life" (Phil. 2:16), and at the same time they shine forth as witnesses of the gospel (cf. Matt. 5:16). If the Philippians persevere in the faith, Paul will exult with joy because then his work on their behalf wasn't futile (Phil. 2:16). He was willing to endure any sacrifice (like Christ! 2:6–11) if it led to their salvation, for in doing so he maximizes his joy, and the Philippians will be full of joy as well.

The Example of Timothy and Epaphroditus (2:19–30)

The divisions fracturing the church are overcome when people live for the glory of God and for the good of others. The supreme example is Jesus Christ, who did not cling to the honor he had but humbled himself to face death on a cross. Paul also functions as an example of such self-giving love, which is motivated by the gospel. Here Paul turns to two other examples: Timothy and

Epaphroditus. We consider Timothy first (2:19–24), whom Paul hopes to send to the Philippians. Timothy stands out because he wasn't self-absorbed and narcissistic; he truly cared and fretted (in the best sense of the word) about the well-being of the Philippians. Most people are consumed with their own lives and worries, but Timothy was concerned about the things of Jesus Christ (cf. 2:5–11). Paul hopes to send Timothy as his beloved son, then, to minister to and care for the Philippians.

Epaphroditus also comes in for high praise (2:25–30), as Paul designates him as his "brother, coworker, and fellow soldier" (2:25). In addition, he was a messenger sent from the Philippians and one who acted like Christ in ministering to Paul's need. In the course of his ministry, Epaphroditus fell ill; the illness was so severe that he almost died, and thereby he risked his life for the sake of love. Incidentally, we learn from Paul's response to the sparing of Epaphroditus's life that he didn't view the matter of life and death simplistically. He didn't respond to Epaphroditus's healing by saying it would have been better if he died (cf. 1:21)! Instead, he says that God showed mercy both to Epaphroditus and to Paul by sparing Epaphroditus's life. Yes, to die is gain, but death is also the last enemy and something to be grieved and lamented (1 Cor. 15:26; Rom. 12:15). In any case, Epaphroditus should be welcomed and honored when he returned to Philippi because he lived for the sake of Christ: he gave his life for the sake of others.

Watch Out for Bad Examples (3:1–6)

Chapter 3 seems to move into a different orbit with a discussion of false teachers, whom the Philippians must avoid, but we see indications throughout the chapter that link chapter 3 with the first two chapters. To put it another way, the teachers function as bad examples, and Paul doesn't want the Philippians to imitate them but to imitate him and his coworkers.

Verse 1 is transitional and not easy to interpret. At the very least we can say that the call to rejoice guards the congregation against division and perhaps against the false teachers. The shift to false teachers is abrupt, and they weren't necessarily in the congregation, for Paul warns the Philippians to be on the lookout for these teachers who were disrupting churches elsewhere. Since these teachers advocated circumcision and observance of the law (so 3:2–9), they represent the same profile as the Judaizers in Galatia. They advocated keeping the law to obtain salvation. Paul turns the tables on them, identifying them as dogs, evil workers, and mutilators. "Dogs" is a term Jews regularly used for unclean gentiles (cf. Matt. 7:6; 15:26–27). Dogs weren't loveable animals in Jewish culture but were considered to be unclean, like pigs (Exod. 22:31;

Luke 16:21). Paul sarcastically identifies the Jewish teachers as dogs, unclean before God. So too, the Judaizers believed that they did good works, but Paul rejects them as "evil workers" (Phil. 3:2). Finally, they were proud of their circumcision, thinking that it commended them before God, but Paul engages in a play on the word "circumcision" (*peritomē*), a wordplay obvious in Greek but not clear in English. Paul compares *peritomē* (circumcision) to *katatomē*, a pagan right of mutilation (Deut. 23:1; cf. Gal. 5:12). The verb for mutilating (*katatemnō*) is used to describe the pagan gashings and cuttings of the prophets of Baal (1 Kings 18:28 LXX). Paul once prized his circumcision as a sign of his devotion to the Lord, but if people clung to the ritual as a way of claiming favor with God, he lampooned it as pagan.

Believers are the true circumcision (cf. Rom. 2:25–29), and true circumcision is spiritual (Deut. 30:6), not physical, so that those who are truly circumcised worship the one true God through the Holy Spirit (Phil. 3:3). They don't place confidence in themselves but in Christ Jesus. The opponents were apparently very proud of their qualifications and their heritage, but Paul says that if they want to play that game (cf. 2 Cor. 11), then he will play too, and he will win! (Phil. 3:4–6). Paul was the quintessential Jew, circumcised the eighth day according to the law (Lev. 12:3). Not only was he from the nation of Israel, but he also knew what tribe he was from: Benjamin. From Benjamin came the first king of Israel (Saul), after whom Paul was presumably named. When Paul says he was "a Hebrew of Hebrews" (Phil. 3:5 NASB), he probably means that he spoke the native language, Aramaic.

Up to this point the qualifications were Paul's by birth, but he goes on to list what he has accomplished. He joined the sect of the Pharisees; as he says in Acts (26:5), the Pharisees were "the strictest sect of our religion," and they were probably the most popular among the common people as well. Paul's zeal, as noted earlier, was patterned after Phinehas (Num. 25:11), Elijah (1 Kings 19:10, 14), and Mattathias (1 Macc. 2:23–27, 50, 54, 58); that was evident in his persecution of the church. Before his conversion Paul didn't feel guilty about persecuting the church but considered his zeal to be pleasing to the Lord. Finally, Paul says he was "blameless" regarding "righteousness that is in the law" (Phil. 3:6). Blameless does not mean the same thing as sinless. Paul was exceptionally devoted to the Torah, but part of that devotion included offering sacrifices for sin.

Gaining Christ (3:7–11)

Paul's ethnic heritage and his accomplishments relative to the law made him stand out among his contemporaries, and they seemed to be a "gain" to him, especially in terms of his relationship with God. Still, they are all "loss" for Christ's sake. Paul picks up the same words for "gain" and "loss" that Jesus used when speaking about "gaining" the entire world but "losing" one's soul (Mark 8:36). Earlier Paul appeared to have gained the world with his heritage and zeal, but he was actually losing his soul. So all the "gains" he had were "loss" in comparison to the incomparable privilege of knowing Jesus Christ (Phil. 3:7). Indeed, Paul didn't regret becoming a believer, as if he looked back fondly at what he achieved and what he was before he encountered Christ on the road to Damascus. Instead, knowing Christ was so entrancing that he considered his past gains to be garbage or excrement compared to knowing Christ.

Paul's goal on the final day was to "be found" in Christ, and the metaphor is legal here, denoting the findings of a judge (3:9). On what basis would Paul be found by the divine judge to be in the right on the day of judgment? Here he contrasts himself with the Judaizers and with what he believed before his conversion. The righteousness that suffices could not be his own, based on his observance of the law. Though Paul doesn't say so here, we know from elsewhere that righteousness from keeping the law isn't adequate since all sin and fail to keep what God commands (cf. Rom. 1:18–3:20; 3:23; 5:20; 7:7–25; Gal. 3:10; 5:3). Thus a right relation with God, right standing with God, comes through faith in Christ, not through achieving but believing. Paul's aim in life was to know Christ and his resurrection power, and this becomes a reality when Paul shares in his sufferings, so that suffering comes first and then glory (Phil. 3:10). By whatever means possible it was Paul's desire to obtain the final resurrection and the life of the age to come (3:11).

Run to Win the Prize (3:12–16)

Paul's goal was the resurrection, which is another way of saying that the goal is perfection, because on the day of resurrection believers will be perfected. Perhaps the Judaizers claimed some kind of perfection via the law, but it is difficult to be sure about this point. In any case, Paul poured all his energies toward grasping the goal, but the emphasis even here isn't on his own effort, for he only made that effort because Christ grasped him first (3:12). Paul recognized that he had not yet attained perfection; he was a pilgrim on a journey. Still, he didn't linger on the past but strained forward like a runner to win the eschatological prize to which God called him (3:13–14). Again we see the delicate balance between Paul's effort and the grace of God that sustains his effort (cf. 2:12–13). Verse 15 is ironic: those who are "perfect" (*teleioi*), those who are "mature," recognize that they aren't perfect! Some were confused on this matter, but if they were Christians of goodwill, Paul was confident that

God would reveal to them, as they continued to grow in their own faith, that perfection is obtained only in the eschaton, the very end of history.

Keep Imitating the Right People (3:17–4:1)

One of the central themes of Philippians is imitating the right people, as we have seen in chapters 1–2. Paul picks up that subject again in this paragraph, instructing the readers to follow those who are like him and to flee from those who proclaim a different message. The identity of the opponents in 3:18–19 has been the subject of debate: are they the same opponents as those described in 3:2–9? In that case they would have been Judaizers. Some argue that we have a new set of opponents because those described seem to be libertines and licentious in contrast to Judaizers, who were law observant. Certainty is difficult, but I incline toward the view that the opponents here are the same as those mentioned earlier in chapter 3. The simplest hypothesis is that the same group is in view, and I will attempt to show why this reading is plausible below.

Paul begins with a call to imitate him, but the invitation wasn't restricted to imitating Paul (3:17). The Philippians are to imitate all believers who follow the pattern set by Paul. Paul wasn't trying to set up a cult of followers who subjugated themselves to Paul's every whim. We have already seen that Timothy and Epaphroditus are lifted up as examples (2:19–30). The readers need to observe and to follow good examples because there were many going in the other direction, many who were "enemies of the cross" (3:18). It is no surprise to characterize Judaizers as enemies of the cross. We saw in Galatians that their insistence on circumcision denigrated the cross (cf. 2:21; 3:1; 5:11; 6:12–14). Believers are to imitate those who know that their righteousness is not in themselves but in Christ crucified and risen.

The errors of the opponents were not minor: their destiny was eschatological destruction (3:19). Saying "their god is their stomach" doesn't necessarily mean that they were libertines; it is probably just a way of saying that their god is themselves, or that they were focused on food laws. What they boast in is shameful because they end up worshiping the creature rather than the Creator (Rom. 1:25), and in this way they set their hearts and minds on earth rather than in heaven.

And heaven is where the Philippian believers find their citizenship (Phil. 3:20), which may strike a blow to those who were proud of the fact that Philippi was a Roman colony. The true Savior is Jesus, not Caesar, and believers await Jesus's coming and don't put their hope in Rome or any other earthly kingdom. The weakness of our bodies and their corruptibility humbles us, showing that the kingdom awaited by believers will not arrive until Jesus comes and transforms our bodies so that they are glorious and powerful like his (3:21). Death and sin must be conquered and subjected fully to Christ. Of course, the victory is sure, and thus the Philippians should hold on to their faith with confidence, as Paul reminds them that they are his joy, his beloved, his crown (4:1).

Exhortations to Peace and Joy (4:2-9)

In this section we find several admonitions that are loosely related, though the injunction to harmony seems to be the theme. The call to unity now becomes specific. Two women, Euodia and Syntyche, apparently had a falling out (4:2–3). These women had played a significant role in ministry, probably as missionaries or evangelists in the city. They were "coworkers" and labored together with Paul in the gospel. We shouldn't think that they were brought up as those who were particularly evil; actually, they stood out for their goodness. Other believers like Clement should play a role in seeing that harmony is restored.

Joy takes center stage as the believers are twice exhorted to rejoice (4:4). If a congregation is joyful, it will be united and free from division. Similarly, believers are to be gracious and reasonable and adaptable, remembering that the Lord is coming soon (4:5). Some matters that often seem so important on earth (and life on earth is important!) are not worth fighting over when seen in the light of eternity. Life on earth is stressful and fills us with concerns, and Paul in one of his most famous admonitions summons believers to refrain from worry and to bring their requests to God in prayer (4:6). Such prayers should be offered "with thanksgiving," for believers know that God loves them and is the almighty God, watching and ruling over every circumstance in their lives. When believers rest in God in this way, then God's peace will fill and fortify their hearts, and it truly will be a peace "which surpasses all understanding" since there is no human reason not to worry and fret (4:7). Where there is peace, there is unity, and in verses 8–9 exhortations are given to ensure that "the God of peace" will continue to dwell with the Philippians. The believers are to set their minds on the true, the beautiful, the right, the pure, and the lovely (4:8). If the instruction seems vague, Paul himself functions as their example. A congregation that lives in such a way will be harmonious and attractive.

Thank You and Goodbye (4:10-23)

Paul returns to what was mentioned at the outset of the letter (1:3–8), the Philippians' partnership in the gospel. Here he particularly thanks them for the gift they sent to assist him in ministry. One scholar said that we have a "thankless thanks" here, but it is better to say that the thanks is nuanced, and there are good reasons for the nuance, as we shall see. Paul begins with the joy that filled him when the Philippians renewed their concern for him by giving him a gift, though he realized that their affection for him had not flagged at any point; they had simply "lacked the opportunity" to send him a gift (4:10).

Paul was thankful, but then he immediately says that he didn't really need the gift, for he had learned how to be content in every situation, whether he had little or much (4:11–12). Christ had given him the strength, the grace, to endure in every circumstance (4:13). Paul didn't say this to detract from the gift the Philippians gave him but to give them a right perspective on money and material possessions. He wasn't desperate for their gift, as many health-and-wealth preachers are today. Still, he was thankful for the assistance and grateful for their love, so he returns to thanking them for helping him in his difficulty (4:14). Indeed, the Philippians stood out for giving to him repeatedly for the sake of the ministry (4:15–16). Paul backtracks again in 4:17. What was most important wasn't the gift he received, though he was grateful for it, but what it showed about the heart of the Philippians. Giving the gift profited the Philippians the most! But they shouldn't take what he said too far, for he is full and happy now that he has received a gift from them (4:18). Using OT language, their gift is "a fragrant offering" and "an acceptable sacrifice." The Philippians should not ultimately think of themselves as noble, however, for God "will supply all your needs" from his inexhaustible glory (4:19). In other words, God will give them everything they need, and since all good things come from God, he receives the glory forever (4:20).

Paul says a quick goodbye in the letter, sending greetings to the church (4:21). Those with him sent their greetings, and he highlights the greetings from "Caesar's household" (4:22). Presumably these people became believers through the witness of Paul when he was in prison. We know what Paul would talk about if he was confined to a guard for several hours! The letter ends with a prayer for grace, which is a signature of Paul's gospel and is communicated through the Letter to the Philippians.

Philippians: Commentaries

Barth, Karl. *The Epistle to the Philippians*. 40th anniversary ed. Edited by Bruce L. McCormack and Francis Watson. Louisville: Westminster John Knox, 2002.

Beare, F. W. *A Commentary on the Epistle to the Philippians*. 2nd ed. BNTC. London: Black, 1969.

Bockmuehl, Markus. *The Epistle to the Philippians*. BNTC. London: A&C Black, 1997.

Bruce, F. F. *Philippians*. NIBC. Peabody, MA: Hendrickson, 1989.

Calvin, John. *The Epistles of Paul the Apostle to the Galatians, Ephesians, Philippians and Colossians*. Translated by T. H. L. Parker, edited by David W. Torrance and Thomas F. Torrance. Calvin's Commentaries. Grand Rapids: Eerdmans, 1965.

Carson, D. A. *Basics for Believers: An Exposition of Philippians*. Grand Rapids: Baker, 1996.

Collange, Jean-François. *The Epistle of Saint Paul to the Philippians*. Translated by A. W. Hethcote. London: Epworth, 1979.

Cousar, Charles B. *Philippians and Philemon: A Commentary*. New Testament Library. Louisville: Westminster John Knox, 2009.

Eadie, John Young William. *A Commentary on the Greek Text of the Epistle of Paul to the Philippians*. Edinburgh: T&T Clark, 1884. Reprinted, Birmingham, AL: Solid Ground Christian Books, 2005.

Fee, Gordon D. *Paul's Letter to the Philippians*. NICNT. Grand Rapids: Eerdmans, 1995.

Fowl, Stephen E. *Philippians*. THNTC. Grand Rapids: Eerdmans, 2005.

Hansen, G. Walter. *The Letter to the Philippians*. PNTC. Grand Rapids: Eerdmans, 2009.

Harmon, Matthew. *Philippians: A Mentor Commentary*. Ross-shire, UK: Christian Focus, 2015.

Hawthorne, Gerald F., and Ralph P. Martin. *Philippians*. Rev. ed. WBC. Nashville: Thomas Nelson, 2004.

Holloway, Paul A. *Philippians*. Hermeneia. Minneapolis: Fortress, 2017.

Kennedy, H. A. A. "The Epistle to the Philippians." In *The Expositor's Greek Testament*, edited by W. Robertson Nicoll, 397–474. London: Hodder & Stoughton, 1897.

Kent, Homer A. "Philippians." In *Ephesians through Philemon*, vol. 11 of *The Expositor's Bible Commentary*, edited by Frank E. Gaebelein, 95–159. Grand Rapids: Zondervan, 1978.

Lightfoot, J. B. *Saint Paul's Epistle to the Philippians*. London: Macmillan & Co., 1898.

Martin, Ralph P. *Philippians: An Introduction and Commentary*. TNTC. Downers Grove, IL: InterVarsity, 2007.

Melick, Richard R. *Philippians, Colossians, Philemon*. NAC 32. Nashville: Broadman & Holman, 1991.

Michael, John Hugh. *The Epistle of Paul to the Philippians*. MNTC. London: Hodder & Stoughton, 1928.

Motyer, Alec. *The Message of Philippians*. BST. Downers Grove, IL: InterVarsity, 1997.

O'Brien, Peter T. *The Epistle to the Philippians: A Commentary on the Greek Text*. NIGTC. Grand Rapids: Eerdmans, 1991.

Reumann, John H. P. *Philippians: A New Translation with Introduction and Commentary*. AB 33. New Haven: Yale University Press, 2008.

Silva, Moisés. *Philippians*. 2nd ed. BECNT. Grand Rapids: Baker Academic, 2005.

———. "Philippians." In *Commentary on the New Testament Use of the Old Testament*, edited by G. K. Beale and D. A. Carson, 835–39. Grand Rapids: Baker Academic, 2007.

Thompson, James, and Bruce W. Longenecker. *Philippians and Philemon: A Commentary*. PCNT. Grand Rapids: Baker Academic, 2016.

Thurston, Bonnie B., and Judith M. Ryan. *Philippians and Philemon*. SP. Collegeville, MN: Liturgical Press, 2005.

Vincent, Marvin R. *A Critical and Exegetical Commentary on the Epistles to the Philippians and to Philemon.* ICC. New York: C. Scribner's Sons, 1897.

Witherington, Ben, III. *Paul's Letter to the Philippians: A Socio-Rhetorical Commentary.* Grand Rapids: Eerdmans, 2011.

Philippians: Articles, Essays, and Monographs

Bertschmann, Dorothea H. "Is There Kenosis in This Text? Rereading Philippians 3:2–11 in the Light of the Christ Hymn." *JBL* 137 (2018): 235–54.

Bockmuehl, Markus. "'The Form of God' (Phil. 2:6): Variations on a Theme of Jewish Mysticism." *JTS* 48 (1997): 1–23.

Briones, David. "Paul's Intentional 'Thankless Thanks' in Philippians 4.10–20." *JSNT* 34 (2011): 47–69.

Burk, Denny. "On the Articular Infinitive in Philippians 2:6: A Grammatical Note with Christological Implications." *TynBul* 55 (2004): 253–74.

Capper, B. J. "Paul's Dispute with Philippi: Understanding Paul's Argument in Philippians 1–2 from His Thanks in 4.10–20." *TZ* 49 (1993): 193–214.

Croy, N. Clayton. "'To Die Is Gain' (Philippians 1:19–26): Does Paul Contemplate Suicide?" *JBL* 122 (2003): 517–31.

Fabricatore, Daniel J. *Form of God, Form of a Servant: An Examination of the Greek Noun μορφή in Philippians 2:6–7.* Lanham, MD: University Press of America, 2010.

Fee, Gordon D. "Philippians 2:5–11: Hymn or Exalted Pauline Prose?" *BBR* 2 (1992): 29–46.

Geoffrion, Timothy C. *The Rhetorical Purpose and the Political Military Character of Philippians: A Call to Stand Firm.* Lewiston, NY: Mellen Biblical Press, 1993.

Gundry, Robert H. "Style and Substance in 'The Myth of God Incarnate' according to Philippians 2:6–11." In *Crossing the Boundaries: Essays in Biblical Interpretation in Honour of Michael D. Goulder*, edited by Stanley Porter, Paul Joyce, and David E. Orton, 271–93. Leiden: Brill, 1994.

Hawthorne, Gerald F. *Word Biblical Themes: Philippians.* Word Biblical Themes. Waco, TX: Word, 1987.

Heil, John Paul. *Philippians: Let Us Rejoice in Being Conformed to Christ.* Society of Biblical Literature: Early Christianity and Its Literature. Atlanta: SBL, 2010.

Hellerman, Joseph H. *Reconstructing Honor in Roman Philippi: Carmen Christi as Cursus Pudorum.* SNTSMS. New York: Cambridge University Press, 2005.

Holloway, Paul A. *Consolation in Philippians: Philosophical Sources and Rhetorical Strategy.* SNTSMS 112. New York: Cambridge University Press, 2001.

Hoover, Roy W. "*Harpagmos* Enigma: A Philological Solution." *HTR* 64 (1971): 95–119.

Jewett, Robert. "Conflicting Movements in the Early Church as Reflected in Philippians." *NovT* 12 (1970): 362–90.

Keown, Mark J. *Congregational Evangelism in Philippians: The Centrality of an Appeal for Gospel Proclamation to the Fabric of Philippians.* PBM. Milton Keynes, UK: Paternoster, 2008.

Martin, Ralph P. *A Hymn of Christ: Philippians 2:5–11 in Recent Interpretation and in the Setting of Early Christian Worship*. Downers Grove, IL: InterVarsity, 1997.

Oakes, Peter. *Philippians: From People to Letter*. SNTSMS 110. New York: Cambridge University Press, 2001.

Palmer, D. W. "To Die Is Gain (Philippians 1:21)." *NovT* 17 (1975): 203–18.

Perkins, Pheme. "Philippians: Theology for the Heavenly *Politeuma*." In *Pauline Theology*, vol. 1, *Thessalonians, Philippians, Galatians, Philemon*, edited by Jouette M. Bassler, 89–104. Minneapolis: Fortress, 1991.

Peterman, Gerald W. "'Thankless Thanks': The Epistolary Social Convention in Philippians 4 (1997): 10–20." *TynBul* 41 (1991): 261–70.

Pilhofer, Peter. *Philippi*. WUNT 87. Tübingen: Mohr Siebeck, 1995.

Rapske, Brian. *The Book of Acts and Paul in Roman Custody*. The Book of Acts in Its First-Century Setting. Grand Rapids: Eerdmans, 1994.

Reed, Jeffrey T. *A Discourse Analysis of Philippians: Method and Rhetoric in the Debate over Literary Integrity*. JSNTSup 136. Sheffield: Sheffield Academic, 1997.

Reumann, John H. P. "Philippians 3.20–21—A Hymnic Fragment?" *NTS* 30 (1984): 593–609.

Strimple, Robert B. "Philippians 2:5–11 in Recent Studies: Some Exegetical Conclusions." *WTJ* 41 (1976): 247–68.

Sumney, Jerry L. *Philippians: A Greek Student's Intermediate Reader*. Peabody, MA: Hendrickson, 2007.

Tellbe, Mikael. "The Sociological Factors behind Philippians 3.1–11 and the Conflict at Philippi." *JSNT* 55 (1994): 97–121.

Ware, James P. *Paul and the Mission of the Church: Philippians in Ancient Jewish Context*. Grand Rapids: Baker Academic, 2011.

Witherington, Ben, III. *Friendship and Finances in Philippi: The Letter of Paul to the Philippians*. NTC. Valley Forge, PA: Trinity Press International, 1994.

Wright, N. T. "*Harpagmos* and the Meaning of Philippians 2:5–11." *JTS* 37 (1986): 321–52.

CHAPTER EIGHT

Colossians

Introduction

Some scholars doubt that Paul wrote Colossians, and the purpose of this book isn't to examine such questions. Still, I believe good arguments exist to support Pauline authorship, and it will be assumed in the discussion that follows. The place from which Paul wrote the letter is also disputed. Some posit Ephesus, and this is certainly a possibility, but I incline to the traditional view that it was written from Rome; if that's the case, the letter was written in AD 60–62.

What has provoked even more discussion is the situation that called forth the letter. Colossae was a smaller city, and apparently Paul didn't evangelize it himself, nor had he ever met the Colossians (2:1). Epaphras, probably from Colossae, likely became a Christian through Paul's ministry. As Paul's delegate, he established the church there (1:7; 4:12–13). He probably visited Paul, informing him about what was going on in Colossae and soliciting Paul's help. What was happening in Colossae that precipitated Epaphras to visit Paul? Most agree that some kind of false teaching threatened the church, and Paul wrote to counter the deviant philosophy (2:8). Actually, a minority voice claims that Paul does not counter false teaching in the letter, but when we look at 2:6–23, it seems evident that Paul countered an alternative version of his gospel.

What did the false teachers propound and promulgate? I read one book that said there are forty-four different views on the identity of the false teachers in Colossae. The number is exaggerated, but we immediately see from this that discerning the nature of the false teaching isn't easy. Only three theories will be mentioned here, and I support the last of the three. First, it was once quite popular to say that the false teaching was gnostic, but that view is rarely heard today because developed gnostic teachings didn't emerge until the second century AD. Second, the false teaching was a blend of Jewish and local pagan folk belief, which was informed by magic, initiation rites from mystery religions, and certain Jewish practices. Such a reading is certainly possible and may indeed be the most plausible background.

Third, I believe, however, that the most likely solution is that the false teaching was a form of Jewish mysticism. This reading has much to commend it, for Paul refers to circumcision (2:11), Sabbath, new moon, and festivals (2:16). The regulations regarding food also fit with a Jewish background (2:20–23). The teaching certainly emphasized angels (1:16; 2:8, 10, 18, 20), and there was significant interest in angels in Second Temple Judaism. Seeing the false teaching as Jewish fits the actual content of the letter. Magic may have been important in the false teaching, but the problem is that Paul never mentions such in the letter. The false teachers probably emphasized the importance of knowledge (2:4–5, 8), of following particular regulations (2:16–23), and venerating angels (2:8, 10, 18, 20). It is difficult to determine how this should all be put together, and various theories are suggested that won't be detailed here. I will tentatively make some suggestions in the exposition below, but it must be recognized that certainty about these matters is impossible.

If we wanted a rough sketch of Colossians (the details are filled out in the headings below), we could outline the letter as follows.

Outline

Thanksgiving for new life and prayer for discernment	1:1–12
The greatness of Jesus Christ and the call to persevere	1:13–23
Paul's ministry to the gentiles	1:24–2:5
Realize you are complete in Christ	2:6–23
Living out one's new life in Christ	3:1–4:6
Final greetings	4:7–18

Greeting and Thanksgiving (1:1–8)

The greeting in the letter has typical elements and lacks surprises (1:1–2). Paul as an apostle and Timothy as a brother are named, but the letter comes from Paul's hand, not Timothy's. The believers in Colossae are saints but are also "faithful brothers and sisters," and Paul wants them to remain such.

Paul gives thanks for their faith and love, for these are the staples of the Christian life (1:3–4). Faith and love are generated by hope (1:5). Clearly faith and hope are closely related, and those who have hope are assured that God has secured eternal life for them. Love also depends on hope, since people are liberated to love when they know that their own needs will be met, and God promises them a happy future forever. Hope is rooted in the gospel proclaimed to the Colossians, the gospel of Christ crucified and risen, and the Colossians have heard and embraced that message. The gospel, wherever it is proclaimed, bears fruit and increases (1:6), which reminds us of the commission given to human beings to "be fruitful and increase in number" (Gen. 1:28 NIV), but here the new-creation power of the gospel is in view. We are reminded of Paul's claim that the gospel is God's power leading to salvation (Rom. 1:16). The Colossians learned about this gospel from Epaphras as Paul's delegate (Col. 1:7), and the love that is in them comes from the Holy Spirit (1:8).

Prayer for Discernment and Growth (1:9–14)

The false teachers were propounding a variant gospel, and thus the Colossians needed discernment and wisdom, which is precisely what Paul prays for, since true wisdom is a gift from God. Paul wasn't interested in wisdom for its own sake, and he isn't praying for abstract understanding. The goal is for the Colossians to live in a way that befits their calling and to please the Lord in their everyday life, which means that they would grow in their "knowledge of God" (1:10). Human beings don't have the inherent capacity to grow in such a way, and so Paul prays for God's power to strengthen them since, according to his glory, he has all the resources that they need. God's strength provides endurance and patience, and believers are full of joy and thanksgiving when they realize the grace poured out upon them. They are now in the realm of light and enjoy an inheritance, a hope (1:5!) that nothing can shake.

The end of verse 12 transitions from Paul's prayer to the great salvation enjoyed by believers, and in verses 12–13 we see the light-darkness contrast that so aptly describes the new and old life of believers. Believers have been "rescued" and delivered from the realm of "darkness," in which they lived under the authority of the devil. Now they have been "transferred" into the Son's kingdom. Believers live under a new king and are members of a new kingdom. The kingdom here isn't a future but a present reality, showing that the Son already reigns, though, of course, not in all his fullness. The rescue, or what is identified in verse 14 as the "redemption" and liberation of God's people, is exodus and new-exodus language. We have seen before that God's rescue and redemption of his people reaches back to the great deliverance of Israel from Egypt (e.g., Exod. 6:6; 14:30) and to the promises of deliverance in the new exodus (e.g., Isa. 48:20; 49:25). Remarkably, redemption here doesn't focus on an external enemy, but on one's own guilt and sin. Redemption consists in forgiveness, in freedom from the guilt and shame activated by one's own sin.

Christ as Lord of Creation and Lord of the Church (1:15–20)

Here we come to one of the most important texts in the letter and in all of Paul's Letters. Most scholars agree that we have an early Christian hymn, and scholars debate whether it was written by Paul or by someone else with possible Pauline adaptations and additions. I slightly lean to a Pauline composition, though for our purposes the matter isn't of fundamental importance since our task is to interpret it in context. The hymn is split up in various ways, and here two main divisions will be defended: Christ is the Lord of creation (Col. 1:15–17), and Christ is the Lord of the church (1:18–20). The false teaching evidently undermined the centrality and sufficiency of Jesus Christ, and thus we could say that the theme of Colossians is Christ's all-sufficiency.

We begin by considering Christ as the Lord of creation (1:15–17). The Son is "the image of the invisible God" (1:15; cf. 2 Cor. 4:4), which means that Jesus Christ represents who God is to human beings. As John says, he explains the invisible God to those who have never seen him (John 1:18). Human beings are created "in the image of God" (Gen. 1:26–27), but the Son *is* the image of God, perfectly representing who God is to human beings. The Son, then, is fully human and fully God. Paul probably draws on wisdom traditions here. We read in Wisdom 7:26 that wisdom "is a reflection of eternal light, a spotless mirror of the working of God, and an image of his goodness" (NRSV).

The next line identifies Christ as "the firstborn over [literally, "of"] all creation" (Col. 1:15). Arius in the past and Jehovah's Witnesses today understand from this and other texts that Jesus is not fully God, that he was created, and that there was a time when he did not exist. In using the word "firstborn" here, however, Paul does not think of temporal priority, or if he does, it is eternal and everlasting temporal priority. Still, the primary idea is sovereignty and rule. Positional priority is in mind here. The firstborn in Hebrew culture enjoyed authority and sovereignty. We see this very plainly in Psalm 89:27, where the psalmist reflects on the Lord's promise to David, "I will also make him my firstborn, greatest of the kings of the earth." David wasn't the first king: that was Saul. Nor was David the oldest in his family. In fact, he was the youngest. He is identified as firstborn to designate his sovereignty, his rule. So too, Jesus as the firstborn of creation points to his rule and authority over all of creation. Jesus isn't merely the authority over all kings, but he is also the ruler of all created reality!

Colossians 1:16 confirms that as the Son, Jesus is not a created being since he created everything. In fact, Paul goes to great lengths to clarify that "everything" really means everything. It includes both what is in heaven and what is on earth; there is no realm of reality that came into existence apart from the Son. In case there is any question, the words "visible" and "invisible" are added to certify that no particle of creation sprang into being autonomously. Finally, "thrones or dominions or rulers and authorities" are said to be created by the Son. These terms could refer to earthly rulers, but almost all scholars rightly say that they designate angelic powers, which played a fundamental role in the theology of the false teachers. We don't know exactly what they taught, but they apparently stressed the importance of placating or worshiping angels (2:18). Paul emphasizes that all angels, both good and bad, were created by Christ (though evil angels turned against God after they were created). Thus the Colossians should not become preoccupied with angels but should remain centered on Jesus Christ. It is difficult, by the way, to establish any clear delineation among the different categories of angels listed here since we lack enough information to make distinctions.

Verse 17 concludes the theme of Christ as Lord of creation. He is "before all things." Since he is the creator, he existed before all things came into being, and thus is sovereign over all things. Furthermore, he holds "all things together." All of created reality, every atom and every molecule, is sustained and held in place by the Son. The Son didn't only create everything; he also continues to rule over everything. He isn't a deistic god, who created everything and then watches as everything unfolds in the natural world. On the contrary, at every moment he sustains, upholds, guides, and controls what is happening in the universe (cf. Heb. 1:3).

Christ is not only the Lord of creation but also Lord of the church (Col. 1:18–20). He is "the head of the body, the church" (1:18). "Head" could mean source here, but in this context (cf. 2:10) it almost certainly means authority. Jesus is not only the sovereign ruler over all creation but also supreme in the church of Jesus Christ. Here the church stands for the universal church, which by virtue of its union with Christ is assembled in heaven. We are also told that Jesus is "the beginning" (1:18), and given where this appears it probably means that Jesus is the beginning of the new creation, which at the same time signals that he is the sovereign and ruler of the new creation. Jesus is the progenitor of the new creation as "the firstborn from the dead" (cf. Rev. 1:5). Here the word "firstborn" has the idea of temporal priority, showing that the new creation has come. The resurrection of the dead is an eschatological, last-days event (cf. Isa. 25:8; 26:19; Ezek. 37:4–14; Dan. 12:1–2; Hosea 6:2). The last days have begun in Jesus Christ, and yet the very end of history hasn't arrived yet. The purpose of Christ's resurrection is so that he would be first in everything, so that he would stand out as "preeminent" (Col. 1:18 ESV). Again we see the central theme of Colossians: Christ is all that believers need, and there is no room for Jesus "plus" something else.

Jesus is preeminent because "God was pleased to have all his fullness dwell in him" (1:19). As we see in 2:9, "The entire fullness of God's nature dwells bodily in Christ." Perhaps the false teachers were saying that fullness could be or should be achieved in some way through angels or by observing certain regulations about food and drink. Paul emphasizes that all fullness resides in Christ. The Lord was pleased to reside in the tabernacle in the OT (Ps. 68:16), but Jesus is the new temple and fulfills in a more profound way what the temple pointed toward.

Since all of God's fullness resides in Jesus, and since he is fully divine, God was pleased to reconcile everything to himself through Jesus. We see here that Jesus could accomplish what he did on the cross because of who he was. Paul didn't merely hold to a functional Christology, for ontology (Jesus's deity) is clearly the basis for Jesus's work. Peace and reconciliation were achieved through his blood, through his death on the cross. No one could enjoy the fullness of God's presence in Jesus without resting in the work accomplished on the cross. What is striking here is that what the reconciliation accomplished is universal, including both heaven and earth, angels and human beings. To put it another way, evil angels are included in this reconciling work. Some have concluded from this that Paul teaches universalism here, that all will finally be reconciled to God so that no one will be alienated from him. But the very next verses indicate that one must persevere to the end for final salvation (Col. 1:21–23), and so universalism is ruled out. Furthermore, the many texts about judgment in Paul can't be so easily explained away. Many interpreters have rightly seen that what Paul teaches here is that all things will be reconciled in that all human beings who gladly submit to the Lord in faith and repentance will enjoy peace with God, but those who resist his rule will be subjugated, domesticated, and pacified. The whole universe will be reconciled in the sense that no outpost of evil will remain undefeated; evil will be defanged, restrained, and detained.

Persevere to the End (1:21–23)

What reconciliation involves in the case of believers and what is required of them is explained in 1:21–23. Before conversion believers were not at peace with God but hostile toward him. They weren't reconciled to God but alienated from him, and their hostility and alienation manifested itself in the evil carried out in their lives. As we have seen so often in Paul, he contrasts "then" and "now" with the words "But now" (1:22). Now believers are reconciled, now they are friends with God, now they are at peace with him, but such peace came at a tremendous cost. Jesus endured suffering and death in his physical body, and the purpose is so that believers would on the last day be presented as "holy, faultless, and without blemish." Such an eschatological presentation, however, requires perseverance. Believers must continue to endure and stand fast in "the hope of the gospel" (1:23). Saving reconciliation is not automatic, and we should not understand perseverance to be anything other than continuance in the grace of God. The same gospel heard by the Colossians has been proclaimed "in all creation under heaven," and this definitely does not mean that everyone in the world has heard the gospel. We see a parallel idea in Romans 10:18, and thus Paul probably intends to say that the gospel has reached all of creation in being extended to the gentiles.

Paul's Role in the Colossians' Faith and Perseverance (1:24–2:5)

Verse 23 concluded with Paul identifying himself as a "servant" of the gospel, and Paul expands upon his role in 1:24–2:5. What is the function of this section? The false teachers were questioning or at least supplementing the Pauline gospel. When we recall that the Colossians had never met Paul, we understand why he explains his unique role as the apostle to the gentiles, for the salvation of the Colossians is tied to the gospel Paul proclaimed. Paul was imprisoned, probably in Rome, and he informs the Colossians that his sufferings are for their sake! (1:24). Indeed, for the sake of the church, Christ's body, he was filling up or "completing" in his sufferings what was lacking in "Christ's afflictions." Such words seem to be over the top in self-importance: how could Christ's sufferings be lacking in any way? The theme of Colossians is that Christ in his person and his work (his death and resurrection) is all that the Colossians need. Nothing and no one can supplement or improve upon what they have in Jesus Christ.

Paul is not calling into question the sufficiency of Christ, nor is he boasting. He had received a unique commission as an apostle, and his sufferings were a corollary of Christ's. He proclaimed the word and suffered in the process, and hence by making "the word of God fully known" (1:25) in and through his sufferings, he filled up what is lacking in Christ's afflictions. In other words, Paul's preaching became *the means* by which the gospel went to the whole of creation (1:23). The sufferings of Jesus, the death of Jesus, reconcile people to the Lord, but Paul's ministry was the means by which the message of Christ was extended to the gentiles. The Lord appointed Paul to play a particular role in disclosing the mystery, which was concealed in the past but was disclosed with the coming of Christ. The mystery centers on Christ (as in Ephesians), but here the mystery is Christ residing in both Jews and gentiles (1:27). Once again Paul emphasizes the hope of believers, for Christ in them is "the hope of glory."

In verse 28 Paul emphasizes that his ministry was for all people everywhere. In a new and distinctive way, the mystery disclosed to Paul included the gentiles in the circle of God's saving purposes, and Paul's mission was to teach and proclaim the good news about Jesus Christ so that all would come to maturity. Paul was animated by divine strength to endure the labor and hardship that characterized his ministry (1:29). Paul happily expended his energy for the sake of the Colossians, the Laodiceans, and all those who had never met him (2:1), so that believers would be encouraged and "united in love" (2:2 NIV). In particular, given the false teaching circulating, he wanted them to have a full and complete understanding that God's mystery centers on Jesus Christ. It would be easy to look elsewhere for wisdom and insight, but "in him are hidden all the treasures of wisdom and knowledge" (2:3). Once again the main theme of Colossians surfaces; the Colossians have everything in Christ: all the wisdom and all the knowledge they need are in Christ, and thus they don't need to worship angels or to engage in asceticism or to abstain from foods.

Paul now informs them why he stressed that God's mystery and all wisdom and knowledge are in Christ. Some teachers were out and about trying to peddle another perspective, and their arguments had a certain ring of truth, a kind of plausibility (2:4). Still, the Colossians must not be deceived even though Paul wasn't present with them. He was with them in spirit, and the power of the Spirit was among them. Paul knew from Epaphras that the believers in Colossae were doing well, and he rejoiced in their good order and their "faith in Christ" (2:5). Paul didn't write because the Colossians were failing; he was fundamentally pleased with where the Colossians were spiritually. He wrote to keep them on track, to deter them from siding with the false teachers.

Stay the Course! (2:6–10)

The false teaching beckoned, but Paul admonishes the Colossians to keep walking in the direction they started. As believers they confessed and "received Christ Jesus as Lord," and they should continue to march in the same direction (2:6) by living under Jesus's lordship and rule. They should not lose their roots (Christ!), and they don't need a new foundation, and so they should continue to be "built up" in Christ (2:7). Establishment "in the faith" here doesn't focus on trust, though trust is certainly implied, but on understanding, on the doctrinal profile of their faith. The Colossians won't totter if they continue to grow in their knowledge of the gospel. At the same time, thanksgiving should overflow in their lives; they won't depart from Christ if they have grateful hearts, if they continually remember the great reconciliation accomplished for them at the cross.

For the first time, in 2:8 we see a clear indication that some teachers were at least trying to get the attention of the Colossians. They were trying to kidnap them and capture them with an alien philosophy. The word "philosophy" isn't inherently negative, but in context we see the problem with the philosophy being advertised. The fundamental problem was that it wasn't Christ-centered; instead, it was in accord with human tradition and could not deliver on its promises. Paul says that it was "based on the elements of the world." The word "elements" (*stoicheia*), as we saw in Galatians (4:3, 9), is quite difficult to interpret. It could refer to elementary principles, to angelic spirits, or most commonly to the constituent elements of the universe, such as earth, air, fire, and water. All of these are possible, but the emphasis on spiritual powers makes elementary principles less likely. The word *stoicheia* isn't clearly identified with demonic spirits until the third century AD. Still, the physical elements of the world are conceived, as we saw in Galatians, as under the dominion of spiritual powers. The notion that spiritual powers are involved fits with the emphasis on angels, which play such an important role in the letter.

Verses 9–10 explain why the alien philosophy should be repudiated. All of God's fullness resides "bodily in Christ" (cf. 1:19). Believers are full and complete in him (2:10), and since they are full in him, and all the fullness of God dwells in Christ, the philosophy being promulgated should be rejected. Since Jesus is the "head," the authority over every angelic "ruler and authority," believers don't need any supplementation from angelic powers. Jesus rules over angels because he created them. They would only turn to something or someone else if they forget all that they have in Jesus Christ.

New Life and Victory in Christ (2:11–15)

Paul explains what completeness in Christ involves, what sufficiency in Christ entails. Believers enjoy new life and have left the old life behind; their sins are forgiven. In addition, Christ has triumphed over evil spiritual powers. The Colossians have received something far better than physical circumcision (2:11). Some think circumcision here depicts the death of Christ. It is more likely that Paul refers to putting off the old Adam, the unregenerate person, and Christ is envisioned as the one who circumcised or cut off the sinful nature. The notion that Jesus's flesh was removed at his death sounds rather docetic, and the emphasis instead is on what Christ accomplished for believers. They are sufficient in Christ because the old Adam has been dealt a death blow at Christ's death.

Verse 12 elaborates on this reality. Believers in baptism were buried and raised with Christ. Since believers are united with Christ, his death was their death, and his resurrection was theirs as well. Baptism doesn't sacramentally save, for it is accompanied by faith in the God who raised Christ from the dead. Baptism here is linked with spiritual circumcision, with the new life granted by God's grace (cf. Deut. 30:6). The Colossians had no reason to pay heed to the philosophy being advocated because they already had new life in Christ; their old self had died, and now they were risen with Christ.

Previously the Colossians were spiritually dead, and their uncircumcised flesh testified that they weren't in covenant with the one true God (Col. 2:13), but since their conversion they were alive in Christ. Their trespasses had been forgiven, and Paul emphasizes freedom from guilt in two striking ways in 2:14. First, the debt owed to God by human beings is depicted as an IOU. They didn't keep the "obligations," the demands of God, written in the law. Those obligations, however, were "erased" at the cross. Second, to put it another way, the debt we owed God has been nailed to the cross, which means that the debt has been decisively and forever removed. The fundamental problem with human beings is sin, and believers are complete in Christ in that their sins are forgiven.

The philosophy was certainly fascinated with angels, and perhaps it emphasized mollifying evil angels. Whatever they taught, the focus should not be on angels but on Jesus, for Jesus stripped and removed the evil "powers and authorities" at the cross and resurrection (2:15). The evil spiritual powers have been publicly shamed and discredited. Paul uses the picture of a triumphal procession where the Romans celebrated victory over a defeated foe with a victory parade through the streets of Rome. At the end of the procession, the foes would be put to death. The Colossians had no reason to fear or to specially reverence angels, for Jesus defeated the spiritual powers opposed to him. They are actually weak and pitiable when compared to Jesus Christ. The theme of the section is clear: Christ is all-sufficient.

Freedom in the Death of Christ (2:16–23)

Since believers have become new persons in Christ, since their sins are forgiven, and since demonic powers have been decisively defeated, they need not worry if anyone passes judgment upon them about foods or the observance of days. The false teachers must have espoused such regulations, and they are apparently derived from the OT since festivals, new moons, and Sabbaths reflect OT customs (cf. Exod. 12:14; 20:8–11; 23:15, 16, 18; Num. 28:11). Such a judgment is confirmed by Colossians 2:17, for the foods and days are identified as a "shadow" of what is "to come." In Hebrews 10:1 the same word "shadow" is used of OT sacrifices, which anticipated the sacrifice of Christ. We have no evidence that Paul would designate pagan rituals regarding foods and days as a shadow of coming things, and thus we are on secure ground in saying that OT regulations are in view. Observing certain food laws and days was quite appropriate before Christ's coming, but Christ is the "substance" or the "reality" to which they pointed. Now that he has come, requiring the observance of certain food laws or days travels backward in salvation history and denigrates Christ's sufficiency.

We learn more about the false philosophy in Colossians 2:18, though the meaning of what Paul says here is quite difficult and therefore contested. Since we don't have space for details, we will have to be content with setting forth the view I think is most probable without investigating the details. The false teachers were trying to impose on the Colossians a regimen of asceticism, which included the forbidding of certain foods (2:16), and they may have also mandated fasting. Perhaps they believed that such an approach would enable one to draw closer to God. They were also entranced by "the worship of angels." Some scholars think what is described here is *worship by angels*, and the Colossians would participate in such worship. Still, the phrase more likely refers to *the worship of angels by the Colossians*. Given the Jewish background of the philosophy, such a scenario seems odd since Jews believed that worship should be reserved for the one true God. Some conclude from this that the false philosophy was syncretistic and mixed with pagan elements. Such a reading is certainly possible, but I incline to the notion that the opponents didn't think of themselves as actually worshiping angels. They probably claimed that they venerated angelic powers, but in Paul's eyes the inordinate attention and importance given to angels amounted to worship. Perhaps it is analogous to the dispute between Roman Catholics and Protestants. Roman Catholics say they *venerate* Mary but don't worship her, but many Protestants think that such a distinction is lost in practice. Apparently those espousing the false philosophy believed that it was crucial for one's spiritual life to practice asceticism and venerate angels.

What Paul says next is difficult to discern, but most agree that the philosophy advocated the importance of visions. Perhaps they said that those who were truly spiritual had access to the visionary realm and that through visions, the veneration of angels, and fasting from certain foods, they received divine fullness. They were doubtless impressed by their spirituality and devotion, but Paul dismisses such notions as the idle and "inflated" concepts of a mind without the Spirit (2:18–19).

As Paul counteracts the false philosophy, he reminds the Colossians of who they are in Christ (2:20–23). Jesus's death was their death, and thus they were no longer bound to "the elements of this world" (cf. 2:8, 11, 20). The world and the spiritual powers that exercise control over it have no authority over the Colossians, since their old self, the old Adam, died with Christ. The decrees and regulations insisted upon by the opponents are superficial. Commands not to taste or touch certain things because they are unclean are simply "human commands and doctrines" (2:22). Food shouldn't be made much of, for it just passes through the human digestive system and is eliminated! The philosophy of the teachers seemed to be spiritual and demanding, but it was actually a religion invented by human beings and included requirements for fasting and asceticism. Even though such requirements appealed to human beings and appeared to be religious, they do not curb "self-indulgence." In fact, they promote self-satisfaction because they pander to human pride.

Focusing on Things Above (3:1-4)

The Colossians have died with Christ (2:11–12; 3:3), but they have also been raised to life with him (2:13; 3:1). They have no need for venerating angels, for asceticism, and for observing certain days to obtain fullness, because they have all the fullness they need in Jesus Christ. These regulations are actually "earthly" (3:2), and heavenly realities, the "things above," are what believers enjoy in Jesus Christ. He is the risen and reigning Christ, and believers rule and reign with him. The regulations proposed attempt to give life to the dead, but believers already participate in life in Jesus Christ. Their life is "hidden with Christ in God" (3:3), and thus there is an eschatological reservation present here. A day is coming, however, when Christ will appear, and then believers will enjoy the fullness of glory. Still, even now, Christ is "your life" (3:4) as the all-sufficient one.

Putting to Death and Putting Away (3:5-11)

Death and life in Jesus Christ have practical implications; the new life is to manifest itself in concrete ways in one's daily life. In the next verses Paul condemns certain vices and praises certain virtues. Those who have died with Christ (2:11–12, 20; 3:3) are to put to death what is earthly in their lives. Paul uses several terms to refer to sexual sin, indicating that the desire for sex outside the bounds God has set is idolatry since it makes pleasure one's god. Nor is such sin a minor matter, for God's wrath will be poured out on those who pursue it (3:6). The Colossians lived in such a way when they were dead, but now they are alive and should leave such things behind (3:7).

They are to put away a fiery temper and all evil speech, including lying (3:8–9). Paul doesn't forget the gospel in giving admonitions, for the call to put off evil finds its roots in the truth that they have already put off "the old self with its practices" (3:9). The old self, the old Adam, the unregenerate self, has died with Christ (2:11–12, 20; 3:3), and thus believers are called to be what they are in Jesus Christ. Indeed, believers haven't just put off the old self: they have also "put on the new self" (3:10). They have died with Christ and have risen with him. They aren't perfect, since they are "being renewed," in that they are becoming more like God, who created them. In Christ they are being fashioned into what God intended in creating them. The new person, the new self, is Christ himself, and in Christ ethnic categories no longer matter (whether one is "Greek or Jew"), and religious practices like circumcision are also inconsequential (3:11). Even those who are outside the cultural mainstream, the barbarian and the Scythian, who were considered to be the lowest of the low, are united in Christ. The same goes for "slave and free." We are not surprised by words that capture the theme of Colossians: "Christ is all," and he is "in all" who are believers.

Putting On (3:12-17)

Believers have died with Christ and are risen with him (2:13; 3:1), and thus they are new in him (3:10). Not only that; now the church occupies the place Israel did in the OT. Now believers are God's "chosen ones," the elect of the Lord. Like Israel, they are also "holy" and the object of God's love (3:12). Believers aren't exhorted to live a new life *so that* God will love them, but they are to live in a new way *because they have already been loved* by the Lord. Since the Lord has loved them, they are to show that same love to others, living with "compassion" and "kindness." They are also to be humble and gentle and patient with others. Since the Lord has forgiven them and borne their own sin, they are to forgive others, putting up with those who are difficult (3:13).

We are not surprised to see that love is prized as the virtue that binds all the virtues together and thus sums up the human response to God's kindness in Christ (3:14). In the congregation, in the one body of Christ, in relationships with one another, peace should rule, and thankfulness should also characterize the community (3:15). Christ's word, the message of the gospel, should deeply impact the life of the church, and this message will become a reality as the members instruct and admonish each other with various songs and hymns (3:16). Christ's word is also disseminated through glad singing, as believers together praise God corporately. We see here that the word of Christ dwelling richly isn't an individual experience but becomes a reality as the church meets corporately. Colossians emphasizes that Christ is all (3:11), that he is our life (3:4), that all fullness is in him (2:9–10), and so we are not surprised to learn that everything a person does, whether in speech or in action, is to be done in Jesus's name (3:17), as believers give thanks and praise to God the Father through Jesus.

Household Relations (3:18–4:1)

Colossians matches Ephesians in many ways, though the admonitions to family members are much briefer (cf. Eph. 5:22–6:4). Ephesians says to be filled with/by the Spirit (5:18), but Colossians says to be filled with the word (3:16). In the discussion of family relationships (Col. 3:18–21) and the relationship between masters and slaves (3:22–4:1), we see the consequences of being richly indwelt with the word. As we saw in Ephesians (5:22–24), wives are exhorted to submit to their husbands since such behavior is fitting "in the Lord" (Col. 3:18). As in Ephesians, a loving and nurturing leadership is assigned to husbands, and women are to adapt to and support their leadership (Col. 3:19). Husbands are particularly enjoined not to grow bitter against their wives. Wives recognize and inevitably point out weaknesses in the lives of their husbands, and such observations by wives aren't to be rejected: husbands must not turn against their wives and nurse resentment against them. Children need to learn to obey the Lord; they learn to do so by obeying their parents in all respects, and in so doing they please the Lord (3:20). Fathers, who in the ancient world and probably today as well tend not to be as nurturing and caring as mothers, need to be careful that they don't exasperate children by pointing out to an excessive degree the many faults of children (3:21). Children could end up being "discouraged" and frustrated.

We saw in Ephesians 6:5–9 Paul's admonitions to slaves and masters, and we see similar commands here. In Ephesians we discussed the role of slavery in the ancient world, and we won't repeat that discussion here except to say that slavery was never endorsed by Paul or any scriptural writer. It is regulated but never commended. Still, Paul was no revolutionary, as these instructions show (3:22–4:1). Slaves are to do their work in the fear of the Lord, which means that they obey their masters' instructions comprehensively, and they don't only work hard when their master is watching. They are to serve "from the heart" since they are serving the Lord in their work (3:23). Slaves don't get an inheritance on earth, but they will receive a far better inheritance than any earthly king, since they will receive the inheritance of eternal life. Their true master, the only one they ultimately serve, is Jesus Christ himself! On the other hand, the slave who does wrong will suffer for the wrong perpetrated, for the Lord is an impartial judge. In the household codes of the ancient world, it was typical for the subservient member to be addressed and not the ones who enjoyed social advantages. But Paul addresses husbands, parents, and masters! Masters don't have unlimited authority; they are slaves of Christ too, for he is their "Master in heaven" (4:1), and so they must live as those under Christ's authority. They are to treat their slaves with justness and fairness.

Prayer and Wisdom (4:2–6)

As Paul nears the end of the letter, he calls the church to pray, as he commonly does, encouraging them to give regular attention to prayer. They are to be alert and vigilant and remain thankful for all that God has given them. Paul also solicits prayer for his mission, asking them to pray for opportunities for him to proclaim the gospel (4:3–4). He longs to speak of "the mystery of Christ," for which he was imprisoned. In particular, they should pray for the ability to speak it clearly. The believers are exhorted to exercise wisdom in their relationships with unbelievers, availing themselves of opportunities (4:5). Given the emphasis on proclaiming the gospel in 4:3–4, he probably has in mind occasions where the gospel may be communicated to those who haven't heard it or haven't yet believed it. More specifically, it is imperative that the speech of believers is gracious and winsome so that they are adept at responding to people in a way that is fitting.

Final Greetings (4:7–18)

The final greetings in Colossians are longer than in any other letter except for Romans, and it is fascinating to consider that Colossae and Rome are the two locales Paul had not visited, and thus the greetings are a way of introducing and commending Paul to the church by another means. These verses may be divided into the following sections:

Sending Tychicus and Onesimus	4:7–9
Greetings from those of the circumcision	4:10–11
Greeting from and commendation of Epaphras	4:12–13

Colossians
Final Greetings (4:7–18)

Greetings from Luke and Demas	4:14
Greetings and instructions regarding Laodicea	4:15–16
Exhortation to Archippus	4:17
Paul's greeting and grace benediction	4:18

Paul begins by commending Tychicus, who almost certainly carried the letter (4:7–8). Paul lavishes praise on Tychicus, identifying him as a "dearly loved brother, faithful minister, and fellow servant in the Lord" (4:7). The Colossians, therefore, should put their full trust in him as he conveys the news about Paul, and as he encourages them. Paul was also returning Onesimus, about whom we learn much more in the Letter to Philemon. Onesimus was well known to the congregation, showing that Philemon was a member of the Colossian church. Onesimus also receives high praise. We have no clue from Colossians that he was Philemon's slave, for here he is commended as "a faithful and dearly loved brother" (4:9). Paul prepares the way for Onesimus to be embraced upon his return.

Greetings are sent from three Jewish coworkers who are with Paul in Rome (4:10–11). Aristarchus (Acts 19:29; 20:4; 27:2; Philem. 24) was probably imprisoned with Paul in Rome, sharing his suffering. Mark, who is identified as Barnabas's cousin, sends greetings, and it is interesting to see that he receives commendation after the previous falling out between Paul and Mark (Acts 13:13; 15:37–39; cf. 2 Tim. 4:11; Philem. 24). Paul anticipates that John Mark might arrive in Colossae and encourages the church to welcome him. The last person mentioned is Jesus Justus, but we don't know anything more about him. All of these men have comforted Paul.

Epaphras (cf. Col. 1:7), who probably planted the Colossian church and according to Philemon was in prison with Paul (Philem. 23), also sends greetings as a faithful servant of Christ (4:12–13). Epaphras prayed ardently for the Colossians that they would continue to be complete and whole in the faith until the end, and thus they would fulfill God's will. Paul vouches that Epaphras labored hard for the sake of believers in Colossae, Laodicea, and Hierapolis. A key indication of love is the exertion of labor and the spending of time, and we see such in the ministry of Epaphras.

In verse 14 greetings are passed along from Luke and Demas, and since they aren't included among the circumcision, they both presumably were gentiles. Only here are we told that Luke was a doctor, and he is actually only mentioned on two other occasions in the NT (2 Tim. 4:11; Philem. 24). He is famous because (rightly, in my judgment) many argue that he was the author of the Gospel of Luke and the Acts of the Apostles. Demas is also mentioned in 2 Timothy 4:10 and Philemon 24, and in 2 Timothy we are told that he abandoned Paul.

332

Greetings were also to be conveyed to believers in Laodicea and to the church that met in Nympha's house (Col. 4:15–16). Paul believed his letter had wider implications and authority because he instructed the Colossians to pass it on (probably by copying) to the church in Laodicea as well, and the letter was to be read publicly in both churches. Apparently a letter was sent to the Laodiceans that Paul also wanted to have read in Colossae. Unfortunately, we have no knowledge of this letter, and it is lost in the sands of history.

Paul believed that Archippus needed special encouragement to carry out his ministry, and thus he appended a note for him in this letter, to be read before the entire church (4:17). It is difficult for us to say more about Archippus's role since we don't know details, but apparently the public word, in Paul's view, would motivate Archippus, who is also referred to in Philemon (v. 2), to do the right thing. At the conclusion of the letter, Paul took up the pen to specially greet the church (Col. 4:18), calling on them to remember his imprisonment, which was for the sake of the gospel. They would remember his chains if they continued to follow Jesus as Lord and if they didn't capitulate to the false teachers. Paul closes with a grace benediction, and the letter itself is a means of grace for the readers.

Colossians: Commentaries

Abbott, Thomas K. *A Critical and Exegetical Commentary on the Epistles to the Ephesians and to the Colossians*. ICC. Edinburgh: T&T Clark, 1897.

Barth, Markus, and Helmut Blanke. *Colossians*. AB 34B. New Haven: Yale University Press, 2007.

Beale, G. K. *Colossians and Philemon*. BECNT. Grand Rapids: Baker Academic, 2019.

Bird, Michael F. *Colossians and Philemon*. NCCS. Eugene, OR: Cascade, 2009.

Bruce, F. F. *The Epistles to the Colossians, to Philemon, and to the Ephesians*. NICNT. Grand Rapids: Eerdmans, 1984.

Calvin, John. *The Epistles of Paul the Apostle to the Galatians, Ephesians, Philippians and Colossians*. Grand Rapids: Eerdmans, 1965.

Campbell, Constantine R. *Colossians and Philemon: A Handbook on the Greek Text*. BHGNT. Waco: Baylor University Press, 2013.

Dunn, James D. G. *The Epistles to the Colossians and to Philemon*. NIGTC. Grand Rapids: Eerdmans, 1996.

Eadie, John. *Commentary on the Epistle of Paul to the Colossians*. Richard Griffin, 1856. Reprinted, Grand Rapids: Zondervan, 1957.

Foster, Paul. *Colossians*. BNTC. New York: Bloomsbury, 2016.

Garland, David E. *Colossians and Philemon*. NIVAC. Grand Rapids: Zondervan, 1998.

Gorday, Peter. *Colossians, 1–2 Thessalonians, 1–2 Timothy, Titus, Philemon*. ACCS 9 (NT). Downers Grove, IL: InterVarsity, 2000.

Harris, Murray J. *Colossians and Philemon*. EGGNT. Grand Rapids: Eerdmans, 1991.

Hay, David M. *Colossians*. ANTC. Nashville: Abingdon, 2000.

Lightfoot, J. B. *Saint Paul's Epistles to the Colossians and to Philemon*. London: Macmillan, 1897. Reprinted, Grand Rapids: Zondervan, 1971.

Lincoln, Andrew T. "The Letter to the Colossians." In *The New Interpreter's Bible*, edited by Leander E. Keck et al., 11:553–669. Nashville: Abingdon, 2000.

Lohse, Eduard. *Colossians and Philemon*. Hermeneia. Philadelphia: Fortress, 1971.

Lucas, R. C. *The Message of Colossians and Philemon: Fullness and Freedom*. BST. Downers Grove, IL: InterVarsity, 1980.

MacDonald, Margaret Y. *Colossians and Ephesians*. SP 17. Collegeville, MN: Liturgical Press, 2000.

Martin, Ralph P. *Colossians and Philemon*. NCB. Grand Rapids: Eerdmans, 1973.

McKnight, Scot. *The Letter to the Colossians*. NICNT. Grand Rapids: Eerdmans, 2018.

Melick, Richard R., Jr. *Philippians, Colossians, Philemon*. NAC 32. Nashville: Broadman, 2000.

Moo, Douglas. *The Letters to the Colossians and to Philemon*. PNTC. Grand Rapids: Eerdmans, 2008.

Moule, C. F. D. *The Epistles of Paul the Apostle to the Colossians and to Philemon*. CGTC. Cambridge: Cambridge University Press, 1968.

O'Brien, Peter T. *Colossians, Philemon*. WBC. Waco: Word, 1982.

Pao, David W. *Colossians and Philemon*. ZECNT. Grand Rapids: Zondervan, 2012.

Pokorný, Petr. *Colossians: A Commentary*. Peabody, MA: Hendrickson, 1991.

Schweizer, Eduard. *The Letter to the Colossians: A Commentary*. Minneapolis: Augsburg, 1982.

Seitz, Christopher R. *Colossians*. BTCB. Grand Rapids: Brazos, 2014.

Thompson, Marianne Meye. *Colossians and Philemon*. THNTC. Grand Rapids: Eerdmans, 2005.

Wall, Robert W. *Colossians and Philemon*. IVPNTC. Downers Grove, IL: InterVarsity, 1993.

Wilson, R. McL. *A Critical and Exegetical Commentary on Colossians and Philemon*. ICC. Edinburgh: T&T Clark, 2005.

Wright, N. T. *The Epistles of Paul to the Colossians and to Philemon*. TNTC. Leicester, UK: Inter-Varsity, 1986.

Colossians: Articles, Essays, and Monographs

Beetham, Christopher A. *Echoes of Scripture in the Letter of Paul to the Colossians*. BIS 96. Leiden: Brill, 2008.

Bevere, A. R. *Sharing in the Inheritance: Identity and the Moral Life in Colossians*. JSNTSup 226. Sheffield: Sheffield Academic, 2003.

Bockmuehl, M. "A Note on the Text of Colossians 4:3." *JTS* 39 (1988): 489–94.

Bornkamm, G. "The Heresy of Colossians." In *Conflict at Colossae: A Problem in the Interpretation of Early Christianity Illustrated by Selected Modern Studies*, edited by F. O. Francis and W. A. Meeks, 123–45. Missoula, MT: Scholars Press, 1973.

Bruce, F. F. "Colossian Problems, Pt. 1: Jews and Christians in the Lycus Valley." *BSac* 141 (1984): 3–15.

———. "Colossian Problems, Pt. 2: The 'Christ Hymn' of Colossians 1:15–20." *BSac* 141 (1984): 99–111.

———. "Colossian Problems, Pt. 3: The Colossian Heresy." *BSac* 141 (1984): 195–208.

———. "Colossian Problems, Pt. 4: Christ as Conqueror and Reconciler." *BSac* 141 (1984): 291–302.

Cannon, G. E. *The Use of Traditional Material in Colossians*. Macon, GA: Mercer University Press, 1983.

Carr, W. "Two Notes on Colossians." *JTS* 24 (1973): 492–500.

Craddock, F. B. "'All Things in Him'—A Critical Note on Col 1:15–20." *NTS* 12 (1965): 78–80.

Crouch, J. E. *The Origin and Intention of the Colossian Haustafel*. FRLANT 109. Göttingen: Vandenhoeck & Ruprecht, 1972.

DeMaris, R. E. *The Colossian Controversy: Wisdom in Dispute at Colossae*. JSNTSup 96. Sheffield: JSOT Press, 1994.

Ellis, E. Earle. "Colossians 1:12–20: Christus Creator, Christus Salvator." In *Interpreting the New Testament Text: Introduction to the Art and Science of Exegesis*, edited by D. L. Bock and B. M. Fanning, 415–28. Wheaton: Crossway, 2006.

Evans, Craig A. "The Colossian Mystics." *Bib* 63 (1982): 188–205.

Ferguson, Everett. "Spiritual Circumcision in Early Christianity." *SJT* 41 (1988): 485–97.

Fossum, J. "Colossians 1:15–18a in the Light of Jewish Mysticism and Gnosticism." *NTS* 35 (1989): 183–201.

Francis, F. O. "The Background of *Embateuein* in Legal Papyri and Oracle Inscriptions." In *Conflict in Colossae: A Problem in the Interpretation of Early Christianity Illustrated by Selected Modern Studies*, edited by F. O. Francis and W. A. Meeks, 197–206. Missoula, MT: Scholars Press, 1973.

———. "Humility and Angelic Worship in Col. 2:18." In *Conflict in Colossae: A Problem in the Interpretation of Early Christianity Illustrated by Selected Modern Studies*, edited by F. O. Francis and W. A. Meeks, 163–95. Missoula, MT: Scholars Press, 1973.

Gardner, P. D. "'Circumcised in Baptism—Raised through Faith': A Note on Col. 2:11–12." *WTJ* 45 (1983): 172–77.

Hartman, Lars. "Code and Context: A Few Reflections on the Parenesis of Col 3:6–4:1." In *Tradition and Interpretation in the New Testament*, edited by G. F. Hawthorne, 237–47. Grand Rapids: Eerdmans, 1987.

Helyer, Larry R. "Colossians 1:15–20: Pre-Pauline or Pauline?" *JETS* 26 (1983): 167–79.

———. "Cosmic Christology and Col 1:15–20." *JETS* 37 (1994): 235–46.

Hollenbach, B. "Col 2:23: Which Things Lead to the Fulfillment of the Flesh." *NTS* 25 (1979): 254–61.

Hooker, Morna D. "Were There False Teachers in Colossae?" In *Christ and Spirit in the New Testament: Studies in Honour of Charles Francis Digby Moule*, edited by B. Lindars and S. S. Smalley, 315–31. Cambridge: Cambridge University Press, 1973.

Hunt, J. P. T. "Colossians 2:11–12, the Circumcision/Baptism Analogy, and Infant Baptism." *TynBul* 41 (1990): 227–44.

Kiley, M. C. *Colossians as Pseudepigraphy*. The Biblical Seminar. Sheffield: JSOT Press, 1986.

Lamp, J. S. "Wisdom in Col 1:15–20: Contribution and Significance." *JETS* 21 (1998): 213–20.

Leppä, O. *The Making of Colossians: A Study on the Formation and Purpose of a Deutero-Pauline Letter*. Publications of the Finnish Exegetical Society 86. Göttingen: Vandenhoeck & Ruprecht, 2003.

Lightfoot, J. B. "The Colossian Heresy." In *Conflict in Colossae: A Problem in the Interpretation of Early Christianity Illustrated by Selected Modern Studies*, edited by F. O. Francis and W. A. Meeks, 13–59. Missoula, MT: Scholars Press, 1973.

Lincoln, A. T. "The Household Code and Wisdom Mode of Colossians." *JSNT* 74 (1999): 93–112.

Lyonnet, S. "Paul's Adversaries in Colossae." In *Conflict in Colossae: A Problem in the Interpretation of Early Christianity Illustrated by Selected Modern Studies*, edited by F. O. Francis and W. A. Meeks, 147–61. Missoula, MT: Scholars Press, 1973.

Martin, Ralph P. "An Early Christian Hymn (Col. 1:15–20)." *EvQ* 36 (1964): 195–205.

Martin, Troy. *By Philosophy and Empty Deceit: Colossians as Response to a Cynic Critique*. JSNTSup 118. Sheffield: Sheffield Academic, 1996.

Motyer, Stephen. "The Relationship between Paul's Gospel of 'All One in Christ Jesus' (Galatians 3:28) and the 'Household Codes.'" *Vox Evangelica* 19 (1989): 33–48.

Moule, C. F. D. "New Life in Colossians 3 :1–17." *RevExp* 70 (1973): 481–93.

O' Brien, Peter T. "The Church as a Heavenly and Eschatological Entity." In *The Church in the Bible and the World*, edited by D. A. Carson, 88–119. Exeter: Paternoster, 1987.

———. "Col 1:20 and the Reconciliation of All Things." *RTR* 33 (1974): 45–53.

Rowland, Christopher. "Apocalyptic Visions and the Exaltation of Christ in the Letter to the Colossians." *JSNT* 19 (1983): 73–83.

Salter, Martin C. "Does Baptism Replace Circumcision? An Examination of the Relationship between Circumcision and Baptism in Colossians 2:11–12." *Themelios* 35 (2010): 15–29.

Sappington, T. J. *Revelation and Redemption at Colossae*. JSNTSup 53. Sheffield: JSOT Press, 1991.

Schweizer, E. "Christ in the Letter to the Colossians." *RevExp* 70 (1973): 451–67.

———. "Traditional Ethical Patterns in the Pauline and Post-Pauline Letters and Their Development." In *Text and Interpretation: Studies in the New Testament Presented to Matthew Black*, edited by E. Best and R. Wilson, 195–209. New York: Cambridge University Press, 1979.

Smith, I. K. *Heavenly Perspective: A Study of the Apostle Paul's Response to a Jewish Mystical Movement at Colossae*. LNTS 346. Edinburgh: T&T Clark, 2006.

Stettler, Hanna. "An Interpretation of Colossians 1:24 in the Framework of Paul's Mission Theology." In *The Mission of the Early Church to Jews and Gentiles*, edited by J. Ådna and H. Kvalbein, 185–208. WUNT 127. Tübingen: Mohr Siebeck, 2000.

Sumney, Jerry L. "Those Who 'Pass Judgment': The Identity of the Opponents in Colossians." *Bib* 74 (1993): 366–88.

Thornton, T. G. C. "Jewish New Moon Festivals, Galatians 4:3–11 and Colossians 2:16." *JTS* 40 (1989): 97–100.

Thurston, Bonnie Bowman. *All the Fullness of God: The Christ of Colossians.* Eugene, OR: Cascade, 2017.

Wilson, W. T. *The Hope of Glory: Education and Exhortation in the Epistle to the Colossians.* NovTSup 88. New York: Brill, 1997.

Yates, R. "Colossians and Gnosis." *JSNT* 27 (1986): 49–68.

———. "Colossians 2:15: Christ Triumphant." *NTS* 37 (1991): 573–91.

CHAPTER NINE

1 Thessalonians

Introduction

Paul visited Thessalonica and established a church there in about AD 49 or 50 (Acts 17:1–9). The city was large, with a population of 65,000 to 100,000. Thessalonica was the mother city of Macedonia, enjoying the advantage of having a harbor on the Aegean Sea and being situated on one of the major east-west road routes in the Roman Empire called the Via Egnatia. As in most major cities, many different cults and religions were present, and the imperial cult was quite prominent. Christians were a distinct minority, and both 1 and 2 Thessalonians portray the minority status reflected in the persecution the believers encountered. The first letter was written a short time after the church was planted, perhaps in AD 50, and thus it is one of Paul's earliest letters. If one accepts a later date for Galatians, then 1 Thessalonians is the first Pauline letter, though I incline toward an earlier date for Galatians. Paul wrote the first letter to express thanksgiving to God for the Thessalonians' faith as they endured trials and opposition. At the same time, he wanted to strengthen them in some areas where they were lacking. Overall, however, he was very happy with the progress of the church.

For a big picture of 1 Thessalonians, we provide the following outline.

Outline

Thanksgiving for the Thessalonians' conversion	1:1–10
Paul's godly example	2:1–12
Thanksgiving for the Thessalonians' perseverance	2:13–3:13
Exhortations for spiritual growth	4:1–5:28

Greeting and Thanksgiving (1:1-10)

Three cosenders are named (1:1): Paul, Silvanus/Silas, and Timothy, though Paul alone wrote the letter, which is confirmed by the final charge in the letter (5:27) and the presence of the first-person singular in 2:18. Paul probably includes Silvanus and Timothy because Silas played a fundamental role in establishing the church, and Timothy helped strengthen and sustain it. Including them as cosenders increases Paul's credibility and adds to his authority, for Paul wasn't writing them as a private individual. The Thessalonians are designated as an assembly, a church that was united to God the Father and the Lord Jesus Christ. We see Christ's stature in that he is placed on the same level as the Father.

The joyful tone of the letter commences at the outset as Paul gives thanks for them, and the presence of the thanksgiving after the greeting is standard in Pauline letters, though we shouldn't conclude from this that the thanksgiving lacks significance. Paul was truly thankful to God for the response of the Thessalonians to the gospel, and he focuses particularly on their faith, love, and hope (1:3). Faith, love, and hope are not merely abstract qualities in the lives of believers. They make a profound difference in everyday life. Faith, for instance, produces work, and thus the fruit of faith becomes visible in concrete ways. Love begets labor, glad but arduous pouring out of one's life for others. Hope gives birth to endurance. Those who have hope for the future are able to withstand hard times and difficulties since they know better days are ahead. The Thessalonians' faith, hope, and love are evidence of their election. Just as Israel was God's elect people in the OT (e.g., Deut. 7:7–8), now the church of Jesus Christ is the elect people of God (1 Thess. 1:4). They belong to God's people because of his gracious choice of them.

Paul knows the believers are elect because when he ministered among them, the gospel came to them not only "in word" but also "in power": the Holy Spirit was working through the message of the cross that Paul proclaimed (1:5; cf. 1 Cor. 1:18; 2:4). Paul's message was backed up by his life, for he himself was transformed by the gospel, and thus the message and the man were congruent, which testified to the truth of the Pauline gospel. Paul's example rubbed off on the Thessalonians, for they imitated both him and the Lord in suffering persecution for God's sake, and yet in the midst of such persecution the Holy Spirit produced a supernatural joy in them (1 Thess. 1:6). The Thessalonians' own joy in turn became an example for believers in the provinces of Macedonia and Achaia so that the gospel reverberated in Macedonia and Achaia and in many other churches as well (1:7–8). The vibrancy and authenticity of their faith could not be denied, for they endured persecution joyfully.

Paul reflects further on their conversion and the fact that he didn't need to report it to others: people everywhere were talking about the time when Paul and Silas visited (Acts 17:1–9). It has often been pointed out that 1 Thessalonians 1:9–10 aptly describes conversion. The Thessalonians turned away from idols, even though worship of many gods and many lords was exceedingly common in Thessalonica (cf. 1 Cor. 8:5). Repudiating idols had social and economic consequences. The Thessalonians had given themselves wholly to the one true God, to the living God, for idols are nonentities, fantasies that have no real existence or power (1 Thess. 1:9; cf. Ps. 96:5). The Thessalonians were not only serving the true God, but they had put their hope entirely in him, and thus they were longing and waiting for the return of his Son, Jesus Christ (1 Thess. 1:10). The Son is the risen and reigning Lord, and the day of his coming will be one of wrath and judgment, but on that day he would spare believers from his wrath. Paul doesn't ever mention justification in 1 Thessalonians, but we have the same basic concept here. Believers will be rescued from punishment through Jesus Christ, and doubtless Paul has in mind Jesus's atoning death and his resurrection.

Defense of Paul's Ministry (2:1–16)

Paul defends his ministry in these verses, and we see three main themes: (1) his integrity, (2) his love, and (3) his gospel. In other words, Paul's ministry was marked by ethos, pathos, and logos (though this last theme bleeds into the next section; see 2:13). Does Paul defend himself against opponents here, or is he merely presenting himself as an ethical example to the Thessalonians? It is difficult to be sure, but a response to adversaries seems to be preferable since both Paul and the Thessalonians were persecuted. As usual, persecution begins with criticism, and if the Thessalonians were rejected by their peers, it makes sense that adversaries would raise questions about the integrity of Paul, Silvanus, and Timothy. Paul emphasizes the positive effect of his ministry and the joyful reception of his message (2:1). The courage of Paul and Silvanus is supported by their response to their suffering in Philippi, where they were "beaten with rods" (Acts 16:19–23). Still, they boldly proclaimed the gospel when they arrived in Thessalonica, even though opposition was present there as well, because of the riot that ensued and the quick exit of Paul and Silas (17:1–10).

How do we account for Paul's boldness? Paul points to his integrity. The appeal, the exhortation to believe, wasn't an attempt to deceive or mislead people. Paul's life was pure and clean and honorable (1 Thess. 2:3). God had tested and approved him, and thus he had the imprimatur of God himself in his proclamation of the gospel (2:4). Many itinerant speakers circulated in the Greco-Roman world, trying to impress crowds with their brilliant and flashy rhetoric. Paul stood in remarkable contrast to them; his goal wasn't to please people, and the persecution meted out to him showed that! One way to please others is flattery, for if we flatter others, they may compliment us, but Paul was willing to speak hard truths as necessary, and he did not use the ministry as a platform for financial advancement (2:5). Nor did Paul use the ministry to coerce others, to subject others to his selfish will (2:7). On the contrary, he was as innocent as an infant. Actually, we have a textual variant here: most English texts read "gentle" instead of "infants" (2:7, CSB footnote). The reading "gentle" makes good sense, but the reading "infants" is more likely. Paul's innocence and lack of guile demonstrates that he didn't take advantage of the Thessalonians.

Paul switches the metaphor to a nursing mother, showing his deep love and affection for the Thessalonians (2:7–8). He wasn't like a speaker who breezed into town to show off his abilities while lacking any concern for the lives of those addressed. Paul didn't only proclaim the gospel; he also revealed his love by giving the Thessalonians his time and energy. Paul's love was verified by his hard work; to avoid taking money from others, he labored as a tentmaker, especially when he first evangelized a city. The elite class in the Greco-Roman world looked down on manual labor, and Paul came from the scholarly elite himself. Still, he didn't despise hard work but gave himself to labor, to ensure that his preaching of the gospel was not misunderstood to be a means of personal enrichment (2:9).

Paul did not claim to be perfect, but he did insist that his public ministry was without reproach (2:10). His behavior was holy, righteous, and without blame. Paul compared himself to infants and to a nursing mother and also to a father (2:11–12). The Thessalonians were his beloved children, and like any father worthy of the name, he longed for the best for his children, and so he exhorted them to live worthily of God's kingdom.

Paul emphasizes his integrity but reaffirms anew (cf. 1:2–10) his grateful- ness for the faith of the Thessalonians (2:13–16). The Thessalonians' reception of God's word and their willingness to be persecuted also confirms Paul's apostolic authority and integrity. When the Thessalonians heard God's word, the gospel of Christ, from the lips of Paul and Silas, they recognized that the words from these human beings were not merely human words. The gospel Paul and Silas preached was actually God's message to the world, and as such it worked powerfully in those who believed (2:13).

Some scholars think verses 14–16 were not written by Paul but were a later interpolation, but there is no textual evidence for this view since these verses are in all the manuscripts. Perhaps scholars desire to save Paul from what they perceive to be a hate-filled statement, but we will see that what Paul says here isn't hateful or surprising. First, Paul doesn't indict all Jews here but just those who participated in killing Jesus, those who killed the prophets, those who persecuted the church, and those who hindered the gentile mission. Indeed, Paul's indictment is comparable to the words of the OT prophets who upbraided fellow Jews for apostasy. The judgment proclaimed by the OT prophets didn't mean that they hated their fellow Jews. Love sometimes has to say difficult things. Actually, Paul's main purpose wasn't to criticize the Jews but to affirm that the Thessalonians had faced the same kind of opposition "from people of your own country" (2:14). There was solidarity in persecution. We also see that punishment isn't swift or immediate; it only strikes when sin has reached its "limit" (2:16). We think of Genesis 15:16, where the punishment of the Amorites was delayed for four generations until their sin had "reached its full measure."

What Paul means in saying that "wrath has overtaken them at last" is disputed (1 Thess. 2:16). Paul uses an aorist verb "overtaken" (*ephthasen*), which many think relates to a particular judgment in history, such as the famine that occurred under Claudius (Acts 11:28). Such readings are certainly possible, but the parallel with Genesis 15:16 suggests a final and decisive judgment, and the aorist tense isn't necessarily limited to past time. So a reference to the final judgment at the very end of history is more persuasive. After all, Paul draws a parallel with the judgment of the Amorites, which refers to their annihilation. Paul's point is that persecutors won't ultimately triumph, and we should not forget the main purpose of the paragraph: Paul was thankful that the Thessalonians embraced the gospel, even though they experienced the same suffering as believers in Judea (1 Thess. 2:14).

Paul's Frustration at Being Unable to Visit (2:17–20)

Paul begins a section here that continues through 3:10. He reflects on his inability to visit the Thessalonians (2:17–20), his sending of Timothy instead (3:1–5), and his joy at receiving news from Timothy (3:6–10). Paul's flight from Thessalonica is recorded in Acts 17:5–9. The mob charged Paul and his companions with exalting Jesus and diminishing Caesar, and the city officials took a bond from Jason to defuse the situation, which was probably a promise that Paul and Silas would leave the city. Paul made every effort thereafter to see the Thessalonians face-to-face but was thwarted (2:17). In the political machinations taking place, which made it impossible for him to return to Thessalonica, he sees the work of Satan (2:18). Paul explains his intense longing to see the Thessalonians (2:19–20). They were his joy, hope, glory, and "crown of boasting" on the day of judgment.

Timothy's Visit (3:1–5)

Paul's love for the Thessalonians is evident in that he was willing to be isolated and alone in Athens, yet he longed to hear news about how the Thessalonians were doing with their newfound faith. In sending Timothy, he wasn't sending just anyone but his trusted brother and coworker in the gospel, who he hoped would encourage and strengthen the Thessalonians in their faith. They needed encouragement because, just as Paul warned, they were suffering in their new life as Christians. Such sufferings were no accident but were ordained by God himself. Presumably the Thessalonians suffered socially because they no longer participated in pagan festivals and rites, and they were probably looked on with suspicion as those who worshiped a king rival to Caesar. Such experiences could shake and disturb their faith, and Paul was eager to know how they were doing, especially since they were relatively new believers. Paul sent Timothy to ascertain their situation because he was concerned that Satan had tempted the Thessalonians and that perhaps they had even abandoned the faith. If that were the case, Paul's labor was in vain. We see here that Paul believes perseverance in faith is necessary for salvation; an initial decision doesn't alone suffice if believers don't continue in the faith. Since Paul wasn't granted a God's-eye view of the Thessalonians' faith, he wasn't certain whether it was genuine until he saw their response to the pressures of life.

Paul's Joy at Timothy's Report (3:6–10)

Paul was filled with joy at receiving Timothy's report about the Thessalonians, for their affection and longing for Paul revealed their love for Christ and his message. So even though Paul was suffering, he was encouraged and filled with joy about the Thessalonians' faith: their standing in the Lord made life worth living! Ultimately, Paul was thankful to God for the Thessalonians, and the deep affection and love he had for them shines through the letter. The first section of the letter is coming to an end: Paul voices his thanks for the faith of the Thessalonians, but he prays that he will be able to visit them (3:10). Even though they were doing well, it was not as if the Thessalonians had arrived: there was still room for growth in their lives, and thus Paul hopes with his visit "to complete what is lacking in [their] faith." Some deficiencies still existed, and since Paul could not visit immediately, he hoped to remedy some of those deficiencies in the following instructions.

Prayer for Love and Holiness (3:11–13)

Paul longed to come and fill up what was lacking in the Thessalonians' faith, and thus he prays that he will be able see them again and fulfill that very aspiration. Satan may have hindered Paul (2:18), but ultimately the Father and Jesus rule, and if God wills, Paul would return to Thessalonica. Some have attempted to establish the divinity of Christ from Paul's use of a singular verb with two subjects (the Father and Jesus) in 3:11. A better argument for Christ's deity, however, is the fact that the prayer is addressed to both the Father and the Lord Jesus. As a Pharisee who was nurtured in monotheism, Paul only prayed to God, and thus the inclusion of Jesus in the prayer is significant. Paul prayed that the Lord would increase the love of the Thessalonians both for one another as believers and for unbelievers as well (3:12). We see from this that growth in holiness is fundamentally growth in love. If they grew in love, they would be without blame at Jesus's return, and Paul's concern, as we have seen throughout the letter, is for the Thessalonians' perseverance (3:13).

Introduction to Exhortations (4:1–2)

Paul hoped to visit the Thessalonians to supply what was lacking in their faith (3:10–13). Meanwhile, in the remainder of the letter he gives exhortations that, if carried out, will supply what is lacking in their faith. What it means to please God is to fulfill the "commands" that Paul relayed "through the Lord Jesus" (4:2). Grace for Paul becomes the basis for a new life, a life of obedience. Paul wasn't instructing the Thessalonians because he was unhappy with them, for they were already pleasing God in their lives. Still, they had not arrived at perfection, and they could grow even more in holiness as believers.

Live in Sexual Purity (4:3–8)

Sexual immorality was exceedingly common in the Greco-Roman world. We noted earlier the comment by Athenaeus, "We keep mistresses for pleasure, concubines for daily concubinage, but wives in order to produce children legitimately and to have a trustworthy guardian of our domestic property" (*Deipn.* 13.573B). In many ways, the Greco-Roman world was much like Western culture today, where people take umbrage at anyone telling them what to do with their bodies. Believers, however, are not to pursue their own desires and will but are to seek "God's will," and his will is their "sanctification." Thus they should be devoted and consecrated to what is good and pure (1 Thess. 4:3). The sanctification that Paul has in mind is abstention "from sexual immorality." The Greek word for "sexual immorality" (*porneia*) is a general term for sexual sin, including incest, premarital sexual relationships, adultery, same-sex erotic behavior, pornography, and any other illicit sexual behavior.

The meaning of verse 4 is debated, and scholars dispute the meaning of two words in particular: *ktasthai* and *skeuos*. The first word can be translated as "take/acquire" or "possess." The second word is literally translated "vessel," and the vessel may be one's wife or one's body/sexual organ. The first interpretation is represented by the RSV, "that each one of you know how to take a wife for himself in holiness and honor." According to this reading, holiness in sexual relations pertains to acquiring a wife. In the second interpretation Paul uses the verb *ktasthai* to exhort believers *to live* with their wives in an honorable and holy way. The third interpretation is supported by most other English versions: "that each of you knows how to control his own body in holiness and honor." The arguments become rather technical, but I think the last reading is the most convincing. It is harder to know if the specific referent is the body or one's sexual organ, but the difference between these two options is one of specificity. Paul probably doesn't give instructions on how to acquire wives, since it is also hard to know what it could mean for someone "to know" how to acquire a wife; it almost sounds as though special classes should be taken on the subject! Also, since many marriages were arranged, such a reading seems unlikely. The second interpretation has more to commend it, but it is more natural to understand vessel to refer to one's own body or sexual organ instead of one's wife. Since believers know God in a saving way, their knowledge of God is to be reflected in their sexual lives, in the holiness and honor with which they conduct themselves, so that they don't fall captive to lust "like the Gentiles" (1 Thess. 4:5).

If a man sins sexually, he takes advantage of or transgresses against a brother, either a father or a husband. Paul wrote in a patriarchal world, and today we can legitimately apply Paul's words more broadly, but he thinks of the impact on a husband and father especially. Such sin isn't a light matter, because the Lord will take vengeance and judge those who offend (4:6). God has called believers for the purpose of purity and to live in holiness (4:7). Rejecting the sexual ethic mandated here isn't optional, for those who reject such are turning against the Holy Spirit, who is called Holy for a reason. Orthodoxy is meaningless without orthopraxy, and Paul doesn't compromise on the matter of sexual purity.

Love in Everyday Life (4:9–12)

The Thessalonians are called to love and to work in these verses. In one sense, they don't need instruction on loving one another since they "are taught by God to love one another." Paul draws on Isaiah 54:13, which is in the context of the Lord restoring Israel and Jerusalem from exile. Israel's return from exile is based on the atoning work of the Servant (Isa. 52:13–53:12), and being taught by God is a result of the servant's work as well. The instruction of all the Lord's children fits with the new-covenant promise in Jeremiah 31:31–34, where the Lord writes the law on the hearts of his people. The Thessalonians love one another because the eschaton has dawned, because the new covenant has arrived. We see an already-but-not-yet dimension in the fulfillment of the covenant. The Thessalonians were genuinely loving brothers and sisters, and yet they had not arrived. They were not yet perfectly loving, and there was room for improvement in love (cf. 1 Thess. 3:12). Paul also calls upon the Thessalonians to work instead of being slackers, and the issue surfaces again in 5:14 and comes to the forefront in 2 Thessalonians 3:6–12. Failure to work hard was a small flame in 1 Thessalonians, but it had become a full-blown fire by the time we get to 2 Thessalonians. Dependence on others because of unwillingness to work generates criticism from unbelievers, and one way the Thessalonians testify to the gospel is by working hard.

Hope for the Believing Dead (4:13–18)

What precipitates Paul's words here was a concern voiced by believers in Thessalonica. Apparently the believing Thessalonians still alive were convinced that believers who died before Jesus's return would be at some disadvantage when Jesus came again. Many theories have been advanced as to why they thought the believing dead were at a disadvantage, and space is lacking to rehearse those options. Most of the proposals are speculative and quite improbable, and we must admit that we don't know *why* they had such a conviction. They were confused in some way and thought the believing dead would be handicapped by dying before the parousia.

What Paul hopes to achieve in the discussion is stated in both verses 13 and 18. He doesn't want living believers to grieve about the believing dead in the same way as unbelievers do. Certainly believers grieve at the death of beloved fellow believers (cf. Rom. 12:15; Phil. 2:27), but their grief differs from the sorrow of unbelievers since the latter lack hope. Paul isn't thinking of subjective hope, for some unbelievers who die are full of confidence and hope. What he has in mind is objective hope: any dreams unbelievers have about the future are fantasies, while believers have true hope (1 Thess. 4:13). Verse 18 represents the same truth: believers are to be encouraged by hearing what Paul has taught in verses 14–17. The passage is like a sandwich: though believers are sorrowful, their grief is mingled with hope (v. 13). In other words, in the midst of their pain, they should find encouragement (v. 18). In verses 14–17 Paul gives the reasons why they should be encouraged and hopeful; these verses are the meat in the sandwich.

The basis for hope and encouragement, not surprisingly, is the death and resurrection of Christ (4:14). Those who belong to Jesus—those who "have fallen asleep," which for Paul always indicates believers—will be with Jesus when he returns. How does Paul know they will be with Jesus? Because of the word of the Lord. It is difficult to find any particular saying of Jesus that fits here, so some think Paul appeals to an unwritten saying of Jesus or to a private revelation. It is more likely that Paul appeals in a general way to Jesus's words in Matthew 24:29–31, 40–41 and perhaps also to 25:1–13. The word of the Lord verifies that those who are alive when the Lord returns will not precede the believing dead. Incidentally, some scholars think that Paul errs here, since he places himself as among the "we" who would be alive when Jesus returns. This is a flat-footed reading if there ever was one, for Paul identifies with living believers because he was still alive! He hardly claims that he will certainly be alive at the parousia.

Paul then relates what will happen when Jesus returns. The Lord will descend from heaven with a shout, with the voice of an archangel (perhaps Michael), and with a trumpet. Some think that all three of these descriptions have the same referent. They are probably distinct, but the matter is of little importance; what is ruled out is a secret rapture since the event reverberates with sound! The main point for the Thessalonians is that the believing dead rise *first*, and only afterward are living believers snatched up (raptured) to meet the Lord in the air (1 Thess. 4:17). Paul definitely teaches a rapture here, yet the rapture isn't distinct from the second coming but occurs at the second coming. The word "meet" (*apantēsis*) is often used to designate citizens going out to meet a dignitary, and then they escort the honored person back into the city. The saints are snatched into the air and return to the earth in triumph with their Lord and will reign forever in the new creation with those raised from the dead.

Be Encouraged by the Day of the Lord (5:1–11)

Eschatology plays a vital role in the Thessalonian letters, and Paul turns to "the day of the Lord" (5:1–11). He has just explained that the believing dead won't suffer any disadvantage, and now he explains further why the day is one that believers should look forward to. The purpose again is pastoral, for these instructions were given to encourage and edify the Thessalonians (5:11). No detailed eschatological chart is provided, but comfort about the final outcome is conveyed. Paul had taught them about "the times and the seasons," which designate end-time events (Acts 1:7), but they needed further reminders about what they had already received (1 Thess. 5:1). He reminds them that "the day of the Lord," which is a very common expression in the OT (e.g., Isa. 13:6, 9; Joel 1:15; 2:1, 11, 31; Amos 5:18, 20; Obad. 15; Zeph. 1:7, 8, 14, 18; 2:2, 3; Mal. 4:5), will come like "a thief in the night" (1 Thess. 5:2). Of course, in saying this he picks up on the words of Jesus himself (Matt. 24:43; Luke 12:39; cf. 2 Pet. 3:10; Rev. 3:3; 16:15).

When unbelievers are saying, "Peace and security," which was a common expression of what Rome had accomplished, then eschatological destruction will strike without warning (1 Thess. 5:3). A woman doesn't know when her labor pains will begin; so too the onset of the day of the Lord, which is a day of judgment and salvation, will spell the ruin of unbelievers. For believers, on the other hand, the day won't engulf them in darkness. Even if they don't know the exact time, it won't be like the arrival of a thief (5:4). The reason is that believers are people of the day and of the light: they have left behind the evil and gloom of darkness (5:5).

The exhortation matches what we see in Jesus's end-time discourses. Believers must not fall into spiritual slumber but be awake and vigilant (cf. Matt. 24:42, 43; 25:13; 26:41; Mark 13:34, 35, 37; Luke 12:37). "Sleep" is used as a metaphor for evil; those who engage in evil are those who are of the night and the darkness (1 Thess. 5:6–7). Spiritual alertness, then, doesn't mean anticipating the precise time of Jesus's return; it denotes readiness for his return, and this readiness is evident if one has put on the spiritual armor of faith, hope, and love (5:8; cf. 1:3). Hope dominates as believers look forward to life after death, since God did not appoint believers to suffer the wrath that will be poured out on the day of the Lord. Instead, Jesus spares them from that wrath and grants them salvation (5:9; cf. 1:10). Paul changes the meaning of the metaphor in 5:10, perhaps casting a backward glance at 4:13–18. Jesus died for believers so that whether one is alert (alive) or asleep (dead), believers will live with him. No wonder believers should be encouraged. Jesus has guaranteed that on the day of the Lord they won't face wrath but will "obtain salvation" (5:9); they are not in the darkness but in the light and have an eternal future of sunny days.

Community Exhortations (5:12–24)

As the letter draws to a close, Paul includes a series of exhortations, which are also designed to fill up what is lacking in the lives of the Thessalonians, representing areas of their lives in which they need regular reminders. He begins with the relationship between leaders and the congregation (5:12–13). Titles are not specified for leaders like pastors, elders, or overseers. Instead, they are recognized for their labor, leadership, and instruction, which should motivate the congregation to honor and love them. Paul recognizes that division easily creeps in between leaders and a congregation, and so he calls on all to live in peace with one another.

General practical exhortations follow. Those who are slackers need a strong word of admonition to work (cf. 1 Thess. 4:11–12; 2 Thess. 3:6–11). On the other hand, those who are disheartened and weak need to be encouraged and helped; they don't need warnings and admonition but comfort. Living with the redeemed isn't yet paradise, and thus patience must be extended to all. Revengeful anger has no place, and instead believers must devote themselves to what is good in their lives with both believers and unbelievers (1 Thess. 5:15). Three commands come in staccato fashion (5:16–18). With all the sufferings and pressures in life, believers should always rejoice, pray constantly (which means regularly and often), and give thanks in every situation. All of these things are God's will in Christ for believers.

Verses 19–22 focus on charismatic gifts in the congregation, and particularly prophecy. Those who prophesy give a specific word of God to address situations in the churches. Paul warns the congregation not to despise prophetic utterances, for in doing so they would stifle the work of the Spirit in the church. At the same time, prophecies must be evaluated and assessed, for believers will go astray if they accept what is said uncritically. They must avoid all evil. Believers are to be open but not naive, humble but not credulous, both simple and shrewd, innocent and discerning.

In 5:23–24 Paul prays for the Thessalonians' holiness, asking that the God who grants peace would sanctify them wholly and that they would be kept until the coming of Jesus Christ (5:23). Some have read out of this a trichotomous understanding of the human person (spirit, soul, and body), but Paul's intention isn't to delineate the elements of the human person but to highlight that holiness is comprehensive. Such perfection in holiness will not be attained before the parousia: since God is faithful, he will complete the work of sanctification in human beings on the last day.

Final Words (5:25-28)

The closing words in 1 Thessalonians are remarkably brief. Paul solicits prayer, probably for his mission. He also enjoins the church to greet one another with a holy kiss, which indicates the warmth of family relationships present in the congregation. The admonition to have the letter read publicly, which was the practice with the OT writings that were authoritative (cf. Exod. 24:7; Deut. 17:19; 31:11; Josh. 8:34–35; Neh. 8:3, 8, 13; 9:3; 13:1), signaled that the Pauline instructions were authoritative and were not merely his private opinion. The letter ends with a grace benediction, and the letter itself is the means of such grace.

See after 2 Thessalonians for a combined bibliography of 1 and 2 Thessalonians.

CHAPTER TEN

2 Thessalonians

Introduction

Second Thessalonians was likely written a short time after 1 Thessalonians, and we see in the letter that the church continued to struggle with eschatology. Some scholars argue that the letter is pseudonymous for various stylistic and theological reasons. It isn't the purpose of this book to adjudicate such matters, but I don't find the objections against Pauline authorship to be compelling, and many scholars defend the authenticity of the letter. Paul actually criticizes those who send pseudonymous letters (2:2) and guarantees the authenticity of 2 Thessalonians at the close of the letter (3:17), which is clearly deceit of the highest order if the author wasn't Paul. Such deceit doesn't fit with the devotion to truth enshrined in the NT documents. For a rough outline of the letter, I suggest the following.

Outline

Thanksgiving for faith, hope, and love of believers	1:1–4
Judgment for the wicked and deliverance for the godly	1:5–12
Instructions about the day of the Lord	2:1–12
Thankfulness for election and prayer for perseverance	2:13–17
Prayer for missions	3:1–5
Admonition to slackers	3:6–18

Greeting and Thanksgiving (1:1–4)

Paul begins by greeting the congregation and giving thanks for God's work among them. The division made here after verse 4 isn't for structural reasons, for there is no clear indication for a break here. The separation is for content reasons since it serves as a convenient place of division for the sake of discussion. The greeting is very similar to 1 Thessalonians, with a few minor additions. Grace and peace, for instance, are now attributed specifically to God the Father and the Lord Jesus Christ. Some think the thanksgiving, which begins in verse 3, is colder than what we find in 1 Thessalonians, since Paul says it is a duty to give thanks—but obligation doesn't mean that the thanksgiving is constrained or less authentic. Paul simply argues that such thanksgiving is warranted, since their faith was growing by leaps and bounds and their love for one another was increasing. The lavish description of their faith and love shows that the thanksgiving was heartfelt. Indeed, Paul bragged about the Thessalonians when he was with other churches because they were enduring persecutions and pressures. Since their faith and love flourished in suffering, they were truly putting their hope in God.

God's Terrifying Judgment and Glorious Salvation (1:5–10)

Paul transitions to the judgment deserved by unbelievers, and we will see the main reason he does so in the course of our discussion. It should be noted at the outset that the *target* of these words is *unbelievers*, but the *audience* is *believers*. In other words, Paul didn't write these words for the sake of non-Christians but for the sake of Christians, and we want to discern the reason he has such strong words about unbelievers. The word "evidence" in verse 5 is disputed, but Paul probably means that the persecution of believers by unbelievers is "evidence" that God's judgment of unbelievers is just. At the same time, the suffering of believers makes them worthy of God's kingdom. Now this doesn't mean that the believers merit or earn their way into the kingdom, since entrance is by God's grace. At the same time, no one enters the kingdom who isn't transformed by the grace of God.

Paul has especially in mind those who were pressuring and mistreating the Thessalonians, but God is "just," and he will "repay" those who are harming believers (1:6). Some say that there is no retributive ethic in Paul's theology, but here we see clearly the notion that the punishment fits the crime, which is a common teaching in the OT (e.g., Exod. 21:24, 27; Lev. 24:20; Deut. 19:21). Paul doesn't explain yet in 2 Thessalonians 1:6 what the affliction of unbelievers will be, but as the argument develops, the nature of the punishment is delineated. He threatens affliction for the wicked and promises relief for believers: this relief and punishment will take place at Jesus's coming, when he is revealed from heaven, and his "powerful angels," or "the angels of his power," return with him (1:7; cf. Matt. 16:27; 25:31). We should note that since the relief and

2 Thessalonians
God's Terrifying Judgment and Glorious Salvation (1:5-10)

the judgment occur at the same time, there is no basis for a rapture taking place seven years before the judgment described here. The rapture of the saints and the second coming occur at the same time.

It is clear that the affliction refers to the final judgment, when the Lord comes to punish the wicked and to reward the righteous (2 Thess. 1:8). The words "flaming fire" describe how the Lord comes when he metes out "vengeance" (i.e., justice) to those who don't know or obey the gospel. Paul alludes to Isaiah 66, which describes God's saving work for his people and the punishment of those who oppose him. Jerusalem will be full of joy, peace, and comfort (Isa. 66:10–14). But in words that anticipate the description of judgment in 2 Thessalonians, Isaiah says, "Look, the LORD will come with fire—his chariots are like the whirlwind—to execute his anger with fury and his rebuke with flames of fire" (66:15). The next verse reprises the theme: "For the LORD will execute judgment on all people with his fiery sword, and many will be slain by the LORD" (66:16).

If there was any doubt about the nature of the affliction that unbelievers will face, 2 Thessalonians 1:9 removes them. The destruction and punishment are "eternal," and it isn't annihilation because unbelievers are excluded "from the Lord's presence" and his "strength," which implies that they are permanently and continually excluded from his gracious presence. Here Paul picks up the language of Isaiah 2, which recounts the awesome and terrifying day of the Lord, and in the LXX the judgment is away "from the presence of the fear of the Lord" (2:10, 19, 21). The punishment is clearly retributive, eternal, and horrifying, and fits with OT revelation (Deut. 32:41; Lev. 26:25; Ezek. 25:12).

Now we need to return to the reason for this long description of the punishment of the wicked, and we also recall the distinction between *target* and *audience*. Since the letter wasn't sent to unbelievers, they are the *target* for what is said but not the *audience*. Why does Paul recount the eternal punishment of the wicked when addressing believers? The answer is so that believers will persevere in their sufferings. Believers need to know that enduring suffering and persecution is worth it. They could easily think about repudiating their faith and aligning themselves with their pagan friends and neighbors. Paul reminds them that those who are persecutors now will be punished later, and their punishment will never end. On the other hand, those who are being persecuted now will find eternal relief later. The destruction of the wicked is brought up, then, to motivate suffering saints to endure and persevere until the end.

The eschatological relief of believers is also described further in 2 Thessalonians 1:10. The day of the Lord isn't only a day of judgment but also a day of salvation. Jesus will be "glorified" and "marveled at" on that day. It won't merely be a day of relief but of unparalleled and stunning beauty (cf. Ps. 89:7). The Thessalonian readers will be filled with joy because of their faith, because of their belief in the gospel. Paul emphasizes that *all* believers will share in this blessing, comforting them with the promise that none of them will be left out.

Paul's Prayer (1:11–12)

Since the final day is coming, a day of judgment and salvation, Paul prays for the Thessalonians, asking that they would truly persevere and live godly lives so that they will be worthy of their calling as Christians. The Thessalonians can't and won't accomplish such by their own strength, and thus Paul prays that the Lord would strengthen them so that they would have desires for goodness, showing that a new life starts in the realm of the inner person, in the motivations and aspirations of the heart. Still, Paul doesn't stop there, for he goes on to pray that their faith will produce works (cf. 1 Thess. 1:3). By God's grace, then, the name of Christ will be glorified and honored among the Thessalonians (cf. Isa. 66:5).

Jesus Is Coming, and Satan's Man Will Be Slain (2:1–12)

Virtually all agree that these verses are among the most difficult to understand in all of the Pauline literature. The purpose is to encourage and strengthen the Thessalonians to persevere. They should hang on to the faith because even though evil will get stronger, Jesus will return and vanquish evil, and believers will triumph forever.

The subject of the paragraph is Jesus's coming and the gathering of believers to him (2:1). Jesus's coming and the gathering of believers are complementary descriptions of the same event, told from two different perspectives. On the one hand, Jesus will be present with his people; on the other hand, believers will be gathered to him. Paul revisits the coming of Jesus, which he already discussed (see 1:7, 10) in the First Letter to the Thessalonians as well.

Paul addresses the subject because the Thessalonians have been thrown off or confused by a prophecy, an oracle, or by a letter supposedly deriving from Paul (2:2). The reference to the "spirit" (KJV, *pneuma*) or oracle probably refers to a prophetic word. It is possible that all three things mentioned—prophecy, word, and letter (see 2:2 NIV)—were understood to be from Paul, or perhaps only the letter was alleged to be from Paul. The wording used is cryptic for us, but not for Paul or the readers, since they both knew what

Paul was talking about. Perhaps Paul mentions three possibilities because he didn't know the exact source of the Thessalonians' confusion. In any case, the Thessalonians needed to be on guard so that they weren't deceived (2:3).

Apparently, some of them believed the day of the Lord had already come (2:2). According to many interpreters, the problem was that they believed the day was impending, since it was obvious that the day hadn't yet come. But the word "has come" (*enestēken*) is in the perfect tense, which almost certainly denotes an existing reality. The word used always refers to events that are present, not events that are near or impending (Rom. 8:38; 1 Cor. 3:22; 7:26; Gal. 1:4; Heb. 9:9). Another problem with the first view is this: the notion that the day of the Lord was near or impending was the standard Christian view, and so it is difficult to see why it was a problem. The entire NT teaches that Jesus is coming soon. The main objection to the idea that the Thessalonians thought the day of the Lord had come was that it seems completely bizarre to think that they thought the end had come. In this case, we should let the natural meaning of the term determine what Paul was saying. Apparently the Thessalonians thought the end had arrived, that the second coming of Christ had already taken place; how they could think this is puzzling to us, and we find it hard to piece together. We face again the frustration of listening to one end of a phone conversation, where we aren't told everything, since Paul and the Thessalonians knew what was happening, and thus Paul doesn't elaborate.

Paul goes on to explain as clearly as he can why the Thessalonians could be certain that the day of the Lord hadn't arrived. Before that day arrives, two things must happen: apostasy and the coming of the man of lawlessness (2:3). We will take these up in turn. Apostasy refers to departure from the things of God (cf. Josh. 22:22; 1 Chron. 29:19; Jer. 2:19; Acts 21:21; cf. 1 Macc. 2:15). Is the apostasy religious or political? The focus in the Scriptures is certainly on the former reality, though a sharp separation between the religious and the political doesn't fit the ancient world, where the religious and political spheres were often merged. Some interpreters think the apostasy is a sharp rejection of the things of God, not necessarily by professing Christians, but by a society that knows God through the created order (cf. Rom. 1:18–32). They point out that Paul expected the Thessalonian church to persevere and to thrive, not to fall away. Others argue that the apostasy will be in the church, where those who professed faith depart from the faith. They maintain that the word "apostasy" means departure from something once held, and some other texts describe believers as falling away from what they once adhered to (1 Tim. 4:1–5; 2 Tim. 3:1–9; 2 Pet. 2:1–22). Since Paul is so terse, knowing what he had in mind isn't easy to discern. What we do know is that there will be a climactic turning away from the Christian faith before the end, whether in the church, outside the church, or both, though it is likely he thinks of apostasy within the church.

The end will not arrive before "the man of lawlessness" steps on the scene, "the son of destruction" (2 Thess. 2:3 ESV). The meaning of this latter expression is nicely captured by the CSB, "the man doomed to destruction," and the destruction here designates final and permanent destruction, which will occur on the day of judgment (1:5–9). He will experience destruction because he will give himself to lawlessness; in other words, he will not subject himself to God and to his will but will pursue his own selfish desires and reject what God has ordained. This is the same person who is elsewhere called "antichrist" (1 John 2:18, 22; 4:3; 2 John 7), and Jesus also warned of "false messiahs" (Matt. 24:5, 23–24; Mark 13:21–22; Luke 21:8).

Parenthetically, before we proceed further, we have implicit evidence that Paul didn't believe in a pretribulation rapture. After all, the Thessalonians believed that the end had come, and the clearest and most unambiguous refutation of such a notion, if Paul believed in a pretribulation rapture, would be for him to say, "Obviously, the end hasn't come. Believers haven't been raptured. I am still here!" Since Paul doesn't mention it, and since he wanted to convince the Thessalonians in the clearest way that the end had not arrived, the dog that doesn't bark is quite significant.

The man of lawlessness, who is destined to be destroyed, shows his selfish will in exalting himself and in not countenancing worship of any other deity, which includes, of course, the worship of the one true God. We are reminded of the king of Babylon who aspired to "ascend to the heavens" "above the stars of God" (Isa. 14:13) since he wanted to "make [himself] like the Most High" (14:14). And the man of lawlessness is like the ruler of Tyre who said, "I am a god; I sit in the seat of gods in the heart of the sea" (Ezek. 28:2; cf. 28:6). Ultimately, this person demands the worship of all people everywhere. He actually takes his seat in God's temple and proclaims that he is God (2 Thess. 2:4). In doing so, he fulfills the prophecy of Daniel, who speaks of "the king," patterned after Antiochus Epiphanes (175–164 BC), who "will do whatever he wants. He will exalt and magnify himself above every god, and he will say outrageous things against the God of gods" (Dan. 11:36). As the next verse says, "He will magnify himself above all" (11:37).

This "antichrist" will also sit in God's temple, proclaiming himself as God (2 Thess. 2:4). One possibility is that the temple of God refers to the church, which fits with how Paul refers to the temple elsewhere (e.g., 1 Cor. 3:16–17; 2 Cor. 6:16; Eph. 2:21), and Paul envisions a great apostasy in the church of Jesus Christ. Despite the attractiveness of this view, the context suggests a reference to the Jerusalem temple, though it doesn't follow from this that a literal referent is required. We see antecedents of this notion in Ezekiel 28:2, Isaiah 14:13–14, and Daniel 11:36–37, cited above. Paul may have had in mind Pompey's desecration of the temple when he entered it in 63 BC (Josephus, *Ant.* 14.69–76; Pss. Sol. 17.11). The emperor Caligula also filled the land with terror in his desire to set up statues of himself in the temple, though his intention never became a reality (Josephus, *J.W.* 2.184–85; *Ant.* 18.261–309; Philo, *Embassy* 203–346). Dispensationalists believe this prophecy will be fulfilled literally in the future with a rebuilt temple. More likely, the prophecy should be understood apocalyptically, and thus it will be fulfilled in a general sense so that a reference to a literal temple isn't required. A person is coming who will demand absolute worship and authority. When kings obtain power, they gravitate toward absolute authority, and the man of lawlessness will fulfill in himself all the madness we have seen in Hitler, Stalin, Mao Zedong, and every megalomaniac in history.

Since the Thessalonians were confused, Paul gently reminds them that he had instructed them on these matters in the past (2 Thess. 2:5). We are also reminded again why this text is so difficult for us. Paul relies on his previous conversations and teaching so that the wording is elliptical. For instance, he says that the Thessalonians know what is restraining the man of lawlessness from appearing, but a look at any modern commentary reveals that we don't know for certain who the restrainer is, which explains why there are so many theories about the restrainer's identity. Before we discuss the restrainer in more detail, we should note a couple of other things about verses 6–7. What Paul says here is part of his argument against the notion that the day of the Lord had already arrived. In other words, the day can't be present because the restraint hasn't been removed. Yes, evil is present now, for "the mystery of lawlessness is already at work," but it hasn't yet reached its culmination and zenith. The full extent and depravity of evil is now hidden since it is being restrained. When the restraint is removed, evil will manifest itself fully.

This brings us to the identity of the restrainer. We have neuter (2:6) and masculine (2:7) forms so that the restrainer is both a thing (2:6) and a person (2:7). Many different proposals have been offered in history, showing that we don't know for certain the restrainer's identity, though, as noted above, the Thessalonians certainly knew. Some have taken the restrainer to be the Roman Empire and emperor, but since the emperor no longer exists, some apply what Paul says to government and to governors (Rom. 13:1–7). This view has much to commend it, though it doesn't explain the singular well since the Roman emperor no longer exists and plural governors don't fit with the singular restrainer. Furthermore, if government restrains evil, how do we explain Revelation 13, where evil is promoted by government? We also see that government can be a force for evil, as in the crucifixion of Christ and the persecution of believers by governing authorities.

Less convincing is the notion that the reference is to the preaching of the gospel and the person of Paul. By extension, one could say that preachers and preaching are what restrains evil today. The problem with this reading is that Paul didn't anticipate dying when he wrote the letter, and thus there is not a clear indication that Paul was the one to be taken "out of the way" (2 Thess. 2:7). The same problem applies to preachers in the plural; we lack any evidence for Paul thinking that preachers would be removed from the scene. Some dispensationalists think Paul points to the Holy Spirit, who is referred to with both masculine and neuter pronouns in Greek. This view fails to convince, for nowhere does *Paul* ever describe the Spirit by using neuter pronouns, nor is it clear that the Spirit will ever be removed from the scene as the Third Person of the Trinity. This view is also bound up with the notion of a pretribulational rapture, but as we have seen, 1 Thessalonians 4:13–18 and 2 Thessalonians 1–2 don't fit with a pretribulational rapture. Others understand the verb *katechō* to mean "rules" or "holds sway," and they think Paul speaks of the power of evil and Satan, which rules until the man of lawlessness arrives. This view doesn't convince: most scholars rightly argue that the verb *katechō* means "restrains." Plus, it doesn't make much sense to say that the man of lawlessness will only appear after Satan has been removed from the scene. In Revelation 13 the beast and Satan operate at the same time, and the beast receives his power from Satan.

We have to admit that we don't know for sure what and who is restraining evil. Ultimately, God is using some means to prevent evil from reaching its full potential, and thus even if we don't know *what* is restraining evil, we know *that* it is being restrained, and that God in his sovereignty rules over what is happening. Perhaps the best candidate for what restrains evil is Michael the archangel, whose *actions* (neuter) and *person* are the means God uses to restrain evil. Paul likely draws on Daniel 10–12, where Michael acts to restrain evil angels of Persia and Greece (10:13, 20–21). We see elsewhere that angels have a restraining role (Rev. 7:1; 20:1–3). Perhaps Daniel 12:1 anticipates the removal of Michael from the scene, signaling the loosening of his restraint and thus opening the door for apostasy and the coming of the man of lawlessness. What follows, then, is a period of great suffering for the people of God.

When the restraint and restrainer are removed, the man who opposes God and is lawless "will be revealed" (2 Thess. 2:8). Paul can't wait to get to the end of the story, and so he immediately records his downfall, for "the Lord Jesus will destroy him with the breath of his mouth and will bring him to nothing at the appearance of his coming." Here Paul alludes to a messianic text from Isaiah 11, where we are told that a shoot from Jesse "will strike the land with a scepter from his mouth, and he will kill the wicked with a command from his lips" (Isa. 11:4). Paul's purpose here is to comfort the Thessalonians. Yes, evil exists and is real, but it won't triumph, and its hour of rule is brief. The kingdom of evil is finally weak and temporary, and thus believers should continue to persevere even if they are persecuted.

Paul concentrates first on the defeat of the lawless one, but he tacks back and talks about his coming (2 Thess. 2:9). The lawless one's arrival is due to the work of Satan and is attested by remarkable power, by signs and wonders. In saying that the signs and wonders are "false," Paul isn't suggesting that they are "fake" miracles, miracles that aren't truly authentic. The signs and wonders are truly miraculous, but they are animated and inspired by evil. Elsewhere in Scripture we see that genuine miracles may stem from the forces of evil (cf. Exod. 7:22; 8:7; Deut. 13:1–2; Matt. 24:24; Mark 13:22; Rev. 13:13–15; 19:20). Those who are perishing, those headed toward eschatological destruction, will be fooled and led astray by these signs and wonders (2 Thess. 2:9–10). At first glance this seems unfair, for they would seem to have a good reason for following these evil powers since miracles verify the claims of wickedness. But Paul explains that the root problem, the reason unbelievers are not saved and "perish," is "because they did not accept the love of the truth" (2:10). They don't perish because it is so difficult to discern between truth and error. No, they give themselves to evil because they don't love the truth. They find evil convincing because they *want to find it convincing*. The convictions of the mind stem from the love of the soul.

Recognizing that people pursue what they love is crucial in interpreting 2:11–12, for it could seem perverse that God sends delusion upon unbelievers so that they believe what is a lie. But we must recognize that God confirms unbelievers in what they love. He doesn't send a spirit of delusion on those pursuing the truth, but on those who, as verse 12 says, "delighted in unrighteousness." The text reminds us of 1 Kings 22, where the Lord put a "lying spirit" in false prophets to ensure the death of Ahab (22:20–23). Ahab and the false prophets weren't neutral and passive objects; they were already opposed to the Lord. So, why would Paul write these words to the Thessalonians? First, they should not be surprised if miracles are done by the powers of evil, and thus such miracles should not shake their faith. Second, they are reminded that those who embrace evil do so because of the desire of their hearts. Third, they are also reminded that those who practice evil will perish, and thus they don't want to follow their path.

Stand Firm in Election (2:13–15)

The question that arises is: How do we account for the Thessalonian believers standing in a different position from unbelievers who delight in and love what is evil? It is not the case that believers are fundamentally different in their character since they were also sinners by nature. In other words, the Thessalonian believers can take no credit for their salvation, but all praise goes to God since he elected them "from the beginning" or as the "firstfruits" (ESV, NIV) to be saved (2 Thess. 2:13). Such salvation is due to the electing love of God and the work of the Spirit in setting apart believers to the Lord. It isn't as if the Thessalonians didn't do anything; they did put their belief in the truth of the gospel, but their belief was a result of the Spirit's work in setting them apart and God's electing work. Election took place before history began, but calling occurs in history, as people hear the gospel and believe. The Thessalonians should be encouraged since they are chosen and called, and in response they should hold on to and keep the traditions Paul gave them.

Prayer for Encouragement (2:16–17)

The purpose of the entire chapter is to encourage the Thessalonians, who were suffering from persecution, so that they would continue to endure until the end. Paul prays, then, that both the Lord Jesus Christ and God the Father would grant encouragement and strengthen the believers in deed and word. It is quite remarkable that Jesus Christ is mentioned before the Father in the prayer, perhaps because of the prominent role Jesus plays in chapter 2. In any case, prayer to both Christ and the Father shows the divine stature of Jesus. The Thessalonians are reminded again of God's love, and in Paul, God's love is often tied to election (cf. Rom. 1:7; 9:13; Col. 3:12; 1 Thess. 1:4; 2 Thess. 2:13). For the Thessalonians to endure, they need to be encouraged, and encouragement comes from knowing God's eternal love for them, and at the same time they have a hope that nothing can shake. Such love and hope are gifts of God and totally undeserved, and they are a bulwark in the midst of persecutions and affliction.

Prayer and Confidence (3:1–5)

This paragraph (3:1–5) contains an exhortation to pray, expressions of confidence, and a prayer. It is rather loosely structured and anticipates the last section of the letter. Paul calls upon the Thessalonians, asking them to pray for his mission, specifically that "the word of the Lord," the gospel, would have free course so that it would spread to many peoples and localities (2 Thess.

3:1). Paul also asks that the word would "be honored," that it would be believed and embraced as it is proclaimed. The preaching of the gospel arouses opposition and persecution, which is designed to hinder its proclamation, and thus the Thessalonians should also pray that Paul doesn't fall into the clutches of evil adversaries. After all, as Paul reminds the Thessalonians, there are many who don't believe.

Paul turns from his situation to the life situation of the Thessalonians. Dangers lurk on every side, but "the Lord is faithful" (3:3). In Paul, the faithfulness of the Lord is regularly linked with his promise to preserve his people (1 Cor. 1:9; 10:13; 1 Thess. 5:24; 2 Tim. 2:13), and such is the case here. Paul almost certainly thinks of the persecution suffered by the Thessalonians, and Satan is the likely source. Still, the Lord will fortify believers and protect them so that they persevere to the end. On the one hand, believers are urged to pray for deliverance from Satan (Matt. 6:13), but they are also promised, as we see here, that they will be delivered from the evil one.

Since the Lord is faithful, Paul is confident that the Thessalonians will carry out what he has commanded (3:4). The wording here is rather general, and so it should be understood in a general sense. The believers will persevere if they know God's love, and thus Paul prays that they will experience God's love. At the same time, he prays for "Christ's endurance," which doesn't signify the endurance Christ gives, but the endurance that marked Christ's life.

Admonitions regarding Slackers (3:6–15)

Evidently some in Thessalonica had ceased working; there are a number of guesses as to why they quit working. The best guess is that they abandoned their work because of their view of eschatology, that the end had arrived or was about to arrive. Still, we don't know for sure why they refrained from working, and any theory has to remain hypothetical. It is imperative to see that the admonition is addressed to those who *refused to work*. Paul isn't thinking of those who are unable to find work or those who are unable to work because of illness or old age. Paul begins solemnly, commanding them "in the name of our Lord Jesus Christ" (3:6). The believers should shun those who are slackers and don't follow the tradition handed down, and here the tradition is the admonition to work. In the ancient world, where honor and shame played a major role, refusal to fellowship with those who refused to work would have a great effect.

Paul then appeals to his own example (3:7–9). When he first came to a city, Paul's practice was not to receive payment but to work at his trade as a tentmaker to support himself. The work, as Paul explains, was tiring, exhausting, and constant: "night and day." Paul didn't want to be a financial burden to the Thessalonians, and thereby he distinguished himself from itinerant speakers who fleeced the people as they traveled. Paul actually believed he had a right to be supported financially, but as we saw in 1 Corinthians 9 and 2 Corinthians 11, he didn't avail himself of his rights in order to serve as an example and to preserve the purity of the gospel.

Paul reminds the Thessalonians of a rule he taught them during his ministry: those who refused to work should not be fed (2 Thess. 3:10). It is important to remind ourselves again that the directive is addressed to those unwilling to work, not to those unable to find work or to those who were physically incapacitated so that they could not work. The growling of the stomach, Paul believes, will serve as a good motivation to work. The report has come to Paul that some are slackers and refusing to work, and the CSB nicely catches the play on words in Greek: they "are not busy but busybodies" (3:11), meddling in the lives of others when their own house isn't in order.

Paul directly addresses the slackers in 3:12, and the introductory words, "Now we command and exhort such people by the Lord Jesus Christ," signify the authority and seriousness accompanying the command. For Paul, the refusal to work isn't a trivial matter, and thus those who are slackers are commanded to return to work and to provide for their own needs. Those who refuse to work should not be given assistance (3:10), but at the same time the recognition that some are lazy and refuse to work should not dampen the generosity of believers (3:13). They must not fall into the trap of saying that everyone is lazy so that they refuse to help.

What should be done if the exhortations about work are ignored or contradicted? The believers should take note of that person and refuse to associate with him. The refusal to associate with him is a form of discipline within the community of faith, which should lead the person behaving in this way to feel shame and remorse. We might think not associating with others betrays the pride of Pharisees, yet the purpose here isn't self-praise but the good of the person who refuses to work. Paul hopes that the church's response will lead to repentance and reformation. Indeed, Paul was worried that his admonition could be misunderstood (3:15). There is no room or place for hatred in the heart toward the slacker, as though he or she were an enemy. Instead, the admonition and reproof stems from a heart of love to one who is a sibling.

Final Words (3:16-18)

The congregation was afflicted by persecution, confused by eschatology, and divided since some refused to work. Paul puts a special emphasis on peace then, praying that "the Lord of peace," who is almost certainly Jesus Christ, would grant them peace in every situation and "in every way" (3:16). We see another remarkable example of a prayer to Jesus, which confirms again Jesus's divine identity. Such peace will be theirs when the Lord Jesus Christ is with them all, and Paul prays it will be so.

Paul takes up the pen at this point, appending his signature in his own hand (3:17). Apparently this was his practice in every letter. Such a signature verified the authenticity of the letter (cf. 2:2) and its authority. We don't have a private missive here. Paul concludes as he regularly does with a prayer that the grace of Christ would be with each and every one of them (3:18).

1–2 Thessalonians: Commentaries

Beale, G. K. *1–2 Thessalonians.* IVPNTC. Downers Grove, IL: InterVarsity, 2003.

Best, E. K. *Commentary on the First and Second Epistles to the Thessalonians.* BNTC. London: Black, 1997.

Bruce, F. F. *1 & 2 Thessalonians.* WBC. Waco: Word, 1982.

Eadie, J. K. *Commentary on the Greek Text of the Epistle of Paul to the Thessalonians.* Edited by W. Young. London: Macmillan, 1877.

Elias, J. W. *First and Second Thessalonians.* BCBC. Scottdale, PA: Herald Press, 1995.

Fee, Gordon D. *The First and Second Letters to the Thessalonians.* NICNT. Grand Rapids: Eerdmans, 2009.

Findlay, G. G. *The Epistles to the Thessalonians.* Cambridge Bible for Schools and Colleges. Cambridge: Cambridge University Press, 1891.

Fowl, S. E. *A Critical and Exegetical Commentary on the Epistles of St. Paul to the Thessalonians.* ICC. Edinburgh: T&T Clark, 1912.

Furnish, Victor P. *1 Thessalonians, 2 Thessalonians.* ANTC. Nashville: Abingdon, 2007.

Gaventa, Beverly R. *First and Second Thessalonians.* Interpretation. Louisville: John Knox, 1998.

Green, Gene L. *The Letters to the Thessalonians.* PNTC. Grand Rapids: Eerdmans, 2002.

Hobbs, H. H. "1–2 Thessalonians." In *The Broadman Bible Commentary*, edited by C. J. Allen, 11:257–98. Nashville: Broadman, 1971.

Holmes, Michael W. *1 and 2 Thessalonians.* NIVAC. Grand Rapids: Zondervan, 1998.

Kim, Seyoon, and F. F. Bruce. *1 & 2 Thessalonians.* Rev. ed. WBC. Dallas: Word, 2019.

Laub, F. *1. und 2. Thessalonicherbrief.* Würzberg: Echter, 1998.

Malherbe, Abraham J. *The Letters to the Thessalonians: A New Translation with Introduction and Commentary.* AB 32B. New York: Doubleday, 2000.

Marshall, I. Howard. *1 and 2 Thessalonians: Based on the Revised Standard Version.* NCBC. Grand Rapids: Eerdmans, 1983.

Martin, D. M. *1, 2 Thessalonians.* NAC 33. Nashville: Broadman & Holman, 1995.

McKinnish Bridges, L. *1 and 2 Thessalonians*. SHBC. Macon, GA: Smyth & Helwys, 2008.

Milligan, G. *St. Paul's Epistles to the Thessalonians: The Greek Text with Introduction and Notes*. London: Macmillan, 1908.

Moore, A. L. *1 and 2 Thessalonians: Based on the Revised Standard Version*. NCBC. London: Nelson, 1969.

Morris, Leon. *First and Second Epistles to the Thessalonians*. Rev. ed. NICNT. Grand Rapids: Eerdmans, 1991.

Plummer, A. *A Commentary on St. Paul's First Epistle to the Thessalonians*. London: Robert Scott, 1918.

Reese, J. M. *1 and 2 Thessalonians*. New Testament Message. Wilmington, DE: Michael Glazier, 1979.

Richard, E. J. *First and Second Thessalonians*. SP. Collegeville, MN: Liturgical Press, 1995.

Shogren, Gary S. *1 and 2 Thessalonians*. ZECNT. Grand Rapids: Zondervan, 2012.

Thomas, Robert L. "1–2 Thessalonians." In *Ephesians through Philemon*, vol. 11 of *The Expositor's Bible Commentary*, edited by F. E. Gaebelein, 227–337. Grand Rapids: Zondervan, 1978.

Walvoord, John F. *The Thessalonian Epistles*. Grand Rapids: Zondervan, 1976.

Wanamaker, Charles A. *The Epistles to the Thessalonians: A Commentary on the Greek Text*. NIGTC. Grand Rapids: Eerdmans, 1990.

Ward, R. A. *Commentary on 1 and 2 Thessalonians*. Waco: Word, 1973.

Weatherly, J. A. *1 and 2 Thessalonians*. CPNIVC. Joplin, MO: College Press, 1996.

Weima, Jeffrey A. D. *1–2 Thessalonians*. BECNT. Grand Rapids: Baker Academic, 2014.

Williams, D. J. *1 and 2 Thessalonians*. NIBC. Peabody, MA: Hendrickson, 1992.

Witherington, Ben, III. *1 and 2 Thessalonians: A Socio-Rhetorical Commentary*. Grand Rapids: Eerdmans, 2006.

1–2 Thessalonians: Articles, Essays, and Monographs

Ascough, R. *1 and 2 Thessalonians: Encountering the Christ Group at Thessalonike*. PGNT 13. Sheffield: Sheffield Phoenix, 2014.

———. *Paul's Macedonian Associations: The Social Context of Philippians and 1 Thessalonians*. WUNT 161. Tübingen: Mohr Siebeck, 2003.

Aune, David E. "Trouble in Thessalonica: An Exegetical Study of I Thess 4:9–12, 5:12–14 and II Thess 3:6–15 in Light of First Century Social Conditions." Master's thesis, Regent College, 1989.

Bailey, J. A. "Who Wrote II Thessalonians?" *NTS* 25 (1978–79): 131–45.

Barclay, John M. G. "Conflict in Thessalonica." *CBQ* 55 (1993): 512–30.

Bassler, Jouette M. "The Enigmatic Sign: 2 Thessalonians 1:5." *CBQ* 46 (1984): 496–510.

Baumert, N. "*Homeiromenoi* in 1 Thess 2:8." *Bib* 68 (1987): 552–63.

Benson, G. P. "Note on 1 Thessalonians 1.6." *ExpTim* 107 (1996): 143–44.

Black, David Alan. "The Weak in Thessalonica: A Study in Pauline Lexicography." *JETS* 5 (1982): 307–21.

Boers, Hendrikus. "The Form Critical Study of Paul's Letters: I Thessalonians as a Case Study." *NTS* 22 (1975): 140–58.

Burke, T. J. *Family Matters: A Socio-Historical Study of Kinship Metaphors in 1 Thessalonians.* JSNTSup 247. London: T&T Clark, 2003.

———. "Pauline Paternity in 1 Thessalonians." *TynBul* 51 (2000): 59–80.

Callow, J. *A Semantic Structure Analysis of Second Thessalonians.* Dallas: Summer Institute of Linguistics, 1982.

Caragounis, Chrys. "Parainesis on ἉΓΙΑΣΜΟΣ (1 Thess. 4:3–8)." *Filología neotestamentaria* 15 (2002): 133–51.

Carras, George P. "Jewish Ethics and Gentile Converts: Remarks on 1 Thes 4,3–8." In *The Thessalonian Correspondence*, edited by R. F. Collins, 306–15. BETL 87. Leuven: Leuven University Press, 1990.

Chadwick, Henry. "1 Thess. 3:3: σαίνεσθαι." *JTS* 1 (1950): 156–58.

Chapa, J. "Is First Thessalonians a Letter of Consolation?" *NTS* 40 (1994): 150–60.

Collins, Raymond F. "The Function of Paraenesis in 1 Thess 4,1–12; 5,12–22." *ETL* 74 (1998): 398–414.

———. *Studies on the First Letter to the Thessalonians.* BETL 66. Leuven: Leuven University Press, 1994.

———. "'This Is the Will of God: Your Sanctification' (1 Thess 4:3)." *LTP* 39 (1983): 27–53.

Cranfield, Charles E. B. "A Study of 1 Thessalonians 2." *Irish Biblical Studies* 1 (1979): 215–26.

Crawford, C. "The 'Tiny' Problem of 1 Thessalonians 2:7: The Case of the Curious Vocative." *Bib* 54 (1973): 69–72.

Delobel, J. "One Letter Too Many in Paul's First Letter? A Study of (ν)ηπιοι in 1 Thess 2:7." *Louvain Studies* 20 (1995): 126–33.

Dixon P. S. "The Evil Restraint in 2 Thess 2:6." *JETS* 33 (1990): 445–49.

Donfried, Karl P. "The Cults of Thessalonica and the Thessalonian Correspondence." *NTS* 31 (1985): 336–56.

———. "The Imperial Cults of Thessalonica and Political Conflict in 1 Thessalonians." In *Paul and Empire: Religion and Power in Roman Imperial Society*, edited by R. A. Horsley, 215–23. Harrisburg, PA: Trinity Press International, 1997.

———. "Paul and Judaism: 1 Thessalonians 2:13–16 as a Test Case." *Interpretation* 38 (1984): 242–53.

———. *Paul, Thessalonica, and Early Christianity.* Grand Rapids: Eerdmans, 2002.

———. "2 Thessalonians and the Church of Thessalonica." In *Origins and Method: Towards a New Understanding of Judaism and Christianity; Essays in Honour of John C. Hurd*, edited by B. H. McLean, 128–44. JSNTSup 86. Sheffield: JSOT Press, 1993.

———. "The Theology of 1 and 2 Thessalonians." In *The Theology of the Shorter Pauline Letters*, edited by J. D. G. Dunn, 1–113. NTT. Cambridge: Cambridge University Press, 1993.

———. "War Timotheus in Athen? Exegetische Überlegungen zu 1 Thess 3,1–3." In *Die Freude an Gott—unsere Kraft: Festschrift für Otto Bernhard Knoch zum 65. Geburtstag*, edited by J. J. Degenhardt, 189–96. Stuttgart: Katholisches Bibelwerk, 1991.

Dunham, Duane A. "2 Thessalonians 1:3–10: A Study in Sentence Structure." *JETS* 24 (1981): 39–46.

Edgar, T. R. "The Meaning of 'Sleep' in 1 Thessalonians 5:10." *JETS* 22 (1979): 345–49.

Elgvin, T. "'To Master His Own Vessel': 1 Thess 4:4 in Light of New Qumran Evidence." *NTS* 43 (1997): 604–19.

Ellingworth, Paul. "Which Way Are We Going? A Verb of Movement, Especially in 1 Thess 4:14b." *BT* 25 (1974): 426–31.

Esler, Philip. "2 Thessalonians." In *The Oxford Bible Commentary*, edited by J. Barton and J. Muddiman, 1213–20. Oxford: Oxford University Press, 2000.

Evans, Craig A. "Ascending and Descending with a Shout: Psalm 47.6 [47.5 ET = 46.6 LXX] and 1 Thessalonians 4.16." In *Paul and the Scriptures of Israel*, edited by C. A. Evans and J. A. Sanders, 238–53. JSNTSup 83. SEJC 1. Sheffield: JSOT Press, 1993.

Evans, R. M. *Eschatology and Ethics: A Study of Thessalonica and Paul's Letters to the Thessalonians*. Princeton, NJ: McMahon Printing, 1968.

Fee, Gordon D. "On Text and Commentary on 1 and 2 Thessalonians." In *SBL 1992 Seminar Papers*, edited by E. H. Lovering Jr., 165–83. Atlanta: Scholars Press, 1992.

———. "Pneuma and Eschatology in 2 Thessalonians 2.1–2: A Proposal about 'Testing the Prophets' and the Purpose of 2 Thessalonians." In *To Tell the Mystery: Essays on New Testament Eschatology in Honor of Robert H. Gundry*, edited by T. E. Schmidt and M. Silva, 196–215. JSNTSup 100. Sheffield: JSOT Press, 1994.

Foster, Paul. "Who Wrote 2 Thessalonians? A Fresh Look at an Old Problem." *JSNT* 35 (2012): 150–75.

Gaventa, Beverly R. "Apostles as Babes and Nurses in 1 Thessalonians 2:7." In *Faith and History: Essays in Honor of Paul W. Meyer*, edited by J. T. Carroll, C. H. Cosgrove, and E. E. Johnson, 193–207. Atlanta: Scholars Press, 1991.

Getty, M. A. "The Imitation of Paul in the Letters to the Thessalonians." In *The Thessalonian Correspondence*, edited by K. F. Collins, 277–83. BETL 87. Leuven: Leuven University Press, 1990.

Giblin, Charles H. "2 Thessalonians 2 Re-read as Pseudepigraphical: A Revised Reaffirmation of *The Threat to Faith*." In *The Thessalonian Correspondence*, edited by K. F. Collins, 459–69. BETL 87. Leuven: Leuven University Press, 1990.

———. *The Threat to Faith: An Exegetical and Theological Reexamination of 2 Thessalonians 2*. AnBib 31. Rome: Pontifical Biblical Institute, 1967.

Gilliard, F. D. "Paul and the Killing of the Prophets in 1 Thess. 2:15." *NovT* 36 (1994): 259–70.

———. "The Problem of the Antisemitic Comma between 1 Thessalonians 2:14 and 15." *NTS* 35 (1989): 481–502.

Gillman, J. "Paul's *Eisodos*: The Proclaimed and the Proclaimer (1 Thes 2,8)." In *The Thessalonian Correspondence*, edited by R. F. Collins, 62–70. BETL 87. Leuven: Leuven University Press, 1990.

———. "Signals of Transformation in 1 Thessalonians 4:13–18." *CBQ* 47 (1985): 263–81.

Gregson R. "Solution to the Problems of the Thessalonian Epistles." *EvQ* 38 (1966): 76–80.

Gundry, R. H. "A Brief Note on 'Hellenistic Formal Receptions and Paul's Use of ΑΠΑΝ-ΤΗΣΙΣ in 1 Thessalonians 4:17.'" *BBR* 6 (1979): 39–41.

Hannah, D. D. "The Angelic Restrainer of 2 Thessalonians 2.6–7." In *Calling Time: Religion and Change at the Turn of the Millennium*, edited by M. Percy, 28–45. Sheffield: Sheffield Academic, 2000.

Heil, J. H. "Those Now 'Asleep' (Not Dead) Must Be 'Awakened' for the Day of the Lord in 1 Thess 5.9–10." *NTS* 46 (2000): 464–71.

Hendrix, H. L. "Archaeology and Eschatology at Thessalonica." In *The Future of Early Christians: Essays in Honor of Helmut Koester*, edited by B. A. Pearson, 107–18. Minneapolis: Fortress, 1991.

———. "Thessalonica." In *Archaeological Resources for New Testament Studies: A Collection of Slides on Culture and Religion in Antiquity*, edited by H. Koester and H. L. Hendrix, 1:1–49. Philadelphia: Fortress, 1987.

Hodges, Zane C. "The Rapture in 1 Thessalonians 5:1–11." In *Walvoord: A Tribute*, edited by D. K. Campbell, 67–79. Chicago: Moody, 1982.

Holland, G. S. "'A Letter Supposedly from Us': A Contribution to the Discussion about the Authorship of 2 Thessalonians." In *The Thessalonian Correspondence*, edited by R. F. Collins, 394–402. BETL 87. Leuven: Leuven University Press, 1990.

———. *The Tradition That You Received from Us: 2 Thessalonians in the Pauline Tradition*. Hermeneutische Untersuchungen zur Theologie 24. Tübingen: Mohr Siebeck, 1988.

Holtz, T. "On the Background of 1 Thessalonians 2:1–12." In *The Thessalonians Debate: Methodological Discord or Methodological Synthesis?*, edited by K. P. Donfried and J. Beutler, 69–80. Grand Rapids: Eerdmans, 2000.

Hooker, Morna D. "1 Thessalonians 1:9–10: A Nutshell—but What Kind of Nut?" In *Frühes Christentum*, 435–48. Vol. 3 of *Geschichte—Tradition—Reflexion: Festschriften für Martin Hengel zum 70. Geburtstag*, edited by H. Cancik, H. Lichtenberger, and P. Schäfer. Tübingen: Mohr Siebeck, 1996.

Horbury, W. "1 Thessalonians 2:3 as Rebutting the Charge of False Prophecy." *JTS* 33 (1982): 492–508.

House, H. Wayne. "*Apostasia* in 2 Thessalonians 2:3: Apostasy or Rapture?" In *When the Trumpet Sounds*, edited by T. Ice and T. J. Demy, 261–95. Eugene, OR: Harvest House, 1995.

Howard, T. L. "The Literary Unity of 1 Thessalonians 4:13–5:11." *Grace Theological Journal* 9 (1988): 163–90.

Hughes, F. W. *Early Christian Rhetoric and 2 Thessalonians*. JSNTSup 30. Sheffield: JSOT Press, 1989.

———. "The Rhetoric of 1 Thessalonians." In *The Thessalonian Correspondence*, edited by R. F. Collins, 94–116. BETL 87. Leuven: Leuven University Press, 1990.

Jewett, Robert. "Enthusiastic Radicalism and the Thessalonian Correspondence." *1972 Proceedings of the Society of Biblical Literature* 1 (1972): 181–232.

———. *The Thessalonian Correspondence: Pauline Rhetoric and Millenarian Piety*. Foundations and Facets. Philadelphia: Fortress, 1986.

Johanson, B. C. *To All the Brethren: A Text-Linguistic and Rhetorical Approach to 1 Thessalonians*. Coniectanea biblica: New Testament Series 16. Stockholm: Almqvist & Wiksell, 1987.

Kim, Seyoon. "The Jesus Tradition in 1 Thess 4.13–5.11." *NTS* 48 (2002): 225–42.

———. "Paul's Entry (εἴσοδος) and the Thessalonians' Faith (1 Thessalonians 1–3)." *NTS* 51 (2005): 37–47.

Koester, Helmut. "From Paul's Eschatology to the Apocalyptic Schemata of 2 Thessalonians." In *The Thessalonian Correspondence*, edited by R. F. Collins, 441–58. BETL 87. Leuven: Leuven University Press, 1990.

———. "Imperial Ideology and Paul's Eschatology in 1 Thessalonians." In *Paul and Empire*, edited by R. A. Horsley, 158–66. Harrisburg, PA: Trinity Press International, 1997.

———. "The Text of 1 Thessalonians." In *The Living Text: Essays in Honor of Ernest W. Saunders*, edited by D. E. Groh and R. Jewett, 219–27. Lanham, MD: University Press of America, 1985.

Krodel, G. A. "The 'Religious Power of Lawlessness' (*Katechon*) as Precursor of the 'Lawless One' (*Anomos*): 2 Thess 2:6–7." *Currents in Theology and Mission* 17 (1990): 440–46.

Lambrecht, Jan. "Loving God and Steadfastly Awaiting Christ (2 Thessalonians 3,5)." *ETL* 76 (2000): 435–41.

———. "A Structural Analysis of 1 Thessalonians 4–5." In *The Thessalonian Debate: Methodological Discord or Methodological Synthesis?*, edited by K. P. Donfried and J. Beutler, 163–78. Grand Rapids: Eerdmans, 2000.

———. "Thanksgivings in 1 Thessalonians 1–3." In *The Thessalonian Correspondence*, edited by R. F. Collins, 183–205. BETL 87. Leuven: Leuven University Press, 1990.

Malherbe, Abraham J. "Exhortation in First Thessalonians." *NovT* 25 (1983): 238–56.

———. *Paul and the Thessalonians: The Philosophic Tradition of Pastoral Care*. Philadelphia: Fortress, 1987.

Marshall, I. Howard. "Election and Calling to Salvation in 1 and 2 Thessalonians." In *The Thessalonian Correspondence*, edited by R. F. Collins, 259–76. BETL 87. Leuven: Leuven University Press, 1990.

———. "Pauline Theology in the Thessalonian Correspondence." In *Paul and Paulinism: Festschrift for C. K. Barrett*, edited by M. D. Hooker and S. G. Wilson, 173–83. London: SPCK, 1982.

McGehee, M. "A Rejoinder to Two Recent Studies Dealing with 1 Thess 4:4." *CBQ* 51 (1989): 82–89.

Mearns, C. L. "Early Eschatological Development in Paul: The Evidence of I and II Thessalonians." *NTS* 27 (1981): 137–57.

Míguez, Néstor O. *The Practice of Hope: Ideology and Intention in 1 Thessalonians*. Minneapolis: Fortress, 2012.

Nicholl, Colin R. *From Hope to Despair in Thessalonica: Situating 1 and 2 Thessalonians*. SNTSMS 126. Cambridge: Cambridge University Press, 2004.

Otto, R. E. "The Meeting in the Air (1 Thess. 4:17)." *HBT* 19 (1997): 192–212.

Pearson, B. A. "1 Thessalonians 2:13–16: A Deutero-Pauline Interpolation." *HTR* 64 (1971): 79–94.

Plevnik, Joseph. "1 Thess 5:1–11: Its Authenticity, Intention and Message." *Bib* 60 (1979): 71–90.

———. "The Taking Up of the Faithful and the Resurrection of the Dead in 1 Thessalonians 4:13–18." *CBQ* 46 (1984): 274–83.

Powell, C. E. "The Identity of the 'Restrainer' in 2 Thessalonians 2:6–7." *BSac* 154 (1997): 320–32.

Robinson, D. W. B. "II Thess. 2,6: 'That Which Restrains' or 'That Which Holds Sway'?" In *Studia Evangelica*, vol. 2, *Papers Presented to the Second International Congress on New Testament Studies Held at Christ Church, Oxford, 1961*, part 1, *The New Testament Scriptures*, edited by F. L. Cross et al., 635–38. TUGAL 87. Berlin: Akademie, 1964.

Roetzel, Calvin J. "1 Thess 5:12–28: A Case Study." In *SBL 1972 Proceedings*, edited by L. C. McGaughy, 2:367–83. Chico, CA: Society of Biblical Literature, 1972.

Ross, J. M. "1 Thessalonians 3.13." *BT* 26 (1975): 444.

Russell, R. "The Idle in 2 Thess 3:6–12: An Eschatological or a Social Problem?" *NTS* 34 (1988): 105–19.

Schlueter, C. J. *Filling Up the Measure: Polemical Hyperbole in 1 Thessalonians 2:14–16.* JSNTSup 98. Sheffield: JSOT Press, 1994.

Schmidt, D. D. "1 Thess 2:13–16: Linguistic Evidence for an Interpolation." *JBL* 102 (1983): 269–79.

———. "The Syntactical Style of 2 Thessalonians: How Pauline Is It?" In *The Thessalonian Correspondence*, edited by R. F. Collins, 383–93. BETL 87. Leuven: Leuven University Press, 1990.

Stephenson, A. M. G. "On the Meaning of ἐνέστηκεν ἡ ἡμέρα τοῦ κυρίου in 2 Thessalonians 2,2." In *Studia evangelica*, vol. 4, *Papers Presented to the Third International Congress on New Testament Studies Held at Christ Church, Oxford, 1965*, part 1, *The New Testament Scriptures*, edited by F. L. Cross et al., 442–51. TUGAL 102. Berlin: Akademie, 1968.

Still, Todd D. *Conflict at Thessalonica: A Pauline Church and Its Neighbours.* JSNTSup 183. Sheffield: Sheffield Academic, 1999.

Theodoret, Bishop of Cyrrhus. "I and II Thessalonians." In *Commentary on the Letters of St. Paul*, translated by R. C. Hill, 2:107–35. Brookline, MA: Holy Cross Orthodox Press, 2001.

Trudinger, P. "The Priority of 2 Thessalonians Revisited: Some Fresh Evidence." *Downside Review* 113 (1995): 31–35.

Wallace, Daniel B. "A Textual Problem in 1 Thessalonians 1:10: Ἐκ τῆς Ὀργῆς vs. Ἀπὸ τῆς Ὀργῆς." *BSac* 147 (1990): 470–79.

Walton, Steve. "What Has Aristotle to Do with Paul? Rhetorical Criticism and 1 Thessalonians." *TynBul* 46 (1995): 229–50.

Ware, James P. "The Thessalonians as a Missionary Congregation: 1 Thessalonians 1,5–8." *ZNW* 83 (1992): 126–31.

Warfield, B. B. "The Prophecies of St. Paul, I: 1 and 2 Thessalonians." *The Expositor*, 3rd series, 4 (1886): 30–44.

Weatherly, J. A. "The Authenticity of 1 Thessalonians 2.13–16: Additional Evidence." *JSNT* 42 (1991): 79–98.

———. "Responsibility for the Death of Jesus in Paul: 1 Thessalonians 2:14–16." In *Jewish Responsibility for the Death of Jesus in Luke-Acts*, 176–94. JSNTSup 106. Sheffield: Sheffield Academic, 1994.

Weima, Jeffrey A. D. "An Apology for the Apologetic Function of 1 Thessalonians 2.1–12." *JSNT* 68 (1997): 73–99.

———. "'But We Became Infants among You': The Case for NHΠΙΟΙ in 1 Thess 2.7." *NTS* 46 (2000): 547–64.

———. "The Slaying of Satan's Superman and the Sure Salvation of the Saints: Paul's Apocalyptic Word of Comfort (2 Thessalonians 2:1–17)." *CTJ* 41 (2006): 67–88.

Weima, Jeffrey A. D., and Stanley E. Porter. *An Annotated Bibliography of 1 and 2 Thessalonians*. New Testament Tools and Studies 26. Leiden: Brill, 1998.

Whitton, J. "A Neglected Meaning for *Skeuos* in 1 Thessalonians 4.4." *NTS* 28 (1982): 142–43.

Wilson, G. B. *I and II Thessalonians: A Digest of Reformed Comment*. Edinburgh: Banner of Truth Trust, 1975.

Winter, Bruce W. "The Entries and Ethics of Orators and Paul (1 Thessalonians 2:1–12)." *TynBul* 44 (1993): 55–74.

———. "'If a Man Does Not Wish to Work . . .': A Cultural and Historical Setting for 2 Thessalonians 3:6–16." *TynBul* 40 (1989): 303–15.

Witmer, Stephen E. "Θεοδίδακτοι in 1 Thessalonians 4.9: A Pauline Neologism." *NTS* 52 (2006): 239–50.

Yarbrough, Robert W. "Sexual Gratification in 1 Thess 4:1–8." *TJ* 20 (1999): 215–32.

CHAPTER ELEVEN

1 Timothy

Introduction

The Pastoral Letters were written to individuals, with two written to Timothy and one to Titus. In critical scholarship they are often identified as pseudonymous for literary, theological, and historical reasons. It isn't the purpose of this work to discuss such questions, but I believe with many that the Pastoral Epistles were actually written by Paul, though he may have used an amanuensis (secretary). Many modern commentators support Pauline authorship, including Luke Johnson, Gordon Fee, Donald Guthrie, Earle Ellis, George Knight, William Mounce, Andreas Köstenberger, Robert Yarbrough, D. A. Carson, and Douglas Moo. Establishing a date for 1 Timothy isn't easy. It could have been written at some point during Paul's ministry before his imprisonment, but I incline to the traditional view that Paul was released from his first Roman imprisonment, so perhaps he wrote 1 Timothy in AD 64–65, before his martyrdom in AD 67. The letter was written to Timothy, who actually wasn't a pastor of the church but an apostolic emissary for the church at Ephesus. We see that in the mid-60s the Ephesian church was struggling with false teaching, and Paul writes to Timothy, who will teach and instruct and correct the Ephesian church on such matters. First Timothy isn't easy to outline in one sense, and in another sense it is rather simple, as Paul covers the topics below. One simple outline is as follows.

Outline

Beware of false teachers	1:1–20
Pray for all	2:1–7

Set up appropriate structures in the church	2:8–3:16
By your life and teaching counter false teachers	4:1–16
Instructions for widows, elders, and slaves	5:1–6:2
Final exhortations for Timothy	6:3–21

Greeting (1:1–2)

Paul designates himself as an apostle because he wasn't writing merely for Timothy but also for the church of Ephesus, and thus what is written here is authoritative. The authority of Paul is particularly stressed since God's command and appointment of him as an apostle is mentioned. Paul had in mind the appearance of Jesus Christ on the road to Damascus, where he was commissioned as an apostle. Salvation and God as Savior (along with Christ) are repeated themes in the Pastorals, and we see up front that they are among the primary themes of 1 Timothy. Hope is also a prominent theme, showing that eschatology hasn't been left behind in these letters.

The letter is addressed to Timothy as an apostolic delegate. Timothy was a confidant, coworker, and perhaps the closest person to the apostle Paul (Acts 16:1, 3; 17:14–15; 18:5; 19:22; 20:4; Rom. 16:21; 1 Cor. 4:17; 16:10; 2 Cor. 1:1, 19; Phil. 1:1; 2:19; Col. 1:1; 1 Thess. 1:1; 3:2, 6; 2 Thess. 1:1; 1 Tim. 1:2, 18; 6:20; 2 Tim. 1:2; Philem. 1). Paul trusted him completely, appointing him to carry out sensitive and crucial tasks for the sake of the ministry. Here Timothy is described as Paul's "true son in the faith" (1 Tim. 1:2) and is called upon to address what is happening in Ephesus as Paul's emissary. We have a typical grace benediction, but mercy is added to grace and peace. Grace and mercy are quite similar in meaning. Both refer to God's love in forgiving the misdeeds of human beings, though grace also points to God's strength for the future. Those who are the recipients of God's grace and mercy also enjoy his peace.

Instructions regarding False Teachers (1:3–11)

We would love to know more of the historical details, but apparently Paul had to leave for Macedonia (sometime after he was released from his first Roman imprisonment in AD 62), and he asked Timothy to stay in Ephesus to deal with the situation. Certain unnamed people were teaching wrong doctrines, and Paul commissioned Timothy to counteract and correct them. What these false teachers taught is frustratingly vague, as Paul refers to "myths and endless genealogies" (1:4). Probably the myths and genealogies were rooted in the OT since these teachers were entranced with the law (1:7–8). In speaking of "endless" genealogies, Paul probably speaks hyperbolically, suggesting that the genealogies were tiring and speculative. The gospel Paul preached is based on history instead of myths, tales, and legends. Paul doesn't describe the false teaching with any precision, because it was useless and a waste of time. Instead, Paul concentrates on God's plan, which centers on faith.

The "goal" of Pauline teaching is love, which is a central theme in Paul's thought (cf. Rom. 12:9; 13:8–10; 1 Cor. 8:1–3; 13:1–13; Gal. 5:14, 22; Eph. 5:2, 25; Phil. 1:9–11; Col. 3:14). Love comes from a "pure heart" (cf. Ps. 24:4), which describes a heart centered on God, but it also comes from a "good conscience," so that no sin is left unconfessed and evil is not allowed a place in one's life. Finally, love stems from a "sincere faith" (1 Tim. 1:5), where faith expresses itself in love (Gal. 5:6). Paul was interested in the transformation of people, not the "fruitless discussion" precipitated by the concerns of the false teachers (1 Tim. 1:6). In fact, they were so interested in arcane matters because they had no concern for love, purity, good conscience, and faith. These teachers longed to instruct, and they especially desired to teach the Mosaic law (1:7), but unfortunately they wanted to teach on matters about which they were invincibly ignorant. They were dogmatic and unbending in their assertions, though they actually didn't know what they were talking about.

Paul wasn't against the law, and his comments are brief because Timothy could explain to the Ephesians Paul's theology of the law, which is quite complex. The problem with the teachers is that, in a play on words, they don't use the law "lawfully" (ESV), "legitimately" (1:8). There is more than one purpose for the law, and it is difficult to know how the errant teachers were using the law. Still, we can understand what Paul says about the law. The law isn't for the righteous person, which probably means that the law doesn't make one righteous (1:9). Such righteousness, as the next paragraph attests (1:12–17), comes from faith in Jesus Christ, not the law. Perfect people don't need the law, but since all are sinners, the law plays an important role. The law is intended for those who are "lawless," "rebellious," "ungodly," and "sinful" (1:9). The law defines what sin is, revealing the lawlessness of those who are wicked. Perhaps Paul also has in mind the idea that the law also increases sin (Rom. 5:20), or it is even possible the notion that the law, when accompanied by quick punishments, restrains sin.

Paul then goes on to detail particularly egregious violations of the law, with sins that match the commandments in the Decalogue.

Texts from 1 Timothy	Texts from Decalogue
Kill fathers and mothers (1:9)	Honor your father and mother (Exod. 20:12)
Murderers (1:9)	Do not murder (Exod. 20:13)

Sexually immoral and homosexuals (1:10)	Do not commit adultery (Exod. 20:14)
Slave traders (1:10)	Do not steal (Exod. 20:15)
Liars, perjurers (1:10)	Do not give false testimony against your neighbor (Exod. 20:16)

Paul doesn't just indict dishonoring parents but also murdering them. Instead of limiting himself to adultery, he refers to sexual immorality in general, which would include fornication, rape, and sexual relations with animals. The word for homosexuality (*arsenokoitai*), which we also saw in 1 Corinthians 6:9, comes from Leviticus (LXX): "Do not have sexual relations with a man as one does with a woman" (18:22 NIV), and "If a man has sexual relations with a man as one does with a woman, both of them have done what is detestable" (20:13 NIV). The universal Jewish view of same-sex relations is that they are always wrong. The law also criticizes slave trading, which is another indication that Paul didn't endorse slavery. Paul also, in accord with the Ten Commandments, proscribes murder, lying, and perjury.

No law is needed for a person who is entirely holy. God, for instance, doesn't need a law. A right understanding of the law is in accord with "sound teaching" (1 Tim. 1:10). And sound teaching in turn conforms to the gospel, which features the stunning splendor and glory of "the blessed God" (1:11). The gospel was "entrusted" to Paul, and he fulfills his duty by guarding it against false teachers. The law can't make human beings right before God since it reveals that all are sinners. Only the gospel can grant new life and truly change human beings.

Paul Gives Thanks for Mercy and Ministry (1:12-17)

Paul gives thanks for the great mercy and ministry that he received from Christ Jesus. Why is this passage here, especially since in 1:18 Paul returns to Timothy's need to resist false teaching? The link with the previous paragraph is the gospel (1:11), and it seems likely that Paul introduces this topic because the false teachers have strayed from the gospel of grace. Paul doesn't dwell on his own life and ministry without purpose, and thus he probably includes this section to correct and counter false teachers.

Paul gives thanks for the strength granted to him through Christ. As one who was faithful, he was inducted into the ministry (1:12). Paul wasn't bragging since, as he says in 1 Corinthians 7:25, his faithfulness is ascribed to the Lord's mercy. Paul rehearses his past life (cf. also Gal. 1:13–14; Phil. 3:4–6), when he reviled God's name and violently persecuted God's assembly, the true people of God (1 Tim. 1:13). Still, God granted him mercy because he was ignorant in his unbelief. Paul isn't saying that ignorance is an excuse for sin, for his ignorance was certainly culpable. Nevertheless, Paul wasn't guilty of defiant sin, for which there was no forgiveness (cf. Num. 15:30).

Paul lists the first of the faithful and trustworthy sayings in the Pastoral Epistles (cf. 1 Tim. 3:1; 4:9; 2 Tim. 2:11; Titus 3:8). Here he shares a fundamental truth of the gospel, which should be accepted by all. "Christ Jesus came into the world to save sinners" (1 Tim. 1:15). It is possible that the false teachers were excluding some people groups from salvation with their genealogical fantasies, and Paul describes himself as the "worst" of sinners because it captures his self-estimate. At the same time, what he says testifies that the grace of God, the mercy of God, reaches down to the lowest of the low. Everyone who looks up for mercy finds it. And this fits beautifully with what Paul says next. Paul as the worst of sinners was granted patience for exemplary reasons (1:16). The salvation of Paul is paradigmatic and instructive for all, showing Christ's patience (an indication of his deity, by the way) toward all those who put their faith in him. The remarkable emphasis on Christ's love for all sinners seems to confirm that the false teachers had wandered from the centrality of the gospel and God's desire to save sinners.

As Paul reflects on the mercy extended to him, his heart fills with praise to God as the sovereign King of all (1:17). No one is like him, for he rules over all of history, and his reign will never end since he is "immortal." Per OT revelation, he is the "invisible" God (Exod. 33:20; Deut. 4:12; cf. also John 1:18; 6:46; Col. 1:15). He is the one and only true God; all the other so-called gods are fantasies of the human imagination, deserving mockery (Isa. 44:9–20). Since God is so great, and since he shows such kindness and mercy to sinners, he deserves all "honor and glory forever and ever."

Charge to Timothy (1:18-20)

Paul picks up the instruction from 1 Timothy 1:5 (using the same word "instruction") and continues to exhort Timothy regarding the false teachers. Timothy was equipped and gifted to deal with the situation he was facing, which was confirmed by the prophecies that were uttered over him when he was installed into the ministry (1 Tim. 4:14; 2 Tim. 1:6–7). Since Timothy was adequately equipped, he should be courageous in withstanding the false teachers and in fighting "the good fight" (1 Tim. 1:18). The fight isn't waged with fleshly weapons, for Timothy must keep trusting God and keep his conscience clear (1:19). The false teachers, however, have abandoned a good conscience.

"Hymenaeus and Alexander" are named as false teachers (1:20), and naming such is rare in Paul. Hymenaeus is listed as denying the resurrection, along with Philetus in 2 Timothy 2:17–18, and perhaps the same Alexander is in view in 2 Timothy 4:14–15. Paul delivered these men over to Satan, just as the man who committed incest in Corinth was turned over to Satan (1 Cor. 5:5). We have an OT antecedent where Job was handed over to Satan (Job 2:6), though in Job's case it wasn't because of any sin he committed. To hand someone over to Satan means that they are outside the church, and once someone isn't in the church, they are in Satan's sphere since he is "the god of this age" (2 Cor. 4:4), "the spirit now working in the disobedient" (Eph. 2:2). Such an action isn't vindictive or mean-spirited, for the hope is that they won't "blaspheme" (1 Tim. 1:20), which is probably another way of saying that the desire is for their salvation (cf. 1 Cor. 5:5). The severe discipline, then, ultimately has a merciful purpose.

Prayer and Salvation (2:1-7)

The instructions that Timothy should pass on to the Ephesian churches begin in earnest in chapter 2. By following Paul's instructions, the Ephesians would be strong in the faith and prepared to stand against the false teaching. Paul uses various terms for prayer, which include both the ideas of petition and thanksgiving. Here petitions and thanksgivings are offered for all people, and given the subject of the paragraph, Paul probably has in mind praying especially for salvation. No people group should be left out or excluded. Paul shifts to prayer for kings and other governing authorities (2:2). Believers should pray for those who exercise governing authority so that life in society will be peaceful and orderly. God is pleased when human society is ruled with justice, wisdom, and equity.

Salvation is for all people everywhere, and perhaps the false teachers were using genealogies to restrict the saved to certain people groups. When Paul says God desires all to be saved, he probably thinks in terms of Jewish and gentile people groups. Verse 7 seems to support this reading since Paul affirms his role as a herald and apostle of the gentiles and then adds that he isn't lying. The statement that he isn't lying is remarkably out of place unless the gentile mission had become controversial in at least some circles in Ephesus. In any case, God doesn't promise universal salvation for all people without exception, for it is quite clear that many won't be saved. Salvation is given to those who believe.

Paul also explains the basis of salvation. The oneness of God—the credo for Jews in Paul's day, reflecting the Shema of Deuteronomy 6:4—points to one way of salvation. Paul makes this very point in Romans 3:29–30, emphasizing that both the circumcised and uncircumcised are saved by faith. He isn't quite so direct here, but the same conception is in view. Since there is only one God, then there can be only "one mediator between God and humanity," and that is "the man Christ Jesus" (1 Tim. 2:5). Paul emphasizes Christ's humanity because he thinks of his death on the cross, where he died as a man (without surrendering his deity) for the sake of human beings. Christ's death wasn't restricted to certain peoples but was for all peoples everywhere. Verse 6 reaffirms and extends this truth, indicating that he was "a ransom for all" so that his death was the means by which people are freed from sin. His death came at the right time, the time God intended and sovereignly planned.

Instructions for Men and Women at Worship (2:8–15)

The paragraph before us is one of the most controversial in Paul and in the entire Bible. Clearly, we can't do justice to all the arguments that swirl around these verses. There is only space to briefly mention some different readings and my own interpretation of the text. The context is public worship, proper behavior when the church gathers for worship. Paul begins by addressing the men (2:8). In every congregation they are to lift up "holy hands" in prayer (cf. Ps. 134:2). Isaiah indicts Israel since when they lift up their hands in prayer their hands are defiled with blood (Isa. 1:15). Paul is not saying that only men are to pray in the congregation (cf. 1 Cor. 11:5), nor is he denying that women might get angry as well. Still, there is probably more of a tendency for men to fall prey to anger and quarreling, which may explain the admonition here.

Paul turns to the women in 1 Timothy 2:9–15, and it seems probable that these words were written because some of the women were violating what Paul here prescribes. Perhaps they applied Galatians 3:28 to their situation and argued that there were no role differences between men and women. The adornment of women is discussed in 1 Timothy 2:9–10. Some think the gathered congregation isn't in view, since appropriate dress is important in every situation, and that is certainly true, but the context suggests that Paul concentrates on the corporate gathering. For modern readers the instructions found here may sound prudish and extreme, but we should recognize that exhortations regarding proper adornment for women were common in the Greco-Roman world (Juvenal, *Sat.* 6.352–65, 457–73; Plutarch, *Mor.* 142ab). Given their social location, the readers of 1 Timothy would not have been astonished or surprised upon reading these words.

Some interpreters read Paul's admonition woodenly, as if he prohibited wearing any jewelry. The key to interpreting what Paul says here can be found in the phrases "modest clothing," "elaborate hairstyles," and "expensive apparel" (2:9). What Paul opposes is ostentatious and seductive dress, which still speaks today, for church may become a fashion show, and immodest dress isn't relegated to the past. The point isn't that women should wear the poorest clothes possible. Paul's target is an unhealthy preoccupation with one's clothing (cf. Isa. 3:16–24). Men may fall into the same trap, and the directives would be the same if they do. Women should adorn themselves with "good works" (1 Tim. 2:10), and such good works demonstrate that women "worship God."

Paul then addresses women teaching in public worship. We know that women prayed and prophesied in the assembly (1 Cor. 11:5), and thus Paul's instructions should not be construed as an absolute prohibition of women speaking. Indeed, he begins by encouraging women to learn (cf. Luke 10:38–42), which was contrary to the views of some rabbis in Jesus's day. Paul believes women should be educated and trained in the Scriptures, and men who think women should not be in seminary or receive biblical training fail to grasp the import of this exhortation. At the same time, women should learn submissively (cf. 1 Cor. 14:34). Submission has a bad reputation today, but all believers are called upon to submit to God's authority and rule in their lives. Ultimately, women are enjoined to submit to God's authority, which is mediated through the elders/overseers (cf. 1 Tim. 3:1–7; 5:17; Titus 1:5–9) in the congregation. The elders/overseers were fallible, of course, and correction may be in order (cf. 1 Tim. 5:19–20). Still, we must recognize in our antiauthoritarian culture that God has ordained certain structures.

In 2:12 Paul says he doesn't "permit" (ESV) women "to teach or to have authority over a man." Virtually every word is contested today. Some think the prohibition is temporary since Paul uses a present-tense first-person singular form of the verb "permit." This claim should be rejected since Paul often uses first-person singular forms for commands that have ongoing authority (e.g., Rom. 12:1; 1 Cor. 1:10; 1 Tim. 2:1, 8). Whether the command is limited in its extent must be discerned from context, not its tense.

Debating the meaning of the verb "to have authority" (*authentein*) is a virtual cottage industry. Scholars today dispute whether the verb has a positive or negative nuance: does it mean "have authority" or "domineer"? If it means domineer, then there would be a place for women to exercise authority in a fitting way. Still, recent research shows that the verb means "exercise authority," and not "usurp authority" or even "assume authority" (NIV). It has been shown in paired constructions where we have two items closely related ("teach" and "have authority") that both items are either negative or positive. In other words, Paul is either saying: "I don't permit a woman to teach false doctrine or domineer men," or "I don't permit a woman to teach or have authority over a man." Since the word "teach" is always a positive word in the Pastoral Epistles, it is clear that the latter is in view. In other words, both teaching and exercising authority are good in and of themselves, but women are prohibited from doing such in the congregation. Instead of teaching and exercising authority, they are to be "quiet," which doesn't mean that they are to be absolutely silent, but they are to have "a gentle and quiet spirit" (1 Pet. 3:4).

Does this injunction still apply today? Some matters in Scripture don't apply in the same way in our context today. Slaves are enjoined to submit to masters, but virtually no one today would endorse slavery as a social system. Many interpreters think the prohibition here should be treated in a similar way. It is important, however, to recognize differences between slavery and what is said here. Slavery is an evil human institution, which is not endorsed in the Scriptures. To put it another way, slavery is regulated but never recommended. The relationship between men and women, however, was established by God at creation. So, it is telling that Paul appeals to creation, to Adam being formed before Eve, which clearly draws on the creation account in Genesis 2:21–23. Since Paul supports the notion that women should not teach or have authority over men from God's good creation, the command here represents a transcendent norm. When biblical writers appeal to creation, we have a norm that still applies today. Thus, Jesus points to the creation of Adam and Eve to teach that marriage is between one man and one woman for life (Matt. 19:3–12). Paul draws on creation to argue that same-sex relations are contrary to God's will (Rom. 1:26–27), that marriage is good (1 Tim. 4:3–5), and that food is a gift from God (1 Cor. 10:25–26).

Some argue that the prohibition against women teaching was temporary, arguing that women were not allowed to teach since they were led astray by the heresy, or they were propagating the false teaching, or they were uneducated. The defect with all of these solutions is that they ignore the reason given in the text (the created order) and substitute a reason not in the text, a reason that could have easily been stated. In fact, the only false teachers mentioned in 1 Timothy are men (1:20), and in a city like Ephesus it is highly unlikely that all the women were uneducated.

The second reason for the prohibition in 2:14 is more difficult to assess. Some have said that women are more prone to deceit than men, and that is why they should not teach. If this is the case, though, we wonder why women can teach other women and children (cf. Titus 2:3). Also, it is difficult to see how Adam's sin was free from deceit since no one sins with their eyes wide open; it seems no one would sin knowing the full consequences. In other words, all sin involves deceit. It seems more likely that Paul, who is writing in brief strokes to his coworker Timothy, is making the point that Eve was deceived first, and yet Adam was held responsible for sin entering the human race (Rom. 5:12–19). The primary responsibility of Adam, in other words, points to the particular role men have in teaching and exercising authority. Satan attempted to subvert male leadership by tempting Eve first.

First Timothy 2:15 doesn't get any easier. The statement that a woman "will be saved through childbearing" is one of the strangest things Paul ever said and seems to contradict the idea that we are saved by grace. Some have tried to solve this by suggesting that Paul thinks of physical preservation, of the lives of women being spared when they give birth. There are two major problems with this reading. First, the verb "saved" is one of Paul's favorites in the Pastoral Epistles, and it always refers to spiritual salvation. Second, many women die in childbirth. Others have suggested that the childbirth is Christ, seeing a fulfillment of the promise of Genesis 3:15. This is a very attractive idea, but if that is what Paul had in mind, he was remarkably unclear in making his point, since most commentators (rightly, in my judgment) have missed the connection!

What does Paul have in mind? The word "saved" means spiritual salvation, but Paul isn't teaching that women must have children to be saved. This would blatantly contradict 1 Corinthians 7, where he recommends that women remain single. We need to remember the situation addressed here, where the differences between men and women are considered. What separates men from women most dramatically, to put it bluntly, is that women can have babies and men can't. What it means for a woman to be saved is to live out her life as a woman, fulfilling her calling, which often means having children. The reference to babies is an example of the part for the whole, and thus Paul immediately explains that what is necessary for salvation is perseverance. Those who "continue in faith, love, and holiness" and are sensible will be saved.

Qualifications for Overseers (3:1–7)

If the church is to manage the storms precipitated by false teachers, if it is to maintain the gospel, it needs godly leaders. We have the second trustworthy statement here, and Paul commends those who have the desire to be an overseer. The word "overseer" describes the same office as the term "elder" (cf. Acts 20:17, 28; Titus 1:5, 7). The desire to be an overseer, which Paul commends, isn't a selfish desire to rule over others or to be noticed or to live a comfortable life. It is a noble desire since it reflects eagerness to serve and help others in the gospel of Jesus Christ.

It is quite remarkable that Paul says very little about what overseers *do* and focuses on character qualifications for the office, showing that godly character is the most important requirement for serving. Two qualities are required of overseers that aren't mentioned with deacons: the ability to teach (1 Tim.

3:2) and managing the church (3:5). Remarkably, these are the two actions forbidden for women in 2:12, showing that women should not function as overseers. Overseers must have the ability to teach the Scriptures, and they are to lead and manage the church. Such leadership must not be tyrannical and overbearing; Paul compares it to caring for one's own household, and he warns elsewhere against exasperating children (Eph. 6:4; Col. 3:21). Overseers should be leaders, but there is both a toughness and a tenderness in the leadership, strength and conviction, and love and gentleness.

If we back up to the character qualifications, we see the overarching need: overseers must be "above reproach" (1 Tim. 3:2). The requirement should not be confused with perfection; it means that there are no evident grounds for denial of the office, and there are many positive reasons to commend the person. The character qualifications represent quick bullet points, which Timothy can fill in from his knowledge of and ministry with Paul. The list isn't intended to be comprehensive, and what is listed is actually expected of all Christians. The list shouldn't be interpreted in a rigid way. For instance, Paul doesn't require that all elders be married, for he would hardly think that Jesus and he were disqualified from serving, especially when he recommends the single life! (1 Cor. 7).

The meaning of "the husband of one wife" is disputed (1 Tim. 3:2). Some think Paul disallows polygamy, and that is surely included, though it probably wasn't at the forefront of his mind since polygamy was rare in Paul's day. Another argument against a direct reference to polygamy is the parallel phrase in 1 Timothy 5:9, "the wife of one husband." In making this comment Paul certainly wasn't thinking of polyandry, for it was nonexistent, and thus we have good grounds to think that he had something else in mind in saying that a husband should be a "one-woman man." Others think he disallows one who is divorced and remarried, and that is certainly possible. It is more likely, however, that divorce and remarriage don't automatically rule someone out. After all, Paul also says that one must not be a drunkard (3:3), but by this he doesn't mean that one was never enslaved to alcohol, but that they have had a good track record for a number of years with respect to that issue. He probably has the same idea in mind regarding marriage: a man is qualified to serve as an overseer if he has been a faithful husband for a number of years, and if his marriage is respected in the church and in the community.

A quick look at the character qualities indicates the nature of those who are to be appointed as overseers. They exercise self-control and are respectable and sensible (3:2). Some might think these qualities are rather ordinary, but those who day in and day out live in such a way stand out for their consistency and godliness. Overseers should also be hospitable, indicating that they are willing to sacrifice their time and privacy for the sake of assisting others. An overseer must have control of his appetites; Paul did not practice abstinence, but those who drink too much wine and live for pleasure are excluded. In the same way, an overseer must not be an authoritarian bully (like Diotrephes in 3 John 9–10!), and they are to be strong but gentle and humble too. If they regularly fight and quarrel and are always drawn into arguments, they aren't fit for the office. Believers are to contend for the truth, but they are not to be contentious. Those who have a love for money should be rejected, for overseers are to be generous and giving, not inclined to hoard their money.

Earlier we mentioned that overseers are to manage their household well, and their children should be obedient (1 Tim. 3:4–5). This should not be understood to say that their children are perfect and that the family has a joyless and cheerless martinet-like feeling. Healthy families are full of joy and obedience, happiness and order. If a child is wild and regularly out of control, if people in the church dread their presence, the household isn't in order. Paul isn't requiring perfect probity but healthy and joyful obedience.

New converts should be avoided because they are prone to pride: they don't have enough experience to recognize their own sinfulness and weakness, and they may begin to believe, to use an old saying, their own press clippings. The devil sinned because of pride as well, and it is the root sin, and thus refusing to appoint someone who is a relatively new believer will spare them from a potential downfall. Last, it is important that overseers have a good reputation with outsiders. If unbelievers are aware that the overseer appointed cheats in business or acts in unprofessional ways with others, they scorn the church and bring reproach upon it.

Qualifications for Deacons (3:8–13)

The order and structure of the church continues to be explained, as Paul outlines the qualifications for deacons. It is remarkable that we know so little about the tasks of deacons (cf. Phil. 1:1), and once again, the character of those who serve receives the emphasis. Two things are said about overseers that are omitted with reference to deacons: the ability to teach and to lead the church. Certainly the list is representative and not exhaustive, but the omission of these two qualifications is significant. Deacons serve the church in numerous ways, and the lack of specificity gives churches freedom today to appoint deacons to serve in finances, ordinances, hospitality, care of the sick, and all sorts of practical ministries.

The character required is not a cut below what is expected of overseers but reaches the same level. Their lives should match their profession of faith, and they should not be enslaved to alcohol or the love of money (1 Tim. 3:8). Doctrinally, they must hold on to the faith with a whole heart and gladness (3:9). The church must be careful about appointing someone to serve without testing and examining them. Those who serve as deacons should be proven and well known in their character.

We see in verse 12 that male deacons have the same requirements as overseers with regard to their families. They must be faithful husbands and guide their children so that they are not running out of control. Those who serve as deacons "acquire a good standing for themselves" (3:13). It is difficult to know if Paul has in mind this life or the life to come, or perhaps both, and serving in such a way will also increase their boldness and confidence.

Scholars dispute whether wives or female deacons are referred to in verse 11. I think a reference to female deacons is more likely. Such a reference doesn't violate the admonition in 1 Timothy 2:12 since deacons don't teach or exercise authority but serve the congregation in a multitude of ways, and anyone who has been in churches knows how women serve sacrificially and remarkably. The arguments supporting female deacons are as follows: (1) The character requirements are the same that are mandated for men. (2) The word "too" or "likewise" most naturally means that the women, just like the men, were deacons. (3) If Paul wanted to specify "wives," he could have easily added, as he does elsewhere, the words "their" or "their own." The lack of such possessives tilts us to seeing a reference to deacons. (4) We would expect Paul, above all, to emphasize the character qualities required for the wives of overseers, since overseers manage the church and serve as teachers. It is quite strange that he would only emphasize wives of deacons, but if he refers to female deacons, then what we have here makes perfect sense. (5) Phoebe was almost certainly a deacon of the church in Cenchreae (Rom. 16:1). (6) There were female deacons very early in the second century (Pliny the Younger, *Letters* 10.96).

The requirements for female deacons are restricted to four items, but we have to remember that Paul wrote in bullet points to his trusted friend and confidant. In the middle of his discussion on male deacons, he reminds Timothy of the role of female deacons (1 Tim. 3:11). Like the men they are to be respectable, and they must not slander and tear down the reputations of others. Like men who hold office, they should exhibit self-control and be reliable and trustworthy.

Right Conduct in God's House (3:14-16)

Paul wrote with the hope that he could come soon, but if delayed, he wanted Timothy and others to have a short handbook so that they would "conduct themselves" well in "God's household." The "household" here probably refers to the temple, as is often the case in the OT (e.g., 2 Sam. 7:5, 6, 7; 1 Kings 3:2; 5:18; 6:2; 1 Chron. 22:1; Ezra 6:3; Ps. 122:1; Hosea 8:1; Joel 1:13; Mic. 1:2; etc.), but now God's temple "is the church of the living God" (1 Tim. 3:15). The church, as "the pillar and foundation of the truth," is a bulwark for the gospel in the world. The gospel creates the church, and yet the church preserves the gospel; and if the church swerves from the truth, the witness of the gospel suffers.

The truth of the gospel leads Paul to a confessional or hymnic statement (3:16), written by him or perhaps someone else. Godliness is a mystery that has now been revealed in Jesus Christ, which perhaps means that it is now clear that the only way to godliness is through Jesus Christ, that human beings need God to be godly! The confessional statement has six lines and begins with the incarnation: Jesus came in the flesh, with a human body. One of the most wondrous truths of all is that God became man, that he assumed humanity in the flesh and blood of Jesus Christ. Paul doesn't dwell on the cross but on Jesus's vindication, which was accomplished "in the Spirit." Jesus's resurrection verifies his "justification," functioning as the public statement that God acknowledged his messianic status and his righteousness. As the risen one, as the one who reigns over all, he was "seen by angels," and Jesus is heralded among the nations as the crucified and risen Lord. He is the only Lord, and there is salvation in no one else (Acts 4:12). Not everyone everywhere believes, but the preaching of Jesus as Lord leads to belief in him as Messiah and Lord throughout the world. Paul concludes with Jesus's ascension, the glory he now enjoys at the Father's right hand.

Warning about Demonic Teaching (4:1-5)

One reason the church needs leaders it can trust both morally and doctrinally is the advent of false teaching. The mystery of godliness summarized in 1 Timothy 3:16 is unfortunately denied by many. The Holy Spirit specifically taught, perhaps in a prophecy given to Paul, that "in later times some will depart from the faith" (4:1). The last days had arrived with Jesus's death and resurrection (cf. Acts 2:17; 1 John 2:18; Heb. 1:2), and thus Paul wasn't looking to a far-off future day; some teachers were deviating from the truth of the gospel in his day, influencing people who likely thought that what they believed was true and good. Yet Paul identifies it as stemming from "deceitful spirits" and "demons." The invisible source for their deception was demons, but the immediate source was false teachers who were hypocrites and liars (1 Tim. 4:2). They had become so accustomed to evil that their "consciences [were] seared."

They believed they were pure because they advocated asceticism, prohibited marriage, and banned the eating of certain foods (4:3). Actually, however, marriage and foods are both good and beautiful, and Paul appeals to God's creation in support. The foods "God created" are to be received with thanksgiving and praise by believers, who embrace the truth of the gospel. In saying that everything "God created is good . . . if it is received with thanksgiving" (4:4), Paul isn't arguing that taking drugs or using pornography is permissible if one is grateful. We have to stick with the context, and his point is that marriage and foods are good gifts given to believers and to all people by the creator God. Foods are "sanctified," set apart and consecrated as good, by God's word (4:5), which most likely refers back to Genesis 1:31 and God's declaration that all that he created was "very good." In Jewish circles it was also a typical practice to give thanks for food, and by giving thanks it is acknowledged that every good gift comes from God's hand.

Timothy's Responsibility to Teach (4:6–16)

Timothy was Christ's "servant" and didn't rule over the Ephesian church, but he had a particular responsibility to remind them of the truth. A right understanding of the faith is nourishing and strengthening. Unfortunately, those with seared consciences were fascinated with "myths" that are "pointless and silly" (1 Tim. 4:7). We wish we knew more about their teaching, but Paul doesn't bother to give us more information, probably because he thought it was quite useless. Timothy should focus on and "train" himself in "godliness" (4:7). Some intellectual teaching is practically worthless, and one way to determine this is if it has no effect on or detracts from godly living.

Physical training and exercise have some value, especially in a world where some Christians are overweight or fall prey to gluttony. Still, godliness is far more important, which is a word that speaks to many who worship health and physical fitness. Godliness is more important because those who are godly through faith in Jesus Christ enjoy now the life of the age to come and are also promised life in the future (4:8). Putting one's focus on a body that will die is massively shortsighted when compared to eternity. It is difficult to discern the content of the faithful saying in verse 9: is Paul pointing backward or forward? Perhaps resolving this issue doesn't matter since both verses refer in one way or another to life in the age to come. Paul didn't labor and strive in athletics or physical competitions. He set his sights and fixed his hopes on "the living God" (4:10). God is "the Savior of all," especially believers. What Paul means by this is disputed. We can rule out universalism, for there would be no need to add that believers are especially saved if all people are saved! Some have argued that "Savior" doesn't refer to spiritual salvation here, but that is quite improbable, for the word refers to spiritual salvation everywhere else in the Pastorals, and salvation is one of his favorite themes in this letter. Paul probably means that salvation is available for all people groups, Jews and gentiles, but only becomes a reality for believers.

Once again, Timothy is enjoined to "command and teach these things" (4:11), which probably goes back to the instructions in verses 7–10. Timothy can't prevent anyone from despising him for his youthfulness, yet the admonition wasn't just for Timothy's ears but for the entire congregation (4:12). What it means to be young is relative since different cultures have different estimates of the matter. Paul was probably in his 60s, and Timothy may have been, if converted when a teenager, in his early 30s. If Timothy conducted himself in a way that was notable and praiseworthy, he would win people's respect. When the congregation meets, the Scriptures should be read publicly, for what was publicly read was considered to be authoritative (4:13). It is fascinating today, and lamentable, that so many churches conduct services without reading the Scriptures publicly. The gathered congregation should also give time for "exhortation," which is probably a designation for preaching. Attention must also be given to "teaching" since the church needs regular and edifying instruction.

The reading, preaching, and teaching were to be carried out by Timothy himself, and Paul reminds him of the gift bestowed on him when the elders laid hands on him (4:14; cf. 2 Tim. 1:6). A prophecy given at the same time confirmed that Timothy was gifted in such a way, and he must not allow his gift to lie fallow. Timothy must give himself to these matters wholly and be absorbed in ministry, and his spiritual progress will be obvious. Verse 16 nicely sums up Paul's concern. Timothy (and all who minister) must guard his life and his teaching. Both are of prime importance, for right understanding of truth and application of truth to life are essential for ministry and the Christian life. Perseverance and endurance are imperative, and they are necessary for eschatological salvation. Paul is scarcely talking about earning one's salvation, since he has made it more than clear that Christ saves sinners (1 Tim. 1:12–17). Still, no one will be saved on the last day who abandons the faith and who gives themselves over to sin. The false teachers had turned astray, and unless they repented, they would not inherit an eternal reward. Timothy's perseverance in these matters wasn't for himself alone, but his ministry would also be the means by which those who heard him would be saved.

The Church as a Family (5:1–2)

Relationships in the church are like relationships in the family, and the extended family is a model for how we should treat one another as believers. Here the instructions are given to Timothy as a younger man, but each person can apply the text, taking into consideration their own age and gender. As a younger person, Timothy should respect older men, and thus he should not upbraid or reprove them sharply. Instead, he should entreat and appeal to them gently. Younger men should not be reproved harshly either, but the relationship is different, and they should be treated as brothers. Older women should be treated with the respect, honor, and deference granted to mothers. Younger women are to be exhorted as sisters, but here Paul wisely adds "with all purity." Sexual desires continue, and lust is a common temptation, thus Timothy should guard his heart and his actions so that he doesn't give way to sin.

Honor Widows (5:3–16)

What it means for a church to be a caring family is evident by the concern for widows and their well-being in 1 Timothy 5:3–16. The importance of providing for the needs of widows and ensuring that they are treated justly is prominent in the OT (e.g., Exod. 22:22; Deut. 10:18; 26:12–13; Job 22:9; 31:18; Pss. 68:5; 146:9; Jer. 7:6; 22:3; Ezek. 22:7; Zech. 4:10; Mal. 3:5; cf. also James 1:27). The honoring of widows focuses on but is not restricted to their need for financial support. The church, however, should not be the first line of support for widows. Family members of the widows are obligated to provide for the needs of widows before turning to the church (1 Tim. 5:3–4, 16). Circles of responsibility are established so that a family with sufficient funds cares for widows instead of absolving themselves of responsibility and transferring the widow to the church's care. If a family has the funds, they should not pawn off care for their own family circle to the church. They show their godliness by caring for the everyday needs of loved ones. The extraordinary importance of the whole matter surfaces in verse 8. Those who do not provide for widows have "denied the faith" and are "worse than an unbeliever." Those who refuse to help a widow in the family deny Christ and are repudiating the Christian faith.

Not all widows can depend upon family members for assistance. If widows are devoted to the things of God and in need of daily provisions, the church should step in and render aid. Discerning whether two different categories of widows are in view in 1 Timothy 5:3–16 is difficult. Some believe that needy widows are discussed in verses 3–8, and in verses 9–15 a special order of widows, those involved in ministry, are in view. The widows in verses 9–15 are even seen by some as wealthy widows, who function as patronesses. Arguments supporting an order of widows are as follows: (1) An age limit is prescribed in verses 9–15 but not in verses 3–8, suggesting a distinction between the two groups. (2) The language of enrolling (v. 9) and refusing to enroll (v. 11) may refer to a process by which qualified widows were placed on a list. (3) The qualifications for widows in verses 9–10 are similar to the qualifications for elders and deacons (3:1–13), suggesting some kind of official ministry. (4) Younger widows are prohibited (vv. 11–15) because they are unable to sustain their vows of celibacy, and such vows were required to enter the order.

Detecting a separate order of widows is quite attractive, and it solves some problems in the text. It seems on balance, however, that the same group of widows is in view in both verses 3–8 and 9–16, so that a separate order of widows is not in view. Several arguments support this interpretation: (1) Evidence for a break between the widows of verses 3–8 and verses 9–15 is difficult to discern. It is scarcely clear that a new category of widows is addressed in verse 9. (2) The words "enrolled" and "refuse" (vv. 9, 11) more likely refer to being put on the list to receive financial support. Some kind of official action of the church is contemplated, but these words in themselves don't necessitate a reference to an official order of widows devoted to ministry. (3) The sixty-year age limit indicates an age in which the energy of women was decreasing, so that their need for support was increasing. Before the age of sixty, presumably, Paul feels that other sources of support were possible for most widows. Paul doesn't absolutely prohibit helping widows less than sixty years of age. Here we have a guideline, not an inflexible rule. Thus, being at least sixty years old speaks against an order of ministry, for such widows had less energy for ministry, not more. (4) The reference to character qualities (vv. 9–10) doesn't necessarily suggest an office, for verse 5 indicates that widows worthy of support must be devoted to prayer and to set their hope on God. Verses 9–10 elaborate, then, the character requirements already suggested in verse 5. (5) The strongest argument for seeing an order of widows is the vow of celibacy pledged by the younger women (5:11–15). But it is also possible that by remarrying, such women gave up a life of prayer enabled by the financial resources of the church. Paul has learned that these younger women are devoting themselves to activities other than prayer, so he counsels remarriage and the raising of children (vv. 13–15).

If the reference is to needy widows throughout, we see how important such support was for Paul. Older widows, who are godly, are to be helped financially. We might wonder why Paul doesn't include all widows who are older and in need. Why the character qualifications? Perhaps to ensure that only widows who were genuine believers in Christ received the assistance. Funds were presumably limited, and the church had to concentrate on meeting specific needs since it lacked the finances to meet all needs. It is not that in principle Paul opposes helping needy unbelievers. He advocates (as we have seen in both Galatians 6:10b and 1 Timothy 5:3–16) circles of responsibility.

Believers should first support their own family members and fellow believers, and then if funds permit, support for others should be given. Such an approach is not selfish. Any community that doesn't care for its own will eventually cease caring for anyone.

Another word should be said about character qualifications. Since resources are limited, women who have a long track record of faithfulness should be supported (5:9–10). They had faithful marriages, were recognized for raising their children well, were generous and hospitable, and devoted themselves to good work. It seems that some younger widows (5:12) had promised not to marry and had received church funds, and then turned around and got married. Some of these younger women who had energy and time on their hands (since they were supported by the church) turned to gossip and meddling in the lives of others. We might think Paul frowned upon them marrying (5:11–12), but he actually wanted them to marry and to raise children (5:14). What bothered him is that they promised one thing and did another, yet all the time they were receiving church funds. The witness of the church was compromised when some gave themselves over to sin and Satan (5:14–15).

Honoring Elders (5:17–25)

Paul's concern in the letter is that the church be the church, that leaders guide the church in a wise and godly way so that the church would be a vibrant witness to the world. He returns to the matter of elders, which is the same office as "overseer" (cf. Acts 20:17, 28; Titus 1:5), presumably because elders play such a vital role in the life of the church. Elders, as we saw earlier, are distinctive in that they lead and teach, and the entirety of the Pastoral Epistles shows how important teaching and preaching are in this whole venture. In any case, those who carry out this ministry well should receive "double honor," which probably means adequate pay and respect (not double pay!). The payment of elders is supported from Deuteronomy 25:4, and this must have been a favorite verse of Paul regarding financial support since he also quotes it in 1 Corinthians 9:9. The argument is from the lesser to the greater. If oxen shouldn't be restrained from eating while working, then ministers certainly deserve support. The second Scripture, which reflects the authority of Jesus's words, passes on the instruction of Jesus to those whom he sent out for mission: "The worker is worthy of his wages." The saying is closer to the wording of Luke 10:7, but is not far from Matthew 10:10. We see an early indication of the authority of Jesus's words, and they confirm the idea that churches should attempt to support financially at least one person to preach the word.

Life as a leader is complicated and fraught with controversy. Accusations may fly, and Paul appeals to the OT requirement for two or three witnesses (cf. Deut. 17:6; 19:15), which ensures that no charge will be accepted unless it is substantiated by evidence. Lies, libel, and slander are sadly common, and churches must be careful before accepting a false report about a leader. On the other hand, elders who sin in a way that warrants rebuke and correction should be reproved publicly. Significant and blatant sins by leaders (sexual infidelity, financial corruption, abuse of others) should not be excused or swept under the rug. When the congregation sees that sin is taken seriously, the rest, which probably means the entire congregation, will fear. The congregation will recognize that the leaders take sin seriously, and this will provoke them to do the same.

Paul's instructions might seem prosaic, but they are to be taken with the utmost seriousness, and thus the instructions in 5:17–20 are to be carried out without favoritism or partiality. This could operate on a number of levels. An elder whom someone likes could be granted more pay, or conversely personal animus could deprive an elder of pay that is warranted. On the other hand, sometimes leadership in a church becomes cocooned and corrupted. It becomes an "old boys' club," which becomes self-protective, and thus leaders who sin are protected out of partiality.

Leaders play a crucial role in the church, and thus elders should not be appointed rashly and quickly. A person's life should be carefully evaluated, and he should be known before being selected (1 Tim. 3:1–7). If someone who is not qualified takes office, those who appointed him share in some of the responsibility for the missteps of the one appointed. Purity doesn't merely involve one's own life but also has to do with how one relates with others. The reference to purity leads Paul to make a comment to Timothy. For whatever reason, Timothy was abstaining from wine (perhaps for ascetic reasons?), and Paul encourages him to drink some wine to ameliorate his stomach problems, which apparently bothered him frequently.

Understanding Paul's point in 5:24–25 isn't easy. He teaches that some evil and good works are easy to discern, but in other cases what is evil and good will only be discerned later. Perhaps Paul's point is that God will reveal and make all things right in the end. Others think he assures Timothy that appointing a good person as a leader is in some cases rather obvious, but in other instances the goodness or badness of a person will only be apparent later on. Timothy should not fret about appointing a person to be a leader if everything seems to be in order, and then that person apostatizes later.

Instructions to Slaves (6:1–2a)

Some brief instructions are given to slaves here. It has been noted earlier that Paul never endorses or commends slavery but regulates an existing evil institution. If slaves are able to get their freedom, they should do so (1 Cor. 7:21). Within the existing society, Paul doesn't advocate societal revolution but a transformation of society from within. Slaves, therefore, are instructed to honor their masters, and in doing so to fulfill their responsibility. The purpose for the admonition is so that God's name and the teaching of the gospel should not be reviled. If masters are believers, it might be tempting to think that brotherhood and equality in the gospel lessen the call to serve. Slaves might even be inclined to treat their masters with disrespect. Actually, however, they should serve their masters all the more since the masters, who are the beneficiaries of their service, are themselves believers and beloved by God.

Warning regarding False Teachers (6:2b–10)

Reproduced in the table below is Robert Yarbrough's chart showing how the end of 1 Timothy recalls matters addressed at the beginning. The beginning and end of the letter feature the same themes, impressing their importance on the readers.

1:3 Charge to stay at Ephesus	6:2b Charge to teach and uphold the faith
1:4–7 Issue (false teachers) and commendation of love	6:3–6 Issue (false teachers) and commendation of godliness
1:8–10 Proper use of the OT (law)	6:7–10 Proper regard for money (see also vv. 17–19)
1:11–16 Testimony: Paul was saved by Christ, not law	6:11–15a Appeal: Timothy should lay hold of eternal life in Christ, who also made the good confession
1:17 Doxology	6:15b–16 Doxology
1:18–20 Application: charge to Timothy confirmed, with warning regarding those who have rejected the faith	6:17–19 Application: charge confirmed to the wealthy under Timothy's leadership and to Timothy himself, with warning regarding those who have rejected the faith

Source: Robert W. Yarbrough, *The Letters to Timothy and Titus*, PNTC (Grand Rapid: Eerdmans, 2018), 305.

As the letter comes to a close, Paul reminds Timothy of a major theme in the letter: he must teach and encourage people regarding the things Paul has said in the letter. This teaching is important because some are teaching false doctrines (cf. 1 Tim. 1:3). They aren't eating and drinking from the healthy words that come from the Lord Jesus Christ, but they are paying attention to words that are sick and diseased, which don't lead to godliness (6:3). The root problem can be traced to the life of such teachers; they are "conceited," and though they are proud of their knowledge, they really know nothing at all (6:4). They mistake their love for debates and disputes as knowledge, but actually they are giving birth to jealousy, fighting, evil talk, wicked conjectures, and ongoing disagreements. Their minds are "depraved and deprived" (6:5). And behind it all is a desire for advancement and prosperity.

True advancement, true gain, is when there is "godliness with contentment" (6:6). Those who are discerning and wise realize that we will leave the world the same way we entered it: with nothing at all (6:7). Thus we should be content with food and clothing during this present life (6:8). The desire for riches poses a great danger since it can take over one's life and lead one to eternal destruction (6:9). Here Paul reminds us of Jesus, who gave so many warnings about the peril of riches, teaching that one could gain the world but lose one's soul (Matt. 16:26). Making money, even enjoying the fruits of money, isn't evil, but loving money begets "all kinds of evil" (6:10). By desiring money, some have fallen away from the faith, from the gospel, and they have impaled themselves—lanced themselves, so to speak—with sorrow upon sorrow (cf. Matt. 13:22).

Admonition to Timothy (6:11–16)

Given the great danger before him, Paul turns to Timothy and warns him to keep pursuing the right way. In calling him "man of God," we are reminded of some of the notable leaders in the OT who are called "man of God," such as Moses (Deut. 33:1; Josh. 14:6), various prophets (1 Sam. 2:27; 1 Kings 12:22; 13:1, 2, 4; 20:28), Samuel (1 Sam. 9:6, 7, 8, 10), Elijah (1 Kings 17:18, 24; 2 Kings 1:9), Elisha (2 Kings 4:7, 9; 5:8), and David (Neh. 12:24). Paul isn't saying that Timothy has the stature of these men, but he does point to the important role Timothy plays as a spokesman for the Lord. As God's man, Timothy should flee from any desire to get rich: instead he should "pursue righteousness, godliness, faith, love, endurance, and gentleness" (1 Tim. 6:11). Character qualities are of much more importance than riches, and their benefit is eternal. Timothy must "fight the good fight of the faith" and "take hold of eternal life" (6:12). In other words, he must actively maintain what he already has and continue to make a "good confession," as he did on the day he confessed Jesus Christ in the presence of others. The validity of the confession made at the beginning is ratified by a confession continually made until the end.

The solemnity and awesomeness of the charge to Timothy is underscored by invoking the presence of the creator God and Jesus Christ, which is another striking example of putting Jesus on the same level as God himself

(6:13). God is the creator, and Christ is adduced here as an example, for he made the "good confession" before Pontius Pilate, who was the procurator of Judea in AD 26–36. Paul doesn't often refer to events in the earthly life of Jesus, and the good confession here includes the idea of testifying to the truth when under duress and threat. Since Timothy lives in the presence of God and Christ, and since Christ functions as his example, Timothy is enjoined "to keep this command" without blemish (6:14), which probably is another way of saying that he should keep the good confession until Christ appears. The end will come at the time God ordains and sees fit, at the perfect time, in accord with his own wisdom (6:15). Paul is moved to doxology (cf. 1:17), recognizing God's blessedness and his sovereignty over all rulers and kings and lords. Inherent and intrinsic immortality is reserved for God alone, for he is the God who gives life and takes life (6:16). And he is so glorious, majestic, and splendid that no one can approach the blinding light and beauty of his presence apart from grace. He is the matchless God, whom no creature can see, and thus all glory and power belong to him.

Words for the Rich (6:17–19)

Those who are rich and successful can fall into thinking that they rule over life since their riches protect them from many ills, and thus they must be vigilant and not give way to pride, as if they have secured their own lives and their future. Riches can easily become an idol on which people set their hope, but they are a vain and unstable god since wealth can vanish quickly. Instead, people should put their hope for the future entirely on God, and God doesn't demand that people live a world-denying life, for he "richly provides us with all things to enjoy" (6:17). Those who are rich have a special opportunity to be generous with others, to help those who are deprived and suffering, and thus riches are to be enjoyed, but they must not become a means by which one focuses on one's own comforts. By giving generously to others, the rich store up treasure for the age that never ends (6:19), which reminds us of Jesus's teaching about storing up treasures in heaven (Matt. 6:19–20). Then they will take hold of true life, everlasting life. Eternal life is a gift that shows itself in the generous way of life of the rich.

Final Admonition to Timothy (6:20–21)

The ending of the letter is remarkably abrupt, and perhaps its brevity can be chalked up to Paul's situation and to his relationship with Timothy. Timothy has received a rough sketch from Paul and can fill in the details. Paul's affection for Timothy surfaces in the words "O Timothy" (1 Tim. 6:20 ESV). With false teachers threatening, Timothy must "guard what has been entrusted" to him: he must guard the gospel. The words of the false teachers may be "called knowledge" by them, but for Paul they were nothing but "godless chatter" (6:20 NIV), and such words have nothing to do with true knowledge. Those who embrace their teaching have swerved from the faith, and Timothy is called upon to be a bulwark and a steadying hand amid the tumult. For that he will need God's grace, and that grace is conveyed through the letter and was Timothy's constant need for the whole of life.

See after Titus for a combined bibliography of the Pastoral Letters (1 and 2 Timothy, Titus).

CHAPTER TWELVE

2 Timothy

Introduction

As stated in the introduction to 1 Timothy, I understand all the Pastoral Epistles to be authentically written by Paul. We can only speculate about the precise circumstances of 2 Timothy. Along with many, I support the traditional view that Paul was released from his first Roman imprisonment and then was arrested again and imprisoned in Rome. Second Timothy reflects his second imprisonment, and Paul realizes that this time, in contrast to his first imprisonment in Rome (cf. Phil. 1:22–24; Philem. 22), he won't be released. Paul was probably executed with a Roman sword around AD 67, and thus this letter was his last literary offering. One outline for 2 Timothy could be as follows, but see the headings for more precision.

Outline

Guard the gospel	1:1–18
Suffer for the gospel	2:1–26
Avoid those who are evil and imitate those who are good	3:1–17
Proclaim the word until the end	4:1–18

Greeting (1:1–2)

Even though Paul writes a personal letter to Timothy, he identifies himself as an apostle because the letter is for the church (perhaps in Ephesus again) as well and bears all the marks of apostolic authority. Paul's apostolic authority isn't self-generated but expresses God's will, which is an allusion to what happened on the road to Damascus: in that event Paul was called to be an apostle. Paul's calling was to spread and further "the promise of life in Christ Jesus." It is hard to imagine a greater calling than to be able to tell people where true life may be found. Paul writes to Timothy, whom we discussed in the opening of 1 Timothy. Timothy was especially beloved by Paul and was a "son" to him in the faith, and certainly their relationship was closer than what we find in many families. Paul prays for grace, mercy, and peace from God the Father and the Lord Jesus Christ.

Thanksgiving (1:3–5)

As usual the greeting is followed by a thanksgiving, and here Paul gives personal and heartfelt thanks for Timothy, whom he regularly remembers in his prayers. We would love to know the occasion for Timothy's tears, but unfortunately Paul felt no need to elaborate since both Timothy and he knew exactly what he was talking about. What does come across is the remarkably close relationship between Paul and Timothy, and thus Paul longs to see Timothy again so that he will be filled with joy.

History also plays a role here. Paul is thankful that his conscience is clear and that he belongs to a long lineage of ancestors before him who served God. Clearly, Paul doesn't think that the Christian faith is cut off from the OT. Instead, it finds its roots in and fulfills OT revelation. Timothy was part of that history, too, because the faith he has can be traced back to his grandmother and mother. There is a baton of faith that has been passed down from generation to generation, from family to family. The history of Israel is often characterized by unfaithfulness, and yet God's truth survived and continues to be proclaimed from generation to generation.

Guard the Gospel (1:6–14)

Since Timothy follows in the path of his ancestors who suffered greatly for their faithfulness, he is summoned to stir up afresh the gift he received when Paul laid hands on him. We probably have the same event noted in 1 Timothy 4:14, relayed here from a more personal perspective. We don't have a call for autonomous courage and strength since God has granted courage, power, love, and sensibility to those who are his (2 Tim. 1:7). Given God's promise to strengthen his own, to give courage instead of fear and love instead of hate, Timothy should not "be ashamed" of the testimony *about* the Lord, or perhaps it means the testimony *given* by the Lord (1:8). Since Paul languished in prison, it would be tempting, especially in an honor-shame culture, to conveniently forget that one knew him. Timothy must, by God's strength and grace, give himself to suffering for the sake of the gospel, the message that brings life to the world.

In verses 9–10, where there is a creedal-type statement, the nature of the gospel is unpacked. God saves and calls, he delivers from sin, and he draws people to himself. Believers are called to holiness, but salvation is not based on works but on God's sovereign purpose, will, and grace. Truly, salvation is of the Lord, since he planned to grant grace to those who are his before history began. What was planned so long ago has now been manifested through the appearance of Jesus Christ in history, who has come as the Savior. The gospel is good news because death, the great enemy of human beings (1 Cor. 15:26), has been conquered, and "life and immortality" have dawned through the gospel (2 Tim. 1:10). We can see why Paul calls upon Timothy to suffer for the sake of the gospel, since suffering opens the door to life that will never end. We also understand why it was such a privilege and joy for Paul to be called as an apostle, a herald, and a teacher of this gospel.

Paul wasn't ashamed to suffer for the sake of a message that promises life and salvation. God had entrusted Paul with the gospel, and Paul rested in the truth that God would protect and defend the gospel until the last day (1:12). Since the gospel is the way of life and salvation, Timothy must also hold on to the healthy teaching that Paul taught him (1:13). The same deposit, the same gospel that Paul taught and guarded, must by the power of the Holy Spirit be guarded also by Timothy (1:14). Since the Spirit indwelt Timothy, he had the strength and power to do so.

Onesiphorus: An Example of One Who Was Not Ashamed (1:15–18)

Timothy must not be ashamed of the Lord or of Paul, and Onesiphorus stands out as an example of one who was not ashamed of Paul. Actually, many others deserted Paul in the province of Asia, perhaps when he was arrested, and "Phygelus and Hermogenes" receive dishonorable mention for doing that (1:15). By way of contrast, Onesiphorus, in a day when prisoners needed to be sustained by friends to live, often visited Paul in prison and refreshed him (1:16). He expended effort and time to find out where Paul was held; presumably he could have used the excuse that he didn't know where Paul was "in chains." Onesiphorus's care for and ministry to others was attested by his time in Ephesus. By associating with a prisoner, Onesiphorus could be accused himself, and thus Paul prays that, because of the courage of Onesiphorus, the Lord would show mercy to his household and to One-siphorus himself (1:18).

Call to Suffer (2:1–13)

Imperatives permeate this section, as Timothy is called upon to suffer. He is to follow the pathway of Onesiphorus and be willing to suffer as Christ's messenger. As Paul's dear and beloved son, he needs the strength and the grace that is in Christ to carry out the task before him (2:1). The task is too great for Timothy, so divine enabling is needed. Paul has faithfully passed on to Timothy the gospel, and Timothy has often heard Paul's teaching. Now that Paul is going to be with the Lord, Timothy must take up the challenge and pass on the gospel to those who are reliable and trustworthy, and these in turn will pass on the faith to still others. Faithful teaching will produce new links in the chain generation after generation!

We must not envision a classroom where information is communicated in a safe environment. These instructions are given to those called upon to suffer, and Timothy must join the ranks of those who suffer as soldiers of Christ (2:3). Illustrations from the life of a soldier, athlete, and farmer are given to buttress the point (2:4–6). Soldiers are not called upon to live an easy life. Their goal is to please their commanding officer, and so they must live in a disciplined way and be ready to die for their cause. Similarly, Timothy must not get distracted so that he loses his grip on the gospel. In the same way, athletes don't win a prize if they violate the rules. They must train arduously and strain with every effort to triumph. The emphasis on labor and work continues, for the farmer who labors intensively enjoys the fruit of his labor. The call to think about what is said indicates that Paul wants Timothy to meditate on the illustrations, to let them sink deep into his consciousness (2:7). At the same time, true under-standing comes only from the Lord. We see a marvelous example of divine sovereignty and human responsibility here. On the one hand, we must reflect and think hard with the minds that God has given to us. On the other hand, if we do come to understand what is being said, it is a gift of God. We are reminded of Proverbs 2:1–5, where we are to seek wisdom with all our might, and yet the Lord ultimately is the one who gives wisdom.

The injunction to remember Jesus Christ as the risen one and the son of David is integral to Paul's gospel (2 Tim. 2:8). Paul probably mentions Jesus's resurrection here as the answer to suffering, showing that suffering isn't the last word. Jesus now reigns as the Davidic king, and thus suffering will give way to glory. Meanwhile Paul suffers and is chained as if he were a criminal, though God's word, the gospel of Jesus Christ, isn't bound or restricted (2:9).

Indeed, Paul's suffering actually furthers the gospel, and so he endures suffering for the sake of God's elect, because Paul's suffering becomes a means by which the gospel is proclaimed, and thus the elect through Paul's ministry enjoy salvation and are promised eschatological glory (2:10).

Verses 11–13 constitute a trustworthy statement. Believers have died with Christ, his death is their death and his life is their life, and so they will also live with him. Salvation is by grace, but those who reign and rule with Christ must persevere to the end to enjoy such a role. Those who deny Jesus fully and finally will also be denied by him (Matt. 10:33). The saying should not be interpreted simplistically, for Peter denied Christ but was forgiven when he repented (cf. John 21). Hence Paul (and Jesus) teach that those who deny Jesus and never turn back from that denial (they never deny their denial) will be repudiated on the last day. The meaning of 2 Timothy 2:13 is disputed. Some think that those who are faithless are in the same category as those who deny Jesus, and God's faithfulness is reflected in his rejection of those whose faith fails since God can't deny himself. Such a reading is certainly possible and fits nicely with the statement on denying Jesus. Still, it seems more likely that the last line envisions another reality. There is a kind of faithlessness— that is, there is sin in the lives of believers that doesn't constitute a rejection of Jesus. Such faithlessness, which all believers experience to some extent or another, doesn't mean that a person will be repudiated by God. God remains faithful because he can't deny himself and the promises he has made to his own (Phil. 1:6). The strongest support for this interpretation, which inclines me to think it is correct, is that God's faithfulness in Paul is tied elsewhere to the promise to preserve believers until the end (cf. 1 Cor. 1:9; 10:13; 1 Thess. 5:24; 2 Thess. 3:3). We must distinguish between cases when, on the one hand, someone denies Jesus, and on the other hand a person has temporary faithlessness and defection.

A Proper Response to False Teachers (2:14–26)

Paul turns now to the problem raised by the false teachers. Believers need to be regularly reminded of the truths articulated in 2:8–13 and avoid word battles, which are useless and even eternally destructive. The false teachers promoted that which is empty and profane, and the fruit is even more godlessness. Timothy, and all those who want to be faithful, must be diligent to conduct their ministries in a way approved by God, and there will be such approval and no basis for eschatological shame if the "word of truth," the gospel, is faithfully taught (2:15). False teaching spreads like a cancer (2:17), eating away at what is healthy and turning lives to rot. False teachers aren't often named, but Hymenaeus and Philetus are mentioned here, and it seems likely that we have the same Hymenaeus noted in 1 Timothy 1:20. This is the only occasion in which Philetus is named. Both of these men strayed from the truth of the gospel (2 Tim. 2:18), affirming that the resurrection had already occurred. Apparently they didn't believe in a future physical resurrection, and Paul makes it plain in 1 Corinthians 15:12–19 that such a view is outside the bounds of orthodoxy. Unfortunately, the cancerous teaching and the denial of the resurrection were having an impact, and the faith of some was overturned.

The denial of the faith by some raises the question whether those who belong to God can turn back and abandon the salvation they once had. Paul answers that question starting in 2 Timothy 2:19. God's house, God's temple, stands firm, and this is verified by the citation of Numbers 16:5: "The Lord knows those who are his." The OT context is crucial because here we find the story of Korah, Dathan, and Abiram, who rebelled against the leadership of Aaron and Moses. The account in Numbers 16 reveals who were the Lord's spokesmen and leaders, and the destruction of Korah and his allies demonstrated that they were not the Lord's. Paul's point here is similar. Discerning who belongs to the Lord takes time, but those who gave up their faith were not truly part of God's household, just as Korah and his friends demonstrated that they did not truly belong to the Lord.

Those who truly belong to the Lord, those who are truly his, will turn from wickedness. Here we likely have an allusion to the same story and to Numbers 16:26–27. The people of Israel were instructed to stay away from Korah, Dathan, and Abiram and their families since they had rebelled against the Lord and were about to experience judgment. If any Israelites joined with them, they would face the same fate. So too, believers must not form an alliance or support Hymenaeus and Philetus or their teaching. They are to turn decisively away from their evil.

An illustration from vessels in a house is presented in 2 Timothy 2:20–21, to emphasize further the need to live in a way that pleases God. Houses have valuable dishes made of silver and gold, but also dishes that are used for common work and made of wood and clay. Paul applies this homely illustration to Timothy and all the readers. Only the honorable and pure vessels will remain in God's household forever. If believers give themselves to evil and follow the words and ways of the false teachers, they won't be used in the house. Paul's point in the illustration is that perseverance in goodness indicates whether one truly belongs to the Lord.

The admonition that follows in 2:22 fits beautifully, then, for believers must run from "youthful passions" and "pursue righteousness, faith, love, and peace." Those who cry out to the Lord "with a pure heart" show purity and authenticity by such qualities. There certainly are times to refute publicly wrongheaded teaching, but there are also times when one should desist from arguing since it can lead to interminable disputes that end up helping no one. Those who are the Lord's servants must not become quarrelsome (2:24). They are to oppose error strenuously without becoming contentious. They are to be gentle and strong, patiently pointing out the errors of those who have gone astray. Anger doesn't accomplish the Lord's work, and the hope is that those who are errant can be recovered (2:25–26). God can overcome their resistance and error and "grant them repentance," which leads them to conversion—that is, knowledge of the truth of the gospel. Unbelievers are trapped by the devil and subservient to the devil's will, but God in his grace can awaken them out of their spiritual slumber so that they come to life, as they are gently but firmly and without compromise taught the way of truth.

Avoid Those Who Are Evil (3:1–9)

This is the final occasion on which Paul warned Timothy about deleterious influences. As usual in the NT, the last days are conceived of as present (cf. Acts 2:17–18; Heb. 1:2; 1 John 2:18); thus Paul talks about what was happening in his day. The problem was caused by people who claimed to be godly, and their claim was buttressed by at least an outward appearance of godliness (2 Tim. 3:5). A deeper look, however, reveals that these so-called religious teachers were dangerous (3:1–4). Their religion is actually narcissism and self-obsession, and Paul strips away their veneer by detailing their true nature. They weren't in love with God but with money. They weren't humble but braggarts and arrogant. They were verbally abusive, flouted parental authority, complained constantly, rejected holiness, spurned natural ties and affection, refused to forgive, lacked self-control, savaged others, hated goodness and purity, abandoned their friends, and made pleasure their god. No wonder Paul says they should be avoided.

The defects of these men unfortunately weren't restricted to themselves alone; they influenced others, especially "gullible women" (3:6). Paul is scarcely saying that all women are gullible; he gives one example of the deleterious impact of the false teachers. Apparently they visited houses and took advantage of women who were captivated by their own sins and swayed by evil desires. These women thought they were learning, but they were actually learning nothing at all (like many people today!) since their education did not lead them to the truth of the gospel (3:7). Here Paul summons the names, conveyed by Jewish tradition, of "Jannes and Jambres," who resisted Moses. Following their infamous example, some false teachers of Paul's day were showing that their thinking was corrupt and that they were unapproved with respect to the faith, thus they were not believers (3:8). Verse 9 isn't easy to interpret, but the reference is probably eschatological since false teachers may make significant "progress" in deceiving others during this present age. Eventually, on the last day, these teachers will be revealed to be foolish, as was the case with the magicians who stood against Moses.

Follow Paul and the Scriptures (3:10-17)

Timothy is to avoid those described in 3:1–9 and to continue to follow Paul as he did in the past (3:10), which includes Paul's teaching, way of life, his purpose, faith, patience, love, and endurance. Timothy witnessed and heard about the persecutions that Paul experienced on his first missionary journey in Pisidian Antioch, Iconium, and Lystra (Acts 13–14). The Lord, however, preserved Paul in every situation. Every believer, Paul affirms, will be persecuted (2 Tim. 3:12). Today believers are being persecuted all over the world: some are killed, some are beaten, some are verbally abused, and some lose their jobs. The level of persecution varies: sometimes it is verbal rejection (cf. 1 Pet. 4:3–4), and on other occasions believers are put to death for their faith. All of this takes place in a context in which others promote evil and are nothing other than "imposters" (2 Tim. 3:13).

Timothy should quietly persevere in what he was taught, learned, and came to believe (3:14). He knew the lives of those who taught him, which included his grandmother Lois, his mother, Eunice, and certainly the apostle Paul (1:5). Seeing his teachers' godly lives and their willingness to face suffering should fortify Timothy in the truth. The Scriptures were known to Timothy from his earliest years, and they are invaluable because they grant the wisdom that leads to salvation "through faith in Christ Jesus" (3:15). Paul goes on to say, in a famous statement, and rightly so, that "all Scripture is inspired by God" (3:16). The thought isn't that Scripture is inspiring. Instead, it is objectively inspired, as the word of God. The practical benefit of Scripture is explained: it is the basis for teaching, sets people right so that we are "[trained] in righteousness." Scripture equips and prepares "the man of God," which, as we saw in 1 Timothy 6:11–16, is a common OT term for those who are God's servants and teachers.

Preach the Word (4:1-5)

Paul has just reminded Timothy about the truthfulness and usefulness of the Scriptures, exhorting him to continue in what he was taught from a young age. Since Scripture is truth and useful, the exhortation to "preach the word" (4:2) follows naturally from the preceding paragraph (3:14–17). The injunction to preach is needed for the salvation and wholeness of his hearers and also to stave off the blandishments of false teachers. The call to proclaim the word is an awesome responsibility, and Paul gives Timothy a solemn injunction to do so in the presence of God and Christ. Preaching is to be done with the recognition that Christ will be the judge of all on the last day; life in this age doesn't last forever since Jesus will come again and establish his kingdom.

Those who preach the word must be prepared to proclaim it whether the hearers are friendly or opposed. What does preaching involve? It is fascinating to see patience and teaching put together. Change doesn't always occur instantly, and thus preachers must patiently teach and herald the word month in and month out, year in and year out. Preaching includes rebuking and exposing evil, correcting and adjusting where people are, and constant encouragement. Such preaching is necessary since many do not want to pay attention to sound teaching. They are attracted to teachers who say what they want to hear, teachers who tickle their ears (4:3). Instead of paying attention to the truth of the gospel, they give themselves to myths (4:4). What Paul means by myths isn't precisely clear, but it refers to fabricated ideas of some kind in contrast with the gospel, which brings salvation. In this situation Timothy must be sober and keep his head; he must be prepared to suffer, to continue to preach the gospel, and to fulfill the ministry that God has called him to do.

Paul as an Example (4:6–8)

Paul's life is pictured as a drink offering, poured out on the ground to symbolize the giving up of his life for the sake of others (Phil. 2:17). Paul recognizes that the hour of his death is near. He calls upon Timothy to fulfill his ministry, knowing that his days of ministry have drawn to a close. He doesn't look back with regret but with thankfulness for what he accomplished by God's grace. He fought the fight and finished the race, which is another way of saying that he kept the faith, that he didn't apostatize. The images used demonstrate that the Christian life isn't easy. It is compared to an arduous fight or competition and to an exhausting race. Every effort expended is worth it because the crown, which is righteousness, awaits Paul for his faithfulness. God is righteous; he repays people according to their works, and thus the crown of righteousness, which is another way of describing eternal life itself, will be granted to all those who love "his appearing."

Final Greetings (4:9-22)

The final words in 2 Timothy are particularly poignant since they are the final words written by Paul. Paul was imprisoned, waiting for the final judicial decision from Nero Caesar, and he anticipated the verdict going against him. He asks Timothy to come as soon as possible (4:9). Demas (see Col. 4:14; Philem. 24) had abandoned Paul, and not for a neutral reason, for "he loved the present world" (2 Tim. 4:10). The defection of Demas probably represents apostasy. Others like Crescens (mentioned only here) and Titus (often mentioned by Paul: 2 Cor. 2:13; 7:6, 13, 14; 8:6, 16, 23; 12:18; Gal. 2:1, 3; Titus 1:4) traveled to Galatia and Dalmatia (southern Croatia today), respectively, probably for ministry reasons. Luke, as Paul's faithful friend and as the one who shared many journeys with Paul, according to the "we" passages of Acts, remained with Paul in his hour of need. We also see that at the end of his life, Paul commends John Mark as useful: the one once rejected by Paul as unfaithful was a dear friend as his life was drawing to a close (Acts 13:13; 15:37–39; Col. 4:10; Philem. 24). Interestingly, Mark and Luke are mentioned in the same verse, and the second and third Gospels are traditionally ascribed to them (2 Tim. 4:11).

Paul sent Tychicus to Ephesus, almost certainly for ministry, and he was a trusted coworker, but though he is mentioned several times, we don't know much about him (4:12; see Acts 20:4; Eph. 6:21; Col. 4:7; Titus 3:12). Paul returns to Timothy's visit, asking him to bring a coat and parchments. The coat was almost certainly needed for warmth during a cold winter in prison, which explains why he urges Timothy to come before winter. We don't know the content of the parchments, but they probably included scriptural texts that Paul would read for edification and encouragement.

Perhaps Alexander harmed Paul by testifying against him, leading to his imprisonment, though we don't know for certain how he opposed Paul (2 Tim. 4:14). There was apparently some venue where he took issue with Paul's teaching (4:15). It may be the same Alexander handed over to Satan in 1 Timothy 1:20. Some think it may even be the same Alexander the Jew who wanted to defend the Jews over against Paul and his companions during the riot that took place in Ephesus (Acts 19:33–34). Paul recognizes that a final judgment is coming and that Alexander will be repaid according to his works. Judgment according to works is a common OT theme (Job 34:11; Pss. 28:4; 62:12; Prov. 24:12; Jer. 17:10; 25:14; 32:19; 51:24; Ezek. 33:20) and is taught elsewhere in Paul (Rom. 2:6; 2 Cor. 5:10; 11:15). Paul was also concerned about Alexander's opposition to Timothy, warning him to beware of Alexander since he might hatch a plot against Timothy as well (2 Tim. 4:15).

Paul turns to his trial (4:16), which, as was noted above, may have been pre-cipitated by Alexander's charges. Apparently Paul had an initial defense, a first hearing. In saying, "No one stood by me," Paul may have his legal defense in view. In any case, he was forsaken and abandoned by all, because identifying with a prisoner could expose one to the same fate as that prisoner. Yet Paul, like Jesus (Luke 23:34) and Stephen (Acts 7:60), did not hold it against those who turned their backs on him, praying that their cowardice would not be held against them. Even though friends forsook him, the Lord did not, granting Paul strength and courage to proclaim the gospel fully and freely. The goal that the gentiles would hear the word, and that Paul would preach before kings (Acts 9:15), perhaps the emperor Nero himself, was fulfilled. Paul's deliverance from the lion's mouth could mean that Nero didn't put him to death immediately (2 Tim. 4:17), but it is more likely that the lion represents Satan here (cf. 1 Pet. 5:8), and Satan stood behind Nero. Paul's deliverance didn't mean that his life was spared but that in a pressure-packed situation he didn't commit apostasy and deny the Lord. This makes more sense of the next verse (2 Tim. 4:18), where Paul affirms that the Lord will rescue him from all evil and bring him into the "heavenly kingdom." Paul didn't envision escaping death, but he was confident that he would not deny Christ even if Nero Caesar condemned him to die. He will be preserved from apostasy and saved forever. Since Christ will preserve his faith, all the glory goes to him forever.

The letter closes with a few greetings, news, a request, and a grace benedic-tion (4:19–22). Apparently Paul's beloved friends Prisca and Aquila were back in Ephesus (cf. Acts 18:2, 18, 26; Rom. 16:3–5; 1 Cor. 16:19). The reference to the household of Onesiphorus, who came in for such commendation earlier in the letter (2 Tim. 1:15–18), may indicate that Onesiphorus was no longer alive, but such an inference is uncertain. Paul left Erastus in Corinth, and we don't know for sure if he is the same Erastus mentioned in Acts 19:22 and Romans 16:23. Presumably he was left in Corinth to do ministry. Paul left Trophimus (Acts 20:4; 21:29) "sick at Miletus" (2 Tim. 4:20), which shows that Paul couldn't and didn't heal everyone. There is no suggestion here that Trophimus was sick because of his sin. After urging Timothy to come before winter, we see greetings from fellow believers in Rome, and Eubulus, Pudens, Linus, and Claudia are specifically mentioned, about whom we know nothing else (4:21). Paul closes his last letter with a prayer that the Lord would continue to be with Timothy and that "grace" would be with the church as a whole (4:22). The Greek plural here for "your" shows that the letter wasn't intended for Timothy alone.

See after Titus for a combined bibliography of the Pastoral Letters (1 and 2 Timothy, Titus).

CHAPTER THIRTEEN

Titus

Introduction

As mentioned in the introduction to 1 Timothy, many scholars reject the notion that Paul wrote Titus as one of the Pastoral Letters. I mentioned there, however, that many scholars today affirm the genuineness and authenticity of the letter, and that is the view supported here. Paul probably wrote Titus sometime after his release from his first Roman imprisonment, in AD 62. Apparently Titus and Paul traveled to Crete together, and perhaps churches were planted in Crete for the first time on this occasion (Titus 1:5). As noted, the letter was written to Titus in Crete, which is a large island in the Mediterranean. Paul left Titus in Crete to set things in order, and he hoped by the time winter arrived that Titus could join him in Nicopolis (3:12).

Titus was a trusted coworker of Paul. He first appeared on the scene in Galatia, from which he traveled to Jerusalem with Paul and Barnabas, and he became, intentionally or not, a test case as a gentile for whether circumcision was required for salvation (Gal. 2:1–5). Paul won that battle, of course, and preserved the truth of the gospel. Titus played an especially critical role in Corinth, as 2 Corinthians testifies. After Paul sent a severe letter (perhaps 1 Corinthians) to that church, he dispatched Titus to discern their response. We see Paul's trust in Titus, shown by sending him on such a delicate and difficult mission (2 Cor. 2:13; 7:6, 13–14). Paul was filled with joy because Titus brought back news of the Corinthians' repentance and sorrow over their sin. Paul also sent Titus to encourage the Corinthians to give toward Paul's collection for the poor in Jerusalem (2 Cor. 8:6, 16, 23), and he had complete faith in Titus's integrity. The last occasion when Titus is mentioned is 2 Timothy 4:10, where Paul, shortly before his death in Rome, sent Titus to Dalmatia, showing that Titus remained a faithful coworker and friend until the end of Paul's life.

Outline

Appoint elders to preserve the gospel	1:1–16
Adorn salvation with a godly life	2:1–15
Live as children who have received mercy	3:1–15

Greeting (1:1–4)

The opening and greeting stand out in Titus as one of the longer openings in Paul's Letters. Only Romans and Galatians have a longer opening than Titus. Paul identifies himself as both a servant and an apostle, and Romans is the only other place where we see both of these designations (Rom. 1:1). With authority as an apostle of Christ, he is commissioned to serve Christ. Paul's ministry was to further "faith" in the elect and to bring them to saving knowledge of the truth, and the consequence of such knowledge is godliness. Central themes of the letter are anticipated here since Titus was left in Crete so that the faith and the truth that lead to godliness would be preserved in Crete. In the letter Paul especially emphasizes that genuine conversion leads to a changed life, that faith results in and leads to good works.

The truth, the gospel that Paul proclaimed, brings hope (Titus 1:2), and the hope is identified as "eternal life." In a world where the future is uncertain and death is coming, the promise of eternal life is an anchor for the life of godliness. The question would naturally arise whether such a promise was too good to be true, and Paul assures them by affirming that God "cannot lie"; God's truthfulness is also declared in the OT (Num. 23:19; 1 Sam. 15:29). What God had determined to carry out before time even began, he will certainly fulfill.

One of the central themes of the Pastorals is that God is "our Savior" (Titus 1:3), and the hope of eternal life rests on God's saving work. We see in verse 3 that Paul was entrusted as an apostle, commissioned on the Damascus road to proclaim God's saving work, a work that has been revealed at a particular time in salvation history. Indeed, the saving work heralded by Paul had been revealed by God in the ministry, death, and resurrection of Jesus Christ. Paul wanted the churches in Crete to know the hope, the promise, the salvation that is in Jesus Christ, and then to live according to this hope. Titus was Paul's "true son," which probably means he was converted by Paul (1:4). They shared a "common faith," and it is this faith that Paul longed to see thrive in Crete. The gospel prospers at God's initiative, and so Paul prays for grace and peace from both God the Father and Christ Jesus. Significantly, he adds that Christ Jesus is "our Savior," impressing upon Titus and the readers that salvation and eternal life are secured through Christ alone.

Appoint Elders (1:5–9)

Titus could serve well in many places but presently he was needed in Crete, specifically to straighten up and finish what was left undone. Even more specifically, this task would be accomplished if he appointed "elders in every town" (1:5). Probably there was a single church in every town, and so we see evidence that there was a plurality of elders, a plurality of church leaders, in every church. There were twenty towns or so in Crete, and we don't know if every one of them had an established church, but this text shows that at least some of them did. We saw in Acts 14:23 that appointing a plurality of elders was Paul's practice from his first missionary journey. As leaders of the congregation, the elders should guide the congregation in both right thinking and right living.

As we read in 1 Timothy 3:1–7, the most important qualification for elders to serve is that they are "blameless" (NKJV). This doesn't mean that they are sinless, since then no one could serve. It means that the men appointed live a godly life, and there is no blatant or hidden sin ruling over them. The list here is representative and not comprehensive; as in 1 Timothy, we have bullet points that Titus could fill in as Paul's coworker and longtime friend. The mistake of being overly literal and rigid surfaces with the next point. Being "the husband of one wife" (Titus 1:6) doesn't mean that one must be married, for otherwise people like Paul and Jesus would be excluded, and Paul's advice to remain single for ministry in 1 Corinthians 7 would be quite strange. Nor is polygamy Paul's central concern (though it is certainly included, it is rare). In 1 Timothy 3:2 we saw that the parallel in 5:9 rules out a focus on polygamy. Nor do divorce and remarriage automatically rule out someone as an elder. The issue is whether a man has a faithful track record in his marriage, whether he is respected and honored in the church and the wider community for his marriage.

Having "faithful children" (Titus 1:6) could mean children who profess to believe, but if that is the case, it relates to children when they are younger and in the home (probably twelve and under in Paul's day). If children of such a young age had a different view than their parents, that would be a matter of concern. Perhaps the point in any case is that children are "faithful," which is explained in the next clause—they are not wild and rebellious. Certainly Paul isn't saying that elders must have perfect children, as if they are little martinets marching according to their parents' commands. His point is that the children of elders are generally well-behaved; they are not notorious "little terrors" in the church.

Paul glides from "elders" (1:5) to "an overseer" (1:7). The office of elder and overseer are not distinct. They refer to the same office (see Acts 20:17, 28); the word "elder" refers to the dignity and respect belonging to the office, and "overseer" to the function and responsibility required. The shift to the singular is generic and should not be interpreted to say that there was only one overseer in a church. We see the same generic singular use of "overseer" in 1 Timothy 3:1, but Paul shifts to the plural term "elders" in 1 Timothy 5:17.

Other character qualities fill in what it means to be blameless, though again the list is scarcely comprehensive. Arrogance, a hot and blazing temper, drunkenness, acting pugnaciously like a bully, and living for money—all such rule a person out as an overseer (Titus 1:7). Paul proceeds to some positive qualities (1:8). Overseers must be hospitable and warmly welcome people. The qualities aren't extreme or stunning: leaders should love goodness, be sensible, live in righteous and holy ways, and exercise self-control. The list may not amaze us, but churches that have such steady and stable leaders are very grateful.

Character is a nonnegotiable for elders/overseers, but they must also have a gift for teaching (cf. 1 Tim. 3:2; 5:17). Before they can teach, they must know and hold fast to the teaching, to the gospel, which is "the faithful message" (Titus 1:9). Overseers who know the faithful message and hold on to it should encourage and strengthen their congregation with the teaching that is healthy and builds them up. The situation in Crete shows, however, that they are not only to build up but also to correct. Overseers must also have the ability to patiently, gently, and firmly show the errors of those who propound false doctrine.

Silence the Rebellious (1:10–16)

The reason Titus needs to set things in order in Crete and to appoint elders/overseers of good character and sound teaching is that there are many who were rebellious and deceptive, moving away from the hope that grants eternal life. Apparently they were Jewish since they were from "the circumcision party" (1:10). Saying they were of the circumcision party doesn't necessarily mean, and actually probably doesn't mean, that they advocated circumcision. We see from verse 14 that the adversaries seemed to be quite similar to the opponents in 1 Timothy (1 Tim. 1:4). They propounded "Jewish myths" and enforced other "commands" contrary to the truth (Titus 1:14). We can't nail down precisely what they taught, but saying that "nothing is pure" to them reminds us of 1 Timothy 4:3, where false teachers "forbid marriage" and denounce the eating of certain foods. Here in Titus they were teaching something similar about impurity, drawing on fabricated Jewish myths and other inanities to promulgate their view. Their mistaken theology had its roots in their own lives, for they were unbelievers and "defiled" in their thinking and conscience (Titus 1:15). Those who were pure recognized that "everything is pure," but the false teachers lacked such purity, and thus their lives and teaching were askew.

We might think these teachers would be devoted to good works, but Paul says they were motivated by financial gain (1:11). They professed to know God, yet their evil works and lives contradicted their claim (1:16). They were "detestable, disobedient, and unfit for any good work." Titus needs to silence them, and so do the future elders who would be appointed (1:11). They were throwing "entire households" into disarray, probably referring to house churches (cf. Rom. 16:5; 1 Cor. 16:19; Col. 4:15; 1 Tim. 3:15; Philem. 2). Paul worries that the Cretans will be prone to listen to such false teachers, quoting a line from one of their writers, whom Paul identifies as a prophet (Titus 1:12). He is probably merely saying that the word spoken here is true, and most think it stems from Epimenides of Crete (6th cent. BC), though the source isn't of great importance.

The saying in verse 12 grates on the ears of people today who are sensitive to cultural denigration. It has also been pointed out that the statement is internally contradictory. Since a Cretan wrote it, it must be a lie because "Cretans are always liars"! Such a literalistic reading of "always" shows that the critic has no idea of how to read poetry. Every culture has strengths and weaknesses, and people in a culture may celebrate certain behavior characteristics that are contrary to God's will. Apparently, lying, laziness, and wickedness were promoted in Crete, and such characteristics aren't limited to Cretans in human history. Paul doesn't believe that such patterns are irremediable, for Titus is to rebuke the Cretans "sharply" so that their understanding of the faith would be solid and stable (1:13–14).

Healthy Teaching for All (2:1–10)

Sound teaching leads to healthy living, and what this means is unpacked for older men (2:2), older and younger women (2:3–5), young men (2:6), Titus (2:7–8), and slaves (2:9–10). Those belonging to the circumcision party displeased God by their evil, and right doctrine is matched by right living. Older men (which doesn't designate the office of elders here) are to be dignified, respectable, and sensible. Paul wasn't plugging what today is called bourgeois values, nor are the virtues here to be interpreted as stuffy and stiff. He refers to a sensibility and dignity that befit an older man. At the same time, older men should show solidity in their trust in God, in their love, and in their perseverance.

Paul then turns toward older and younger women (2:3–5). Older women should also live in a reverent and godly way, being free from slanderous talk and addiction to wine or any other substance. The older women have a particular responsibility to teach younger women: they should urge younger women to love their husbands and their children. The instructions may sound prosaic, but when such love is actually lived out, the consequences are far-reaching. The younger women should be sensible, pure in body and spirit, managers of their homes, and submissive to their own husbands. We have seen elsewhere that such submission doesn't mean the negation of a wife's personality, and certainly a wife should not submit if the husband wants her to sin, to violate her conscience, or to suffer abuse. When wives live in ways that please God, the gospel is commended.

Somewhat surprisingly, only one verse is addressed to young men (2:6), though perhaps the call to self-control sums up everything they needed to hear. Paul shifts to Titus, who was probably young himself (2:7–8). Titus should live an exemplary life with good works, and his teaching should be unimpeachable. If the lives and teaching of believers are congruent, opponents will find no grounds for criticism and will end up being ashamed.

Elsewhere we have discussed the instructions given to slaves (cf. 1 Cor. 7:21–23; Eph. 6:5–9; Col. 3:22–4:1; 1 Tim. 6:1–2; Philemon). Here slaves are told to submit to their masters, to serve them well, and not to engage in arguments with them (Titus 2:9–10). They must not be found guilty of stealing but should be known for their reliability, and in this way "the teaching of God our Savior" will be commended.

The Power of God's Grace (2:11–15)

The basis for the new life, which has been sketched out for various people in various stations of life (2:1–10), is now explained (2:11–15). Paul doesn't merely give admonitions to people to live in a new way. The new way of living finds its grounding in the grace of God, and God's grace "appeared" and has brought salvation to all people groups, to both Jews and gentiles. The grace of God has been manifested particularly in the ministry, death, and resurrection of Jesus Christ. Human beings don't have the resources, as the sons and daughters of Adam, to live new lives. God's grace both instructs and empowers believers so that they are strengthened to reject godlessness and "worldly lusts" (2:12). During "the present age," an age ravaged by evil, grace strengthens so that believers live sensibly, righteously, and reverently. Still, the present age isn't perfect, nor are Christians perfected. They await the consummation, "the blessed hope" (2:13), when Jesus Christ will gloriously appear, who is "our great God and Savior." The grammar of this last statement clearly demonstrates that Jesus Christ is God. We have what is called the Granville Sharp rule, named after the person who first proposed it. When there are two singular personal nouns that are not proper nouns, and there is one article with the two nouns that are joined by the word "and," then the two nouns refer to the same entity. We have this construction in verse 13, and thus it is clear that Jesus Christ is identified as God and Savior. Jesus was truly human, of course, but we are reminded that only God could save us from our sins.

That only God saves us from our sins is indicated in the next verse (2:14). Jesus Christ surrendered his life for our sake; he died the death we should have died. He liberated us, freeing believers from rebellion and the selfish will that dominated our lives, cleansing believers of all their sins so that they are his special possession. As those who are loved and redeemed by the Lord, believers are "eager to do good works," not to win God's favor but to express joy and thankfulness for being freed from all evil. Titus's role is to teach and encourage all in such truths (2:15): Paul commissions Titus to exercise his authority to lead in such a way.

Live a New Life as Those Who Are Saved (3:1–8)

The new life of believers, Paul continues to emphasize, is rooted in God's grace. We don't have dry and dusty moralism, for the exhortations are grounded in the amazing grace of God (3:4–7). Paul begins by instructing the Cretans to submit to and to follow ruling authorities (3:1). We see a similar admonition in more detail in Romans 13:1–7 (cf. also 1 Pet. 2:13–17). Human beings are predisposed to resist and to contradict authority. Of course, there are exceptions to what is commanded here, but the admonition focuses on what is generally the case. God's grace changes us so that believers are eager and "ready for every good work" (Titus 3:1). It is human to criticize and verbally abuse others and to quarrel and contend, but it is divine to be gentle and humble (3:2). This is not a counsel for spineless wimpiness that kowtows out of fear of others. Such gentleness and humility come from a strength and power that is restrained for the sake of others, for it stems from the love of Christ.

We have one of Paul's famous contrasts between "then" and "now," between the time before salvation and the time of salvation (3:3–7). Believers should not look down on those who don't know God and those who sin, since they know their own history. We were "foolish" as well, for we didn't know the truth about God and about the meaning of life. We were also disobedient, refusing to respond to God's authority. Unbelievers aren't conscious of the wrong paths they have taken; they are "deceived," which means that they are convinced that their beliefs, decisions, and actions are justified. They think they are free, but they are actually enslaved to sin (cf. John 8:34; Rom. 6:6, 17, 20) and are led, like those addicted to sugar, by their passions and desires. Hatred, envy, and malice characterize their lives. Of course, Paul's point in all this is that before conversion all believers lived like this; there is no basis for moral superiority.

What accounts for the new life of believers? It can't be ascribed to their own wisdom or moral strength. We saw a reference earlier to God's grace appearing (Titus 2:11) and here to the appearing of God's saving love and kindness (3:4–5). Paul drills down further: human beings are not saved "by works of righteousness that we had done" (3:5). No space is given to human goodness, and thus pride in our moral transformation is completely ruled out. Salvation is undeserved and finds its origins in God's mercy. Believers are saved through the work of the Holy Spirit, who regenerates and renews believers at baptism when they are washed and cleansed from their sins. Paul's words here should not be interpreted to support baptismal regeneration, since baptism belongs to a whole complex of events that include confessing Jesus as Lord, trusting in Christ, receiving the Spirit, and so forth. In fact, the next verse makes this clear. God has given the Spirit to all believers "through Jesus Christ our Savior" (3:6).

The Trinity shines through in these verses, showing that the Father, the Son, and the Holy Spirit all play a vital role in salvation. The Father planned it, the Son accomplished it, and the Spirit applied it. Those who are saved are also "justified by his grace," which decisively counters the notion that the Pastoral Epistles are bereft of the Pauline gospel (3:7). Paul's famous teaching—enshrined in Romans, Galatians, and Philippians—is likewise in Titus! Justification, being declared right by God, standing in the right before him, is by grace! And those who are right with God are "heirs" and thus enjoy the sure "hope of eternal life" (3:7). Those who are regenerated, renewed, saved, and justified should "devote themselves to good works" (3:8).

Avoiding and Rejecting (3:9-11)

We see another indication that the adversaries in Titus are rather similar to the opponents in 1 Timothy. They were entranced with inane debates and disputations and found value in arcane genealogies (cf. 1 Tim. 1:4; 6:4; cf. also 2 Tim. 2:23). Furthermore, they were making their case from "the law," as we also see in 1 Timothy 1:7–11. Titus needed to steer clear of these theological debates because they were "unprofitable and worthless" (see 1 Tim. 1:6 and Titus 1:10). We shouldn't glean from this that any theological dispute is a waste of time. A believer needs discernment to determine whether one should expend energy to identify and refute error. In some cases (cf. Galatians) such refutation is helpful, and in other instances it isn't. Some engage in theological argumentation because they are fundamentally "divisive," fractious, peevish, and grumpy (Titus 3:10). If such a person continues to engage in fruitless disputes, they should be rejected after they have been warned a couple of times. The person is condemned because of his own actions and behavior, and his sin creates disunity and unhappiness.

Final Words (3:12–15)

As with the rest of Paul's Letters, the letter closing contains some final instructions, greetings, and a grace benediction. Paul was sending Artemas and Tychicus to Crete, probably to keep up the work that Titus had started. We don't know anything else about Artemas, but Tychicus, who was "from the province of Asia" (Acts 20:4), was the letter carrier for both Ephesians (Eph. 6:21) and Colossians (Col. 4:7). Shortly before Paul's death, he sent Tychicus to Ephesus for ministry (2 Tim. 4:12). Upon the arrival of these two men, Titus is asked to join Paul in Nicopolis since Paul had decided to spend the winter there. The distance from Crete to Nicopolis is around three hundred miles, and so this wasn't an easy journey. Nicopolis was the capital of the province of Epirus, which was on the west coast of Greece. The city was known for its milder winters, and perhaps this was one reason Paul decided to winter there, though certainly the dissemination of the gospel was Paul's primary motive.

Zenas and Apollos were probably going out for mission work, and Paul asks that their needs be met (Titus 3:13). Zenas was probably a jurist in the Roman world, and Apollos was famous for his eloquence (cf. Acts 18:24; 19:1; 1 Cor. 1:12; 3:4, 5, 6, 22; 4:6; 16:12). The changed life produced by the gospel is a major theme in the letter, and so we aren't surprised that Paul mentions again the importance of good works to meet the needs of others. True grace, as Paul says repeatedly in the letter, is transforming. The letter closes with family affection (3:15). Those with Paul send their greetings to Titus and the churches in Crete. Those who love Paul in the faith, in the truth of the gospel, are also greeted. Finally, as is customary with Paul, the letter concludes with a prayer for grace to be with all.

Pastorals: Commentaries

Barrett, Charles K. *1 Timothy, 2 Timothy, Titus*. ANTC. Nashville: Abingdon, 1996.

———. *The Pastoral Epistles in the New English Bible*. Oxford: Clarendon, 1963.

Baugh, S. M. "1 and 2 Timothy, Titus." In *1 and 2 Thessalonians, 1 and 2 Timothy, Titus*, edited by J. A. D. Weima and S. M. Baugh, 444–511. ZIBBC 3. Grand Rapids: Zondervan, 2002.

Belleville, Linda. *1 Timothy*. Cornerstone Biblical Commentary. Carol Stream, IL: Tyndale, 2009.

Bernard, J. H. *The Pastoral Epistles*. Grand Rapids: Eerdmans, 1980.

Calvin, John. *The Second Epistle of Paul the Apostle to the Corinthians and the Epistles to Timothy, Titus and Philemon*. Translated by T. A. Smail. Edited by D. W. Torrance and T. F. Torrance. Grand Rapids: Eerdmans, 1964.

Collins, Raymond F. *1 and 2 Timothy and Titus*. NTL. Louisville: Westminster John Knox, 2002.

Dibelius, Martin, and Hans Conzelmann. *The Pastoral Epistles*. Translated by P. Buttolph and A. Yarbro. Hermeneia. Philadelphia: Fortress, 1972.

Gloer, W. Hulitt. *1 and 2 Timothy–Titus*. SHBC. Macon, GA: Smyth & Helwys, 2010.

Guthrie, Donald. *The Pastoral Epistles*. Rev. ed. TNTC. Leicester, UK: Inter-Varsity, 1990.

Hanson, A. T. *The Pastoral Epistles*. NCB. Grand Rapids: Eerdmans, 1982.

Johnson, Luke T. *The First and Second Letters to Timothy*. AB 35A. New York: Doubleday, 2001.

———. *Letters to Paul's Delegates: 1 Timothy, 2 Timothy, Titus*. NTC. Harrisburg, PA: Trinity Press International, 1996.

Kelly, J. N. D. *The Pastoral Epistles*. BNTC. Peabody, MA: Hendrickson, 1998.

Knight, George W., III. *The Pastoral Epistles*. NIGTC. Grand Rapids: Eerdmans, 1992.

Köstenberger, Andreas. *Commentary on 1–2 Timothy and Titus*. Biblical Theology for Proclamation Series. Nashville: Holman Reference, 2017.

Krause, Deborah. *1 Timothy*. Readings: A New Biblical Commentary. Sheffield: Sheffield Academic, 2004.

Laansma, J. *2 Timothy, Titus*. Cornerstone Biblical Commentary 17. Carol Stream, IL: Tyndale, 2009.

Long, T. G. *1 and 2 Timothy and Titus*. Belief: A Theological Commentary on the Bible. Louisville: Westminster John Knox, 2016.

Luther, Martin. *Commentaries on 1 Corinthians 7, 1 Corinthians 15, Lectures on 1 Timothy*. Edited by H. C. Oswald. LW 28. St. Louis: Concordia, 1973.

Marshall, I. Howard, and Philip H. Towner. *The Pastoral Epistles*. ICC. Edinburgh: T&T Clark, 2004.

Montague, G. T. *First and Second Timothy, Titus*. CCSS. Grand Rapids: Baker Academic, 2008.

Mounce, William D. *Pastoral Epistles*. WBC. Nashville: Thomas Nelson, 2000.

Ngewa, S. *1 and 2 Timothy and Titus*. Africa Bible Commentary Series. Grand Rapids: Zondervan, 2009.

Oden, Thomas C. *First and Second Timothy and Titus*. IBC. Louisville: Westminster John Knox, 1989.

Quinn, J. D. *The Letter to Titus*. AB 35. New York: Doubleday, 1990.

Quinn, J. D., and W. C. Wacker. *The First and Second Letters to Timothy*. Vol. 1. Grand Rapids: Eerdmans, 1999.

Ramsay, W. R. *Historical Commentary on the Pastoral Epistles*. Edited by M. Wilson. Grand Rapids: Kregel, 1996.

Saarinen, R. *The Pastoral Epistles with Philemon and Jude*. Brazos Theological Commentary on the Bible. Grand Rapids: Brazos, 2008.

Smith, Craig A. *2 Timothy*. Readings: A New Biblical Commentary. Sheffield: Sheffield Phoenix, 2016.

Spencer, A. B. *2 Timothy and Titus*. NCCS. Eugene, OR: Cascade, 2014.

Stott, J. R. W. *The Letters to Timothy and Titus*. NICNT. Grand Rapids: Eerdmans, 2006.

———. *The Message of 1 Timothy and Titus: Guard the Truth*. BST. Downers Grove, IL: InterVarsity, 1996.

Thomas Aquinas. *Commentaries on St. Paul's Epistles to Timothy, Titus, and Philemon*. Translated and edited by C. Baer. South Bend, IN: St. Augustine's Press, 2007.

Trebilco, P., C. Caradus, and S. Rae. *2 Timothy and Titus*. ABCS. Singapore: Asia Theological Association, 2009.

Trebilco, P., and S. Rae. *1 Timothy*. ABCS. Singapore: Asia Theological Association, 2006.

Wall, Robert W., with Richard B. Steele. *1 and 2 Timothy and Titus*. THNTC. Grand Rapids: Eerdmans, 2012.

Witherington, Ben, III. *Letters and Homilies for Hellenized Christians*. Vol. 1, *A Socio-Rhetorical Commentary on Titus, 1–2 Timothy and 1–3 John*. Downers Grove, IL: IVP Academic, 2006.

Wright, N. T. *Paul for Everyone: The Pastoral Letters; 1 and 2 Timothy and Titus*. 2nd ed. London: SPCK, 2004.

Yarbrough, Robert W. *The Letters to Timothy and Titus*. PNTC. Grand Rapids: Eerdmans, 2018.

Zehr, P. *1 and 2 Timothy, Titus*. BCBC. Scottdale, PA: Herald Press, 2010.

Pastorals: Articles, Essays, and Monographs

Aageson, James W. *Paul, the Pastoral Epistles, and the Early Church*. Peabody, MA: Hendrickson, 2008.

Balla, Peter. *The Child-Parent Relationship in the New Testament and Its Environment*. WUNT 155. Tübingen: Mohr Siebeck, 2003.

Bassler, Jouette. "A Plethora of Epiphanies: Christology in the Pastoral Letters." *Princeton Seminary Bulletin* 17 (1996): 310–25.

Batten, Alicia J. "Christology, the Pastoral Epistles, and Commentaries." In *On the Writing of New Testament Commentaries*, edited by S. E. Porter and E. J. Schnabel, 317–36. Leiden: Brill, 2013.

———. "Neither Gold nor Braided Hair (1 Timothy 2:9; 1 Peter 3:3): Adornment, Gender and Honour in Antiquity." *NTS* 55 (2009): 484–501.

Baugh, S. M. "A Foreign World: Ephesus in the First Century." In *Women in the Church: An Interpretation and Application of 1 Timothy 2:9–15*, 3rd ed., edited by A. J. Köstenberger and T. R. Schreiner, 25–64. Wheaton: Crossway, 2016.

Burk, Denny. "New and Old Departures in the Translation of Αὐθεντειν 1 Timothy 2:12." In *Women in the Church: An Interpretation and Application of 1 Timothy 2:9–15*, 3rd ed., edited by A. J. Köstenberger and T. R. Schreiner, 279–96. Wheaton: Crossway, 2016.

Christensen, Sean M. "The Pursuit of Self-Control: Titus 2:1–14 and Accommodation to Christ." *JSPL* 6 (2016): 161–80.

Cooper, M., and J. Cabellero. "Reasoning through the Creation Order as a Basis for the Prohibition in 1 Timothy 2:12." *Presb* 43 (2017): 30–38.

Couser, Greg. "'Prayer' and the Public Square: 1 Timothy 2:1–7 and Christian Political Engagement." In *New Testament Theology in Light of the Church's Mission: Essays in Honor of I. Howard Marshall*, edited by J. Laansma, G. Osborne, and R. Van Neste, 277–94. Eugene, OR: Wipf & Stock, 2011.

———. "'The Testimony about the Lord,' 'Borne by the Lord,' or Both? An Insight into Paul and Jesus in the Pastoral Epistles (2 Tim. 1:8)." *TynBul* 52 (2004): 295–316.

Doriani, Daniel. *Women and Ministry: What the Bible Teaches*. Wheaton: Crossway, 2003.

Edwards, J. Christopher. "The Christology of Titus 2:13 and 1 Timothy 2:5." *TynB* 62 (2011): 141–47.

Elliott, J. H. "Jesus Was Not an Egalitarian: A Critique of an Anachronistic and Idealist Theory." *Biblical Theology Bulletin* 32 (2002): 75–91.

Elliott, J. K. *The Greek Text of the Epistles to Timothy and Titus*. Studies and Documents 36. Salt Lake City: University of Utah Press, 1968.

Faber, Riemer. "'Evil Beasts, Lazy Gluttons': A Neglected Theme in the Epistle to Titus." *WTJ* 67 (2005): 135–45.

Feltham, Martin. "1 Timothy 2:5–6 as a Christological Reworking of the Shema." *TynB* 68 (2017): 241–60.

Grudem, Wayne. *Evangelical Feminism: A New Path to Liberalism?* Wheaton: Crossway, 2006.

Harrill, J. Albert. "'Without Lies or Deception': Oracular Claims to Truth in the Epistle to Titus." *NTS* 61 (2018): 451–72.

Harris, Murray J. *Slave of Christ*. Downers Grove, IL: InterVarsity, 1999.

Harrison, P. N. *The Problem of the Pastoral Epistles*. London: Oxford University Press, 1921.

Hubbard, Moyer V. "Kept Safe through Childbearing: Maternal Mortality, Justification by Faith, and the Social Setting of 1 Timothy 2:15." *JETS* 55 (2012): 743–62.

Hübner, J. "Revisiting the Clarity of Scripture in 1 Timothy 2:12." *JETS* 59 (2016): 99–117.

Hutson, Christopher R. "'Saved by Childbearing': The Jewish Context of 1 Timothy 2:15." *NovT* 56 (2014): 392–410.

Johnson, Alan F. "Dissertation and Monograph Summary: 'Pastoral Rule or Lesson on Assimilation?'" *JSPL* 3 (2013): 263–67.

————, ed. *How I Changed My Mind about Women in Leadership: Compelling Stories from Prominent Evangelicals.* Grand Rapids: Zondervan, 2010.

Knight, George W., III. *The Faithful Sayings in the Pastoral Letters.* Grand Rapids: Baker, 1979.

Köstenberger, Andreas, and Thomas R. Schreiner, eds. *Women in the Church: An Interpretation and Application of 1 Timothy 2:9–15.* 3rd ed. Wheaton: Crossway, 2016.

Köstenberger, Margaret E. *Jesus and the Feminists: Who Do They Say That He Is?* Wheaton: Crossway, 2008.

Kruger, Michael. "First Timothy 5:18 and Early Canon Consciousness: Reconsidering a Problematic Text." In *The Language and Literature of the New Testament: Essays in Honour of Stanley E. Porter's 60th Birthday*, edited by L. Dow, C. Evans, and A. Pitts, 680–700. Leiden: Brill, 2017.

Levine, Amy-Jill, with M. Blickenstaff, eds. *A Feminist Companion to the Deutero-Pauline Epistles.* Cleveland: Pilgrim Press, 2003.

Marshall, I. Howard. "The Pastoral Epistles in Recent Study." In *Entrusted with the Gospel*, edited by A. J. Köstenberger and T. L. Wilder, 268–312. Nashville: B&H Academic, 2010.

Naselli, Andrew, and J. D. Crowley. *Conscience: What It Is, How to Train It, and Loving Those Who Differ.* Wheaton: Crossway, 2016.

O'Donnell, Tim. "The Rhetorical Strategy of 1 Timothy." *CBQ* 79 (2017): 455–75.

Pao, David. "Let No One Despise Your Youth: Church and the World in the Pastoral Epistles." *JETS* 57 (2014): 743–55.

Payne, Philip B. *Man and Woman, One in Christ.* Grand Rapids: Zondervan, 2009.

Perry, G. R. "Phoebe of Cenchreae and 'Women' of Ephesus: 'Deacons' in the Earliest Churches." *Presb* 36 (2010): 9–36.

Porter, Stanley E. "Family in the Epistles." In *Family in the Bible: Exploring Customs, Culture, and Context*, edited by R. S. Hess and M. D. Carroll R., 148–66. Grand Rapids: Baker Academic, 2003.

————. "What Does It Mean to be 'Saved by Childbirth' (1 Tim. 2.15)?" *JSNT* 49 (1993): 87–102.

Poythress, Vern S. "The Meaning of μάλιστα in 2 Timothy 4:13 and Related Verses." *JTS* 53 (2002): 523–32.

Robinson, John A. T. *Redating the New Testament.* Philadelphia: Westminster, 1976.

Sanders, E. P. *Paul.* Minneapolis: Fortress, 2015.

Sandom, Carrie. *Different by Design: God's Blueprint for Men and Women.* Ross-shire, UK: Christian Focus, 2012.

Schnabel, Eckhard J. "Paul, Timothy, and Titus: The Assumption of a Pseudonymous Author and of Pseudonymous Recipients in the Light of Literary, Theological, and Historical Evidence." In *Do Historical Matters Matter to Faith?*, edited by J. Hoffmeier and D. Magary, 383–403. Wheaton: Crossway, 2012.

Smith, Claire S. *God's Good Design: What the Bible Really Says about Men and Women.* Kingsford, Australia: Matthias Media, 2012.

————. *Pauline Communities as "Scholastic Communities": A Study of the Vocabulary of "Teaching" in 1 Corinthians, 1 and 2 Timothy and Titus.* WUNT 335. Tübingen: Mohr Siebeck, 2012.

Still, Todd D. "Did Paul Loathe Manual Labor? Revisiting the Work of Ronald F. Hock on the Apostle's Tentmaking and Social Class." *JBL* 125 (2006): 781–95.

Stout, Stephen O. *Preach the Word: A Pauline Theology of Preaching Based on 2 Timothy 4:1–5*. Eugene, OR: Pickwick, 2014.

Swinson, L. Timothy. *What Is Scripture? Paul's Use of "Graphe" in the Letters to Timothy*. Eugene, OR: Wipf & Stock, 2014.

Thornton, Dillon T. *Hostility in the House of God: An Investigation of the Opponents in 1 and 2 Timothy*. Bulletin for Biblical Research Supplement 15. Winona Lake, IN: Eisenbrauns, 2016.

Towner, Philip H. *The Goal of Our Instruction*. JSNTSup 34. Sheffield: Sheffield Academic, 1989.

Tracy, S. "What Does 'Submit in Everything' Really Mean? The Nature and Scope of Marital Submission." *TJ* 29 (2008): 285–312.

Treggiari, S. "Marriage and Family in Roman Society." In *Marriage and Family in the Biblical World*, edited by K. Campbell, 132–82. Downers Grove, IL: InterVarsity, 2003.

Twomey, Jay. *The Pastoral Epistles through the Centuries*. BBC. Chichester, West Sussex (UK): Wiley-Blackwell, 2009.

Wieland, George M. "Roman Crete and the Letter to Titus." *NTS* 55 (2009): 338–54.

Winter, Bruce. "The 'New' Roman Wife and 1 Timothy 2:9–15: The Search for a *Sitz im Leben*." *TynBul* 51 (2000): 285–94.

Wolters, Al. "ΑΥΘΕΝΤΗΣ and Its Cognates in Biblical Greek." *JETS* 52 (2011): 719–29.

———. "An Early Parallel of Αὐθεντεῖν." *JETS* 54 (2011): 673–84.

Yarbrough, Robert. "Schlatter on the Pastorals: Mission in the Academy." In *New Testament Theology in Light of the Church's Mission: Essays in Honor of I. Howard Marshall*, edited by J. Laansma, G. Osborne, and R. Van Neste, 295–316. Eugene, OR: Wipf & Stock, 2011.

Young, Frances. *The Theology of the Pastoral Letters*. NTT. Cambridge Cambridge University Press, 1994.

Zamfir, K. *Men and Women in the Household of God: A Contextual Approach to Roles and Ministries in the Pastoral Epistles*. NTOA/SUNT 103. Göttingen: Vandenhoeck & Ruprecht, 2013.

CHAPTER FOURTEEN

Philemon

Introduction

Philemon is the smallest Pauline letter, but it is a beautiful example of Christian love and diplomacy as Paul exhorts Philemon regarding his slave Onesimus. When we compare Colossians and Philemon, it is clear that both letters were sent to the same destination since Onesimus is mentioned in both, as is Archippus. A few scholars have argued that Philemon was actually written to Archippus, but in Greek letters the first person addressed was the recipient, and so we can be confident that the letter was addressed to Philemon. Apphia was probably the wife of Philemon, and Archippus was possibly his son, though he may also have been a partner in ministry.

The letter may have been written from Ephesus since Rome is so far from Colossae, and we can easily see why Onesimus would seek Paul in Ephesus: it was nearby. Certainty is impossible, but I incline to the view that Paul wrote the letter from Rome while imprisoned there in AD 60–62. We know from other sources that people actually traveled quite often and far in the Greco-Roman world, and thus such a journey by Onesimus is quite conceivable. Fortunately, the interpretation of the letter doesn't depend on the date of its composition or place of origin.

The circumstances of the letter to Philemon are difficult to trace in detail. I suggest that we know the following about Onesimus and Philemon:

- Onesimus was Philemon's slave (v. 16).
- Onesimus probably sought out Paul to get his help.
- Onesimus was converted by Paul (v. 10).

- Paul was sending Onesimus back to Philemon (v. 12).
- Onesimus was previously useless to Philemon (v. 11).
- Onesimus probably wronged Philemon in some way (v. 18).

Perhaps Onesimus fled to Paul, asking him to adjudicate a dispute between him and Philemon. Or perhaps he was a fugitive and sought out Paul because he had met Paul previously and respected and looked up to him. In any case, Onesimus had become a Christian, and Paul was sending him back to Philemon with a cover letter, exhorting and encouraging Philemon to receive Onesimus as a brother in Christ.

In 1 Corinthians 7 we have discussed slavery in the Greco-Roman world, and more briefly in Ephesians 6 and Colossians 3. We need to remember that slavery was not racially based in the ancient world. Most people became slaves as a result of war or even sold themselves into slavery to pay debts. Manumission was also possible, and thus slavery was not necessarily a permanent condition. Slaves, as we noted earlier, could be doctors, teachers, and architects. This is not to deny for a moment that slavery was terribly inhumane and vicious, since masters had absolute authority over slaves and had permission to abuse them with callous disregard for the most elementary human rights. Furthermore, some slaves served in mines, which were horrible places to work and live, and thus the lives of some slaves were absolutely miserable from dawn to dusk. More will be said about Paul's response to slavery in the exposition of the letter.

Outline

Thankful for Philemon's past encouragement	1–7
Request for Philemon to be a future encouragement	8–25

Another outline could be as follows:

Greeting	1–3
Thanksgiving and prayer	4–7
Basis of appeal	8–16
The appeal: welcome Onesimus	17–21
Final words	22–25

Greeting (1–3)

What stands out immediately in the greeting is that Paul identifies himself as "a prisoner of Christ Jesus" (v. 1). In fact, Paul mentions his imprisonment quite often for such a brief letter (also vv. 9, 10, 13, 23). Typically Paul describes himself as an apostle, and in no other letter does he introduce himself as Christ's prisoner. Paul doesn't want to appeal to his apostolic authority in a coercive way, for we see his courtesy and diplomacy throughout the letter in addressing Philemon. Still, his authority shines through, since Paul speaks of what Philemon owes him (v. 18) and the confidence that Philemon will obey the directives in the letter (v. 21). The designation "prisoner" adds an emotional and persuasive dimension to what Paul writes, since he was asking Philemon to give up his rights for the sake of the gospel, just as Paul had. Timothy is introduced as the cosender, and here we have a subtle indication of Paul's authority, for Timothy as his partner in ministry concurred with what Paul wrote.

Philemon is identified as Paul's coworker in the gospel; they shared the same passion for the gospel of Christ, and it is for the sake of the gospel that Paul writes. He also describes Philemon as beloved, and this anticipates one of the key themes in the letter as Paul repeatedly appeals to Philemon's love in making the case for Onesimus (vv. 5, 9, 16; cf. also vv. 7, 12, 20). The reference to the church and to Apphia and Archippus indicates that the letter was not merely private. Philemon's response to Onesimus wasn't an individualistic matter just between him and Onesimus; it wasn't merely his own business, but it had implications for the entire church and for the reputation of Christians. Paul prays for grace and peace from the Father and the Lord Jesus Christ (v. 3). Philemon needed grace to respond rightly to the situation facing him, and Paul also prays that he will have peace and a settled heart as he thinks and prays about Paul's admonitions.

Thanksgiving (4–7)

In Paul's Letters we have seen that after the greeting there is typically thanksgiving, and we see this same pattern in Philemon, for Paul gives thanks in verses 4–5, which morphs into a prayer in verse 6. Constantly Paul thanked God for Philemon in his prayers as he recalled his love for the saints and his faith in the Lord Jesus Christ. Paul anticipated that his love and faith would continue to be exercised in the situation regarding Onesimus. Given Philemon's past faithfulness, Paul was confident as he considered the future. Verse 6 is almost certainly a prayer, but translating the Greek and grasping its meaning is no easy task. I understand Paul to ask that the participation in the faith, in the gospel, which he and Philemon shared, would bear fruit. In other words, Philemon's participation in the faith should make a concrete difference in his life, since by virtue of his union with Christ, Philemon enjoyed every good gift. Paul prays that the good shared will result in Christ's praise and honor (cf. v. 14). In verse 7 the encouragement and joy Paul derived from Philemon is celebrated, particularly because Philemon had "refreshed" "the hearts of the saints." The word for "hearts" is literally "entrails" or "insides" (*splanchna*), but English versions naturally translate it as "hearts." Philemon had regularly refreshed and helped believers, and Paul wanted to see this continue (vv. 12, 20). To sum up, three themes anticipate what is coming in verses 4–7: (1) Philemon's love for the saints, (2) his partnership in the gospel, and (3) his refreshing the hearts of believers.

Appeal for Onesimus (8–20)

The main purpose of the letter now emerges: Paul urges Philemon to welcome his returning slave, Onesimus (though not until v. 17). We see the delicacy and diplomacy with which Paul exhorts his friend and coworker in the gospel. If some of what Paul says strikes us as alien, we need to recognize that we inhabit a different culture, which has different social norms and expectations. Paul could boldly order Philemon about what is fitting regarding Onesimus, whom he hasn't named yet (v. 8). Instead, however, he urges him because of "love" (v. 9), the very love that Philemon had so often expressed in his life. The appeal is grounded as well in Paul's old age and his being a prisoner. In our cultural context we would value an appeal that tugs at Philemon's sympathy. But in the ancient world old age signified that one should be respected and honored (Lev. 19:32; Prov. 20:29; Lam. 5:12). Paul also should be honored and respected and loved as one who is a prisoner of Christ. He doesn't primarily appeal to sympathy here but to his status as an older man, as a prisoner for the gospel.

Finally, the nature of the appeal emerges: Paul entreats Philemon about Onesimus; apparently Onesimus visited Paul in prison and became Paul's son, meaning that he was converted (Philem. 10). As noted in the introduction, we don't know for certain why Onesimus visited Paul. I suspect that he traveled to meet Paul because he was upset with or had wronged Philemon in some way. He traveled to meet Paul since he had met Paul previously and respected him. We are not surprised to learn that Paul shared the good news with Onesimus, and Onesimus believed the gospel of Christ. Onesimus had probably wronged Philemon in some way since Paul, in a play on the name Onesimus, concedes that Onesimus was "useless" to Philemon in the past (v. 11). But now that he was converted, he was "useful" (the meaning of his name) to both Philemon and Paul. He was not only useful to Paul but incredibly dear to and beloved by him. In sending Onesimus back to Philemon, Paul was sending "my very own heart." Again we see the word for "insides" or "entrails" (*splanchna*), which occurred in verse 7. Onesimus ministered to the very core of Paul's being, and sending him back was an enormous sacrifice.

Paul continues to explain to Philemon why Onesimus was beloved and valuable (v. 13). Indeed, Paul wanted to keep him in Rome, and he could have kept him there by asking Philemon to let him stay. After all, Onesimus was fulfilling a function Philemon could not, in that he was ministering to Paul, who was imprisoned for the sake of the gospel. Again, we might think Paul was trying to evoke pity, but since he nowhere else mentions his imprisonment to gain sympathy, his chains should be understood as providing further motivation for Philemon to grant his request. Paul recognizes and celebrates the "good" in Philemon for Christ's sake, and he clarifies why he didn't keep Onesimus with him. Such a move would have been coercive and manipulative and would force Philemon's hand (v. 14). Certainly, Paul wrote to motivate Philemon to grant his request, but he wanted Philemon's response to be authentic and free from compulsion. The good that Paul requested needs to come from Philemon's heart: it needs to be free and unconstrained.

Paul then reflects on God's providence in the whole situation. Onesmius may have abandoned Philemon, which testified to his uselessness, but the temporary situation was all for the good because now Philemon could enjoy friendship with Onesimus forever (v. 15). Paul isn't saying that Onesimus will be a slave forever. Instead, Philemon and Onesimus were now members of the same family, the family of God, forever. Some think Paul explicitly calls upon Philemon to free Onesimus in verse 16 since he says that he should be welcomed "no longer as a slave." Such an interpretation, however, over-reads the text, for the point is that the fundamental relationship between Philemon and Onesimus is no longer master-slave. They are now brothers in the Lord; the family relationship "in the Lord" takes precedence over earthly relationships. Still, there is recognition that earthly relationships exist "in the flesh." "In the flesh" here stands for the earthly relationship between Philemon and Onesimus, since Philemon, in the realm of the flesh in everyday life, still remains Onesimus's master. Social standing and social location, however, aren't fundamentally important (cf. 1 Cor. 7:21–23); what matters to Paul is one's relationship to Christ, and thus relationships that matter so much in the world were irrelevant to Paul. The implications for slavery will be discussed shortly.

Paul aligns himself with Onesimus as his child in the faith and as a beloved brother. He is now ready to make the appeal that was anticipated in Philemon 11. The idea of partnership is also picked up from verse 6: Paul and Philemon were partners in the faith. Paul asks Philemon to welcome Onesimus as he would welcome Paul himself (v. 17). The request is extraordinary to ask on behalf of a slave, showing that Paul subverted the social fabric of the Greco-Roman world. Perhaps Philemon would think of the losses incurred from Onesimus leaving, and so Paul adds that if any injury or loss was incurred, Philemon should put it on Paul's account (v. 18). Paul solemnly promises, affixing his signature, that he would repay anything owed (v. 19). On the one hand, he puts some pressure on Philemon, reminding him that he owed Paul everything! Apparently Philemon came to faith through Paul. On the other hand, Paul was willing to pay what was owed, but he also challenges Philemon to think about whether he would try to cash in, since he owed Paul a debt that could never really be repaid.

Paul addresses Philemon as "brother," reminding him again of their relationship as Christians (v. 20). Paul plays off the name of Onesimus again, asking Philemon to "benefit" him in the Lord by responding graciously to Paul's request. Philemon should "refresh my heart in Christ." For the third time we see the word *splanchna* for one's insides (vv. 7, 12). Paul also picks up the word "refresh" from verse 7, where he affirmed that the hearts of believers had been refreshed by Philemon. In verse 12 Paul claims that Onesimus is so bound together with Paul that he represents his very heart (*splanchna*). Here Paul urges Philemon to do what he had done so often in the past: to refresh Paul's heart by welcoming Onesimus as a brother, as a forgiven sinner, as a beloved friend.

Final Words (21-25)

Paul wanted Philemon to respond freely (v. 14), but he also wrote expecting his "obedience"! (v. 21). In fact, Paul was sure Philemon would respond to his overtures. Paul's expectation of obedience might seem awkward to us, but we need to recall our cultural distance from the world in which these words were written. Furthermore, Paul and Philemon knew and loved each other; these are words between beloved friends, not a missive sent to a person alienated from Paul.

Paul was certain that Philemon would exceed his expectations and do more than he says. Was Paul suggesting that Philemon free Onesimus without saying so precisely? A number of hints in the letter could be read along these lines: (1) Paul could command him "to do what is right" (v. 8); (2) Paul wanted to keep Onesimus with him (v. 13); (3) Paul needed Philemon's consent (v. 14); (4) Onesimus is "no longer a slave" but a "brother" (v. 16); (5) Paul counsels Philemon to welcome Onesimus as he would welcome Paul, and Paul would repay any loss (vv. 17–19). A number of interpreters have defended such a conclusion, and it is certainly possible. Perhaps Paul was implicitly asking

Philemon to send Onesimus back to Paul for the sake of ministry, which would in effect free him from slavery. It was quite common for masters to assist in manumitting slaves. Still, going by the vague wording in the letter, I am not persuaded that Paul gave such specific advice. Paul, in other words, granted leeway to Philemon to carry out the Pauline exhortations in a way that was fitting.

Why didn't Paul come out and tell Philemon to free Onesimus, since they were brothers in the Lord? We have to remember that the Christian movement was exceedingly small and that its fundamental purpose wasn't social reformation. A general policy of freeing slaves was not practical, for some people voluntarily sold themselves into slavery to ameliorate their own economic situation. We must not impose a modern capitalistic society on the ancient world, as if all freed slaves could immediately find other jobs. Paul doesn't endorse slavery but regulates it and reforms it from within, though he does counsel slaves to get their freedom if possible (1 Cor. 7:21). Still, we must constantly beware of imposing our cultural moment and social location onto those who lived in the Greco-Roman world two thousand years ago. It is even possible that Onesimus preferred to be Philemon's slave instead of working elsewhere. Perhaps this was a better situation for him. Obviously, we don't know, but we must avoid judging NT writers as if such situations are easily resolved.

Paul hopes that he will be released from prison, though prayer will play a vital role in the entire enterprise (Philem. 22). If Paul was in Rome, his release would be from his first Roman imprisonment. Epaphras, who played such a prominent role in Colossians and apparently was in prison with Paul (or possibly previously a prisoner) greeted Philemon, and doubtless they were closely allied and presumably friends in the gospel (v. 23). It is also possible that Epaphras voluntarily shared in Paul's imprisonment for a season. Others sent greetings (as in Col. 4:10, 14): "Mark, Aristarchus, Demas, and Luke," designated as Paul's coworkers (Philem. 24). Jesus Justus (Col. 4:11) is left out, but perhaps he departed for some reason before Philemon was completed. The letter concludes with a grace benediction (Philem. 25), for grace was needed to fulfill the Pauline instructions.

Philemon: Commentaries

Barth, Markus, and Helmut Blanke. *The Letter to Philemon: A New Translation with Notes and Commentary.* Eerdmans Critical Commentary. Grand Rapids: Eerdmans, 2000.

Beale, G. K. *Colossians and Philemon.* BECNT. Grand Rapids: Baker Academic, 2019.

Bird, Michael F. *Colossians and Philemon*. NCCS. Eugene, OR: Cascade, 2009.

Bruce, F. F. *The Epistles to the Colossians, to Philemon, and to the Ephesians*. NICNT. Grand Rapids: Eerdmans, 1984.

Campbell, Constantine R. *Colossians and Philemon: A Handbook on the Greek Text*. BHGNT. Waco: Baylor University Press, 2013.

Dunn, James D. G. *The Epistles to the Colossians and to Philemon*. NIGTC. Grand Rapids: Eerdmans, 1996.

Fitzmyer, Joseph. *The Letter to Philemon: A New Translation with Introduction and Commentary*. AB 34C. New York: Doubleday, 2000.

Garland, David E. *Colossians and Philemon*. NIVAC. Grand Rapids: Zondervan, 1998.

Gorday, Peter, ed. *Colossians, 1–2 Thessalonians, 1–2 Timothy, Titus, Philemon*. ACCS 9 (NT). Downers Grove, IL: InterVarsity, 2000.

Harris, Murray J. *Colossians and Philemon*. EGGNT. Grand Rapids: Eerdmans, 1991.

Lightfoot, J. B. *Saint Paul's Epistles to the Colossians and to Philemon*. London: Macmillan, 1897. Reprinted, Grand Rapids: Zondervan, 1971.

Lohse, Eduard. *Colossians and Philemon*. Hermeneia. Philadelphia: Fortress, 1971.

Martin, Ralph P. *Colossians and Philemon*. NCB. Grand Rapids: Eerdmans, 1973.

McKnight, Scot. *The Letter to Philemon*. NICNT. Grand Rapids: Eerdmans, 2017.

Melick, Richard R., Jr. *Philippians, Colossians, Philemon*. NAC 32. Nashville: Broadman, 2000.

Moo, Douglas. *The Letters to the Colossians and to Philemon*. PNTC. Grand Rapids: Eerdmans, 2008.

Moule, C. F. D. *The Epistles of Paul the Apostle to the Colossians and to Philemon*. CGTC. Cambridge: Cambridge University Press, 1968.

O'Brien, Peter T. *Colossians, Philemon*. WBC 44. Waco: Word, 1982.

Thompson, James, and Bruce W. Longenecker. *Philippians and Philemon: A Commentary*. PCNT. Grand Rapids: Baker Academic, 2016.

Thompson, Marianne Meye. *Colossians and Philemon*. THNTC. Grand Rapids: Eerdmans, 2005.

Vincent, Marvin R. *A Critical and Exegetical Commentary on the Epistles to the Philippians and to Philemon*. ICC. New York: C. Scribner's Sons, 1911.

Wall, Robert W. *Colossians and Philemon*. IVPNTC. Downers Grove, IL: InterVarsity, 1993.

Wilson, R. McL. *A Critical and Exegetical Commentary on Colossians and Philemon*. ICC. Edinburgh: T&T Clark, 2005.

Wright, N. T. *The Epistles of Paul to the Colossians and to Philemon*. TNTC. Leicester, UK: Inter-Varsity, 1986.

Philemon: Articles, Essays, and Monographs

Banker, J. *A Semantic and Structural Analysis of Philemon*. Dallas: Summer Institute of Linguistics, 1990.

Barclay, John M. G. "Paul, Philemon and the Dilemma of Christian Slave-Ownership." *NTS* 37 (1991): 161–86.

Birdsall, J. N. "Πρεσβύτης in Philemon 9: A Study in Conjectural Emendation." *NTS* 39 (1993): 625–30.

Brogdon, Louis. *A Companion to Philemon*. Eugene, OR: Cascade, 2018.

Burtchaell, J. T. "Paul's Epistle to Philemon: Toward an Alternative *Argumentum*." *HTR* 86 (1993): 357–76.

———. *Philemon's Problem: A Theology of Grace*. Grand Rapids: Eerdmans, 1998.

Church, F. F. "Rhetorical Structure and Design in Paul's Letter to Philemon." *HTR* 71 (1978): 17–33.

Cope, L. "On Rethinking the Philemon-Colossians Connection" *Biblical Research* 30 (1985): 45–50.

De Vos, C. S. "Once a Slave, Always a Slave? Slavery, Manumission and Relational Patterns in Paul's Letter to Philemon." *JSNT* 82 (2001): 89–105.

Frilingos, C. "'For My Child, Onesimus': Paul and Domestic Power in Philemon." *JBL* 119 (2000): 91–104.

Glaze, R. E., Jr. "Onesimus: Runaway or Emissary?" *TTE* 54 (1996): 3–11.

Goodenough, E. R. "Paul and Onesimus." *HTR* 22 (1929): 181–83.

Harrill, J. Albert. "Using the Roman Jurists to Interpret Philemon: A Response to Peter Lampe." *ZNW* 90 (1999): 135–38.

Heil, John P. "The Chiastic Structure and Meaning of Paul's Letter to Philemon." *Bib* 82 (2001): 178–206.

Ip, Alex Hon Ho. *A Socio-Rhetorical Interpretation of the Letter to Philemon in Light of the New Institutional Economics: An Exhortation to Transform a Master-Slave Economic Relationship into a Brotherly Loving Relationship*. WUNT 2/444. Tübingen: Mohr Siebeck, 2017.

Jeal, Roy R. *Exploring Philemon: Freedom, Brotherhood, and Partnership in the New Society*. Rhetoric of Religious Antiquity 2. Atlanta: SBL Press, 2015.

Johnson, Matthew V., James A. Noel, and Demetrius K. Williams, eds. *Onesimus Our Brother: Reading Religion, Race, and Culture in Philemon*. Minneapolis: Fortress, 2012.

Knox, John. *Philemon among the Letters of Paul*. London: Collins, 1960.

Marshall, I. Howard. "The Theology of Philemon." In *The Theology of the Shorter Pauline Letters*, edited by K. P. Donfried and I. H. Marshall, 175–91. Cambridge: Cambridge University Press, 1993.

Mullins, T. Y. "The Thanksgivings of Philemon and Colossians." *NTS* 30 (1984): 288–93.

Nordling, J. G. "Onesimus *Fugitivus*: A Defense of the Runaway Slave Hypothesis in Philemon." *JSNT* 13 (1991): 97–119.

Petersen, Norman R. *Rediscovering Paul: Philemon and the Sociology of Paul's Narrative World*. Philadelphia: Fortress, 1985.

Rapske, Brian M. "The Prisoner Paul in the Eyes of Onesimus." *NTS* 37 (1991): 187–203.

Sanders, L. L. "Equality and a Request for the Manumission of Onesimus." *ResQ* 46 (2004): 109–14.

Seesengood, Robert. *Philemon: Imagination, Labor, and Love*. London: Bloomsbury, 2017.

Still, Todd D. "Philemon among the Letters of Paul: Theological and Canonical Considerations." *ResQ* 47 (2005): 133–42.

Tolmie, D. Francois, ed. *Philemon in Perspective: Interpreting a Pauline Letter.* BZNW 169. Berlin: de Gruyter, 2010.

Winter, S. C. "Paul's Letter to Philemon." *NTS* 33 (1987): 1–15.

Scripture and Ancient Writings Index

Romans

Scripture and Ancient Writings Index

11 424, 426
12 424, 425, 426, 428
13 425, 427, 428
14 426, 427, 428
15 427
16 423, 425, 427, 428
17 426, 427
17–19 428
17–21 424
18 424, 425, 428
19 428
20 425, 426, 428
21 425, 428
22 397, 429
22–25 424
23 332, 425, 429
24 2, 332, 406, 429
25 429

Hebrews
1:2 154, 386, 403
2:2 250
3:7–4:11 197
3:17 160
5:12 252
6:8 158, 168
9:9 357
10:10 141
10:29 141
11:26 96
12:22 255
13:12 141

James
1:2–4 70
1:13–14 162
1:27 389

1 Peter
1:6–7 70
2:5 131
2:8 106
2:13–17 103, 415
3:1–5 147
3:4 381
4:3–4 404
5:1–2 39
5:8 407
5:14 110

2 Peter
2:1–22 357
3:10 349
3:15–16 241

1 John
2:10 106
2:18 358, 386, 403
2:19 156
2:22 358
3:10 252
3:12 252
4:3 358
5:19 199

2 John
7 358

3 John
9–10 384

Jude
5 160

Revelation
1:5 321
2:14 31, 152, 154
2:20 31, 152, 154
3:3 349
3:5 96
3:12 255
4:1 19
7:1 360
11:19 19
12:3 167
13 360
13:13–15 361
16:1 96
16:15 349
19:11 19
19:12 167
19:20 361
20:1–3 360
20:4 139
21:2 255
21:10 255
21:18–21 131

Old Testament Apocrypha

Baruch
4:7 163

2 Esdras
16:53 103

1 Maccabees
1:14–15 148
1:47 105
1:62 105
2:15 357
2:23–25 236
2:23–27 308
2:24 236
2:26 236
2:27 236
2:50 236, 308
2:52 67
2:54 236, 308
2:58 236, 308

4 Maccabees
5:2 152
7:6 105
12:13 252

Sirach
8:10 103
11:32 103
29:21 173
44:19–21 67

Tobit
13:11–13 98

Wisdom
7:26 320
11–15 58

Old Testament Pseudepigrapha

2 Baruch
57.1–2 67

Joseph and Aseneth
8.5–7 146–47

Jubilees
16.28 67
22.16 24
24.10–11 67

Liber antiquitatum biblicarum
10.7 160
11.15 160

Psalms of Solomon
17.11 359
17.30–31 98

Sibylline Oracles
2.96 152

Testament of Benjamin
9.2 98

Testament of Solomon
8.1–2 252
18.1–2 252

Papyri

Oxyrhynchus Papyri
1484 153

Dead Sea Scrolls

4QpNah
5–8 248

11QTemple
64.6–13 24

450

Subject Index

wisdom, 100, 101, 125–26,
129, 132
wrath, 66
See also Trinity
God-fearers. *See* gentiles
godliness, 386, 387
gospel
in Acts, 3–4, 5
and Christ, 39, 55–56, 128
different, 232, 234–35
expansion, 17–18
and hope, 319
and Isaiah, 55
nature of, 399
and Old Testament, 55
and Paul, 5, 32, 39–40, 55,
56–57, 73, 128, 157,
234–35, 238–40, 244,
302, 342, 362–63
and revelation, 94
and sin, 73
government, 103–4, 359–60,
378. *See also* authority
grace
Corinth, 124
and gentiles, 89
God's gift in Christ, 208–9
justification, 65, 84, 416
and Paul, 73–74
power, 414–15
salvation, 278
and sin, 73–74, 76
transformative, 203
Granville Sharp rule, 415
Greco-Roman world, 58, 110,
125, 127, 142, 143, 144,
149, 153, 203, 290, 345,
423, 424
greetings. *See under specific
letters (e.g., Romans)*
grumbling, 161–62, 306

Habakkuk, 28, 58, 247–48
Hagar, 254, 255, 256
headship, 164, 290. *See also*
authority; Jesus Christ:
headship
healing, 28, 171
heaven, 303, 310–11
heir, 251–52
Herod Agrippa I, 25–26
Herod Agrippa II, 42, 43, 44

Holy Spirit
in Acts, 7–8, 9, 11–12, 15
and apostles, 21
and Cornelius, 24–25
and disciples of John the
Baptist, 36
filled by, 289
and flesh, 81
fruit of, 259
and God, 129, 276
and groanings, 82–83
and hope, 82
and the law, 78, 244, 259
and letter, 197
living by, 258, 259–60
and new covenant, 12
Pentecost, 11–12
pouring out of, 12, 15
and prayer, 9, 82–83
promise of, 7–8, 245
reception of, 20–21
and salvation, 416
Samaritans, 20
seal, 275
and sonship, 252–53
spiritual gifts, 169
temple of, 130, 143
unity, 282–83
work of, 199
hope, 81–83, 84, 174, 276,
318–19, 347–48
human race, 35, 59, 71, 72,
277
husbands, 144–45, 146, 147,
152, 164–65, 176, 290,
330, 383, 385. *See also*
marriage; men
Hymenaeus, 377–78, 402

idolatry, 31, 34, 59, 152–53,
154, 155, 161, 162–63,
305, 341
incest, 135–36
inheritance, 275, 276
"I" of Romans 7 and Ga-
latians 2, 76–78, 79,
243–44
Isaac, 86, 250, 254, 255–56
Isaiah
call, 236
God's plan, 100
and gospel, 55

and Israel, 93–94, 100
and Paul, 43–44, 45
prophecy, 26, 43–44, 45, 93,
108, 125
reconciliation, 203–4
shoot of Jesse, 108–9
and tongues, 175
Ishmael, 86–87, 250, 254,
255–56
Israel
all, 97, 99
and Christ, 99
and church, 159, 329
conversion, 99
covenant, 86, 88
ethnic, 86, 97–98, 99
exodus, 17
and gentiles, 94, 96–98, 108–9
and God, 18, 60, 63, 85–88,
90, 94–95, 96, 99, 261
grumbling, 161–62
idolatry, 59, 161
"I" of Romans 7, 77
and Isaiah, 93–94, 100
judgment, 60, 63, 95–96,
179–80
and law, 77
and mystery, 97, 98
olive tree, 96–97
patriarchs, 86
and Paul, 78, 85
privileges, 85–86
promises, 86–87
rejects God's messengers, 19
remnant, 95, 96
restoration, 8–9, 58, 89–90
and sacraments, 160
sacrifices, 162
salvation, 98–99
servant of the Lord, 26
Stephen's speech, 18
and temple, 18
unbelief, 90, 94, 96–97
wilderness generation,
159–61

Jacob, 87–88
James, brother of Jesus,
30–31, 177, 237, 238,
239–40
James, brother of John, 25